THE CUSTER READER

THE
CUS

University of Nebraska Press Lincoln & London

TER
READER

EDITED BY PAUL ANDREW HUTTON

Acknowledgments for previously
published selections appear on pages
575–76.

Library of Congress
Cataloging-in-Publication Data
The Custer reader / edited by Paul
Andrew Hutton.
p. cm.
Includes bibliographical references
and index.
ISBN 0-8032-2351-X (alk. paper)
1. Custer, George Armstrong, 1839–1876.
2. Little Big Horn, Battle of the, 1876.
3. Indians of North America—Wars—
1866–1895.
I. Hutton, Paul Andrew, 1949–
E467.1.C99C85   1992
973.8'2—dc20   91-16845
                                        CIP

To my father,

PAUL A. HUTTON, SR.

and to the memory of my mother,

LOUISE K. HUTTON

CONTENTS

MAPS

E ven though the apologia has long since gone out of literary fashion, it seems nevertheless proper and fitting to offer an explanation for presenting the world with yet another book on the ubiquitous George Armstrong Custer. Despite the incredible bibliographic bulk on America's most famously unfortunate soldier, there is no publication available similar to the one you presently hold. I have attempted to produce a unique volume that will be of particular value to both the new reader on Custer and the experienced Custer student. The reader unfamiliar with the Custer story will find a complete, reliable introduction to this legendary figure's personality, career, and myth within these pages. Here is Custer as he saw himself, as his contemporaries saw him, and as the best scholars have interpreted him. The Custer student will discover new insights within these pages while also rediscovering some familiar sources. Here are the best of the Custer articles, many quite rare, assembled together for easy reference. For both groups of readers, this book will serve as a guide through the oftimes treacherous morass of partisan writing on this ever so controversial cavalryman.

It is rather surprising, considering the incredible array of publications on Custer, that an anthology reprinting classic articles has not appeared before. There have been a few minor anthologies of limited circulation publishing new essays, and Edward S. Godfrey's memoir of the last battle has been reprinted several times, but a Custer reader has not appeared—until now.

This is a somewhat unusual reader, in that it combines first-person narratives, memoirs, reprinted scholarly articles, and photo essays with new essays by the top Custer scholars. These new essays, by Gregory J. W. Urwin, Brian W. Dippie, Robert M. Utley, and Eric von Schmidt, along with the editor's section introductions, provide a modern interpretive context for all the essays in the book. Here, then, is not only the best of what has already been published but also four new essays by leading authorities on Custer.

The book is divided into four sections—the Civil War, the Indian *xiii*

Wars, the Little Big Horn, and the Custer myth. The first two sections contain essays by Custer himself, and three of the sections reprint memoirs by Custer's contemporaries. Each section also features a photographic essay by the editor. The result, it is hoped, is a definitive reader on this complex, contradictory, and eternally fascinating man.

As with all projects, I have been assisted in this book by several people whom it is a pleasure to acknowledge. The editors of various journals kindly granted permission to reprint essays. Malory Ausland and Dorothy Calloway granted permission to reprint the work of their father, Walter Campbell. I would also like to thank Raymond J. DeMallie, D. Teddy Diggs, Paul Fees, Paul Hedren, Vincent Heier, James S. Hutchins, Douglas McChristian, Neil Mangum, Joseph Musso, B. Byron Price, Charles Rankin, William R. Reid, and Tom Swinford for their assistance.

The authors of the new essays—Gregory J. W. Urwin, Brian W. Dippie, Robert M. Utley, and Eric von Schmidt—not only were a delight to work with but also provided constructive criticisms on this anthology and assisted greatly in providing illustrations for the photographic essays.

In particular I must acknowledge the assistance of the late John M. Carroll. He provided advice on which essays to include in the anthology as well as copies of articles and illustrative material from his vast Custeriana collection. With his friend Robert Aldrich, Carroll constructed a fabulous Custer collection that he was always most generous in sharing with other researchers. The contagious enthusiasm he brought to the Custer field, along with his warmth and generosity, will be greatly missed.

Finally I must acknowledge my debt to my own little yellow-haired warrior, Laura. At eight years old, she is just beginning her journey of discovery into our rich historical past, but her wide-eyed enthusiasm reminds me often of why I began this journey myself so long ago. My partner on that journey, Lynn Brittner Hutton, often takes time from her own busy career in the world of Indian art to advise, console, cajole, encourage, and just make every day brighter than the one before.

Major General George Armstrong Custer, May 23, 1865
(Custer Battlefield National Monument)

INTRODUCTION

George Armstrong Custer loved war. It was as a tonic to him. Whereas others shrank from its ghastly carnage, he reveled in it. It often seemed, in fact, that only when dealing in death could he truly come alive. War not only brought him national acclaim and high rank but also gave him a power that peace denied him. For only through displays of the most reckless courage was he able to impress, even inspire, others.

If he had never gone west to die in the most famous frontier battle in history, Custer would nevertheless command attention as a bold, resourceful leader of cavalry. Many proclaimed him second only to Sheridan as a leader of horse. That is debatable, but it is nevertheless beyond dispute that this wild youth contributed far more than many others of his generation to preserving the Union and eradicating the abomination of slavery from the Republic. However he may have tarnished a glowing record by subsequent acts, the facts of his bold deeds during the Civil War speak for themselves quite eloquently.

In the world's first modern war he was already something of an anachronism. A leader of cavalry in the last great conflict before the machine banished the horse from the battlefield, he gloried in those charges of mounted men that looked to a medieval past rather than an iron-and-steam future. Like his Southern opponents whose archaic politics and outmoded racial sensibilities he so admired, he viewed warfare as a romantic escapade. Bedecked with gold braid and scarlet scarf as if a cavalier of old, with flowing locks long out of style, he resembled more his dashing enemy J.E.B. Stuart than his hard-bitten mentor Phil Sheridan. His romanticism, however, was tempered with a cold ruthlessness that scorched the Shenandoah Valley and marked him a willing proponent of the new total warfare advocated by his superiors. Later, on the frontier, he would once again garb himself in romantic trappings while applying the torch with abandon and making cruel war on noncombatants.

It must always be remembered, of course, that he was just a boy. His wild enthusiasms and incredible recklessness were evidence of a youthful sense of immortality. That he emerged relatively unscratched while continuously engaging in some of the hottest combat of America's bloodiest war is truly remarkable. This sense of invulnerability never left him, and helps to explain much of his conduct in the decade after Appomattox. He truly came to believe in "Custer's Luck"—and why not?

Even his friends recognized a dangerously volatile side to his character. Sheridan, who knew Custer best, championed him, protected him, and more than any other, advanced his career, feeling that "if there was any poetry or romance in war he could develop it." But Sheridan also recognized the danger inherent in Custer's personality, characterizing his protégé as "too impetuous, without deliberation; he thought himself invincible and having a charmed life." To Sheridan, Custer "was as boyish as he was brave" and thus "always needed someone to restrain him."[1]

Gregory J. W. Urwin—an associate professor of history at the University of Central Arkansas, the leading authority on Custer's Civil War career, and the author of *Custer Victorious: The Civil War Battles of General George Armstrong Custer* (1983)—surveys Custer's meteoric rise to major general in an original essay that is the first selection in this section. Urwin's incisive essay shows how a combination of personal charm, reckless courage, true talent, and careful political string-pulling led to one of the most remarkable success stories in American military history.

Custer speaks for himself in "From West Point to the Battlefield," first published in the *Galaxy Magazine* for April 1876. Custer wrote seven installments of his Civil War memoirs, completing the last one not long before his fatal encounter on the Little Big Horn. He was already an accomplished author, his *My Life on the Plains* having appeared in 1874. This memoir of Indian warfare first appeared in serial form in *Galaxy* as well, and undoubtedly, had Custer lived, his Civil War memoirs would also have been consolidated into book form. Unfortunately, Custer's seven Civil War articles carry him only to 1862.

The essay published here was the second installment of the memoirs published by *Galaxy*, a popular middle-class literary magazine. It covers Custer's West Point years, his interesting observations on his southern colleagues, his first sad scrape with military justice, his belated graduation, and his journey to the war zone. Although written in a rather stolid style, the article is nevertheless interestingly expressive of the personality and convictions of its author. That a dedicated man of action such as Custer was such a prolific author may surprise many. Others will dismiss his writing as another symptom of his constant hungering after the limelight. Yet the fact remains that before he died at thirty-six he left an impressive body of written work, all the while vigorously pursuing a busy military career. His dedication to writing history while at the same time making it places him squarely in a grand American literary tradition that begins with Benjamin Franklin, includes the frontiersman David Crockett, and most vividly flourishes, if not climaxes, with Theodore Roosevelt.

The third essay is Jay Monaghan's "Custer's 'Last Stand'—Trevilian Station, 1864," from the September 1962 *Civil War History*. Monaghan was a distinguished historian of the American West, best known for *Custer: The Life of General George Armstrong Custer* (1959), for years the standard biography.[2] He served as the state historian of Illinois for several years before becoming the consultant for the Wyles Collection of Lincolniana at the University of California, Santa Barbara. The author of a dozen books, he was recognized as one of the premier authorities on Abraham Lincoln and the Civil War. His essay reflects this mastery of Civil War sources as well as a graceful writing style. Monaghan, whose biography of Custer is quite favorable to its subject, nevertheless sees portents of calamity in the Boy General's bungling at Trevilian Station.

The final essay in this section was written by a captain of New York volunteer cavalry who served under Custer. Harlan Page Lloyd's "The Battle of Waynesboro" describes the March 1865 battle that marked the final defeat of Confederate forces in the Shenandoah Valley. The rebels had already been routed at Cedar Creek the previous October, and much of the intervening time had been occupied with rearguard actions against the partisan rangers of the redoubtable John Singleton Mosby and with scorching the once bountiful Shenandoah Valley. Even though Waynesboro was anticlimactic to the overall Shenandoah campaign, it nevertheless showcased Custer's tactical talents and incredible bravado.

Lloyd's essay vividly displays why this rash youngster was so adored by his troops throughout the Civil War. It is a side to Custer that is often ignored or blithely dismissed by his later critics, yet it is an important measure of the man. Those who served with him in the terrible crucible of Civil War combat could not help but agree with Colonel Frederic Newhall's battle memory of him with "a pistol in his boot, jangling spurs on his heels, and a ponderous claymore swinging at his side—a wild daredevil of a general, and a prince of advance guards."[3]

Notes

1. Quoted in H. C. Greiner, *General Phil Sheridan As I Knew Him, Playmate-Comrade-Friend* (Chicago: J. S. Hayland and Co., 1908), 357–58.

2. Jay Monaghan, *Custer: The Life of General George Armstrong Custer* (Boston: Little, Brown and Co., 1959). The biography is currently still in print as a Bison Book paperback from the University of Nebraska Press. Monaghan also authored *The Great Rascal: The Life and Adventures of Ned Buntline* (Boston: Little, Brown and Co., 1951) and *Civil War on the Western Border, 1854–1865* (Boston: Little, Brown and Co., 1955).

3. [Frederic Cushman Newhall], *With General Sheridan in Lee's Last Campaign, by a Staff Officer* (Philadelphia: Lippincott and Co., 1866), 211–12.

CUSTER: THE
CIVIL WAR YEARS

GREGORY J. W. URWIN

O**n April 16, 1864, as the Army of the Potomac prepared for a spring drive against Richmond, the capital of the Confederacy, Major James Harvey Kidd of the Sixth Michigan Cavalry** wrote a letter to his father. Over the past two years, the Union's largest field army had mounted similar efforts to capture the rebel seat of government, only to be repulsed by outnumbered enemy forces. Despite that humiliating record, Kidd predicted, "This Campaign will squelch rebellion." The source of the major's unflagging optimism was his total faith in his brigade commander, Brigadier General George Armstrong Custer. "We swear by him," Kidd declared. "His name is our battle cry. He Can get twice the fight out of this brigade that any other man Can possibly do."[1]

Less than three weeks later, the Army of the Potomac marched south, unleashing the bloodiest two months in America's deadliest war. Between May 4 and July 1, Custer's brigade lost 776 officers and men, statistics that helped it claim an unenviable honor at the war's end—the highest number of casualties sustained by any mounted organization of equivalent size in the Union army.[2] Yet through all the misery and slaughter, Kidd's admiration for Custer never wavered. From the midst of the mounting carnage, he informed his anxious loved ones:

> For all that this Brigade has accomplished all praise
>   is due to Gen Custer
> So brave a man I never saw and as Competent as brave.
>   Under him a man is ashamed to be Cowardly. Under
>   him our men can achieve wonders.[3]

For all their sincere fervor, Kidd's words are bound to puzzle most modern readers. The only Custer they know is a loser, the man responsible for the United States Army's most famous defeat in an Indian war.

7

Since the 1930s, it has been fashionable to picture Custer as a freak—a cold-blooded scoundrel and egotistical misfit who attained high rank through dumb luck and then recklessly squandered the lives of friends and foes until he received his comeuppance at the Little Big Horn.[4]

The generation that weathered the Civil War knew a different Custer. To those Americans, he was a genuine hero—dashing, brave, and able—a military prodigy whose exploits on horseback materially shortened a tragic, fratricidal conflict. A society caught in the wrenching transition from agrarianism to industrialism embraced Custer as a personification of the comforting belief that war was still a glorious adventure, his deeds apparent proof that individual courage could decide great battles.[5] Largely because of his brilliant Civil War career, the public heralded Custer as the nation's leading Indian fighter, even though his successes on the plains were not as numerous or decisive as those of other officers. And because ordinary citizens invested him with an aura of invincibility, his death at the Little Big Horn left a traumatic impression on their psyches, assuring the Last Stand an enduring place in America's popular consciousness.[6]

In the eleven decades since the Custer fight, the event has assumed a life of its own, eclipsing nearly everything else about its main protagonist. Nevertheless, if Custer had not already been a national hero when he met his doom, his name would be no better known than those of other white commanders killed in Indian battles. Indeed, up to the present time, many paintings and films commemorating the Last Stand have depicted Custer as the Civil War's young "General with the Golden Locks" rather than the short-haired, middle-aged lieutenant colonel who died eleven years after Appomattox. Disaster made Custer's name immortal, but the imagery of his final defeat is inextricably woven with the imagery of his earlier triumphs.[7] His meteoric rise in the Civil War is as much a part of the "Custer Myth" as his fall. Any effort to separate the man from the myth must begin with the conflict that shaped so much of his personal and professional character and determined the direction of his career.

When the Civil War erupted in April 1861, George Armstrong Custer was finishing his fourth turbulent year at the U.S. Military Academy. Long afterward, he frankly admitted that his record as a cadet would never stand as an example to be emulated by those who followed in his footsteps. "Custer's course at West Point may be described in the remark that he merely scraped through," a classmate observed. "He was always loaded down with demerit marks, he was not attentive to his military duties, and he was anything but a good student."[8] Underclassman Peter Michie, who returned to West Point in 1871 to join the faculty, recalled: "Custer . . . was always in trouble with the authorities. . . . He had more fun, gave his friends more anxiety, walked more tours of extra guard, and came nearer to being dismissed more often than any other cadet I have ever known."[9]

Cadet Custer's difficulties stemmed from an immature craving for thrills and attention—not lack of intelligence. He once told Michie that there were only two positions in a class, "head and foot." Since he was disinclined to strive for the former, he aimed for the latter. He studied just enough to keep from flunking out. He flouted regulations with reckless abandon—until his tally neared the limit requiring expulsion. Then he became the model of military decorum. To his delight, when graduation day rolled around on June 24, 1861, he ranked thirty-fourth in a class of thirty-four.

In the tradition of class clowns, Custer was extremely popular with his fellows. Everybody seemed to like the laughing cadet with the blond curls and devil-may-care attitude. Whenever mischief was brewing, Custer emerged as a natural leader. In an institution where hazing plebes was a hallowed custom, he excelled as an ingenious and indefatigable prankster, displaying an uncanny knack for instantly assessing a victim's weaknesses. Moreover, his horsemanship and athletic prowess impressed his more serious-minded peers.[10]

The sudden onset of the secession crisis dampened even Custer's ebullience. As early as November 1860, he predicted that the departure of the slave states would result in war. "You cannot imagine how sorry I will be to see this happen," he wrote his sister, "as the majority of my best friends and all my room mates except one have been from the South." As a Democrat, he sympathized with the white South's resolve to preserve a social order based on slavery, but as an Ohioan, he felt bound by his cadet's oath to defend the Union. The chilling prospect of turning his sword against men he loved as brothers did not prevent him from seeking high rank in one of the volunteer regiments Ohio raised in response to the attack on Fort Sumter. "I would prefer serving with the troops of my native state," he explained, "besides I could get a much higher office [than] in the regular service . . . at least . . . Captain and probably higher."[11]

Custer's dream of entering his profession at the top came to naught. He had to settle for a second lieutenant's commission in the Second U.S. Cavalry, reporting to his company in time to witness the First Battle of Bull Run on July 21, 1861. That debacle convinced Union authorities their troops needed more training and better organization to crush the rebellion. Major General George B. McClellan, a dapper West Pointer credited with routing the secessionists from western Virginia, was summoned to Washington, D.C., to mold a horde of recruits into a respectable field force. The subsequent formation of McClellan's Army of the Potomac deprived Custer of much of the time he should have spent learning about cavalry operations on the company and battalion levels. In that assemblage of amateurs, even a poorly ingested West Point education was a prized commodity, and Custer rotated among the staffs of several minor generals, helping to process the paperwork necessary for the smooth running of military bureaucracies.[12]

In the spring of 1862, McClellan caught the Confederates off guard, slipping one hundred thousand soldiers onto the peninsula formed by the York and the James rivers in an amphibious flanking movement with Richmond as the objective. Eager for some action, Custer took an army transport down Chesapeake Bay, only to be loaned to the Topographical Engineers as the campaign got under way. He soon tired of such tame pursuits as drawing maps and locating roads. Not even the chance to observe the enemy from a gas balloon quenched his thirst for excitement.[13] Whenever he found a spare moment, he would ride off to any spot where combat seemed likely, prompting his colleagues to shout after him, "There goes Custer, as usual, to smell out a fight!"[14]

In an army where the ruling virtue was prudence bordering on timidity, Custer's belligerence stood out and earned him a series of commendations.[15] On May 5, 1862, he entered an engagement near Williamsburg, attaching himself to Brigadier General Winfield S. Hancock as a volunteer aide. Dashing forward to inspire charging Federal infantry, he single-handedly captured six rebels and a large silk flag— the first colors taken by the Army of the Potomac. Twenty days later, after a daring, daylight reconnaissance to the south side of the Chickahominy, he guided a raiding party back across the river to overrun an enemy picket post. "Lieutenant Custer . . . was the first to cross the stream," reported a superior, "the first to open fire, and one of the last to leave the field."[16]

When McClellan heard of the affair, he offered Custer a place on his staff with the temporary rank of captain. His muddy uniform still dripping the Chickahominy, the flabbergasted boy stammered his grateful acceptance. In eleven short months, Custer had progressed from class "goat" to membership in the official family of the Republic's most important soldier. A glittering new world of undreamed opportunities lay within his grasp.[17]

Appropriately enough, the new captain had been a McClellan admirer well before the general plucked him from obscurity. On the eve of his departure for the Peninsular campaign, Custer had testified: "I have more confidence in General McClellan than any man living. I would forsake everything and follow him to the ends of the earth. I would lay down my life for him. . . . Every officer and private worships him. I would fight anyone who would say a word against him." Despite McClellan's penchant for self-delusion, his repeated failure to make proper use of superior numbers, and his aversion to battle, Custer continued to regard him as "our only hope" in saving the Union.[18]

For his part, McClellan found Custer the ideal aide—brave, loyal, untiring, and efficient. "His head was always clear in danger," the general reminisced, "and he always brought me clear and intelligible reports."[19] Indeed, had McClellan acted with greater speed on the intelligence Custer supplied during the Antietam campaign, he might have destroyed the major portion of Robert E. Lee's Army of Northern Virginia before it could concentrate at Sharpsburg, Maryland. As it was, the poorly coordinated assaults that "Little Mac" directed at Lee on September 17, 1862, resulted in the bloodiest day in American history.

As McClellan permitted Lee's divisions, battered but intact, to withdraw into the safety of Virginia, President Abraham Lincoln's patience ran out. McClellan had been given a year to prove himself, and all he had to show for his elaborate efforts were setbacks, excuses, and recriminations. To make matters worse, the little general was an arrogant man, unable to subordinate his conservative Democratic principles to the decisions of his commander-in-chief. He dared to criticize the Lincoln administration's increasingly harsh war policies, particularly the

Emancipation Proclamation. Obstructionism is a luxury no unsuccessful general can afford. On November 7, 1862, McClellan learned of his dismissal as the head of the Army of the Potomac.[20]

For George Armstrong Custer, McClellan's ouster constituted a painful lesson in the principle of civilian control of the military. With other West Pointers, he rebelled against the notion that meddlesome politicians should have the authority to tell professional soldiers how to shape strategy and conduct operations, a resentment that surfaced both immediately in his private correspondence and years later in his Civil War memoirs. In fact, Custer may have belonged to the group of hotheaded young staff officers who urged their beloved chief to march on Washington, seize power, and then deal with the Confederacy on his own terms. Fortunately, McClellan spurned temptation and bid his adoring troops farewell, leaving a deflated Custer with the reduced rank of first lieutenant in the Fifth U.S. Cavalry.[21]

Following an extended winter leave in Monroe, Michigan (where he began courting Elizabeth Bacon, whom he would marry on February 9, 1864), Custer received orders to join his company at Washington. But once again, a kindly superior saved him from the anonymous existence of a lowly subaltern. Sometime that spring, Brigadier General Alfred Pleasonton, the commander of a cavalry division, brought Custer onto his staff. Attending Pleasonton could not compare to the prestige of riding in McClellan's entourage, but the appointment offered sufficient compensations.

To begin with, Pleasonton was a rising star in the North's military firmament, and his staff was bound to share in his good fortune. Seventeen years of frontier service with the Second Dragoons had molded the short, slightly built martinet into one of the few Yankee generals who understood how to use the mounted arm. For the first two years of the Civil War, Federal cavalry units had done little to justify their existence, failing to match their Confederate counterparts in reconnaissance, raiding, and combat. Rebel horsemen derived their edge from General Lee's policy of concentrating them in large strike forces, whereas their blue-clad foes were dispersed in impotent driblets as couriers and escorts for infantry generals. With prophetic wisdom, Pleasonton urged the establishment of a Union cavalry corps of several divisions, buttressing his recommendation with this promise: "Our cavalry can be made superior to any now in the field by organization."

On February 5, 1863, Major General Joseph Hooker, the new head of McClellan's old army, turned Pleasonton's dream into reality, but he presented the coveted command to Brigadier General George Stoneman.[22]

A gifted schemer, Pleasonton strove to weasel his way into Hooker's good graces, disparage Stoneman, and grab control of the Cavalry Corps. Unlike the obstreperous McClellan, Pleasonton courted the favor of President Lincoln and other Republican politicians. He was also a master at manipulating the news media, feeding correspondents skewed accounts that converted his modest successes into spectacular victories. Pleasonton's expertly orchestrated campaign of exaggerating, falsifying, and pulling strings paid quick dividends, gaining him Stoneman's job by May 22. When the prospering commander advanced in grade to major general a month later, Custer could anticipate a corresponding promotion to captain.[23]

Pleasonton proved an outstanding administrator, but he possessed a serious flaw as a soldier—an aversion to risking his life in battle. Lieutenant Custer, on the other hand, relished danger, a trait that attracted his general's notice. Pleasonton quickly came to rely on the blond daredevil to carry instructions to embattled elements of the Cavalry Corps, often empowering Custer to use his personal judgment and issue his own orders to senior officers.[24] Thanks to this growing dependence, the Pleasonton-Custer relationship soon shed the strict formality of master and servant and evolved into something much warmer. The general called the younger man "boy" and took an active interest in his personal life. "I do not believe a father could love his son," Custer boasted, "more than Genl. Pleasanton [*sic*] loves me."[25]

Pleasonton's growing trust and the commencement of the Gettysburg campaign furnished Custer with ample opportunities to display his talent for combat leadership, and his exploits were enhanced by the Union cavalry's newborn willingness to close with the enemy. At Brandy Station on June 9, 1863, Custer rode in the spearhead of one of Pleasonton's columns, distinguishing himself in a surprise attack that foreshadowed the demise of the Confederacy's mounted supremacy in the eastern theater. Eight days later, in a sharp skirmish at Aldie, Custer helped rally the First Maine Cavalry as it recoiled before a rebel thrust, and he then led the regiment in a countercharge. When his skittish horse carried him into the midst of the enemy, Custer kept his head and cut his way clear with his saber, downing three assailants in the process—a feat that won him mention in Northern newspapers.[26]

Thus far, his association with Pleasonton had brought Custer increased responsibilities, several commendations, and the mixed pleasure of seeing his name misspelled in the *New York Times*, but none of that truly satisfied him. Many of his West Point friends were now leading regiments and brigades while Custer remained nothing more than a glorified messenger boy. Bent on securing a command of his own, he focused his attention on the recently raised Fifth Michigan Cavalry, whose colonel had been upgraded to brigadier general. Claiming Michigan citizenship on the basis of a few years' residence with a half-sister in Monroe, he presented himself to the state's Republican governor, Austin Blair, as a candidate for the vacant colonelcy. Heeding Pleasonton's example, Custer prevailed on a prominent Republican politician from Monroe to plead his suit with Blair. At the same time, he rounded up endorsements from seven influential generals, leaking their high opinions of his merits to the Michigan press. Finally, he visited the Fifth Michigan's camp in northern Virginia and asked its officers to petition Blair in his favor. Put off by Custer's youth and impertinence, the officers declined to lend their names to his cause.[27]

Even if Custer had filled his petition with signatures, his chances of impressing Blair would have remained slim. Crass political patronage determined the awarding of commissions in Union volunteer regiments. In Blair's eyes, Custer's liabilities far outweighed his military credentials. The boy was a Democrat and his family came from the wrong side of the tracks. Infinitely worse, Custer was a "McClellan man," a crippling handicap, since McClellan's continuing criticism of the Lincoln administration made him the likely Democratic nominee for the 1864 presidential race. Refusing to deviate from the spoils system, Blair installed a solid Republican lawyer and businessman as the Fifth's colonel on June 11, 1863.[28]

Whatever disappointment Custer felt dissolved before the month's end. On June 28, within hours of succeeding Hooker as the head of the Army of the Potomac, Major General George G. Meade appointed three captains in the Cavalry Corps as brigadier generals in the U.S. Volunteers: Wesley Merritt, Elon J. Farnsworth, and George A. Custer.[29] It was no mere coincidence that the lucky trio were also alumni of Pleasonton's staff; Meade's cavalry chief had pushed hard for their elevation.

Ever protective of his own reputation, Pleasonton hoped to revitalize his command by filling the top slots with "officers with the proper dash to command Cavalry"—young men who were not afraid to fight. "Give me 15000 cavalry," he begged, "let me place my own officers over it—& I will soon place Lee where he now has us[,] on the defensive."[30] Having built his career on intrigue, Pleasonton also wanted to surround himself with senior subordinates who owed their advancement, and hence their loyalty, to him. An inveterate xenophobe, he cleared the way for his protégés by deposing several foreign-born division and brigade leaders.[31] In addition, Pleasonton strengthened his political position by so favoring two of his ex-aides. Elon Farnsworth's uncle was Congressman John Farnsworth, an Illinois Republican, a personal friend of the president's, and Pleasonton's main intermediary at the White House. Wesley Merritt's father edited a Democratic newspaper in southern Illinois, making him a useful connection should the war-weary Northern electorate turn against the Republicans.[32]

Regarding Custer, Pleasonton harbored no ulterior motives. When someone later questioned the wisdom of presenting such an exalted rank to a stripling two years out of West Point, his patron snapped, "Custer is the best cavalry general in the world."[33] However debatable his claim, Pleasonton sincerely believed what he said. He had no other reason to insist on his favorite aide's promotion. As Custer's future father-in-law (as yet no admirer of his daughter's suitor) realized, "No man could be made a general at 23 without [political] influence unless there was something in him as a man and a soldier."[34]

When he traded his captain's bars for a brigadier's star, Custer received command of the Second Brigade of the Third Cavalry Division—known simply as the Michigan Brigade because it was the only such unit in the Cavalry Corps to draw all its regiments (the First, Fifth, Sixth, and Seventh) from the same state. Appealing to local pride to build morale, Custer dubbed the outfit the Wolverine Brigade and vowed, "I would not exchange it for any brigade in the army." Perhaps nothing about his appointment pleased him more than its irony. "The regiment of which I attempted to obtain the colonelcy (5th) belongs to my brigade," he explained, "so that I rather outwitted the Governor who did not see fit to give it to me."[35] But even as he gloated, Custer noted certain deficiencies in his regiments. "When I assumed command," he mused afterward, "few if any of the men . . . had even heard a hos-

tile shot fired, their discipline was lax and organization incomplete."
As soon as a lull occurred in the summer campaigning, Custer meant
to instruct and train his officers and men until they stood "unequalled
in every trait essential to soldiers." But with Lee's second invasion
of the North in full swing, the Michiganders would receive their first
soldiering lesson in the merciless school of combat.[36]

In less than a week, with Custer at the reins, the Wolverine Brigade
justified its fearsome nickname. On the afternoon of July 3, 1863, as the
greatest battle waged on American soil neared its climax, 6,000 Confederate cavalry under Major General J.E.B. ("Jeb") Stuart squared
off against 5,000 blue troopers on rolling farmland three miles east of
Gettysburg, Pennsylvania. Stuart hoped to skirt the Army of the Potomac's right flank and create confusion in its rear while Major General
George E. Pickett and 13,000 rebel infantry were to pierce the Federal
center on Cemetery Ridge. As the senior Union officer present, Brigadier General David McMurtrie Gregg took charge of the force opposing
Stuart, but he confined the two brigades from his Second Cavalry Division to supporting roles. Custer's 2,344 Michiganders would bear the
brunt of the coming duel with the cream of Lee's cavalry.

For more than two hours, Stuart probed Gregg's deployments with
artillery fire and clouds of skirmishers. Then at 4:00 P.M., two rebel
brigades lumbered forward to sweep the Yankees from the field. With
half his brigade disrupted by the previous fighting, Custer had only
one regiment, the veteran First Michigan, in position to meet the approaching masses—five hundred Yankee troopers to stop more than
four times their number. Unwilling to let his men enter an unequal
contest without him, Custer placed himself at their head. As the puny
band moved out, an officer moaned: "Great heavens! We shall all be
swallowed up!" Laying spurs to his steed, Custer shot forward until the
entire regiment could see him, and then—just before he disappeared
among the rebels—he brandished his saber and shouted, "Come on, you
Wolverines!" Cheering like maniacs, the Michiganders bounded after
their intrepid brigadier, slashing, stabbing, and shooting at anyone in
gray. Staggered by the Federals' ferocious impetuosity and by flank
attacks driven home by some squadrons from Gregg's division and regrouped companies of the Fifth and Seventh Michigan, the Confederate
column melted away in retreat.[37]

The Michigan Brigade was properly ecstatic. The cavalry battle east of Gettysburg had been the unit's first major engagement, and the Wolverines had outfought the legendary Jeb Stuart and his vaunted "Invincibles," an exploit that gave the lie to the myth of Southern cavalry superiority. Moreover, any doubts the Michiganders had harbored about their new brigadier had disappeared in the face of his courageous, personal style of leadership.[38] One excited trooper penned this tribute to "Genl. Custerd [*sic*]" on July 9, 1863: "He is a glorious fellow, full of energy, quick to plan and bold to execute, and with us he has never failed in any attempt he has yet made."[39]

Custer attracted additional praise in the eleven days following Gettysburg as the Union cavalry harassed Lee's withdrawal to Virginia. At Falling Waters, Maryland, on the last day of the pursuit, the Michigan Brigade swamped the rebel rear guard, nabbing fifteen hundred prisoners and three battle flags. Amid the final flurry of hand-to-hand combat, a Fifth Michigan private saw "General Koster [*sic*] . . . plunge his saber into the belly of a rebel who was trying to kill him. You can guess how bravely soldiers fight for such a general."[40]

"Gallant officers make good soldiers."[41] That was Custer's motto, and he loved to practice what he preached. "When Custer made a charge, he was the first sabre that struck," confirmed a troop commander, "for he was always ahead."[42] Civil War soldiers expected their officers to behave fearlessly under fire—such displays reassured the men—but Custer exceeded the strict standards of his age. "Whenever he orders a charge he always leads in person," enthused the *New York Herald*.[43] Watching Custer direct a skirmish, an aide marveled, "Through all that sharp and heavy firing the General gave his orders as though conducting a parade or review, so cool and indifferent that he inspired us all with something of his coolness and courage."[44]

To ensure his example did not go unnoticed, Custer designed a special uniform for himself. Known as his "fighting trim," it consisted of a tight hussar jacket and trousers of black velveteen garnished with yards of gold lace, a blue sailor shirt bearing a white star on each side of the collar, a long cravat of flaming scarlet, a black broad-brimmed hat adorned with a gold cord and a silver star, and a pair of high-topped boots sporting gilt spurs. With his blond mustache, imperial, and shoulder-length hair, he looked like the reincarnation of some seventeenth century cavalier. The admiring Northern press christened him the "Boy General with the Golden Locks," and his troopers cheered him as "Old Curly."

Soon every Wolverine was wearing a red necktie, and many officers ordered smart blue jackets festooned with gold. And like their general, the Wolverines became noted for a courage as conspicuous as their appearance.[45]

During the fall of 1863, Union and Confederate cavalry clashed with jarring frequency as Meade and Lee sparred inconclusively in northern Virginia. With each passing engagement, Custer matured as a general. As his confidence grew, he displayed more initiative and won increasing respect from his superiors and subordinates. More than once, his bold assaults extricated the Third Cavalry Division from traps sprung by the crafty Jeb Stuart. Succumbing to a euphoria born of repeated success, Custer blurted to a friend: "Oh, could you but have seen some of the charges that were made! While thinking of them I cannot but exclaim 'Glorious War!' "[46]

In his boyish naiveté, Custer trusted that battlefield exploits alone would please his civilian masters enough to keep them from laying him "on the shelf." In an institution as politicized as the Union army, however, any general craving job security had to keep one eye on the Confederates and the other on Washington. Early in 1864, Custer learned that unnamed enemies were at work in the U.S. Senate to block confirmation of his appointment as brigadier general. Unable to fault his military record, they charged him with being a "McClellan man" and even a "copperhead"—a closet traitor out to sabotage the administration's war policies.[47]

Desperate to clear his name and save his commission, Custer sent an eight-page open letter to Jacob M. Howard, a powerful Michigan Republican who sat on the Senate's Military Affairs Committee. To be sure, Custer's private utterances about the war had reflected the convictions of a McClellan Democrat. "I never heard slavery mentioned as an issue," he informed his father-in-law. "The Union—it was the Union we were fighting for." But now, with so much at stake, he showered Senator Howard with sentiments worthy of a radical Republican: "The President . . . as Commander in Chief of the Army and as my Superior officer Cannot issue any decree or order which will not receive my unqualified *support*. . . . But I do *not* stop here. . . . All his acts, proclamations and decisions embraced in his war policy have received not only my support, but my most hearty, earnest and cordial *approval*." Touching on Lincoln's controversial Emancipation Proclamation, Custer asserted, "My friends . . . *can* testify that I have insisted that so long as a single slave was held in bondage, I for *one*, was opposed to peace on any terms, and to show that my acts agree with my words I can boast of having liberated more slaves from their Masters than any other General in this Army." As for the possibility of ending the war through negotiation rather than conquest, Custer protested, "I would *offer* no compromise except that which is offered at the point of the bayonet."[48]

This flawlessly disingenuous performance made Custer the darling of the Republican majority in Congress, and his confirmation sped through the Senate. In fact, such highly placed radicals as Ohio's Senator Ben Wade spoke of raising him to major general "as soon as a vacancy occurs."[49]

While the war lasted, Custer took special pains to retain the goodwill of his Republican patrons. Later in 1864, after a superior told him to expect the conferral of a division command, the Boy General defused possible political opposition by writing a strong, pro-Lincoln letter that just happened to find its way into the press. The fact that this letter appeared a few weeks before the presidential election endeared Custer all the more to the ruling party. But the young cavalryman had possibly become too consummate a careerist to bet all his money on one horse. Even as Custer backed Lincoln in public, one of his former aides escorted a McClellan campaign official on an expedition to canvass votes from soldiers at the front.[50]

Ingratiating himself with Congress did not render the Boy General immune to all strains of army politics, an unpleasant truth that became evident in the wake of his confirmation victory. Desiring to personally supervise the annihilation of Lee's ragged but resilient Confederate army, Lieutenant General Ulysses S. Grant, the conqueror of Vicksburg and newly appointed "General in Chief of the Armies of the United States," attached his headquarters to the Army of the Potomac in March 1864. Grant liked to surround himself with cronies, and he rearranged the upper echelons of the Cavalry Corps to provide places for two "pets" from the western theater.

Custer's closest associates fell victim to Grant's manipulations. Pleasonton was banished to the Department of Missouri, one of the war's backwater sectors. Brigadier General Hugh Judson Kilpatrick, Custer's division commander, was posted to the Army of the Cumberland for the Atlanta campaign. Pleasonton's transfer deprived Custer of a valued friend and protector, and he brooded over the ungrateful treatment accorded a general "who never lost a battle and who was the first to give a character and reputation to the cavalry."[51] Kilpatrick's fate, on the other hand, elicited no such misgivings. A shameless braggart and grandstander, Kilpatrick was known as "Kill-Cavalry" because of his reckless tactics and utter disregard for the lives of those serving under him—defects that had cost him Custer's respect the previous autumn.[52]

As Kilpatrick's senior subordinate, Custer felt entitled to inherit the command of the Third Cavalry Division, a sentiment shared by General Meade. But the prize went to a bright, young engineer from Grant's staff, Brigadier General James H. Wilson. Conveniently forgetting the role that partiality had played in his own rise, Custer denounced Wilson as "this Court favorite," an "imbecile and upstart" who had "never even commanded a company of men." Custer added, "Since assuming command of the Division . . . [he] has made himself ridiculous by the ignorance he displays in regard to cavalry."[53] Furthermore, Wilson was Custer's junior in rank by four months. To avoid undue friction and other complications, the Michigan Brigade and its fuming Boy General were shifted to the First Cavalry Division.[54]

Though unable to disguise his contempt for Wilson, Custer developed an instant liking for Pleasonton's successor, Major General Philip H. Sheridan. No pampered paper-shuffler, "Little Phil" was a hot-blooded fighting general, renowned for his valor at Perryville, Stones River, and Missionary Ridge. The charismatic Irishman also harbored some ambitious plans for his corps. He wanted to employ his troopers as an independent combat arm rather than as mere auxiliaries for Meade's infantry.[55]

On May 9, 1864, less than a week after Grant opened his spring offensive, Sheridan cut loose from the Army of the Potomac with ten thousand blue horsemen, skirted Lee's left flank, and headed straight for Richmond. He calculated that a lunge at the rebel capital would draw the Confederate cavalry into the open for a showdown. Snapping at the bait on May 11, Jeb Stuart threw forty-five hundred gray riders across Sheridan's path at a crossroads called Yellow Tavern. As the three Yankee divisions deployed for battle, Custer spotted a vulnerable point in Stuart's line. Taking his own brigade and part of another,

Custer overran an enemy battery in a brilliantly conducted charge. When Stuart galloped up to seal the breach, a dismounted Wolverine shot him in the abdomen, inflicting a mortal wound.[56]

Having humbled and weakened his Southern foes, Sheridan turned homeward, but General Wilson, who held the van, lost his way and blundered into the Richmond defenses. To Custer's glee, Sheridan sent him to extricate the bumbling engineer and create an escape route for the Cavalry Corps. The Boy General executed his order with skill and speed, and Sheridan expressed his satisfaction in no uncertain terms: "Custer is the ablest man in the Cavalry Corps."[57]

As superiors went, Sheridan proved a harsh master—a general who demanded results and tolerated no excuses. Even so, he was quite generous to subordinates who met his expectations, and since he had Grant's ear, he could be a powerful patron. The Richmond raid showed Sheridan that Custer was one of his "most gallant and efficient officers," but such regard carried a high price.[58] Sheridan depended on Custer as his main troubleshooter, utilizing the crack Michigan Brigade and its leader to contain emergencies and carry out dangerous duties. Custer neatly summarized service under Sheridan when he wrote: "We have passed through days of carnage and have lost heavily. . . . The Michigan Brigade has covered itself with undying glory." Upset by newspaper accounts of her husband's recurring brushes with death, Custer's new bride complained, "Why is it your Brigade has to do everything?"[59]

In August 1864, Grant dispatched Sheridan to the Shenandoah Valley to dispose of Lieutenant General Jubal A. Early's impudent Confederate army, which had recently menaced Washington. Incorporated into Sheridan's forty-thousand-man Army of the Shenandoah were the First and Third Cavalry Divisions. With its open fields and rolling hills, the valley was ideal cavalry country, and here Custer attained his apex as a soldier. At the climactic moment in the Battle of Winchester on September 19, 1864, Custer rallied five hundred of his Wolverines and rode down an entrenched brigade of sixteen hundred infantry, taking seven hundred prisoners as he turned Early's left flank and threw the rebels into a panic. In a war where the increased range of infantry weapons threatened the saber charge with obsolescence, Custer's achievement merited a substantial reward. On September 30, after the hapless Wilson departed for the western theater to salvage his reputation, Sheridan presented Custer with the Third Cavalry Division.[60] But the Third had deteriorated badly during Wilson's tenure. "Wilson was universally considered to be an unlucky man," acknowledged an Ohio sergeant. "We never had confidence in him or ourselves." [61]

Welcoming the challenge, Custer wasted no time in restoring the division's morale and effectiveness. On October 9, he routed a larger rebel cavalry division led by an old friend from West Point days, Brigadier General Thomas L. Rosser, and captured all the enemy's guns and wheeled transport. "With Custer as a leader," crowed an elated Yankee captain, "we are all heroes and hankering for a fight." Speaking for the rank and file, Wilson's Ohio critic added: "Each member felt proud to be known as one of Custer's Division. . . . With Custer . . . we never began but we felt sure of victory." [62]

Ten days later, in Sheridan's decisive victory at Cedar Creek, Custer plunged through a gap in Early's left wing just as the Confederate line started to crumple. Pursuing the stampeding foe, Custer's cheering troopers picked up forty-five cannon and swarms of prisoners. Sheridan signified his pleasure by brevetting the young daredevil to major general. Custer returned the favor on March 2, 1865, when he smashed the remnants of Early's army at Waynesboro. [63]

Eager to return to the control of their beloved Boy General, hundreds of officers and men from the Michigan Brigade petitioned for transfer to the Third Cavalry Division—but to no avail. [64] Meeting with one of Custer's sergeants, a Wolverine voiced his frustration: "Why, since Custer left the 1st Division it has done nothing. . . . Now, all you hear about is the 3d Division. The 3d Division captured so many battle flags, nothing but the 3d Division, while the 1st Division is scarcely heard of. The fact is you have Custer now." [65]

With the Shenandoah Valley pacified, Sheridan rode east to assist Grant in prying Lee out of the earthworks guarding Richmond and Petersburg. Marshaling a mixed force of cavalry and infantry, Little Phil chopped up the right wing of the Army of Northern Virginia at Five Forks on April 1, 1865, severing the last two railroads feeding supplies to the besieged Confederates. To save his troops from starvation and encirclement, Lee abandoned Richmond and darted west to elude Grant. Urged on by the relentless Sheridan, four Union cavalry divisions galloped in pursuit, lashing the weary rebels every step of the way. Intoxicated with the spirit of the chase, Custer outdid his colleagues in carving away chunks of Lee's shrinking army. By April 6, the fourth day of the epic race, the bronzed bluecoats composing the Boy General's escort bore thirty-one rebel battle flags—each tattered banner a mute symbol of a destroyed regiment.[66]

As dusk fell on April 8, Custer headed off his desperate quarry at Appomattox Station, the jubilant Federal troopers seizing four trains crammed with munitions and supplies meant for the exhausted rebel fugitives. Leading the retreat, Lee's reserve artillery—thirty guns—attempted to blast the Third Cavalry Division out of the depot. Amid the intermittent glare of shells bursting in the fading light, Custer regrouped his scattered squadrons and led a series of small assaults. "We expected Custer would be killed every time," reported an enlisted man in the Second Ohio Cavalry, "but he was not scratched, tho [sic] he had a horse or two killed under him. He really appeared to lead a charmed life." Before darkness forced an end to the fighting, Custer had two dozen fieldpieces in his possession.[67]

Bringing up his other three horse divisions, Sheridan held Lee in place until the next morning, when the arrival of three corps of Federal infantry robbed the rebels of their last hope of escape. Custer received the enemy's first flag of truce, and a few hours later, Lee surrendered in the parlor of the Wilmer McLean house.[68] After the Virginian left to confront his heartbroken followers, Sheridan purchased the table on which the articles of capitulation had been drafted. Little Phil sent the precious trophy to Elizabeth Custer, along with the following note: "I respectfully present to you the small writing-table on which the conditions for the surrender of the Confederate Army of Northern Virginia were written by Lt. General Grant—and permit me to say, Madam, that there is scarcely an individual in our service who has contributed more to bring this about than your very gallant husband."[69]

No soldier could desire a finer tribute.

Whatever errors he later committed as an Indian fighter, George Armstrong Custer shone in the conventional, set-piece battles that decided the Civil War in the eastern theater. As a cavalryman, he rated second only to Sheridan. Custer possessed an eye for picking out an opposing formation's weaknesses and the ruthless nerve to exploit what he saw. He knew when to charge on horseback and when to defend on foot. Surrounded by soldiers who did not shy from hardship or danger, he proved an inspiring and considerate commander. He brought out the best in his troopers with his fearless example, firm but humane discipline, compassionate treatment for his sick and wounded, and the promise of medals, furloughs, or promotions in recognition of valorous conduct. Most important of all, his tactical decisions usually resulted in victory at a reasonable cost. "Custar [*sic*] was . . . a man extremely careful to give his soldiers every advantage of position that could be obtained," wrote Quartermaster Sergeant Roger Hannaford of the Second Ohio Cavalry, "but when that was done he struck hard & swift. He was by no means the reckless harum scarum so many represent him to be." Judging from the numerous accolades found in the memoirs, letters, and diaries left by his followers, Custer was one of the most popular generals in the Army of the Potomac. Even infantrymen, who habitually jeered the cavalry, could not suppress their hurrahs when Old Curly cantered by. To the continuing bewilderment of his biographers, the Custer recalled by Civil War veterans bears little resemblance to the petty, impulsive tyrant described by so many Seventh Cavalrymen who knew him later in the West.[70]

The Civil War, the grandest tragedy in America's annals, was the most fulfilling period in Custer's life. Blessed with a combination of personal charisma, physical stamina, martial talent, and political savvy, he climbed to the summit of his profession before his twenty-fifth birthday. Both on the battlefield and behind the lines, he made the right moves and pleased the right people. He would spend the eleven remaining years of his life in a futile quest to match the deeds that had earned him such acclaim in 1863, 1864, and 1865.

Perhaps if he had not succeeded so well as the Boy General, George Armstrong Custer might have died a less driven, less controversial man.

Notes

1. James Harvey Kidd to "Dear Father," April 16, 1864, James Harvey Kidd Papers, Michigan Historical Collections, Bentley Historical Library, University of Michigan, Ann Arbor.

2. Custer's Michigan Cavalry Brigade suffered a total of 525 battle-related deaths in the course of the Civil War. However, a significant number of brigade fatalities occurred when Custer was not in command. U.S. War Department, *The War of the Rebellion:*

A *Compilation of the Official Records
of the Union and Confederate Armies*,
130 vols. (Washington, D.C.: Government Printing Office, 1880–1901), 1st
ser., vol. 36, pt. 1, p. 811 (hereafter
cited as *OR*); Gregory J. W. Urwin,
" 'Come on, You Wolverines!': Custer's
Michigan Cavalry Brigade," *Military
Images* 7 (July–August 1985): 7–15;
William F. Fox, *Regimental Losses
in the American Civil War, 1861–1865*
(Albany: Fort Orange Press, 1898),
120, 376–78.

3. Kidd to "Dear Father & Mother,"
June 3, 1864, Kidd Papers.

4. Frederic F. Van de Water's
Glory-Hunter: A Life of General Custer
(Indianapolis: Bobbs-Merrill Co., 1934)
set the pattern for Custer debunkers.
For the latest in that line, see Evan S.
Connell, *Son of the Morning Star* (San
Francisco: North Point Press, 1984).

5. For what Custer symbolized to
nineteenth-century Americans, see
Richard Slotkin, *The Fatal Environment: The Myth of the Frontier in the
Age of Industrialization, 1800–1890*
(New York: Atheneum, 1985). For the
refusal of the Civil War generation to
acknowledge the realities of modern
warfare, see Gerald F. Linderman,
*Embattled Courage: The Experience
of Combat in the American Civil War*
(New York: Free Press, 1987).

6. Ever at variance with the pre-
vailing sentiment of his time, William
Tecumseh Sherman felt that Custer's
Indian campaigns were "more valuable
in the great cause of civilization" (i.e.,
American expansion) than were the
young cavalier's "more appreciated and

brilliant actions around Richmond in
1864, 5." William T. Sherman to Elizabeth Bacon Custer, January 24, 1889,
Elizabeth B. Custer (hereafter cited
as EBC) Collection, Custer Battlefield
National Monument, Crow Agency,
Montana. For a comparison of Custer's
accomplishments with those of other
Indian fighters, see Paul Andrew Hutton, ed., *Soldiers West: Biographies
from the Military Frontier* (Lincoln:
University of Nebraska Press, 1987).

7. Custer entered his final battle
equipped with a hunting rifle, two
revolvers, and a knife, but numerous
scriptwriters and artists have armed
him with a saber (his trademark in the
Civil War) for their restagings of the
Last Stand. A few have even dressed
him in a Civil War uniform instead of
buckskins. See Harrison Lane, "Brush,
Palette, and the Little Big Horn," *Montana the Magazine of Western History*
23 (July 1973): 66–80; Brian W. Dippie,
"Brush, Palette, and the Custer Battle:
A Second Look," *Montana the Magazine of Western History* 24 (January
1974): 55–67; and Paul A. Hutton,
"Hollywood's General Custer: The
Changing Image of a Military Hero in
Film," *Greasy Grass* 2 (1986): 15–21.

8. J. M. Wright, "West Point before the War," unidentified magazine
article, ca. 1880, EBC Collection.

9. Peter Michie, "Reminiscences of
Cadet and Army Service," in A. Noel
Blakeman, ed., *Personal Recollections
of the War of the Rebellion* (New York:
G. P. Putnam's Sons, 1897), 194.

10. W. Donald Horn, ed., *"Skinned":
The Delinquency Record of Cadet*

George Armstrong Custer, U.S.M.A. Class of June 1861 (Short Hills, N.J.: Privately printed, 1980), 1–21; Wright, "West Point"; Michie, "Reminiscences," 194–95; Morris Schaff, The Spirit of Old West Point, 1858–1862 (Boston: Houghton, Mifflin and Co., 1907), 25–28, 66–67, 115–16, 159, 193–94; Joseph Pearson Farley, West Point in the Early Sixties (Troy, N.Y.: Pafraets Book Co., 1902), 21–22, 75; James Harrison Wilson, Under the Old Flag, 2 vols. (New York: D. Appleton and Co., 1912), 1:101; E. Van A. Andruss to Elizabeth Bacon Custer, September 27, 1905, EBC Collection.

11. George A. Custer to Lydia Ann Reed, November 10, 1860, April 10, 26, 1861, EBC Collection.

12. Marguerite Merington, ed., The Custer Story: The Life and Intimate Letters of General George A. Custer and His Wife Elizabeth (New York: Devin-Adair, 1950), 11–13, 25.

13. For Custer's short career as a pioneer aeronaut, see Lawrence A. Frost, "Balloons over the Peninsula: Fitz John Porter and George Custer Become Reluctant Aeronauts," Blue and Gray Magazine 2 (January 1985): 6–12; OR, 1st ser., vol. 11, pt. 1, pp. 107–11, 152–54.

14. Detroit News Tribune, May 15, 1910.

15. For the persistent timidity of the Army of the Potomac and the inferiority complex that inspired it, see Michael C. C. Adams, Our Masters the Rebels: A Speculation on Union Military Failure in the East, 1861–1865 (Cambridge: Harvard University Press, 1978). According to Theodore Lyman, an aide at Army of the Potomac headquarters, this voracious love of battle continued to distinguish Custer from most other Union officers in the eastern theater: "There are not many officers who of their own choice and impulse will dash in on formidable positions. They will go anywhere they are ordered and anywhere they believe it is their duty to go; but fighting for fun is rare; and unless there is a little of this in a man's disposition he lacks an element. Such men as . . . Custer and some others, attacked wherever they got a chance, and of their own accord. . . . The ordeal is so awful that it requires a peculiar disposition to 'go in gaily,' as old [Philip] Kearny used to say." Theodore Lyman to his wife, June 2, 1864, in George R. Agassiz, ed., Meade's Headquarters, 1863–1865 (Boston: Atlantic Monthly Press, 1922), 139.

16. OR, 1st ser., vol. 11, pt. 1, pp. 111, 525–28, 536, 543, 651–54; Custer to Lydia Ann Reed, May 15, 1862, EBC Collection; O. S. Barrett, Reminiscences, Incidents, Marches, and Camp Life of the Old Fourth Michigan Infantry in War of Rebellion, 1861 to 1864 (Detroit: W. S. Ostler, 1888), 13–14; William H. Powell, The Fifth Army Corps (New York: G. P. Putnam's Sons, 1896), 60–61.

17. Edward H. Wright to Elizabeth Bacon Custer, April 30, 1888, EBC Collection; OR, 1st ser., vol. 11, pt. 3, pp. 198–99.

18. Custer to his parents, March 17, 1862, and to Daniel S. Bacon, May 20,

1863, in Merington, *Custer Story,*
27–28, 52.

19. George Brinton McClellan,
McClellan's Own Story (New York:
Charles L. Webster Publishing Co.,
1887), 365.

20. For the Antietam campaign
and McClellan's political differences
with Lincoln, see Stephen W. Sears,
*Landscape Turned Red: The Battle
of Antietam* (New York: Ticknor and
Fields, 1983). Custer's dispatches,
some of which are cited in the above
study, may be found among the McClellan Papers in the Manuscript Division
of the Library of Congress in Washington, D.C.

21. Frederic E. Ray, *Alfred R.
Waud: Civil War Artist* (New York:
Viking Press, 1974), 38–39; Wilson,
Under the Old Flag 1:126–27.

22. Edward G. Longacre, "Alfred
Pleasonton: 'The Knight of Romance,'"
Civil War Times Illustrated 13 (December 1974): 13–14; Stephen Z. Starr,
The Union Cavalry in the Civil War,
3 vols. (Baton Rouge: Louisiana State
University Press, 1979–85), 1:327, 337–
40; Gregory J. W. Urwin, *The United
States Cavalry: An Illustrated History* (Poole, Dorset: Blandford Press,
1983), 114–20; Special Orders, No. 174,
War Department, Adjutant General's
Office, April 16, 1863, EBC Collection;
Merington, *Custer Story*, 53.

23. For a reconstruction of Pleasonton's devious machinations, see
Edward G. Longacre, *The Cavalry
at Gettysburg: A Tactical Study of
Mounted Operations during the Civil
War's Pivotal Campaign, 9 June–*

14 July 1863 (Rutherford, N.J.: Fairleigh Dickinson University Press,
1986), 48–49, 90; Starr, *Union Cavalry*
1:313–14, 367–69; Merington, *Custer
Story,* 56; Lawrence A. Frost, *General Custer's Libbie* (Seattle: Superior
Publishing Co., 1976), 65.

24. Merington, *Custer Story,* 58;
Longacre, *Cavalry at Gettysburg,* 49,
56–57.

25. Custer to Annette Humphrey,
October 1863, in Merington, *Custer
Story,* 69; Custer to Lydia Ann Reed,
May 16, 27, 1863, EBC Collection.

26. *OR,* 1st ser., vol. 27, pt. 1,
pp. 905, 1046; *Monroe Commercial,* July 23, 1863; *New York Times,*
June 20, 1863; *Detroit Free Press,*
July 10, 1863; Henry C. Meyer, *Civil
War Experiences under Bayard, Gregg,
Kilpatrick, Custer, Raulston, and
Newberry, 1862, 1863, 1864* (New York:
Privately printed, 1911), 33, 48; Frederick Whittaker, *A Complete Life of
Gen. George A. Custer* (New York:
Sheldon and Co., 1876), 155–60.

27. In addition to Hooker, Pleasonton, and Stoneman, Custer's military
references included Major General
Ambrose E. Burnside (Hooker's predecessor as the head of the Army of the
Potomac), Brigadier General Joseph T.
Copeland (the first colonel of the Fifth
Michigan Cavalry and original commander of the Michigan Cavalry Brigade),
Brigadier General Julius Stahel (the
commander of a cavalry division assigned to the defense of Washington),
and Brigadier General Andrew A.
Humphreys (McClellan's former Chief
Topographical Engineer, who had

overseen some of Custer's work in the Peninsular campaign). Custer's politician friend from Monroe was Issac P. Christiancy, an associate justice on the Michigan Supreme Court and a member of the West Point Board of Visitors. *Monroe Commercial*, July 2, 1863; Issac P. Christiancy to Custer, February 10, 1875, Marguerite Meringmton Papers, New York Public Library, New York; *Record of Service of Michigan Troops in the Civil War*, vol. 35: *Fifth Michigan Cavalry* (Kalamazoo: Ihling Bros and Everard, 1905), 1–2; Samuel Harris, *Personal Reminiscences of Samuel Harris* (Chicago: Rogerson Press), 17, 23–24; Meyer, *Civil War Experiences*, 49; Frost, *Libbie*, 41.

28. Blair's choice for the colonelcy, Russell A. Alger, would translate his military record into a long political career, serving two years as the governor of Michigan, two years as the commander-in-chief of the Grand Army of the Republic, five years as a U.S. senator, and as William McKinley's controversial secretary of war during the Spanish-American War. For the politicized nature of officer procurement in the Union army, see Fred Albert Shannon, *The Organization and Administration of the Union Army*, 2 vols. (Cleveland: Arthur H. Clark Co., 1928), 1:158–73.

29. *OR*, 1st ser., vol. 27, pt. 3, p. 373.

30. Alfred Pleasonton to John F. Farnsworth, June 23, 1863, Alfred Pleasonton Papers, Manuscript Division, Library of Congress, Washington, D.C.; Starr, *Union Cavalry* 1:416–17; Longacre, *Cavalry at Gettysburg*, 166.

31. The foreign-born officers Pleasonton marked for oblivion were Julius Stahel (Hungarian), Luigi Palma di Cesnola (Italian), Alfred N. Duffie (French), and Sir Percy Wyndham (English). Longacre, *Cavalry at Gettysburg*, 91, 161.

32. Elon J. Farnsworth to John F. Farnsworth, June 23, 1863, Pleasonton Papers; Don E. Alberts, *Brandy Station to Manila Bay: A Biography of General Wesley Merritt* (Austin, Tex.: Presidial Press, 1980), 1–5.

33. On a more calm occasion, Pleasonton stated, "I regard Custer as one of the finest cavalry officers in the world." C. J. Woods, *Reminiscences of the War* (N.p.: Privately printed, [1880]), 212; Edward Bailey Eaton, *Original Photographs Taken on the Battlefields during the Civil War of the United States by Matthew Brady and Alexander Gardner* (Hartford, Conn.: Privately printed, 1907), 61.

34. Frost, *Libbie*, 106.

35. Custer to Lydia Ann Reed, July 26, 1863, EBC Collection; *OR*, 1st ser., vol. 27, pt. 3, p. 376; J. H. Kidd, *Personal Recollections of a Cavalryman with Custer's Michigan Cavalry Brigade in the Civil War* (1908; reprint, Grand Rapids, Mich.: Black Letter Press, 1969), 53; *Detroit Free Press*, July 10, 1863.

36. Custer to Daniel S. Bacon, September 2, 1864, EBC Collection.

37. Gregory J. W. Urwin, *Custer Victorious: The Civil War Battles of General George Armstrong Custer*

(Rutherford, N.J.: Fairleigh Dickinson University Press, 1983), 73–81; Starr, *Union Cavalry* 1:431–38; Longacre, *Cavalry at Gettysburg*, 220–31, 237–39, 244; Urwin, *United States Cavalry*, 121–22; Asa B. Isham, *An Historical Sketch of the Seventh Regiment Michigan Volunteer Cavalry* (New York: Town Topics Publishing Co., 1893), 28.

38. R. C. Wallace, *A Few Memories of a Long Life* (Helena, Mont.: Privately printed, 1916), 19; *Detroit Free Press*, July 15, 1863.

39. Edwin R. Havens to "Dear Father, Mother, & Nell," July 9, 1863, Edwin R. Havens Papers, Historical Collections, University Archives, Michigan State University, East Lansing.

40. Victor E. Comte to "Dear Elise," July 16, 1863, Victor E. Comte Papers, Michigan Historical Collections, Bentley Historical Library, University of Michigan, Ann Arbor; Urwin, *Custer Victorious*, 89–94.

41. Custer to Daniel S. Bacon, November 20, 1864, Merington Papers.

42. *Chicago Tribune*, July 7, 1876.

43. *New York Herald*, May 17, 1864; Linderman, *Embattled Courage*, 20–28, 35–60, 76–79.

44. James I. Christiancy to Daniel S. Bacon, August 27, 1863, EBC Collection.

45. Urwin, *Custer Victorious*, 57–59, 82; *Chicago Tribune*, July 7, 1876; *New York Herald*, May 17, 1864; *Detroit News Tribune*, May 15, 1910; Meyer, *Civil War Experiences*, 49; Urwin, "Custer's Michigan Cavalry Brigade," 7–15; Elizabeth B. Custer to her parents, May 1, 1864, in Merington, *Custer Story*, 94.

46. Custer to Annette Humphrey, October 12, 1863, in Merington, *Custer Story*, 66; Urwin, *Custer Victorious*, 95–113.

47. Custer suspected that Governor Blair and Brigadier General Joseph T. Copeland (whom Custer had displaced as commander of the Michigan Cavalry Brigade) were behind the effort to discredit him. This was never proven. Custer to Daniel S. Bacon, January 19, 1864, Merington Papers; Custer to Annette Humphrey, August 13, 1863, in Merington, *Custer Story*, 63.

48. Custer to Jacob M. Howard, January 19, 1864, in Hamilton Gay Howard, *Civil War Echoes: Character Sketches and State Secrets* (Washington, D.C.: Howard Publishing Co., 1907), 306–13; Merington, *Custer Story*, 56. Custer was more an anxious rationalizer than a cold-blooded hypocrite. Less than a month before his wedding, he sent his future father-in-law, Daniel S. Bacon, a private letter proclaiming his loyalty to the Lincoln administration, and Judge Bacon detested Lincoln. Custer to Daniel S. Bacon, January 19, 1864, Merington Papers.

49. Among Custer's other new boosters were Senator Schuyler Colfax of Indiana and Representative F. W. Kellogg of Michigan. In October 1864, Kellogg published a letter about Custer and concluded, "He has no superior as a cavalry officer in the Union army, and it is astonishing that he has not been made a Major General before now."

Detroit Advertiser and Tribune, October 19, 1864; Elizabeth B. Custer to her parents, March 28, 1864, and to Custer, early June 1864, in Merington, *Custer Story*, 88, 101.

50. Custer to Daniel S. Bacon, September 2, 1864, EBC Collection; *Detroit Advertiser and Tribune*, October 19, 1864; Roberta E. Fagan, "Custer at Front Royal: 'A Horror of the War,'" in Gregory J. W. Urwin and Roberta E. Fagan, eds., *Custer and His Times: Book Three* (Conway: University of Central Arkansas Press, 1987), 32, 71–72.

51. *OR*, 1st ser., vol. 33, pp. 721, 732–33; Custer to Daniel S. Bacon, April 23, 1864, EBC Collection; Starr, *Union Cavalry* 2:73–76.

52. Theodore Lyman to his wife, February 24, 1864, in Agassiz, *Meade's Headquarters*, 76; Kidd, *Personal Recollections*, 164–65; *Chicago Tribune*, July 7, 1876; Custer to Annette Humphrey, October 20, 1863, in Merington, *Custer Story*, 68; Frost, *Libbie*, 98. For more on Kilpatrick, see John Edward Pierce, "General Hugh Judson Kilpatrick in the American Civil War: A New Appraisal" (Ph.D. diss., Pennsylvania State University, 1983).

53. Custer to Daniel S. Bacon, April 23, 1864, EBC Collection; Custer to Elizabeth Bacon Custer, July 1, 1864, in Merington, *Custer Story*, 111. For more on the Custer-Wilson relationship, see Roberta E. Fagan, "James Harrison Wilson and George Armstrong Custer," *Research Review: The Journal of the Little Big Horn Associates* 1 (June 1987): 34–43, and Edward G. Longacre, *From Union Stars to Top Hat: A Biography of the Extraordinary James Harrison Wilson* (Harrisburg, Pa.: Stackpole Books, 1972).

54. *Detroit Advertiser and Tribune*, April 29, 1864; Custer to Elizabeth Bacon Custer, April 16, 1864, in Merington, *Custer Story*, 89; Starr, *Union Cavalry* 2:76.

55. Philip H. Sheridan, *Personal Memoirs of P. H. Sheridan, General, United States Army*, 2 vols. (New York: Charles L. Webster and Co., 1888), 1:354–57; Custer to Daniel S. Bacon, April 23, 1864, EBC Collection. For a complete picture of Sheridan's long military career, consult both Richard O'Connor, *Sheridan the Inevitable* (Indianapolis: Bobbs-Merrill, 1953), and Paul Andrew Hutton, *Phil Sheridan and His Army* (Lincoln: University of Nebraska Press, 1985).

56. Starr, *Union Cavalry* 2:95–110; Urwin, *Custer Victorious*, 134–45; Urwin, *United States Cavalry*, 125.

57. Custer to Elizabeth Bacon Custer, May 16, 1864, in Merington, *Custer Story*, 97; Urwin, *Custer Victorious*, 145–48; Starr, *Union Cavalry* 2:110–13.

58. Philip H. Sheridan to Edwin M. Stanton, April 6, 1866, EBC Collection.

59. Custer to Elizabeth Bacon Custer, May 14, 1864, and Elizabeth Bacon Custer to Custer, Fall 1864, in Merington, *Custer Story*, 97, 118. Sheridan once told a major in the Sixth Michigan Cavalry that

whenever his troops ran into trouble, "they all wanted to see Custer and the Michigan Brigade." *Chicago Tribune*, July 7, 1876; *New York Times*, June 2, August 12, 20, 25, 27, 29, 31, September 5, 1864; *New York Herald*, June 21, 1864; *New York Daily Tribune*, August 22, 24, 1864; *Detroit Free Press*, July 17, 1864.

60. *OR*, 1st ser., vol. 43, pt. 1, pp. 455–58, pt. 2, pp. 158, 177, 218; *Chicago Tribune*, July 7, 1876; Harris H. Beecher, *Record of the 114th Regiment N.Y.S.V.* (Norwich, N.Y.: J. F. Hubbard, Jr., 1886), 426–28; Kidd, *Personal Recollections*, 390–94; Grady McWhiney and Perry D. Jamieson, *Attack and Die: Civil War Military Tactics and the Southern Heritage* (University: University of Alabama Press, 1982), 126–39.

61. Stephen Z. Starr, "The Last Days of Rebellion," *Cincinnati Historical Society Bulletin* 35 (1977): 11.

62. Custer to Daniel S. Bacon, September 2, 1864, EBC Collection; Publication Committee of the Regimental Association, eds., *History of the Eighteenth Regiment of Cavalry Pennsylvania Volunteers* (New York: Privately printed, 1909), 59–60; Henry Norton, *Deeds of Daring; or, History of the Eighth N.Y. Volunteer Cavalry* (Norwich, N.Y.: Chenango Telegraph Printing House, 1889), 93–95; Starr, "Last Days of Rebellion," 9; Luman H. Tenney, *War Diary of Luman Harris Tenney, 1861–1865* (Cleveland: Evangelical Publishing House, 1914), 132; Starr, *Union Cavalry* 2:297–301.

63. Robert G. Athearn, ed., "The Civil War Diary of John Wilson Phillips," *Virginia Magazine of History and Biography* 62 (January 1954): 118; *OR*, 1st ser., vol. 43, pt. 1, p. 34; *New York Tribune*, October 25, 1864; Urwin, *Custer Victorious*, 205–30.

64. Three such petitions (dated November 18, November 27, and December 7, 1864), bearing hundreds of signatures, are preserved in the EBC Collection.

65. Starr, "Last Days of Rebellion," 9.

66. James H. Stevenson, *"Boots and Saddles": A History of the First Volunteer Cavalry Regiment of the War Known As the First New York (Lincoln) Cavalry, and Also As the Sabre Regiment* (Harrisburg, Pa.: Patriot Publishing Co., 1879), 345; Starr, *Union Cavalry* 2:425–88; *OR*, 1st ser., vol. 46, pt. 1, pp. 1132, 1136.

67. *OR*, 1st ser., vol. 46, pt. 1, pp. 1109, 1132; Starr, "Last Days of Rebellion," 11–18; William H. Beach, *The First New York (Lincoln) Cavalry from April 19, 1861, to July 7, 1865* (New York: Lincoln Cavalry Association, 1902), 506; Luman H. Tenney to his mother and sisters, April 8, 1866, in Tenney, *War Diary*, 158–59.

68. Starr, *Union Cavalry* 2:480–86.

69. Sheridan to Elizabeth Bacon Custer, April 10, 1865, in Merington, *Custer Story*, 159.

70. Roger Hannaford, "Reminiscences," Box 3, Folder 3, pp. 3–4, Roger Hannaford Papers, Cincinnati Historical Society, Cincinnati, Ohio.

For appraisals of Custer's Civil War generalship, see Starr, *Union Cavalry* 2:294–95, 487–88; Urwin, *Custer Victorious*, 265–86. For instances where Union infantrymen cheered Custer, see *Providence Daily Journal*, September 30, 1864; *New York Times*, April 14, 1865; Athearn, "John Wilson Phillips," 119; Publication Committee, *Eighteenth Regiment*, 60.

FROM WEST POINT TO THE BATTLEFIELD

G. A. CUSTER

In June, 1857, I entered the Military Academy at West Point as a cadet, having received my appointment thereto through the kindness of the Hon. John W. Bingham, then representing in Congress the district in Ohio in which I was born, and in which I had spent almost my entire boyhood. The first official notification received by me of my appointment to the Military Academy bore the signature of Jefferson Davis, then Secretary of War in the cabinet of President James Buchanan. Colonel Richard Delafield, one of the ablest and most accomplished officers of the Engineer Corps, occupied the position of superintendent of the Academy, and Lieutenant-Colonel Wm. J. Hardee, of the cavalry, afterward lieutenant-general in the Confederate army, was the commandant of the Corps of Cadets.

During the four years spent by me at West Point there were stationed there, either as officers in the capacity of instructors, or as cadets, several who afterward became more or less distinguished in the war of rebellion. Of these I now recall Lieutenant James B. Fry, post adjutant; Lieutenant John Gibbon, post quartermaster; Lieutenants George L. Hartsuff and Charles L. Griffin, instructors of artillery; Lieutenants John M. Schofield and Cyrus B. Comstock, instructors of natural philosophy, etc.; Lieutenants Wm. B. Hazen and Alex. McD. McCook, instructors of infantry tactics; Lieutenant Godfrey Weitzel, instructor of engineering. These all achieved, a few years later, the rank of major-general in the Union armies, and commanded either armies or corps, or filled equally responsible and honorable positions. Of those whom I remember as instructors, and who, casting their fortunes with the forces of the South, afterward attained high rank, and who were then captains or lieutenants, were Charles W. Field, John Pegram, Fitzhugh Lee, Cadmus Wilcox, and John Forney. Of those who were cadets with me between the years of 1857 and 1861, there were quite a number who became more or less distinguished during the war. Of those who fought for the Union were Hardin, Merritt, Kilpatrick, Ames, Upton, and McKenzie, each of whom within less than three years from the date of his departure from the Academy won by bravery and distinguished conduct on the field of battle the star of brigadier-general. Most of these attained before the termination of the war the high grade of major-general. Among those joining the Confederate force who rose to distinction were Wheeler, Rosser, Young, Robertson, and Kelley, all of whom became general officers and rendered highly important service in the cause for which they battled. It is somewhat remarkable that these five general officers held commands in the cavalry, as did also three of the six—Merritt, Kilpatrick, and McKenzie—named on the Union side—to which list I might add my own name—thus showing that the cavalry offered the most promising field for early promotion.

A few months prior to the breaking out of the war, Beauregard, then a major of Engineers, was ordered to West Point as superintendent of the Academy; but whether because he foresaw the events of the near future, or from other motives, he applied to be relieved from the effect of the order. His application was granted, and he took his departure after a sojourn of but a few days.

Among the noticeable features of cadet life as then impressed upon me, and still present in my memory, were the sectional lines voluntarily established by the cadets themselves; at first barely distinguishable, but in the later years immediately preceding the war as clearly defined and strongly drawn as were the lines separating the extremes of the various sections in the national Congress. Nor was this fact a strange or remarkable one. As each Congressional district and territory of the United States had a representative in Congress, so each had its representatives at the Military Academy. And there was no phase of the great political questions of the times, particularly the agitation of the slavery question as discussed and maintained by the various agitators in Congress, but found its exponents among the cadets. In fact the latter as a rule reflected the political sentiments of the particular member who represented in Congress the locality from which the cadet happened to hail. Of course there were exceptions to this rule, but in the absence of any clearly formed political sentiment or belief of his own, it seemed to be the fashion, if nothing more, that each particular cadet should adopt the declared views and opinions of his representative in Congress. Hence it was no difficult matter to find exponents of the greatest political extremes; from the sturdy and pronounced abolitionist, hailing from New England, or perhaps the Western reserve in Ohio, to the most rabid of South Carolina nullifiers or Georgia fire-eaters. While the advocates for and against slavery were equally earnest and determined, those from the South were always the most talkative if not argumentative. As the pronounced abolitionist was rarely seen in Congress in those days, so was his appearance among the cadets of still rarer occurrence; besides it required more than ordinary moral and physical courage to boldly avow oneself an abolitionist. The name was considered one of opprobrium, and the cadet who had the courage to avow himself an abolitionist must be prepared to face the social frowns of the great majority of his comrades and at times to defend his opinions by his physical strength and metal. The John Brown raid into Virginia stirred the wrathful indignation of the embryonic warriors who looked upon slavery as an institution beyond human interference; while those of the opposite extreme contented themselves by quietly chuckling over the alarm into which the executive and military forces of the entire State were thrown by the invasion led by Brown, backed by a score or two of adherents.

The Presidential campaign which resulted in the election of Abraham Lincoln was not more hotly argued and contested by the regular stump speakers of either party than by the Northern and Southern cadets in their efforts to re-echo the political sentiments of their respective sections. The Republicans of course espoused the cause championed by Lincoln and Hamlin and the extreme Democrats announced themselves as under the banner of Breckinridge and Lane. A son of the latter was a member of my class, and occupied an adjoining room. The more moderate of the Democrats declared for Douglas and Johnson, while a few neutrals from the border States shouted feebly for Bell and Everett. The Breckinridge army of Southern Democrats did not hesitate to announce, as their seniors in and out of Congress had done, that in the event of Lincoln's election secession would be the only resource left to the South. So high did political feeling run among the cadets, or a portion of them, that Mr. Lincoln was hung in effigy one night to a limb of one of the shade trees growing in front of cadet barracks. The effigy was removed early in the morning—so early that few of the cadets or professors even knew of the occurrence.

It seemed to have been part of the early teaching of the Southern youth, that the disruption of the Union was an event surely to be brought about. As an illustration of this I remember that Congress had appointed a committee in 1859, I believe, to visit West Point, and determine whether the course of study should continue to be five years, or be reduced to four. This committee was composed of two United States Senators, two members of the House, as many officers of the Army. Jefferson Davis, then a Senator from Mississippi, and a member of the Military Committee of the Senate, was a member of this special committee. The cadets, anxious to render their detention at the Academy as brief as possible, were warmly interested in the result of the committee's labors and investigation, and hoped ardently that the report would induce Congress to shorten the term of study from five to four years. To their great disappointment, however, it was soon after announced that the committee had reported in favor of continuance of the five-year system of instruction. It was believed by the cadets that this conclusion had been reached through the great influence of Jefferson Davis in the committee; an influence which his military ability, and particularly his experience and high reputation won while filling the office of Secretary of War, had properly given him. Whether justly or not, the disappointment of the cadets was loudly expressed when in groups by themselves. In one instance when the subject was being discussed a Georgia cadet, afterward distinguished in the war, indulged in the most bitter invectives against Davis, whom he charged with being the person responsible for detaining us an additional year in the Academy, concluding his execration by verbally consigning the object of his youthful ire to a locality hotter even than his native State. The next moment, however, he corrected himself in the most solemn manner by remarking, "No, I'll take that all back; for I believe the day is coming when the South will have need of Mr. Davis's abilities."

In looking back over the few months and years passed at West Point immediately preceding the war some strange incidents recur to my mind. When the various State conventions were called by the different States of the South with a view to the adoption of the ordinance of secession, it became only a question of time as to the attempted

withdrawal of the seceding States. And while there were those representing both sections in Congress who professed to believe that war
would not necessarily or probably follow, this opinion was not shared in
even by persons as young and inexperienced as the cadets were. War
was anticipated by them at that time and discussed and looked forward
to as an event of the future with as much certainty as if speaking of
an approaching season. The cadets from the South were in constant
receipt of letters from their friends at home, keeping them fully advised of the real situation and promising them suitable positions in the
military force yet to be organized to defend the ordinance of secession.
All this was a topic of daily if not hourly conversation. Particularly was
this true when we assembled together at meal time, when, grouped in
squads of half a dozen or more, each usually found himself in the midst
of his personal friends.

I remember a conversation held at the table at which I sat during
the winter of '60–'61. I was seated next to Cadet P.M.B. Young, a gallant young fellow from Georgia, a classmate of mine, then and since the
war an intimate and valued friend—a major-general in the Confederate forces during the war and a member of Congress from his native
State at a later date. The approaching war was as usual the subject
of conversation in which all participated, and in the freest and most
friendly manner; the lads from the North discoursing earnestly upon
the power and rectitude of the National Government, the impulsive
Southron holding up pictures of invaded rights and future independence. Finally, in a half jocular, half earnest manner, Young turned to
me and delivered himself as follows: "Custer, my boy, we're going to
have war. It's no use talking: I see it coming. All the Crittenden com-
promises that can be patched up won't avert it. Now let me prophesy
what will happen to you and me. You will go home, and your abolition
Governor will probably make you colonel of a cavalry regiment. I will
go down to Georgia, and ask Governor Brown to give me a cavalry
regiment. And who knows but we may move against each other during the war. You will probably get the advantage of us in the first few
engagements, as your side will be rich and powerful, while we will be
poor and weak. Your regiment will be armed with the best of weapons,
the sharpest of sabres; mine will have only shotguns and scythe blades;
but for all that we'll get the best of the fight in the end, because we will
fight for a principle, a cause, while you will fight only to perpetuate the

abuse of power." Lightly as we both regarded this boyish prediction, it was destined to be fulfilled in a remarkable degree. Early in the war I did apply, not to the abolition Governor of my native State, but to that of Michigan, for a cavalry regiment. I was refused, but afterward obtained the regiment I desired as a part of my command. Young was chosen to lead one of the Georgia cavalry regiments. Both of us rose to higher commands, and confronted each other on the battlefield.

On December 20, 1860, South Carolina formally led the way by adopting the ordinance of secession; an example which was followed within the next few weeks by Mississippi, Alabama, Florida, Georgia, Louisiana, and Texas, in the order named. As soon as it became evident that these States were determined to attempt secession, the cadets appointed therefrom, imitating the action of their Senators and representatives in Congress, and influenced by the appeals of friends at home, tendered their resignations, eager to return to their homes and take part in the organization of the volunteer forces which the increasing difficulties and dangers of the situation rendered necessary. Besides, as the Confederate Congress was called to meet for the first time at Montgomery, Alabama, February 6, 1861, and would undoubtedly authorize the appointment of a large number of officers in the formation of the Confederate armies, it was important that applicants for positions of this kind should be on the ground to properly present their claims.

No obstacle was interposed by the Government to prevent the departure of the cadets from the South, although it seemed to me then, as it does now, strange that the Government did not adopt measures which would prevent the opponents of the national authority from availing themselves of the services and abilities of those who had been educated at the public expense. They knew the purpose of these cadets, like that of the many officers of the army who resigned, was to serve against the Government, and had a just and unquestioned claim, according to the terms of their oath of office, upon their loyalty and faithful service until freed from their allegiance by the acceptance of their resignation or their discharge. They could have refused to accept the resignations of all persons in the military service when there was reason to believe that such persons intended to aid the public enemy. Without the exercise of any greater or more questionable authority than that frequently exercised at a later period of the war, the Government could have promptly arrested and confined every person, of whatever rank in the military service, who tendered his resignation in the face of the enemy or in anticipation of a coming conflict. Thus the South would have been shorn of its chief military strength by being deprived of all its great military leaders. A few rash, thoughtless men might have fled to the seceded States, but the vast majority, being bound to the National Government by the solemn obligations of their oaths, would have rendered obedience, even if distasteful, to the demands of the national authority, until that authority should consent to release them from their obligations of duty, as it did by accepting their resignations. To have done otherwise would have been to commit the double offense of perjury and desertion; and I have too high an opinion of the sense of honor which governed the men who afterward became the gallant but mistaken leaders of the Confederate armies, to suppose them capable of this.

One by one the places occupied by the cadets from the seceding States became vacant; it cost many a bitter pang to disrupt the intimate relations existing between the hot-blooded Southron and his more phlegmatic schoolmate from the North. No schoolgirls could have been more demonstrative in their affectionate regard for each other than were some of the cadets about to separate for the last time, and under circumstances which made it painful to contemplate a future coming together. Those leaving for the South were impatient, enthusiastic, and hopeful. Visions filled their minds of a grand and glorious confederacy, glittering with the pomp and pageantry which usually characterizes imperial power, and supported and surrounded by a mighty army, the officers of which would constitute a special aristocracy.

Their comrades from the North, whom they were leaving behind, were reserved almost to sullenness; were grave almost to stoicism. The representatives of the two sections had each resolved upon their course of action; and each in a manner characteristic of their widely different temperaments, as different as the latitudes from which they hailed. Among the first of the cadets to leave West Point and hasten to enroll themselves under the banner of the seceding States, were two of my classmates, Kelley and Ball of Alabama. Kelley became prominent in the war, and was killed in battle. Ball also attained a high rank, and is now a prominent official in one of the most extensive and well-known business enterprises in this country. They took their departure from the Academy on Saturday. I remember the date the more readily as I was engaged in—to adopt the cadet term—"walking an extra," which consisted in performing the tiresome duties of a sentinel during the unemployed hour of Saturday; hours usually given to recreation. On this occasion I was pacing back and forth on my post, which for the time being extended along the path leading from the cadets' chapel toward the academic building, when I saw a party of from fifteen to twenty cadets emerge from the open space between the mess hall and academic building, and direct their steps toward the steamboat landing below. That which particularly attracted my attention was the bearing aloft upon the shoulders of their comrades of my two classmates Ball and Kelley, as they were being carried in triumph from the doors of the Academy to the steamboat landing. Too far off to exchange verbal adieux, even if military discipline had permitted it, they caught sight of me as step by step I reluctantly paid the penalty of offended regulations, and raised their hats in token of farewell, to which, first casting my eyes about to see that no watchful superior was in view, I responded by bringing my musket to a "present."

The comrades who escorted them were Southerners like themselves, and only awaiting the formal action of their respective States on the adoption of the secession ordinance to follow their example. It was but a few weeks until there was scarcely a cadet remaining at the Academy from the Southern States. Many resigned from the border States without waiting to see whether their State would follow in the attempt at secession or not; some resigned who had been appointed from States which never voted to leave the Union; while an insignificant few, who had resolved to join the Confederate forces, but desired to obtain their diplomas from the academic faculty, remained until the date of their graduation. Some remained until long after the declaration and commencement of hostilities; then, allowing the Government to transport them to Washington, tendered their resignations, and were dismissed for doing so in the face of the enemy. Happily the number that pursued this questionable course did not exceed half a dozen.

At no point in the loyal States were the exciting events of the spring of 1861 watched with more intense interest than at West Point. And after the departure of the Southern cadets the hearts of the people of no community, State, town, or village beat with more patriotic impulse than did those of the young cadets at West Point. Casting aside all questions of personal ambition or promotion; realizing only that the Government which they had sworn to defend, the principles they had been taught from childhood, were in danger, and threatened by armed enemies, they would gladly have marched to battle as private soldiers, rather than remain idle spectators in the great conflict.

As the time for the inauguration of Mr. Lincoln approached, rumors prevailed, and obtained wide belief, to the effect that a plot was on foot by which the inauguration of Mr. Lincoln was to be made the occasion on the part of the enemies of the Government, of whom great numbers were known to be in Washington, for seizing or making away with the executive officers of the nation, and taking possession of the people's capital. Whether or not such a scheme was ever seriously contemplated, it was deemed prudent to provide against it. The available military resources of the Government amounted to but little at that period. Lieutenant-General Scott, then commander-in-chief of the army, issued orders for the assembling at Washington of as large a military force as circumstances would permit. Under this order it became necessary to make a demand upon the regular military forces then employed at West Point. A battery of artillery was hastily organized from the war material and horses kept at the Academy for the purpose of instruction to the cadets. The horses were supplied by taking those used by the cadets in their cavalry and artillery drills. The force thus organized hastened to Washington, where, under the command of Captain Griffin— afterward Major-General Griffin—it took part in the inaugural ceremonies. Then followed the firing upon Sumter, the intelligence of which waked the slumbering echoes of loyalty and patriotism in every home and hamlet throughout the North.

It is doubtful if the people of the North were ever, or will ever be again, so united in thought and impulse as when the attack on Sumter was flashed upon them. Opponents in politics became friends in patriotism; all differences of opinion vanished or were laid aside, and a single purpose filled and animated the breast of the people as of one man— a purpose unflinching and unrestrained—to rush to the rescue of the Government, to beat down its opposers, come from whence they may. In addition to sharing the common interest and anxiety of the public in the attack upon Sumter, the cadets felt a special concern from the fact that among the little band of officers shut up in that fortress were two, Lieutenant Snyder and Hall, who had been our comrades as cadets only a few months before.

As already stated, the time of study and instruction at West Point at that period was five years, in the determination and fixing of which no one had exercised greater influence than Jefferson Davis—first as Secretary of War, afterward as United States Senator and member of a special Congressional committee to consider the question as to whether the course should extend to five years or only include four. There was no single individual in or out of Congress, excepting perhaps the venerable Lieutenant-General at the head of the army, whose opinions on military questions affecting the public service had greater weight than those of Jefferson Davis up to the date of his withdrawal from the Senate in January, 1861. As a Secretary of War he displayed an ability and achieved a reputation which has not since been approached by any of the numerous incumbents of that office, if we except Secretary Stanton. It is doubtful, however, if his administration of the duties of the war office in time of a great war like that of the rebellion, would have been successful. His strong prejudices for and against particular individuals, as illustrated in later years, would have tended to embarrass rather than promote a great cause.

In the general demand in 1861, not only from the National Government, but from States, for competent and educated officers to instruct and command the new levies of troops then being raised, in response to the call of the President, to oppose the rebellion, it was decided by the authorities at Washington to abandon the five years' course of instruction at the Military Academy, and reestablish that of four years. The effect of this was to give to the service in that year two classes of graduates for officers instead of but one. By this change the class of which I was a member graduated, under the four years' system, in June, while the preceding class was graduated, under the five years' rule, only a couple of months in advance of us. The members of both classes, with but few exceptions, were at once ordered to Washington, where they were employed either in drilling raw volunteers or serving on the staffs of general officers engaged in organizing the new regiments into brigades and divisions. I was one of the exceptions referred to, and the causes which led me in a different direction may be worthy of mention. My career as a cadet had but little to commend it to the study of those who came after me, unless as an example to be carefully avoided. The requirements of the academic regulations, a copy of which was placed in my hand the morning of my arrival at West Point, were not observed by me in such manner at all times as to commend me to the approval and good opinions of my instructors and superior officers. My offences against law and order were not great in enormity, but what they lacked in magnitude they made up in number. The forbidden locality of Benny Havens possessed stronger attractions than the study and demonstrations of a problem in Euclid, or the prosy discussion of some abstract proposition of moral science. My class numbered upon entering the Academy about one hundred and twenty-five. Of this number only thirty-four graduated, and of these thirty-three graduated above me. The resignation and departure of the Southern cadets took away from the Academy a few individuals who, had they remained, would probably have contested with me the debatable honor of bringing up the rear of the class.

We had passed our last examination as cadets, had exchanged barrack for camp life, and were awaiting the receipt of orders from Washington assigning us to the particular branches of the service for which we had been individually recommended by the academic faculty. The month of June had come, and we were full of impatience to hasten to the capital and join the forces preparing for the coming campaign. It is customary, or was then, to allow each cadet, prior to his graduation, to perform at least one tour of duty as an officer of the guard, instead of the ordinary duties of a private soldier on guard. I had not only had the usual experience in the latter capacity, extending over a period of four years, but in addition had been compelled, as punishment for violations of the academic regulations, to perform extra tours of guard duty on Saturdays—times which otherwise I should have been allowed for pleasure and recreation. If my memory serves me right, I devoted sixty-six Saturdays to this method of vindicating outraged military law during my cadetship of four years. It so happened that it fell to my detail to perform the duties of officer of the guard in camp, at a time when the arrival of the order from Washington officially transforming us from cadets to officers was daily expected. I began my tour at the usual hour in the morning, and everything passed off satisfactorily in connection with the discharge of my new responsibilities, until just at dusk I heard a commotion near the guard tents. Upon hastening to the scene of the disturbance, which by the way was at a considerable distance from the main camp, I found two cadets engaged in a personal dispute, which threatened to result in blows. Quite a group of cadets, as friends and spectators, had formed about the two bellicose disputants.

I had hardly time to take in the situation when the two principals of the group engaged in a regular set-to, and began belaboring each other vigorously with their fists. Some of their more prudent friends rushed forward and attempted to separate the two contestants. My duty as officer of the guard was plain and simple. I should have arrested the two combatants and sent them to the guard tents for violating the peace and the regulations of the Academy. But the instincts of the boy prevailed over the obligation of the officer of the guard. I pushed my way through the surrounding line of cadets, dashed back those who were interfering in the struggle, and called out loudly, "Stand back, boys; let's have a fair fight."

I had occasion to remember, if not regret, the employment of these words. Scarcely had I uttered them when the crowd about me dispersed hurriedly, and fled to the concealment of their tents. Casting about me to ascertain the cause of this sudden dispersion, I beheld approaching at a short distance two officers of the army, Lieutenants Hazen and Merrill (now Major-General Hazen and Colonel Merrill of the Engineer Corps). I sought the tent of the officer of the guards promptly, but the mischief had been done. Lieutenant Hazen was the officer in charge on that particular day, whose duty it was to take cognizance of the violations of the regulations. Summoning me to his presence, near the scene of the unfortunate disturbance, he asked me in stern tones if I was not the officer of the guard; to which I of course responded in the affirmative. He then overwhelmed me by inquiring in the same unrelenting voice, "Why did you not suppress the riot which occurred here a few minutes ago?" Now, it had never been suggested to me that the settlement of a personal difficulty between two boys, even by the administering of blows, could be considered or described as a riot. The following morning I was required to report at the tent of the commandant (Lieutenant-Colonel John F. Reynolds, afterward General Reynolds, killed at Gettysburg). Of course no explanation could satisfy the requirements of military justice. I was ordered to return to my tent in arrest. The facts in the case were reported to Washington, on formal charges and specifications, and a court-martial asked for to determine the degree of my punishment.

Within a few hours of my arrest the long-expected order came, relieving my class from further duty at West Point, and directing the members of it to proceed to Washington and report to the Adjutant-

General of the Army for further orders. My name, however, did not appear in this list. I was to be detained to await the application of the commandant for a court-martial to sit on my case. The application received approval at the War Department, and a court was assembled at West Point, composed principally of officers who had recently arrived from Texas, where they served under General Twiggs, until his surrender to the Confederate forces. The judge advocate of the court was Lieutenant Benet, now Brigadier-General and Chief of the Ordnance Corps. I was arraigned with all the solemnity and gravity which might be looked for in a trial for high treason, the specification setting forth in stereotyped phraseology that "He, the said cadet Custer, did fail to suppress a riot or disturbance near the guard tent, and did fail to separate, etc., but, on the contrary, did cry out in a loud tone of voice, 'Stand back, boys; let's have a fair fight,' or words to that effect."

To which accusations the accused pleaded "Guilty," as a matter of course, introducing as witnesses, by way of mitigation, the two cadets, the cause of my difficulty, to prove that neither was seriously injured in the fray. One of them is now a promising young captain in the Engineer Corps.

The trial was brief, scarcely occupying more time than did the primary difficulty.

I dreaded the long detention which I feared I must undergo while awaiting not only the verdict, but the subsequent action of the authorities at Washington to whom the case must by law be submitted.

My classmates who had preceded me to Washington interested themselves earnestly in my behalf to secure my release from further arrest at West Point, and an order for me to join them at the national capital. Fortunately some of them had influential friends there, and it was but a few days after my trial that the superintendent of the Academy received a telegraphic order from Washington, directing him to release me at once, and order me to report to the Adjutant-General of the Army for duty. This order practically rendered the action and proceedings of the court-martial in my case nugatory. The record, I presume, was forwarded to the War Department, where it probably lies safely stowed away in some pigeonhole. What the proceeding of the court or their decision was, I have never learned.

I left West Point on the 18th of July for Washington, delaying a few hours that afternoon on my arrival in New York to enable me to purchase, of the well-known military firm of Horstmann's, my lieutenant's outfit of sabre, revolver, sash, spurs, etc. Taking the evening train for Washington, I found the cars crowded with troops, officers and men, hastening to the capital.

At each station we passed on the road at which a halt was made, crowds of citizens were assembled provided bountifully with refreshments, which they distributed in the most lavish manner among the troops. Their enthusiasm knew no bounds; they received us with cheers and cheered us in parting. It was no unusual sight, on leaving a station surrounded by these loyal people, to see matrons and maidens embracing and kissing with patriotic fervor the men, entire strangers to them, whom they saw hastening to the defence of the nation.

Arriving at Washington soon after daylight, Saturday morning, the 20th of July, I made my way to the Ebbit House, where I expected to find some of my classmates domiciled. Among others whom I found there was Parker, appointed from Missouri, who had been my room and tent-mate at West Point for years. He was one of the few members of my class who, while sympathizing with the South, had remained at the Academy long enough to graduate and secure a diploma. Proceeding to his room without going through the formality of announcing my arrival by sending up a card, I found him at that early hour still in bed. Briefly he responded to my anxious inquiry for news, that McDowell's army was confronting Beauregard's, and a general engagement was expected hourly. My next inquiry was as to his future plans and intentions, remembering his Southern sympathies. To this he replied by asking me to take from a table near by and read an official order to which he pointed.

Upon opening the document referred to, I found it to be an order from the War Department dismissing from the rolls of the army Second Lieutenant James P. Parker, for having tendered his resignation in the face of the enemy. The names of two others of my classmates appeared in the same order. Both the latter have since sought and obtained commissions in the Egyptian army under the Khedive. After an hour or more spent in discussing the dark probabilities of the future as particularly affected by the clouds of impending war, I bade a fond farewell to my former friend and classmate, with whom I had lived on terms of closer intimacy and companionship than with any other being. We had eaten day by day at the same table, had struggled together in the effort to master the same problems of study; we had marched

by each other's side year after year, elbow to elbow, when engaged
in the duties of drill, parade, etc., and had shared our blankets with
each other when learning the requirements of camp life. Henceforth
this was all to be thrust from our memory as far as possible, and our
paths and aims in life were to run counter to each other in the future.
We separated; he to make his way, as he did immediately, to the seat
of the Confederate Government, and accept a commission under a flag
raised in rebellion against the Government that had educated him, and
that he had sworn to defend; I to proceed to the office of the Adjutant-
General of the Army and report for such duty as might be assigned me
in the great work which was then dearest and uppermost in the mind
of every loyal citizen of the country.

It was not until after two o'clock in the morning that I obtained an
audience with the Adjutant-General of the Army and reported to him
formally for orders, as my instructions directed me to do. I was greatly
impressed by the number of officials I saw and the numerous messengers to be seen flitting from room to room, bearing immense numbers of
huge-looking envelopes. The entire department had an air of busy occupation which, taken in connection with the important military events
then daily transpiring and hourly expected, and contrasted with the
hum-drum life I had but lately led as a cadet, added to the bewilderment
I naturally felt.

Presenting my order of instructions to the officer who seemed to be
in charge of the office, he glanced at it, and was about to give some
directions to a subordinate near by to write out an order assigning me to
some duty, when, turning to me, he said, "Perhaps you would like to be
presented to General Scott, Mr. Custer?" To which of course I joyfully
assented. I had often beheld the towering form of the venerable chieftain during his summer visits to West Point, but that was the extent
of my personal acquaintance with him. So strict was the discipline at
the Academy that the gulf which separated cadets from commissioned
officers seemed greater in practice than that which separated enlisted
men from them. Hence it was rare indeed that a cadet ever had an
opportunity to address or be addressed by officers, and it was still more
rare to be brought into personal conversation with an officer above the
grade of lieutenant or captain; if we except the superintendent of the
Academy and the commandant of the corps of cadets. The sight of a
general officer, let alone the privilege of speaking to one, was an event

to be recounted to one's friends. In those days the title of general was not so familiar as to be encountered on every hotel register. Besides, the renown of a long lifetime gallantly spent in his country's service had gradually but justly placed General Scott far above all contemporary chieftains in the admiration and hero worship of his fellow countrymen; and in the youthful minds of the West Point cadets of those days Scott was looked up to as a leader whose military abilities were scarcely second to those of a Napoleon, and whose patriotism rivalled that of Washington.

Following the lead of the officer to whom I had reported, I was conducted to the room in which General Scott received his official visitors. I found him seated at a table over which were spread maps and other documents which plainly showed their military character. In the room, and seated near the table, were several members of Congress, of whom I remember Senator Grimes of Iowa. The topic of conversation was the approaching battle in which General McDowell's forces were about to engage. General Scott seemed to be explaining to the Congressmen the position, as shown by the map, of the contending armies. The Adjutant-General called General Scott's attention to me by saying, "General, this is Lieutenant Custer of the Second Cavalry; he has just reported from West Point, and I did not know but that you might have some special orders to give him." Looking at me a moment, the General shook me cordially by the hand, saying, "Well, my young friend, I am glad to welcome you to the service at this critical time. Our country has need of the strong arms of all her loyal sons in this emergency." Then, turning to the Adjutant-General, he inquired to which company I had been assigned. "To Company G, Second Cavalry, now under Major Innes Palmer, with General McDowell," was the reply. Then, addressing me, the General said, "We have had the assistance of quite a number of you young men from the Academy, drilling volunteers, etc. Now what can I do for you? Would you prefer to be ordered to report to General Mansfield to aid in this work, or is your desire for something more active?" Although overwhelmed by such condescension upon the part of one so far superior in rank to any officer with whom I had been brought in immediate contact, I ventured to stammer out that I earnestly desired to be ordered to at once join my company, then with General McDowell, as I was anxious to see active service. "A very commendable resolution, young man," was the reply; then, turning to the Adjutant-General, he added,

"Make out Lieutenant Custer's orders directing him to proceed to his company at once"; then, as if a different project had presented itself, he inquired of me if I had been able to provide myself with a mount for the field. I replied that I had not, but would set myself about doing so at once. "I fear you have a difficult task before you, because, if rumor is correct, every serviceable horse in the city has been bought, borrowed, or begged by citizens who have gone or are going as spectators to witness the battle. I only hope Beauregard may capture some of them and teach them a lesson. However, what I desire to say to you is, go and provide yourself with a horse if possible, and call here at seven o'clock this evening. I desire to send some dispatches to General McDowell, and you can be the bearer of them. You are not afraid of a night ride, are you?" Exchanging salutations, I left the presence of the General-in-Chief, delighted at the prospect of being at once thrown into active service, perhaps participating in the great battle which every one there knew was on the eve of occurring; but more than this my pride as a soldier was not a little heightened by the fact that almost upon my first entering the service I was to be the bearer of important official dispatches from the General-in-Chief to the General commanding the principal army in the field.

I had yet a difficult task before me, in procuring a mount. I visited all the prominent livery stables, but received almost the same answer from each, the substance of which was, that I was too late; all the disposable horses had been let or engaged. I was almost in despair at the idea that I was not to be able to take advantage of the splendid opportunity for distinction opened before me, and was at a loss what to do, or to whom to apply for advice, when I met on Pennsylvania avenue a soldier in uniform, whom I at once recognized as one of the detachment formerly stationed at West Point, who left with those ordered suddenly to the defence of Washington at the time of Mr. Lincoln's inauguration, when it was feared attempts would be made to assassinate the President elect. Glad to encounter any one I had ever seen before, I approached and asked him what he was doing in Washington. He answered that he belonged to Griffin's battery, which was then with McDowell's forces at the front, and had returned to Washington, by Captain Griffin's order, to obtain and take back with him an extra horse left by the battery on its departure from the capital. Here then was my opportunity, and I at once availed myself of it. It was the intention of this man to set out on his return at once; but at my earnest solicitation he consented to defer his departure until after seven o'clock, agreeing also to have the extra horse saddled and in readiness for me.

Promptly at seven o'clock I reported at the Adjutant-General's office, obtaining my dispatches, and with no baggage or extra clothing to weight down my horse, save what I carried on my person, I repaired to the point at which I was to find my horse and companion for the night. Upon arriving there I was both surprised and delighted to discover that the horse which accident seemed to have provided for me was a favorite one ridden by me often when learning the cavalry exercises at West Point. Those who were cadets just before the war will probably recall him to mind when I give the name, "Wellington," by which he was then known.

Crossing Long bridge about nightfall, and taking the Fairfax C.H. road for Centreville, the hours of night flew quickly past, engrossed as my mind was with the excitement and serious novelty of the occasion as well as occasionally diverted by the conversation of my companion. I was particularly interested with his description, given as we rode in the silent darkness, of a skirmish which had taken place only two days before at Blackburn's ford, between the forces of the enemy stationed there and a reconnoitring detachment sent from General McDowell's army; especially when I learned that my company had borne an honorable part in the affair.

It was between two and three o'clock in the morning when we reached the army near Centreville. The men had already breakfasted, and many of the regiments had been formed in column in the roads ready to resume the march; but owing to delays in starting, most of the men were lying on the ground, endeavoring to catch a few minutes more of sleep; others were sitting or standing in small groups smoking and chatting. So filled did I find the road with soldiers that it was with difficulty my horse could pick his way among the sleeping bodies without disturbing them. But for my companion I should have had considerable difficulty in finding my way to headquarters; but he seemed familiar with the localities even in the darkness, and soon conducted me to a group of tents near which a large log fire was blazing, throwing a bright light over the entire scene for some distance around. As I approached, the sound of my horse's hoofs brought an officer from one of the tents nearest to where I halted. Advancing toward me, he inquired who I wished to see. I informed him that I was bearer of dispatches from General Scott to General McDowell. "I will relieve you of them," was his reply; but seeing me hesitate to deliver them, he added, "I am Major Wadsworth of General McDowell's staff." While I had hoped from ambitious pride to have an opportunity to deliver the dispatches in person to General McDowell, I could not decline longer, so placed the documents in Major Wadsworth's hands, who took them to a tent a few paces distant, where, through its half-open folds, I saw him hand them to a large, portly officer, whom I at once rightly conceived to be General McDowell. Then, returning to where I still sat on my horse, Major Wadsworth (afterward General Wadsworth) asked of me the latest news in the capital, when I replied that every person at Washington was looking to the army for news, he added, "Well, I guess they will not have to wait much longer. The entire army is under arms, and moving to attack the enemy to-day." After inquiring at what hour I left Washington, and remarking that I must be tired, Major Wadsworth asked me to dismount and have some breakfast, as it would be difficult to say when another opportunity would occur. I was very hungry, and rest would not have been unacceptable, but in my inexperience I partly imagined, particularly while in the presence of the white-haired officer who gave the invitation, that hunger and fatigue were conditions of feeling which a soldier, especially a young one, should not acknowledge. Therefore, with an appetite almost craving, I declined the kind proffer of the Major. But when he suggested that I dismount and allow my horse to be fed I gladly assented. While Major Wadsworth was kindly interesting himself in the welfare of my horse, I had the good fortune to discover in an officer at headquarters one of my recent West Point friends, Lieutenant Kingsbury, aide-de-camp to General McDowell. He repeated the invitation just given by Major Wadsworth in regard to breakfast, but I did not have the perseverance to again refuse. Near the log fire already mentioned were some servants busily engaged in removing the remains of breakfast. A word from Kingsbury, and they soon prepared for me a cup of coffee, a steak, and some Virginia corn bread, to which I did ample justice. Had I known, however, that I was not to have an opportunity to taste food during the next thirty hours, I should have appreciated the opportunity I then enjoyed even more highly.

As I sat on the ground sipping my coffee, and heartily enjoying my first breakfast in the field, Kingsbury (afterward Colonel Kingsbury, killed at the battle of Antietam) informed me of the general movement then begun by the army, and of the attack which was to be made on Beauregard's forces that day. Three days before I had quitted school at West Point. I was about to witness the first grand struggle in open battle between the Union and secession armies; a struggle in which, fortunately for the nation, the Union forces were to suffer defeat, while the cause for which they fought was to derive from it renewed strength and encouragement.

CUSTER'S "LAST STAND"—
TREVILIAN STATION, 1864

JAY MONAGHAN

"**A**gain I am called on to bid you adieu for a short period," Brigadier General George Armstrong Custer wrote his bride in June, 1864. ". . . Need I repeat to my darling that while living she is my all, and if Destiny wills me to die, wills that my country needs my death, my last prayer will be for her, my last breath will speak her name and that Heaven will not be Heaven till we are joined together." He ended the letter with, "Yours through time and eternity, Autie."[1]

At the moment he penned this rare prose, young Custer had been married less than four months and had just been ordered to join the expedition to Trevilian Station. Having been on active service since his marriage, he carried in his field desk a packet of love letters and an ambrotype of Mrs. Custer. Along with these cherished memorabilia, two devoted civilian waifs ornamented Custer's headquarters. One was Johnnie Cisco, a white boy who washed the General's shirts, waited table, and led his extra horses during battle. Custer's other ragamuffin retainer, Eliza, was an escaped slave girl who followed him with a special cooking outfit in an antique carriage which had been "requisitioned" on some plantation, presumably because the picturesque contraption would not take an oath of allegiance to the Union. In any event the old rattletrap caused much good-natured amusement in Federal ranks and undoubtedly prompted other daring cavalry officers to forage far and wide in search of more grandiose and disreputable vehicles. Eliza thoroughly enjoyed her position in Custer's Michigan Brigade, and her chuckling quips about her erstwhile masters and war in general were often repeated by the troopers, who called her "the Queen of Sheba."

Custer's bride, Libbie, had succeeded so far in making only one change in her eccentric and resplendent husband. For the wedding he had cut off his long golden locks which had earned him the informal title of "the Boy General with the flowing yellow curls."

Custer's rise in the army had been as miraculous as the nickname implied. While he was a lieutenant on the staff of General Alfred Pleasonton in 1863, that cavalryman jumped him all the way to brigadier general. Captains, majors, and colonels complained that the promotion showed rank favoritism, and when Pleasonton was transferred to the West the following spring, some prophesied the Boy General's downfall. Custer himself feared that his good fortune—"Custer Luck" he called it—might end as tough, hard-fighting Phil Sheridan assumed Pleasonton's command in Virginia in April, 1864.

Sheridan's first act was to reorganize the cavalry corps. Custer's Michigan Brigade—which included the 1st, 5th, 6th, and 7th Michigan regiments—together with Colonel Tom Devin's and Brigadier General Wesley Merritt's brigades, became the new First Division. Brigadier General Alfred T. A. Torbert, a slow but competent regular army infantryman inclined to be unappreciative of Custer's reckless aggressiveness, assumed command. Brigadier General David McMurtrie Gregg, under whom Custer had fought at Gettysburg, headed the Second Division. The Third was assigned to Brigadier General James H. Wilson. Like Custer, Wilson had risen rapidly. He was destined for a long and distinguished military career, but did not show it during the weeks ahead.

U.S. Grant had just arrived from the West, and he and George Meade mounted the 1864 spring offensive against Richmond and Lee's Army of Northern Virginia. Early in May the Union troops pushed into the Wilderness, with Custer guarding the wagon trains—scarcely the place for a cavalryman to show Sheridan his mettle. Wilson, assigned an advance position, promptly led the army into a trap. During the fighting which followed, neither the Confederate nor the Federal forces won much of a victory, and the cavalry had little opportunity for action except as dismounted troops. On the fourth day, May 9, Sheridan obtained permission to ride away from the army and raid toward Richmond. Jeb Stuart overtook this expedition two days later at Yellow Tavern, six miles from the capital, and was killed in a charge by Custer's Wolverines. Young Wilson failed once more to distinguish himself.

After this fight Sheridan skirted Richmond and joined Benjamin F. Butler's army on the James. Navy ships brought supplies here regularly and on their return to Washington carried Sheridan's wounded. With them, Custer sent a letter to his bride, describing the Yellow Tavern fight and enlarging on the number of cannon he had captured. He also claimed that "Wilson proved himself an imbecile and . . . nearly ruined the corps with his blunders. Genl Sheridan sent me to rescue him."[2]

After two days' rest Sheridan marched north across enemy country to rejoin Grant. He entrusted the van to Custer, who had now attracted his admiration.[3] Several skirmishes were fought, but Sheridan felt too weak and too far from supplies to challenge the enemy. He ordered his corps to keep on the defensive—and on the march. Every horse that failed the pace would be killed by the rear guard. Perhaps 300 animals were thus kept from falling into enemy hands.[4]

Custer came upon the Union Army above the North Anna River. It had fought its way south thirty miles during the two weeks since the cavalry left and now sprawled near the Chesterfield station on the railroad running between Fredericksburg and Richmond. On May 24 Sheridan's blue riders shuffled into the great Union encampment. Little Phil's first act was to report to Grant; Custer's was to scratch a letter to Libbie. "When I think how successful I have been of late," he rejoiced, "and how much has been said of my conduct and gallantry I think, '*She* will hear of it, and will be proud of her Boy!' That is all the reward I ask."[5]

The Boy General soon found his next opportunity for glory. The Union Army had now penetrated tidewater Virginia where the land was flat and the streams were sluggish inlets from Chesapeake Bay, uncrossable except on pontoons. Custer was selected to construct such a bridge across the Pamunkey. On May 27, 1864, the Second Division, under Gregg, crossed here and the next day, in dense woods and swamps around Haw's Shop, was stopped by Confederate cavalry entrenched behind log fortifications. Repeated attacks failed to drive out the enemy. Gregg's men became disheartened. In the evening Custer's brigade arrived.[6] The Confederate position looked impregnable. Leaves and twigs cut from the trees by bullets lay like a carpet on the ground between the two forces.[7] No creature, it appeared, could hope to cross that area alive.

Custer, with characteristic optimism, dismounted his brigade behind Gregg's discouraged line, formed them in column of platoons, commanded the band to play, and ordered them forward. As his Michigan

Brigade reached the center of Gregg's, the tired troopers saw Custer, so young, so confident, so gay. They took fresh grasps on their carbines, and the two divisions surged forward, sweeping the enemy before them, breaking the defenders' line into dozens of battles within the battle. The 5th Michigan lost five officers. Custer's home-town friend and fellow officer, Jim Christiancy, was wounded—thigh and thumb. Custer's horse was shot from under him. His adjutant, Jacob Greene, was hit in the head by a spent bullet but survived. Fighting lasted until it was too dark to aim but by then enemy resistance had been shattered. During the night the dead were buried, among them Private John A. Huff, a 5th Michigan sharpshooter credited with killing Jeb Stuart at Yellow Tavern sixteen days earlier. He was one of the footmen who slipped in when the mounted regiments charged.[8]

Grant's army now sidled massively toward Cold Harbor and some of the severest fighting of the entire war. Custer's troopers, on the move, constantly fended off Confederate cavalry thrusts. Pausing a moment under enemy fire the General dashed off the usual report to Libbie. "I am well and unhurt," he wrote. "We had a fight yesterday. . . . Our Brigade lost heavily but was victorious!"[9]

On June 3, Lee decisively repulsed the Army of the Potomac before Cold Harbor, exacting frightful losses. Grant grudgingly changed his strategy. He decided to move across the James River and starve out Richmond by cutting its main supply routes. He ordered General Sheridan to destroy the vital Virginia Central Railroad to the west, and then join General David Hunter's marauding cavalry force for the return march.

For this maneuver Sheridan chose his First and Second Divisions, leaving Wilson to serve with Grant's advance. Once again Custer was to have an opportunity to demonstrate his ability to the commanding general. The raid was scheduled to last five days. For this, three days' rations for the men and two days' forage for the horses were issued at the Newcastle Ferry on the south bank of the Pamunkey. Each trooper received 100 rounds of ammunition—forty in his bandoleers, sixty in the ammunition wagons. Two flying batteries, Heaton's and Pennington's, accompanied the column, which also contained one medical wagon, eight ambulances, and eight pontoons.[10]

Thus heavily laden, the column started up the north bank of the North Anna River. The Virginia Central Railroad ran some ten miles south of that stream. On June 10 Sheridan passed the bridge which led south to Trevilian Station. A few miles beyond it he crossed the river by Carpenter's Ford.[11] The road south cut through brushy country with sporadic clearings. Halfway to Trevilian Station the Union force camped in the woods and ragged fields around Clayton's store where a road branched to the east, leading to Louisa Court House.

Lee learned of the raiders and sent the divisions of Generals Wade Hampton and Fitzhugh Lee to intercept them. Sheridan had two days' start but the Confederates' interior route was shorter. On the day that Sheridan forded the North Anna, Hampton reached Trevilian Station, a loading point with water tank and a few other buildings. He established his headquarters in a Mr. Netherland's house near the railroad embankment half a mile east. That same night Fitzhugh Lee encamped at Louisa Court House, a hamlet of some 400 people several miles farther down the track.[12]

Both Wade Hampton and Phil Sheridan reckoned that a battle would be fought next day, June 11, and each planned to take the initiative. Two roads led from Trevilian Station to Sheridan's encampment—one of them the Clayton's store road, the other a woods road to the east. A third road from Trevilian meandered down the railroad track to Louisa Court House. A fourth route branched off the Clayton's store road and crossed the track west of Trevilian. A fifth road connected Louisa Court House and Clayton's store. Such a maze of connecting roads, interspersed with woodlands, promised some interesting exercises in tactics.

Wade Hampton's plan of battle was to move in force up the direct road from Trevilian Station to Clayton's store. As he did so Fitzhugh Lee was to advance from Louisa Court House to the store. Between them they would hit Sheridan, front and flank. To prevent Little Phil from getting around the Confederate left flank in a counterstroke, Hampton stationed Thomas Lafayette Rosser and his Laurel Brigade on the road which crossed the tracks west of Trevilian.[13]

While Hampton made plans for this offensive, Sheridan decided on his own course of action. He would advance down the direct road from Clayton's store to Trevilian Station. Custer was flattered when assigned the special duty of guarding against a flank attack from Louisa Court House. His orders also told him to feel his way along the woods road into Trevilian Station, where he might strike Hampton in the flank or rear. Custer never liked to work with others and he was happy to note that his orders gave this part of the field to himself alone.

During the night of June 10–11, as these plans were explained to the Union division commanders, Hampton's vedettes groped through the woods uncovering Sheridan's pickets, leaving them uncertain as to where the main Confederate blow would fall. Sheridan, always an aggressive fighter, did not wait to find out. As dawn approached, Hampton warned his officers against any undue noise. No bugle calls must be sounded. Sheridan, on the other hand, set the night ringing with call after call, and as soon as it was light enough to shoot he started Merritt's Reserve Brigade down the Clayton's store road. The 2nd U.S. Cavalry led the way at a trot.[14]

A mile off, at the column's left, Custer advanced more cautiously. He had seen parties of Fitzhugh Lee's men on the road to Louisa Court House and was not sure whether they presaged an attack from that direction or were only scouts.[15] To handle them he left the 1st and 7th Michigan regiments. Both were veteran organizations which had distinguished themselves at Gettysburg and had made the mounted charge at Yellow Tavern when Jeb Stuart was killed.

With the remainder of the brigade—the 5th and 6th Michigan—and Pennington's attached battery, Custer proceeded down the woods road toward Trevilian Station. The 5th led, with its 3rd Battalion deployed as advance guard under Captain Smith H. Hastings.[16] Custer and his staff came next—all excellently mounted, all with red neckties tossed over one shoulder. Custer, like Sheridan, believed that a commander should be out front. Behind his staff rode the rest of the Fifth Brigade, under Colonel Russell A. Alger. Then came Pennington's battery. Behind the guns, and out of Custer's sight, the 6th Michigan was supposed to be following. It had camped that night in the thick brush back off the road, and before dawn the men had saddled. When they received the order to march, they started toward the road in single file, the only formation possible in the underbrush. As each troop emerged on the road it lined up, company front, and waited.

This was the situation when a messenger from the deployed van galloped back to Custer with information that they had come to the clearings around Trevilian Station. In the roads, along the railroad tracks, and on the route leading off into the woods to the west, they could see hundreds of canvas-covered wagons as well as great numbers of led horses. Custer realized at once that he had penetrated Hampton's rear. He turned to his aide-de-camp, F. Stewart Stranahan, and told him to have Colonel Alger charge with the 5th.[17]

Custer and his staff moved to the roadside as the regiment cantered past. Pennington's artillery then rumbled up, filling the road behind them for over a hundred yards. Six horses stood hitched to each gun and caisson. The sultry sun beat down, making the animals switch, stamp, and rub against one another. Custer presumed that the 6th Michigan was in the road behind them, out of sight. He sent an aide to its commander, Major J. H. Kidd, with orders to "gallop and pass the battery."[18]

That morning Kidd rode an unusually spirited black horse. A fellow officer had asked him to "take the ginger" out of his fractious mount. Astride the prancing animal, Kidd was waiting for the entire regiment to emerge from the woods and form column when he received Custer's command. He knew that an order from the Boy General must be acted upon at once and no excuses made. Without waiting for the regiment to assemble he commanded the men already aligned company front to "Form fours, gallop, *march!*"

Down the road past the artillery dashed the first four troops of the 6th Michigan, while the remainder of the regiment—two-thirds of it—continued to trickle out of the brush. Custer had galloped away to the front but Kidd's squadron overtook him and his staff, in the open fields near the road junction east of Trevilian Station. Custer was exchanging pistol shots with an enemy toward the west. He turned to Kidd, pointed, and shouted, "Charge them!"

Kidd, on his prancing black horse, slowed the column for a few moments to let his squadron close ranks, then commanded, "Draw sabers, *charge!*"

The enemy made little resistance and seemed to be in small numbers. The charging column followed the road around a stand of woods. Kidd did not know that Alger was ahead of him until he met detachments coming back with prisoners. Some 250 wagons, three caissons of Confederate ammunition, probably a thousand led horses, and 350 prisoners had already been taken.[19]

Kidd's fractious black had outrun his battalion. There was obviously nothing ahead to attack. Kidd returned his revolver to its holster and with two hands free sawed the black's mouth until the animal slowed down. While he was battling with his horse, his squadron caught up and rocketed past him. Kidd shouted *"Halt!"* but the column did not hear his command. It clattered across the tracks and passed the station and water tank. Kidd's own prancing charger thrashed off into the brush on the right out of sight of the road. In the woods on all sides he heard a sudden firing. Something unexpected had happened. Kidd guided his horse toward the road but before he reached it Confederate soldiers appeared among the green leaves in the thickets and took him prisoner.

The sudden change in the fortunes of battle which permitted Kidd's capture was equally disturbing to Custer. He had watched the lead squadrons of Kidd's 6th gallop past the station. Dust had hardly settled behind their flying hoofs, when he saw horsemen in unmistakable Confederate uniforms appear on the road behind them. The sight of these troops, in addition to those at whom he had been shooting, convinced him that the enemy had arrived in large and dangerous numbers. He also noticed gray-clad soldiers around the old hotel which commanded the road to the east.[20] Obviously the Confederates had slipped into Trevilian Station after his command had galloped through it, thus cutting his small force in two.

As a matter of fact, Wade Hampton, on hearing that Custer was in his rear, ordered Rosser in from the west. Hampton also about-faced as many of his men as he dared to recapture their led horses and train. These were the forces which cut off Alger's 5th and a third of Kidd's 6th. Neither unit took any further part in the fight. Some forty of them rejoined the command later by making a twenty-mile detour.[21]

Custer's command was now reduced to the Michigan 1st and 7th, the remnant of Kidd's 6th, the artillery, and the wagon train.[22] Though closely pressed by the enemy on all sides, Custer remained confident. He planned first to retake the station. To do this he ordered a field gun into position near the railroad track, concealed behind a high board fence. It was loaded with grape and canister. Custer hoped that a surprise blast from this piece so close to the Confederates' position would confuse them. The explosion was also to be the signal for a charge by the 1st Michigan, his favorite regiment. Then the 7th, which had tarried to build barricades across the Louisa Court House road, was to sweep in on the enemy's flank.

All was ready, and the hidden gun's Number One man raised his axe to knock off the boards when Custer saw something which made him stop the fellow. Across a field to the right about 100 yards away a long gray line of men had vaulted the fence and was rapidly approaching the gun.

Custer ordered gun and crew to withdraw on the double![23]

With the sound of clanking chains and pounding hoofs the gun lurched away. But Custer's trouble had just begun. A messenger from the 7th, which was to reinforce the action he planned, dashed in with word that his regiment was being pounded by Confederates coming down the Louisa Court House road.

Custer's proposed offensive turned immediately into a desperate defense. Not only did the Confederates hold Trevilian Station to his front, but Custer's two and two-thirds regiments were hemmed in, flanks and rear, by two enemy divisions well protected by timber. The force pressing in on him consisted of Rosser's brigade, Hampton's rear, and Fitzhugh Lee's division which was filtering in on both the woods and the Louisa Court House roads. Custer's men relinquished their positions in the woods grudgingly, and the fighting became confused. Units got behind each other's lines. Sometimes troopers heard men stumbling in the brush and called across to learn if they confronted friend or foe. At least one Union group escaped by claiming to be Confederate. In the midst of these blind and blundering maneuvers, Pennington rode up to Custer and announced dismally, "They's taken one of my pieces, sir, and I think they intend to keep it."

"I'll be damned if they do," the Boy General replied. He called for volunteers. Thirty men spurred forward, eager to follow their chief into any adventure. Away they all went after the captured cannon. An enemy volley set the charging horses on their haunches, emptied some saddles. The survivors retreated. Custer dismounted them and, waving his saber, led them forward on foot. This time they passed through the fusillade and overtook the gun. Enemy footmen were hauling it off with prolonges, but they dropped the ropes and scampered away. Custer's men trundled the gun back to their lines.[24]

With every isolated thrust by the converging enemy Custer was pushed back. He formed his men for a "last stand" in a great circle, within which he hoped to maneuver his artillery to disperse enemy formations preparing to attack him. His brigade stood now in open country somewhat resembling Western prairieland. Nowhere could his men find cover from enemy fire. The officer in charge of wagons moved toward a wood lot where he hoped to be protected. Instead of finding shelter, however, he ran into Fitzhugh Lee's column, and his entire train was captured, including Custer's headquarters wagon with his field desk, clothes, and general's commission. Worst of all, he lost that precious ambrotype of Libbie and a packet of letters from her. His three spare horses had been captured. Lost, too, was Eliza with her cooking outfit and the antique carriage which so amused the soldiers. Poor Eliza might be back in slavery for life now.

Custer ordered the 7th forward and, leading it himself, tried to retake the wagons. He succeeded only in retrieving two caissons, three ambulances, and a few forage wagons.[25] The midsummer weather was sultry, with a scorching sun beating down on roads ankle-deep in dust. Barrels of the repeating carbines, when fired rapidly, became too hot for the men to touch. The artillery raced from place to place, wherever the enemy seemed to be concentrating for a charge. Custer's color-bearer, Sergeant Mitchell Beloir, rode up to him white and trembling. "General," he said, "they have killed me. Take the flag."[26]

Custer tore the cloth from the tottering staff and stuffed it inside his jacket. The wounded man died before morning. Custer himself was struck twice by spent balls, which raised welts on his shoulder and arm. Once he dismounted and ran forward to carry away a dying man. A glancing bullet momentarily stunned him, but he got back to his lines.[27] Always the Boy General displayed bravery under fire.

Years later John Kelly, a 2nd Cavalry veteran, described the fight as witnessed by Merritt's men from positions near the Clayton's store road. The charge on Trevilian Station by Custer's troops, he remembered, "was a splendid sight and how vividly it called to mind Tenysons description of the charge at Balacklava, and it came near being as fatal. . . ." As the force penetrated their lines, the Confederates, he recalled,

> changed front to the rear, and wheeling their then right flank so as to form two sides of a square, and their troops which still kept poring out from the woods formed on the other flank, thus leaving no opening for escape but towards the rear of their position, and even this soon closed in, actually closing Custer in on the inside of a living triangle, and now his men charged madly from one side to another, but to no purpose. They could not penetrate those ranks

which ware gradualy closing in on them. When this body of the enemy first made their appearance Merrit had sent a mesenger to headquarters for instructions, and now every eye was turned in that direction, but no mesenger returned. And now we could destinguish Custers movements by the direction of his brigade flag of which those boys used to be so proud. Directly we saw their flag go down and thought it was all up with them, but one thing at least was in their favor, the rebels could not do much firing, as they ware just as likely to hit their own men as not, so the[y] calculated to overpower them and cause them to surender. But those hardy wolverines determined to sell their liberty dearly, for it was now a question of liberty or death with them in earnest.[28]

Finally, hearing the prolonged firing from Custer's position, General Sheridan ordered Torbert to push forward with Merritt's and Devin's brigades. With them went one of Gregg's. That general's other brigades were engaged with Fitzhugh Lee to the east.[29] Back near the Clayton's store road Merritt's men, watching the annihilation of their embattled comrades, had become nearly unmanageable. When the order to attack at last arrived their commander, trooper Kelly recalled,

took his brandy flask from his saddle bags and took a good long pull at [it], and who would blame him, for there was a fair prospect of its being the last he would ever take. Handing it to one of his staff he turned to his men and addressed them saying, men we have got to cut out a road to let them Michigan men out of that scrape. We advanced well into the opening when the trumpeters was ordered to sound the charge. We had now sumthin less than half a mile of open ground to charge over, and at them we went with a yell which more resembled the Indian war whoop than a cheer from civelized troops. . . .[30]

The attackers sliced through to Custer's perimeter, saving the remainder of his force and splitting the Confederates in half.

Both Hampton and Sheridan had miscalculated events on the Clayton's store road. Hampton was not prepared for the resistance he met there when marching north at dawn and was completely disconcerted when Custer captured his horses in the rear. In his battle report he said that he was stopped on his first forward thrust by Federal breastworks in the woods. The Union reports mentioned no construction of works. On the contrary, they claimed that they were stopped by Hampton's works, which prevented them from coming through in time to join Custer at Trevilian Station. In all probability neither side had any works other than the fences, downed timber, and tree stumps which soldiers wisely had learned to use for cover and concealment.

The first day's battle was a draw. The Union forces had retaken Trevilian Station, and Sheridan's entire command encamped there.[31] The Confederates occupied the railroad track both east and west of them. During the night prisoners were interrogated. Sheridan learned that it was useless to go on and try to join Hunter at Charlottesville.[32] That general was west of the Blue Ridge at or near Lexington, presumably moving toward Lynchburg. Custer learned that Rosser, one of his best friends at West Point, had been painfully wounded late in the afternoon's fight. One Confederate told an amusing story which flattered the Boy General. The prisoner said that when Captain J. L. Greene had been captured and compelled to surrender his spurs he boasted, "You have the spurs of General Custer's Adjutant General."[33]

Before morning Eliza trudged in out of the night. She wore a grin on her shining black face and carried a satchel in her hand, saying she had escaped from her captors. When asked how, she only chuckled and replied that a Confederate cavalryman ordered her to mount his horse behind him and she replied, "I don't see it." Then according to Eliza, the disgruntled trooper said to a companion, "Ain't she damned impudent," and as they discussed this she disappeared.[34]

In the morning, June 12, Sheridan ordered his troops to feel their way westward along the track. Within two miles they came to lines of hastily-constructed fortifications in open fields, along fences, and behind the railroad embankment.[35] During the night Fitzhugh Lee had circled around Trevilian Station and joined Hampton in the west. The united forces were now ready to stop Sheridan's advance. Little Phil did not attack until 3:00 P.M.[36] Then he struck the enemy line seven times without success. The fighting was more desperate this second day, but Custer's brigade was only a part of the line and avoided another spectacular "last stand." At ten o'clock that evening Sheridan ordered a withdrawal. He lacked sufficient ammunition for another day's fight, and he had already torn up the railroad track behind him and destroyed Trevilian Station.[37] Ties had been burned and rails properly twisted around trees and poles. Sheridan considered this a fulfillment of his mission since he could not meet Hunter at Charlottesville. Technically it may have been, but had Sheridan joined Hunter, thus cutting off Richmond's connections with the northwest, the war might have ended a year earlier.

During the warm summer night the Union army drew back toward the North Anna and crossed at Carpenter's Ford after daylight on June 13. With this obstacle behind them to check the enemy, Sheridan called a halt. His horses were turned into green pastures. The poor animals had eaten nothing for forty-eight hours,[38] and when horses are without food for that length of time they begin to bite wooden boards and chew one another's manes and tails.

Sheridan had lost 575 men, 490 of them wounded. In ambulances, farm wagons, and carts taken from nearby plantations, he loaded 377 men able to travel. The remainder lay with the Confederate wounded who had fallen into his hands. Surgeons and attendants with suitable medical supplies were left with them.[39]

For Sheridan the situation was still critical, and he pushed on as fast as his horses and men could go. The dilapidated wagons carrying his wounded became a problem but he exerted every effort to keep them rattling along. Men with wounded legs sat in drivers' seats. Men with one disabled arm held whips in their sound members.[40] As on other raids Sheridan ordered his rear guard to kill all the horses that dropped out. At every crossroad escaping slaves joined the procession. Their number grew daily until there were 2,000 of them—a nuisance for Sheridan. He marveled that the country, in peacetime, had supported so many.

The battered horsemen finally reached the Federal supply depot at White House Landing on the Pamunkey but the enemy had closed in on them more dangerously every day, and it took sharp fighting to get within the protection of the big guns at the depot. Grant and Meade were no longer there, having marched the army twenty-five miles farther south to City Point on the James to establish headquarters for the siege of Petersburg. Custer, with the First Brigade, dismounted near the charred ruins of the ancestral mansion belonging to the families of Mrs. George Washington and Mrs. Robert E. Lee. McClellan had ordered it protected when he was here in 1862, but it burned as he moved his base to the James during the Seven Days battle. Custer found the lawn green and pleasant, but he could still hear shooting out beyond the Union lines. Yes, Lee would give them plenty of trouble when they started south, running the gauntlet to join Grant.

Locating a shady place under a big tree and with his staff lounging about him, he wrote Libbie while Eliza cooked dinner. He told his bride about the Trevilian defeat, said he had lost everything "except my toothbrush," even her letters which would probably cause coarse laughter in Confederate camps. He closed by asking her to write his parents for him. "Tell them I am too busy. Our men and horses are completely wearied out. Write the boy who adores his darling little one."[41]

Grant and Meade had left an order for Sheridan to bring their wagons, some 900 of which remained behind. Little Phil grumbled. He hated guard duty and obeyed with ill grace. He knew Lee would fight for those wagons every foot of the way, and that the Union horses were already exhausted. The prospect held nothing but fatigue, wounds, death, and no glory. In a bad humor he ordered the column to start south next day. It was a slow, grinding fight for twenty-five miles with none of the cavalry charges which he and Custer enjoyed, but the wagons were duly delivered on the north bank of the James. Here, at last, the cavalrymen turned out their tired mounts on fresh feed and settled down for a much-needed rest.

At Trevilian Station Custer had suffered the worst defeat thus far in his career. He had survived what had threatened to become a last stand, but the fight had cost him 416 casualties—more than he had lost at Haw's Shop and Cold Harbor combined. His troopers said his luck had changed since he cut off his curls.[42] But as it turned out, the glory-hungry young cavalry officer had enjoyed far better luck than he was to know at a second—and more famous—last stand, on an oddly similar June day twelve years later.

Notes

1. Marguerite Merington, ed., *The Custer Story: The Life and Intimate Letters of General George A. Custer and His Wife Elizabeth* (New York: Devin-Adair, 1950), 103.

2. Ibid., 97.

3. U.S. War Department, *The War of the Rebellion: A Compilation of the Official Records of the Union and Confederate Armies*, 130 vols. (Wash-

ington, D.C.: Government Printing Office, 1880–1901), 1st ser., vol. 36, pt. 1, pp. 792, 819 (hereafter cited as *OR*, with all references being to 1st ser.). See also Theo. F. Rodenbough, comp., *From Everglade to Cañon with the Second Dragoons* (New York: D. Van Nostrand, 1875), 308.

4. *OR*, vol. 36, pt. 1, p. 792.

5. Merington, *Custer Story*, 99.

6. *OR*, vol. 36, pt. 1, pp. 793, 854.

7. Rodenbough, *Second Dragoons*, 309.

8. Ibid.; *OR*, vol. 36, pt. 1, pp. 804, 829, 861; Robert Underwood Johnson and Clarence Clough Buel, eds., *Battles and Leaders of the Civil War*, 4 vols. in 8 (New York: Century, 1884–88), 4:193 (hereafter cited as *B&L*).

9. Merington, *Custer Story*, 99–100.

10. J. H. Kidd, *Personal Recollections of a Cavalryman* (Ionia, Mich.: Privately printed, 1908), 342.

11. *OR*, vol. 36, pt. 1, p. 1095.

12. *B&L* 4:237; George Michael Neese, *Three Years in the Confederate Horse Artillery* (New York: Neale Publishing Co., 1911), 283–84.

13. Daniel Amon Grimsley, *Battles in Culpeper County, Virginia 1861–1865* (Culpeper, Va.: Exponent Printing Office, 1900), 33.

14. Douglas S. Freeman, *Lee's Lieutenants: A Study in Command*, 3 vols. (New York: Charles Scribner's Sons, 1942–44), 3:520.

15. *OR*, vol. 36, pt. 1, p. 823.

16. Ibid., 830.

17. Ibid.

18. Kidd, *Personal Recollections*, 352.

19. Ibid., 254; *OR*, vol. 36, pt. 1, pp. 796, 1095.

20. Grimsley, *Battles in Culpeper County*, 34.

21. *OR*, vol. 36, pt. 1, p. 831.

22. Ibid., 823–24; Kidd, *Personal Recollections*, 357.

23. *B&L* 4:233.

24. Ibid., 234.

25. *OR*, vol. 36, pt. 1, p. 824.

26. Ibid., 823–24; Merington, *Custer Story*, 105.

27. Merington, *Custer Story*, 104–5; *B&L* 4:234; Joseph Mills Hanson, "The Civil War Custer," *Cavalry Journal* 43 (1934): 29.

28. John Patrick Kelly to Patrick Kelly, May 26, 1876, Wyles Collection, University of California at Santa Barbara.

29. Philip H. Sheridan, *Personal Memoirs of P. H. Sheridan, General, United States Army*, 2 vols. (New York: Charles L. Webster and Co., 1888), 1:420–21.

30. Kelly to Kelly, Wyles Collection.

31. Kidd, *Personal Recollections*, 361.

32. Rodenbough, *Second Dragoons*, 313.

33. Merington, *Custer Story*, 103.

34. Ibid., 104.

35. *B&L* 4:238; Kidd, *Personal Recollections*, 362.

36. *OR*, vol. 36, pt. 1, p. 808; *B&L* 4:238.

37. *OR*, vol. 36, pt. 1, pp. 797, 824, 842.

38. Rodenbough, *Second Dragoons*, 314.

39. Sheridan, *Personal Memoirs* 1:423, 425.

40. Rodenbough, *Second Dragoons*, 313–14.

41. Merington, *Custer Story*, 104–5.

42. Frederick Whittaker, "General George A. Custer," *Galaxy* 22 (1876): 365.

THE

BATTLE OF

WAYNESBORO

HARLAN PAGE

LLOYD

The battle of Waynesboro, Virginia, was fought on the second day of March, 1865. Judged by the numbers engaged on either side, or by the number of killed and wounded, it was not one of the great battles of the war. But it was a memorable battle in this, that it resulted in the capture of the last organized Confederate force in the Shenandoah Valley, a valley which, in one part or another, was one continuous battle-field from 1861 to 1865. It was important also in this, that it left General Sheridan free to move, with his two divisions of veteran cavalry, over the Blue Ridge, through the heart of Virginia, to march to the James to rejoin our gallant comrades of the Army of the Potomac, and to take a leading part in that wonderful series of movements which culminated at Appomattox.

At the close of the brilliant campaign of General Sheridan in the Valley of the Shenandoah, in 1864, his headquarters were established in the City of Winchester. But in order that the enemy might have no time for recuperation, the Federal cavalry was kept constantly employed in active operations until the close of December. Early in January, 1865, we were permitted to erect huts for ourselves and sheds for the horses on the hills west of Winchester. These huts were occupied about six weeks. The resting time was short. The Sixth Corps, which had shared the fortunes and the glories of the Valley Campaign, had been sent to the James River, leaving the Army of the Shenandoah, under General Sheridan, composed of two divisions of cavalry, with a few batteries of horse artillery attached thereto.

On an open plain north of Winchester, a magnificent review of the cavalry was held about the 20th of February, previous to which a thorough inspection had been made to ascertain the exact condition of the entire command.

Early on the morning of February 27, 1865, we broke camp, set fire to our huts, formed a marching column, and started up the valley pike with our faces southward, with the grim determination in the heart of every officer and every man to make that the last campaign, not only in the Shenandoah Valley, but of the war. The chief of cavalry was General Wesley Merritt, an able and accomplished soldier, who had been a successful brigade commander during the previous year, and later had commanded the First Division. General Thomas C. Devin succeeded to the command of the First Division. The First Brigade was commanded by Colonel Stagg, the Second Brigade by Colonel Fitzhugh, and the Reserve Brigade by General Alfred Gibbs.

The Third Cavalry Division was under the command of General George A. Custer, next to Sheridan the idol of the cavalry corps, the dashing, brave, and successful chevalier, a born master of the horse, an ideal leader of cavalry, a genial and accomplished gentleman.

His First Brigade was commanded by Colonel Pennington, the Second Brigade by General William Wells, and his Third Brigade, which had been sent to us from the Army of West Virginia, was commanded by Colonel Capehart. My regiment, the Twenty-second New York Cavalry, was in the Second Brigade of the Third Division. My own position was on the staff of General Wells. I had been wounded in one of the fights in the valley several months before. I had at this time an open wound, and I was really in no physical condition for field service, especially in a winter campaign. But I felt sure that we were about to enter upon the last struggle of the war, and I was determined to be in at the death.

No finer body of men ever rode forth than those bronzed veterans of the cavalry corps. They were the men who had fought under Stoneman, and afterward under Pleasonton at Aldie, at Chancellorsville, and at Gettysburg. They had fought under Sheridan at the Wilderness, at Trevillian, and at Cold Harbor. The Third Cavalry Division, under General Wilson, had made the raid toward Danville, in June, 1864, and had made its own glorious fights at Nottaway and Dinwiddie. The First Division and the Third had gone together from the James River to the Potomac for the defense of Washington against Early in August, 1864, and afterward entered upon that wonderful campaign of the Shenandoah, when, after three hotly contested battles, to use the graphic language of the commanding general, "Early was sent whirling up the valley."

They were men who had known in their campaigns in distant fields, both success and failure. But for them, the Valley of the Shenandoah had always been lighted with the bonfires of victory, and their flashing sabers had carved the way, time and again, through cavalry, infantry and artillery, until the Third Cavalry Division, under Custer's command, was able to say, in regard to the valley campaign of 1864, what had never been said by any other in the land, that it had literally captured every piece of cannon whose fire had been directed against it. All the troopers were bold, rough riders. It was a conspicuous example of the survival of the fittest, and there was no man in the command at that time who could not be depended upon in any emergency, and to the last extremity.

We knew where the armies of Grant and Meade lay, and how they longed for the next act in the great drama of war. We knew where were the armies of the Tennessee and the Cumberland, and how eager they were to do their part in the great closing struggle. We would be worthy of companionship with such heroes.

Under wintry skies, with the snow lying in shrunken drifts by the roadside, and in great masses on the mountains, with a drizzling rain, which froze as it fell, the dark column stretched to its full length, and wound slowly up the familiar pike. I can well imagine that each man's thoughts were busy with the past, from General Sheridan, who might have been recalling the steps of his famous ride to Cedar Creek, to the humblest private in the ranks, who had marched up and down the old pike so often, that every stone, and stump, and tree had become as familiar as the face of a friend.

We marched thirty miles to Woodstock and bivouacked for the night on a sloping hillside half covered with ice and snow. The blazing fires set little rills of water running, which added to the picturesqueness but not to the comfort of the situation. The next morning found us in the saddle early, and we marched to Lacey's Springs, then and still a famous fountain, bubbling from beneath the rock, in a volume large enough to make a small river. The night was bitterly cold, and we were glad enough to be up early on Wednesday morning and hurry on toward Staunton.

At Mount Crawford we had first struck a small body of rebels under General Rosser, who disputed the passage of the river, and who had barricaded the bridge and afterward attempted to burn it. But a battalion plunged into the water, icy cold, above the bridge, made its way across, flanked the rebel position, and saved the bridge. An important thing for us, as the loss of the bridge, would have detained us for several hours. We captured a gun and thirty prisoners.

Thursday morning, March 2d, found us within four miles of Staunton, with a dismal storm of rain, and sleet, and hail, which made us thoroughly uncomfortable, and made the roads almost impassable; but we rushed into the town hoping to catch the rear guard of Early's army. In this we were disappointed, for the wily old general had moved easterly with Wharton's division of infantry, Nelson's artillery, and Rosser's cavalry, first to Fisherville, and finally to Waynesboro, where he carefully selected a position admirably adapted for defense. Having learned from scouts of our movement up the valley, he had summoned by telegraph all of his staff officers, and had gathered his available force to dispute our passage. Wharton's division, though reduced in numbers, was the same steady body of brave and determined men, whom we had encountered so often in previous years, and the Confederacy had no better. Rosser was the classmate of General Custer at West Point, and our frequent encounters with him and his men had made us feel that we would rather capture Early and Rosser than any other two men in the Confederate army.

The instructions given to General Sheridan before he left Winchester were very general in their character. He was to go to Staunton, and thence to Lynchburg; he was to destroy the railway communications, and, if deemed expedient, to push on southward until he effected a junction with Sherman's army; or, at his discretion, he was to move to South-western Virginia, or return to Winchester. The principal idea was, that he should thoroughly clean out the Shenandoah Valley, and put an end to the fighting there. All other matters were largely left to his discretion. When he arrived at Staunton and learned that Early was strongly intrenched at Waynesboro, he thought it unwise to move southward toward Lynchburg, leaving so large a force upon his flank and rear, especially as the Shenandoah Valley was then left almost unprotected, and a rapid movement by Early could place his men at Harper's Ferry, or still further north, at a time when all the available troops were needed for the final struggle about Petersburg. Therefore, General Custer was ordered to push at once with his division for

Waynesboro, and to reconnoiter Early's position, so as to ascertain his numbers, and any points which might present a favorable opening for attack.

Through rain, and sleet, and hail, and storm, through mud which rendered the roads almost impassable, through streams without bridges, we pushed on with an eagerness inspired by the hope of capturing Early, the route running near the present track of the Chesapeake and Ohio Railroad, from Staunton eastward through Fisherville to Waynesboro.

Our advance consisting of a squadron of the Twenty-second New York Cavalry, under Captain Lusk, struck the rear guard of the rebels about three miles from Staunton. A sharp skirmish ensued, and the rebels fled to Fisherville, a small hamlet where Early's commissary stores had been piled, before they were hastily removed to Waynesboro. My own duties for the day kept me with the advance of our column, and we eagerly pressed on, exchanging shots at frequent intervals, until we came in sight of Early's position at Waynesboro.

The town lies upon the south side of the Chesapeake and Ohio Railroad, and immediately west of the South River, a branch of the South Fork of the Shenandoah. It is near the base of the Blue Ridge Mountains, and the town occupies an elevation of about three hundred feet above the adjacent plain, with a road from Staunton leading gradually up a slope to the crest of the hill. Early had seized the salient points of the elevation west of the town, had erected earthworks, and planted his artillery so as to sweep, by a concentrated fire, the only road leading to his position; while the open fields in his front were so soft with the heavy rains and upheaving frosts that he deemed them utterly impassable for cavalry. These fields constituted a deep, miry mass of mud.

The Twenty-second New York was immediately deployed in a skirmish line and engaged the rebel infantry which was thrown out in front, and drove it back within the earthworks. This regiment was ordered to hold its position until the remainder of the brigade and division could come up. Riding back rapidly, I reported the situation to General Wells, who ordered me to ride at once to General Custer giving him the same information.

With his characteristic vigor, General Custer immediately ordered General Wells to send a regiment to the support of the Twenty-second New York on the skirmish line, ordered the First and Third Brigades to be massed in column of squadrons in the woods on either side of the road, and just beyond the range of the enemy's guns. The rebel artillery was firing rapidly, and our skirmish line was so completely mired in the mud that it was difficult either to advance or retreat. General Custer rode quickly to the front, made a hasty but careful reconnoisance, ordered a section of Woodruff's battery of horse artillery to advance rapidly and fire a few rounds, and then move slowly back as if we had found the rebel position too strong to attack.

Within the rebel lines, General Long commanded the right wing, General Wharton the left, while Nelson's artillery was in the center behind hastily-constructed breastworks, with the guns so placed as to sweep the fields. Rosser's cavalry was on the extreme rebel right to protect it from a flank movement by way of the railroad track. The weak point in Early's position was, that General Wharton's left flank did not extend to and rest upon South River, as it should have done. The keen eye of Custer quickly discovered this vulnerable point, and his plan was instantly made to turn the left flank of the rebel position, while a vigorous attack was made in front. General Custer sent a courier to General Sheridan at Staunton to advise him of Early's position and probable strength, and that Custer was about to attack, and had no doubt of his ability to carry the position. The courier had not traversed more than half the distance before the battle was fought and won.

General Custer sent Colonel Whittaker of his personal staff, with three regiments of the First Brigade, dismounted, to pass under cover of the woods to the rebel left, extending our line as far as the banks of the South River, with orders that when in position a signal should be given, so that a simultaneous attack might commence in front. Meantime, General Wells, with two regiments of the Second Brigade was moving forward, and Woodruff's battery was again ordered to the front, and opened a rapid fire upon the rebel lines. General Custer directed me to put the Eighth New York, from the Second Brigade, in column of fours, in the road just outside of the woods, ready to charge up the road when he gave the command with his bugle, and General Wells directed me to lead the regiment. The First Connecticut was directed to follow us in column of fours; and we were scarcely in position when Custer's bugles, which had been trained to sound no other notes but those of the charge, rang out sharp and clear, and we started along that muddy road to make the last fight of the Shenandoah.

What a wild ride that was! The condition of the road was past description. We started at full gallop, with the mud and water flying in every direction, and our movement was the signal for the rebel artillerists to concentrate their fire upon the narrow road along which we were hurrying. In a moment the shot and shell came tearing through our ranks, splashing the mud and water even worse than the horses had already done; and the Eighth New York soon presented the appearance of men who had been soaked bodily in the soft mire of the road. A shell struck a few feet in front of my horse and exploded as it struck. I felt a sharp concussion on the left side of my head, which almost stunned me, and for a moment I supposed I had been hit with a piece of the exploding shell. With an instinctive movement I put up my hand, and was relieved to find that it was not obdurate iron, but a plaster of soft mud driven with great rapidity, unpleasant, but not dangerous. It was not a time or place for one to be fastidious about his toilet; and, allowing the horses to choose their footing for themselves, we galloped up to the Confederate breastworks, sabers in hand, with ringing cheers rode down the artillerists, stopped the firing of their guns, crowded through the lines of the infantry, and into the town, hoping to capture General Early at his headquarters.

Meantime, our dismounted men had successfully turned the left of General Wharton's division, and were forcing his men rapidly back in the greatest confusion. The mounted regiments which I have before named also assaulted the lines in front, and carried them at every point. Colonel Capehart's brigade came handsomely up to our support and prevented the escape of any portion of the enemy's infantry upon the right of its line.

Learning that General Early, General Long, and General Wharton, all well mounted, with several staff officers, had fled across the South River east of Waynesboro, and along the road leading to Rock Fish Gap, we pushed on with the Eighth New York and First Connecticut, dashed pell-mell into the South River, crossed it, and, immediately facing about, formed a line on the east bank, which effectually cut off the further escape of any portion of the Confederate troops in that direction.

Still we were not satisfied; General Early had not been captured, and, surmising that he would naturally take the road through Rock Fish Gap, as the one most available for escape, with Captain Lusk and half a dozen men from my own regiment, and as many more from the Eighth New York, we dashed along the stony road leading up to the gap. The roadway was filled by the transportation wagons of Early's command, the ordnance, commissary, and medical supplies having been hastily ordered to Greenwood Station, when Early discovered that Custer's attack was to be a serious one.

How hard we rode, and how hard we struggled, to capture our able and wily foe. We had fought him so often, and had chased him back and forth so many times, that it seemed but justice that the last crowning touch should be given to our victory by the capture of the rebel chieftain of the valley. Alas, that it was not so to be. General Rosser, with a few of his horsemen, had escaped to the northward along the west bank of the South River, starting to escape before any of our men were near enough to intercept him. A few mounted men were seen on the road in advance of our small party, urging their horses to their utmost speed toward Rock Fish Gap in the Blue Ridge Mountains.

I was well mounted on a splendid Virginia horse of the old hunter stock, fleet as a deer and eager for the chase. Captain Lusk, also well mounted, was by my side, and was sure that he recognized General Early in one of the fleeing rebel horsemen. Our steeds needed no spurs, for they fairly flew over the ground. In five minutes Captain Lusk and I, with a sergeant of the Twenty-second New York Cavalry, were entirely separated from our comrades, and had overtaken and passed so many orderlies, and mounted men, that it suddenly occurred to me to look over my shoulder and see whether any of our men were near. At least fifty armed rebels were behind us, and not one of our command in sight. The road in front was still blockaded with wagons, and stragglers of Early's army were flying along the road. My revolver had been emptied in our charge upon the artillery; my hands were so benumbed with cold that it was impossible to reload it, and I had no resource but my saber, in case the numerous rebels around us should take in the situation, conclude to capture us, and take our horses for escape.

Communicating these facts to Captain Lusk, in an undertone, I suggested that there was but one course for us to adopt, which was to press on, as if we had five hundred men at our immediate back. He agreed with me, and being a stalwart officer, with a tremendous voice, he kept up a continual shouting, and ordered every man whom we overtook to dismount and go to the rear. This in an imperious tone which did not admit of dispute. Just before us I saw a towering form, which I believed to be General Early. We had a hot race and I did my best to overtake him. He was mounted on a beautiful gray, which was quite the equal of mine. I finally overtook him and got him out of the saddle, but he proved to be a staff officer and not the general.

Learning from this officer that General Early was not on the Rock Fish Road, we made this capture the occasion for a short halt, to enable some of our men to catch up with us; for it was not pleasant to be in command of so large a portion of the Confederate army without staff officers or orderlies to assist. We soon had a small detachment of our own men gathered about us, and immediately pushed on up the rocky road, making captures of men, horses, and material at every step.

The rain of sleet, which froze as it fell, had continued to fall since the early morning, and, as we had been without food since our hasty cup of coffee at 4 A.M., I found myself at the top of the gap in a physical condition where food was absolutely necessary. Halting for a moment by the side of one of the captured medical supply wagons, I secured a few necessary articles, and went into a neighboring house to get warm. I was delighted to find a large blazing log-fire. Ten minutes enjoyment of its genial warmth metamorphosed me; I remounted my horse and pushed on with the column to Brookville, where our division was halted for the night.

Meantime, that portion of our division which had remained at Waynesboro had gathered the prisoners together, placed a strong guard about them, had secured such supplies as could be used, and destroyed the remainder, with a large portion of the captured arms. We found in our possession nearly one thousand eight hundred prisoners, eleven pieces of artillery, seventeen captured battleflags, a train of more than one hundred wagons and ambulances, including the headquarters wagon of General Early, with all his official books, papers, and records.

General Sheridan reached Waynesboro late in the evening after the battle, and directed that the prisoners should be sent back to Winchester, under a strong guard commanded by Colonel Thompson of the First New Hampshire Cavalry, while the battle flags were carried immediately in rear of General Custer's flag during the remainder of the great raid.

The capture of Rock Fish Gap was of immense advantage to us, as there was no way of flanking the position, and if Early's army had been advantageously posted in the most available position of the gap, he could have held it against a cavalry force indefinitely. Early was an able commander, with the instincts of a soldier, as he had proven on many a hard-fought field. He had a very quick eye for the advantage of a position, and he could arrange an army with marvelous skill. His position at Waynesboro was carefully chosen, and his force admirably arranged for defense. His only mistake was in his over-confidence. He threw his left flank so far to the front, in the hope of sweeping with an infantry fire the entire open space intervening between his position and the woods on the west, that he neglected to protect the flank by refusing its extreme wing. It was a repetition on a small scale of the fearful blunder at Chancellorsville.

Immediately after the war, General Early wrote a small memoir in which he declared that he had no doubt that he could hold our army in check at Waynesboro until night, and then he intended to cross the South River and take up his position in Rock Fish Gap. This was a costly blunder for him, and a rare piece of good fortune for us. General Early's only solution of his great misfortune was, that we fought much better than he anticipated; and that his own men did not fight as he had expected them to do. The man who had won and afterward had lost a battle on the same day at Cedar Creek, who had seen the terrible rout of his army at Fisher's Hill, whose infantry, cavalry and artillery had melted away under the quick saber strokes of Custer's men, should not have underrated at that late period of the war the fighting qualities of his enemy.

Once upon the summit of Rock Fish Gap, it was easy for us to push forward to Brookville, and Greenwood Station, and early on the morning of the 3d, our division was in the saddle on the march for Charlottesville. As our division was twelve miles in advance of the First Division, General Custer still had the lead, and we were glad to be the first to enter the old university town of Charlottesville, where General Custer was met by the Mayor of the city, the President and Professors of the University, and a deputation of old citizens, who stood, with bowed heads, as the column approached the corner of the college campus, and in the most respectful manner tendered the keys, and besought the general that he would not permit the spoilation of the town, and especially the burning of the University. The old University of Virginia was dear to the heart of every citizen of the state. It had been the educational nursery of her most distinguished sons, and its renown had filled the whole country. General Custer immediately placed a strong provost guard around the entire University property, with the strictest orders that neither officer nor man should be permitted to set foot within the lines during the entire stay of our troops.

We then marched on through the city, passing on our way the immense rebel hospitals which had there been erected. Those who were able to walk had gone South at the news of our approach; but a long line of mutilated men, armless or legless, were arranged along the outside of the hospital buildings, and with sad, pathetic eyes, watched the victorious column as it swept proudly by. In their hearts they must have suffered some of the misery which afterward covered the Southland like a pall, when they realized the full meaning of the words "LOST CAUSE."

At Charlottesville our division was engaged for three days in destroying the railroad tracks and bridges, and burning such war material as was gathered there.

On the morning of the 7th, the command was divided, the Third Cavalry Division moving in the direction of Lynchburg, parallel with the line of the railroad, while the First Division moved by a shorter route toward Columbia.

On the morning of our departure, a little incident occurred so characteristic of General Custer that I must mention it here. On the evening of the day of our arrival, we had captured a captain belonging to a Virginia regiment in Lee's army. He was sent to the division headquarters, and was perfectly astonished to find his own house occupied for that purpose by General Custer. The scene when the captive captain met his wife in General Custer's presence was most affecting, and the general, taking him aside immediately after, placed him upon his parole of honor that he would not attempt to escape, and then gave him the freedom of the house during our stay. His wife was a polished and cultivated lady, who extended many courtesies to General Custer and the members of his staff, and during the ensuing three days the relations were most pleasant. As we were about to depart, a horse was brought by one of the provost guard for the rebel captain, and his agonized wife stood upon the front porch saying her tearful goodbye. The captain was about to mount, when General Custer, still standing by the porch, called him back, and turning to the lady, said: "Madam, I am under great obligations for your kindness during our stay with you. To show my appreciation, and as the best return which I can make, allow me to present you your husband." The general instantly sprang into the saddle, then lifting his hat with knightly courtesy, and bowing very low to the captain and his wife, he rode on, leaving them in an ecstacy of happiness and wonder that a Yankee soldier could be such a gallant cavalier.

Time does not permit me to follow, in detail, the route of march from Charlottesville through the long and difficult circuit of the great raid. Our course was marked with the destruction of railroads and of the locks of the James River Canal, and of such supplies as were most needed by Lee's army. It was a most difficult and toilsome march for men and horses; the rain still fell in torrents every day; the weather was bitterly cold for marching; the roads were as bad as possible. We were in a section of the country not hitherto traversed by our armies. Topographical maps were unknown, and it was difficult to find the way to many points which General Sheridan desired to reach. We had one rendezvous at Columbia, and we examined the James River at many points, hoping to find a possible fording place, but were unable to cross the river without pontoons. Turning eastward, our division was moved to Goochland, and then northward to Frederick Hall, on the line of the Virginia Central Railroad, where we captured a large amount of stores and a few prisoners. We destroyed the railroad tracks in both directions, burned the buildings at the station, and several large ware-houses filled with supplies for Lee's army. Passing eastward, we drove a small hostile force in our front to Ashland, on the Richmond Road. General Lee took the alarm and sent out Pickett's division, a portion of General Longstreet's command, to intercept us. General Sheridan turned northward, crossed the South Anna, and Pennington's brigade of Custer's division was sent forward in the direction of Richmond to deceive the enemy and hold them in check, while our main column passed a critical point. Pennington did his work admirably, and with his single brigade held the enemy back until the main body had crossed the North Anna, when, under cover of the night, he withdrew his men, without loss, crossed the two rivers safely, and after midnight came into camp with us.

A cavalry force had been sent by General Lee, hoping to intercept us at Hanover. We, therefore, moved early on the ensuing morning, marched as rapidly as the nature of the roads would permit, and pushed our way against a small opposing force until we reached the north bank of the Pamunkey River at White House Landing, on the evening of March 18th. General Fitzhugh Lee was close in our rear, but General Sheridan managed to cross the entire command on a skeleton railroad bridge, which was hastily covered with such lumber as could be found in the vicinity, and on the 19th we were met with supplies on the south bank of the Pamunkey at White House Landing.

The horses were badly worn out, and the men were very tired, but all hearts were jubilant, and soldiers were never known in better spirits than were we. We had had a hard march; we had made the longest and most successful cavalry raid of the war; we had fought a decisive battle; we had captured an entire army; we had deprived a noted Confederate general of his last command; we had captured a large number of railroad trains; had burned fifty bridges; had blown up twenty canal locks; had burned immense quantities of supplies for Lee's army; had destroyed many miles of railroad track, burning ties and bending the rails; had been within eight miles of Richmond on the west, where federal troops had never trod before, and had planted ourselves in a position where we could easily rejoin the Army of the Potomac, giving to Grant, and to the country, the services of Sheridan, Custer and Merritt, with a score of other able leaders of less renown, with two divisions of cavalry, whose superiors had never marched. A few days later we had crossed the James River at Bermuda Hundred; Sheridan was on board a small steamer in consultation with President Lincoln, General Grant and General Meade; we were upon the left flank of the army which had fought so long in front of Petersburg, and were ready for the final movement, whose story you know so well, which culminated in the surrender at Appomattox.

February 3, 1892.

PHOTOGRAPHIC ESSAY

The freckle-faced boy brandishing a puny Colt side-hammer revolver does not look very imposing in this July 1861 ambrotype (top). Although Cadet George Armstrong Custer soon left the West Point uniform behind, the boyishness would prove more difficult to shed (National Portrait Gallery, Smithsonian Institution). Not quite a year later, Second Lieutenant Custer wades into the Chickahominy River on May 22, 1862, to scout Confederate lines (bottom). This action, coupled with his part in cutting off an enemy picket post three days later, led to Custer's appointment to the staff of Major General George B. McClellan, then the commander of the Army of the Potomac. Sketch by the combat artist Alfred R. Waud (Library of Congress).

Captain Custer (top), aide-de-camp to General McClellan, had this portrait taken during an April 1863 visit to Monroe, Michigan (Monroe County Historical Commission). Landing on his feet after McClellan's dismissal, Custer was soon aide-de-camp to General Alfred Pleasonton. At Aldie, Virginia, on June 16, 1863 (bottom), the young captain rode forth to rally the faltering brigade of Colonel Hugh Judson Kilpatrick (unhorsed behind Custer) and caught everyone's attention. Thirteen days later he was appointed brigadier general. Alfred R. Waud drawing from Frederick Whittaker, *A Complete Life of Gen. George A. Custer* (1876) (Author's Collection).

Brigadier General Custer, resplendent with flowing locks and velveteen uniform, sits beside the man who gave him his star, Major General Alfred Pleasonton (top), at Warrenton, Virginia, October 9, 1863 (Custer Battlefield National Monument). Three months earlier, at Gettysburg on July 3, 1863 (bottom), the twenty-three-year-old brigadier had proven the wisdom of that promotion by triumphing over Stuart's cavalry with a vital victory that protected the flank of the Union center, then battling against Pickett's Charge. The contemporary artist Joseph Musso's *Custer's Charge at Hanover Pike Near Gettysburg* captures the fury of that battle (Courtesy Joseph Musso).

On October 9, 1864, Custer faced his old West Point comrade Brigadier General Thomas Rosser at Tom's Brook in the Shenandoah. To the astonishment of all, just before the battle began, Custer trotted out between the lines, swept off his hat and bowed gracefully in the saddle. Rosser smiled and remarked, "That's General Custer, the yanks are so proud of, and I intend to give him the best whipping today that he ever got." But it was Rosser's forces that were soundly whipped in a battle called the "Woodstock Races" by the triumphant Yankees. Alfred R. Waud drawing from Whittaker, *A Complete Life* (Author's Collection).

No other man proved more important to Custer's career than black-eyed, hard-bitten, profane Major General Philip H. Sheridan (top). He championed Custer, protected him, and always relied on him. "If there was any poetry or romance in war he could develop it," said Sheridan of his protégé. Custer, in turn, was devoted to Sheridan, once gushing to his wife on receiving a commendation from him, "Oh, is it not gratifying to be so thought of by one whose opinion is above all price?" (Library of Congress). Their bond was forged in the hot crucible of battle and nourished by the blood of friend and foe alike. At Cedar Creek on October 19, 1864, after Sheridan had rallied his stricken army to counterattack and rout the Confederates, Custer pursued the retreating rebels well past nightfall. Returning to Sheridan's camp, he jumped from his saddle, picked up his mentor, and gleefully waltzed him around the campfire. "By God Phil!" he exclaimed. "We've cleaned them out of their guns and got ours back!" (bottom). The combat artist James E. Taylor captured the moment (Western Reserve Historical Society).

Custer presents the rebels' battle flags captured at Cedar Creek by Sheridan's Army of the Shenandoah in a ceremony held at the War Department, Washington, D.C., on October 23, 1864 (top). It was during this ceremony that Secretary of War Edwin M. Stanton announced Custer's promotion to major general. Sketch by Alfred R. Waud (Library of Congress). Major General Custer with his wife, Elizabeth Bacon Custer, and their housekeeper, Eliza Brown, posed for this portrait on April 12, 1865 (bottom). Elizabeth sports a military dress of her own. Sheridan told her that her husband was the only one of his officers "who had not been spoiled by marriage" (Custer Battlefield National Monument).

Custer, ever in the advance, receives the Confederate flag of truce on April 9, 1865 (top). Later that day he would watch as Lee surrendered to Grant at Appomattox. Alfred Waud made this eyewitness sketch (Library of Congress). The changes wrought in Custer by four years of war were captured brilliantly by Matthew Brady's camera on May 23, 1865, the day of the Grand Review in Washington, D.C. The tanned general with the piercing eye is hardly recognizable as the pale cadet of 1861. But the freckles remain (National Archives).

Lieutenant Colonel George Armstrong Custer, February 9, 1869
(Custer Battlefield National Monument)

Suddenly, the cheering stopped. Although Custer was handsomely rewarded for his Civil War services with an impressive promotion from captain in the regular army to lieutenant colonel, it was nevertheless a bittersweet advancement. Everyone continued to refer to him as "general," for he held the brevet rank of major general in the regular army, but he could no longer wear the twin stars of a major general of volunteers. His regiment, the Seventh Cavalry, was newly created in the postwar growth of regular army forces meant to aid national expansion by meeting the challenge posed by the powerful western Indian tribes. Phil Sheridan's own brother, Michael, held a captaincy in the Seventh—a clear sign of the regiment's elite status. Yet Custer, without the constant crucible of battle to overawe his soldiers, could never win his regiment's devotion. The one great battle they fought, on the Washita in 1868, resulted only in further bitterly dividing the regiment rather than uniting it.

Nor was there much glory in this frustrating warfare in the West. Custer's first campaign against the Indians won him only a court-martial. His second made him a hero in the West, but from the East came a rising chorus of condemnation. "This shameless disregard for justice has been the most foolhardy course we could have pursued," preached an Episcopal bishop from Minnesota, Henry Whipple. One of Custer's own officers, Captain Frederick Benteen, fiercely criticized him in a letter published in the St. Louis Democrat and the New York Times.[1] "I only know the names of three savages upon the Plains," thundered the famed abolitionist Wendell Phillips of Boston, "Colonel Baker, General Custer, and at the head of all, General Sheridan."[2]

Custer was himself torn by the requirements of Indian warfare. His writings portray the natives as heroic defenders of their rights on the one hand and as base savages of unparalleled cruelty on the other. Like many of his military contemporaries, he was both repulsed and attracted by them, but unlike other officers, he clearly identified himself with the Indians and the West and relished the role of Indian fighter. His first efforts at writing did not concern his exploits in the Civil War but instead dealt with his hunting and Indian-fighting adventures in the West. Raised on tales of Indian warfare himself, he now quickly adopted the buckskin clothing of the frontiersman and began to act out a role that had already become a violent ritual in America. Not unlike the nation's first pioneer hero, Captain John Smith, Custer also found his Pocahontas-like Indian princess on the plains and made her his mistress in 1868–69.[3] He embraced the western wilderness and, above all, wished the public, and posterity, to view him as a frontiersman. He got his wish, but at an unexpected price.

Brian W. Dippie, a professor of history at the University of Victoria, British Columbia, and a distinguished western historian best known for his work on Indian policy and western art, has long been fascinated by Custer. His first book, *Custer's Last Stand: The Anatomy of an American Myth* (1976), is a classic of Custeriana, but in the original essay published here he deals not with his favorite topic, the Custer myth, but rather with the Custer of fact. Broadly interpretive, Dippie's essay follows Custer from court-martial in 1867 to triumph at the Washita in 1868, from the Yellowstone country to the Black Hills, and finally to the eve of the Battle of the Little Big Horn, always with an eye toward how each event might help explain the continuing enigma of Custer's Last Stand.

The late Minnie Dubbs Millbrook, a premier "grassroots historian," contributed articles on Kansas history to newspapers and magazines and was the author of a history of her county, *Ness, Western County, Kansas* (1955). Her interest in writing a biography of Elizabeth Custer led her to engage in extensive research on the Custers' time on the southern plains. A series of excellent articles followed that marked Millbrook as the leading authority on Custer in Kansas.[4] The best of them, "The West Breaks in General Custer," was published in the summer 1970 issue of the *Kansas Historical Quarterly* and is reprinted here. It recounts Custer's sad initiation into Indian warfare during General Winfield Scott Hancock's bungled 1867 campaign against the Cheyennes and Sioux. The campaign resulted in Custer's court-martial and suspension from the army.

Custer, recalled to service by Sheridan, retrieved his sullied reputation with a smashing victory over the Cheyennes at the Battle of the Washita on November 27, 1868. Humanitarian critics at the time, and historians since, characterized this battle as a massacre of innocents.

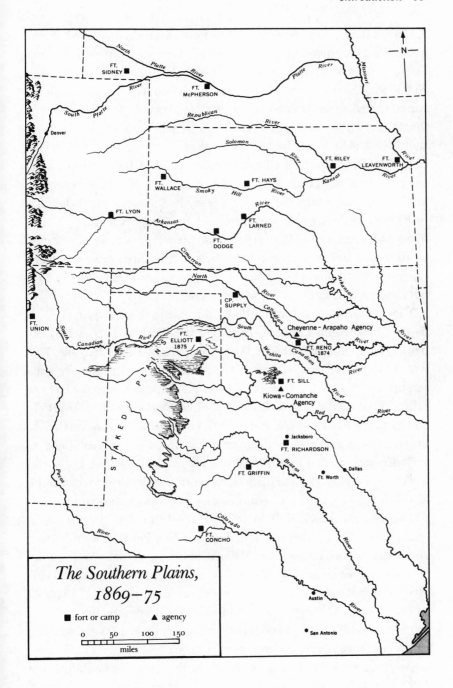

The Southern Plains,
1869–75

■ fort or camp ▲ agency

0   50   100   150
miles

Although the fight on the Washita was most assuredly one-sided, it was not a massacre. Black Kettle's Cheyennes were not unarmed innocents living under the impression that they were at peace. Although Black Kettle was the leading peace chief among the Cheyennes, several of his warriors had earlier raided the Kansas settlements and had recently fought the white soldiers. The chief had been informed by military authorities that he would be attacked unless he surrendered to General Sheridan. Black Kettle's village was a mixture of Indians representing both war and peace factions. After Custer's attack, government mail, army mules, and domestic property and photographs belonging to Kansas settlers were recovered from the camp. Nor were the soldiers under orders to kill everyone, for Custer personally intervened to stop the slaying of noncombatants, and fifty-three prisoners were taken by the troops. The battle, although a sad and tragic affair, does not deserve the harsh epithet of *massacre*.[5]

The best account of that battle by a participant is Edward S. Godfrey's "Some Reminiscences, Including the Washita Battle, November 27, 1868," first published in the October 1928 *Cavalry Journal*. This was the third, and final, memoir of the southern plains Indian wars written by Godfrey for the *Cavalry Journal*.[6] Although this essay has not attained the classic status of Godfrey's 1892 *Century Magazine* article on the Little Big Horn (reprinted in the next section), it nevertheless presents an equally clear and eloquent description of the Washita fight.

Godfrey graduated from West Point in June 1867 and was appointed a second lieutenant in Company G, Seventh Cavalry. He was with the Seventh Cavalry at the Washita, during the 1873 Yellowstone expedition, into the Black Hills in 1874, at the Little Big Horn in 1876, during the 1877 pursuit of Chief Joseph's Nez Perce (where he was severely wounded and won the Medal of Honor), and in the final conflict at Wounded Knee in 1890. He retired as a brigadier general in 1907, after over forty years of service, and did not die until April 1, 1932.[7]

The Seventh Cavalry, scattered to various Reconstruction posts in the South in 1871, was pulled together again early in 1873 and ordered to the northern plains. Nonreservation Sioux had disrupted the work of survey parties for the transcontinental Northern Pacific Railroad in 1872, and the transfer of the Seventh to Dakota was meant to overawe these Indians. Such hardly proved to be the case, for despite the formidable size of the military escort provided to the railway survey crews in

1873, the clearly unimpressed Sioux clashed with the troops on several occasions.

Custer's introduction to the northern plains is cogently chronicled in a series of letters from Second Lieutenant Charles W. Larned of the Seventh Cavalry to his mother. Compiled and edited by the historian George Frederick Howe, the letters were first published in the December 1952 *Mississippi Valley Historical Review*. Lieutenant Larned, who graduated from West Point in 1870, served only briefly with the Seventh Cavalry before returning to West Point in 1874 as a drawing instructor. He remained at the military academy for the rest of his career. This detached duty saved his life when his company was wiped out at the Little Big Horn.[8] In his letters home, this young officer echoes the sentiments of several of his fellow officers in his clear disdain for Custer, who he portrays as a nepotistic, egotistical, petty tyrant.

A considerably different viewpoint is evident in George A. Custer's own account of the Yellowstone expedition, "Battling with the Sioux on the Yellowstone," first published in the July 1876 *Galaxy Magazine*. Custer begins his narrative with a brief editorial in favor of government support of railroad expansion. He, like most of his fellow officers, was a warm friend to the railroaders.[9] Conspicuously absent from the narrative is any sense of the tense relationship that existed between Custer and the expedition's commander, Colonel David S. Stanley. Their quarrel, resulting from Custer's determination to exercise independent command and from Stanley's near constant drunkenness, climaxed with Custer being placed under arrest for two days and banished to the rear of the column. Stanley, drunk at the time he ordered Custer's arrest, was so chagrined once he sobered up that he virtually abdicated command thereafter to the more vigorous, able, and always sober cavalryman.[10]

Custer's narrative is quite the rousing adventure tale but must have seemed disturbingly ironic and deeply poignant when first published just after his own death at the hands of the Sioux on the Little Big Horn. It is marked by several interesting literary conceits worthy of a twentieth-century motion-picture script: the loyal Indian companion (the real Bloody Knife, later to die at the Little Big Horn, assuming the fictional Chingachgook/Tonto role); the hero-author's dashing younger brother (Lieutenant Tom Custer, here referred to by his brevet rank of colonel); the laughing exchange between Irish troopers in the heat

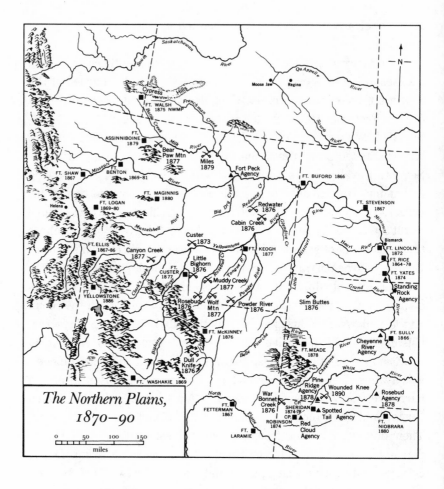

The Northern Plains,
1870–90

of combat (so reminiscent of later dialogue between Victor McLaglen and Jack Pennick in a John Ford cavalry film); the tiny band of determined troopers surrounded by a savage foe; and the climactic rush of the rescuing troops of cavalry, guidons dancing in the western wind. No doubt, three years later on the Little Big Horn only a few miles to the southwest, Custer and his desperate troopers again turned their eyes to distant hills in search of those dancing guidons—but this time the flags would not appear.

Notes

1. Quoted in Paul Andrew Hutton, *Phil Sheridan and His Army* (Lincoln: University of Nebraska Press, 1985), 95–96.

2. Quoted in Robert Winston Mardock, *The Reformers and the American Indian* (Columbia: University of Missouri Press, 1971), 73.

3. Custer's relationship with Mo-nah-se-ta (or Me-o-tzi), the daughter of the Cheyenne leader Little Rock, is well documented. She figures prominently in Custer's memoirs and in Elizabeth Custer's *Following the Guidon* (New York: Harper and Brothers, 1890) as an attractive and able intermediary between the soldiers and the Indians. Although six or seven months pregnant at the time of her capture during the November 1868 Battle of the Washita, she was Custer's mistress that winter and early spring. Cheyenne oral tradition, as reported independently in the works of Thomas Marquis, Charles Brill, Mari Sandoz, and David Miller, identified her as such. This is further corroborated by Ben Clark, Custer's chief scout during the Washita campaign, and by Captain Frederick Benteen of the Seventh Cavalry. Thomas B. Marquis, *Custer on the Little Bighorn* (Lodi, Calif.: Kain Publishing Co., 1969), 35, 43; Mari Sandoz, *Cheyenne Autumn* (New York: Hastings House, 1953), xvii; Charles J. Brill, *Conquest of the Southern Plains: Uncensored Narrative of the Battle of the Washita and Custer's Southern Campaign* (Oklahoma City: Golden Saga Publishers, 1938), 22, 45–46; David Humphreys Miller, *Custer's Fall: The Indian Side of the Story* (New York: Duell, Sloan and Pearce, 1957), 67–68, 237; John M. Carroll, ed., *The Benteen-Goldin Letters on Custer and His Last Battle* (New York: Liveright, 1974), 271; Ben Clark Interview, Field Notes, Folder 4, Box 2, Walter Camp Papers, Lilly Library, Indiana University.

4. See Minnie Dubbs Millbrook: "Custer's First Scout in the West," *Kansas Historical Quarterly* 39 (Spring 1973): 75–95; "Mrs. General Custer at Fort Riley, 1866," ibid. 40 (Spring 1974): 63–71; "Big Game Hunt-

ing with the Custers, 1869–1870," ibid. 41 (Winter 1975): 429–53; and "Rebecca Visits Kansas and the Custers: The Diary of Rebecca Richmond," ibid. 42 (Winter 1976): 366–402. For more on Custer in Kansas, see Brian W. Dippie, ed., *Nomad: George A. Custer in Turf, Field, and Farm* (Austin: University of Texas Press, 1980); Blaine Burkey, *Custer, Come at Once! The Fort Hays Years of George and Elizabeth Custer, 1867–1870* (Hays, Kans.: Thomas More Prep, 1976); Robert M. Utley, ed., *Life in Custer's Cavalry: Diaries and Letters of Albert and Jennie Barnitz, 1867–1868* (New Haven: Yale University Press, 1977); Lawrence A. Frost, *The Court-Martial of General George Armstrong Custer* (Norman: University of Oklahoma Press, 1968); and Henry M. Stanley, *My Early Travels and Adventures in America and Asia,* 2 vols. (New York: Charles Scribner's Sons, 1895).

5. For the Battle of the Washita, see Hutton, *Phil Sheridan and His Army,* 56–100. A harsh critique of Custer's role can be found in Brill, *Conquest of the Southern Plains,* and Jess C. Epple, *Custer's Battle of the Washita and a History of the Plains Indian Tribes* (New York: Exposition Press, 1970). More balanced, although the author still labels the Washita a massacre despite the fact that his own evidence proves otherwise, is Stan Hoig, *The Battle of the Washita: The Sheridan-Custer Indian Campaign of 1867–69* (Garden City, N.Y.: Doubleday and Co., 1976). A valuable compilation of documents concerning the

battle is John M. Carroll, ed., *General Custer and the Battle of the Washita: The Federal View* (Bryan, Tex.: Guidon Press, 1978).

6. E. S. Godfrey, "Reminiscences of the Medicine Lodge Peace Treaties," *Cavalry Journal* 37 (January 1928): 112–15; "Some Reminiscences, Including an Account of General Sully's Expedition against the Southern Plains Indians, 1868," *Cavalry Journal* 36 (July 1927): 417–25.

7. Francis B. Heitman, *Historical Register and Dictionary of the United States Army, from Its Organization, September 29, 1789, to March 2, 1902,* 2 vols. (Washington, D.C.: Government Printing Office, 1903), 1:461; Kenneth Hammer, *Biographies of the Seventh Cavalry: June 25th, 1876* (Fort Collins, Colo.: Old Army Press, 1972), 187–88.

8. Hammer, *Biographies of the Seventh,* 122.

9. For Custer's relationship with the railroads and his active promotion of their cause in the West, see Paul Andrew Hutton, "'Fort Desolation': The Military Establishment, the Railroad, and Settlement on the Northern Plains," *North Dakota History* 56 (Spring 1989): 21–30; Marvin E. Kroeker, "Deceit about the Garden: Hazen, Custer, and the Arid Lands Controversy," *North Dakota Quarterly* 38 (Summer 1970): 5–21; John M. Carroll, "A Short Evaluation of the Custer-Hazen Debates," in John M. Carroll, *4 On Custer by Carroll* (Bryan, Tex.: Guidon Press, 1976), 40–44; and Edgar I. Stewart, ed., *Penny-an-Acre Empire in the West* (Norman:

University of Oklahoma Press, 1968). Custer's business connections are also a central theme of Richard Slotkin, *The Fatal Environment: The Myth of the Frontier in the Age of Industrialization, 1800–1890* (New York: Atheneum, 1985), and Richard Slotkin, "'. . . & Then the Mare Will Go!': An 1875 Black Hills Scheme by Custer, Holladay, and Buford," *Journal of the West* 15 (July 1976): 60–75. Slotkin, in this essay and his later book, identifies former confederate General Abraham Buford as Custer's partner in a proposed business enterprise in the Black Hills, but he misread the signature on a key letter. The actual author of the letter was Colonel Rufus Ingalls, the acting quartermaster general of the army. The Custer-Ingalls relationship makes much more sense than a Custer-Buford relationship, which Slotkin had to construct through tortured logic.

The overall points made in the book and essay, however, remain valid.

10. There is no good monograph on the 1873 Yellowstone expedition, but for useful overviews, see Alan Rolston, "The Yellowstone Expedition of 1873," *Montana the Magazine of Western History* 20 (April 1970): 20–29, and Lawrence A. Frost, *Custer's Seventh Cav and the Campaign of 1873* (El Segundo, Calif.: Upton and Sons, 1986). For accounts by participants, see Charles Braden, "The Yellowstone Expedition of 1873," *Journal of the U.S. Cavalry Association* 16 (October 1905): 218–41; D. S. Stanley, *Personal Memoirs of Major General David S. Stanley* (Cambridge: Harvard University Press, 1917); and D. S. Stanley, *Report on the Yellowstone Expedition of 1873* (Washington, D.C.: Government Printing Office, 1874).

CUSTER:
THE INDIAN
FIGHTER

BRIAN W.

DIPPIE

A fter making a valiant stand against an overwhelming force of Indians, the soldiers had been wiped out to a man. A letter of condolence to a grieving parent described the battlefield:

From the large number of arrows picked up . . . and from other indications to be observed, it was evident that a desperate struggle had ensued before the Indians were successful in over-powering their victims. . . . The ground near which the bodies . . . lay was thickly strewn with exploded metallic cartridges, showing conclusively that they had defended themselves a long time and most gallantly too, against their murderous enemies. . . . the bodies, which were probably found as they fell, were lying near each other, thus proving that none had endeavored to flee or escape, but all died nobly fighting to the last. . . . no one is left to tell the tale, but from the evidence and circumstances before us we can imagine what determination, what bravery, what heroism must have inspired this devoted little band of martyrs, when, surrounded and assailed by a vastly overwhelming force of bloodthirsty barbarians, they manfully struggled to the last equally devoid of hope or fear.[1]

Custer's Last Stand? In fact, the letter writer was George A. Custer himself, reporting from Fort Riley, Kansas, on August 23, 1867, on the fate of a party of eleven men under Lieutenant Lyman S. Kidder. For Custer, the "Kidder Massacre" was a stark introduction to the dangers of plains warfare. The years from 1867 to 1869 marked the most intensive Indian campaigning of his entire career as he chased a

103

scattered, mobile foe over a vast expanse of land. Physical demands were as great as opportunities for decisive action were few. Kansas would reshape the Boy General of Civil War fame into the buckskin-clad Indian fighter whose death on the Little Big Horn River in 1876 brought mythic immortality.

By all accounts Custer came out of the Civil War peacock-proud and brimming with confidence, admired, even idolized, by many of his countrymen. A brevet major general when the war ended, Custer had experienced nothing but success as he had led brigades, then divisions of cavalry. Reconstruction duty in Texas through January 1866 prolonged the perks of high rank, but the volunteer troops were restive and peacetime duty an irritant. At twenty-six, Custer's glory days seemed behind him, and he pondered his future over the summer of 1866. He landed on his feet when, effective that September, he was appointed lieutenant colonel of the newly formed Seventh Cavalry regiment, a promotion, since his regular army rank was that of captain. But it must have seemed a demotion of sorts, and it accurately foretold what service in the postwar army would be like: a man who had enjoyed meteoric rise during the Civil War was still lieutenant colonel of the Seventh Cavalry when he died on the Little Big Horn a decade later.

Custer reported for duty at Fort Riley in October, was settled there by December, and was inducted into plains service the following spring as commander of cavalry in General Winfield S. Hancock's fourteen-hundred-man expedition. Intended to overawe the southern plains tribes by a show of force and, if need be, to punish them for their raids on white settlers, the expedition was a failure: counterproductive if peace was the goal, since it exacerbated hostilities by destroying a Sioux and Cheyenne village; ineffective if war was the goal, since the village was deserted and the Indians outraged, not cowed, by Hancock's action. Even as the expedition was disbanding in early May the Indians were retaliating. Custer both learned and suffered through it all. He was to follow the "hostiles" who had fled the village, protect the stage route, prevent depredations, and mete out punishment. But he could not even catch them. Instead he passed a sulky spring, moody, irritable, and despondent over the long separation from his wife. Everything was a frustration: supplies and forage that failed to arrive; the dreary stretches of sunbaked wastes that broke horses and men and made desertion an epidemic; an elusive quarry whose mobility mocked the army's plodding pursuit.

As spring stretched into summer and the frustrations only mounted, Custer made a bad decision: he would reunite with his wife at Fort Riley whatever the cost. In May he had confessed he was tempted to "desert and fly" to her. On July 15, with an escort of four officers and seventy-two men, he simply left his command at Fort Wallace, the westernmost in the string of posts along the Smoky Hill road in Kansas, and set off at a punishing pace for Fort Riley, 275 miles to the east. Custer would argue military considerations in his defense, but the Seventh's commanding officer, Colonel Andrew J. Smith, was unconvinced and preferred charges for absence without leave from command and for conduct prejudicial to good order and military discipline. A disgruntled officer filed additional charges relating to an incident in July when Custer, incensed by repeated desertions, had ordered a group of men making off in broad daylight to be ridden down and shot. Three had been wounded, one fatally, and Custer had made a public display of denying them medical aid.[2]

On October 11, the court-martial at Fort Leavenworth found Custer guilty as charged on all specifications, with no criminality attached to the most serious, and on November 20 he was sentenced to suspension from rank and pay for one year. Nonchalant in his public reaction, Custer had much to mull over in private. Clearly, he had not done well as an Indian fighter in 1867, but what had he learned? He had seen one sight on the Hancock expedition that could not fail to impress—several hundred Indians "formed in line of battle upon the open plain, about one mile in our advance." The moment passed, and Custer would never see another quite like it again—unless the dust at the Little Big Horn lifted long enough for him to peer through it at the village stretched along the river and the hundreds of warriors racing toward him, affording a fleeting glimpse of his own mortality. He had also learned one hard truth about Indian campaigning: "I am of the opinion, . . . justified by experience, that no cavalry in the world, marching, even in the lightest manner possible, unencumbered with baggage or supply trains, can overtake or outmarch the Western Indian, when the latter is disposed to prevent it." He had also seen, in the grisly remains of Kidder's men, what could happen when a small force of soldiers stumbled onto a larger one of Indians not disposed to flee. Indian campaigning, an infantryman observed in 1876, was reminiscent of an illustration showing the Prince of Wales on a tiger hunt: "First the prince gets a rear view of the tiger; Then a front view, then the tiger gets a rear view of the Prince of Wales." When the terrain was right, the odds favorable, or the situation desperate enough, plains Indians could be formidable fighters. But ordinarily they did their best fighting by not fighting at all. For the soldiers, war was business; for the Indians, it was a matter of survival. Defeats were temporary setbacks for the army, but for the Indians, they could mean confinement and the end to independence.[3]

These considerations dictated military strategy as it unfolded in 1868. Generals William Tecumseh Sherman and Philip H. Sheridan, commanders respectively of the Military Division of the Missouri and the Military Department of the Missouri within it, determined to visit total war on the Indians. A winter campaign and unremitting pursuit would tax the Indians' will to resist and would end hostilities on the plains. No one, Sheridan believed, could do the job better than Custer, and on September 24 he wired Custer in Monroe: "Generals Sherman, Sully, and myself, and nearly all the officers of your regiment, have asked for you, and I hope the application will be successful. Can you come at once? Eleven companies of your regiment will move about the 1st of October against the hostile Indians." It was a jubilant Custer who telegraphed back that he was on his way to Kansas. Despite his public indifference over his suspension, the enforced idleness had been a torment. "It is said that blessings sometimes come in disguise," he later wrote. "Such proved to be true in this instance, although I must say the disguise for some little time was most perfect."[4]

Custer's return to the Seventh Cavalry on October 11 reinvigorated the whole regiment. One officer recalled, "We had unconsciously fallen into a state of inertia, and appeared to be leading an aimless sort of existence, but with his coming, action, purpose, energy and general strengthening of the loose joints was the order of the day." Certainly the dispensation from on high had reinvigorated Custer. Gone was the lethargy that had afflicted him in 1867. He had patrols in the field at once and could barely contain his impatience for another crack at the Indians. The inevitable delays this time only fed his eagerness, and on the morning of November 23, from Camp Supply on the North Canadian River in Indian Territory, Custer led the Seventh through a blizzard due south toward the Washita River, where the Cheyennes, Comanches, Kiowas, and Arapahos were wintering. His pace never slackened, and the early hours of November 27 found him on a bluff above the Washita with Black Kettle's village of Cheyennes at hand. Custer could not smell the wood smoke an Osage scout detected, nor see the ponies grazing in the distance, but he heard a dog bark, a bell tinkle, and a baby cry. "Savages though they were," he acknowledged, ". . . I could not but regret that in a war such as we were forced to engage in, the mode and circumstances of battle would possibly prevent discrimination." Soldiers who had helped bury Kidder's men or heard stories of torture and mutilation felt no such compunction. A coordinated attack at dawn caught the Indians still sleeping; within minutes the camp was in the soldiers' possession, and when the fighting ended, 103 Cheyenne men, women, and children were dead on the ground, another 53 taken captive. In the spirit of total war, 875 Indian ponies were slaughtered and all the captured property—lodge skins, robes, weapons, and the like—destroyed. Custer could not linger to relish victory. Warriors from nearby villages were arriving in unexpected numbers, and the situation was growing ominous. Although the Seventh's casualties were light, in keeping with a surprise attack (only one officer and one enlisted man were killed in the initial charge), Major Joel H. Elliott had led seventeen men on an unwise chase after fleeing Indians and had not been seen again. Tradition demanded that Custer make a thorough search, but darkness and the uncertainty of the situation dictated a withdrawal from the field and a return to base camp.[5]

Sheridan applauded the victory on the Washita as decisive, and Custer found himself acclaimed as a great Indian fighter. "The sad side of the story," as Custer delicately put it at the time, was the loss of Elliott and his men. What Custer did not fully grasp was the effect Elliott's "abandonment" would have on the Seventh Cavalry, cleaving it into factions, one uncritically loyal to him, the other perpetually critical. Captain Frederick W. Benteen, whose mocking contempt for Custer's conduct of the battle became public knowledge, still despised him seven and a half years later, when the regiment rode to disaster on the Little Big Horn. The Washita taught Custer something else about Indian fighting: Sheridan and the western press might cheer him, but eastern opinion was nowhere near so favorable. The former abolitionist firebrand Wendell Phillips declared Custer and his kind the only savages on the plains, and humanitarian reformers uniformly condemned the Washita battle as an indiscriminate slaughter. Still, buoyed by victory and the esteem of his superiors, Custer pressed on.[6]

With the major battle over, he wanted the campaign over too. He was "as impatient as a crazed animal" to start for home, but the Indians were as elusive as ever, and only a grueling pursuit, the troops sometimes subsisting on horseflesh, brought the campaign to an inconclusive end in late March. It would be fall before the southern plains were calm, and the Custers settled into a routine of hosting guests, hunting buffalo, and savoring the colonel's new prominence as an Indian fighter. The western plains that had once represented only failure and humiliation had become "dear to us," Elizabeth Custer recalled, "because of the happy hours spent there."[7]

The idyll ended in March 1871 when the Seventh was transferred from Kansas to the Department of the South and scattered to various points, principally in South Carolina and Kentucky. Custer found Reconstruction duty uncongenial and was delighted in February 1873 when the regiment was reassigned to the Department of Dakota for service against the Sioux. The transfer was by steamboat, railroad, then horseback (proof positive that civilized amenities were being left behind once again) from Yankton, Dakota Territory, to Fort Rice, the staging point for a major expedition into Sioux country. Ten days after the Seventh Cavalry's arrival, on June 20, the Yellowstone expedition under the command of Colonel David S. Stanley set off. More formidable than Hancock's, with a combined strength of almost two thousand cavalry, infantry, artillery, scouts, and civilian employees, the expedition was to serve the Sioux notice that resistance to construction of the Northern Pacific Railroad would be futile.

The Yellowstone expedition provided Custer his second direct experience in Indian fighting. First, though, he had a preliminary skirmish with Colonel Stanley. Custer was not an easy man to deal with. Charming and ingratiating in his social relations, he managed to alienate civilians who encountered him in an official capacity. Joseph La Barge, the master of a steamboat contracted to ferry the Seventh across the Missouri in 1873, remembered Custer's imperious "Stand aside, sir," when La Barge had insisted on loading his own vessel, and the postmistress at Bismarck clashed with Custer over his assumption that mail destined for Fort Abraham Lincoln had priority. A squabble over the government key and a mailbag slit in a fit of pique were evidence of a petty streak and an overbearing manner. "Custer seemed to me to be generally unpopular, that is, I rarely heard him well spoken of," La Barge remarked. Certainly his officers did their share of complaining. Custer was high-handed, demanding, unreasonable, and unfair. Such grumbling was a staple of army life, but Edward S. Godfrey, who generally respected Custer, related a revealing incident that had occurred on the march from Yankton to Fort Rice. An evening gathering around Godfrey's campfire, informal and merry, broke up as soon as Custer put in an appearance. With yawns and polite excuses, the officers extinguished their pipes and slipped away one by one until only Godfrey was left. Mortified, Custer stayed on late into the night talking compulsively. His relations with certain superiors were equally strained. Custer thrived on independent command and preferred giving orders to taking them. Others had already found him a reluctant subordinate, and Colonel Stanley had been forewarned. The expedition was barely out of Fort Rice before they collided. Abstemious himself, Custer regarded Stanley as a drunken incompetent. Stanley, in turn, resented Custer's assumption that as the commander of the cavalry he was free to come and go as he pleased, scouting ahead of the main column, chasing after game, generally enjoying what everyone seemed to consider a great lark. The two eventually sorted out their differences, and Custer was permitted to make the return march from the Yellowstone on his own, arriving at Fort Lincoln, the Seventh's new headquarters on the Missouri just upriver from Fort Rice, on September 21. Though all ended well, no account of the 1876 Great Sioux War and the issue of disobedience of orders can ignore Custer's track record on earlier Indian campaigns. The habit of command was not one he ever willingly relinquished.[8]

Two battles with the Sioux on the Yellowstone added to Custer's reputation as an Indian fighter, but worrisome tendencies were also in evidence. On August 4 Custer and a small advance party had a hot brush with several hundred Sioux who failed to decoy them into an ambush; seven days later a general battle ensued when the Indians attacked the cavalry encampment at daybreak. Custer's management of both battles has been praised. But he tempted fate on August 4 by reconnoitering on his own in the face of a concealed enemy and was almost cut off by the charging Sioux as he dashed for safety. The ambush "came near being a surprise to Custer," an officer noted, whereas the fight on the eleventh might have been avoided had Custer heeded a scout's warning that the Indians were massing for a dawn attack. Custer seemed to have trouble taking the Sioux seriously. When he described his race for life on the fourth he borrowed race-track parlance to embellish the tale. His brother-in-law, Lieutenant James Calhoun, described the episode as a "little game" the Indians had "intended to play," not realizing Custer held "the winning hand." The entire expedition struck one observer at the outset as "a picnic on a grand scale," and even casualties never dampened the festive mood. Caught up in the excitement of the battle on the eleventh, some civilians with the command "enjoyed themselves immensely" and declared Indian fighting "the best sport in the world." It was a strange kind of "sport"—official reports placed the military's casualties at four wounded and four killed. But the next day Custer, with a small party, galloped off eight miles in pursuit of elk. It was all a glorious adventure, and when it ended, nothing gave Custer more pleasure than toting up his hunting score.[9]

A year's reflection did not change Custer's attitude. In July 1874, the Seventh Cavalry was off again, this time on its own, to explore the Black Hills, determine possible locations for a military post, and investigate persistent rumors of gold. The hills were Sioux country, confirmed to them by treaty in 1868, and the expedition would be proceeding at risk. Nevertheless, Custer had no hesitation in inviting a New York friend along for the fun:

> I say that our object is a peaceful one but I have no idea that our trip will be. The Indians have long opposed all efforts of white men to enter the Black Hills and I feel confident that the Sioux will combine their entire strength and endeavor to oppose our progress. I will have a well equipped force, strong enough to take care of itself . . . ten full companies of the best cavalry in Uncle Sam's service. . . . [You will] be exposed to no danger whatever.[10]

The prospect of Sioux resistance was offered as an inducement, not a warning. It would add a little tang to a two-month western excursion.

The Black Hills expedition turned out to be in truth a lark. Indian opposition never materialized. Custer, with the independent command he coveted, was generally in a coltish mood. And the hills were spectacular. The column of wagons, soldiers, and civilians, almost one thousand strong, wended its way through lush valleys bedecked with wild-flowers and watered by ice-cold crystalline streams, "a very paradise." The enlisted men played baseball. Officers fished and hunted to their hearts' content, Custer adding a grizzly bear (or so he claimed) to his tally. The scientific corps studied the flora, fauna, and geology, the correspondents filed euphoric dispatches, and two prospectors found gold.[11]

The expedition was back at Fort Lincoln by the end of August, just as the furor created by the news of gold was beginning. The army was relatively successful in upholding the Sioux title and keeping the area clear of miners through the summer of 1875. But that September the government began negotiations with the Sioux to purchase either mining rights or the Black Hills proper, and when that failed, it took the position that it could do no more for the Indians. A full-blown gold rush followed, precipitating a series of events that would find Custer in May 1876 in the saddle again, leading the Seventh Cavalry to another rendezvous with the Sioux. He was, by then, a veteran Indian campaigner with nine years of intermittent experience. But what had he learned since 1867?

The memory of the Kidder party's fate may have faded a little, but Custer should have known the Sioux were a foe to be reckoned with. Besides his own encounters on the Yellowstone, there was the sobering lesson provided by Captain William Judd Fetterman. Fetterman had boasted that he could ride through the whole Sioux nation, and he got his chance on December 21, 1866, when he took eighty men with him to their deaths near Fort Phil Kearny in Wyoming. The "Fetterman Massacre," the worst defeat inflicted on troops by the Indians after the Civil War, had set the army abuzz. It would undoubtedly have been a primary topic of conversation even as Custer was settling into his quarters at Fort Riley before his first Indian campaign. In its lethal mixture of arrogance and inexperience, it was reminiscent of the disaster that befell British General Edward Braddock's army of regulars and colonial militia en route to Fort Duquesne in 1755, when it was cut to pieces by ambuscaded French and Indian allies. "Who would have thought it?" a mortally wounded Braddock repeatedly asked his attendants. Not Fetterman, certainly. None accompanying him survived to record *his* dying words, but Custer reconstructed the likely scenario in his 1874 reminiscences, *My Life on the Plains*:

It is stated that the Indians were massed to resist Colonel Fetterman's advance along Peno creek . . . ; that Colonel Fetterman formed his advanced lines on the summit of the hill overlooking the creek and valley . . . ; that the Indians in large force attacked him vigorously in this position, and were successfully resisted for half an hour or more; that the command then being short of ammunition and seized with a panic at this event and the great numerical superiority of the Indians, attempted to retreat . . . ; that the mountaineers and old soldiers, who had learned that a movement from Indians in an engagement was equivalent to death, remained in their first position and were killed there; that immediately upon the commencement of the retreat the Indians charged upon and surrounded the party, who could not now be formed by their officers and were immediately killed. Only six men of the whole command were killed by balls, and two of these, Colonel Fetterman and Captain Brown, no doubt inflicted this death upon themselves, or each other, by their own hands.[12]

Such in outline was the strategy Custer likely had in mind when he faced his own day of decision on the Little Big Horn.

The Fetterman fiasco was a compelling precedent. Custer recognized the decoy tactics employed by the Sioux in their encounter on August 4, 1873, as the very ones that had brought Fetterman to grief. Officers present commented that before the battle on the eleventh, the Sioux had taunted Custer's scouts with the memory of Fetterman's fate, whereas afterward, Indians who had fancied themselves "a terror and dread to all whites" since their victory over Fetterman were "thunder-struck and amazed" by the cavalry's "perfect indifference" to their reputation. Just months before starting on his final campaign, Custer rehashed the whole Fetterman affair with the officer commanding Fort Phil Kearny at the time. He drew from it the lesson that once plains Indians settled on war, they could conduct it "with astonishing energy and marked success." But the key lesson offered by Fetterman, and Kidder for that matter, was tactical: when the Indians enjoyed numerical superiority and were determined to fight, it was fatal to turn your backs on them and attempt to flee; only a resolute stand, such as Custer had made on the Yellowstone in 1873, offered any hope.[13]

The precedents were there, in short, as were the lessons to be learned. But though the memory of finding the mangled corpses of Kidder's men could even at a distant day make Custer's "very blood curdle," it was hard to keep such precedents in mind when the real fear in 1876 was not that the Indians would make a successful resistance, but that they would make a successful escape, stymieing the army and prolonging the campaign. Only weeks before the Battle of the Little Big Horn, an officer with General George Crook's command, writing from a camp 190 miles from the fort in Wyoming named after the ill-fated Fetterman and having just passed over the "very ground" where Fetterman had been killed, was unimpressed by the portents to caution. "Dont you belive all the rumors you hear about the warriors leaving to fight us," he comforted his wife. "All we are afraid of [is] that we wont find them." And one of the Seventh Cavalry's medical officers wrote to his wife just four days before he died on the Little Big Horn, "I think it is very clear that we shall not see an Indian this summer."[14]

Knowing what happened next, we can hardly credit such complacency today. But when it came to Indian fighting lessons were always easier to come by than to learn. Impetuosity was not the problem; experience was, when the Indians failed to act as they were supposed to. Then it could prove actively, even fatally, misleading. And so Custer could ride to the Little Big Horn weighed down by the prospect of futile weeks in the saddle in pursuit of an elusive foe, dreading an inconclusive campaign, hoping against hope for a decisive encounter—with Kidder and Fetterman in his head, perhaps, but with the Washita still warm in his heart.

Notes

1. Custer letter in Barton R. Voight, "The Death of Lyman S. Kidder," *South Dakota History* 6 (Winter 1975): 15.

2. G. A. Custer to E. B. Custer, May 6, 1867, in Marguerite Merington, ed., *The Custer Story: The Life and Intimate Letters of General George A. Custer and His Wife Elizabeth* (New York: Devin-Adair, 1950), 202. For Custer in 1867 and his court-martial, see Minnie Dubbs Millbrook, "The West Breaks in General Custer," reprinted in this volume, and Minnie Dubbs Millbrook, "Custer's First Scout in the West," *Kansas Historical Quarterly* 39 (Spring 1973): 75–95; Robert M. Utley, ed., *Life in*

Custer's Cavalry: Diaries and Letters of Albert and Jennie Barnitz, 1867–1868 (New Haven: Yale University Press, 1977); Brian W. Dippie, ed., *Nomad: George A. Custer in Turf, Field, and Farm* (Austin: University of Texas Press, 1980); Gary M. Thomas, *The Custer Scout of April 1867* (Kansas City: Westport Printing, for the author, 1987); and Lawrence A. Frost, *The Court-Martial of General George Armstrong Custer* (Norman: University of Oklahoma Press, 1968).

3. "On the Plains," *Turf, Field, and Farm*, November 9, 23, 1867, in Dippie, *Nomad*, 21, 28; Gregory J. W. Urwin, "'Custar Had Not Waited for Us': One of Gibbon's Doughboys on the Custer Battle," in Gregory J. W. Urwin and Roberta E. Fagan, eds., *Custer and His Times: Book Three* (Conway: University of Central Arkansas Press and the Little Big Horn Associates, 1987), 188.

4. Sheridan quoted in George Armstrong Custer, *My Life on the Plains; or, Personal Experiences with Indians* (New York: Sheldon and Co., 1874), 125; ibid., 23. And see Paul Andrew Hutton, *Phil Sheridan and His Army* (Lincoln: University of Nebraska Press, 1985), 28–114.

5. Francis M. Gibson (E. S. Luce, ed.), "The Battle of the Washita," in John M. Carroll, ed., *Washita!* (Bryan, Tex.: John M. Carroll, 1978), 8; Custer, *My Life on the Plains*, 159. See also Stan Hoig, *The Battle of the Washita: The Sheridan-Custer Indian Campaign of 1867–69* (Garden City, N.Y.: Doubleday and Co., 1976), and John M.

Carroll, ed., *General Custer and the Battle of the Washita: The Federal View* (Bryan, Tex.: Guidon Press, 1978).

6. Custer quoted in Elizabeth B. Custer, *Following the Guidon* (New York: Harper and Brothers, 1890), 45; [F. W. Benteen], "The Battle of the Washita," *Missouri Democrat* (St. Louis), February 9, 1869. On Wendell Phillips, see Robert Winston Mardock, *The Reformers and the American Indian* (Columbia: University of Missouri Press, 1971), 71–72.

7. Custer, *Following the Guidon*, 49; ibid., 308. And see Dippie, *Nomad*, 41–71.

8. Hiram Martin Chittenden, *History of Early Steamboat Navigation on the Missouri River: Life and Adventures of Joseph La Barge*, 2 vols. (New York: Francis P. Harper, 1903), 2:431–32; Jessamine Slaughter Burgum, *Zezula; or, Pioneer Days in the Smoky Water Country* (Valley City, N.D.: Getchell and Nielsen, 1937), 102–5; E. S. Godfrey quoted in John M. Carroll, ed., *The Yellowstone Expedition of 1873* (Mattituck, N.Y., and Bryan, Tex.: J. M. Carroll and Co., 1986), 70–71 n. 12. And see Lawrence A. Frost, *Custer's Seventh Cav and the Campaign of 1873* (El Segundo, Calif.: Upton and Sons, 1986).

9. Robert M. Utley, *Cavalier in Buckskin: George Armstrong Custer and the Western Military Frontier* (Norman: University of Oklahoma Press, 1988), 119–22; Charles Braden, "The Yellowstone Expedition of 1873," *Journal of the U.S. Cavalry Association* 16 (October 1905), reprinted in

Carroll, *Yellowstone Expedition of 1873*, 55, 58; Dippie, *Nomad*, 105–6; Lawrence A. Frost, ed., *Some Observations on the Yellowstone Expedition of 1873* (Glendale, Calif.: Arthur H. Clark, 1981), 61; Charles W. Larned quoted in Roger Darling, *Custer's Seventh Cavalry Comes to Dakota* (El Segundo, Calif.: Upton and Sons, 1989), 191; Frost, *Some Observations*, 76, 78.

10. "Custer to Barrett: Come, Join Our Fun in the Black Hills!" *Pacific Historian* 12 (Winter 1968): 39. Lawrence Barrett could not find the time to join the expedition, but he and Custer were intimates in New York, and he recalled Custer's mood before the 1876 campaign: "The thought that he was going into action, into certain peril, did not make me fearful. He was so associated with success . . . that he seemed invincible. He predicted a severe campaign, but was not doubtful of the result. His plans were well laid, his command efficient; and he joyfully obeyed the summons to return to his duty. . . . As he rode out of Fort Lincoln for the last time, he was as full of glee as a child; his duty lay before him, his glory, of which no enemy could rob him." "Personal Recollections of General Custer," in Frederick Whittaker, *The Complete Life of Gen. George A. Custer* (New York: Sheldon and Co., 1876), 641–42.

11. Herbert Krause and Gary D.

Olson, *Prelude to Glory: A Newspaper Accounting of Custer's 1874 Expedition to the Black Hills* (Sioux Falls, S.D.: Brevet Press, 1974), 23. See also Donald Jackson, *Custer's Gold: The United States Cavalry Expedition of 1874* (New Haven: Yale University Press, 1966), and Dippie, *Nomad*, 160–61 n. 2.

12. *The Autobiography of Benjamin Franklin* (New York: Washington Square Press, 1964), 175–77; Custer, *My Life on the Plains*, 84–85. And see Dee Brown, *Fort Phil Kearny: An American Saga* (New York: G. P. Putnam's Sons, 1962).

13. Frost, *Some Observations*, 123; ibid., 74 (Calhoun's recollection); Charles W. Larned in Darling, *Custer's Seventh Cavalry Comes to Dakota*, 101; Henry B. Carrington, letter in *New York Times*, July 12, 1876; Custer, *My Life on the Plains*, 83.

14. Custer, *My Life on the Plains*, 77; James H. Nottage, "The Big Horn and Yellowstone Expeditions of 1876 As Seen through the Letters of Captain Gerhard Luke Luhn," *Annals of Wyoming* 45 (Spring 1973): 32; Edward S. Luce, ed., "The Diary and Letters of Dr. James M. DeWolf, Acting Assistant Surgeon, U.S. Army; His Record of the Sioux Expedition of 1876 As Kept until His Death," *North Dakota History* 25 (April–July 1958): 81.

THE
WEST
BREAKS IN
GENERAL
CUSTER

MINNIE DUBBS

MILLBROOK

According to legend Gen. George Armstrong Custer took to the West as a seal to the sea, glorying in its hardships and its dangers. Mrs. Custer would write reminiscently, "General Custer was such an enthusiast over our glorious West. . . ."[1] Actually this enthusiasm took some time to develop. From all indications the first year of Custer's service in Kansas and Nebraska was not a happy one and the young general had no liking for the country or the army service in it.

The adjustment from the lofty realm of major general down to lieutenant colonel in a regiment was no doubt difficult. Custer's extraordinary success in the Civil War[2] had enabled him to skip the arduous years of training by which a young lieutenant usually came up through officer ranks. Thus he had little experience in the close, direct command of men. He had not had an independent command; his orders came down to him from above and he handed them on to the regimental officers below. His willingness to fight, his brilliance in leading men in battle and his quick eye in selecting strategic points of attack earned him much praise, quick promotion, and generous leaves of absence. He had enjoyed all the perquisites of a general's headquarters, first as an aide and then as a general himself. The Army of the Potomac was the best-supplied, best-equipped army in the world and it operated so near to the capital city that its officers were often a part of the social scene in Washington. Custer's wife was with him when there was no other woman in camp. The newspapers were full of his exploits and crowds cheered at the sight of him.

After the war, followed by a year of leave and service in Louisiana and Texas, Custer was sent to the "American Siberia"—that vast, empty Plains region where there were no crowds and no one remembered his glory. There was not even any comfort. The weather was harsh and unpredictable; there was little water to drink, no trees to shelter a soldier from the pitiless sun or the driving rain. The food was bad and insufficient and inevitably on the march the officer was reduced to the trooper's monotonous ration. Even the enemy—the scruffy, slippery Indian—was an unworthy and inglorious foe. For Custer the summer of 1867 was a season of dispirit, privation, and indignity.

The year had opened rather auspiciously for the United States army in Kansas. The volunteer soldiers of the Civil War had all been mustered out and the regular army would take over its old task of policing the trails, protecting the settlers, and punishing the Indians if necessary. It would have an extra duty that year for a railroad—the Union Pacific, Eastern division—was building up the Smoky Hill river valley and the surveyors and tracklayers would have to be guarded against Indian attack. Several new cavalry regiments had been allowed by congress and one of them, the U.S. Seventh, had been trained at Fort Riley and was ready for duty. Three well-known generals would direct and command operations. Gen. Winfield S. Hancock[3] commanded the Department of the Missouri[4] which included the states of Kansas, Colorado, New Mexico, and Indian territory. Gen. Andrew J. Smith,[5] colonel of the Seventh cavalry, would also direct the District of the Upper Arkansas,[6] with the Santa Fe and Smoky Hill trails his special concern. Gen. George Armstrong Custer, lieutenant colonel of the Seventh, would lead the cavalry striking force that would pursue the Indians into their fastnesses and smite them in their camps if necessary.

Gen. William T. Sherman, commanding the Division of the Missouri,[7] was anxious for the army in Kansas to get out into the Indian country early. It had been a bad, snowy winter and the wet inclement weather continued on into the spring. Early in March it was evident that the expedition to the west under General Hancock, planned to impress the Plains tribes, would be unable to start as scheduled. From Fort Riley General Smith wrote Hancock at Fort Leavenworth:

> The Republican [river] is booming and full of ice . . . a pontoon
> bridge could not live an hour. . . . Old Moses himself could not
> stay the coming flood or assure us passage dry shod between us
> and Harker. There are trains between here and Harker that have
> been waterbound for one month. . . . The present state of affairs is
> unusual and occurs but once in many years. I remember seeing it
> in 1844.[8]

The quartermaster at Fort Riley, Cpt. George W. Bradley, wrote
to his superior on March 3, reporting what such weather meant to his
operation:

> I have worked day and night to get the stores forward. I have
> built four different bridges across the Republican at this point. Two
> have been sunk and two destroyed by ice. I have a ferry in opera-
> tion here which can transport one team at a time. It was stopped
> by the ice. The commissary and ordnance stores for Fort Harker,
> Hays, Larned and Dodge are all water bound between this place
> and the Solomon River.[9]

The fact of this unusual wet, miserable weather which continued
right down to July, needs to be taken into consideration in any account
of the summer because it made the supply problem of the army very
difficult, almost impossible at times. As the railroad along the Smoky
Hill advanced, it helped, but in June, though the railroad had reached
beyond Salina, there were no trains for 11 days due to the washing out
of bridges and tracks.[10] The long overland supply trains, oxen or mule
drawn, were stuck again for days in the bottomless mud.

The expedition to the west got off on March 26. It was made up of
six companies of the Seventh cavalry, seven companies of the 37th infantry and a battery of the Fourth artillery, aggregating eventually
1,400 soldiers.[11] Hancock, Smith, and Custer were along. Altogether it
was quite an impressive army and the Western newspapers spoke of
it as "the grand advance" or the "expedition de Hancock."[12] Hancock
hoped the Indians, too, would be impressed. In martial array the cortege proceeded to Fort Larned where the Cheyennes had been asked
to meet the general.[13] The railroad was to be built through Cheyenne
country and the attitude of the Indians had been a matter of comment
and conjecture throughout the winter.

At Fort Larned the troops endured an eight-inch snowstorm on April 9 and cold so severe that Custer considered taking his mare, Fanchon, into his tent for shelter. The storm delayed the Indians, adding to the tensions and misunderstandings of the meeting. Dissatisfied because so few of the chiefs had come and because of their stolid lack of response, Hancock decided to go on out to the Indian village on Pawnee fork so that all the people might see his mighty army and be deterred from any overt actions later. He found a large encampment of both Sioux and Cheyennes.[14] As he approached the village the frightened people ran away and on their flight to and across the Smoky Hill, killed three station keepers on the trail as they passed.

Custer, sent with the cavalry to bring them back, failed to come up with even one Indian but was treated instead to a magnificent demonstration of the way the Indian, even on his winter-weakened ponies, burdened with his women and children, could evade the U.S. cavalry. Following the Indian sign, Custer marched obliquely northwest towards the Smoky Hill river, and came around eventually to discover the burned and mutilated bodies of the station men slightly northeast of the camp on the Pawnee from which the Indians had fled.[15] When Hancock heard of the atrocity, he burned the village the Indians had forsaken. Thus the season began.

Custer, his horses worn out by his fast scout—150 miles in four and a half days—came into Fort Hays to find no forage for his horses and sat down to wait for it. Hancock and Smith went on to Fort Dodge to talk to chiefs of other tribes and inspect the condition of the post. To his embarrassment Hancock also ran short of forage. The weather had continued adverse and at Dodge on April 22 more snow had fallen. One of the frontier newspapers that had been observing with interest the meeting of the ponderous army with the nimble Indian, reported, "His [Hancock's] mules are in very precarious circumstances . . . his hay exhausted, and a courier was dispatched to Fort Harker for a supply. He has with him about seventeen hundred mules." [16]

Always sensitive to public criticism, Hancock wrote to General Sherman:

> I have seen some notices in the newspapers, stating that the expedition has been detained for want of forage, and that our animals are suffering, &c. There is not a word of truth in such state-

ments. . . . The hay contractors failed almost entirely, owing to high water, bad roads, &c., and we have consequently only had hay sufficient for the animals during the most inclement weather. . . . The only serious trouble we have met in respect to forage was that when General Custer arrived at Fort Hays from Pawnee Fork he found there was only a sufficient supply for his command for one or two days, and was unfortunately delayed on that account. . . .[17]

This shortage of supplies troubled Hancock greatly for he was a careful planner, a master of army red tape as well as a master of army supply. Before the Civil War he had been a quartermaster in the Western districts and during the war the Second Corps, which he commanded, was known as the best-organized, best-supplied corps in the Army of the Potomac.

The expedition had accomplished little. Perhaps for the lack of a little hay an opportunity had been lost. Had Custer been able to follow and catch the Indians and bring them back this ambiguous condition of neither war nor peace would not have existed.

In their swing around to talk to Indians as well as to arrange for the rebuilding of the Western posts, Smith and Hancock arrived at Fort Hays on May 3. Though by that time Hancock well knew that Custer had not been able to go on north after the Indians, he asked for a written report of the matter. The methodical general liked to have everything written down. Custer's report of May 4 shows a tinge of resentment:

> I have the honor to acknowledge the receipt of your communication of this date, calling upon me for my "reasons in detail for not making any movement" with my command since my arrival at this point. In reply, I would state that I reached this post on the 19th ultimo, expecting to find forage and subsistence stores for my command. Upon the contrary, no provision had been made for its supply. . . .[18]

A full supply was not forthcoming until April 27. By that time his horses were out of condition, having subsisted for some days upon "dry prairie grass." Also "subsistence stores expected daily at this post have been small and insufficient, but about two days supply being on hand."[19] Though as soon as the shortages were known the orders had gone out that all supply trains, even those bound for Santa Fe, should be rerouted to Custer at Hays, it took some time for the deficiencies to be made up. Custer never forgave what he called the "neglect" of the quartermaster's department and some years later excoriated it thus: "Dishonest contractors at the receiving depots further east had been permitted to perpetrate gross frauds upon the Government, the result of which was to produce want and suffering among the men."[20]

Mrs. Custer would further charge in her memoirs that the rations were inferior in quality and that the subsistence supplies had been sent out to the frontier posts during the Civil War, had lain in poorly constructed storehouses and then, moldy and spoiled, were issued to the men throughout 1867.[21]

Custer's own report of May 4 refutes this statement. There was no backlog of bacon and hardtack molding in the storehouse at Fort Hays, since "but about two days supply" was on hand. In some measure this condition existed at all the outlying forts throughout the summer. They never had any great accumulation of subsistence stores and reported frequently how many days' supply was on hand. But no one actually ran out, nor did any report that the rations were old and unfit for consumption.

There was, however, a shortage of fine stores for officers. For the first time, as an experiment, in 1867 the quartermaster's department proposed to send and keep at each post a supply of canned goods, hams, etc., for purchase by officers and their families. Heretofore officers had had to provide their own food, either taking a supply along to their stations or buying it from the high-priced sutler's store. Unfortunately the new system did not work very well under the exigencies of 1867 transportation and the officers were thrown back onto the monotonous hard bread, bacon, and beans of the trooper. On May 4 there were no fine stores at Fort Hays and Hancock ordered some sent at once.

It should be remembered that when Custer made his complaints about the provisioning of the troops he was accounting for the many desertions from his regiment, 90 altogether while he was at Hays. Besides the rations he noted that there was cholera about and scurvy in the ranks. There was no cholera in Kansas in April and May—it would come later—but there were 13 cases of scurvy, a condition that is not caused by bad bread and does not develop in a month. It could have been prevented by a more diversified diet through the winter at Fort Riley. On May 4 Hancock ordered antiscorbutics—potatoes and onions—sent out at once.

Whatever the cause of the desertions, the cavalry camp near Fort Hays was certainly grim and miserable. The post possessed only a few small shacks, inadequate even for the shelter of the men stationed there.[22] The weather was cold and Custer's regiment lived in tents pitched on soggy ground that never dried out. A rainstorm, "which promised permanence," had set in "to make the mud more bottomless than that which the army of the Potomac wallowed through during the Burnside mud march at Fredericksburg." Theodore R. Davis, a reporter with the regiment, spoke of the Custer moodiness and "sombre mien following the enforced anchorage of his command in the muddy camp at Big Creek." As Davis sat whistling in his little A tent while he sketched by the light of a candle, Custer burst in with the demand, "Stop this cheerfulness in purgatory or I'll have you out here in the flood walking post."[23]

Custer's boredom and depression was expressed in his letters to his wife. "The inaction to which I am subjected now, in our present halt, is almost unendurable. It requires all the buoyancy of my sanguine disposition to resist being extremely homesick."[24] He wanted nothing so much as to get an appointment to Fort Garland out in the mountains of Colorado where the hunting and weather would be better and he could have his wife with him.[25] As always when the young general was sick or depressed he turned to his wife for comfort and renewed assurance.

Custer had also lost any interest he might have had in Indian fighting. The fiercest Indians of the Plains had not impressed him as a foe— they were timid and had run away. He had written to his superiors stating that the redskins were frightened and peaceful and he could see no reason for any war.[26] He reassured his wife as to the danger, "The chances are, however, that I shall not see any of them, it being next to impossible to overtake them when they are forewarned and expecting us, as they now are."[27] He would more or less act on this belief the rest of the summer.

When the weather permitted Davis took Custer out for a buffalo hunt. He suggested a contest between two teams of officers to see which could kill the most buffalo in one day. All the fresh meat thus obtained must have been a welcome addition to the troopers' diet. Foot races were organized for the men. A courier system was set up to bring the mail from Fort Harker more expeditiously than it came by stage. Hancock agreed that Mrs. Custer might come to Hays and General Smith insisted that the tent carried by General Hancock on the expedition should be allotted to her use. The Seventh cavalry band was sent out from Riley by General Gibbs.[28] Everyone did his best to allay the Custer malaise.

Although the Cheyennes signified their hostile intent by killing a few settlers in Kansas in May they concentrated more on harassing the stage line and railroad workers along the Platte river. Sherman recast his plans for the summer. Though certain of the so-called friendly bands of Sioux had been granted permission to hunt between the Platte and the Smoky Hill, word was sent to them to come in to the forts along the Platte or return north of the river to avoid involvement in the war that seemed imminent. Custer would be sent to patrol the area.[29] He would be ideal for the assignment—aggressive, "willing to act and fight."[30] Sherman wanted a man who would go after the Indians, not stand back and wait for them to come to him. On May 13 Gen. C. C. Augur, commanding on the Platte wrote: "All the friendly bands have left the Republican and gone north of the Platte. They report two hundred fifty lodges of Cheyennes, and sixty lodges of Sioux, on Turkey Creek, a tributary of the Republican, about eighty miles south of Fort McPherson."[31]

On the 15th Hancock wrote to Smith about the proposed patrol. Subsistence supplies had been placed at all points in case Custer might need them. "I do not know how long the cavalry will be absent. It does not much matter, they can go leisurely, unless they meet trails of Indians when they should pursue. When they come back they can rest at Hays. The commander should report progress frequently by telegraph or otherwise. Send the odometer."[32]

But when days went past and Custer still did not move Hancock became impatient. Smith explained that Custer was waiting for shelter tents which were absolutely necessary. They had had extremely cold weather in the West and "some of the most terrific storms I have ever witnessed on the plains."[33] Smith also sent a special courier down to Harker for officers' stores for Custer since Hancock's order for them had not been filled.[34] Finally on June 1 when the grass was up and Custer was prepared to his own satisfaction he left Fort Hays with six cavalry troops and 20 supply wagons for Fort McPherson on the Platte. His orders of May 31 stated:

> The object of the expedition is to hunt out and chastise the Cheyennes and that portion of the Sioux who are their allies, between the Smoky Hill and the Platte. It is reported that all friendly Sioux have gone north of the Platte and may be in the vicinity of Forts McPherson or Sedgwick. You will as soon as possible, inform yourself as to the whereabouts of these friendly bands and avoid a collision with them.[35]

Sherman in Nebraska wrote hopefully to Gov. Alexander C. Hunt of Colorado, who was worried for fear the Indian attacks might close the trail to Denver: "It is barely possible the Cheyenne camp, stampeded by Hancock on Pawnee fork is now on the Republican, south of this. General Custer may strike them in coming across. . . ."[36]

On the sixth day of its march the contingent struck the four-day-old trail of a small party of Indians but "after following it far enough to determine the futility of pursuit, the attempt was relinquished."[37] On the seventh day in the vicinity where the reports had indicated the Cheyennes might be, the troopers "suddenly came in full view of about a hundred mounted warriors, who . . . set off as fast as their horses could carry them. One squadron was sent in pursuit, but was unable to overhaul the Indians."[38] While the tracks might not have been sufficiently plain to follow, they were plain enough to show that the warriors were mounted on horses stolen from the stage company. The inference was that since the stage horses were so superior to army horses extended pursuit was useless.

The Seventh cavalry column arrived at Fort McPherson on June 10 having marched 229 miles in 10 days, an average of 23 miles a day,[39] despite the delays of Indian trails, a heavy rain storm and the necessity of corduroying some creek banks and cutting down ridges to get the wagons over. Unluckily no Indian camps had been discovered.

Shortly after he reached the Platte Custer held a pow-wow with Pawnee Killer, one of the Sioux chiefs, who had been camped with his band alongside the Cheyennes on Pawnee fork in April. He and others of the Sioux had made protestations of friendliness, which had been accepted. The Sioux had fled with the Cheyennes but as Custer's orders were to "avoid collision" with friendly bands, he was pleasant. Only later would it be found out that it had been the Sioux who had killed the station keepers on the Smoky Hill. Custer wrote to his wife, "six of the principle Sioux Indians have just come in to see me to sue for peace for their whole tribe. . . . I encouraged peace propositions. . . ."[40]

Sherman, old and wise in the ways of the wily Indian, did not agree with Custer's handling of the situation. When he came in next day to the cavalry camp, he suggested that Custer might rather have taken some hostages that would have insured the behavior of Pawnee Killer's band. Sherman remained with the young general for two days talking at length with him about his next movement. Though the orders were verbal,[41] there has since been no disagreement as to their content. Custer was to go down to the forks of the Republican river and scout the region thoroughly for Indians. He was to come up to Fort Sedgwick for supplies and further orders, then make a long march to the west along the Republican, coming out on the Platte somewhere west of Fort Sedgwick. Contingencies might arise for which Custer would have to use his own judgment; if he found Indians he could go anywhere—to hell or Denver and not a word said if he marched his horses to death when he found a hot trail. Sherman was anxious to have the Indians harried out of the area.[42]

Custer arrived at the forks of the Republican June 21, having marched 107 miles "over very bad country" in four days.[43] The next day he dispatched D company under Lt. Samuel M. Robbins to accompany a train of 12 wagons commanded by Lt. William W. Cook[44] to Fort Wallace on the Smoky Hill for supplies. Along with the wagons and escort he sent Company K under Cpt. Robert M. West with instructions to stop at Beaver creek and scout it while D company went on into Fort Wallace.

The only explanation of this early need for supplies and in the opposite direction from which his orders indicated is given in the Custer memoirs:

> Circumstances seemed to favor a modification . . . at least as to marching the entire command to Fort Sedgwick. . . . My proposed change of programme contemplated a continuous march, which might be prolonged twenty days or more. To this end additional supplies were necessary. The guides all agreed in the statement

that we were then about equidistant from Fort Wallace on the south and Fort Sedgwick on the north, at either of which the required supplies could be obtained; but that while the country between our camp and the former was generally level and unbroken . . . that between us and Fort Sedgwick was almost impassable for heavily-laden wagons.[45]

The real reason for going so quickly to Fort Wallace was to pick up Mrs. Custer who had been instructed by letter as early as June 17 to come to that post where a squadron would be sent for her. There was no danger—the Indians were pretty well scared and peace had been made with Pawnee Killer. The marching would not be too hard for her. In the note he sent along by Lieutenant Cook the devoted husband wrote, "I never was so anxious in my life." Not anxious for her safety and comfort but anxious to have her with him.[46]

Custer's facile decision not to obey Sherman's express orders to draw his supplies from Fort Sedgwick was evidence of his rather casual view of the whole expedition and its purpose. There was good reason for Sherman's instructions. The primary purpose of the scout was to protect the Platte trail and railroad and the appearance of the troop at Fort Sedgwick near the railroad would be a warning to hostile Indians. Furthermore Fort Sedgwick was easily provisioned by rail while Fort Wallace could only be supplied with difficulty by wagon trains.

Maj. Joel Elliott was given the duty of getting Custer's report to Sedgwick and bringing back any further orders from General Sherman. Allowed to make his own arrangements he elected to depend on speed rather than numbers and took with him but one scout and 10 men on fast horses. He left the camp at three A.M. the morning of June 23.

Then, when more than a third of Custer's command was gone on their errands, the "monotony of idleness"[47] was broken at daybreak on June 24 by a party of 50 Indians, all gaudily painted and accoutered as a war party. The picket was shot down but the quick response of the troopers foiled an attempt to drive off the cavalry horses. While everybody in camp considered the Indian action an attack, Custer would not have it so. He sent his scout to give the sign for a parley. As he said:

> I was extremely anxious . . . to detain the chiefs near my camp . . .
> and keep up the semblance at least of friendship. . . . I was particu-
> larly prompted to this desire by the fact that the two detachments

which had left my command the previous day would necessarily continue absent several days, and I feared that they might become the victims of an attack from this band if steps were not taken to prevent it.[48]

The parley was attended by seven officers and seven chiefs, one of whom was Pawnee Killer, who had been specifically warned to go north of the Platte or remain near Fort McPherson or otherwise be liable to attack. The parley was inconclusive. The reporter, Davis, gives a somewhat different account of this episode than does Custer in his memoirs:

> The circumstance was an afternoon peace talk with some Sioux chiefs who had that morning made an attack of small moment upon Custer's camp, and later with considerable impudence accorded to the General an opportunity to talk the matter over—stipulating that the meeting should be a friendly affair and to this end the parties to it must appear unarmed, in fulfillment of which the individuals on both sides were so loaded down with weapons that an indifferent concealment of their armament gave rise to observable stiffness of movement especially on the part of the most prominent members of the peace congress.
>
> It was discovered when too late to avoid the session, that notwithstanding what seemed a sufficient precaution—the Indians really controlled the situation and were obviously aware of the fact—and it is my firm conviction, that our little party escaped, and the affair ended without a sanguinary conclusion, mainly by the peculiar influence of Custer's presence.[49]

Custer told Pawnee Killer he would follow him to his camp. "We followed as rapidly as our heavier horses could travel, but the speed of the Indian pony on this occasion, as on many others, was too great for that of our horses."[50] Lt. Henry Jackson, who was supervising the odometer, mapping, and recording each day's journey, also gave a laconic account of the pursuit: "At 12 M., struck camp and moved out after Indians[,] crossing the north Fork [of the Republican] and marching S.W. along south Fork and marched 2 M. when we turned N.E. by E. and returned to our old camp. Found Indians had been in our camp while we were away."[51]

The Indians continued their fun and games, luring away from camp a detachment under Cpt. Louis M. Hamilton. After some maneuver and skirmish Hamilton came back with the loss of only one horse. The most thrilling event of the afternoon was the chase by a half-dozen well-mounted warriors after Dr. I. T. Coates who for some reason or another found himself about four miles out of camp on a jaded horse. The doctor out-ran his pursuers and arrived safely in camp because as Custer said, "our domestic horses, until accustomed to their presence, are as terrified by Indians as by a huge wild beast, and will fly from them. . . ."[52]

After the encounter with Pawnee Killer Custer was truly anxious for his wife's safety. On the morning of June 25 he sent out another full company, E, under Cpt. Edward Myers, who was to march without halting to Captain West on the Beaver and then with him proceed on towards Fort Wallace to further protect the supply train and Mrs. Custer. Now one half of the Custer command was committed to this duty of replenishing the supplies and bringing out Mrs. Custer.

So expeditiously did Myers move that by the morning of the 26th, he and Captain West were able to pick up the supply train about 30 miles out of Fort Wallace and frighten away a party of several hundred Cheyennes and Sioux, who had been attacking the train for about three hours. The train was doing quite well by itself. Commanded by Lieutenant Robbins the troopers had been dismounted and deployed in a circle on foot on all sides of the wagons which advanced in parallel columns. The horses were led between the wagons. This was the standard defense posture for wagon trains under Indian attack. The red warriors circled around at some distance exchanging shots with the troopers. No one was killed on either side though the cavalry was sure that a few of the Indians had bit the dust. Mrs. Custer had not come to Fort Wallace and was not with the train.[53] Escorted from then on by three companies of cavalry the supply wagons arrived at the camp on the Republican on the morning of June 27. A quick trip had been made.

The scout, William Comstock, who had gone with the train, had cherished for some time the belief that the Indian camps, which it was hoped Custer would find, were located somewhere on Beaver creek. This was undoubtedly the reason Captain West had been sent to scout there though his orders from Custer "contemplated a friendly meeting between his forces and the Indians should the latter be discovered."[54]

When the wagons and escort arrived at Fort Wallace they were greeted with the news that the Cheyennes had for a month been raiding the stage stations along the Smoky Hill almost nightly. On June 21 the fort itself had been attacked, two men had been killed and others wounded.[55] So as was very evident the Indians were hostile and probably camped not a great distance to the north.

Lt. Joseph Hale, Third U.S. infantry, commanding at Wallace, reported on June 27:

> Lieutenants Robbins and Cook, 7th Cavalry arrived at this post on the 24th. Inst. from Genl. Custars command, with about twenty wagons, for rations and q. m. stores. They returned on the evening of the 25th. Comstock, the guide who accompanied these officers, thinks that Indian villages can be found on "Beaver Creek."[56]

Hancock sending this report on to Sherman phrased it differently, "Comstock . . . reports crossing a trail of seven hundred warriors going toward Beaver Creek."[57]

The attack on the wagon train by both the Sioux and the Cheyennes, mostly Sioux, must have reinforced Comstock's belief that the hostiles could be found somewhere on the Beaver if anyone cared to seek them out.[58]

As for the supplies, the large amount drawn by Custer depleted the store at Fort Wallace. Lieutenant Hale noted in his report, "I would also respectfully state that the supply of commissary stores will soon be exhausted, officers supplies are entirely out."[59] Custer would later complain bitterly about the dearth of officers' supplies.

The supply wagons returned to the camp on the Republican on June 27 and Major Elliott came back from Fort Sedgwick on the 28th, reporting the distance therefrom to be 105 miles. He brought no new orders from Sherman, only a reiteration from General Augur:

> I infer from a dispatch recd. from Gen. Sherman that he will order you again to the Smoky Hill route. If not, proceed to carry out such instructions as you have already recd. from him concerning your present scout, and having completed it, return to Sedgwick. . . . I think it very important to get Pawnee-Killer and all other Indians who desire to be friendly, out of the Republican country, and wish you to do all you can to accomplish it. If your

instructions from Gen. Sherman will allow it, pitch into the Cheyenne Villages by all means. . . . If you do not meanwhile receive orders from Gen. Sherman, I will have none for you on your arrival at Sedgwick. Meantime scout the country well. . . .[60]

Despite Sherman's and now Augur's emphasis on the importance of getting the friendly Indians out of the country and attacking the hostile ones, together with Comstock's freely expressed opinion as to where the camps were, Custer now decided to follow the letter of Sherman's earlier instructions, when no one knew anything about the Indians on the Beaver. On June 29 he took off, marching for more than two days along the south side of the South fork of the Republican, which in that area turns rather sharply to the southwest. On the third day they "crossed an Indian trail going up it" and before they camped that night crossed the river itself. After that they went northnorthwest until they reached the Platte. On July 3 they encountered some difficulty in finding a crossing over Black Tail Deer creek and in the afternoon and evening suffered a terrible wind and hail storm which blew down most of the tents and did much damage to the camp. On July 4, they marched but five miles and then paused to rest for the final journey to the Platte. Just why Custer proposed to travel this great distance in one prolonged effort is not known. Since it would go over a divide he might have feared he would find little water. Perhaps he did not realize the distance would be so long or perhaps he was impatient to get the orders that might send him back to the Smoky Hill.

The march began at midnight on the 4th and continued until eight o'clock in the evening of the 5th. On the journey the column found water in several places and stopped to water its horses at the last arroyo, where water lay in pools or could be obtained by digging. They were then about 24 miles from the Platte. On its return the detail would camp overnight at this spot. Nevertheless the trip was grueling, the latter part of the 60 miles under a hot July sun and through masses of cacti.[61] While Custer's later comments on this day differed in a number of details from Lieutenant Jackson's careful notes on the spot, it was more graphic. Many of the dogs with the column died from thirst and exhaustion. The indefatigable Custer with three companions rode ahead of the rest to select a good camping ground. But when they reached the river they were so spent that instead of going back to guide the troops behind, they all lay down on the bare ground and slept through the night unawakened by a shower of rain. The tired troopers found their own way to the river, camping almost three miles below their commander's bivouac.[62]

At nearby Riverside station Custer telegraphed for orders. He found that the next day after Major Elliott had left Sedgwick on June 26, new orders had come from Sherman. These had been entrusted to Lt. Lyman S. Kidder, Second U. S. cavalry, and an escort of 10 men and a scout with instructions to find Custer and deliver the orders to him. Kidder had not yet caught up with the column. A copy of the orders was transmitted to Custer and they gave him instructions to return to Fort Wallace. They also gave an intimation of Sherman's surprise that the young general had drawn supplies from Fort Wallace.

> I don't understand about General Custer being on the Republican awaiting provisions from Fort Wallace. If this be so, and all the Indians be gone south, convey to him my orders that he proceed with all his command in search of the Indians towards Fort Wallace, and report to General Hancock, who will leave Denver for same place today.[63]

Sherman's shift of this his striking force down to the Smoky Hill was due not so much to the relative quiet on the Platte but to the great need on the Smoky Hill. The stage stations to the west had been under almost constant attack. The Indians came at night, stealing the horses and burning the buildings and the hay. Cpt. Myles W. Keogh[64] at Fort Wallace pleaded constantly for more guards both for the stations and the fort. Musicians and mechanics had to be pressed into service. When Hancock went through on his way to Denver on June 18 he took Keogh and I company of the Seventh cavalry along as escort, leaving the post defended by an assortment of infantry and dismounted cavalrymen. Then the Indians attacked the post in broad daylight on June 21 and again on the 26th. Lt. Frederick H. Beecher, Third U. S. infantry, quartermaster at Fort Wallace, wrote to his mother after the June 21 attack. They had taken

> . . . into the field one hundred and twenty-five infantry, unhorsed cavalry and citizens. We sit up nights and sleep by turns during the day. Really, I think we are not in danger of losing life and limb. We

are only surrounded, and thereby much inconvenienced and tried. My stone quarry has fallen into the enemies' hands and my work, thereby, almost stopped. Don't get up any alarm for my safety, but condole with me that the government will give us so few troops to fight so many Indians.[65]

The Indian raids spread to the east. The surveying teams began coming in to the forts as their escorts had to be reduced. Though the attacks in the west had been attributed to the Cheyennes and the Sioux, the Kiowas took a hand and on June 12 ran off all the government stock at Fort Dodge. Company A of the Seventh cavalry stationed there lost all its horses and was afoot. On June 16 a large train at Cimarron crossing was attacked, two men killed and the wagons plundered.[66] Some of the advance Union Pacific, Eastern Division, railroad workers were killed and the rest of the men fled from their work.[67] Demands for more protection came raining in on the army. Railroad officials bothered little to complain to the local post commanders but concentrated on the governor of Kansas and officials at Washington.[68] Hancock was in Denver or on the road. General Smith at Fort Harker in the center of the pressure did everything he could, cutting the guards where least necessary and maintaining them where they were vital. He had to keep the supply trains running for the very life of the forts to the west depended upon them. At the same time he pleaded to Sherman for more help. As early as June 19 he had asked that Custer be sent back to his district.[69] Gov. Samuel Crawford of Kansas made a great fuss about the inadequacy of the army and offered to raise a regiment of local cavalry.

Sherman had been determined not to allow the use of local troops as he considered them prone to act irresponsibly as Chivington had done at Sand creek.[70] He had managed to avoid accepting them in Minnesota, Montana, and Colorado. In Kansas he vacillated, first giving permission and then withdrawing it. Finally on July 1 he gave Governor Crawford permission to enlist six or eight companies and having decided to allow them, wanted them by July 6. This was impossible. Recruits gathered quickly at Harker but had difficulty in finding horses.

Meanwhile fate threw another bolt at the straining army and its laboring General Smith at Fort Harker. Some companies of the 38th U. S. infantry coming from Jefferson Barracks to go with Maj. H. C. Merriam to New Mexico brought with them the deadly seeds of cholera.

The first case was identified at Fort Harker on June 28. That same day the Merriam cortege left the fort for the southwest and as it went distributed the fatal disease it carried to every fort and camp at which it stopped—Fort Zarah, Fort Larned, Fort Dodge, and Fort Lyon. The surgeon and his wife with the contingent were both victims.

At Fort Harker the same day the disease appeared in the 38th infantry another fatal case was noted in an employee of a beef contractor. For a few days the infection was confined to the troops camped about the post rather than in the garrison itself but the sickness soon engulfed not only the post but the town of Ellsworth as well. Dr. George M. Sternberg of the post eventually reported 79 cases in his hospital with 29 deaths but he agreed that probably as many as 200 died at and in the vicinity of Fort Harker.[71] Mrs. Sternberg and her cook died on two successive days.[72] The Catholic priest, Father Louis Dumortier, who served the area is said to have died alone, along the road, while his mule wandered away.[73]

The frontier newspapers, always booster minded, first ignored the epidemic. "The cholera rumors from Harker only increase in proportions and frightfulness. They are so conflicting and unsatisfactory . . . we will not attempt any notice of it."[74] But eventually they had to notice it. A dispatch from Ellsworth dated July 26 read: "Everyone who was not tied here has left and no labor is performed at all. It is hard to get graves dug, or people to sit by corpses or to dress them for the grave. Long trains of loaded cars stand on the track with no one to unload them."[75]

The 18th Kansas cavalry—four companies of them, that being all that horses could be provided for—were mustered in on July 15. They too suffered from the cholera: "When the battalion was in line, being mustered into service at Fort Harker, the cholera was raging in the garrison and three of the Kansas boys were striken down while the oath was being administered. The remainder, however, stood firm and when the ceremony was over, marched off the parade ground with a steady step."[76]

Starting out on an assignment to scout between the Smoky and the Arkansas, they made a long march, all apparently well until after supper in camp: "In another hour the camp became a hospital of screaming cholera patients. Men were seized with cramping of the stomach, bowels, and muscles of the arms and legs. The doctor and his medicine were powerless to resist the disease. . . . The morning of the 17th found five dead and thirty-six stretched on the ground in a state of collapse."[77] Such was the savage onset of the disease.

Worried by the situation at Harker, General Sherman came out on July 5 and remained until the 12th when Hancock came through on his way back from Denver. General Smith then and later refused to be relieved.[78] He knew the problems and he knew the territory and the disposition of the troops in the posts and along the trail. He would stick with the job until the situation eased. Sherman had done what he could to relieve the pressure for more troops—he had ordered Custer back to the Smoky Hill and much against his judgment had allowed the recruitment of the local cavalry. As for the cholera he could only send more doctors.

Custer on the Platte did not linger long, scarcely 24 hours. Despite the punishing march and the need of rest for both horses and men, the command was forced to move quickly out into the wastes again. The temptation of the busy, well-traveled trail along the river was too much for the tired, beaten men and in that one night on the Platte about 30 of them deserted.[79] Even when the company, 12 miles out paused for dinner, the men slipped away in groups of two or three. Outraged at such open flouting of oaths and duty, Custer impulsively ordered officers out after them "to bring none in alive." In the hurried chase to stop the deserters, three were shot, one, Charles Johnson of Company K, was fatally wounded by a ball through his head and chest. An army wagon was sent out to bring in the injured. When it returned to the column and the doctor started towards it, the commander ordered him to stop and "not to go near those men." This denial of medical attention was apparently to be a warning against further desertion. As the troopers passed the wagon, some threw their overcoats into its bed so that the wounded would not have to lie on the bare, rough boards.

A bit later Custer privately told Dr. Coates to attend the deserters but to not let it be known that he had had second thoughts. The result was a rather bizarre situation and much conflicting testimony later. According to the doctor the wounds were not dressed for two days because there was no good water available and besides gunshot wounds often dried up better by themselves without being dressed. The men were left in the wagon because it was more comfortable than the ambulances which had weak springs. The men had been given opiates within two hours after they were shot and this repeated medication had kept them relatively comfortable throughout the journey. None of the wounds had been considered serious though Johnson's was worse than the others. The doctor would swear that Johnson died of his wound and not from any lack of medical attention but some of the troopers and officers would continue stubbornly to believe that the wounded men had been inhumanely treated.[80]

Custer was short on supplies. He could have gone on up to Fort Sedgwick where they had been waiting for him for some time but that would have put him back at least a day and would also have run the risk of more desertions. Moreover he was anxious on account of Lieutenant Kidder as well as anxious to get back to the Smoky Hill and his wife. So out they went through the dust, heat, and cactus beds, still carrying in their bones the weariness of that awful march of July 5. Each day they must march a little farther than they thought they could because they must get to Wallace before the supplies gave out.[81]

On the way they found the remains of Lieutenant Kidder and his party, 12 men dead and well cut up, near the Beaver creek where Comstock had been so sure the Indians were camped.[82] There was no doubt about it; this was the work of the Sioux, the answer to Custer's forbearance. It was ironic too that had Custer sent to Sedgwick for supplies as ordered, Kidder might not have died. The road to Sedgwick from the Republican fork being, as Custer said, more difficult and the wagon train slower than Elliott's stripped down party, the supply train might well have brought down the new orders and saved that long march to the west which had been so hard on the men and the horses and so barren of results. Custer could not but have been discouraged and depressed by his summer's work.

As history now records it, Pawnee Killer's band was responsible for the killing of the station men in April which started the war.[83] The party that attacked the wagon train out of Fort Wallace had been mostly Sioux.[84] It was Pawnee Killer who had made the pass at Custer's camp on the Republican. Finally it was the Sioux with a few Cheyennes who had killed and mutilated the Kidder party.[85] This was the way the Indians made war—friendly on the surface but ready to use a knife in the back at the first opportunity. Every young army officer had to learn this. Half-Cheyenne George Bent told the Indian story of the summer. "All through June, July and August the Indians continued to raid . . . easily avoiding the large bodies of troops sent against them and attacking the small detachments." [86]

Custer arrived at Fort Wallace on July 13, camping several miles out in order to have good grazing for the horses. On this last lap he had marched 181 miles in seven days to average 26 miles a day. His overall rate for the entire patrol was a little more than 25 miles a day.

There had been an easing of the Indian attacks within Fort Wallace's jurisdiction. General Hancock had come back from Denver, dropping off Keogh and his company at Wallace and distributing in turn his infantry escort at the stations along his way east. The two surveying parties, Greenwood's and Wright's, that had been at the post several weeks hoping to get a larger escort from Hancock, plucked up their courage and went on with what they had. [87] The mail stages, running double, were coming through about once a week. [88] Some of the stage stations had been abandoned and travel on the trail had been reduced mainly to supply or immigrant trains of at least 20 wagons and 30 men. There was apparently no forage and little grain at the fort, nor were there enough horseshoes to refit Custer's horses. [89] Fortunately for history Keogh was still writing his frequent reports to headquarters, always with some complaint of shortages. On July 8 he was low on arms and ammunition because he had had to supply every train from the east that demanded them. The supply trains too had to return east without any protection and he had not received a single man "to carry out the instructions in regard to reinforcing the stations." He had only 50 men at the post and his cavalry was in bad shape. Perhaps he hoped some of Custer's men would be allotted to relieve the manpower stringencies of his command. He wrote:

> The horses of I troop are in no better condition than those of the remainder of the regiment just come in with General Custer and without grain they will not be fit to do any duty as they are all broken down.
>
> I have the honor to state that rations will last only until the 15th of August and until then only in case no more troops come here needing them. [90]

So it was explicit that when Custer arrived at Fort Wallace there was no shortage of rations. Still the post was dreary enough to a man who had been out in the wilderness for six weeks.

It was Sherman's expectation, when he instructed Custer to go to Fort Wallace, that he would get there about the same time as General Hancock, who would give him further orders. But since Custer had not received those orders until two weeks after they were issued he had missed Hancock and was now at Wallace without orders. Not that this made any practical difference—his men and his horses were so exhausted that they would not be ready for further duty for some time.

Custer did not know where his wife was since no letters from her were at Fort Wallace to explain why she had not come there as he had hoped.[91] He was naturally much concerned. If only he had some way to quickly contact General Smith, he could reasonably ask for a short leave while his command recuperated. General Smith was sympathetic with his officers in such matters. In a telegram to Custer on June 18 on army business, General Smith, rather against army practice, had contrived to let the cavalryman know that his wife was well and safe. "The people are here with me and all well."[92]

Unfortunately, with no telegraph and the stages running but once a week, there was no hope for quick communication to solve Custer's dilemma. He resolved on another course. He explained to Major Elliott, to whom he left his command, that being without orders he felt it was his duty to follow his superior commander to headquarters or at least to go to the nearest telegraph office and report to him.[93] This sounded plausible and as it proved later if Custer had gone down by stage or with a returning supply train his action would not have been unduly questioned. Instead he ordered his company officers to select each from his own company 12 men with the best horses for a journey down to Fort Harker. When later called on to explain the need for such a huge escort which required practically every horse that was in fit condition, he said: "I expected to apply for Quartermasters' supplies that were actually required . . . and besides, I needed a large number of fresh animals. . . . It was well-known and conceded that I required these animals and therefore I supposed that they would be ready for me."[94]

Considering Custer's experience with the quartermasters corps in the spring it is to wonder how he could believe that the horses would be ready for him just because they had been promised and he needed them. As for the horseshoes to be applied for, they would not fill more than one wagon. Altogether his excuses were rather weak and when he wrote his memoirs a few years later he set forth more compelling reasons for going down to Fort Harker, with a large detail. He wrote that when he reached Fort Wallace on July 13, he found it in dire straits:

> Stages had been taken off the route. . . . No despatches or mail had been received at the fort for a considerable period, so that the occupants might well have been considered as undergoing a state of siege. Added to these embarrassments . . . a more frightful danger stared the troops in the face. . . . The reserve of stores at the post were well-nigh exhausted. . . . Cholera made its appearance among the men, and deaths occurred daily.[95]

No one of these statements was true. The post was in better shape than it had been in June and certainly did not now consider itself besieged. There was food for a month and there was no cholera. It would not reach the Seventh cavalry until July 22 and then it would be frightful. Confined to the cavalry camp, the mortality would be higher than anywhere else—11 deaths out of 17 cases—because the men were so worn by the hard marching.[96] But Custer was not there to see it. Probably on July 13 Fort Wallace was not even aware of the cholera at Harker. Yet historians would repeat and repeat again that Custer had gathered together his best troops and horses to break through a trail swarming with fierce Indians in order to bring back badly needed medicine for the sick and food supplies for the beleaguered and hungry post.

The contingent of four officers and 72 men started down the trail on the evening of July 15. The weather had turned dry and hot now and the night march would be more comfortable. With them Keogh sent a supply wagon to provision the several stations to the east that were under his supervision. After a march of 32 miles they reached Smoky Hill station at sunrise, took leave of Keogh's supply wagon and stopped for about two hours, "command unsaddled, and the horses were grazing, and the command were sleeping."[97] Then they went on through the morning hours making about 20 miles more before they stopped near Monument Station.

Here they met a supply train carrying forage for Fort Wallace and obtained enough forage for the horses for the rest of the trip. Cpt. Frederick W. Benteen, Company H, Seventh cavalry, who, detached on other duty, had not been with the regiment, was in charge of the escort for the four large supply trains traveling together.[98] Benteen was going out to join his regiment. He had left Fort Hays on July 12, met the Custer column near the monuments and would be in Fort Wallace on the 19th. He undoubtedly gave Custer all the news of the regiment and other army details. If the general had not known where his wife was and whether she was in danger he would certainly have found out from Benteen. He may have been told of the cholera at Fort Harker but Mrs. Custer was at Fort Riley where there was no cholera. Unknown to everybody somewhere in one of the trains rode the germs of the dreaded disease that would in a few days show its presence in the Seventh cavalry.

Through the afternoon the Custer column went on under the cruel sun making less than 20 miles when near Chalk Bluffs before sundown they "stopped, and made coffee, and rested about three-fourths of an hour."[99] Then they marched steadily through the second night. They marched in the usual cavalry fashion at an ordinary walk for about 50 minutes of each hour. Then the troopers were wheeled into line and dismounted without unsaddling for five or ten minutes. Now in this hourly pause the men fell asleep on the ground and a sergeant had to be sent around to waken them from a slumber so deep that at the command the horses went on without them. The horses began to give out; five of them were left at Grinnell Springs station during the night. When on the trail the played-out beasts were shot at first so the Indians would not get them; later they were just left where they lay.

On this second day two miles east of Castle Rock station the column met two mail stages,[100] which were stopped and Custer searched through the mail bags, finding no letters or orders for himself. Before they went on the general noticed that his mare, Fanchon, and the man who led her were missing. Although until now he had left the management of the column to Captain Hamilton, Custer personally gave Sgt. James Connelly an extra horse and an escort of six men to go back and find Trooper Young and the mare. According to all reports Indians lurked about the trail[101] and yet Custer sent six men on worn-out horses on this dangerous errand.

Young and the mare were found at Castle Rock and as the party came hurrying back to catch up with the main column it was attacked by Indians. One man was shot and fell off his horse; another was wounded. The excited mare pulled her leader several hundred yards off the trail and the Indians moved to cut her off. By the time the mare was back on the trail the wounded man had fallen well back behind the rest. The sergeant wanted to go back and tie the wounded man on his horse and bring him in, but two of the troopers refused to come back and galloped ahead. In the melee of shouting and shooting the wounded man slipped off his horse. With only two effective men left and the Indians closer to the wounded man than he was, the sergeant felt forced to go on and leave him. The Indians followed the party until they were about a mile and a half or 15 minutes from Downer station where the command had stopped.

When the sergeant's party came pounding into Downer's with its tale of Indians it made quite a stir. The men pulled themselves out of their lethargy and waited for the command to go out and find their fellow troopers and drive off the Indians. Hamilton reported to Custer but nothing happened. The griping in the ranks grew loud and mutinous, so much so that Hamilton went again to Custer. The general was not accustomed to consult his officers about his orders, nor did he welcome advice. Now he merely said they would have to go on.[102]

Later Custer would give several accounts of this episode. In his general report of his summer's work on August 6, he wrote:

> My march from Fort Wallace to Fort Harker was made without incident except the killing of two men about five miles beyond Downer's Station. A sergeant and six men had been sent back to bring up a man who had halted at the last ranch; when returning this party was attacked by between forty and fifty Indians, and two of them killed. Had they offered any defense this would not have occurred, instead however they put spurs to their horses and endeavored to escape by flight.[103]

Custer insisted all along that the two men had been reported to him as dead. The fact that he believed them to be dead seems to have removed them from any further consideration. Any further duty he might have had was to punish the Indians. As for this, Custer had learned better: "I well knew, and so did everyone else who knows of Indian warfare, that any party I might send back, by the time it reached the scene of attack, would find no trace of the Indians. The latter would not even leave a trail to follow and it would have been the measure of absurdity to have undertaken such an errand."[104]

In his memoirs the young general again referred to the incident:

Almost at every station we received intelligence of Indians having been seen in the vicinity within a few days of our arrival. We felt satisfied they were watching our movements, although we saw no fresh signs of Indians until we arrived near Downer's station. Here, while stopping to rest our horses for a few minutes, a small party of our men, *who had without authority* halted some distance behind, came dashing into our midst and reported that twenty-five or thirty Indians had attacked them some five or six miles in rear, and had killed two of their number. As there was a detachment of infantry guarding the station, *and time being important,* we pushed on to our destination.[105]

The infantry captain, Arthur B. Carpenter, 37th U.S. infantry provided the sequel. "As Genl. Custer moved on without giving any directions concerning the bodies of these men, I sent out a detail to find them, they found one man killed and one wounded. I had the body buried and the wounded man is at this post under treatment."[106]

The cavalry column went on down the trail, the troopers adding one more sullen resentment to their accumulated misery. There was now only a little more than 40 miles to go. The pace was very slow. Bone-weary and sleep-sodden the men and horses plodded on under the pitiless July sun. Lieutenant Cook remembered a stop somewhere along in the afternoon; Hamilton did not. Sergeant Connelly's horse gave out and he crawled into an ambulance and slept. They reached Big Creek station near Fort Hays on the morning of the 18th, one said at three o'clock, another said daybreak. They had made altogether about 150 miles in from 55 to 57 hours of almost steady marching.[107] Hamilton estimated that they had rested five hours all together, Cook believed it was nearer 10.

Custer had begun his summer's work with a march after fleeing Indians of 150 miles in four and a half days, which both he and Hancock thought very good marching. Now he had ended his summer's work with a march of almost exactly the same distance in two and a half days. And for what purpose? Custer was fond of recounting his fast marches but this one, he always insisted, was not a rapid march; it was "slow— the average being less than three and a half miles an hour, which every cavalryman knows to be a slow and deliberate rate of marching."[108]

When the contingent reached Big Creek station the men rested. That night 20 of them deserted. Custer, his brother Tom, Lieutenant Cook, the reporter Davis and an orderly boarded the two ambulances that had been brought along from Fort Wallace.[109] Four fresh mules were harnessed to the ambulances and off they went down the trail to Fort Harker. All the rest of the day they sped along, the passengers undoubtedly catching up on their sleep. About nine o'clock in the evening near Bunker Hill the ambulances met another supply train under the escort of Cpt. Charles C. Cox, 10th U.S. cavalry.[110] Cox had Custer's orders, the lack of which had brought the general on this wearisome journey. According to his instructions he was to remain based at Fort Wallace and operate between the Platte and the Arkansas. "The cavalry should be kept constantly employed."[111]

The orders were clear and incontrovertible. But Custer was too near his goal; the temptation was too great. The overriding desire that had colored his whole summer and influenced almost every move of his extended scout was still unsatisfied. He would not face another sentence to the dry empty wastes without his comfort and his stay. Within a day or two he could pick up his wife and be back long before his men were able to travel again on the desert patrol. Custer went on into Fort Harker. He arrived about 2:00 or 2:30 A.M. on the morning of July 19. He went at once to awaken General Smith.

It will be remembered that at this time Fort Harker was in the grip of the cholera epidemic. Due to the persistent Indian attacks along the trails and his shortage of manpower, Smith had been struggling to keep the supply trains going and the railroad protected. Surveyors, railroad officials, the newspapers, and the public were clamoring and complaining about the inadequacies of the military. Pressed almost beyond reason by his cares and responsibilities, General Smith was sleeping heavily when Custer arrived. Custer had not been Smith's responsibility; Sherman had made the plans, taken him out of the department and directed his movements. Although Smith knew of Custer's imminent return under Sherman's orders, he could not know but what Sherman had also given the young officer a leave of absence.

This nighttime appearance was confusing to the sleep-fogged Smith. But as usual he was kind and genial. He asked Custer about his summer patrol and went to waken his adjutant, Lt. Thomas B. Weir, to take Custer to the train. Because he already knew, Custer did not ask where

Mrs. Custer was; he talked fast, carefully not asking permission to go to Fort Riley but still making it plain that he was on his way. Smith who always wanted everybody to be happy, called out as his officers left, that Custer should pay his respects to the ladies.[112]

Only the next morning, clear-headed and rested, did Smith again consider and investigate Custer's nighttime appearance:

> Gen. Custer came to my quarters between two and three o'clock at night and I don't know that I asked the question how he came down. It was my impression he came by stage. I learned the next morning from my Adj. Gen. Lt. Weir that he came with an escort part of the way, and in an ambulance from Fort Hays to Ft. Harker, and then I immediately ordered him back to his command. He left for Fort Riley on the three o'clock train and from there I ordered him back the next morning after I learned how he came down.[113]

In Custer's new orders had been a request for an immediate report of his summer's scout. When this was not forthcoming promptly, Smith, knowing Hancock's desire for early information, gathered together as many details as he could and sent them to his superior under date of July 28. In this report he also recited his further action in regard to Custer:

> On the 19th I telegraphed him to return immediately to Fort Wallace and rejoin his command unless he had permission from higher authority to be absent. He telegraphed me to know if he could wait until Monday and I replied that he must return by the first train. He started by the first train but was delayed with no fault of his until the night of the 21st. As soon as he reported to me, I placed him under arrest, his family and baggage were with him and under the circumstances, I deemed it best to send him back to Fort Riley, where he now remains in arrest. . . . Charges against Gen. Custer will be forwarded to you tomorrow.[114]

General Smith did not want Mrs. Custer at Fort Harker where she might contract cholera so, thoughtful as ever, he sent the Custers back to Fort Riley. As he related in the report above, Smith placed Custer in arrest on July 21. General Hancock hearing indirectly of Custer's arrival had his adjutant telegraph Smith on July 22:

The Major General Commanding directs me to say that he presumes you did not allow Genl. Custer to go to Fort Riley. He should have been arrested as his action was without warrant and highly injurious to the service, especially under the circumstances. The General thinks you should have preferred charges against Genl. Custer giving his instructions to his successor in command but if he has gone back without delay from Fort Harker he leaves the matter in your hands.[115]

Hence, though Hancock agreed as to the necessity of discipline, he left the final decision to Smith who had already put Custer under arrest before he received the telegram from Hancock. Custer always blamed Hancock for his arrest and court-martial, saying Smith had signed the charges but Hancock had ordered him to do so.

Though Lieutenant Jackson had kept a careful log of the travels to the Platte and back, a more comprehensive report was due from the commanding officer. While under the circumstances Custer could not have been very busy he put off writing his report until August 6 and 7. By that time Charles Johnson, the wounded deserter had died and Custer's mind was very much on the desertions. On the field of action he always believed attack was the best defense. He blamed the desertions on the commissary:

The march from the Platte to Fort Wallace was a forced one, from the fact that although my train contained rations for my command up to the 20th of the month yet when the stores came to be issued they were discovered to be in such a damaged condition that it would be with difficulty they could be made to last until we should reach Fort Wallace. And I take this opportunity to express the belief, a belief in which I am supported by facts as well as by the opinions of the officers associated under me, that the gross neglect and mismanagement exhibited in the Commissary Department through this District has subjected both officers and men to privations for which there was no occasion and which were never contemplated or intended by the Government when my command left Fort Hays for the Platte.

The officers were only able to obtain hard bread and bacon, coffee and sugar for their private messes although it had been known weeks, if not months, before that a large command was expected to arrive at Fort Hays; in the same manner it was known that an expedition was contemplated to the Platte. On my return march to Fort Wallace all hard bread not damaged was required to subsist the enlisted men, while the officers were actually compelled to pick up and collect from that portion of the hard bread which had been condemned and abandoned, a sufficient amount to subsist themselves to Fort Wallace. That this bread was damaged will not appear remarkable when it is known that some of the boxes were marked 1860.[116]

The core of the complaint seems to be that the officers had to subsist often on the troopers' ration of bacon, hardtack, sugar, and coffee and that the hardtack was damaged. It was true that fine stores for the officers had been nonexistent most of the time at Hays and probably Custer did not get all he ordered when he sent his wagons to Wallace. Certainly this was a deprivation that Custer had not suffered before in his earlier army service and he must have felt it keenly. The ration of the soldier on the Plains was monotonous and unappetizing. If in 1867 it was also generally aged and defective, such evidence does not appear in the reports of any command of the Kansas posts.

The charges made against General Custer by General Smith were first, "Absence without leave from his command," and second, "Conduct to the prejudice of good order and military discipline." Under the second charge, specific allegations were made of "overmarching and damaging the horses" on a march not on public business, using government ambulances and mules on unauthorized business, and failure to take proper measures for the repulse of Indians or for the defense and relief of his detachment near Downer's station.[117]

Captain West of the Seventh cavalry, still angry at the shooting and subsequent death of his trooper, Charles Johnson, preferred additional charges against Custer under that all inclusive head of "Conduct prejudicial to good order and military discipline," which specified particularly that Custer had ordered the shooting of the deserters without trial and afterwards denied them medical attention and care.[118]

Beginning on September 15 the court-martial sat for almost a month at Fort Leavenworth. General Custer was found guilty on all charges,[119] and sentenced "To be suspended from rank and command for one year, and forfeit his pay for the same time."[120]

It seems likely that although the army brass could not refuse to accept and try the charges of Captain West, it was not in sympathy with them. Custer's action in regard to the deserters may have been unwise and unnecessary but the army believed that the commander of a military detachment in the field must be the sole judge of the measures necessary to preserve his command from danger even if he had to shoot someone. This was made clear in the review of the court-martial proceedings by the judge advocate general in Washington. Gen. Joseph Holt wrote first in regard to the charges preferred by General Smith:

> The conclusion unavoidably reached under this branch of the inquiry, is that Gen. Custer's anxiety to see his family at Fort Riley overcame his appreciation of the paramount necessity to obey orders which is incumbent on every military officer; and that the excuses he offers for his acts of insubordination are afterthoughts.
>
> For this offense alone it is believed that the sentences pronounced by the court is in no sense too severe, especially when considered in connection with the finding under specification 4th of charge 2, alleging neglect to pursue and punish certain Indians who had attacked a small party detached from his command, though he was officially informed at the time or within less than an hour after, of the death of one and probably two of his men in consequence of this attack, he is shown to have taken no measures to verify the statement or recover the bodies of the killed, but within half an hour afterwards to have continued his hurried march towards Fort Riley, and to have left this imperative duty to the officer of Infantry in command of the Post at Downer's Station.[121]

Holt then took up the additional charge of a "graver character," the "shooting down without trial of three enlisted men, on the supposition that they were deserters. . . ." This was discussed at great length and dealt with the statistics of desertion from the Custer contingent[122] and whether the loss of so many men placed the command in "the danger of an attack from a powerful enemy" and justified Custer's action by "an imperative necessity."

> Should Gen. Custer's act be considered as an unwarranted exercise of lawless power, the result of habits of thought acquired while controlling in time of open war a large command,[123] and when accus-

tomed to this doing of those duties of military emergency which war sometimes necessitates, and not as justified by the peculiar and difficult circumstances under which this deed was committed, the sentence pronounced by the Court in this case is utterly inadequate and measures should be at once taken for Gen. Custer's trial before a Court of competent jurisdiction.[124]

Custer's superiors thought he needed disciplining but they were not about to take his case any further. General Grant approved the sentence as it stood, though he commented on its leniency. In effect Custer was punished for absence without leave and for flouting the old army tradition that the army saves its wounded, buries its dead, and punishes its enemies; for his impulsive order to shoot the deserters he escaped penalty. When West, still unsatisfied, brought a charge of murder in civil court against his commander and Lieutenant Cook, who actually fired the shot, General Smith and Surgeon Madison Mills, medical director of the Department of the Missouri, came forward to sign Custer's bond.[125] After a few days' testimony the judge dismissed the case because the evidence did not support the charges.[126]

Custer's first reaction to his arrest and the ensuing charges was mild enough for as his wife wrote to her cousin, "When he ran the risk of a court-martial in leaving Wallace he did it expecting the consequences."[127] Therefore it might seem he would not have been too disturbed at his sentence. Such was not the case. In assembling the evidence and constructing a defense he quite convinced himself of his innocence and was indignant at his conviction and sentence. He publicly charged that his judges had been prejudiced rather than judicious. The court had been improperly constituted—too many of the officers were below him in rank and too many were from Hancock's staff, some from the commissary department and therefore hostile towards him for his complaints about army supply. His accusations were printed in the New York newspapers and widely distributed.[128] The higher echelons of the army must have regretted this publicity.

In apparent retaliation, Custer brought charges of "drunkenness on duty" against Captain West. West was undoubtedly a heavy drinker, though according to the testimony of his fellow officers he still managed to be one of the best company commanders in the regiment. Convicted on a part of the charges, West was suspended from rank and pay for two months and confined to the limits of the camp or post occupied by his company.[129] Sadly enough these court-martials, which called on many of the regimental officers for testimony, forced them to take one side or another, creating a schism in the regiment that was not healed for years.

All in all Custer's first year in the West had not been a success. He had displayed none of the aggressiveness and willingness to do and fight that Sherman had expected. A reluctant warrior, his only interest seemed to be in getting over the prescribed course as quickly as possible. He was annoyed at the discomfort of harsh weather and the uncertain supply which was almost inherent in Plains service. Irritated by the continuing desertions he over-reacted by ordering drastic measures. Finally he had fled towards family and civilization in a journey so irrational in its haste that it could not fail to bring down upon him disciplinary charges. Faced with a mild sentence he had reacted publicly and petulantly with accusations of jealousy, bias, and injustice.

Yet who can say but that Custer was well-broken in. After his exile the young general would return to his regiment under the aegis of his former commander, admirer, and friend, Gen. Philip H. Sheridan. He was given every opportunity to show his mettle and responded vigorously. He followed Indian trails doggedly—some weeks' old—and discovered the tribesmen in their camp. When he found the enemy he attacked. He rescued white women captives from the Indians and seized red women as hostages. When on the trail the food supply was reduced to mule meat without bread, the general did not complain. His wife was with him in camp but not on his scouts. The pervasive theme of both of them in their memoirs would be the gayety and fortitude with which they had met the challenges, hardships, and deprivations of army life on the Plains.

Notes

1. Elizabeth B. Custer, *Tenting on the Plains; or, General Custer in Kansas and Texas* (New York: Harper and Brothers, 1887), 595.

2. George Armstrong Custer (1839– 1876) was graduated from West Point in June, 1861, and went immediately into the army as second lieutenant in the Second U.S. cavalry. He spent little time with his regiments, be-

coming an aide successively to Generals Philip Kearny, George McClellan, and Alfred Pleasonton. In June, 1863, Custer received an appointment as brigadier general of volunteers, and in April, 1865, major general. Meanwhile, though his rank in the regular army advanced only to captain, he was awarded for meritorious services several brevets, the highest one of major general in 1865. Brevets were most often honorary ranks, which bestowed the title and the right to wear the insignia upon the officer, but not the pay or duties of the brevet rank except in special assignments. After the Civil War, officers customarily went under the title of their brevet rank. Hence Custer was Brevet Major General Custer though his pay and duty were that of lieutenant colonel of the Seventh U.S. cavalry.

3. Winfield Scott Hancock (1824–1886) was graduated from West Point in 1844. Most of his early service was in California and the West where he worked in the quartermaster corps. When the Civil War opened he was made a brigadier general of volunteers, in recognition of his known ability. He was a handsome man and that together with his able handling of his troops earned him the sobriquet of Hancock the Superb. He was given much credit for the Union victory at Gettysburg where he was wounded on the second day. After the war he was made a major general in the army. He had political ambitions and was nominated for President in 1880 by the Democratic party.

4. The Military Department of the Missouri was only a part of the Division of the Missouri commanded by William T. Sherman.

5. Andrew Jackson Smith (1815–1897) was graduated from West Point in 1838 and became second lieutenant in the First U.S. dragoons. He was in a number of the early cavalry movements in the West—with Stephen Kearny to South Pass in 1845 and with the Mormon battalion in their march from Fort Leavenworth to Santa Fe and on to California in 1846–1847. His Civil War service was primarily in the Western campaigns where he commanded an army corps and several divisions. He was at Vicksburg, on the Bank's Red river campaign and with Thomas against Hood at Nashville. He was one of the few to defeat Nathan B. Forrest, whom he stopped at Tupelo in 1864. He attained the rank of major general of volunteers and major general by brevet in the regular army. He was appointed colonel of the Seventh U.S. cavalry in 1866.

6. The District of the Upper Arkansas was a temporary district created for this one season. Smith reported to Hancock and the records of the District can be found in the National Archives with those of the Department of the Missouri.

7. William Tecumseh Sherman, next to Grant, was the most famous of Union generals. The Military Division of the Missouri covered all the states and territories between the Mississippi and the Rocky mountains except Arkansas, Louisiana, and Texas.

8. Smith to Hancock, March 5, 1867,

"Letters and Telegrams Received, Department of the Missouri, U.S. Army Commands, War Department," National Archives, Record Group 98. (Hereafter, records in the National Archives are indicated by the symbol NA, followed by the record group (RG) number.)

9. Cpt. G. W. Bradley to Brig. Gen. S. C. Easton, March 3, 1867, "Letters Received, Dept. of the Missouri," NA, RG 98. Other sources that stress the bad rainy weather of the spring and early summer of 1867 are: Custer, *Tenting on the Plains*, 614–18; William A. Bell, *New Tracks in North America* (Albuquerque: Horn and Wallace, 1965), 23–27; Theodore R. Davis, "With Generals in Their Camp Homes," Manuscript Division, Kansas State Historical Society.

10. W. H. Cantrill's testimony, in Lawrence A. Frost, *The Court-Martial of General George Armstrong Custer* (Norman: University of Oklahoma Press, 1968), 204. This book contains a transcript of the entire court-martial proceedings.

11. *Reports of Major General W. S. Hancock upon Indian Affairs, with Accompanying Exhibits* (Washington, D.C., n.d.), 17.

12. *Junction City Weekly Union*, March 30, June 1, 1867.

13. For accounts of the Hancock expedition, see *Reports of Major General W. S. Hancock; Difficulties with Indian Tribes*, 41st Cong., 2d sess., 1870, H. Ex. Doc. 240; Henry M. Stanley, *My Early Travels and Adventures in America and Asia*, 2 vols. (New York: Charles Scribner's Sons, 1895), 1:1–96; Theodore R. Davis, "A Summer on the Plains," *Harper's New Monthly Magazine* 36 (February 1868): pp. 292–98; George Armstrong Custer, *My Life on the Plains* (New York: Sheldon and Co., 1874), pp. 20–43; George Bird Grinnell, *The Fighting Cheyennes* (New York: C. Scribner's Sons, 1915), 236–53; Marvin H. Garfield, "Defense of the Kansas Frontier, 1866–67," *Kansas Historical Quarterly* 1 (August 1932): 326–44; Donald J. Berthong, *The Southern Cheyennes* (Norman: University of Oklahoma Press, 1963), 269–81; and Lonnie J. White, "The Hancock and Custer Expeditions of 1867," *Journal of the West* 5, no. 3 (July 1966): 355–78.

14. Camped with the Cheyennes on Pawnee Fork were some Sioux variously designated as of the Brule or Ogallala bands. In number they probably aggregated more than the Cheyennes since they left 140 lodges when they ran away while the Cheyennes left but 111. See *Reports of Major General W. S. Hancock*, 51.

15. For Custer's route in pursuit of the Indians, see Minnie Dubbs Millbrook, *Ness, Western County, Kansas* (Detroit: Millbrook Print. Co., 1955), 55.

16. *Junction City Union*, April 20, 1867.

17. *Difficulties with Indian Tribes*, 107.

18. Custer to Lt. Thomas B. Weir (Smith's acting assistant adjutant), May 4, 1867, *Reports of Major General W. S. Hancock*, 79.

19. Ibid.

20. Custer, *My Life on the Plains*, 46.

21. Custer, *Tenting on the Plains*, 687, 688.

22. There were no new buildings or other improvements at Fort Hays as at the other posts because the fort was to be relocated nearer the route of the railroad.

23. Davis, "With Generals in Their Camp Homes."

24. Custer to Elizabeth, April 22, 1867, in Custer, *Tenting on the Plains*, 570.

25. Custer to Elizabeth, April 8, 1867, in ibid., 527, 528.

26. This letter could not be found among the records but it probably got the same reception as an earlier letter of Custer's to General Hancock stating that the army was too lenient with deserters—the lack of severe punishment encouraged desertion. Hancock answered rather tersely that he did not make the policies of the army—he only followed orders.

27. Custer to Elizabeth, May 2, 1867, in Custer, *Tenting on the Plains*, 578.

28. Alfred Gibbs (1823–1868) was the senior major of the Seventh U.S. cavalry and a major general by brevet. He was from a distinguished New England family and was a West Point graduate, being a classmate of George McClellan and Stonewall Jackson. Like all the young army officers of his time he was sent west and had some service in the Mexican war where he won two brevets. He was badly wounded in an Indian skirmish. Early in the Civil War he was captured along with Maj. Isaac Lynde near Fort Fillmore in New Mexico by the Confederates, and placed on parole for a year. Though he therefore had a late start in the Civil War he rose to become a brigadier general with a brevet of major general in Sheridan's cavalry. Due to the old lance wound his health was poor. An excellent administrator and able handler of men, he played a most important part in the organization of the Seventh cavalry. He was often in command at Fort Riley and Fort Leavenworth and organized the Seventh cavalry band.

29. Custer's first orders in regard to this scout are reproduced in Frost, *Court-Martial*, 124, 125.

30. Gen. W. T. Sherman to John Sherman, February 24, 1867, W. T. Sherman Papers, Library of Congress.

31. *Difficulties with Indian Tribes*, 57.

32. Hancock to Smith, May 15, 1867, Department of the Missouri, United States Army Commands, NA, RG 98.

33. Smith to Hancock, May 23, 1867. (When no other source is indicated for letters and dispatches, they are from Department of the Missouri, United States Army Commands, NA, RG 98.

34. There was a great deal of discussion in the quartermaster corps in regard to this new system of furnishing fine stores for officers to purchase at reasonable prices. It would be impossible to know how much and what items to forward. One comment was that "perhaps it was unfortunate for the Officers of the Army that the authority to the subsistence department

to supply the officers with canned articles was not deferred until all the officers who entered the army since 1860 had an opportunity to learn by experience how officers were supplied before that time." Another thought it could never be satisfactory. "Let the officers of the Subsistence Department try as they will, some officers of the army will expect to be able to procure articles at posts on the Plains as they would in the city."

Like all new systems this one did not work well in the beginning and there were reports during the summer from various posts that the fine stores were exhausted.

35. Smith to Custer, May 31, 1867.

36. *Annual Report of the Secretary of War [1867]*, 40th Cong., 2d sess., H. Ex. Doc. 1, p. 33.

37. Custer, *My Life on the Plains*, 53.

38. Ibid.

39. Custer aimed to average about 25 miles a day "when not in immediate pursuit of the enemy." Ibid., 52. Mrs. Custer wrote, "A cavalry column marches at the rate of four miles an hour, and the length of a day's journey varies from twenty-five to forty miles." Elizabeth B. Custer, *Following the Guidon* (New York: Harper and Brothers, 1890), 328. It would seem that this was considerably in excess of the usual cavalry rate in summer patrols on the Plains, which was governed by the necessity of keeping the horses in condition. "Twenty miles a day, for a horse loaded down with the heavy equipment of a dragoon soldier, is pretty hard traveling. . . ." Samuel J. Bayard, *The Life of George Dashiell Bayard* (New York, 1874), 121. See also "Lieutenant J. E. B. Stuart's Journal, May 15 to August 11, 1860," in Le Roy R. Hafen and Ann W. Hafen, eds., *Relations with the Indians of the Plains, 1857–1861* (Glendale, Calif.: A. H. Clark Co., 1959), 215–44. The extent of the daily march was as carefully kept on this journey as was that of Custer's in 1867. The average daily march was just under 18 miles.

40. Custer to Elizabeth, June 12, 1867, in Frost, *Court-Martial*, 46. Both Sherman and Hancock disapproved of Custer's handling of this situation. On June 26, 1867, Hancock wrote to Smith: "We will have no talks with Indians nor make any terms except absolute submission. . . . Gen. Custer has accepted the surrender of Pawnee Killer and band to be placed at Ft. McPherson what I entirely disapprove, as also does Gen. Sherman."

41. Sherman's attitude towards the Indians, which he must have communicated to Custer, were expressed in a dispatch to Hancock, June 11, 1867: "I hear that Custer is arriving at McPherson. After a very short rest, I will have him to scour the Republican to its source to kill and destroy as many Indians as possible. He will then come into the Platte here or above for orders. Look out on your line in case they run that way. You may reduce to submission all Indians between the Arkansas and Platte or kill them. All are hostile or in complicity. Keep our people as active as possible. . . ."

42. Custer, *My Life on the Plains*, 54, 55; Frost, *Court-Martial*, 191–93; *Annual Report of the Secretary of War [1867]*, 35.

43. Davis, "Summer on the Plains," 302; Custer, *My Life on the Plains*, 55.

44. In Custer's account of this scout, he designates his officers by their brevet rank. That designation is not used here except for the Generals Custer, Smith, and Gibbs, which conforms with the practice of the time. In army correspondence and records regimental officers are usually spoken of as in their regular rank. So too in the Custer court-martial record. Most of the better-known officers of the Seventh cavalry carried the brevet rank of lieutenant colonel, only Cpt. Frederick W. Benteen being a brevet colonel. 1Lt. Samuel Robbins had no brevet rank because, as he wrote General Hancock, he had served in the First Colorado cavalry out west where no brevets had been recommended. Yet he had participated in many stiff engagements and was as deserving as the rest. Hancock recommended him for a brevet.

45. Custer, *My Life on the Plains*, 55, 56.

46. Custer, *Tenting on the Plains*, 581–83; Frost, *Court-Martial*, 54, 55. Frost states this letter shows Custer's anxiety about the spread of cholera. The cholera did not come to Kansas until June 28, so Custer could not possibly have known anything about it at this time.

47. This is Custer's own phrase. *My Life on the Plains*, 56.

48. Ibid., 59.

49. Davis, "With Generals in Their Camp Homes."

50. Custer, *My Life on the Plains*, 60.

51. Lt. Henry Jackson, "Itinerary of the March of the Seventh United States Cavalry," June 24, 1867. This careful record with maps of each day's march and camp is in the National Archives. Though Jackson seldom gave any details beyond his log of distances, his work is a valuable check on other accounts.

52. Custer, *My Life on the Plains*, 61.

53. It has never been satisfactorily explained why Mrs. Custer did not come to Fort Wallace as Custer had asked her to in his letter from Fort McPherson. He said (*My Life on the Plains*, 64) that his letter had miscarried. Mrs. Custer says (*Tenting on the Plains*, 625–27) that she was at Fort Wallace when Cook and Robbins came for supplies and that Hancock, the commanding officer of the department, there temporarily, forbade her going. It is doubtful that Mrs. Custer ever went to Fort Wallace. In fact she had just returned to Fort Riley from Fort Hays around June 18 (ibid., 547–49) and could not possibly have traveled to Fort Wallace in time to have arrived by June 24. Her letter to Custer from Riley, June 27, does not indicate any trip that far west.

54. Custer, *My Life on the Plains*, 63. This is an almost incredible statement since Custer had been sent to attack and kill any Indians found between

the Platte and the Smoky.

55. Lt. Joseph Hale to Weir, June 22, 1867, "Letters Sent," Fort Wallace Records, 1867. A copy of the records from the National Archives is in the Kansas State Historical Society.

56. Hale to Weir, June 27, 1867, ibid.

57. *Difficulties with Indian Tribes*, 62.

58. Davis, "Summer on the Plains," 303, mentions that after the trip to Wallace, Comstock, reading the Indian signs, declared that the Indians had moved west and camped at the head of the Beaver.

59. Hale to Weir, June 27, 1867, "Letters Sent," Fort Wallace Records.

60. C. C. Augur to Custer, telegram, June 25, 1867, in Frost, *Court-Martial*, 209.

61. The account of this march follows Jackson's "Itinerary" rather than that of Custer in his memoirs. Custer would say it was 65 miles long and that the troops did not all reach the river until morning, while Jackson records the day's march as 59 ⅓ miles. He also states that the column arrived at the Platte at eight P.M., one mile west of Riverside station.

62. Custer, *My Life on the Plains*, 69, 70.

63. *Annual Report of the Secretary of War [1867]*, 35; Frost, *Court-Martial*, 200.

64. Captain Keogh commanding at Fort Wallace, gives an excellent account of Fort Wallace and the stations under his superintendence. He reported almost every other day until he went with General Hancock to Den-

ver on June 18. Lt. Joseph Hale, taking Keogh's place as commanding officer, reported the battles of June 21 and 26. See also Bell, *New Tracks*, 52. Cpt. Albert Barnitz of the Seventh cavalry has often been reported in command at Fort Wallace at this time. He was there in command of the escort of the Gen. W. W. Wright surveying party and took part in the battle of the 26th.

65. *Memorial of Lieut. Frederick Henry Beecher, U.S.A.* (Portland, 1870), 31.

66. Maj. Henry Douglas to Brig. Gen. Chauncey McKeever, June 18, 1867, "Letters Sent," Fort Dodge Records, microfilm, Kansas State Historical Society.

67. Just at this time Fort Hays was moving from its first location on the Smoky to a location, 17 miles northwest, on Big creek. This move brought the fort closer to the railroad line and thereafter when frightened by Indian attack the construction men often came into Fort Hays. Fort Hays records are very sparse and reflect this period inadequately.

68. Samuel J. Crawford, *Kansas in the Sixties* (Chicago: A. C. McClurg and Co., 1911), 251–66.

69. *Difficulties with Indian Tribes*, 61; McKeever to Maj. Gen. William A. Nichols, telegram, June 19, 1867.

70. Robert G. Athearn, *William Tecumseh Sherman and the Settlement of the West* (Norman: University of Oklahoma Press, 1956), 126–48. Athearn discusses Sherman's attitude towards local troops.

71. "Epidemic Cholera," *Report of*

Surgeon General's Office, June 10, 1868, Circular No. 1. This careful study records in detail the appearance and progress of the disease of cholera at Kansas posts and in various army details. All statements in this paper in regard to the cholera are taken from this source.

72. Alice Blackwood Baldwin, *Memoirs of the Late Frank D. Baldwin, Major General, U.S.A.* (Los Angeles: Wetzel Publishing Co., 1929), 133, 134.

73. Ibid., 134; Sister M. Evangeline Thomas, "The Rev. Louis Dumortier, S.J., Itinerant Missionary to Central Kansas, 1859–1867," *Kansas Historical Quarterly* 20 (November 1952): 269.

74. *Junction City Union,* July 20, 1867.

75. Ibid., August 3, 1867.

76. Crawford, *Kansas in the Sixties,* 260.

77. Horace L. Moore, "The Nineteenth Kansas Cavalry," *Kansas Historical Collections* 6 (1897–1900): 36.

78. *Leavenworth Conservative,* July 7, August 23, 1867.

79. Frost, *Court-Martial,* 210, 211. It is not plain in this tabulation how many men deserted the night of July 6 or on the 7th. The total for the two days was 34.

80. This episode is covered thoroughly by the testimony of witnesses in the court-martial record. Frost, *Court-Martial,* 150–211. See also Custer, *My Life on the Plains,* 72, 73.

81. Custer's official report, August 6, 1867, of the march from the Platte to Fort Wallace. Ibid., 174–77. While there is no supporting evidence that the troopers' ration was short and damaged, the officers' stores were probably exhausted. See report of Lieutenant Hale to Weir, June 27, 1867, "Letters Sent," Fort Wallace Records, 1867.

82. Custer, *My Life on the Plains,* 75–78; Davis, "Summer on the Plains," 306.

83. George E. Hyde, *Life of George Bent: Written from His Letters,* ed. Savoie Lottinville (Norman: University of Oklahoma Press, 1968), 261.

84. Grinnell, *Fighting Cheyennes,* 251. "These all appeared to be Sioux."

85. Hyde, *Life of George Bent,* 274, 275; Grinnell, *Fighting Cheyennes,* 252.

86. Hyde, *Life of George Bent,* 276.

87. Bell, *New Tracks,* 65–67.

88. Frost, *Court-Martial,* 204, testimony of W. H. Cattrill at the court-martial. Also see *Court of Claims, Indian Depredations; Wells Fargo vs. United States, 1867,* for testimony of various stage employees.

89. Frost, *Court-Martial,* 198, 199, deposition of Major Elliott.

90. Keogh to Weir, July 8, 1867, and Keogh to Cpt. W. G. Mitchell, July 16, 1867, "Letters Sent," Fort Wallace Records, 1867.

91. There is no actual proof that Custer did not find letters from his wife at Fort Wallace though his actions later support that belief. Mrs. Custer in *Tenting on the Plains,* 701, states that he did find letters from her at Fort Hays and Fort Harker, implying that he had had none at Wallace.

92. Telegram, Smith to Custer, June 18, 1867, quoted in Frost, *Court-Martial,* 51.

93. Deposition of Major Elliott, October 6, 1867, in ibid., 199.

94. Custer's defense at his trial, in ibid., 225. General Augur in his dispatch of June 25, 1867 (ibid., 209), wrote: "Gen. Myers is purchasing a hundred and fifty horses for you, how rapidly I cannot say."

95. Custer, *My Life on the Plains*, 79, 80.

96. "Epidemic Cholera," 52, Dr. Lippincott's report. This first cholera infection which appeared on July 22 was confined to the Seventh cavalry. Prompt measures were taken and Major Elliott was given great credit for his management of the command under this affliction. Keogh wrote on July 29, "supplies are coming in promptly. The medical and quartermaster stores have been received and in fact every thing needed is on hand. Everything we have we share with the 7th Cavalry. . . . The work on the Post progresses finely. . . . The stage company are getting their stock in again and propose soon to commence running regularly."

On the 8th of August there arrived at Fort Wallace from New Mexico a battalion of the Fifth U.S. infantry under Cpt. Henry C. Bankhead to take over command of the post from Keogh. The day after it arrived the first case of cholera appeared in the Fifth infantry but since it was camped a mile above the post the garrison was not infected. There were 25 cases and 11 deaths, one of which was Mrs. Bankhead, the captain's wife. Mrs. Custer in *Tenting on the Plains*, 696, mentions this second epidemic.

97. Frost, *Court-Martial*, 117, Lieutenant Cook's testimony.

98. Captain Benteen at Fort Downer to General Gibbs at Fort Hays, July 14, 1867.

99. Frost, *Court-Martial*, 111, Captain Hamilton's testimony.

100. Ibid., 118, Lieutenant Cook's testimony.

101. A. B. Carpenter to Smith, July 18, 1867. The Indians had driven off eight stage horses from Fort Downer on the 12th and 18 horses from Chalk Bluffs on the 14th.

102. Several persons gave testimony on this episode at the court-martial: Sgt. James Connelly, 137–46; Captain Hamilton, 111–13; Lieutenant Cook, 120; Cpt. Arthur Carpenter, 135. Page references are to Frost, *Court-Martial*.

103. Custer's official report of his expedition, August 6, 1867, in ibid., 176, 177.

104. Custer's own defense at his court-martial, in ibid., 231.

105. Custer, *My Life on the Plains*, 82. The italics were added by this writer.

106. Carpenter to Smith, July 18, 1867. See, also, Frost, *Court-Martial*, 134–36. In a letter to his parents from Downer's station, August 15, 1867, Carpenter wrote more fully about the incident: "He [Custer] came through here about the middle of last month on his way to Reilly, and stopped for dinner. While at dinner his rear guard was attacked about 3 miles west of here, and those who came in reported two killed. Custer remained unconcerned—finished his dinner, and moved on with-

out saying a word to me about the bodies, or thinking of hunting the indians. As soon as my wagons came in . . . I sent 10 men and one wagon to recover the bodies to prevent the wolves from eating them. They found one not killed but wounded, shot through the leg, the other was about a half a mile further on killed and scalped, and stripped of everything but his boots. . . . The wounded man . . . says that he would have died before morning if I had not sent out and brought him in." *Western America in Documents*, Catalogue 161 (New York: Edward Eberstadt and Sons, n.d.), 41, quoted by permission.

107. Actually the table of distances introduced at the court-martial shows the distance between Big Creek and Fort Wallace to be 141 miles. Frost, *Court-Martial*, 147. The Big Creek stage station was down on the old trail about eight miles southwest of new Fort Hays.

108. The quotation is from Custer's defensive letter to the *Sandusky* (Ohio) *Register*, December 28, 1867, in which he writes principally in regard to the shooting of the deserters and barely mentions this march. In *My Life on the Plains*, 82, Custer mentions several of his fast marches, and Mrs. Custer repeats them in *Tenting on the Plains*, 700, 701.

109. These must have been the same ambulances that accompanied the expedition to the Platte as they were brought along with the Custer column from Fort Wallace. The wounded deserters were placed in an army wagon because the ambulances were unfit.

110. Frost, *Court-Martial*, 131–34, 223, testimony of Captain Cox, and Custer's comment on it.

111. Ibid., 126–28. The entire order is given in this text.

112. Cpt. Thomas B. Weir's testimony appears in ibid., 128–30, and Custer's version of the meeting is in the same text, 225–27.

113. Smith's testimony before the court-martial, in ibid., 150.

114. Smith to Hancock, July 28, 1867.

115. Telegram, W. G. Mitchell to Smith, July 22, 1867.

116. Frost, *Court-Martial*, 174–77. This general report dated August 6 was entered into the proceedings of the court-martial by the judge advocate. The report of August 7 concerned the Kidder massacre.

117. Ibid., 99, 100.

118. Ibid., 100–102.

119. Although Custer was found guilty of the charge no criminality was attached to the use of government mules and ambulances in his trip from Hays to Harker. This charge probably had its genesis in an earlier order from General Grant concerning "extravagant" practices that had become prominent during the Civil War, two instances noted being the use of ambulances and mounted orderlies at all posts. See *Annual Report of the Secretary of War [1867]*.

The other specification of which Custer was declared guilty but to which no criminality was attached was that of denying immediate medical attention to the wounded deserters and putting them in a wagon.

120. J. Holt, "Review of the Trial of Gen. G. A. Custer," Records of the United States Army Continental Commands, 1821–1920, Judge Advocate General's Office, NA, RG 353.

121. Ibid.

122. The desertions suffered in the two months, April 19–July 13 by the Custer command totaled 156. Ninety of these were from Hays in April and May. Custer started his marches with about 360 men and ended with 296. This does not include the 20 men who left the night after Custer arrived at Big Creek near Hays on July 18. See Frost, *Court-Martial*, 210, 211.

123. With the approval or order of General Sheridan, Custer had executed several deserters during the Civil War, specifically one on January 6, 1865. Ibid., 210. He had also executed one after a court-martial in Louisiana, July 28, 1865. See Custer, *Tenting on the Plains*, 105.

124. Holt, "Review of the Trial."

125. *Leavenworth Conservative*, January 4, 1868.

126. Ibid., January 8–10, 19, 1868.

127. Marguerite Merington, ed., *The Custer Story: The Life and Intimate Letters of General George A. Custer and His Wife Elizabeth* (New York: Devin-Adair, 1950), 212.

128. *Sandusky* (Ohio) *Register*, December 28, 1867. See note 108. This letter was also printed in part in the *New York Times*, December 28, 31, 1867, and in the *Army and Navy Journal*, January 4, 1868.

129. Court-martial of Cpt. Robert M. West, JAGO, NA, RG 353. The charges by General Custer, concerning incidents five or more months earlier, were ordered for trial on December 17. The court was convened on January 15 but was forced to wait to begin proceedings until January 20 as Custer and Cook were still in civil court on West's charges there.

SOME REMINISCENCES, INCLUDING THE WASHITA BATTLE, NOVEMBER 27, 1868

EDWARD S. GODFREY

During our return march to Fort Dodge from General Sully's first expedition, September, 1868, the General would at times relieve his mind by talking of his problems at the headquarters mess and campfires. One of the problems was a commander of his cavalry. For some reason he had come to the conclusion that Major Elliott, then in command of the troops of the 7th Cavalry, had not had sufficient experience to trust him with an independent command.[1] He mentioned the various field officers of cavalry within his jurisdiction as district commander and finally eliminated all of them. He, several times, mentioned the "Triumvirate of S's"—Sherman, Division Commander; Sheridan, Department Commander; and Sully, District Commander[2]—and seemed perfectly satisfied with the results of the expedition. For future operations he intended to ask for a larger force, operate against the Indians till he chastised them, and then return to winter quarters.

On arrival at Fort Dodge, he asked for recruits and horses and equipments for the troops of the 7th Cavalry to the maximum (then one hundred) and for Lieutenant Colonel Custer to command the regiment.

Plan of Campaign and Preparations

A few days later General Sheridan arrived at the post. The plan of campaign was changed to establish a supply camp of a more permanent nature and to make a winter campaign. The supply cantonment was to be at the junction of the Beaver, or North Fork of the Canadian, and Wolf Creek, where General Sully had abandoned pursuit of the hostiles.

Major Alfred Gibbs with the headquarters and band from Fort Leavenworth joined the 7th Cavalry, and, later, the two troops stationed at Fort Harker arrived—eleven troops present. The regiment was sent out to Bluff Creek, about thirty miles southeast of Fort Dodge. General Custer joined the regiment early in October and at once began aggressive operations against the hostiles who had repeatedly attacked the camp.

The troops of the 10th Cavalry were sent north to protect the frontier settlements on the Saline, Solomon and Republican Rivers which the Indians had been raiding since the tenth of August.

General Sheridan established his field headquarters at Fort Hays where he could be in closer touch with communications and energize the forwarding of supplies for the coming campaign. Finding difficulty in getting transportation to forward supplies from Hays City to Fort Dodge, he ordered Number One Depot Train from Fort Leavenworth. This train was the pride of the Quartermaster's Department. It was composed of selected mules, as for many years the best mules sent to the department had been assigned to this train. That woke up the Quartermaster Department!

While at Fort Dodge, he learned that the commissary of the post had asked the families and officers' messes to estimate the amount of officers' stores they wanted for the coming year. These were tabulated and sent to the Chief Commissary, Department Headquarters, as his annual requisition. When the supplies arrived, these canned goods were apportioned according to estimates, or if the garrison had been increased, according to the number of persons in the several messes. General Sheridan found some of the delicacies quite toothsome and drew on the stores until he was informed that he *had* his quota. He was surprised that there was a limit and that special requisitions were taboo. He ordered and approved a special requisition, and further ordered that in the future special requisitions be honored. That woke up the Commissary Department!

In the meantime, General Sully was busy with his requisitions for the new cantonment, or Camp Supply. Finding that mules were scarce, he estimated for a number of yokes of oxen, intending to use them to haul the supplies for the buildings at the supply camp, etc., on the army wagons with trailers to the new post; then use them to "snake" the logs for stockades; and subsequently kill them for beef. That horrified both departments! But he got his oxen, or "bulls," as they were called in the parlance of the West.

The outrages on the Kansas frontier settlers and the capture of women aroused the people of that state to appeal for protection. The Congress authorized the organization of the 18th and 19th Kansas Volunteer Cavalry. The Governor, Honorable S. J. Crawford, resigned to accept the colonelcy of the 19th which rendezvoused at Topeka.

General Sheridan's plan for the winter campaign involved the operations of three columns:

Colonel A. W. Evans with six troops of the 3rd Cavalry and two companies of infantry was to march from a base at Fort Bascom, New Mexico, establish a supply depot at Monument Creek, then scout the Canadian and the North Fork of the Red River Valleys as far as the Red River, the boundary of the Department of Missouri.

A column of seven troops of the 5th Cavalry under the command of Lieutenant Colonel E. A. Carr was to march southeast from Fort Lyon, Colorado, unite with Captain Penrose with five troops of cavalry, then on the north fork of the Canadian, and operate toward Antelope Hills on the Canadian.

The third column, at Fort Dodge under General Sully, was to move southward and establish the cantonment at the fork of Beaver Creek and Wolf Creek. This column consisted of eleven troops of the 7th Cavalry and five companies of the 3rd Infantry. The 19th Kansas Volunteer Cavalry was organized at Topeka, Kansas, and was ordered to join this column at Camp Supply.

All these columns were to march November 1st, but owing to the delays of supplies, the time was changed to November 12.

On the 28th of October, the 7th Cavalry went into camp a short distance below Fort Dodge and named the camp "Camp Sandy Forsyth" in honor of Colonel George A. Forsyth, who, with fifty volunteer scouts, had withstood the attack of about seven hundred hostiles on the Arickaree Fork of the Republican. The arrival of about five hundred recruits and the same number of horses filled the organizations to the maximum. All the horses of the regiment were then arranged according to color on one long picket line and each troop commander, according to rank, was given choice of color for his troop. According to color there were: Four troops of bay horses, three sorrel, one each black, brown and gray, the band and trumpeters gray, and the eleventh troop the odds and ends of all colors, including roans, piebalds, etc. For several years after this, before requisitions for colors were given consideration in purchases, I observed that these ratios obtained.

Drills and target practice were pushed to the limit. Forty of the best shots were selected for a separate organization under the command of Lieutenant Cooke. We youngsters named it the "Corps d'elite" and the name stuck throughout the campaign.

On November 12th the Fort Dodge column assembled on Mulberry Creek, the 7th Cavalry from Camp Sandy Forsyth on the Arkansas River, and the supply train of nearly four hundred army wagons with its infantry escort from Fort Dodge.

Establishing the Base

The next morning we had one of those tedious jobs of crossing a prairie creek; steep, deep banks, doubling of teams, breaking of coupling poles, amid the shouting and cursing of wagon masters and teamsters. The wagon train was assembled in columns of fours—two troops of cavalry as advance guard, three troops with flankers on each flank, and two as rear guard. The infantry companies were distributed along the train, and the beef herd along the train inside the flanking troops. The leading troop on the flanks would march to the head of the train, halt and graze until the rear of the train had passed it, thus alternating so as to save dismounting and yet cover the flanks of the train. The advance guard of one day would be rear guard the next day. The details were by roster so as to equalize the functions. The slow travel of the "bull" train was a handicap to travel and to arrival in camp on a full day's march. The ensemble made an imposing cavalcade.

The march was without special incident till the last day's march down Beaver Creek, when our Osage Indian trailers discovered the trail of a war party of a hundred or more on their way north to raid the frontier. On arrival in camp, General Custer requested permission to take the cavalry on the back trail of this war party and attack the village whence they came. General Sully disapproved the proposal on the ground that since it was absurd to suppose the hostiles were unaware of our presence in the country, the village could not be surprised but would be on the alert. He was obsessed with the idea that all our operations were under the constant surveillance of hostile scouts who kept the tribes fully informed.

On the sixth day of our march we arrived at the fork of Beaver and Wolf Creeks. At once preparations began for the building of the cantonment on which was bestowed the name of Camp Supply. This isolated post became the abode of many "Winners of the West." It was at this place that General Sully had abandoned the pursuit of the hostiles about two months before.

The next day activities began in locating and laying out the cantonment; digging trenches for the stockade and for the quarters and barracks to house the personnel, and digging wells for water supply. Outside parties, guarded by mounted troops, were sent to gather supplies and material for the post. The hum of the mowing machines was accompanied by the ring of the axe, punctuated by the crash of the falling timber. With axes and saws these trees were made into usable parts which the bull teams "snaked" to convenient sites to load in wagons. The mule-whackers hauled them to the cantonment where they were sorted for various uses, as palisades, upright walls for buildings, rafters, etc., etc. What a contrast these pioneer activities were to the centuries of quiet, wild life, yet to the participants it was all in the day's work.

The 19th Kansas Volunteer Cavalry had been ordered to proceed from its rendezvous at Topeka on November 5th. Two troops had gone to Fort Dodge to escort General Sheridan and it was expected that the other eight troops would meet us at the fork of the Beaver and Wolf Creeks. Their absence created much concern.

On the 15th of November, General Sheridan left Fort Hays to join the Fort Dodge column. He relates:

"The first night out a blizzard struck us and carried away our tents; and, as the gale was so violent that they could not be put up again, the rain and snow drenched us to the skin. Shivering from the wet and cold, I took refuge under a wagon, and there spent such a miserable night that, when at last morning came, the gloomy predictions of Old Man Bridger and others rose up before me with greatly increased force." (Bridger had endeavored to dissuade him from making a winter campaign.) "As we took the road the sleet and snow were still falling, but we labored on to Dodge that day in spite of the fact that many mules played out on the way. We stayed only one night at Dodge, and then on the 17th, escorted by a troop of cavalry and Forsyth's scouts, now under the command of Lieutenant Pepoon (10th Cavalry), crossed the Arkansas and camped the night of the 18th at Bluff Creek, where the two troops of the 19th Kansas, previously detailed as my escort were awaiting our coming. As we were approaching this camp some suspicious looking objects were seen moving off at a long distance to the east of us, but as the scouts confidently pronounced them buffalo, we were unaware of their true character till next morning, when we became satisfied what we had seen were Indians, for immediately after crossing Beaver Creek, we struck a trail leading to the northeast of a war party that evidently came up from the headwaters of the Washita River. The evening of November 21st we arrived at the Camp Supply depot, having traveled all day in another snow storm that did not end till twenty-four hours later."

Hearing of the near approach of General Sheridan, General Custer mounted his horse and rode out to meet him.

The arrival of General Sheridan with two troops of the 19th Kansas Volunteers gave rise to an occurrence not mentioned by either General Sheridan or General Custer in their published writings of this campaign. At that time the Rules and Articles of War provided that when troops of the regular army and volunteers came together, brevet rank took effect. Both Sully and Custer were lieutenant colonels. Colonel Crawford of the 19th Kansas was the senior in rank. General Sully issued an order assuming command of the troops by virtue of his brevet rank of brigadier general, U. S. A. When this order reached General Custer, he issued an order assuming command by virtue of his brevet rank of major general, U. S. A. Sully contended that as between officers of the regular army this should not obtain. General Sheridan decided in favor of General Custer. General Sully was relieved from duty with the expedition and ordered to Fort Harker to command the District of the Upper Arkansas. I heard General Custer say that had the question not been raised he would not have taken his stand and would have been perfectly satisfied to have served under Colonel Crawford. During the balance of the campaign General Custer exercised the immediate control of the troops.

"November 22nd, 1868—The morning is cold; it snowed all night and is still snowing. Cleared up at noon and got warmer. We took our horses out to graze at noon and let them pick all they can this Sunday . . . . Still it snows . . . . . ." (From the diary of Blacksmith W. S. Harvey, Troop K, 7th Cavalry, now living at Belle Vernon, Pennsylvania.)

We were grazing the horses in the sand hills on that day when, in the afternoon, orders came to return to camp at once and prepare for thirty days' campaign. It is my recollection that three wagons were assigned to each troop, this for convenience for picket line—one for troop mess, etc., one for officers' mess, extra ammunition, etc., and one for forage. Baggage was limited to necessities.

Finding the Trail

November 23rd—Reveille at 3 o'clock. Snowed all night and still snowing very heavily. The darkness and heavy snowfall made the packing of the wagons very difficult, but at dawn the wagons were assembled in the train and daylight found us on the march, the band playing, "The Girl I Left Behind Me," but there was no woman there to interpret its significance. The snow was falling so heavily that vision was limited to a few rods. All landmarks were invisible and the trails were lost. "We didn't know where we were going, but we were on the way." Then General Custer, with compass in hand, took the lead and became our guide.

As the day wore on the weather became warmer and I have never seen the snowflakes as large or fall so lazily as those that fell that day. Fortunately there was no wind to drift the snow to add to our discomfort. They melted on the clothing so that every living thing was wet to the skin. The snow balled on the feet of our shod animals causing much floundering and adding to the fatigue of travel. About two o'clock we came to Wolf Creek, crossed to the right side of the valley, and continued to march till we came to a clump of fallen timbers and there went into camp with our wagon train far behind. As soon as the horses were unsaddled everyone except the horse holders was gathering fuel for fires. The valley was alive with rabbits and all messes were supplied with rabbit stew. Our rawhide covered saddles were soaked. The unequal drying warped the saddle trees which subsequently caused that bane of cavalry—many sore backs. Snow, eighteen inches "on the level"; distance marched, about fifteen miles.

The snowfall ceased during the night. The sun rose on the 24th with clear skies and with warmer weather. The snow melted rapidly. The glare of the bright sunshine caused much discomfort and a number of cases of snowblindness. Some buffalo were killed and many rabbits. Some deer were seen. We camped on Wolf Creek. Distance marched, about 18 miles.

November 25th we marched some distance up Wolf Creek and then turned in a southerly direction toward the Canadian. As we approached the summit of the divide, the peaks of the Antelope Hills loomed up and became our marker for the rest of the day. We made camp late that evening on a small stream about a mile from the Canadian. The day's march had been tedious. The melting snows balled on our shod animals during the long pull to the divide. A number of horses and mules gave out, but were brought in late that night. Wood was very scarce, but usually the quartermaster sergeants would load some wood in the cook wagon when packing and they usually were on the lookout for fuel on the march.

At daybreak, November 26th, Major Elliott, with troops G, H, and M, some white scouts and Osage trailers, started up the north side of the Canadian to scout for a possible trail of war parties. The remainder of the command and the wagon train marched to the Canadian to cross to the south side. To "California Joe" had been given the task of finding a ford. The river was high and rising, current swift and full of floating snow and slush ice. After much floundering he found a practical ford. The cavalry crossed first and assembled on the plain. Owing to the quicksand bottom, each wagon was double teamed and rushed through without halting. A mounted man preceded each team and other mounted men were alongside to "whoop 'em up."

While this tedious crossing and parking was going on, General Custer and a number of officers went to the tops of the hills to view the country. The highest peak was about three hundred feet above the plain.

Suddenly we were enveloped in a cloud of frozen mist. Looking at the sun we were astonished to see it surrounded by three ellipses with rainbow tints, the axes marked by sundogs, except the lower part of the third or outer ellipse which seemingly was below the horizon, eleven sundogs. This phenomenon was not visible to those on the plain below.

As the last of the wagons had crossed and the rear guard was floundering in crossing, someone of our group on the hills called out, "Hello, here comes somebody." But General Custer had already seen him and had focused his field glasses on the galloping scout, but he said nothing. It was a tense moment when Jack Corbin rode up and began his report.

Major Elliott had marched up the Canadian about twelve miles when he came to the abandoned camp of a war party of about one hundred and fifty; he had crossed the river and was following the trail which was not over twenty-four hours old, and asked for instructions. Corbin was given a fresh horse to return to Major Elliott with instructions to follow the trail till dark, then halt till the command joined him.

Officers' call was sounded and when assembled we were told the news and ordered to be prepared to move as soon as possible. One wagon was assigned to each squadron (two troops), one to Troop G and the teamsters, and one to headquarters; seven in all, and one ambulance under the quartermaster, Lieutenant James M. Bell. These were to carry light supplies and extra ammunition. I cannot recall of just what the limited supplies consisted. Each trooper was ordered to carry one hundred rounds of ammunition on his person. (They were armed with the Spencer magazine carbine and Colt revolver, paper cartridges and caps.) The main train guarded by about eighty men under the command of the officer of the day was to follow as rapidly as possible. For this guard men with weak horses were selected. Captain Louis M. Hamilton, a grandson of Alexander Hamilton, was officer of the day. He was greatly distressed because this duty fell to him and begged to go along to command his squadron, but was refused unless he could get some officer to exchange with him. Lieutenant E. G. Mathey, who was snowblind, agreed to take his place.

Soon the regiment was ready to move and we struck in a direction to intercept the trail of Elliott's advance. We pushed along almost without rest till about 9 P. M. before we came to Elliott's halting place. There we had coffee made, care being taken to conceal the fires as much as possible. Horses were unsaddled and fed. At 10 P. M. we were again in the saddle with instructions to make as little noise as possible,—no loud talking, no matches were to be lighted. Tobacco users were obliged to console themselves with the quid. Little Beaver, Osage Chief, with one of his warriors, had the lead dismounted as trailers; then followed the other Indian and white scouts with whom General Custer rode to be near the advance. The cavalry followed at a distance of about a half mile. The snow had melted during the day but at night the weather had turned cold and the crunching noise could be heard for a considerable distance.

After a couple of hours' march, the trailers hurried back for the command to halt. General Custer rode up to investigate when Little Beaver informed him that he "smelled smoke." Cautious investigation disclosed the embers of a fire which the guides decided from conditions had been made by the boy herders while grazing the pony herds and from this deduced that the village could not be far distant. The moon had risen and there was little difficulty in following the trail and General Custer rode behind the trailers to watch the developments. On nearing the crest of any rise, the trailer would crawl to the crest to reconnoiter, but seeing Little Beaver exercise greater caution than usual and then shading his eyes from the moon, the General felt there was something unusual. On his return the General asked, "What is it?" and Little Beaver replied, "Heap Injuns down there." Dismounting and advancing with the same caution as the guide, he made his personal investigation, but could only see what appeared to be a herd of animals. Asking why he thought there were Indians down there, Little Beaver replied, "Me heard dog bark." Listening intently they not only heard the bark of a dog, but the tinkling of a bell, indicating a pony herd, and then the cry of an infant.

The Plan of Battle

Satisfied that a village had been located, the General returned to the command, assembled the officers, and, after removing sabres, took us all to the crest where the situation was explained or rather conjectured. The barking of the dogs and the occasional cry of infants located the direction of the village and the tinkling of the bells gave the direction of the herds. Returning and resuming our sabres, the General explained his plans and assigned squadron commanders their duties and places.

Major Elliott, with Troops G, H and M, was to march well to our left and approach the village from the northeast or easterly direction as determined by the ground, etc. Captain Thompson, with B and F, was to march well to our right so as to approach from the southeast, connecting with Elliott. Captain Myers, with E and I, was to move by the right so as to approach from a southerly direction. The wagons under Lieutenant Bell and Captain Benteen's squadron—H and M—had been halted about two or three miles on the trail to await the outcome of the investigations.

Just after dismissing the officers and as we were separating, General Custer called my name. On reporting, he directed me to take a detail, go back on the trail to where Captain Benteen and the wagons were, give his compliments to Captain Benteen and instruct him to rejoin the command, and Lieutenant Bell to hold the wagons where they were till he heard the attack which would be about daybreak. "Tell the Adjutant the number of men you want and he will make the detail. How many do you want?" I replied, "One orderly." He then said, "Why do you say that? You can have all you want." I replied that one was all I wanted— "to take more would increase the chances of accident and delay."

I delivered my messages and returned with Captain Benteen's squadron. The camp guard remained with the wagons.

Upon the arrival of Captain Benteen's squadron, Major Elliott proceeded to take position, also Captain Thompson and later Captain Myers.

Before the first streak of dawn, General Custer's immediate command as quietly as possible moved into place facing nearly east, Lieutenant Cooke's sharpshooters in advance of the left dismounted. General Custer and staff were followed by the band mounted. Captain West's squadron was on the right and Captain Hamilton's on the left, the standard and guard in the center. Troop K (West's) was on the right flank and I had command of the first platoon.

With the dawn we were ordered to remove overcoats and haversacks, leaving one man of each organization in charge with orders to load them in the wagons when Lieutenant Bell came up. Following the General, the command marched over the crest of the ridge and advanced some distance to another lower ridge. Waiting till sunrise we began to feel that the village had been abandoned although the dogs continued their furious barkings. Then "little by little" we advanced. Captain West came to me with orders to charge through the village but not to stop, to continue through and round up the pony herds.

The Battle

With all quiet in the early dawn, Major Elliott's command had reached a concealed position close to the village, but was waiting for the signal from headquarters. The furious barking of the dogs aroused an Indian who came from his lodge, ran to the bank of the Washita, looked about and fired his rifle. I was told that a trooper had raised his head to take aim and was seen by this Indian. With the alarm thus given, the command opened fire. The trumpeters sounded the charge and the band began to play "Garry Owen," but by the time they had played one strain their instruments froze up.

My platoon advanced as rapidly as the brush and fallen timbers would permit until we reached the Washita which I found with steep, high banks. I marched the platoon by the right flank a short distance, found a "pony crossing," reformed on the right bank, galloped through the right of the village without contact with a warrior, and then proceeded to round up the pony herds.

As I passed out of the village, Captain Thompson's and Captain Myers' squadrons came over the high ridge on my right. Both had lost their bearings during their night marching and failed to make contacts for the opening attack.

At the opening of the attack, the warriors rushed to the banks of the stream. Those in front of Custer's command were soon forced to retire in among the tepees, and most of them being closely followed retreated to ravines and behind trees and logs, and in depressions, where they maintained their positions till the last one was killed. A few escaped down the valley. This desperate fighting was carried on mostly by sharpshooters, waiting for a head to show. Seventeen Indians were killed in one depression.

Lieutenant Bell, when he heard the firing, rushed his teams to join the command and while loading the overcoats and haversacks was attacked by a superior force and the greater part of them had to be abandoned. His arrival with the reserve ammunition was a welcome reinforcement.

While the fighting was going on, Major Elliott seeing a group of dismounted Indians escaping down the valley called for volunteers to make pursuit. Nineteen men, including Regimental Sergeant Major Kennedy responded. As his detachment moved away, he turned to Lieutenant Hale waved his hand and said: "Here goes for a brevet or a coffin."

After passing through the village, I went in pursuit of pony herds and found them scattered in groups about a mile below the village. I deployed my platoon to make the roundup and took a position for observation. While the roundup was progressing, I observed a group of dismounted Indians escaping down the opposite side of the valley. Completing the roundup, and starting them toward the village, I turned the herd over to Lieutenant Law who had come with the second platoon of the troop and told him to take them to the village, saying that I would take my platoon and go in pursuit of the group I had seen escaping down the valley.

Crossing the stream and striking the trail, I followed it till it came to a wooded draw where there was a large pony herd. Here I found the group had mounted. Taking the trail which was well up on the hillside of the valley, and following it about a couple of miles, I discovered a lone tepee, and soon after two Indians circling their ponies. A high promontory and ridge projected into the valley and shut off the view of the valley below the lone tepee. I knew the circling of the warriors meant an alarm and rally, but I wanted to see what was in the valley beyond them. Just then Sergeant Conrad, who had been a captain of Ohio volunteers, and Sergeant Hughes, who had served in the 4th U. S. Cavalry in that country before the Civil War, came to me and warned me of the danger of going ahead. I ordered them to halt the platoon and wait till I could go to the ridge to see what was beyond. Arriving at and peering over the ridge, I was amazed to find that as far as I could see down the well wooded, tortuous valley there were tepees—tepees. Not only could I see tepees, but mounted warriors scurrying in our direction. I hurried back to the platoon and returned at the trot till attacked by the hostiles, when I halted, opened fire, drove the hostiles to cover, and then deployed the platoon as skirmishers.

The hillsides were cut by rather deep ravines and I planned to retreat from ridge to ridge. Under the cavalry tactics of 1841, the retreat of skirmishers was by the odd and even numbers, alternating in lines to the rear. I instructed the line in retreat to halt on the next ridge and cover the retreat of the advance line. This was successful for the first and second ridges, but at the third I found men had apparently forgotten their numbers and there was some confusion, so I divided the skirmishers into two groups, each under a sergeant, and thereafter had no trouble.[3]

Finally the hostiles left us and we soon came to the pony herd where the group we had started to pursue had mounted. I had not had a single casualty. During this retreat we heard heavy firing on the opposite side of the valley, but being well up on the side hills we could not see through the trees what was going on. There was a short lull when the firing again became heavy and continued till long after we reached the village, in fact, nearly all day.

In rounding up the pony herd, I found Captain Barnitz' horse, *General*, saddled but no bridle. On reaching the village I turned over the pony herd and at once reported to General Custer what I had done and seen. When I mentioned the "big village," he exclaimed, "What's that?" and put me through a lot of rapid fire questions. At the conclusion I told him about finding Captain Barnitz' horse and asked what had happened. He told me that Captain Barnitz had been severely and probably mortally wounded.

Leaving the General in a "brown study" I went to see my friend and former Captain, Barnitz. I found him under a pile of blankets and buffalo robes, suffering and very quiet. I hunted up Captain Lippincott, Assistant Surgeon, and found him with his hands over his eyes suffering intense pain from snowblindness. He was very pessimistic as to Barnitz' recovery and insisted that I tell him that there was no hope unless he could be kept perfectly quiet for several days as he feared the bullet had passed through the bowels. I went back to Captain Barnitz and approached the momentous opinion of the surgeon as bravely as I could and then blurted it out, when he exclaimed, "Oh hell! they think because my extremities are cold I am going to die, but if I could get warm I'm sure I'll be all right. These blankets and robes are so heavy I can hardly breathe." I informed the first sergeant and the men were soon busy gathering fuel and building fires.

In the midst of this, the General sent for me and again questioned me about the big village. At that time many warriors were assembling on the high hills north of the valley overlooking the village and the General kept looking in that direction. At the conclusion of his inquiry, I told him that I had heard that Major Elliott had not returned and suggested that possibly the heavy firing I had heard on the opposite side of the valley might have been an attack on Elliott's party. He pondered this a bit and said slowly, "I hardly think so, as Captain Myers has been fighting down there all morning and probably would have reported it."

Mopping Up

I left him and a while later he sent for me again, and, on reporting, told me that he had Romeo, the interpreter, make inquiries of the squaw prisoners and they confirmed my report of the lower village. He then ordered me to take Troop K and destroy all property and not allow any looting—but destroy everything.

I allowed the prisoners to get what they wanted. As I watched them, they only went to their own tepees. I began the destruction at the upper end of the village, tearing down tepees and piling several together on the tepee poles, set fire to them. (All tepees were made of tanned buffalo hides.) As the fires made headway, all articles of personal property—buffalo robes, blankets, food, rifles, pistols, bows and arrows, lead and caps, bullet molds, etc.—were thrown in the fires and destroyed. I doubt but that many small curios went into the pockets of men engaged in this work. One man brought to me that which I learned was a bridal gown, a "one piece dress," adorned all over with bead work and elks' teeth on antelope skins as soft as the finest broadcloth. I started to show it to the General and ask to keep it, but as I passed a big fire, I thought, "What's the use, 'orders is orders'" and threw it in the blaze. I have never ceased to regret that destruction. All of the powder found I spilled on the ground and "flashed."

I was present in August, 1868, at Fort Larned, Kansas, when the annuities were issued, promised by the Medicine Lodge Peace Treaties of 1867, and saw the issue of rifles, pistols, powder, caps, lead and bullet molds to these same Cheyennes.

While this destruction was going on, warriors began to assemble on the hill slopes on the left side of the valley facing the village, as if to make an attack. Two squadrons formed near the left bank of the stream and started on the "Charge" when the warriors scattered and fled. Later, a few groups were seen on the hill tops but they made no hostile demonstrations.

As the last of the tepees and property was on fire, the General ordered me to kill all the ponies except those authorized to be used by the prisoners and given to scouts. We tried to rope them and cut their throats, but the ponies were frantic at the approach of a white man and fought viciously. My men were getting very tired so I called for reinforcements and details from other organizations were sent to complete the destruction of about eight hundred ponies. As the last of the ponies were being shot nearly all the hostiles left. This was probably because they could see our prisoners and realized that any shooting they did might endanger them.

Searching parties were sent to look for dead and wounded of both our own and hostiles. A scout having reported that he had seen Major Elliott and party in pursuit of some escapes down the right side of the valley, Captain Myers went down the valley about two miles but found no trace.[4]

The Return March

A while before sunset, as the command was forming to march down the valley, the General sent for me to ride with him to show him the place from which we could see the village below. There was no attempt to conceal our formation or the direction of our march. The command in column of fours, covered by skirmishers, the prisoners in the rear of the advance troops, standard and guidons "to the breeze," the chief trumpeter sounded the advance and we were "on our way," the band playing, "Ain't I Glad to Get Out of the Wilderness." The observing warriors followed our movement till twilight, but made no hostile demonstration. Then as if they had divined our purpose there was a commotion and they departed down the valley.

When we came in sight of the promontory and ridge from which I had discovered the lower villages, I pointed them out to the General. With the departure of the hostiles our march was slowed down till after dark, when the command was halted, the skirmishers were quietly withdrawn to rejoin their troops, the advance counter-marched, joined successively by the organizations in the rear, and we were on our way on our back trail. We marched briskly till long after midnight when we bivouacked till daylight with the exception of one squadron which was detached to hurry on to our supply train, the safety of which caused great anxiety. I was detailed to command the prisoners and special guard.[5]

Aftermath

At daylight the next morning, we were on the march to meet our supply train and encountered it some time that forenoon. We were glad that it was safe, but disappointed that Major Elliott and party had not come in. After supper in the evening, the officers were called together and each one questioned as to the casualties of enemy warriors, locations, etc. Every effort was made to avoid duplications. The total was found to be one hundred and three. General Custer then informed us that he was going to write his report and that couriers would leave that night for Camp Supply and would take mail. I visited Captain Barnitz and wrote a letter and telegram to Mrs. Barnitz that he had been seriously wounded but was improving. California Joe and Jack Corbin started with dispatches and mail after dark.

On November 30th, California Joe, Jack Corbin and another scout, rejoined the command with mail and dispatches including General Sheridan's General Field Order No. 6, which embodies the purport of General Custer's official report. The command was formed as it reached camp on Wolf Creek and this order was read:

"Headquarters, Department of the Missouri, in the Field, Depot on the North Canadian, at the Junction of Beaver Creek, Indian Territory, November 29, 1868.

General Field Orders No. 6.

"The Major General commanding, announces to this command the defeat, by the Seventh regiment of Cavalry, of a large force of Cheyenne Indians, under the celebrated chief, Black Kettle, re-enforced by the Arapahoes under Little Raven, and the Kiowas under Satanta, on the morning of the 27th instant, on the Washita

River, near the Antelope Hills, Indian Territory, resulting in a loss
to the savages of one hundred and three warriors killed, including
Black Kettle; the capture of fifty-three squaws and children; eight
hundred and seventy-five ponies; eleven hundred and twenty-three
buffalo robes and skins; five hundred and thirty-five pounds of powder; one thousand and fifty pounds of lead; four thousand arrows;
seven hundred pounds of tobacco; besides rifles, pistols, saddles,
bows, lariats, and immense quantities of dried and other winter
provisions; the complete destruction of their village, and almost
total annihilation of this Indian band.

"The loss to the Seventh Cavalry was two officers killed, Major
Joel H. Elliott and Captain Louis McL. Hamilton, and nineteen
enlisted men; three officers wounded, Brevet Lieutenant Colonel
Albert Barnitz (badly), Brevet Lieutenant Colonel T. W. Custer,
and Second Lieutenant T. J. March (slightly) and eleven enlisted
men.

The energy and rapidity shown during one of the heaviest snow
storms that has visited this section of the country, with the temperature below freezing point, and the gallantry and bravery displayed, resulting in such signal success, reflects the highest credit
upon both the officers and enlisted men of the Seventh Cavalry;
and the Major General commanding, while regretting the loss of
such gallant officers as Major Elliott and Captain Hamilton, who
fell while gallantly leading their men, desires to express his thanks
to the officers and men engaged in the battle of the Washita and his
special congratulations to their distinguished commander, Brevet
Major General George A. Custer, for the efficient and gallant services rendered, which have characterized the opening of the campaign against hostile Indians south of the Arkansas.

"By command of
"Major General P. H. Sheridan.
"(Signed)
"J. Schuyler Crosby,
"Brevet Lieutenant Colonel.
"A.D.C. A.A.A.General."

General Sheridan was informed as to the probable time of our arrival
at Camp Supply and received us in review. Before we came in sight of

the cantonment, the command was formed for the review of triumph. The Osage trailers, painted and in picturesque tribal garb, were at the head of the column, followed by the white scouts in motley frontier dress; then my prisoners blanketed or in buffalo robes. At a distance in the rear came the band, followed by Lieutenant Cooke's sharpshooters, and the regiment in column of platoons, the wagon train in the rear. As we came in sight of the cantonment, the Osages began chanting their war songs and at intervals firing their guns and uttering war whoops with some exhibitions of horsemanship. California Joe and scouts emulated the Osages' exuberance in Western frontier style. The prisoners were awed and silent till the band began playing "Garry Owen" for the review of the regiment when they awakened to conversation.

This pageant and review rivaled and no doubt was the prototype of the modern Wild West Shows. It was the real thing. We camped on the Beaver and that evening buried Captain Hamilton near the camp with all the formalities and solemnity of the military funeral, the Seventh Cavalry and the Third Infantry present in formation. Hamilton had been an officer in the Third Infantry prior to promotion to the Seventh Cavalry and had been its regimental quartermaster. General Sheridan, General Custer, Colonel Crosby, Captain Beebe, and Lieutenant Cooke, Custer and Joseph Hale (3d Infantry) were the pall bearers.

We soon learned that the campaign was to be extended through the winter and began our preparations. I turned my prisoners over to the garrison. Later they were transferred to Fort Hays where they were held for some months as hostages for the safety of white captives known to be in the villages of some of the tribes and to compel the tribes to go to their agencies.

We had the satisfaction that we had punished Black Kettle's band, whose warriors were the confessed perpetrators of the attacks and outrages on the Kansas frontier settlements of August 10th—the originators of the Indian War of 1868.

Notes

1. Major Joel Elliott was younger than all the captains, most of whom had been field officers during the Civil War; some had commanded regiments and brigades. He was younger even than most of his lieutenants. In the

Civil War, the highest rank held by him was that of captain and his highest command had been a squadron (two troops) in his volunteer regiment of cavalry. After the war he taught school and at the time he went before the Casey Board of Examiners for a commission, he was superintendent of the public schools of the City of Toledo, Ohio, intending eventually to study and practice law. He passed such a perfect mental examination that the board recommended his appointment as major of cavalry. He had anticipated an appointment as first lieutenant, or, at most, as captain.

2. Division, department, and district denote geographic jurisdiction of military commands.

3. When on the Tactical Board to devise new Drill Regulations (1881–90) this experience was instrumental in adopting the retreat and advance by alternating groups or units instead of by odd and even numbers.

4. Headquarters Military Division of the Missouri, Chicago, Illinois, April 28, 1870.

Mr. De B. Randolph Keim.

Dear Sir: I have carefully read the proof-sheets sent me of your forthcoming book, (Sheridan's Troopers on the Borders), and think well of it.

Very truly yours,

P. H. SHERIDAN,

Lieutenant General.

From De B. Randolph Keim, *Sheridan's Troopers on the Borders: A Winter Campaign on the Plains* (Philadelphia: Clayton, Remsen and Habbelfinger, 1870), 149–50:

Although the fate of Elliott's party would appear as a gross abandonment by Custer, particularly for not even recovering the bodies, or making some effort to learn what had become of them, when found missing, after the fight, the circumstances of the event were of such a character, that while no attempt was made with that view, the conduct of Custer in ordering a withdrawal was justifiable according to the laws of war. He struck the upper flank of a long range of villages, numbering several thousand warriors. His own force was small, and without supplies. In going into the fight the troopers had divested themselves of overcoats and all unnecessary trappings, leaving them near the field. These fell into the hands of the savage allies. The men, consequently, were without the proper protection, while the weather was cold and wintry. The wagon-train containing the subsistence stores and tents of the entire column, which had been left miles away, had not yet come up. The guard consisted of but eighty men. Custer, after the fight commenced, seeing such an extraordinary display of force, felt a natural anxiety to look after his wagons, for their destruction would involve the loss of the entire command, and probably defeat the whole campaign. He therefore set out for the train, and was hastened by experiencing greater opposition than was anticipated.

It will be seen that there were

reasons, the second, particularly, which would warrant the abandonment of the field, and there being hardly a doubt of the fate of Elliott, when found missing, the safety of the command was certainly more to be considered than the loss of a small fraction of it. The pursuit of the fugitives, by Elliott, was entirely exceptional, as he had his own squadron of attack to look after, this fact has led to the opinion that his horse ran away with him, and seeing him pass, a number of troopers not actually engaged in the fight, joined him and were the companions of his sad end. Major Elliott was an efficient and much esteemed officer, and his loss was deeply deplored by his associates.

5. One day on the march through a mesquite forest, Mahwissa, who was my "go-between" for the prisoners, came to me for permission for a squaw to fall out. This I granted and detailed a guard to remain with her. To this she objected and Mahwissa strenuously sustained the objection and assured me it would be all right to let the woman go alone. With great reluctance I consented. At our next halt I was pacing back and forth with anxious looks on the back trail. I was perturbed not only with the prospective loss of a prisoner, but official action in consequence. Mahwissa came to me as if to reassure me, but receiving scant attention, she turned away with a look of disappointment. Soon there was a shout from the prisoners and looking at the back trail to my great relief, I saw my prisoner galloping toward us. Her countenance was beaming and as she passed me I saw the black head of a pappoose in the folds of a blanket at her back swaying with the motions of the galloping pony. The prisoners gave her a demonstrative welcome.

EXPEDITION TO THE YELLOWSTONE RIVER IN 1873: LETTERS OF A YOUNG CAVALRY OFFICER

CHARLES W. LARNED

Edited by George Frederick Howe

Surveys to establish the route of the Northern Pacific Railroad between Bismarck and Bozeman were undertaken in 1872 and 1873. This portion of the right of way crossed an area inhabited by hostile Sioux tribes and had to be surveyed under substantial military protection. In 1872 one party started eastward on July 27 from Fort Ellis, near Bozeman, escorted by a force of about 400 cavalry and infantry,[1] while a second group made preliminary surveys westward from Fort Rice, near Bismarck, protected by almost 600 infantry, one 12-pounder, and two Gatling guns.[2] The two parties were expected to meet near the junction of the Yellowstone and Powder rivers. The eastern force arrived there on August 18. After a battle at Pryor's Fork on August 14 against a large number of Sioux, the smaller western party turned back when it had continued only as far as Pompey's Pillar. The group from Fort Rice surveyed the route eastward, somewhat harried by Indians, and reached the station on October 15. In effect, the Indians had seriously hampered the project and become correspondingly emboldened.

A second survey during the summer of 1873 was provided with much greater military protection. Nineteen companies of infantry were assembled at Fort Rice from four different regiments stationed along the line of the upper Missouri. The Seventh Cavalry, which had been scattered at southern stations following its earlier service against the Cheyennes, was reassembled to join the expedition to the Yellowstone

River. The ten companies moved by railroad to Camp Sturgis near Yankton during the early spring, and thence by stages (Forts Randall, Thompson, and Sully) along the Missouri River to Fort Rice.[3] At successive points along the river the cavalry column met an accompanying steamboat which carried forage, stores, and, among its passengers, the wives of some of the officers. Three other steamboats later supported the combined cavalry-infantry force, beyond Fort Rice.[4]

One of the young officers of the Seventh Cavalry on the expedition of 1873 was Second Lieutenant Charles W. Larned, then three years out of the United States Military Academy and soon destined to return to it as an instructor. As a correspondent of the Chicago *Inter-Ocean*, he published some letters in that paper; a much more numerous series to his mother is now in the possession of a son, Major Paul Larned, United States army, retired. Selections from this correspondence illuminate the military aspects of the expedition of 1873, the life of the young officer, the lot of the officers' wives, and the roles of various men who were destined only three years later to perish in the famous "Last Stand" on the Little Big Horn.[5] Larned's letters reveal considerable literary craftsmanship, as well as an interest in good literature.

Camp at Yankton, Apr 12, 1873

You will not blame me, I am sure, for having allowed a day to slip by since my last without a letter, when I tell you that my desk with my furniture has been boxed all day awaiting our change of camp. I told you that the five companies under [Major Joseph G.] Tilford[6] had arrived while I was writing. The same day I mailed the letter [Lieutenant Colonel George A.] Custer[7] came with the remaining four troops. His arrival was the signal for an entire change of location, so that ever since, the whole command has been hard at work taking down tents and moving bag and baggage to the new site—about half a mile from our temporary location.

We are now regularly encamped—ten companies in all, and the regular routine of military discipline established. My tent is an admirable one and a model of comfort and neatness. Bed on one side, chest at the end, table and desk in the corner, washstand at foot of bed, trunk opposite and a bit of carpet on the ground to complete the picture of luxury. As I write the wind, which, it seems, never ceases here, shakes my

habitation to its "foundations," and flares the candle in a highly unsatisfactory manner; but all its efforts to distort my equanimity are fruitless,
on the principle that familiarity breeds contempt. The climate is fast
making an aboriginal of me, both as regards complexion and health, so
that I am not disposed to be captious with its eccentricities however
annoying.

More of the ladies than I supposed, from reports at Louisville, are
here, huddled together in the slovenly outrage they call a hotel, and
bewailing the impossibility of going elsewhere. Mrs. Hart, Benteen,
McIntosh, Gibson, Yates, Calhoun, Custer and Godfrey[8] comprise the
circle, all, as I told you, brought by pecuniary necessity, except, perhaps, Mrs. Custer and all in the agony of uncertainty as to their next
move. The last plan suggested is to storm Fort Rice in a body, take
to tents, throw themselves on the charity of the government and the
"ins" at that post, and scramble through the summer in the best manner possible. The officers, however, smile grimly at the project and
say nothing. Yates is going to send his family to St. Paul, he tells
me. The wiser or more fortunate few, as Smith, De Rudio,[9] and myself, congratulate themselves daily on their foresight and good fortune,
and watch the commotion complacently. The little hotel! is crammed to
suffocation and grows fat and greasy from the substance of its comfort-
less guests, absorbed at first class rates. The officers, however, who
are independent of them and can run their camp messes at the first
symptom of extortion, are accommodated with day rates at times as
reasonable as the first are reverse. . . .

Camp at Yankton
April 12th, 1873

. . . Today has been rainy and disagreeable. We have settled into
camp life and await the first news of our movements with impatience.
The ladies are still uncertain and uncomfortable. Those who would go
to St. Paul or elsewhere, as Mrs. Yates, have no one to escort them and
have to submit to bed bugs and anxiety until something turns up. A
circular order has just passed around camp confining the officers very
strictly to its limits after tomorrow. How the married men will like that
is not a question of much uncertainty.

My day is pretty well divided between reveille, morning stables, retreat, tattoo and meals. The latter I shall take at the hotel so long as Custer will permit as I can live much more cheaply there than in a private mess of our own—about $22.00 per month. Craycroft, Hodgson, Braden, Godfrey, Hale and Col. Thompson[10] are among those with us whom you used to know. Very little changed any of them and all very friendly to me. Calhoun, Custer's brother-in-law, is adjutant of the cavalry. . . .

Camp Sturgis, Yankton DA

April 19th, 1873

. . . We have all settled back again into our old camp and everything is running smoothly once more.[11] Weather delightful and snow rapidly disappearing. The character of the soil is so spongy that water stands on it but a very short time, and the constant breeze dries the surface very rapidly. The first morning after the storm was bright, but cold and windy. I left my stable and rode out alone over the prairie to camp. The scene was anything but inspiriting, desolation and silence being the only inhabitants of our lively little cloth village. The white tents [were] half buried in snow with here and there a gap in the line where the wind had proved too strong for guy rope and tent pegs. A few men who had straggled or been sent back from town were busy digging their effects out of the drifts, or shoveling the snow out of the interior of the tents, where it had generally attained the height of four or five feet.

I found my own things perfectly safe and dry, and my tent, strange to say, entirely free of snow. After establishing a guard I returned to the city and hotel and found everybody generally demoralized. Before evening, however, the men were mostly gathered together, marched out to camp and set at the work I have described. Our company was particularly fortunate in having less snow in the company street than any of the other troops, and in a short time the tents and picket line were clear and ready for men and horses. Thursday afternoon, the horses were brought in, and by yesterday evening everything had assumed its former appearance. The damage done to stock and men is not nearly so great as any one would naturally have anticipated who experienced the fury of the storm. Cases of frozen members were quite plentiful and here and there used up a horse, but happily no loss of life. Our escape from severer consequence is solely due to the comparative moderation of the temperature. Ten degrees lower, few if any of those left in camp could have escaped. I never cease to be thankful that I did not bring you with me when I think of the discomforts. . . .

. . . Our squadron mess will be started tomorrow. It consists of four officers, McIntosh, Yates, Wallace [12] and myself. As I have the management of it, I run it as economically as I choose.

.   .   .   .

The only thing that troubles me is the fear that Custer will force us to buy horses. He has already sent an order around directing that all officers desiring to purchase horses shall make their application by Monday morning. I am afraid that some time on the march he will spring a trap similar to the one that caught most of the officers napping during the Kansas Campaign, and forced them to buy horses at ruinous prices. . . .

Custer is not making himself at all agreeable to the officers of his command. He keeps himself aloof and spends his time in excogitating annoying, vexatious, and useless orders which visit us like the swarm of evils from Pandora's box, small, numberless, and disagreeable. However, we are enjoying ourselves hugely. . . .

Camp Sturgis, Yankton
April 25th, 1873

.   .   .   .

Last night we attended the ball given in our honor by the citizens of Yankton. It was a homespun affair, but given and received in the same spirit of cordiality and kindness. It would have amused you, for a short time, to have seen the bumpkins and their sweethearts—the Touchstones and Audreys of this locality—shake the frost out of their heels to the enlivening accompaniment of our band. The army ladies were there in full force taking their last draught from the bowl of dissipation and festivity. I came home among the first, after paying my respects to the fair bluebloods of our own patrician circle.

.   .   .   .

Camp Sturgis, Yankton, DA
April 30th, 1873

.   .   .   .   .   .

Yesterday noon I marched off my tour of officer of the guard. The duty . . . consists lately of a mixture of that of a policeman and detective. He is stationed in the city entirely out of camp, with orders to patrol the streets four times a day, visiting each time all the saloons and pothouses in the place, and arresting all soldiers found therein without a pass. You can imagine the pleasures of such occupation better than I can describe them. Yankton, like all frontier towns, is half composed of gambling halls "et id genus omne" and a midnight tour among them, clothed with an office not congenial to their frequenters and proprietors, is perhaps instructive but not amusing. However, I shall not again be called upon to perform that duty before leaving. Today the best part of daylight, before the storm came on, has been consumed in muster and inspection. The command presents a splendid appearance under arms and is in magnificent condition. Custer, however, wears the men out by ceaseless and unnecessary labor. The police of camp, stables twice a day, water call (involving a 5 mile ride) twice—mounted guard mounting (a guard of 65 men) drills twice, and dress parade composes an exhaustive routine. We all fear that such ill advised and useless impositions will result in large desertions when the command is paid off, as it will be tomorrow morning. Custer is not belying his reputation—which is that of a man selfishly indifferent to others, and ruthlessly determined to make himself conspicuous at all hazards.

We have just heard today to our great joy that Gen. [Samuel D.] Sturgis[13] is to be here this evening and that he will take command. For how long, no one knows; perhaps to Fort Rice—perhaps only for a few days—any time would be a relief. We have received the order from Dept. Hdqrs. organizing the expedition. (Gen. [Absalom] Baird[14] will get you a copy of it.) It does not vary in any particular from the information we have already received. Four battalions of Infantry— numbering some twenty companies in all—our ten companies of cavalry—two Rodman guns, and 75 scouts. In all, including teamsters, some twenty-five hundred men; to leave Fort Rice on the 12th or 15th of June.

. . . We still anticipate leaving here on the 5th, but can make no definite prophecies. Custer, I understand, is not sure that he will be able to arrange about forage so early, and we may linger three or four days after that date before starting. After the receipt of this you had better direct your letters to Fort Sully DA, where we stop for five days, until about the tenth of May, after which direct all to Fort Rice DA. I have received an order appointing me Judge Advocate of that inevitable court martial which follows me so closely. Terry[15] it seems has not forgotten me. There are ten of the officers of my regiment on the court. We sit at Sully. . . .

.   .   .   .

Camp Sturgis, Yankton, DA

May 6th, 1873

. . . The order was . . . sent around today for a start at 12 m. tomorrow. Our allowance of baggage is quite comfortable, much better than we had anticipated. Each officer is allowed to carry one medium trunk. This will give me ample room for all the necessaries and many comforts. I have packed my trunk with all my substantials and transferred all the superfluities to the chest. I am provided with everything I can think of necessary for my physical well being and with a small dictionary and my Shakespeare in the bottom of my trunk shall not suffer mentally. Dick[16] rides in Capt. Yates' wagon and takes charge of the lunch together with my valise. There is a steamboat provided to carry forage, following on the river our march by land, and meeting us at different points whenever practicable. The ladies go on this boat together with the sick. Our first stopping place available for mail will be Fort Randall[17]—four days' march. The condition of the roads between may however delay us several days. From Randall you will hear from me with account of the march etc. etc.

Camp at Fort Sully, DA[18]

May 24, 1873

We camped about five miles from here all day yesterday changing our location this morning to within half a mile of the post. Our last march was a long and tedious one of over thirty miles and it is with no slight feeling of satisfaction that we welcome the prospect of a four or five days' rest.

Since leaving [Fort] Thompson[19] the march has not been characterized by anything unusual, except perhaps a day or two of clear weather. Some of the scenery on the way up has been very fine as we obtained occasional glimpses of the river from the high bluffs bordering it, but as a general rule the monotony of rolling treeless prairie has been uninterrupted.

.   .   .   .

We have ascertained since our arrival some additional facts about the expedition. Gen. [David S.] Stanley[20] is here and has been unreserved in his conversation in reference to it. It seems then that from Rice we strike across to where his expedition terminated last year and make that our base of supplies; i.e. the mouth of Powder River. From there we separate in two detachments, one to go North and Northwest to where Baker had arrived at the time of his repulse, and the other to proceed to the South and Southwest as far as the Montana settlements. It is not expected that we will remain out longer than the 15th of October, leaving Powder River on or about that time for return. . . . Those with whom I have spoken and who were out last year anticipate no trouble whatever from the Indians. One assured me that he would have no hesitation whatever in taking a hundred men and crossing the country from the Missouri to the Pacific. . . .

Fort Rice DA
June 11, 1873

We arrived here the day before yesterday, eleven days from [Fort] Sully—and no mail between. The last week's marching had been fine and enjoyable—pleasant camps and short tramps. We met two Indian camps on the road, one at Grand River Agency, and another some forty or fifty miles from here, comprised of nearly a hundred lodges under Two Bears, a Yankton Sioux. We have had no trouble with any of these gentlemen but have had our fill of their society. Tawdry cavalcades of the rascals, mounted on their little ponies, decked in comical assortments of skins and rags, tin plates, feathers, neckties, beads, earrings, and stove pipe hats, have thronged our camp semi occasionally affording gratification to a mutual but quickly satisfied curiosity.

The Court Martial at Sully was the source of endless annoyance and trouble to all concerned. Custer undertook to bully and insult that body at the start, and, finding that his efforts at control were powerless, did everything in his power to hector and annoy its members. The court has made an indignant protest against his assumption, the which as recorder I have written out and will forward to Dept. Hqrs. On our arrival here we found all of the infantry already in camp and waiting. Stanley [was here] with his staff, and [so was] all our baggage which had been left behind at Yankton for shipment. . . .

.   .   .   .

We are all in a hubbub as yet waiting the arrival of [General] Terry, who is expected tomorrow, before deciding upon the day of departure or even the line of march. It seems that [General Philip H.] Sheridan was opposed to a separation at Powder River and in consequence the plan of campaign from that point is somewhat uncertain as yet. A large number of wagons—part of our train, is yet to arrive as well as 600 head of stock for our consumption.

The infantry officers I have met have not impressed me favorably. They appear to belong to a very inferior class of society. There will be, however, very little necessity for association as the two corps will be quite isolated. . . . The scientific corps has not arrived yet, but are expected tomorrow. They say Stanley has received more orders in regard to them than for all the rest of the expedition. Stanley seems to be very much liked and impressed me very favorably when I met him. Large, handsome and dignified. Since the establishment of the depot at the mouth of Powder River,[21] by means of steamboat communication, our facilities for mail will be very much increased. Boats will make several trips from there in all probability—backwards and forwards and in addition, trains with scouts will be sent back occasionally.

The appearance of things here would seem to indicate a picnic on a grand scale. Three large steamboats lay at the wharf, soldiers, officers, Indians, scouts and guides throng about the post and keep up quite a metropolitan bustle and excitement. Two young English lords are to accompany us and have bought a wagon and team bodily to take them and their effects. . . .

Your wishes in regard to accompanying the ladies up would speedily change into congratulations at having escaped their experience. Only today Mrs. Yates and others were saying that you had acted so wisely in remaining. They have all been more or less sick, cooped up in the small cabin of a rear wheeled boat, living on the most atrocious of boat fare for 34 days. During that time they have succeeded in discovering each other's failings with astonishing distinctness, and, from all I hear, have made the atmosphere pretty warm. Add to this the difficulty of officers communicating with the boat after a hard day's march—forced to go sometimes two or three miles to where she lay, through the woods, and return late in the dark—losing thereby the best part of a much needed night's sleep, and there is but little remaining to make the trip desirable. Here the ladies are all adrift with the prospect of the command leaving in a few days. I never saw such confusion and uncertainty. No two of them think alike or seem to have any definite plan. They were all obliged to hustle off of the boat on its arrival, and seek accommodations on another whose stay is almost as uncertain as the first. Some talk of going back to Yankton and Sioux City, to St. Paul, to Indiana, and even to Canada. . . .

Ft. Rice   June 17, 1873

Taps have just sung our evening lullaby and camp subsides into the drowsy silence of night. . . .

.   .   .   .

We have had two or three intensely hot, dry, dusty days, relieved, however, by the blessing of cool nights. Terry reviewed us yesterday with the thermometer 96°. Whew! A detachment of 25 cavalry under De Rudio and 4 companies of Infantry left two days back for the [Missouri River] crossing,[22] to escort the Engineers from there, and meet us after our start some miles out. They reached [Fort] Lincoln about the time the rumor came to us that the Fort had been "bounced" by the reds. Today, a courier brings tiding that the detachment has been having a little brush with them. The Indians are showing by this their evident intention for the Summer, which will probably be to abandon us to our own sweet will and touch up the posts on the river which have thus been reduced by the expedition. They can do very little harm beyond picking off stragglers and stealing stock.

We are down to fighting trim. Small "pup tents" for the men and A tents for officers. My trunk and chest are packed with all superfluities and the campaign allowance confined to the limits of the valise and whatever I can smuggle into my bedsack. I shall have ample. I have had made for my bedding a long canvas bag, double thickness, drawing together at the top. In the bottom of this I place all the heavy clothing for the Fall return, including warm underclothing, socks, etc. My bedding is then rolled up and slipped in on top the bag, drawn together, buckled and strapped, forming a piece of furniture hard to equal for compactness and variety of uses. In the valise I can carry many conveniences and all the necessaries for the Summer. "Man needs far little etc." The mattress is boxed, and together with trunk, chest etc. stored under charge of an officer left behind in charge. . . .

. . . Terry said in a little speech he made us on the occasion of our call that this was the most interesting of all the Indian campaigns. What with English lords, scientists, and outsiders of every military description you would imagine it a big picnic. . . .

Camp on Heart River   DA
June 25th, 1873

Here we are sixty miles from Rice in a delightful camp with a day's rest before us. We have had a pleasant and interesting march out with a fair proportion of rain and storm, but still altogether delightful. We make an imposing show on these rolling prairies—1500 men, 250 teamsters, 40 scouts, 250 wagons, 800 horses, 600 head of cattle and 1500 mules;[23] too imposing, in fact, for the Indians who have not as yet put in an appearance. The marches have been short and somewhat tedious, on account of the difficulty of moving so large and heavy a train. The average will not exceed 8 miles a day, although some days we have exceeded it largely and on others fallen very much below that mark. The weather, as I have said, has not been uniformly pleasant but then the storms, although terrible and severe while they last, are only of hours instead of days duration. The thunder and lightning I have never seen equalled for intensity and grandeur. Fortunately, we have been in camp, with one exception, before their commencement. . . .

We find the country a perfect wilderness. Grass is the only vegetation with a few scattered trees along the creek and river bottoms. The prairie is broken by ravines and barren stony bluffs which cross and cut it in every direction. We have passed through hundreds of antelope that follow the column and trot curiously along its flanks. Hunters are out every day and keep our mess supplied with their meat which has become quite a drug on the market. The dogs catch the young and afford many an exciting chase. A very pretty young fawn came into my hands through their agency, which I brought into camp with the intention of raising. By evening, it was quite tame and docile, but the difficulties of finding proper nourishment and the want of means for its transportation induced me to let it go. Today, we struck the Heart river, a narrow, rapid stream that empties into the Missouri. . . . We found a lovely bottom quite well wooded for these latitudes, surrounded by high bluffs with a fine rich growth of grass for grazing. Here we have established ourselves for a day in order to send out scouting parties to find the Engineers and [escorting] detachment who left Lincoln a day or two before we started from Rice.

June 26th

This morning at 5 o'clock, Moylan was sent out with his troop for this purpose. He takes a day's rations and no wagons. Is to return by evening. Went over to the Infantry Camp to call on Jones, Grant, etc. Found that Stanley had about decided to divide the command as soon as we reached the Engineers, take five troops of cavalry and two battalions of Infantry (22nd and 17th) and move on ahead by rapid marches for the Yellowstone. He intends leaving Custer in command of the remaining 5 troops and two battalions who stay behind with the Engineers. If he does this we will reach the Yellowstone some 15 or 20 days before the rest, go into camp there, meet the boats, build the depot and have a pleasant time. I say *we*, because the cavalry has been divided into two wings—one under the command of Capt. Hart and the other under Benteen. Hart's wing contains Moylan, Tom Custer and all those related to the "royal family" whom Custer will of course retain with him. We are in Benteen's wing, comprising besides "F" troop, Hale's (K) with Godfrey and Aspinwall, Weston's (L) with Braden, McIntosh's (S) with Wallace, and Benteen's (H) with Gibson and De Rudio. De Rudio, you will remember, was sent, before we left Rice, to Lincoln with twenty-five men and two companies of Infantry to escort these same Engineers until they met us. It was on the day of their start that they had the skirmish with the Indians. This afternoon, about six, he suddenly made his appearance here. He had been sent from their camp yesterday afternoon to find us and after a ride of about 40 miles struck our trail at 10 o'clock this morning and followed us in. He reports that their column was struck two days ago by a furious hail storm while on the march, which stampeded all their horses and mules, upset and smashed the most of their wagons and demoralized them generally. They are camped about 25 miles to the northeast and are awaiting our arrival. The order comes around this evening that the whole of the cavalry will move on ahead and reach them tomorrow. It will take the Infantry and train two days to accomplish the distance. I sincerely hope that Stanley will carry out his idea of moving ahead to the Yellowstone and that we go with him. It will be infinitely pleasanter than poking along with the Engineers. There we will meet the boats, go into camp and have a long, refreshing rest.

.   .   .   .

Fort Lincoln, D. T.

July 6, 1873

My telegram will have taken the edge off of your surprise, so you will expect this as a natural consequence of it. My lucky star must be near the Zenith to have brought about so happy a conjunction of circumstances as has brought me here at so fortuitous a time.

We had reached the crossing of the Heart River and had sent out a detachment to find the locality of the engineers, when De Rudio came in from them and brought accounts of their suffering from the hailstorm. Stanley ordered Custer ahead the next morning with the whole of the cavalry to reach Townsend and the engineers by night, if possible. We accordingly made a long march of it, bridged the Big Muddy and reached their camp an hour before sunset. Here we lay over a day expecting Stanley to come up in the meanwhile. The morning after Custer started off without him on his own hook. We had not gone more than 11 miles before a courier from Stanley brought a peremptory order for him to halt on the spot, and to send back one squadron as escort to a supply train to be sent to Lincoln for forage. We, as good luck would have it, received the order to leave in an hour, which we accordingly did retracing our steps and reaching Stanley at sundown 20 miles back on the Big Muddy exactly where we had crossed two days before. The river had risen ten feet and they found it impossible to cross with 250 heavy wagons. We camped on the opposite side and remained two days while a pontoon bridge was manufactured out of inverted wagon beds filled with kegs. On this structure they crossed in a night and a day. We accompanied them as far on the road to Custer at the old Engineer Camp and from there struck back with 60 wagons for Lincoln. As our train was empty we made the distance in two days and reached here on the 2d at 8 A.M., tired but glad to see once more anything in the semblance of a house.

.   .   .   .

Camp on Yellowstone
July 21st, 1873

. . . Stanley, after joining the engineers who had started from Lincoln, at a point about 20 miles north of the Heart river and 45 miles from the Missouri, concluded to send back such a portion of his train as had become empty for new supplies and ordered a squadron to be detached from Custer to escort it. Col. Baker, Q. M. of the expedition, accompanied us and with young Dashiell and Dr. Ruyer, our surgeon, composed our little party. We left Stanley at 5 o'clock on the morning of July 3d and reached Lincoln at 8 o'clock a.m. July 4th, camping overnight at the crossing of the Heart about 10 miles from our destination. What occurred there you will sufficiently have gathered from my motley letter [of July 6]. . . .

. . . .

We left Lincoln with 53 wagons heavily loaded and have been exactly twelve days in making the journey here—250 miles. Every morning saw us up at 3 o'clock and on the march by 5. Have averaged eleven hours in the saddle. Sometimes marched twelve and once it was fifteen. Our object was to reach Stanley as soon as possible and to accomplish this it was necessary to double up on his marches with a train as heavily loaded as his own. Continuous rains for the first week filled the creeks and ravines and rendered bridging and filling necessary every few miles. We expected to find Stanley encamped on the Little Missouri 140 miles from Lincoln waiting our arrival in case we did not reach him before. On the fourth day we rejoined [the] camp where we had left Custer and came suddenly on a small war party of 11 Sioux quite ignorant of our proximity. They were not long in the neighborhood, some business of a pressing and unexpected nature requiring their attention "over the hills and far away." This was on a small stream called the "Little Muddy" perhaps on your map. On the seventh day we began to approach what are called the "Mauvaises Terres" or Bad Lands. We found a note on the trail left by Adjutant General informing us that Stanley had pushed on to the Yellowstone but had left a body of 100 infantry on the right bank of the Heart river near its source to await our arrival. This was good news as we had but ten days rations. The next day we crossed to the right bank of the Heart and began to keep a lookout for reinforcement. We marched all that day, however, without striking them and went into camp in a ravine by some rain pools. We had made about 24 miles and had ridden eleven hours and were well fatigued. Two hours before sunset four men were sent forward to find the infantry, if possible. They were to return, if unsuccessful, after ten or twelve miles. At dusk our pickets and one of the scouts reported a number of Indians on the horizon. This news made us anxious for the safety of the party sent forward to reconnoitre and I was accordingly ordered out with a detachment of 25 men to follow their trail and bring them back. This I did with some difficulty as the tremendous storm rendered it a very difficult task for two hours at a very rapid gait. I lost the trail several times and only recovered it again by the aid of the vivid and incessant lightning. . . .

The next day we made a long march and reached the infantry who were in an entrenched camp one day's march from the Little Missouri. This river we forded and for the two succeeding days marched through the bad lands. The description of these I must leave to a succeeding letter and more leisure, as Yates is impatiently waiting for me to finish this. It is sufficient to refer you to Doré's[24] "Inferno" for the present. Yesterday morning with the thermometer 103° in the shade we crawled over the bare bluffs that fringe the river and saw its welcome length trailing at our feet. There is a level flat two miles wide on each side rising into high bluffs.

We are encamped in the woods waiting the order to cross. Stanley farther back on the flat. We leave about 100 infantry in a stockade to guard the depot and cross within five days. Expect to be gone on the other side between 40 and 60 days. Are to follow down the river to Pompey's Pillar, return by the "Muscleshell" and hope to reach Lincoln by the middle or end of September.

[Camp on the Musselshell River
August 19, 1873]

Dr. John Hensinger, veterinary surgeon, Seventh Cavalry, and Mr. Balaran, sutler, were [on August 4] the two victims to a want of caution that our long immunity from attack had engendered.[25] They had left the train during the halt for the purpose of watering their horses, and on their way back skirting the foot of the bluffs in order to meet the column in its descent, quite unconscious of danger and the horrible fate awaiting them, were suddenly surprised by a party of three Sioux, who had secreted themselves in a ravine, and shot from behind with arrows.

General Custer in the morning had taken a squadron, A and B troops of the Seventh Cavalry, and moved rapidly ahead of the main body about four miles beyond the point at which this tragedy occurred. There, in a belt of woods, his escort had unsaddled, picketed their horses and were lying under the trees awaiting the arrival of the main body, when a shot from the pickets and their sudden appearance brought everyone to his feet. Quickly and quietly the horses were brought in and saddled, a dismounted detachment thrown out as skirmishers, while the remainder of the command moved in the direction of the attack. But three or four Indians were to be seen, galloping and gesticulating wildly in front of the column, which moved quickly forward at a trot. Hardly, however, had the flank arrived opposite a second belt of dense woods before a long line of Indians suddenly moved in regular order from their midst straight to the attack. They were all in full war costume, mounted on stalwart little ponies, and armed, as are all we have seen, with the best of Henry rifles. As rapidly as possible the command was dismounted and formed in skirmish line in front of the horses, but not a moment too soon, as the enemy came whooping and screeching down upon it. A square volley in their teeth cooled their ardor, and sent them flying back to a respectful distance. For three hours the fight was kept up, the Indians maintaining a perfect skirmish line throughout, and evincing for them a very extraordinary control and discipline. After this desultory fighting had become tiresome, the cavalry mounted suddenly and dashed forward at a charge, scattering their wary antagonists, who were not prepared for such a demonstration, in every direction. Our casualties were one man and three horses wounded. The loss of the enemy, estimated from those seen to fall, must have been something in the vicinity of ten in all, and five ponies.

For the next three days nothing was seen of our friendly neighbors in person, but abundant evidence of their camps, and the heavy trail of a retreating village, numbering, as our Indian scouts told us, in the neighborhood of eighty lodges. Each day General Custer, with two squadrons of cavalry, pushed on in advance, following rapidly on the trail.

It was not, however, until the evening of August 8 that he received orders from General Stanley to push on with the whole of the available cavalry force, make forced night marches, and overtake the village, if possible. . . .

At early dawn on the 10th our efforts to cross [the Tongue River] commenced, and it was not until 4 in the afternoon that they were reluctantly relinquished, after every expedient had been resorted to in vain. The current was too swift and fierce for our heavy cavalry. We therefore went into bivouac close to the river bank to await the arrival of the main body, and slept that night as only men in such condition can sleep. We hardly anticipated the lively awakening that awaited us. Just at daylight our slumbers were broken by a sharp volley of musketry from the opposite bank, accompanied by shouts and yells that brought us all to our feet in an instant. As far up the river as we could see, clouds of dust announced the approach of our slippery foes, while the rattling volleys from the opposite woods, and the "zip," "zip" of the balls about our ears told us that there were a few evil disposed persons close by.

For half an hour, while the balls flew high, we lay still without replying, but when the occasional quiver of a wounded horse told that the range was being acquired by them, the horses and men were moved back from the river edge to the foot of the bluffs, and there drawn up in line of battle to await developments. A detachment of sharpshooters was concealed in the woods, and soon sent back a sharp reply to the thickening compliments from the other side. Our scouts and the Indians were soon exchanging chaste complimentary remarks in choice Sioux— such as: "We're coming over to give you h——l;" "You'll see more Indians than you ever saw before in your life," and "Shoot, you son of a dog" from ours. Sure enough, over they came, as good as their word, above and below us, and in twenty minutes our scouts came tumbling down the bluffs head overheels, screeching: "Heap Indian come." Just at this moment General Custer rode up to the line, followed by a bright guidon, and made rapid disposition for the defense. Glad were we that the moment of action had arrived, and that we were to stand no longer quietly and grimly in line of battle to be shot at. One platoon of the first squadron on the left was moved rapidly up the bluffs, and thrown out in skirmish line on the summit, to hold the extreme left. The remainder of the squadron followed as quickly as it could be deployed, together with one troop of the Fourth Squadron.

On they came as before, 500 or 600 in number, screaming and yelling as usual, right onto the line before they saw it. At the same moment the regimental band, which had been stationed in a ravine just in rear, struck up "Garry Owen." The men set up a responsive shout, and a rattling volley swept the whole line.

The fight was short and sharp just here, the Indians rolling back after the first fire and shooting from a safer distance. In twenty minutes the squadrons were mounted and ordered to charge. Our evil-disposed friends tarried no longer, but fled incontinently before the pursuing squadrons. We chased them eight miles and over the river, only returning when the last Indian had gotten beyond our reach.

No less than a thousand warriors had surrounded us, and we could see on the opposite bluffs the scattered remnants galloping wildly to and fro. Just at the conclusion of the fight the infantry came up, and two shells from the Rodman guns completed the discomfiture of our demoralized foes. Our loss was one killed, Private Tuttle, E Troop, Seventh Cavalry, and three wounded. Among the latter, Lieutenant [Charles] Braden, Seventh Cavalry, while gallantly holding the extreme left, the hottest portion of the line, was shot through the thigh, crushing the bone badly.[26] Four horses were killed and eight or ten wounded, and deserve honorable mention, although noncombatants. Official estimates place the Indian loss at forty killed and wounded, and a large number of ponies.

The troops engaged consisted of the following companies of cavalry: A, Captain Moylan, Lieutenant Varnum; B, Lieutenants Tom Custer and Hodgson; E, Lieutenants McDougall and Aspinwall; F, Captain Yates and Lieutenant Larned; G, Lieutenants McIntosh and Wallace; K, Captain Hale, Lieutenant Godfrey; L, Lieutenants Weston and Braden; M, Captain French, Lieutenant Mathey.[27] A detachment of scouts under Lieutenant Brush, Seventeenth Infantry, were with us and did excellent service. Accompanying headquarters were Lieutenant Ketchum, Twenty-second infantry, Lieutenant Jones, Fourth Cavalry, and Lieutenant Calhoun, Seventh Cavalry.[28] Captain Hart, Seventh Cavalry, was second in command, and in charge of the left wing. We have seen but three or four small parties of half a dozen Sioux at a distance since the fight, and are at present encamped on the upper waters of the Musselshell, hoping to reach the crossing of the Yellowstone by the 10th of September. Until then, au revoir.

Notes

1. Under command of Major E. M. Baker, 2nd Cavalry. See Report of Major General Winfield S. Hancock, CG, Department of Dakota, October 3, 1872, *Annual Report of the Secretary of War* [1872] (Washington, 1872), 1: 39–41. The *Report* is in 42d Cong., 3d sess., H. Ex. Doc. 1, pt. 2.

2. Report of the expedition to the Yellowstone, Colonel David S. Stanley to Assistant Adjutant General, Department of Dakota, St. Paul, Minnesota, October 28, 1872, War Department Records, National Archives, No. 3512 (AGO), 1872. His party consisted of 33 officers, 553 enlisted men, and over 150 armed teamsters, escorting a surveying party of 47. The expedition was threatened by one eloquent Indian who identified himself as Sitting Bull.

3. A vivacious account of this part of the journey forms part of the recollections of Brigadier General George A. Custer's widow, Elizabeth B. Custer, *"Boots and Saddles"; or, Life in Dakota with General Custer* (New York: Harper and Brothers, 1885). She rode with the regiment.

4. One of the engineers in 1873, later chief engineer of the Northern Pacific Railroad, was Thomas L. Rosser, a former Confederate cavalry commander, whose career was somewhat intertwined with that of Custer from the time when both were cadets at West Point, just prior to the outbreak of the Civil War. See Joseph M. Hanson, "Thomas Lafayette Rosser," in Allen

Johnson, Dumas Malone, and Harris E. Starr, eds., *Dictionary of American Biography*, 21 vols. and index (New York: C. Scribner's Sons, 1928–44), 16: 181–82.

5. The story of the Yellowstone expeditions of 1872 and 1873 is available in published accounts of Custer's career: Custer, *"Boots and Saddles"*; Frederick Whittaker, *A Complete Life of Gen. George A. Custer* (New York: Sheldon and Co., 1876), 479–500; and Frederick S. Dellenbaugh, *George Armstrong Custer* (New York: Macmillan Co., 1917), 148–63; in Eugene V. Smalley, *History of the Northern Pacific Railroad* (New York: G. P. Putnam's Sons, 1883); and in reports to William T. Sherman, general of the army, from the Military Division of the Missouri, *Annual Report of the Secretary of War* [1872], 1: 39–41; ibid. [1873], 3 vols. (Washington, 1873), 1: 40–41. The *Report* for 1873 is in 43d Cong., 1st sess., H. Ex. Doc. 1, pt. 2. A search in the National Archives for Colonel Stanley's official report for 1872 was successful, but for 1873 only supplementary reports on the geography of the area and on army administrative matters were discovered.

6. Captain, 3rd Cavalry, 1861; major, 7th Cavalry, 1867; lieutenant colonel, 7th Cavalry, 1883.

7. Custer, after attaining the grade of major general of volunteers on April 15, 1865, was mustered out of the volunteer service, having been brevetted major general for his ser-

vice in northern Virginia. He became lieutenant colonel, 7th Cavalry, on July 28, 1866, and was much of the time thereafter in actual command of the regiment.

8. These ladies were the wives, respectively, of Captains Verling K. Hart and Frederick W. Benteen, First Lieutenants Donald McIntosh and Francis M. Gibson, Captain George W. Yates, First Lieutenant James Calhoun, Custer, and First Lieutenant Edward S. Godfrey.

9. Second Lieutenant Charles C. De Rudio.

10. Second Lieutenants William T. Craycroft, Benjamin H. Hodgson, and Charles Braden, Captains Owen Hale and William Thompson. Thompson had been a colonel of volunteers in 1864.

11. An extremely heavy wind from the Northwest brought a blizzard from April 13 to 16 which buried tents under five to six feet of snow, and drove men and horses to shelter in Yankton. Custer, *"Boots and Saddles,"* 20–29, gives her recollections of this storm.

12. Second Lieutenant George D. Wallace.

13. Samuel D. Sturgis was in 1873 colonel of the 7th Cavalry. He had been a brigadier general of volunteers, and had been brevetted major general for gallant and meritorious service. He did not remain with the expedition after it left Fort Rice.

14. General Absalom Baird was in 1873 assistant inspector general with the permanent grade of lieutenant colonel. In 1864 he had been awarded

the Medal of Honor for gallantry in action and was brevetted a major general.

15. Brigadier General Alfred H. Terry then commanded the Department of Dakota in the Military Division of the Missouri.

16. A servant.

17. Situated on the Missouri River, near the Nebraska border.

18. On the Missouri River, near the mouth of the Cheyenne River.

19. In northern Dakota on the Missouri River at the Crow Creek Agency.

20. In 1873 Stanley was commanding officer of the 22nd Infantry.

21. Following a report by Major George A. Forsyth on his reconnaissance, a site was selected at that point. See Report of Lieutenant General Philip H. Sheridan, CG, Military Division of the Missouri, October 27, 1873, *Annual Report of the Secretary of War* [1873], 1: 41.

22. Near Bismarck, protected in 1873 by Fort Abraham Lincoln.

23. The trains for the Yellowstone expedition of 1873 "consisted of two hundred and two 6-mule teams, nine 4-mule teams for spring-wagons, two 6-mule teams for artillery, and some 12 riding-mules for wagon-masters. In addition, there were one 6-mule team, one 4-mule spring-wagon and team, and nine riding-horses provided for the use of the scientific party accompanying the expedition." They were assembled at Fort Abercrombie, Minnesota, in April and May, 1873. The teamsters were hired in St. Paul and Fort Leaven-

worth, Kansas. See report of Captain G. B. Dandy, assistant quartermaster at Fort Abraham Lincoln, *Annual Report of the Secretary of War* [1873], 1: 112–13.

24. Paul Gustave Doré (1832–83), the famous illustrator of an edition of Dante's *Divine Comedy*.

25. This letter was sent for publication in the Chicago *Inter-Ocean*. The Indian hostilities formed the subject of a report by Custer which was reprinted as an appendix in Custer, *"Boots and Saddles,"* 280–90.

26. Charles Braden was brought back 350 to 400 miles on a litter suspended from long poles between the front and rear axles of an old spring wagon. He survived, retired from the army on June 28, 1878, and was later brevetted first lieutenant for gallantry and meritorious service in the action at Tongue River.

27. In addition to those previously identified, these were Second Lieutenant Charles A. Varnum, First Lieutenants Thomas W. Custer, Thomas M. McDougall, Edward G. Mathey, and Captain Thomas H. French.

28. First Lieutenants Daniel H. Brush, Hiram H. Ketchum, and James H. Jones.

BATTLING
WITH THE SIOUX
ON THE
YELLOWSTONE

G. A. CUSTER

I n the early spring of '73 the officials of the Northern Pacific railroad applied to the Government authorities at Washington for
military protection for a surveying party to be sent out the ensuing summer to explore and mark out the incompleted portion of
the road extending from the Missouri river in Dakota to the interior of
Montana, west of the Yellowstone. This enterprise, which was intended
to open a new highway to travel and commerce between the people of
the Atlantic and Pacific States, had not then encountered the financial
calamities that swept over the country later in that year. It had com-
mended itself to the attention and approval of not only the public, but
to the protection and fostering care of the National Government. It was
seen that the completion of the Northern Pacific road would be a measure which, aside from opening to settlement a large tract of valuable
country, and aiding in the development and successful working of a rich
mineral region otherwise inaccessible, would produce to the Government a large annual saving of money in the way of cost of transportation
of troops and supplies. The experience of the past, particularly that of
recent years, has shown too that no one measure so quickly and effectually frees a country from the horrors and devastations of Indian wars
and Indian depredations generally as the building and successful operation of a railroad through the region overrun. Thus, aside from the
ordinary benefits and purposes which inspire the building of railroads
through the unsettled portions of the West, the Government, simply as
a measure of economy, has ample reason to extend to such enterprises
encouragement and help.

So earnest is my belief in the civilizing and peace-giving influence of railroads when extended through an Indian country, that the idea has often occurred to me, laying aside all considerations and arguments as to whether such a road will ever be required in the interests of trade and commerce, that a railroad established and kept in operation from a point on our extreme northern boundary, somewhere between the 100th and 105th meridian, to a corresponding point on the Rio Grande river in Texas, would for ever after have preserved peace with the vast number of tribes infesting the immense area of country lying between the Rocky mountains and the valley of the Mississippi. A more surprising statement than this, however, and one which will bear investigation, is that the avoidance of wars with the tribes which have occupied this region of the plains lying contiguous to the indicated line of railroad, would have resulted in a saving of money to the Government more than sufficient to build, equip, and place in running order a railroad from British America to the Rio Grande.

Few of our people realize the immense outlay and expense rendered necessary by an Indian war. As an illustration take the following extract from a report to the President of the United States, made in 1868 by a commission of which Generals Sherman, Harney, Terry, and Augur were members. Referring to the alleged "Chevington massacre," and the Cheyenne war of 1867, the report of the commission states: "No one will be astonished that a war ensued which cost the Government *thirty million dollars*."

To extend encouragement and aid to the projectors and builders of the Northern Pacific road, the Government granted the application of the road for a military escort, and gave authority for the organization of what was afterward designated as the Yellowstone expedition. The troops composing the expedition numbered about seventeen hundred men, consisting of cavalry, infantry, an improvised battery of artillery, and a detachment of Indian scouts, the whole under command of Brevet Major General D. S. Stanley, an officer whose well-known ability and long experience on the Plains and with Indians amply qualified him for the exercise of so important a command. Fort Rice, Dakota, on the Missouri river, was selected as the point of rendezvous and departure of the expedition.

To illustrate how our little army, as occasion demands, is frequently shifted from one remote point to another, in order to meet the demands of the service, it may be mentioned that in collecting troops to compose the Yellowstone expedition most of my command, the cavalry, was transported from the extreme southern States, the Carolinas, Florida, and Louisiana, to within a few days' march of the British possessions. When it is remembered that a portion of the immense journey was by rail, a portion by steam transports, and about five hundred miles by marching, the extent of the preliminary preparations rendered necessary in an expedition of this kind will be appreciated.

It was not until July that the Yellowstone expedition assumed definite shape, and began its westward movement from Fort Rice. The engineers and surveyors of the Northern Pacific railroad were under the direction and management of General Thomas L. Rosser. This gentleman deserves a fuller notice than the limits of this article will permit. He and I had been cadets together at the Military Academy at West Point, occupying adjoining rooms, and being members of the same company, often marching side by side in the performance of our various military duties while at the Academy. When the storms of secession broke upon the country in '61, Rosser, in common with the majority of the cadets from the Southern States, resigned his warrant, and hastened to unite his personal fortunes with those of his State— Texas. He soon won distinction in the Confederate army, under Lee, and finally rose to the rank and command of major general of cavalry. I held a similar rank and command in the Union army, and it frequently happened, particularly during the last year of the war, that the troops commanded by Rosser and myself were pitted against each other in the opposing lines of battle, and the two cadets of earlier years became not only hostile foes, but actual antagonists.

When the war was ended Rosser, like many of his comrades from the South who had staked their all upon the issue of the war, at once cast about him for an opportunity to begin anew the battle, not of war, but of life. Possessing youth, health, many and large abilities, added to indomitable pluck, he decided to trust his fortunes amidst his late enemies, and repaired to Minnesota, where he sought employment in one of the many surveying parties acting under the auspices of the Northern Pacific road. Upon applying to the officer of the road for a position as civil engineer, he was informed that no vacancy existed to which he could be appointed. Nothing daunted, he persisted, and finally accepted a position among the axemen, willing to work, and proved to his employers not only his industry, but his fitness for promotion. He at once attracted the attention of his superiors, who were not slow to recognize his merit. Rosser was advanced rapidly from one important position to another, until in a few months he became the chief engineer of the surveying party accompanying the expedition. In this capacity I met him on the plains of Dakota, in 1873, nearly ten years after the date when in peaceful scabbards we sheathed the swords which on more than one previous occasion we had drawn against each other. The manly course adopted by Rosser after the war, his determined and success- ful struggle against adversity, presents a remarkable instance of the wonderful recuperative powers of the American character.

Scarcely a day passed, during the progress of the expedition from the Missouri to the Yellowstone, that General Rosser and I were not in each other's company a portion of the time, either as we rode in our saddles, "boot to boot," climbed together unvisited cliffs, picked our way through trackless cañons, or sat at the same mess table or about the same camp fire. During these strolling visits we frequently ques- tioned and enlightened each other as to the unexplained or but partially understood battles and movements in which each had played a part against the other.

Passing over all this, and omitting the incidents of the march from our starting point, Fort Rice, on the Missouri, we come to the time when we found ourselves encamped on the east bank of the beautiful and swift flowing Yellowstone, about a hundred miles from its mouth. At this point the expedition was met by a steamer, sent for that pur- pose up the Missouri, hundreds of miles above Fort Rice, then up the Yellowstone to the point of juncture. From it fresh supplies of for- age and subsistence stores were obtained. This being done, the entire expedition, save a small detachment left at this point to guard our sur- plus stores, intended for our return march, was ferried by the steamer across the Yellowstone river. Our course for several days carried us up that stream; our tents at night being usually pitched on or near the river bank. The country to be surveyed, however, soon became so rough and broken in places that we encountered serious delays at times in finding a practicable route for our long and heavily laden wagon trains, over rocks and through cañons hitherto unexplored by white men. So seri- ous did these embarrassments become, and so much time was lost in accomplishing our daily marches, that I suggested to General Stanley that I should take with me each day a couple of companies of cavalry and a few of the Indian scouts, and seek out and prepare a practicable road in advance, thereby preventing detention of the main command. This proposition being acceded to, it was my custom thereafter to push rapidly forward in the early morning, gaining an advance of several miles upon the main expedition, and by locating the route relieving the troops and trains in rear of a great amount of fatigue and many tedious detentions. One result of this system was that I and my little party, who were acting as pioneers, usually arrived at the termination of our day's march, our camp ground for the night, at an early hour in the day, several hours in advance of the main portion of the expedition.

This of itself was quite an advantage, as it gave the party in advance choice of camp ground, and enabled themselves and horses to obtain several hours of rest not enjoyed by their less fortunate comrades in rear. We had marched several days after our departure from the point at which we crossed the Yellowstone without discovering any signs or indications of the presence of hostile Indians, although our scouts and guides had been constantly on the alert, as we knew we were traversing a portion of the country infested by savage tribes. On the morning of August 4, with two companies of the Seventh Cavalry, commanded by Captain Moylan and Colonel Custer—who, with my adjutant, Lieutenant Calhoun, and Lieutenant Varnum, composed the officers of the party—and guided by my favorite scout, Bloody Knife, a young Arickaree warrior, the entire party numbering eighty-six men and five officers, I left camp at five o'clock in the morning, and set out as usual to explore the country and find a practicable route for the main column. Soon after we left camp, Bloody Knife's watchful eyes discovered fresh signs of Indians. Halting long enough to allow him to examine the trail, Bloody Knife was soon able to gather all the information attainable. A party of Indians had been prowling about our camp the previous night, and had gone away, travelling in the direction in which we were then marching.

This intelligence occasioned no particular surprise, as we had been expecting to discover the presence of Indians for several days. Bloody Knife's information produced no change in our plans. The hostile party of whose presence we had become aware numbered nineteen; our party numbered over ninety. So, sending intelligence back to General Stanley of the circumstance of the discovery, we continued our march, keeping up if possible a sharper lookout than before, now that we were assured of the proximity of Indians in our neighborhood. Over rock-ribbed hills, down timbered dells, and across open, grassy plains, we wended our way without unusual interest, except at intervals of a few miles to discover the trail of the nineteen prowling visitors of the previous night, showing that our course, which was intended to lead us again to the Yellowstone, was in the same direction as theirs. Bloody Knife interpreted this as indicating that the village from which the nineteen had probably been sent to reconnoitre and report our movements, was located somewhere above us in the Yellowstone valley. About ten o'clock we reached the crest of the high line of bluffs bordering the Yellowstone valley, from which we obtained a fine view of the river and valley extending above and beyond us as far as the eye could reach. Here and there the channel of the river was dotted with beautiful islands covered with verdure and shaded by groves of stately forest trees, while along the banks on either side could be seen for miles and miles clumps of trees varying in size from the familiar cottonwood to the waving osier, and covering a space in some instances no larger than a gentleman's garden, in others embracing thousands of acres.

After halting upon the crest of the bluffs long enough to take in the pleasures of the scene and admire the beautiful valley spread out like an exquisite carpet at our feet, we descended to the valley and directed our horses' heads toward a particularly attractive and inviting cluster of shade trees standing on the river bank and distant from the crest of the bluffs nearly two miles. Upon arriving at this welcome retreat, we found it all that a more distant view had pictured it. An abundance of rich, luxuriant grass offered itself to satisfy the craving appetites of our travelled steeds, while the dense foliage of the forest trees provided us with a protecting shade which exposure to the hot rays of an August sun rendered more than welcome. First allowing our thirsty horses to drink from the clear, crystal water of the Yellowstone, which ran murmuringly by in its long tortuous course to the Missouri, we then picketed them out to graze.

Precautionary and necessary measures having been attended to looking to the security of our horses, the next important and equally necessary step was to post half a dozen pickets on the open plane beyond to give timely warning in the event of the approach of hostile Indians. This being done, the remainder of our party busied themselves in arranging each for his individual comfort, disposing themselves on the grass beneath the shade of the wide-spreading branches of the cottonwoods that grew close to the river bank. Above us for nearly a mile, and for a still greater distance below, the valley was free from timber. This enabled our pickets to command a perfect view of the entire valley, at this point about two miles wide, and almost level, save where here and there it was cut up by deep washes in the soil. Satisfied that every measure calculated to insure our safety had been taken, officers and men—save the trusty pickets—stretched their weary forms on the grassy lawn, and were soon wrapped in slumber, little reckoning that within a few rods there lay concealed more than five times their number of hostile Sioux warriors, waiting and watching for a favorable moment to pounce upon them. For myself, so oblivious was I to the prospect of immediate danger, that after selecting a most inviting spot for my noonday nap, and arranging my saddle and buckskin coat in the form of a comfortable pillow, I removed my boots, untied my cravat, and opened my collar, prepared to enjoy to the fullest extent the delights of an outdoor siesta.

I did not omit, however, to place my trusty Remington rifle within easy grasp—more from habit, it must be confessed, than from antici-pation of danger. Near me, and stretched on the ground sheltered by the shade of the same tree, was my brother, the Colonel, divested of his hat, coat, and boots; while close at hand, wrapped in deep slum-ber, lay the other three officers, Moylan, Calhoun, and Varnum. Sleep had taken possession of us all—officers and men—excepting of course the watchful pickets into whose keeping the safety, the lives, of our little detachment was for the time entrusted. Many of the horses even, having lunched most bountifully from the rich repast which nature had spread around and beneath them, seemed to share in the languor and drowsiness of their riders, and were to be seen here and there repos-ing upon the soft green carpet which to them was both food and couch. How long we slept I scarcely know—perhaps an hour, when the cry of "Indians! Indians!" quickly followed by the sharp ringing crack of the pickets' carbines, aroused and brought us—officers, men, and horses—to our feet. There was neither time nor occasion for questions to be asked or answered. Catching up my rifle, and without waiting to don hat or boots, I glanced through the grove of trees to the open plain or valley beyond, and saw a small party of Indians bearing down toward us as fast as their ponies could carry them.

"Run to your horses, men! Run to your horses!" I fairly yelled as I saw that the first move of the Indians was intended to stampede our animals and leave us to be attended to afterward.

At the same time the pickets opened fire upon our disturbers, who had already emptied their rifles at us as they advanced as if boldly intending to ride us down. As yet we could see but half a dozen warriors, but those who were familiar with Indian stratagems knew full well that so small a party of savages unsupported would not venture to disturb in open day a force the size of ours. Quicker than I could pen the description, each trooper, with rifle in hand, rushed to secure his horse, and men and horses were soon withdrawn from the open plain and concealed behind the clump of trees beneath whose shade we were but a few moments before quietly sleeping. The firing of the pickets, the latter having been reinforced by a score of their comrades, checked the advance of the Indians and enabled us to saddle our horses and be prepared for whatever might be in store for us.

A few moments found us in our saddles and sallying forth from the timber to try conclusions with the daring intruders. We could only see half a dozen Sioux warriors galloping up and down in our front, boldly challenging us by their manner to attempt their capture or death. Of course it was an easy matter to drive them away, but as we advanced it became noticeable that they retired, and when we halted or diminished our speed they did likewise. It was apparent from the first that the Indians were resorting to stratagem to accomplish that which they could not do by an open, direct attack. Taking twenty troopers with me, headed by Colonel Custer and Calhoun, and directing Moylan to keep within supporting distance with the remainder, I followed the retreating Sioux up the valley, but with no prospect of overtaking them, as they were mounted upon the fleetest of ponies. Thinking to tempt them within our grasp, I being mounted on a Kentucky thoroughbred in whose speed and endurance I had confidence, directed Colonel Custer to allow me to approach the Indians accompanied only by my orderly, who was also well mounted; at the same time to follow us cautiously at a distance of a couple of hundred yards. The wily redskins were not to be caught by any such artifice. They were perfectly willing that my orderly and myself should approach them, but at the same time they carefully watched the advance of the cavalry following me, and permitted no advantage. We had by this time almost arrived abreast of an immense tract of timber growing in the valley and extending to the water's edge, but distant from our resting place, from which we had been so rudely aroused, about two miles.

The route taken by the Indians, and which they evidently intended us to follow, led past this timber, but not through it. When we had arrived almost opposite the nearest point, I signalled to the cavalry to halt, which was no sooner done than the Indians also came to a halt. I then made the sign to the latter for a parley, which was done simply by riding my horse in a circle. To this the savages only responded by looking on in silence for a few moments, then turning their ponies and moving off slowly, as if to say, "Catch us if you can." My suspicions were more than ever aroused, and I sent my orderly back to tell Colonel Custer to keep a sharp eye upon the heavy bushes on our left and scarcely three hundred yards distant from where I sat on my horse. The orderly had delivered his message, and had almost rejoined me, when, judging from our halt that we intended to pursue no further, the real design and purpose of the savages was made evident. The small party in front had faced toward us and were advancing as if to attack. I could scarcely credit the evidence of my eyes, but my astonishment had only begun when turning to the wood on my left I beheld bursting from their concealment between three and four hundred Sioux warriors mounted and caparisoned with all the flaming adornments of paint and feathers which go to make up the Indian war costume. When I first obtained a glimpse of them—and a single glance was sufficient—they were dashing from the timber at full speed, yelling and whooping as only Indians can. At the same time they moved in perfect line, and with as seeming good order and alignment as the best drilled cavalry.

To understand our relative positions the reader has only to imagine a triangle whose sides are almost equal; their length in this particular instance being from three to four hundred yards, the three angles being occupied by Colonel Custer and his detachment, the Indians, and myself. Whatever advantage there was in length of sides fell to my lot, and I lost no time in availing myself of it. Wheeling my horse suddenly around, and driving the spurs into his sides, I rode as only a man rides whose life is the prize, to reach Colonel Custer and his men, not only in advance of the Indians, but before any of them could cut me off. Moylan with his reserve was still too far in the rear to render their assistance available in repelling the shock of the Indians' first attack. Realizing the great superiority of our enemies, not only in numbers, but in their ability to handle their arms and horses in a fight, and fearing they might dash through and disperse Colonel Custer's small party of twenty men, and having once broken the formation of the latter, dispatch them in detail, I shouted to Colonel Custer at almost each bound of my horse, "Dismount your men! Dismount your men!" but the distance which separated us and the excitement of the occasion prevented him from hearing me.

Fortunately, however, this was not the first time he had been called upon to contend against the sudden and unforeseen onslaught of savages, and although failing to hear my suggestion, he realized instantly that the safety of his little band of troopers depended upon the adoption of prompt means of defence.

Scarcely had the long line of splendidly mounted warriors rushed from their hiding place before Colonel Custer's voice rang out sharp and clear, "Prepare to fight on foot." This order required three out of four troopers to leap from their saddles and take their position on the ground, where by more deliberate aim, and being freed from the management of their horses, a more effective resistance could be opposed to the rapidly approaching warriors. The fourth trooper in each group of "fours" remained on his horse holding the reins of the horses of his three comrades.

Quicker than words can describe, the fifteen cavalrymen now on foot, and acting as infantry, rushed forward a few paces in advance of their horses, deployed into open order, and dropping on one or both knees in the low grass, waited with loaded carbines—with finger gently pressing the trigger—the approach of the Sioux, who rode boldly down as if apparently unconscious that the small group of troopers were on their front. "Don't fire, men, till I give the word, and when you do fire, aim low," was the quiet injunction given his men by their young commander, as he sat on his horse intently watching the advancing foe.

Swiftly over the grassy plain leaped my noble steed, each bound bearing me nearer to both friends and foes. Had the race been confined to the Indians and myself the closeness of the result would have satisfied an admirer even of the Derby. Nearer and nearer our paths approached each other, making it appear almost as if I were one of the line of warriors, as the latter bore down to accomplish the destruction of the little group of troopers in front. Swifter seem to fly our mettled steeds, the one to save, the other to destroy, until the common goal has almost been reached—a few more bounds, and friends and foes will be united—will form one contending mass.

The victory was almost within the grasp of the redskins. It seemed that but a moment more, and they would be trampling the kneeling troopers beneath the feet of their fleet-limbed ponies; when, "Now, men, let them have it!" was the signal for a well-directed volley, as fifteen cavalry carbines poured their contents into the ranks of the shrieking savages. Before the latter could recover from the surprise and confusion which followed, the carbines—thanks to the invention of breech-loaders—were almost instantly loaded, and a second carefully aimed discharge went whistling on its deadly errand. Several warriors were seen to reel in their saddles, and were only saved from falling by the quickly extended arms of their fellows. Ponies were tumbled over like butchered bullocks, their riders glad to find themselves escaping with less serious injuries. The effect of the rapid firing of the troopers, and their firm, determined stand, showing that they thought neither of flight nor surrender, was to compel the savages first to slacken their speed, then to lose their daring and confidence in their ability to trample down the little group of defenders in the front. Death to many of their number stared them in the face. Besides, if the small party of troopers in the front was able to oppose such plucky and destructive resistance to their attacks, what might not be expected should the main party under Moylan, now swiftly approaching to the rescue, also take part in the struggle? But more quickly than my sluggish pen has been able to record the description of the scene, the battle line of the warriors exhibited signs of faltering which soon degenerated into an absolute repulse. In a moment their attack was transformed into flight in which each seemed only anxious to secure his individual safety. A triumphant cheer from the cavalrymen as they sent a third installment of leaden messengers whistling about the ears of the fleeing redskins served to spur both pony and rider to their utmost speed. Moylan by this time had reached the ground and had united the entire force. The Indians in the mean time had plunged out of sight into the recesses of the jungle from which they had first made their attack. We knew too well that their absence would be brief, and that they would resume the attack, but not in the manner of the first.

We knew that we had inflicted no little loss upon them—dead and wounded ponies could be seen on the ground passed over by the Indians. The latter would not be satisfied without determined efforts to get revenge. Of this we were well aware.

A moment's hurried consultation between the officers and myself, and we decided that as we would be forced to act entirely upon the defensive against a vastly superior force, it would be better if we relieved ourselves as far as possible of the care of our horses, and take our chances in the fight, which was yet to come, on foot. At the same time we were then so far out on the open plain and from the river bank, that the Indians could surround us. We must get nearer to the river, conceal our horses or shelter them from fire, then with every available man form a line or semicircle, with our backs to the river, and defend ourselves until the arrival of the main body of the expedition, an event we could not expect for several hours. As if divining our intentions and desiring to prevent their execution, the Indians now began their demonstrations looking to a renewal of the fight.

This time, however, profiting by their experience on their first attack, they did not come forth in a body, thus presenting a large target to the aim of their opponents, but singly and alone—their favorite mode of warfare—each seeming to act upon his own judgment, yet all governed by one general plan. The troopers, most of them being thoroughly accustomed to Indian fighting, preserved the most admirable coolness from the moment the fight began. Some even indulged in merry-making remarks tinctured at times with the drollest humor. When the savages first made their sudden appearance from the wood, and came rushing down as if to bear everything before them, and the fifteen troopers were kneeling or lying on the ground waiting till the Indians were near enough to receive their fire, a trooper addressed his comrade:

"Say, Teddy, I guess the ball's opened."

"Yis," says Teddy; "and by the way thim rid nagurs is comin' it's openin' wid a grand march."

"Teddy, if we only had the band here, we could play 'Hail to the Chief' for their benefit."

"Begorrah, if they'll come a little closer to this little shootin' inshtrumint, I'll play hell wid their chief for me own benefit."

Of course it was easy to see what had been the original plan by which the Indians hoped to kill or capture our entire party. Stratagem of course was to play a prominent part in the quarrel. The few young warriors first sent to arouse us from our midday slumber came as a decoy to tempt us to pursue them beyond the ambush in which lay concealed the main body of the savages; the latter were to dash from their hiding place, intercept our retreat, and dispose of us after the most approved manner of barbarous warfare.

The next move on our part was to fight our way back to the little clump of bushes from which we had been so rudely startled. To do this Captain Moylan, having united his force to that of Colonel Custer's, gave the order, "Prepare to fight on foot." This was quickly obeyed. Three-fourths of the fighting force were now on foot armed with the carbines only. These were deployed in somewhat of a circular skirmish line, of which the horses formed the centre; the circle having a diameter of several hundred yards. In this order we made our way back to the timber; the Indians whooping, yelling, and firing their rifles as they dashed madly by on their fleet war ponies. That the fire of their rifles should be effective under these circumstances could scarcely be expected. Neither could the most careful aim of the cavalrymen produce much better results. It forced the savages to keep at a respectful distance, however, and enabled us to make our retrograde movement. A few of our horses were shot by the Indians in this irregular skirmish; none fatally however. As we were falling back, contesting each foot of ground passed over, I heard a sudden sharp cry of pain from one of the men in charge of our horses; the next moment I saw his arm hanging helplessly at his side, while a crimson current flowing near his shoulder told that the aim of the Indians had not been entirely in vain. The gallant fellow kept his seat in his saddle, however, and conducted the horses under his charge safely with the rest to the timber. Once concealed by the trees, and no longer requiring the horses to be moved, the number of horseholders was reduced so as to allow but one troop to eight horses; the entire remainder being required on the skirmish line. The redskins had followed us closely step by step to the timber, tempted in part by their great desire to obtain possession of our horses. If successful in this, they believed no doubt that flight on our part being no longer possible we must be either killed or captured.

Taking advantage of a natural terrace or embankment extending almost like a semicircle in front of the little grove in which we had taken refuge, and at a distance of but a few hundred yards from the latter, I determined by driving the Indians beyond to adopt it as our breastwork or line of defence. This was soon accomplished, and we found ourselves deployed behind a natural parapet or bulwark from which the troopers could deliver a carefully directed fire upon their enemies, and at the same time be protected largely from the bullets of the latter. The Indians made repeated and desperate efforts to dislodge us and force us to the level plateau. Every effort of this kind proved unavailing. Several times savages were discovered creeping stealthily toward us through the deep grass in our front, but the whistling of a few carbine bullets about their ears changed their determination. The Indians never ceased during the fight to engage in their favorite mode of warfare, dashing at full speed along our front, firing and draining our fire. Thus they continued so long, that fearing to exhaust our supply of ammunition, an object that our enemies had probably in view, directions were given to the troopers to reserve their fire as much as possible consistent with safety.

Rather a remarkable instance of rifle shooting occurred in the early part of the contest. I was standing in a group of troopers, and with them was busily engaged firing at such of our enemies as exposed themselves. Bloody Knife was with us, his handsome face lighted up by the fire of battle and the desire to avenge the many wrongs suffered by his people at the hands of the ruthless Sioux. All of us had had our attention drawn more than once to a Sioux warrior who, seeming more bold than his fellows, dashed repeatedly along the front of our lines, scarcely two hundred yards distant, and although the troopers had singled him out, he had thus far escaped untouched by their bullets. Encouraged by his success perhaps, he concluded to taunt us again, and at the same time exhibit his own daring, by riding along the lines at full speed, but nearer than before. We saw him coming. Bloody Knife, with his Henry rifle poised gracefully in his hands, watched his coming, saying he intended to make this his enemy's last ride. He would send him to the happy hunting ground. I told the interpreter to tell Bloody Knife that at the moment the warrior reached a designated point directly opposite to us he, Bloody Knife, should fire at the rider and I at the same instant would fire at the pony.

A smile of approval passed over the swarthy features of the friendly scout as he nodded assent. I held in my hand my well-tried Remington. Resting on one knee and glancing along the barrel, at the same time seeing that Bloody Knife was also squatting low in the deep grass with rifle levelled, I awaited the approach of the warrior to the designated point. On he came, brandishing his weapons and flaunting his shield in our faces, defying us by his taunts to come out and fight like men. Swiftly sped the gallant little steed that bore him, scarcely needing the guiding rein. Nearer and nearer both horse and rider approached the fatal spot, when sharp and clear, and so simultaneous as to sound as one, rang forth the reports of the two rifles. The distance was less than two hundred yards. The Indian was seen to throw up his arms and reel in his saddle, while the pony made one final leap, and both fell to the earth. A shout rose from the group of troopers, in which Bloody Knife and I joined. The next moment a few of the comrades of the fallen warrior rushed to his rescue, and without dismounting from their ponies, scarcely pulling rein, clutched up the body, and the next moment disappeared from view.

Foiled in their repeated attempts to dislodge us, the Indians withdrew to a point beyond the range of our rifles for the apparent purpose of devising a new plan of attack. Of this we soon became convinced. Hastily returning to a renewal of the struggle, we saw our adversaries arrange themselves in groups along our entire front. They were seen to dismount, and the quick eyes of Bloody Knife detected them making their way toward us by crawling through the grass. We were at a loss to comprehend their designs, as we could not believe they intended to attempt to storm our position on foot. We were not left long in doubt. Suddenly, and almost as if by magic, we beheld numerous small columns of smoke shooting up all along our front.

Calling Bloody Knife and the interpreter to my side, I inquired the meaning of what we saw. "They are setting fire to the long grass, and intend to burn us out," was the scout's reply, at the same time keeping his eyes intently bent on the constantly increasing columns of smoke. His features wore a most solemn look; anxiety was plainly depicted there. Looking to him for suggestions and advice in this new phase of our danger, I saw his face gradually unbend and a scornful smile part his lips. "The Great Spirit will not help our enemies," was his muttered reply to my question. "See," he continued; "the grass refuses to burn." Casting my eyes along the line formed by the columns of smoke, I saw that Bloody Knife had spoken truly when he said, "The grass refuses to burn."

This was easily accounted for. It was early in the month of August; the grass had not ripened or matured sufficiently to burn readily. A month later, and the flames would have swept us back to the river as if we had been surrounded by a growth of tinder. In a few moments the anxiety caused by the threatening of this new and terrible danger was dispelled. While the greatest activity was maintained in our front by our enemies, my attention was called to a single warrior who, mounted on his pony, had deliberately, and as I thought rashly, passed around our left flank—our diminished numbers preventing us from extending our line close to the river—and was then in rear of our skirmishers, riding slowly along the crest of the high river bank with as apparent unconcern as if in the midst of his friends instead of being almost in the power of his enemies. I imagined that his object was to get nearer to the grove in which our horses were concealed, and toward which he was moving slowly, to reconnoitre and ascertain how much force we held in reserve. At the same time, as I never can see an Indian engaged in an unexplained act without conceiving treachery or stratagem to be at the bottom of it, I called to Lieutenant Varnum, who commanded on the left, to take a few men and endeavor to cut the wily interloper off. This might have been accomplished but for the excessive zeal of some of Varnum's men, who acted with lack of caution, and enabled the Indian to discover their approach and make his escape by a hurried gallop up the river. The men were at a loss even then to comprehend his strange manœuvre, but after the fight had ended, and we obtained an opportunity to ride over and examine the ground, all was made clear, and we learned how narrowly we had escaped a most serious if not fatal disaster.

The river bank in our rear was from twenty to thirty feet high. At its base and along the water's edge ran a narrow pebbly beach. The redskins had hit upon a novel but to us most dangerous scheme for capturing our horses and at the same time throwing a large force of warriors directly on our rear. They had found a pathway beyond our rear, leading from the large tract of timber in which they were first concealed through a cut or ravine in the river bank. By this they were enabled to reach the water's edge, from which point they could move down the river, following the pebbly beach referred to, the height of the river bank protecting them perfectly from our observation. Thus they would have placed themselves almost in the midst of our horses before we could have become aware of their designs. Had they been willing, as white men would have been, to assume greater risks, their success would have been assured. But they feared we might discover their movements and catch them while strung out along the narrow beach, with no opportunity to escape. A few men on the bank could have shot down a vastly superior force. In this case the Indians had sent on this errand about one hundred warriors. Judging from the trail made along the water's edge, they had already accomplished more than two-thirds of the distance which separated them at starting from the coveted prize, when I saw and observed the strange movements of the lone warrior as he deliberately made his way along the river bank. He was acting as the lookout for the party of warriors at the foot of the high river bank, and kept them advised of our movements. Of course when Lieutenant Varnum and his party attempted the capture of the lookout his comrades instinctively supposed that we had discovered their intentions, and they turned and fled up the river when success was almost within their grasp. Even after the flight of the lookout on the bank the Indians below could have continued their movement in the direction of our horses unsuspected and undiscovered by our party. We only learned of their designs after the fight had terminated.

The contest had now been going on almost without interruption for several hours. It had begun about noon, and it was now nearly three o'clock in the afternoon. I knew that we would soon be released from all danger by the arrival of the main body of the expedition; but a serious question presented itself. Many of the men who had been firing most incessantly now began to complain that their stock of ammunition was well-nigh exhausted. They were cautioned to use the few remaining rounds as sparingly as possible. At the same time I sent a couple of non-commissioned officers quickly into the timber, instructing them to obtain every round remaining in the cartridge-boxes of the horsehold-ers and the wounded. This gave us quite a number of rounds, as this supply had not been touched during the fight.

In this chapter, already extended to its full limit, I fear I must omit many interesting minor incidents. The reader can imagine how long-ingly and anxiously both officers and men constantly turned their eyes to the high ridge of hills, distant nearly two miles, over which we knew we would catch the first glimpse of approaching succor. Our ene-mies seemed equally aware of our hopes and fears, and strange to say, their quick eyes, added to better points for observation, enabled them to detect the coming of our friends sooner than did we whose safety depended upon it.

Before we became aware of the fact that succor was near at hand we observed an unusual commotion in the ranks of our adversaries, and soon after a gradual withdrawal from in front of our right and a concentration of their forces opposite our left. The reason for this was soon made clear to us. Looking far to the right and over the crest of hills already described, we could see an immense column of dust rising and rapidly approaching. We could not be mistaken; we could not see the cause producing this dust; but there was not one of us who did not say to himself, "Relief is at hand." A few moments later a shout arose from the men. All eyes were turned to the bluffs in the distance, and there were to be seen, coming almost with the speed of the wind, four separate squadrons of Uncle Sam's best cavalry, with banners flying, horses' manes and tails floating on the breeze, and comrades spurring forward in generous emulation as to which squadron should land its colors first in the fight. It was a grand and welcome sight, but we waited not to enjoy it. Confident of support and wearied from fighting on the defensive, now was our time to mount our steeds and force our enemies to seek safety in flight, or to battle on more even terms. In a moment we were in our saddles and dashing after them. The only satisfaction we had was to drive at full speed for several miles a force outnumbering us five to one. In this pursuit we picked up a few ponies which the Indians were compelled to abandon on account of wounds or exhaustion. Their wounded, of whom there were quite a number, and their killed, as afterward acknowledged by them when they returned to the agency to receive the provisions and fresh supplies of ammunition which a sentimental government, manipulated and directed by corrupt combinations, insists upon distributing annually, were sent to the rear before the flight of the main body. The number of Indians and ponies killed and wounded in this engagement, as shown by their subsequent admission, almost equalled that of half our entire force engaged.

That night the forces of the expedition encamped on the battle-ground, which was nearly opposite the mouth of Tongue river. My tent was pitched under the hill from which I had been so unceremoniously disturbed at the commencement of the fight; while under the wide-spreading branches of a neighboring cottonwood, guarded and watched over by sorrowing comrades who kept up their lonely vigils through the night, lay the mangled bodies of two of our companions of the march, who, although not present nor participating in the fight, had fallen victims to the cruelty of our foes. The description of the manner in which this was brought about, and how by an accident the intelligence of our situation was carried back to the main expedition, resulting in the prompt arrival of the four squadrons to our assistance, must be reserved for a future chapter.

PHOTOGRAPHIC ESSAY

The intrepid plainsman—an image of himself that Custer wished the world to embrace—was perfectly captured in this August 1874 photograph taken by William H. Illingworth during the Black Hills expedition. The frontiersman-soldier sits surrounded by his hounds, his weapons, and his scouts. His favorite Indian scout, Bloody Knife, points to the map (Custer Battlefield National Monument).

In October 1868, a month before the Battle of the Washita, Seventh Cavalry officers gathered for a group photograph at Camp Sandy Forsyth on the Arkansas River. Two of them would die at the Washita, several of the others at the Little Big Horn. Back: Dr. Henry Lippincott; Charley Thompson; 2nd Lt. Thomas March; 2nd Lt. H. Walworth Smith; Capt. Lee Gillette; 1st Lt. Charles Brewster; 1st Lt. Samuel Robbins; Capt. George Yates; Dr. Charles Degraw; Capt. Thomas Weir; 1st Lt. William Cooke; 1st Lt. Owen Hale; 2nd Lt. Edward Law; 2nd Lt. Francis Gibson; 1st Lt. Edward Godfrey. Front: Capt. William Thompson; 1st Lt. Matthew Berry; 1st Lt. David Wallingford; Capt. Albert Barnitz; Capt. Edward Myers; Maj. Joel Elliott (killed at the Washita); 1st Lt. Myles Moylan; Capt. Louis McLane Hamilton (the grandson of Alexander Hamilton, killed at the Washita); Lt. Col. Custer; 1st Lt. Thomas Wallace (Third Infantry); 1st Lt. Thomas Custer; Dr. William Rennick; 2nd Lt. Edward Mathey; 1st Lt. James Bell (Yale Collection of Western Americana, Beinecke Rare Book and Manuscript Library).

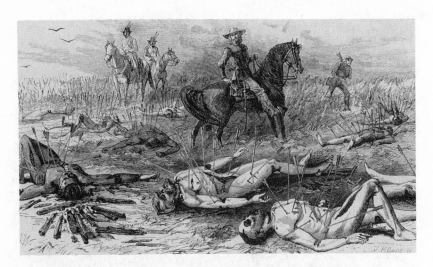

On July 12, 1867, Custer discovered the mutilated remains of Lieutenant Lyman S. Kidder and his eleven-man detachment. Carrying dispatches for Custer, they had been cut off and slaughtered. J. P. Davis drawing from George Armstrong Custer, *My Life on the Plains* (1874) (Author's Collection).

Custer proved a dogged, aggressive pursuer, be the quarry man or beast. In Charles Schreyvogel's *Custer's Demand*, a dramatic confrontation between Custer and Kiowa chiefs on December 17, 1868, is depicted (top). After the Washita battle, Custer's determined pursuit throughout the winter and early spring drove the Kiowas and the Cheyennes onto their reservations. Schreyvogel portrays (left to right) Little Heart, Lone Wolf, Kicking Bird, Satanta, Scout Abner Grover, Custer, Lt. Tom Custer, Lt. Col. John Schuyler Crosby of Sheridan's staff, and General Sheridan in front of the distant troops (Custer Battlefield National Monument). Custer, an avid sportsman, never missed an opportunity to hunt western game, often turning his Indian campaigns into extended hunting expeditions. William Pywell captured the frontier nimrod with an impressive elk on September 6, 1873, during the Yellowstone expedition (Custer Battlefield National Monument).

A contemplative Custer is at work in his Fort Abraham Lincoln study in November 1873 (top). It was here that he would do much of his writing (Custer Battlefield National Monument). But Custer looks far more at home in his buckskins in this July 1875 photograph taken by Orlando Goff at a picnic by the Heart River near the fort (bottom). Left to right: 1st Lt. James Calhoun (Custer's brother-in-law); Leonard Swett; Capt. Stephen Baker (Sixth Infantry); Boston Custer (Custer's brother); 2nd Lt. Winfield S. Edgerly; Emily Watson; Capt. Myles W. Keogh; Margaret Calhoun (Custer's sister); Elizabeth B. Custer; Dr. Holmes Paulding; Custer; Nettie Smith; Dr. George Lord; Capt. Thomas B. Weir; 1st Lt. William W. Cooke; 2nd Lt. Richard Thompson (Sixth Infantry); Nellie Wadsworth; Emma Wadsworth; 1st Lt. Thomas W. Custer (Custer's brother); and 1st Lt. Algernon E. Smith. The three Custer brothers, Calhoun, Keogh, Cooke, Smith, and Lord would all perish a year later at the Little Big Horn (Custer Battlefield National Monument).

THE LITTLE BIG HORN

Here Fell Custer *(detail) by Eric von Schmidt*
(© 1976 Eric von Schmidt).

INTRODUCTION

L
ittle Big Horn—mysterious, romantic, so fittingly contradictory a place-name. There has never been agreement even on its spelling.[1] The battle that raged across the rolling hills above its meandering course has given to that river a universal recognition accorded few places on this earth. And like the enigmatic name of the river, the battle is also marked by endless contradictions, controversies, and mysteries. That is, of course, part of its enduring appeal.

Custer's own striking personality combines with the mystery and drama of the battle to guarantee lasting controversy. The debate over Custer's motives and actions began immediately after the battle and has continued unabated to this day. Did Custer disobey orders? Did he attack in hopes of riding a great victory into the White House? Was he deserted by Reno and Benteen? Did he try to cross the river at Medicine Tail Coulee? Was he the first to fall, killed at the river crossing, or the last, standing alone on the hilltop, as Sitting Bull put it, "like a sheaf of corn with all the ears fallen around him"?[2] Did Custer commit suicide? Which Indian killed Custer? Did Rain-in-the-Face kill him and cut out his heart? Was Custer mutilated or not? The questions have always proliferated more quickly than the answers.

Many of these Custer controversies, such as his presidential ambitions, have been satisfactorily answered for years but nevertheless continue to be repeated. Anyone with even the slightest comprehension of Gilded Age politics understands that it would have been ludicrous for Custer to harbor any presidential ambitions for 1876, but the story has been repeated so often that it is often casually accepted as fact. Ambition was always a powerful motivation for Custer, but at the Little Big Horn that ambition was expressed in military, not political, terms. A great victory might well have assured his promotion to brigadier general if the Democrats captured the White House in November, as many expected them to do. To ascribe presidential ambitions to Custer at the Little Big Horn is wild rhetorical overkill, yet the overblown Custer legend invites such extreme statements.[3]

Without Custer, the Battle of the Little Big Horn would not have retained its grip on the popular imagination. The Little Big Horn would have been just another military debacle, greater perhaps than Fetterman's fight in 1866 but certainly not near the magnitude of St. Clair's defeat in 1791. The collective popular historical consciousness has long since forgotten Fetterman and St. Clair. But the memory of Custer's Last Stand still burns bright. It is that rare combination of Custer's riveting persona and contemporary fame mixing with the natural mystery and high drama of any battle in which one side is annihilated that makes the Little Big Horn so universally compelling an event.

The mystery of exactly what happened to Custer's five companies may never be fully solved. The Indian eyewitness accounts are often frustratingly incomplete or glaringly contradictory. Those who went over the battlefield immediately afterward are divided as to whether it was a complete rout or a heroic defense by disciplined troops. Recent archaeological digs at Custer Battlefield National Monument have added tantalizing bits of new evidence to the story. All of this is considered by Robert M. Utley in the first essay of this section. No other historian is better equipped than Utley to tackle the mystery of exactly what happened that Sunday afternoon in 1876. The acknowledged dean of frontier military studies and the author of the best biography of Custer, *Cavalier in Buckskin: George Armstrong Custer and the Western Military Frontier* (1988), Utley brings a lifetime of careful study to his essay on the Little Big Horn and comes to conclusions that are surprisingly favorable toward Custer.

The best account of the battle by a white participant is undoubtedly Edward S. Godfrey's "Custer's Last Battle," first published in the January 1892 issue of *Century Magazine*. It is *the* classic Custer essay, and the starting point for further study. The essay, although enthusiastically greeted, was not without controversy. Many felt it too favorable to Custer. Godfrey rewrote the essay in 1908 and in his revisions addressed some of the questions raised by his critics. The result, however, is even more laudatory of Custer than the 1892 version. The new version was eventually published as a pamphlet on the forty-fifth anniversary of the Battle of the Little Big Horn to accompany the unveiling of a monument to Custer in Hardin, Montana. It was reprinted in 1974 in a limited edition edited by John M. Carroll. That edition, from which our version is reprinted, also contained Godfrey's hand corrections placed in brackets throughout the text. This gives to the reader the most authoritative, and rare, version of Godfrey's famous narrative.

Godfrey's essay is one of our best sources for the dress of Custer and his soldiers at the Little Big Horn, a topic of enduring interest to military history enthusiasts. Using Godfrey's work and a wide range of other sources, James S. Hutchins dealt with the question of dress and accoutrements in "The Cavalry Campaign Outfit at the Little Big Horn," first published in 1956 in *Military Collector and Historian*. Hutchins, who presently serves as deputy curator and supervisor of the Division of Armed Forces History, National Museum of American History, Smithsonian Institution, is one of the nation's leading authorities on military material culture.[4]

Perhaps no other writer knew the old plains warriors better, nor wrote of their lives more sensitively and insightfully, than did Walter S. Campbell. Writing under the pen name of Stanley Vestal, he produced a remarkable trilogy of classic books on the final days of Sioux power: *Sitting Bull* (1932), *Warpath* (1934), and *New Sources of Indian History* (1934).[5] Following in the path of George Bird Grinnell, he pioneered the combined use of Indian oral narratives and traditional white written sources to produce powerful narratives rich in ethnohistorical detail.

Campbell first interviewed White Bull, Sitting Bull's nephew, in the summer of 1930. They became fast friends, and White Bull eventually adopted Campbell as his son. The White Bull interviews were valuable source material for *Sitting Bull*, but Campbell realized that another great story remained to be told. He returned to the Cheyenne River Reservation in 1932 for more interviews concerning White Bull's warrior days. He used this material to write an epic history of plains Indian warfare, with White Bull's life as its core.

Eventually Campbell became convinced, or he convinced himself, that White Bull was the slayer of Custer. To protect the old chief from harm, Campbell never revealed his discovery until after White Bull's death in 1947. Then, in 1956, Campbell prepared a revision of *Sitting Bull* for the University of Oklahoma Press and included a new section on White Bull's killing of Custer. That material was excerpted in a 1957 *American Heritage* article and caused something of a media sensation. Campbell died on December 25, 1957, with his new edition of *Sitting Bull* selling well and his account of White Bull's death-struggle with

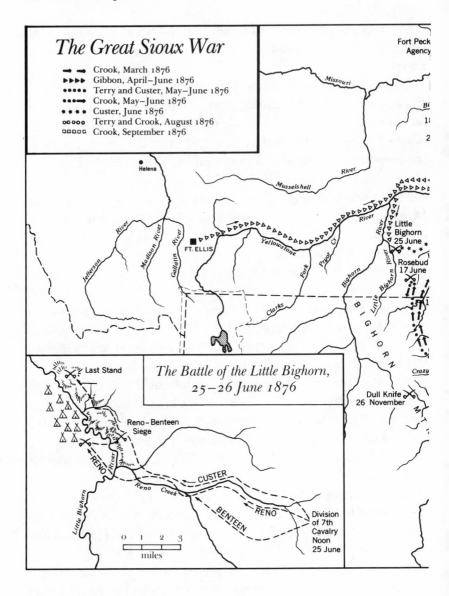

The Great Sioux War

- ➡ ➡ Crook, March 1876
- ▶▶▶▶ Gibbon, April–June 1876
- ●●●●● Terry and Custer, May–June 1876
- ●●●➡ Crook, May–June 1876
- ✦ ✦ ✦ Custer, June 1876
- ∞∞∞∞ Terry and Crook, August 1876
- □□□□ Crook, September 1876

Fort Peck
Agency

Bi
1I
2

Helena

Missouri

River

Musselshell

River

FT. ELLIS

Yellowstone

Fork

Pryor Cr.

Bighorn

Little Bighorn River

Little
Bighorn
25 June

Rosebud
17 June

Clarks

B
I
G
H
O
R
N

Crazy

Last Stand

The Battle of the Little Bighorn,
25–26 June 1876

Reno-Benteen
Siege

Dull Knife
26 November

RENO

River

Little Bighorn

Reno   Creek

CUSTER

BENTEEN

RENO

Division
of 7th
Cavalry
Noon
25 June

0   1   2   3
miles

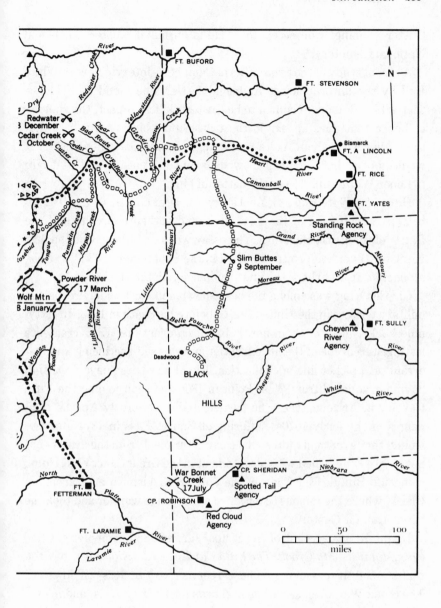

Custer winning wide acceptance. He is buried at Custer Battlefield National Cemetery.[6]

A recent study of the transcripts of Campbell's interviews with White Bull by the anthropologist Raymond J. DeMallie found no evidence that White Bull ever claimed to be Custer's killer. In fact, the sketchy evidence that does appear in the transcripts points to the fact that the soldier with whom White Bull struggled was clearly not Custer. It would appear that Campbell allowed his romantic nature, and his desire to honor White Bull, to get the better of him.[7]

However White Bull's original story was later embellished by Campbell, it remains one of the most vivid and authentic accounts of the Battle of the Little Big Horn. The essay we present here was the first version to ever see print, published in the September 1933 *Blue Book Magazine*. It is perhaps the finest Indian account of the battle.

Charles King was among the best-known and most widely respected military writers in the United States before his death in 1933. In sixty-nine books, most of them novels based on army life, King created a lasting stereotype of the little frontier army as self-sacrificing knights-errant on a picket line of civilization. King knew those days firsthand, having graduated from West Point in 1866 and soon joining the Fifth Cavalry in Arizona. There he participated in the lively Apache campaigns of the early 1870s, suffering at Sunset Pass in 1874 a severe wound that eventually forced his early retirement from the army—but not before King joined with his regiment in the Great Sioux War, riding alongside Buffalo Bill Cody in the July 1876 skirmish at Warbonnet Creek, where the famous scout killed a Cheyenne warrior and took the "first scalp for Custer."[8]

It was King's account of the Sioux War, an 1880 pamphlet entitled *Campaigning with Crook: The Fifth Cavalry in the Sioux War of 1876*, that started the ex-soldier on his career as a writer. It is still in print.[9] The Sioux War often served as backdrop for King's novels, and in one, *Marion's Faith*, there is even a chapter on the Little Big Horn, but Custer makes few substantive appearances. King's acute sense of soldier loyalty prevented him from writing negatively of his fellow officers, especially those who had fallen on the field of battle. Thus he is generally silent on Custer. His 1890 essay for *Harper's*, reprinted here, is as interesting for what it does not contain as for what it does. It requires careful reading between the lines, but King's distaste for Custer, mixed with a melancholy admiration, is apparent. He has no mixed feelings concerning Major Marcus Reno, and his assessment rings damningly clear. He places the battle and its personalities, both Indian and white, in a solid context of the times as seen by a participant. It is a marvelous essay, as fast-paced as a cavalry charge and as eloquent at times as a bugle sounding taps. It makes a particularly fine companion piece, and counterbalance, to the Godfrey essay.

Finally, to close this section, is the narrative of Kate Bighead, a Cheyenne woman who was in the great village on the Little Big Horn and observed much of the battle. She told her story to Dr. Thomas B. Marquis in 1927. Marquis served as the agency physician on the Northern Cheyenne Indian Reservation in 1922–23 and for several years thereafter operated a private practice out of Lodge Grass, not far from the Custer Battlefield. Always fascinated with history and more interested in pursuing a literary career than a medical one, Marquis sought out old-timers among the Cheyennes and Crows who could tell him of the old days and ways. He became obsessed with the Custer fight, and his pioneering research resulted in an impressive body of published work before his death in 1935. A veteran of World War I, he was buried with full military honors at the Custer Battlefield National Cemetery.[10]

Kate Bighead's narrative, as interpreted by Dr. Marquis, gives a concise history of the travail of the Cheyennes during the long years of warfare with the whites. Her compelling account of the Little Big Horn battle, marked by her particular perspective, gives the modern reader important insights into the Indian point of view. Her account of mass suicides by Custer's men, though controversial, is in accord with other Cheyenne narratives of the battle. Dr. Marquis eventually became convinced that these suicides were the key to understanding the Seventh's debacle. Finally, her concluding words are filled with a poignant poetry that form a fitting final note to our section on this epic clash between red man and white.

Notes

1. At the time of the battle, the name of the river was most often spelled Little Big Horn. Modern usage, especially as defined by cartographers, has changed the spelling to Little Bighorn. In this anthology the reprinted

essays use both spellings, and we have left the spellings as they originally appeared. New material in this book uses Little Big Horn. This is done for reasons both historical and sentimental.

2. Quoted in W. A. Graham, *The Custer Myth: A Source Book of Custeriana* (1953; reprint, Lincoln: University of Nebraska Press, 1986), 73.

3. Red Star, the Arikara scout, is the sole source for the story that Custer sought a victory at the Little Big Horn in order to become president. His account, as reported by O. G. Libby, states: "Custer told him that he had been informed that this would be his last campaign in the West among the Indians. He said that no matter how small a victory he could win, even though it were against only five tents of Dakotas, it would make him President, Great Father, and he must turn back as soon as he was victorious. In case of victory he would take Bloody Knife back with him to Washington." O. G. Libby, ed., *The Arikara Narrative of the Campaign against the Hostile Dakotas, June, 1876* (Bismarck: North Dakota Historical Society, 1920), 58–59.

From this slender thread various authors have spun fabulous tapestries. It has been a favorite theme among novelists and moviemakers, reaching its culmination in the 1970 Arthur Penn film *Little Big Man*, where a voice-over narration makes it clear that Custer's presidential ambitions were a "historical fact." But novels and films are fictional contrivances, and such lapses are understandable. The historians

Mari Sandoz and David Humphreys Miller are not so easily forgiven. Sandoz, in her influential *The Battle of the Little Big Horn*, and Miller, in his popular *Custer's Fall*, both greatly embellished Red Star's story. Sandoz went so far as to invent a scheme by Custer to strike on June 25 so his scouts could carry the news of his victory to telegraph stations in time to reach the Democratic national convention so that his partisans could swing the convention to him. (The convention met in St. Louis June 27–29, 1876, and nominated Samuel J. Tilden of New York on the first ballot. Custer's name was never mentioned at the convention or in the contemporary press as even a dark-horse candidate.) This is no minor theme in Sandoz's fictive history. She uses it as Custer's main motivation and repeats it again as the conclusion of her book. The story is not as important a literary device in Miller's book but is nevertheless presented as Custer's direct statement to his scouts at the Crow's Nest. Miller, like Sandoz, engages in an outright fictional contrivance by having Custer conspire with James Gordon Bennett of the *New York Herald* to secure the Democratic nomination once he had defeated the Sioux. That is only one of many inventions in Miller's book. Richard Slotkin recently countered that Custer's ambition was not to be president but rather to accept an appointment as head of the Indian Bureau in the new Democratic administration. That Custer would consider lowering himself to accept a position previously filled by some of the nation's most inept political hacks is pretty far-fetched. Slotkin's thesis can at least be regarded as speculation, whereas Sandoz's and Miller's must be discarded as fiction. Mari Sandoz, *The Battle of the Little Big Horn* (Philadelphia: J. B. Lippincott Co., 1966), 54–55, 181–82; David Humphreys Miller, *Custer's Fall: The Indian Side of the Story* (New York: Duell, Sloan and Pearce, 1957), 13, 37; Richard Slotkin, *The Fatal Environment: The Myth of the Frontier in the Age of Industrialization, 1880–1890* (New York: Atheneum, 1985), 426–27.

Ambition indeed directed Custer at the Little Big Horn, as it had throughout his career. But it was military in nature, not political. James Forsyth, of Sheridan's staff, capsulized Custer's political squabbles with the Grant administration quite succinctly in an 1876 letter to Secretary of War William W. Belknap: "The fact of the matter is that both Hazen, and Custer, are now working to make capital with the Democratic party—*they want stars.*" The same could as easily have been said of Custer's motivation at the Little Big Horn. James W. Forsyth to William W. Belknap, April 5, 1876, Box 45, Philip H. Sheridan Papers, Library of Congress. Also see Craig Repass, *Custer For President?* (Fort Collins, Colo.: Old Army Press, 1985).

4. For more on this topic, see James S. Hutchins, *Boots and Saddles at the Little Bighorn: Weapons, Dress, Equipment, Horses, and Flags of General Custer's Seventh U.S. Cavalry in 1876* (Fort Collins, Colo.: Old Army Press, 1976); John S. du Mont, *Custer Battle Guns* (Fort Collins, Colo.: Old Army Press, 1974); Elwood L. Nye, *Marching with Custer: A Day-to-Day Evaluation of the Uses, Abuses, and Conditions of the Animals on the Ill-Fated Expedition of 1876* (Glendale, Calif.: Arthur H. Clark Co., 1964); and Ernest Lisle Reedstrom, *Bugles, Banners, and War Bonnets* (Caldwell, Idaho: Caxton Printers, 1977).

5. Stanley Vestal, *Sitting Bull: Champion of the Sioux, a Biography* (Boston: Houghton Mifflin, 1932); Stanley Vestal, *Warpath: The True Story of the Fighting Sioux Told in a Biography of Chief White Bull* (Boston: Houghton Mifflin, 1934); Stanley Vestal, *New Sources of Indian History, 1850–1891: The Ghost Dance—The Prairie Sioux: A Miscellany* (Norman: University of Oklahoma Press, 1934). Also see Sherry L. Smith, "Stanley Vestal," in John R. Wunder, ed., *Historians of the American Frontier: A Bio-Bibliographical Sourcebook* (Westport, Conn.: Greenwood Press, 1988), 697–712.

6. Stanley Vestal, "The Man Who Killed Custer," *American Heritage* 8 (February 1957): 4–9, 90–91. The first appearance of the story of White Bull's killing Custer actually came two years before but received little publicity. See Reginald Laubin, "Who Killed Custer?" *Adventure* (September 1955): 27–29, 43–44. It was again repeated in 1968 when White Bull's war record, as prepared for Usher Burdick in 1931, was published as James H. Howard, trans. and ed., *The Warrior Who Killed Custer: The Personal Narrative of*

Chief Joseph White Bull (Lincoln: University of Nebraska Press, 1968).

7. Raymond J. DeMallie, Foreword to Stanley Vestal, *Warpath: The True Story of the Fighting Sioux Told in a Biography of Chief White Bull* (Lincoln: University of Nebraska Press, Bison Book, 1984), v–xxiii. Also see DeMallie's insightful foreword to the 1989 University of Oklahoma Press paperback edition of Vestal's *Sitting Bull*.

8. For Charles King's career, see Don Russell, *Campaigning with King: Charles King, Chronicler of the Old Army*, ed. Paul L. Hedren (Lincoln: University of Nebraska Press, 1991), and Paul L. Hedren, "Charles King," in Paul Andrew Hutton, ed., *Soldiers West: Biographies from the Military Frontier* (Lincoln: University of Nebraska Press, 1987), 243–61. Also see Paul L. Hedren, *King on Custer: An Annotated Bibliography* (Bryan, Tex.: Brazos Corral of the Westerners, n.d.); C. E. Dornbusch, *Charles King: American Army Novelist* (Cornwallville, N.Y.: Hope Farm Press, 1963); and Paul L. Hedren, *First Scalp for Custer: The Skirmish at Warbonnet Creek, Nebraska, July 17, 1876* (Glendale, Calif.: Arthur H. Clark Co., 1980), reprinted as a Bison Book by the University of Nebraska Press in 1987.

9. Charles King, *Campaigning with Crook* (Norman: University of Oklahoma Press, 1964). The fine introduction by Don Russell makes this the best of numerous editions of this work.

10. Thomas B. Marquis also authored *A Warrior Who Fought Custer* (Minneapolis: Midwest Co., 1931); *Memoirs of a White Crow Indian (Thomas H. Leforge)* (New York: Century Co., 1928); *Custer, Cavalry, and Crows: The Story of William White As Told to Thomas Marquis* (Fort Collins, Colo.: Old Army Press, 1975); *Keep the Last Bullet for Yourself: The True Story of Custer's Last Stand* (New York: Two Continents Publishing Group/Reference Publications, 1976); and *The Cheyennes of Montana*, ed. Thomas D. Weist (Algonac, Mich.: Reference Publications, 1978).

THE
LITTLE
BIG
HORN

ROBERT M.

UTLEY

George Armstrong Custer died a spectacular death at the Battle of the Little Big Horn on June 25, 1876, the victim of federal Indian policies that he had played no role in formulating. Yet he was their eager instrument and, fittingly, assumed a major part in the two demonstrations of federal policy that led most directly to his death. First was the government's partnership with the Northern Pacific Railroad to push transcontinental rails through the heart of the buffalo ranges of the northern plains. Second was the government's tortuous complicity in opening the Black Hills to white gold-seekers. Both policies outraged the Sioux and the Cheyenne Indians, whose interests they imperiled.

The Fort Laramie Treaty of 1868 had laid the groundwork for the conflict over these two initiatives. Ending the war between the Sioux and the United States over the Bozeman Trail to the Montana goldfields, this accord conceded victory to the Indians and provided for the withdrawal of the guardian soldiers from the trail. But it also marked out a "Great Sioux Reservation"—all of present South Dakota west of the Missouri River—as a new, much smaller homeland in which the tribes were to settle, abandon the chase, and draw government rations while learning to farm. Since not all cared to give up the free life of the plains, the treaty also vaguely defined an "unceded territory" in which Indians opposed to the reservation might continue to follow the buffalo. This area extended from the western boundary of the new reservation to the summit of the Big Horn Mountains and embraced the valleys of the Powder, Tongue, Rosebud, and Big Horn rivers and the rolling plains and timbered mountains separating them.

Within a few years, most of the Sioux and Cheyennes had moved to the Great Sioux Reservation. Some fifteen thousand people, representing all seven tribes of the Teton Sioux, attached themselves to one of the five agencies established for their control and "civilization." Even Red Cloud, who had led the fight against the Bozeman Trail, joined with the more compliant but equally influential Spotted Tail in the new life of the reservation.

To the west, in the unceded territory, a hard core of holdouts clung to the traditional nomadic life of the horse and buffalo. They numbered about three thousand Sioux from all the Teton tribes and four hundred Cheyennes. The government's term for these people, *nontreaties*, accurately reflected their attitude. They wanted nothing to do with government agents, reservations, or white people. They wanted, in short, simply to be left alone. Each of the nontreaty tribes followed its own noted chiefs, but dominating them all was the stalwart Sitting Bull, whose influence extended beyond his own Hunkpapa tribe and who, year after year, held the various nontreaty groups together in a solid coalition.[1]

Nontreaty and reservation Indians did not stand aloof from each other. Frequently people from the Sitting Bull bands appeared at the agencies to visit friends and relatives, share in the government handouts, and make trouble for the agents. And each summer people from the agencies headed west to join the nontreaties for buffalo hunts and raids on the pony herds of the Crow and other enemy tribes. Along the Platte River road and in Montana's Gallatin Valley, white travelers and settlers also felt the sting of Sioux and Cheyenne raids. Hardly had the ink dried on the Fort Laramie Treaty when the Great Father's officials saw that in the unceded territory they had created a fountain of endless trouble.

Almost at once the discord threatened the Northern Pacific Railroad. In 1873 the rails reached the Missouri River at Bismarck, Dakota Territory, but already surveyors had appeared in the Sioux country west of the river. In the summers of 1871 and 1872, escorted by soldiers, they had run lines through the jumble of colorful badlands cut by the Little Missouri River and had driven stakes along the base of the pine-dappled ridges and bluffs shouldering the valley of Montana's Yellowstone River.

Both at the agencies and out in the unceded territory, the Indians reacted with fury. Railroads disrupted the migrations of buffalo and brought an invasion of white people who ruined the country and doomed the Indian way of life. Although the Treaty of 1868 had left obscure whether the unceded territory reached as far north as the Yellowstone River, the boundary made no difference because the treaty permitted railroads anywhere in Indian country. Such legalisms failed to impress the angry Sioux and Cheyennes, who probably knew nothing about them anyway.

Into this boiling kettle, in the spring of 1873, dropped George Armstrong Custer. Elated at escaping the stagnation of Reconstruction duty in the South, the lieutenant colonel of the Seventh Cavalry led the regiment up the Missouri River to Fort Abraham Lincoln, near Bismarck. His command formed part of the escort for the summer's surveying expedition to the Yellowstone. In two battles with Sitting Bull's warriors, Custer exposed the measure of Indian opposition to the railroad. Afterward, from his new station at Fort Lincoln, he became an effective advocate for the Northern Pacific and the opening to white settlement of the Indian lands through which it would run.[2]

A year later, in the summer of 1874, Custer and the Seventh Cavalry blazed the "Thieves' Road" to the Black Hills. The Sioux treasured these dark and beautiful mountains sprawling across the western quarter of the Great Sioux Reservation. Whites, suspecting the presence of gold as well as the game animals and tipi poles that enticed the Indians, clamored for the opening of the hills to white settlement. The Custer expedition of 1874, ostensibly looking for a suitable site for a military post, confirmed the rumors of gold and set off a mining rush.

No treaty ambiguity surrounded the Black Hills. Lying within the Great Sioux Reservation, they were guaranteed to the Indians by treaty and were plainly forbidden to whites. All Sioux and Cheyennes, reservation and nontreaty alike, were enraged by the gold seekers pouring into the hills. The government made a half-hearted effort to bar them, then tried to buy the coveted territory. The Indians would not sell, largely because wrathful men from the Sitting Bull bands threatened death to any who stepped forward to sign the bill of sale.[3]

The chief obstacle to the cession of the Black Hills lay in the independence of the Sitting Bull bands. If they could be forced to give up the free life of the unceded territory, they, like the reservation Indians, could be made dependent on the government. The task of reaching agreement on "extinguishing Indian title," as government terminology expressed it, would then become easier. Late in 1875, therefore, the government contrived a war against the "renegade" Sioux bands. For two years these Indians had done little to justify a war. On orders from Washington, however, runners set forth through winter snows with an ultimatum to the bands in the unceded territory: report to the agencies by January 31, 1876, or be declared hostile and subject to military action.[4]

They did not report, of course, but even before the deadline, the army had begun to prepare a campaign to enforce the ultimatum. The chief strategist was Lieutenant General Philip H. Sheridan, who commanded the Military Division of the Missouri from headquarters in Chicago. He designed an offensive featuring three columns converging on the country roamed by the Indians now labeled "hostiles." Brigadier General George Crook, the commander of the Department of the Platte, would move north from Fort Fetterman, Wyoming. The other two columns would organize in the Department of Dakota, Brigadier General Alfred H. Terry commanding. Colonel John Gibbon would march east from bases in western Montana. Lieutenant Colonel George A. Custer would push west from Fort Abraham Lincoln. Because of the uncertain location of the enemy, Sheridan did not try to concert the movements of the three columns.[5]

The offensive went badly from the beginning. Conceived as a winter operation to catch the quarry unprepared in their snow-clogged camps, it foundered on the harsh realities of the northern plains winter. On March 17, 1876, Crook's cavalry leader botched an attack on a village on the Powder River, and the entire column, nearly ruined by blizzards and sub-zero temperatures, returned to Fort Fetterman. Custer could not even push off until melting snow unblocked the Northern Pacific Railroad and allowed supplies to be stockpiled. Only Gibbon marched, slowed by snow and mud, and at length he received orders to go into camp on the upper Yellowstone River until the other commands could take the field. Sheridan's winter campaign turned into a spring campaign and finally into a summer campaign.

Also complicating the departure of the Fort Abraham Lincoln column were the tribulations of its commander. Throughout the spring, Custer found himself increasingly drawn into the political storms swirling around the expiring Republican presidency of Ulysses S. Grant. A partisan Democrat with strong ties to prominent party leaders, Custer could not resist making his contribution to the fortunes of his party. Called east in March 1876 to assist in congressional probes of the scandal-ridden Grant regime, he gave testimony about the fraudulent frontier schemes of the administration and even about the presidential family, testimony that snarled him in election-year politics. Furious, Grant deposed Custer as expedition commander and in the end relented, on petition of Generals Sheridan and Terry, only so far as to let him go at the head of the Seventh Cavalry, but subordinate to Terry.[6]

A chastened but bitter Custer led the Seventh Cavalry out of Fort Abraham Lincoln on May 17, 1876, the kindly Terry exercising a considerate and gentle watch over his bruised underling. Terry prized the lieutenant colonel's drive and boldness, and he meant to use Custer and his horsemen as the expedition's striking arm. Terry's column numbered more than a thousand—the Seventh Cavalry, 750 strong, plus infantry, a battery of Gatling guns, a wagon train, and a beef herd. Other infantry companies would join the column on the Yellowstone.

Terry and Custer did not know where the Indians were. Neither did Crook, who headed north for the second time on May 29. Curiously, Gibbon knew where they were but failed to inform Terry. On May 16 Gibbon's Crow scouts spotted the main Sioux and Cheyenne village in the valley of the Tongue River. Two weeks later they found it again on the Rosebud. Gibbon could not get his command across the swollen Yellowstone to launch an attack.[7]

Nor did the generals know how many Indians they faced. They had accurate estimates of the size of the nontreaty bands—about four hundred lodges, three to four thousand people, eight hundred fighting men. They did not know how many reservation Indians would come out for the summer, or when they would arrive. In fact, the strategists did not much care about enemy strength. From experience, they worried more about finding and catching the Indians than about defeating them.

For their part, the Indians were not looking for a fight, although not avoiding one either. As usual, the bands had passed the winter in snug camps scattered across eastern Montana and western Dakota. Crook's attack on the Powder River village in March had come as a declaration of war, prompting the dispersed groups to begin uniting for the summer. As the village moved slowly west, across the Powder and the Tongue rivers to the Rosebud, its size remained stable. Not until the prairie grass greened, providing forage for the ponies, could many of the agency Indians find their way to the lodges of their western kin.

On June 9, aboard the chartered river steamer *Far West*, Terry and Gibbon at last met, and Terry learned for the first time where the Indians were. Establishing a supply base at the mouth of the Powder River, he moved his command up the Yellowstone to meet with Gibbon's column of 450 men of the Seventh Infantry and Second Cavalry. Further scouting disclosed the Indian trail leading up Rosebud Creek to the south.

On the afternoon of June 21, Terry gathered his principal subordinates in the cabin of the *Far West*, moored to the Yellowstone's bank at the mouth of the Rosebud, to work out final details of plans that he had already formulated. The scouts guessed that the quarry would turn west from the Rosebud and be found camped in the valley of the Little Big Horn River. Custer would ascend the Rosebud and sweep down the Little Big Horn. Gibbon would retrace his march up the Yellowstone, ascend the Big Horn, and assume a blocking position at the mouth of the Little Big Horn. With Terry accompanying, he would be there by June 26.

This was not designed as a concerted movement, any more than Sheridan had intended the convergence of Terry, Crook, and Gibbon to be concerted, and for the same reason: the uncertain location of the Indians. Custer's mission was to attack the Indians, wherever and whenever he might find them. With luck, this might occur on June 26, with Custer, the hammer, driving the enemy against Gibbon, the anvil. The notion that Terry intended his two subordinates to attack from different directions at the same time, however, arose only after disaster demanded a scapegoat. As a matter of fact, Gibbon did not get into position until late on June 26.

At noon on June 22, the Seventh Cavalry passed in review before Terry and other senior officers. Badly under strength initially, still further reduced by details to the Powder River base, it numbered 31 officers and 566 enlisted men in 12 companies, 35 Arikara and Crow Indian scouts, about a dozen packers, guides, and other civilians, and a train of pack mules bearing rations, forage, and reserve ammunition. Each man carried a Springfield single-shot carbine and a Colt six-shooter, with one hundred cartridges for the former and twenty-four for the latter. Sabers had been left behind as cumbersome and useless in Indian combat.

Full of veterans, the Seventh was a good outfit, almost as good as Custer thought. Even so, its officer corps suffered a damaging factionalism. As always either beloved or detested, Custer himself stood at the center of the disharmony. Some of the officers formed a "royal family," blindly loyal to their commander. Others, excluded from his favor or contemptuous of his pretensions, made up the opposition. An accomplished nepotist, Custer numbered among his loyalists four members of his own family: his brother Tom, captain of C Company; his brother-in-law James Calhoun, first lieutenant commanding L Company; his brother Boston, a civilian hired as a forage master; and his nephew Armstrong Reed, listed on the rolls as "guide."

Ominously, Custer's two ranking subordinates stood with his antagonists. Major Marcus A. Reno, a besotted, socially inept mediocrity, commanded little respect in the regiment and was the antithesis of the electric Custer in almost every way. Captain Frederick W. Benteen, a fearless combat leader and able but crotchety company commander, had despised and obstructed Custer from the day they had first met nearly ten years earlier.

Up the Rosebud marched the Seventh, twelve miles the first day, thirty each of the next two. The Indian trail appeared to be several weeks old and evidenced roughly four hundred lodges, the approximate size of the nontreaty bands. But on the afternoon of June 24 the trail suddenly turned fresh and scarred by movements and activities that left the officers bewildered. Whatever the explanation, Indians had to be nearby, possibly within striking distance.

They were. In fact, their village sprawled along the banks of the Little Big Horn River just across the Wolf Mountains, only thirty miles distant. It contained a fighting force vibrating with elation and confidence, for less than a week earlier several hundred painted and befeathered warriors had fallen on General Crook's command on the upper Rosebud and sent him reeling back to his base camp crying for reinforcements.

Even more portentous, the village no longer represented only the

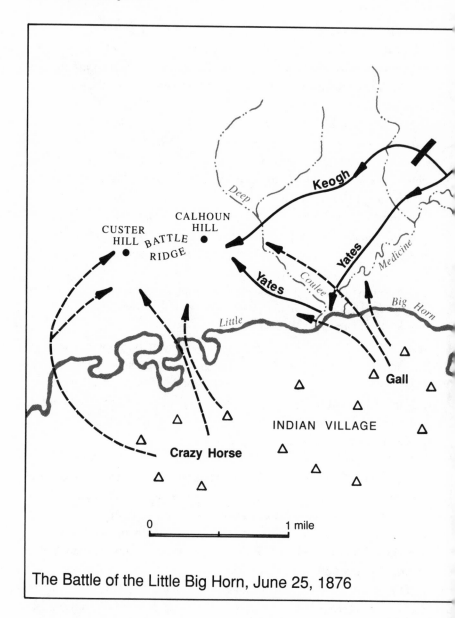

CUSTER
HILL
CALHOUN
HILL
BATTLE
RIDGE

Keogh

Yates

Yates

Medicine

Coulee

Deep

Little

Big Horn

Gall

INDIAN VILLAGE

Crazy Horse

0   1 mile

The Battle of the Little Big Horn, June 25, 1876

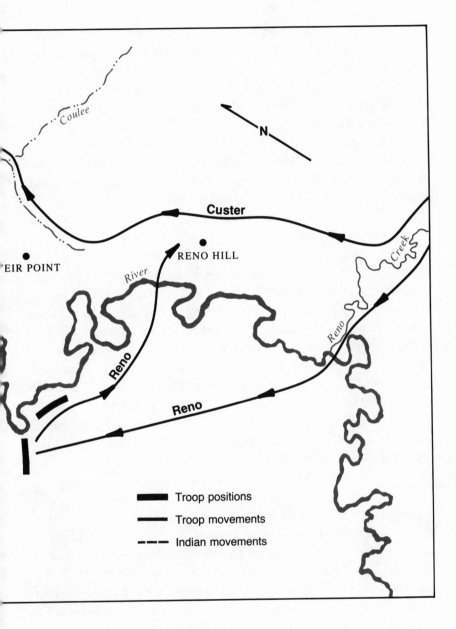

Coulee

N

Custer

RENO HILL

EIR POINT

River

Reno

Creek

Reno

Reno

Reno

■■■ Troop positions

── Troop movements

--- Indian movements

nontreaties. Within the past few days, agency Indians had begun to arrive in large numbers, swelling Sitting Bull's following from three thousand to nearly seven thousand people, with fighting men numbering two thousand or more instead of eight hundred. The tipis of six separate tribal circles, five of Sioux and one of Northern Cheyenne, crowded the narrow valley of the Little Big Horn.

Custer's Indian scouts must have known why the Sioux trail abruptly turned fresh and confused: a big influx of agency Indians suddenly converging on the Sitting Bull camp and obliterating the old trail. But apparently Custer did not ask the scouts and did not guess himself. He knew only that he now had Indians in his immediate front and that he had better attack as quickly as he could or they would discover his approach and flee. A night march, he announced to his officers late on June 24, would take the regiment across the mountains. There he would spend the next day resting the men, searching out the location of the objective, and devising a plan for attacking on June 26, the day Gibbon had predicted that he would reach the mouth of the Little Big Horn.

But at dawn on June 25 these plans fell into disarray. From a mountaintop later named the Crow's Nest, scouts spotted the Sioux and Cheyenne village some fifteen miles in the hazy distance. They also spotted parties of Sioux observing the military activities. To Custer, this meant that the enemy had discovered him and, unless prevented, would strike their tipis and escape. Actually, these Sioux were on their way to the agencies and did not report back to the village. But Custer did not know this, and he resolved to move at once to the attack.

What he did not know shaped Custer's plan. He did not know exactly where in the Little Big Horn Valley the Indians were camped, and he did not know the character of the terrain on which he would have to fight. He had intended to gather these critical items of intelligence on June 25. Now he had to seek them out at the same time that he advanced to the attack. The answer to the problem was a reconnaissance in force: push the entire regiment forward in components that could be employed, separately or in concert as unfolding circumstance required, in reconnaissance, maneuver, or combat.

As the Seventh Cavalry topped the divide between the Rosebud and the Little Big Horn valleys at noon on June 25, Adjutant William W. Cooke split the regiment into battalions. Major Reno commanded one, of Companies A, G, and M, 140 officers and enlisted men. Captain Benteen received another, Companies D, H, and K, 125 strong. Two more, Companies E and F under Captain George W. Yates and C, I, and L under Captain Myles W. Keogh, with a total of about 225, remained under Custer's immediate command. Captain Thomas M. McDougall with Company B brought up the rear, escorting the packtrain.[8]

At once Custer began the reconnaissance phase of the operation. The view from the Crow's Nest had revealed the general location of the Sioux village in the lower valley of the Little Big Horn. Now Custer had to make certain that no Indians were camped in the upper valley, above the point where he would enter it and therefore in his rear as he moved on the objective. He dispatched Captain Benteen with his battalion to find a ridge line to the left, or south, from which he could scan the upper Little Big Horn Valley. Benteen was then to swing back to Custer's trail, which lay down the valley of a small stream later named Reno Creek. Custer's two battalions took the right bank of Reno Creek, Reno's battalion the left bank.

A march of ten miles down Reno Creek brought Custer and Reno to a point about four miles above its confluence with the Little Big Horn. Here, at the site of an abandoned village marked by a single tipi containing the body of a slain warrior, the reconnaissance in force uncovered further intelligence. Ahead in the creek valley some forty Indian warriors galloped toward the Little Big Horn, and to the right front a wall of dust rose from behind an intervening ridge line.

To Custer, the dust cloud undoubtedly signified the Indian village, its inhabitants scrambling to get away from the oncoming soldiers. Even though Benteen remained somewhere back on the trail, the findings of his scout unknown, Custer had to attack before the Indians escaped. Instantly, he ordered Reno to pursue the warriors fleeing down the creek and to charge them, and he promised to support Reno with the whole outfit.

Fording the Little Big Horn at the mouth of the creek, Reno's battalion, accompanied by the Arikara scouts, advanced down the open valley. Ahead, indistinct in the dust boiling from behind a timbered bend of the river, warriors raced their mounts in preparation for battle. Reno signaled a charge, and his little command spurred to the attack.

As the galloping troopers neared the point of timber jutting into the valley, they saw the blurred shapes of tipis in the murk and yelping warriors by the hundreds rushing forth on ponies to defend their families. At the same time, backward glances revealed none of the support Custer had promised. Afraid of plunging into overpowering Sioux numbers, Reno flung up his arm and shouted the command to fight on foot. The charge ground to a halt, horse holders dashed to the rear with four mounts each, and a thin skirmish line, anchored on the nose of the river bend, stretched across the valley. A ragged curtain of carbine fire spat at the fleeting forms of Indian horsemen.

Custer, meantime, had not ridden into the Little Big Horn Valley as he had led Reno to expect. Instead he had turned right and ascended a long gentle slope toward the dust cloud. Just short of the skyline, he halted the column and, with his orderly trumpeter and a few Crow scouts, rode to the summit.

Below, at his very feet, Custer had his first glimpse of the Indian village and the battlefield terrain. Bluffs cut by ravines fell steeply three to four hundred feet to the winding, tree-fringed river. From the sweeping river bend, tipis clustered in tribal circles extended down the valley for three miles. Warriors raced toward the upper end of the village to meet Reno, who was stringing his skirmish line across the valley, while others ran for their ponies pastured in a vast herd on the benchland beyond. Swinging his hat overhead, Custer returned to his two battalions.

What Custer planned must be surmised. Almost certainly he meant to find a break in the bluffs that would allow him to cross the river and thrust into the village. This would confront the enemy with attacks from two directions and allow him to cut off Indians fleeing from Reno. As the five companies rode north, descending a ravine angling away from the bluff tops, Custer sent a courier on the back trail with orders for Captain McDougall to hurry forward the ammunition packs. Later, approaching a broad coulee pointing toward the river, Custer dispatched another courier, his orderly trumpeter, with a written message to Benteen to hasten forward, bringing the packs.

The five companies had reached a drainage later named Medicine Tail Coulee. Nearly three miles to the west it joined with a smaller drainage cutting in from the north, Deep Coulee, to empty into the Little Big Horn at a wide and easy ford. In these two coulees and amid the hills and ridges separating them occurred critical phases of the battle. Sending Yates's two-company battalion down Medicine Tail to the river,

Custer, with Keogh's three-company battalion, formed a dismounted skirmish line on the north slope of Medicine Tail. His motives can only be speculated. Most likely, he intended Yates to secure the ford while he covered Benteen's approach route. Strengthened by Benteen, he would then lead all eight companies in a charge across the river into the village.[9]

Whatever Custer's purpose, it foundered on developments elsewhere. Most critical were Benteen's actions. His scout to the left had quickly confirmed the absence of Indians in the upper Little Big Horn Valley, and Benteen had rejoined the main trail. He did not send word of his findings to Custer, however, nor did he hurry to catch up. The arrival of Custer's first courier failed to quicken the pace. Only after the second appeared, his horse bleeding from a bullet wound, did Benteen exhibit any sense of urgency, and even then not much.

Reno's actions also proved critical. His skirmish line at the upper end of the village lasted hardly fifteen minutes before Sioux horsemen spilled around its left flank and got in his rear. He then took up new positions in the timber on his right flank. Trees and dense underbrush interfered with a coherent defense and made control difficult. Warriors fired from all directions and began to infiltrate the area. Within half an hour, even though he had taken few casualties, Reno decided that he could not hold this position either. He ordered a withdrawal back up the valley.

The movement turned into a bloody disaster. Those who had heard the command gathered on horseback at the edge of the timber. In a loose column, with Reno in the van, they spurred back on their trail. Mounted warriors closed in to press them toward the river. Working the levers of their Winchester repeaters and plunging into hand-to-hand combat with knives and lances, the Indians took a fearful toll. With no organized covering force, the withdrawal turned into a rout, every man for himself. Across the river the troopers splashed as Indians crowded the banks and fired into the tangle of struggling horses and riders.

Only on the bluff tops above the river, from which Custer had scanned the valley less than an hour earlier, did the demoralized troopers find relief. Here Benteen came up to bring order out of chaos, and at the same time the Indians began to draw off. Of Reno's 140 men, 40 had been killed and 13 wounded. Sixteen, who had not heard the order to retreat, were missing, left in the timber below. The Arikara scouts had vanished.

Thus, for sound reasons or not, both Benteen and Reno helped pronounce the death sentence on Custer and his five companies. Benteen did not hurry forward to join Custer as ordered but instead threw in with Reno, to whom, as senior officer, fell further responsibility. Reno, by abandoning his valley position, freed the warriors defending the village to meet the new threat downstream. Leaving Reno, they now concentrated their entire strength on Custer.

Under the Hunkpapa chief Gall, warriors confronted Captain Yates at the mouth of Medicine Tail Coulee. As his two companies fell back up Deep Coulee, fighting a rearguard action, large numbers of Indians streamed across the Little Big Horn. Some pressed Yates while others veered up Medicine Tail against Keogh's three companies, strongly posted on the heights where they awaited Benteen. Well-directed volley fire easily kept these attackers at bay, but the prospect of the two battalions becoming cut off from each other prompted a fighting retreat north across the divide between the two coulees. The two commands united on the flat southern nose of a northward trending height since called Battle Ridge.

Here on Calhoun Hill, named for his brother-in-law, the commander of L Company, Custer beheld growing numbers of Indians gathering in his rear and, to his left front, others pouring across the Little Big Horn to meet his advance. To counter these, he flung out Captain Tom Custer's C Company in an offensive left oblique, but the Indians drove the unit back. Along the ridgeline the command made its way, L Company holding Calhoun Hill against the warriors moving up its southern face.

In addition to the swarms in Custer's rear and on his left flank, another large force, under the Oglala chief Crazy Horse, crossed the Little Big Horn below the village and swung in a wide arc up the slope at the northern point of Battle Ridge. This move, completing the encirclement of Battle Ridge, doomed Custer. Calhoun and his men died defending Calhoun Hill. Keogh and I Company fell in clusters in a shallow ravine east of Battle Ridge, victims of Crazy Horse's rolling assault. Remnants of all the companies gathered with Custer at the northern end of the ridge—Custer Hill. They shot their horses, formed a rough circular barricade, and fought to the last. Near the end, some of Companies C and E broke for the river but were cut to pieces at the foot of Custer Hill. In less than one hour after the first shot at the mouth of Medicine Tail, every trooper of Custer's command lay dead or wounded on the grassy slopes of Battle Ridge. Those not killed outright fell victim to the knives and hatchets of the women who thronged the field in search of plunder while the men turned to other matters.[10]

Where was Custer? the traumatized soldiers on Reno Hill asked. The sound of the volleys Keogh fired from his position above Medicine Tail gave a clue, but neither Reno nor Benteen made a move in the direction of the firing. Captain Thomas B. Weir did, and his company followed without orders. Hesitantly, Reno brought the other companies out on Weir's trail. From a high hill now named Weir Point, the troopers saw the final stages of the fighting on Battle Ridge, though so shrouded in dust and smoke as to obscure all detail. Hit by warriors returning from the Custer field, the surviving companies fought a rearguard action back to Reno Hill.

Surrounded, the seven companies held off the Sioux and Cheyennes until dusk brought relief. During the night the officers established a defense perimeter, enclosing a saucer-shaped depression in which the hospital and pack train were placed. Soldiers scooped out shallow pits to shelter themselves during the next day's battle.

At first light, a single rifle shot signaled renewed fighting. Throughout the day Indians and soldiers exchanged fire. Warriors pressed Benteen's sector so closely that he led a counterattack. The same occurred on the sector held by Reno, who also led a counterattack. Thirst tormented the wounded, and volunteer water parties made their way under fire down a steep ravine to the river. Men suffered and died, displayed heroism and cowardice, and held their hill through a long, scorching day.

Late in the afternoon the Indians pulled back. A wall of smoke rose from the valley, hiding the village. At dusk a great procession of Sioux and Cheyennes emerged from behind the smoke and crawled off to the southwest, leaving the exhausted soldiers to wonder what would happen next. Throughout the night of June 26 they waited. Details descended to the river for water. Reno's missing, who had spent a terrifying night and day hiding in the timber, found their way into his lines on the hilltop.

The next morning the reason for the Indians' exodus materialized in the blue column of Colonel Gibbon, marching up the valley to the village site. His Crow scouts, probing the east side of the river, discovered the stripped and mutilated bodies of Custer and his men and brought word of the tragedy to their comrades. The scouts had found no living man or beast on the bloody field. Later, Captain Keogh's horse, Comanche, near death from many wounds, would be discovered and nursed back to health to become the only military survivor of the catastrophe.

The Sioux and Cheyennes had won a stunning victory, the greatest in all the history of conflict between whites and the Indians of the Great Plains. All five of Custer's companies, 225 men, had perished. Reno and Benteen had lost 53 killed and 60 wounded. How many Indians paid with their lives will never be known; estimates range from 30 to 300.

Although the Indians won the battle, they lost the war. An outraged nation demanded vengeance. Reinforcements poured into the Sioux country. Within a year, most of the nontreaties had surrendered. Sitting Bull and a small following found sanctuary in Canada, but they too gave up in 1881. With the unceded territory no longer harboring troublemakers, the government could now dictate a final resolution of the Black Hills controversy. The Sioux sold. No portions of the tribes retained their independence. All submitted to the reservation.

For Indians and whites alike, however, the Little Big Horn remained a vibrant memory. Long after the last old warrior passed away, the Sioux and the Cheyennes would recall with pride and satisfaction the day they had rubbed out Long Hair. And for the white people, nagging questions of how and why would dog the memory of Custer, Reno, Benteen, and the men they had led. Endless deliberation and controversy will forever swirl around the battle called simply Custer's Last Stand.

Little Big Horn is embedded for all time in the history and folklore of the two peoples.

Notes

1. The standard biography is Stanley Vestal, *Sitting Bull: Champion of the Sioux* (Norman: University of Oklahoma Press, 1957). The Treaty of 1868 and its aftermath is the subject of a voluminous literature, but an authoritative account, based on Indian and white sources, is James C. Olson, *Red*

Cloud and the Sioux Problem (Lincoln: University of Nebraska Press, 1965).

2. Besides Custer's own "Battling with the Sioux on the Yellowstone," reprinted in this volume, see Charles Braden, "The Yellowstone Expedition of 1873," *Journal of the U.S. Cavalry Association* 16 (October 1905): 218–41. A recent history, including much original material, is Lawrence A. Frost, *Custer's Seventh Cav and the Campaign of 1873* (El Segundo, Calif.: Upton and Sons, 1986). I deal with Custer's further service to the Northern Pacific in *Cavalier in Buckskin: George Armstrong Custer and the Western Military Frontier* (Norman: University of Oklahoma Press, 1988), 103–27.

3. For the Black Hills expedition and its aftermath, see Donald Jackson, *Custer's Gold: The United States Cavalry Expedition of 1874* (New Haven: Yale University Press, 1966); Watson Parker, *Gold in the Black Hills* (Lincoln: University of Nebraska Press, 1982); and Herbert Krause and Gary D. Olson, *Prelude to Glory: A Newspaper Accounting of Custer's 1874 Expedition to the Black Hills* (Sioux Falls, S.D.: Brevet Press, 1974). The attempt to buy the Black Hills is set forth in Olson, *Red Cloud and the Sioux Problem*, chap. 11.

4. For a revealing debate over the motives for the war, see Mark H. Brown, "Muddled Men Have Muddied the Yellowstone's True Colors," *Montana the Magazine of Western History* 11 (January 1961): 28–37, and Harry H. Anderson, "A Challenge to Brown's

Sioux Indian Wars Thesis," ibid. 12 (January 1962): 40–49.

5. Mountains of commentary deal with the campaign of 1876 and the Battle of the Little Big Horn. Long standard has been Edgar I. Stewart, *Custer's Luck* (Norman: University of Oklahoma Press, 1955). However, by all measures the best synthesis is John S. Gray, *Centennial Campaign: The Sioux War of 1876* (Fort Collins, Colo.: Old Army Press, 1976). Important too are W. A. Graham, *The Story of the Little Big Horn* (1926; reprint, Harrisburg, Pa.: Military Service Publishing Co., 1945), reprinted as a Bison Book by the University of Nebraska Press in 1988, and W. A. Graham, *The Custer Myth: A Source Book of Custeriana* (Harrisburg, Pa.: Stackpole Co., 1953), reprinted as a Bison Book by the University of Nebraska Press in 1986. Official documents are reprinted in John M. Carroll, ed., *General Custer and the Battle of the Little Big Horn: The Federal View* (Bryan, Tex.: J. M. Carroll Co., 1986). A day-by-day account is James Willert, *Little Big Horn Diary: Chronicle of the 1876 Indian War* (La Mirada, Calif.: N.p., 1977).

6. An authoritative and balanced treatment of Custer's political troubles is Gray, *Centennial Campaign*, chap. 6. Though highly partisan, another illuminating account, quoting liberally from official records, is Robert P. Hughes (General Terry's aide), "The Campaign against the Sioux in 1876," *Journal of the Military Service Institution of the United States* 18 (1896), reprinted in

Graham, *Story of the Little Big Horn*.

7. The movements of Gibbon's column, and especially the activities of his scouts, are well documented in the diary of his scout commander: "Journal of James H. Bradley: The Sioux Campaign of 1876 under Command of General John Gibbon," *Montana Historical Society Contributions* 2 (1896): 302–13.

8. Amid the mountains of literature dissecting the Battle of the Little Big Horn, the analysis that stands above all others is Gray, *Centennial Campaign*, chaps. 13–16. My construction directly reflects Gray's. Accounts of participants, both white and Indian, are in Graham, *Custer Myth*, and Kenneth Hammer, ed., *Custer in '76: Walter Camp's Notes on the Custer Fight* (Provo, Utah: Brigham Young University Press, 1976). Indispensable is the testimony of whites elicited in 1879 in the official inquiry into Major Reno's conduct in the battle: *The Reno Court of Inquiry: The Chicago Times Account* (Fort Collins, Colo.: Old Army Press, 1972). My own most recent thinking is set forth in greater detail in *Cavalier in Buckskin*, chaps. 8–9, and in *Custer Battlefield: A History and Guide to the Battle of the Little Bighorn*, National Park Service Handbook no. 132 (Washington, D.C.: Government Printing Office, 1988).

9. The action in this quarter is ably analyzed and intelligently speculated in Jerome A. Greene, *Evidence and the Custer Enigma: A Reconstruction of Indian-Military History* (Kansas City: Kansas City Posse of the Westerners, 1973), and Richard G. Hardorff, *Markers, Artifacts, and Indian Testimony: Preliminary Findings on the Custer Battle* (Short Hills, N.J.: W. Donald Horn, Publisher, 1985).

10. There have been many attempts to reconstruct the action on Battle Ridge. The above represents my own reading of the evidence but in general reflects the most recent thinking. The evidence, dauntingly voluminous, falls into two main categories. First are the tangible remains on the field: (1) the placement of the bodies as described by the men who buried them and as now roughly represented by white marble headstones; (2) the pattern of firing positions and targets as developed through forty years of mapping the location of expended cartridge cases and spent bullets recovered through random discoveries and systematic surveys, of which the archaeological work of 1984–85 represents the most recent. Second is the testimony of Indian participants. Because of barriers of language and culture, this is extremely difficult to use. By selective culling from the huge number of Indian accounts, one may find eyewitness evidence to support almost any reconstruction. Because the evidence can be read in so many ways, speculation and debate over what happened along Battle Ridge is unlikely ever to subside.

CUSTER'S LAST BATTLE

EDWARD S.
GODFREY

Foreword

Although it happened a generation ago, the public interest in Custer's last battle seems to continue unabated. When in the field it was my custom to keep a diary of events, etc. This sometimes was made in the form of a letter to my family, in which case, only the more important military events were noted in my book. After the battle of the Little Big Horn, I made notes of some of the stories, anecdotes, etc., told by comrades.

In 1879 my brother officers at West Point asked me to write a paper on the subject to be read at the Lyceum. With the aid of my diary, letters, notes and with events fresh in my mind, I wrote up a very sizable pile of manuscripts. I then cut out much that I know now would be of quite general interest. The rejected material, together with notes and some letters were destroyed. This destruction has been regretted many times since, as much of it [bore]* on subjects of controversy as to the campaign and the conduct of individuals.

In 1886 I was enabled to get former hostile Indians to talk to me of the battle. The account given me by Mrs. "Spotted Horn Bull" and her husband was by all odds the most circumstantial, comprehensive and straightforward, particularly her relation to that part of the battle that resulted in the annihilation of General Custer's Command. I told her I wanted only the facts and as they occurred: I have every reason

*The brackets in this article indicate the hand corrections of General Godfrey to his record copy of *Custer's Last Battle.*

to believe that she and her husband told the truth as they knew it. We had a map of the field before us and I took notes of her narrative. Then I got Chief Gall's story on the field and afterward in garrison through interpreters. The material facts were given as related in the text and agreed substantially with the story of Spotted Horn Bull and wife. In the light of these new facts the version of the fight of Custer's immediate command was rewritten.

"Custer's Last Battle" was first published in the Century Magazine, January, 1892, and its [cordial] reception by public and particularly by my comrades, who were fellow-participants in the battle, has induced me to publish it with added material, and again submit it to the public.

1908   E. S. GODFREY

On the 16th of April, 1876, at McComb City, [Mississippi], I received orders to report my troop ("K" 7th Cavalry) to the Commanding General of the Department of Dakota, at St. Paul, Minnesota. At the latter place about twenty-five recruits fresh from civil life joined the troop, and we were ordered to proceed to Fort Abraham Lincoln, Dakota, where the Yellowstone Expedition was being organized. This expedition consisted of the 7th United States Cavalry, commanded by General George A. Custer, 28 officers and about 700 men; two companies of the 17th United States Infantry, and one company of the 6th United States Infantry, 8 officers and 135 men; one platoon of Gatling guns, 2 officers and 32 men (of the 20th United States Infantry); and 40 "Ree" Indian scouts. The expeditionary forces were commanded by Brigadier-General Alfred H. Terry, the Department Commander, who, with his staff arrived several days prior to our departure.

On the 17th of May, at 5 a.m., the "general" (The signal to take down tents and break camp.) was sounded, the wagons were packed and sent to the Quartermaster, and by six o'clock the wagon-train was on the road escorted by the Infantry. By seven o'clock the 7th Cavalry was marching in column of platoon around the parade-ground of Fort Lincoln, headed by the band playing "Garry Owen," the Seventh's battle tune, first used when the regiment charged at the battle of Washita. The column was halted and dismounted just outside the garrison. The officers and married men were permitted to leave the ranks to say "good-bye" to their families. General Terry, knowing the anxiety of the ladies, had assented to, or ordered, this demonstration in order to allay their fears and satisfy them, by the formidable appearance we made, that we were able to cope with any enemy that we might expect to meet. Not many came out to witness the pageant, but many tear-filled eyes looked from the latticed windows.

During this halt the wagon-train was assembled on the plateau west of the post and formed in column of fours. When it started off the "assembly" was sounded and absentees joined their commands. The signals "mount" and "forward" were sounded and the regiment marched away, the band playing "The Girl I Left Behind Me."

The 7th Cavalry was divided into two columns, designated right and left wings, commanded by Major Marcus A. Reno and Captain F. Benteen. Each wing was sub-divided into two battalions of three troops each. After the first day the following was the habitual order of march: one battalion was advance guard, one was rear guard, and one marched on each flank of the train. General Custer with one troop of the advance guard, went ahead and selected the route for the train and the camping places at the end of the day's march. The other two troops of the advance guard reported at headquarters for pioneer or fatigue duty, to build bridges and creek crossings. The rear guard kept behind everything; when it came up to a wagon stalled in the mire, it helped to put the wagon forward. The battalions on the flanks were kept within five hundred yards of the trail and not to get more than half a mile in advance or rear of the train, and to avoid dismounting any oftener than necessary. The march was conducted as follows: One troop marched until about half a mile in advance of the train, when it was dismounted, the horses unbitted and allowed to graze until the train had passed and was about half a mile in advance of it, when it took up the march again; each of the other two troops would conduct their march in the same manner, so that two troops on each flank would be marching alongside the train at all times. If the country was much broken, a half dozen flankers were thrown out to guard against surprise. The flankers regulated their march so as to keep abreast of their troops. The pack animals and beef herd were driven alongside the train by the packers and herders.

One wagon was assigned to each troop, and transported five days' rations and forage and the mess kit of the troop; also the mess kit, tents, and baggage of the troop officers and ten days' supplies for the officers' mess. The men were armed with the carbine and revolver; no one, not even the officer of the day, carried the sabre. Each troop horse carried, in addition to the rider, between eighty and ninety pounds. This additional weight included all equipments and about one hundred rounds of ammunition, fifty in the belt and fifty in saddlebags.

The wagon-train consisted in all of about one hundred and fifty wheeled vehicles. In it were carried thirty days' supplies of forage and rations (excepting beef), and two hundred rounds of ammunition per man. The two-horse wagons, hired by contract, carried from fifteen hundred to two thousand pounds. The six-mule government wagons carried from three to five thousand pounds, depending on the size and condition of the mules. The Gatling guns were each hauled by four condemned cavalry horses and marched in advance of the train. Two light wagons loaded with axes, shovels, pick-axes and some pine boards and scantling, sufficient for a short bridge, accompanied the "pioneer" troops. The "crossings" as they are termed, were often very tedious and would frequently delay the train several hours. During this time, the cavalry horses were unbitted and grazed, the men holding the reins. Those men not on duty at the crossing slept, or collected in groups to spin yarns and take a whiff at their "dingy dudeens." The officers usually collected near the crossing to watch progress, and passed the time in conversation and playing practical jokes. About noon the "strikers" who carried the haversacks, were called, and the different messes had their luncheon, sometimes separately, sometimes clubbing together. When the haversacks were opened the horses usually stopped grazing and put their noses near their riders' faces and asked very plainly to share their hardtack. If their polite request did not receive attention they would paw the ground, or even strike their riders. The old soldier was generally willing to share with his beast.

The length of the day's march, varying from ten to forty miles, was determined in a great measure by the difficulties or obstacles encountered, by wood, water and grass, and by the distance in advance where such advantages were likely to be found. If, about two or three o'clock in the afternoon, a column of smoke was seen in the direction of the trail and a mile or two in advance, it was a pretty sure indication that a camp had been selected. The cavalry, excepting the rear guard, would then cut loose from the train and go directly to camp. The rear guard would send details to collect fuel and unpack their wagons. The adjutant showed the wing commanders the general direction their lines or tents were to run, and the latter then directed the battalion or troop commanders to their camping places. Generally, one flank of each line would rest near the creek. The general form of the command was that of a parallelogram. The wings camped on the long sides facing each other, and the headquarters and guard were located at one end nearest the creek. The wagon train was packed to close the other end and was guarded by the infantry battalion. The troops, as they arrived at their places were formed in line, facing inward, dismounted, unsaddled, and, if the weather was hot and the sun shining, the men rubbed the horses' backs until dry. After this the horses were sent to water and put out to graze, with side-lines and lariats, under charge of the stable guard, consisting of one non-commissioned officer and three or six privates. The men of the troop then collected fuel, sometimes wood, often a mile or more distant from the camp; sometimes "buffalo chips." The main guard, or camp guard, consisting usually of four or five non-commissioned officers and twelve or fifteen privates, reported mounted at headquarters, and were directed to take posts on prominent points overlooking the camp and surrounding country, to guard against surprise. Each post consisted of one non-commissioned officer and three privates. The officer of the day, in addition to his ordinary duties in camp, had charge of the safety of the cavalry herds. Sometimes this latter duty was performed by an officer designated as "Officer of the Herd." To preserve the grazing in the immediate vicinity of the camp for evening and night grazing, all horses were required to be outside of the camp limits until retreat. When the train arrived, the headquarters and troop wagons went directly to the camping-place of their respective commands. The officers' baggage and tents were unloaded first; then the wagons went near the place where the troop kitchen was to be located, always on that flank of the troop farthest from headquarters. The teamsters unharnessed their mules and put them out to graze. The old stable guard reported to the troop commander for fatigue duty to put up the officers' tents and collect fuel for their mess. The troop officers' tents were usually placed twenty-five yards in rear of the line of men's tents and facing toward them. Their cook or mess tent was placed about ten or fifteen yards further to the rear. The "striker" made down the beds and arranged the "furniture," so to speak, which generally consisted of a camp-stool, tin washbasin, and a looking glass. The men put up their tents soon after caring for their horses. The fronts of their tents were placed on a line established by stretching a picket rope. The first sergeant's was on that flank of the line nearest to the headquarters. The horse equipments were placed on a line three yards in front of the tents. The men were not prohibited from using their saddles as pillows. A trench was dug for the mess fire, and the grass was burned around it for several yards to prevent prairie fires. After this the cooks busied themselves preparing supper. Beef was issued soon after the wagon train came in, and the necessary number of beeves were butchered for the next day's issue; this was hauled in the wagons. Stable call was sounded about an hour before sunset. The men of each troop were formed on the parade and marched to the horse herds by the first sergeant. Each man went to his own horse, took off the sidelines and fastened them around the horse's neck, then pulled the picket pin, coiled the lariat, noosed the end fastened to the head halter around the horse's muzzle, mounted, and assembled in line at a place indicated by the first sergeant. The troop was then marched to the watering place, which was usually selected with great care because of the boggy banks and miry beds of the prairie streams. After watering, the horses were lariated outside the vicinity of the camp. The ground directly in the rear of the troop belonged to it, and was jealously guarded by those concerned against encroachment by others. After lariating their horses, the men got their curry-combs, brushes, and nose-bags and went to the troop wagon where the quartermaster sergeant and farrier measured, with tin cups, the forage to each man, each watching jealously that he got as much for his horse as those before him. He then went at once to feed and groom his horse. The officer whose duty it was to attend stables and the first sergeant superintended the grooming, examining each horse's back and feet carefully to see if they were all right. When a horse's back got sore, through the carelessness of the rider, the man would generally be compelled to lead his horse until the sore was well. Immediately after stables, the cooks announced in a loud tone "Supper!" The men with haversack and tincup went to the mess fire and got their hardtack, meat, and coffee. If game had been killed the men did a little extra cooking themselves.

The troop officers' mess kits consisted of a sheet-iron cooking stove, an iron kettle, stewing, frying, baking, and dish pans; a small Dutch oven, a camp-kettle, a mess-chest holding tablewear for four persons, and a small folding table. The table in fair weather was spread in the open air. The early part of the meal was a matter of business, but after the substantials were stowed away, the delicacies were eaten more leisurely and time found for conversation. After supper the pipes were lighted, and the officers, if the weather was cold, went to the windward side of the camp fire. Each man, as he took his place, was sure to poke or kick the fire, turn his back, hitch up his coat tail, and fold his hands behind him.

Retreat was sounded a little after sunset and the roll was called, as much to insure the men having their equipments in place as to secure their presence, for it was not often we were near enough to any attraction to call the men away. (In 1876 there was not a ranch west of Bismarck, Dakota, nor east of Bozeman, Montana.) The stable guards began their tours of duty at this time. The non-commissioned officers reported to the troop commander for instructions for the night; these usually designated whether the horses were to be tied to the picket line or kept out to graze, and included special instructions for the care of sick or weak horses. At dusk all horses were brought within the limits of the camp. The picket-line was stretched over three wagons in front of the men's tents, or three posts were used when remaining in camp over a day.

During the evening, the men grouped about the fires and sang songs and spun yarns until "taps." The cooks prepared breakfast, which usually consisted of hard bread, bacon and coffee. If beans or fresh meat were to be cooked, the food was put into the Dutch ovens or camp-kettles, which were placed in the fire trench, covered over with hot ashes and coals, and a fire was built over them. If the wind blew hard all fires were extinguished, to prevent prairie fires. The cooks were called an hour or an hour and a half before reveille. At the first call for reveille, usually 4:20 a.m., the stable guard awakened the occupants of each tent and the officer whose duty it was to attend the roll-call. Stable call followed reveille and was superintended by an officer. This occupied about three-quarters of an hour. Two hours after reveille, the command would be on the march. Of course, there were incidents that occasionally relieved the monotony.

Antelope were plentiful, and the men were encouraged by troop commanders to hunt. General Custer had a number of stag-hounds, which amused themselves and the command in their futile attempts to catch them. One morning they started up a large buck near where the column was marching; Lieutenant Hare immediately followed the hounds, passed them, drew his revolver, and shot the buck. Nothing of special interest occurred until the 27th of May, when we came to the Bad Lands of the Little Missouri River. On the 30th, General Custer was sent with four troops to make a scout up the Little Missouri, for about twenty miles. He returned the same day, without having discovered any recent "Indian signs." On the 31st we crossed the Little Missouri without difficulty. On the 1st and 2nd of June we were obliged to remain in camp on account of a snow-storm.

We remained in camp on the Powder River for three days. General Terry went to the Yellowstone to communicate with the supply steamer *Far West*, which was at the mouth of the Powder River. He also went up the Yellowstone to communicate with General Gibbon's command, known as the "Montana Column," composed of four troops of the 2nd Cavalry and several companies of the 7th Infantry. Before General Terry left it was given out that the 7th Cavalry would be sent to scout up the Powder River, while the wagon-train, escorted by the infantry, would be sent to establish a supply camp at the mouth of the Powder.

Eleven pack-mules, saddle and aparejos, were issued to each troop for this scout. This was a new departure; neither officers, men nor mules had had any experience with this method of transportation. There were a few "packers" (civilian employees) to give instructions. Short, compactly built mules, the best for the purpose, were selected from the teams. A non-commissioned officer and four men of each troop were detailed for packers. After some instruction had been given by the professionals, especially how to tie the "diamond hitch," we concluded to make our maiden attempt by packing two empty water casks. The mule was blinded and he submitted, with some uneasiness, to the packing. We supposed the packs were securely fastened and did not anticipate any trouble; but it is always the unexpected that happens with a mule. The blind was lifted, the mule gave a startled look first to one side, then to the other, at the two casks bandaged to his sides. He jumped to one side causing to rattle a bung-plug that had fallen inside one of the casks. This startled him still more, and with head and tail high in the air he jumped again. He snorted and brayed, bucked and kicked until the casks fell off. One was fastened to the saddle by the sling-rope. He now began to run, braying and making such a "rumpus" that the camp turned out as spectators. The affair excited serious concern lest all the animals in the camp would be stampeded. When the cask was loosed we got him back and made a second attempt with two sacks of grain. These he soon bucked off and then regaled himself with the spilt grain. As a final effort, we concluded to try the aparejo, and pack two boxes of ammunition. This done, the mule walked off with as little concern as if he had been a pack-mule all his life. The pack saddles were usually of the "saw-buck" variety. The "aparejo" or Spanish pack saddle is made of heavy sole leather; it is double except about twelve inches in the center thus making two pockets, not unlike a pair of huge saddle bags. General Terry, having returned, orders were issued on the tenth for the right wing, six troops under Major Reno, to make a scout up the Powder, provided with twelve days' rations.

The left wing was ordered to turn over all forage and rations; also the pack-mules, except four to each troop. Major Reno left at 3 p.m., and the next day the rest of the command marched to the mouth of the Powder. My troop was rearguard, and at times we were over three miles in rear of the wagon-train waiting on the packets, for we had taken this opportunity to give them practical instruction.

Up to this time we had not seen an Indian, nor any recent signs of them, except one small trail of perhaps a half-dozen tepees, evidently of a party of agency Indians on their way to join the hostile camp. The buffalo had all gone west; other game was scarce and wild. The indications were that the Indians were west of the Powder, and information from General Gibbon placed them south of the Yellowstone. Some of the officers of the right wing before they left expressed their belief that we would not find any Indians, and were sanguine that we would all get home by the middle of August.

Major Reno was ordered to scout to the forks of the Powder, then across to Mizpah Creek, follow it down to near its confluence with the Powder; then cross over to Pumpkin Creek, follow it down to the Tongue River, scout up that stream and then rejoin the regiment at the mouth of the Tongue by the time his supplies were exhausted; unless, in the meantime, he should make some discovery that made it necessary to return sooner to make preparations for a pursuit. A supply depot was established at the mouth of the Powder, guarded by the infantry, at which the wagon-train was left.

General Terry, with his staff and some supplies, took passage on the supply steamer *Far West*, and went up to the mouth of the Tongue. General Custer with the left wing, marched to the mouth of the Tongue, where we remained until the 19th waiting tidings from Reno's scout. The grounds where we camped had been occupied by the Indians the previous winter. (Miles City, Montana, was first built on the site of this camp.) The rude shelters for their ponies, built of driftwood, were still standing and furnished fuel for our camp fires. A number of their dead, placed upon scaffolds or tied to the branches of trees, were disturbed and robbed of their trinkets. Several persons rode about exhibiting their trinkets with as much gusto as if they were trophies of their valor, and showed no more concern for their desecration than if they had won them at a raffle. Ten days later I saw the bodies of these same persons dead, naked, and mutilated.

On the 19th of June tidings came from Reno that he had found a large trail that led up the Rosebud River. The particulars were not generally known. The camp was full of rumors; credulity was raised to the highest pitch, and we were filled with anxiety and curiosity until we reached Reno's command, and learned the details of their discoveries. They had found a large trail on the Tongue River, and had followed it up the Rosebud about forty miles. The number of lodges in the deserted villages was estimated by the number of campfires remaining to be about three hundred and fifty. The indications were that the trail was about three weeks old. No Indians had been seen nor any recent signs. It is not probable that Reno's movements were known to the Indians, for on the very day Reno reached his farthest point up the Rosebud, the battle of the Rosebud, between General Crook's forces and the Indians, was fought. The two commands were then not more than forty miles apart, but neither knew nor even suspected the proximity of the other. We reached the mouth of the Rosebud about noon of the 21st and began preparations for the march, and for the expected battle or pursuit.

The "Black Hills of Dakota," so called in contradistinction from the "Black Hills of Wyoming," was regarded as the Indian "watering" place, where they would go for camping and hunting in small parties. To all white men it was a land of mystery. Reynolds and Warren of the U.S. Topographical Engineers had explored around them, but the Indians were jealous of any white men entering the interior. Not infrequently they would pay traders for supplies in gold nuggets, but never would they tell where these nuggets were found. Whenever attempts were made to "pump" the Indians about the Black Hills country they would maintain a mysterious silence; naturally this mystery excited great curiosity. Stories and traditions of fabulous wealth there hidden were bandied about among the frontiersmen, but none had dared to go there.

In 1874 General Custer had asked permission to make an exploration of this region. General Sheridan granted authority, but limited the period of absence from the regular stations to sixty days, and with the understanding that only the military, the necessary employees, and a few selected scientists and several newspaper correspondents should go with the expedition. The proposed expedition created intense excitement in the Northwest, and there were applications by the hundreds from all over the country. Miners, adventurers and men looking for business opportunities flocked to Bismarck, then the terminus of the Northern Pacific Railroad. We had a large wagon train and a number of this crowd were hired as teamsters and herders for our cattle.

The expedition left Fort Abraham Lincoln July 2d and returned August 31. At one camp near where Custer City is now located the miners reported "color." From this camp we turned north for our return journey. As we left Charlie Reynolds, a noted scout and frontiersman, was sent with dispatches to General Sheridan in which General Custer announced that gold had been found "from the grass roots down." So when we returned to the Missouri River there were crowds waiting to receive confirmations of the "find." Immediate plans were made to rush the country and there followed an immense immigration. The Indians were very angry and demanded the eviction of the trespassers on their reservation. Efforts were made to arrest the rush but to no avail. Trains, stages and stations were attacked, captured and destroyed and of course all barbarities were blamed on the Indians. The Indian agents insisted that the outrages were committed by the hostile Indians and renegade whites posing as Indians.

The Hostiles

There were a number of Sioux Indians who never went to an agency except to visit friends and relatives and to barter. They camped in and roamed about the buffalo country. Their camp was the rendezvous for the agency Indians when they went out for their annual hunts for meats and robes. They were known as the "Hostiles," and comprised representatives from all the different tribes of the Sioux nation. Many of them were renegade outlaws from the agencies. In their visits to the agencies they were usually arrogant and fomenters of discord. Depredations had been made upon the commerce to the Black Hills, and a number of lives taken by them or by others, for which they were blamed. The authorities at Washington had determined to compel these Indians to reside at the agencies—hence the Sioux War.

Major James McLaughlin, United States Indian Agent, stationed at the Devil's Lake Agency, Dakota, from 1870 to 1881, and at Standing Rock Agency, Dakota, from 1881 to 1895, and to the present time Inspector in the Bureau of Indian Affairs, has made it a point to get estimates of the number of Indians at the hostile camp at the time of the battle. In his opinion, and all who know him will accept it with confidence, about one-third of the whole Sioux nation, including the northern Cheyennes and Arapahoes, were present at the battle; he estimated the number present as between twelve and fifteen thousand; that one out of four is a low estimate in determining the number of warriors present; every male over fourteen years of age may be considered a warrior in a general fight, such as was the battle of the Little Big Horn; also considering the extra hazards of the hunt and expected battle, fewer squaws would accompany the recruits from the agencies. The minimum strength of their fighting men may then be put down as between twenty-five hundred and three thousand. [Crazy Horse stated afterwards when he surrendered to General Crook at the agency that he had no less than 6500 men in the fight.] Information was despatched from General Sheridan that from the agencies about 1800 lodges had set out to join the hostile camp; but that information did not reach General Terry until several days after the battle. [July 14th.] The principal warrior chiefs of the hostile Indians were "Gall," "Crow King" and "Black Moon," Huncpapa Sioux; "Low Dog," "Crazy Horse" and "Big Road," Ogallala Sioux; "Spotted Eagle," Sans-Arc Sioux; "Hump" of the Minneconjous; and "White Bull" and "Little Horse" of the Cheyennes. To these belong the chief honors of conducting the battle. However, "Gall," "Crow King" and "Crazy Horse" were the ruling spirits. [June 8th despatches were received by General Crook notifying him that all able-bodied male Indians had left the Red Cloud Agency.]

Sitting Bull

"Sitting Bull," a Huncpapa Sioux Indian, was the chief of the hostile camp; he had about sixty lodges of followers on whom he could at all times depend. He was the host of the Hostiles, and as such received and entertained their visitors. These visitors gave him many presents, and he was thus enabled to make many presents, in return. All visitors paid tribute to him, so he gave liberally to the most influential, the chiefs, *i.e.* he "put it where it would do the most good." In this way he became known as the chief of the hostile camp, and the camp was generally known as "Sitting Bull's camp" or "outfit." Sitting Bull was a heavy set, muscular man, about five feet eight inches in stature, and at the time of the battle of the Little Big Horn was forty-two years of age. He was the autocrat of the camp—chiefly because he was the host. In council his views had great weight, because he was known as a great medicine man. He was a chief, but not a warrior chief. In the war councils he had a voice and vote the same as any other chief. A short time previous to the battle he had "made medicine" and had predicted that the soldiers would attack them and that the soldiers would all be killed. He took no active part in the battle, but, as was his custom in time of danger, remained in the village "making medicine." Personally, he was regarded by the Agency Indians as a great coward and a very great liar, "a man with a big head and a little heart."

The War Chief, Gall

Chief Gall was born about 1840, of Huncpapa parents. Until Sitting Bull's surrender, 1881, Gall never lived at the agencies, but was sometimes a guest. When 25 years old he was noted for his bravery and daring. He was so subtle, crafty and daring, that in [1866] the military authorities offered a reward for his body, dead or alive; an outrage had been committed, which for daring and craftiness, it was thought no other Indian was gifted. However, he was innocent. Gall knew of the price laid on his carcass and kept away from the military. At Fort Berthold, while visiting friends at the Agency, his visit was made known to the commanding officer at Fort Stevenson, a few miles away. A detachment was sent to the tepee where he was visiting, to arrest him. On their entrance Gall dropped on his belly and pushed himself backward under the tepee. A soldier on the outside bayonetted him through the body and held him till he fainted. The soldiers supposed him to be dead, and so reported to their commander. They were sent back with transportation to get the body. Great was their astonishment to find that Gall had recovered consciousness and crawled away. The men searched faithfully the woods in which Gall had concealed himself, but he was not discovered. Gall then got back to his people and vowed vengeance. He had it in many a foray and numbers of battles. He lurked about the military posts and pounced on luckless promenadors, even at the very gates of the stockade that enclosed the barracks and quarters. He raided settlements and attacked Black Hill stages and freighters. He it was who followed the "Boseman (sic.) Expedition" about 1874, for days, when they were searching for gold, compelling them at all times to be in readiness for battle. One of their intrenchments may yet be seen on the divide between the Rosebud and Little Big Horn at the head of [North Fork of Reno Creek].

In 1872 he led his braves in a raiding attack on the 2nd Cavalry at "Baker's Battlefield" on the Yellowstone, which by reason of its surprise, came near proving a disaster, as Indians rarely made night attacks. August 4th, 1873 General Custer had gone into bivouac on the north bank of the Yellowstone, just above Fort Keogh, waiting for the main command under General Stanley. The two troops had unsaddled and were resting in the supposed security afforded by the absence of fresh "Indian signs," while Gall made his dispositions for attack. His warriors crawled through woods, down ravines and under the river bank to within 300 yards when an alarm called to arms and a lively battle was kept up until the arrival of troops from the main command which had heard and seen the firing from the mesa several miles away. A week later Gall made an attack on the 7th Cavalry at the head of "Pease Bottom," a few miles below the mouth of the Big Horn. In this fight Gall, dressed in brilliant scarlet and war bonnet, rode back and forth in front of the firing line, the target of hundreds of shots, but escaped unharmed. He was the Great War Chief of all the Sioux at "Custer's Last Battle." In 1877 he went with Sitting Bull to Canada, and in 1881 surrendered at Popular [*sic*] Creek, Montana. The band was taken into Standing Rock Agency, 1882, by steamboat. The boat was met by a great throng of people; the military, settlers and employees and Indians of that Agency were at the landing. When the boat tied up, Gall, in full war paint and regalia ostentatiously walked down the gang plank, halted and surveyed the surroundings. His old mother ran to him and tried to gain his notice; she got on her knees, clasped him about his legs, took hold of and kissed his hand; she moaned and cried. Ignoring her caresses, he stalked dramatically aboard the boat. Later Gall became reconciled to agency life and was a good Indian; wise and conservative, he supported the Agent, Major James McLaughlin, in all his efforts for the good of the people. In the grand councils of all the Chiefs of the Sioux nation, he was the most influential and stood up for what he considered the just rights of his people. He died at Oak Creek, near Standing Rock Agency, in 1895. His features were massive, and in facial appearance was compared to the great expounder, Webster, to Henry Ward Beecher and to Bishop Newman. He was a man of great natural ability, force of character and possessed great common sense.

The Sun Dance

The "Sun Dance" was a semi-religious festival where the young men of the tribes were transformed into warriors, knighted as it were. The Sun Dance lodge was the arena and was constructed of rough cut poles; the center pole, fifteen to twenty feet high, was firmly planted within the ground; a circular framework about thirty to forty feet in diameter was constructed around it, the whole tied together with raw hide thongs. It had no covering. Raw hide thongs fifteen to twenty feet long were tied to the center pole. Buffalo skulls were provided to which raw hide thongs were attached.

The warriors squatted in a circle around the arena, first the chiefs and elders, then the other warriors in rear of them; the squaws assembled standing in rear of the warriors; the tom-toms, the orchestra, as it were, were inside the circle near the opening for the neophytes. The neophytes assembled at the large council tent. When all was in readiness they emerged from the tent clothed only in the loin cloth or "gee string," and their bodies painted in all the hideousness that contrasted brilliant colors could give; some with half the body, from hair tip down, painted in green, the other half yellow or white; or, as the individual fancy could invent. They formed in column and proceeded in slow measured steps, chanting in weird, mournful, sing-song tones, to the arena; the tom-toms were beaten to the time of the chant; as they approached the squaws began in low muffled voices, their plaintive chanting; entering the arena the medicine men made incisions in the skin and flesh of the breast, back or other part of the body of the neophyte and tied one of the thongs fast. Frantic with pain he would dance and yell and plunge his bloody body to break away from this cruel tether that tied him to the frame-work, or from the additional torture of the tied buffalo head. They fasted for a period before and during the ordeal, all of which was to test the fortitude and courage; such as could pass through the test were received as warriors. Those who failed were branded as "squaws" and cowards and were doomed to the association of squaws and to celibacy. During the Sun Dance, the crowd feasted on dog soup—considered a great delicacy. This dance was a ceremony of great importance, and it compared in interest to the Indians with the graduation exercises of our civilized communities. One had taken place about June 5th on the Rosebud. In anticipation of it, the Agency Indians had here joined the Hostiles. We passed this Sun Dance lodge on June 24th, where we halted for a rest.

Preparations

On our arrival at the mouth of the Rosebud, Generals Terry, Gibbon and Custer had a conference on board the steamer *Far West*. It was decided that the 7th Cavalry, under General Custer, should follow the trail discovered by Reno. "Officers call" was sounded in the 7th Cavalry camp as soon as the conference had concluded. Upon assembling, General Custer gave us our orders. We were to transport, on our pack-mules, fifteen days' rations of hard bread, coffee and sugar; twelve days' rations of bacon, and fifty rounds of carbine ammunition per man. Each man was to be supplied with 100 rounds of carbine and 24 rounds of pistol ammunition, to be carried on his person and in his saddle bags. Each man was to carry on his horse twelve pounds of oats.

The pack-mules sent out with Reno's command were badly used up, and promised seriously to embarrass the expedition. General Custer recommended that some extra forage be carried on the pack-mules. In endeavoring to carry out this recommendation some troop commanders (Captain Moylan and myself) foresaw the difficulties, and told the general that some of the mules would certainly break down, especially if the extra forage was packed. He replied in an unusually emphatic manner, "Well, gentlemen, you may carry what supplies you please; you will be held responsible for your companies. The extra forage was only a suggestion, but this fact bear in mind, we will follow the trail for fifteen days unless we catch them before that time expires, no matter how far it may take us from our base of supplies; we may not see the supply steamer again;" and, turning as he was about to enter his tent, he added: "You had better carry along an extra supply of salt; we may have to live on horse meat before we get through." He was taken at his word, and an extra supply of salt was carried. "Battalion" and "wing" organizations were broken up, and troop commanders were responsible only to General Custer. Of course, as soon as it was determined that we were to go out, nearly every one took time to write letters home, but I doubt very much if there were many of a cheerful nature. Some officers made their wills; others gave verbal instructions as to the disposition of personal property and distribution of mementos; they seemed to have a presentiment of their fate.

Instructions

General Custer's written instructions were as follows:

Camp at Mouth of Rosebud River,
Montana Territory, June 22nd, 1876
Lieut.-Col. Custer, 7th Cavalry.
Colonel:

The Brigadier-General Commanding directs that, as soon as your regiment can be made ready for the march, you will proceed up the Rosebud in pursuit of the Indians whose trail was discovered by Major Reno a few days since. It is, of course, impossible to give you any definite instructions in regard to this movement, and were it not impossible to do so, the Department Commander places too much confidence in your zeal, energy, and ability to wish to impose upon you precise orders which might hamper your action when nearly in contact with the enemy. He will, however, indicate to you his own views of what your action should be, and he desires that you should conform to them unless you shall see sufficient reason for departing from them. He thinks that you should proceed up the Rosebud until you ascertain definitely the direction in which the trail above spoken of leads. Should it be found (as it appears almost certain that it will be found) to turn towards the Little Horn, he thinks that you should still proceed southward, perhaps as far as the headwaters of the Tongue, and then turn towards the Little Horn, feeling constantly, however, to your left, so as to preclude the possibility of the escape of the Indians to the south or southeast by passing around your left flank. The column of Colonel Gibbon is now in motion for the mouth of the Big Horn. As soon as it reaches that point it will cross the Yellowstone and move up at least as far as the forks of the Big and Little Horns. Of course its future movements must be controlled by circumstances as they arise, but it is hoped that the Indians, if upon the Little Horn, may be so nearly inclosed by the two columns that their escape will be impossible.

The Department Commander desires that on your way up the Rosebud you should thoroughly examine the upper part of the Tulloch's Creek (NOTE: On the morning of the 24th, some of the command were quite excited over what they thought were "Smoke puffs" as made by Indians when signaling. At our first halt, I called General Custer's attention to this. He replied that our scouts were well out of the divide, and was sure if any such signals were made our scouts would have reported them, but on the contrary, they reported nothing had been seen. Subsequent observations convinced me that these supposed "smoke puffs" were cloudlets of mist formed during the night in the valleys and wafted over the hill tops by the morning breeze.—E.S.G.) and that you should endeavor to send a scout through to Colonel Gibbon's column, with information of the result of your examination. The lower part of this creek will be examined by a detachment from Colonel Gibbon's command. The supply steamer will be pushed up the Big Horn as far as the forks if the river is found to be navigable for that distance, and the Department Commander, who will accompany the column of Colonel Gibbon, desires you to report to him there not later than the expiration of the time for which your troops are rationed, unless in the meantime you receive further orders.

> Very respectfully,
> Your obedient servant,
> E. W. SMITH, Captain, 18th Infantry,
> Acting Assistant Adjutant-General.

These instructions are explicit, and fixed the location of the Indians very accurately. It has been assumed by some writers that General Terry's command would be at the mouth of the Little Big Horn on June 26th, and that General Custer knew of that—also by some that the two commands were to come together about that date at that place. General Terry's instructions do not say when his command would reach that point, and according to the instructions, General Custer was not necessarily expected there before the 5th or 6th of July, being rationed for fifteen days.

The March up the Rosebud

At twelve o'clock, noon, on the 22nd of June, the "Forward" was sounded, and the regiment marched out of camp in column of fours, each troop followed by its pack-mules. Generals Terry, Gibbon and Custer stationed themselves near our line of march and reviewed the regiment. General Terry had a pleasant word for each officer as he returned the salute. Our pack-trains proved troublesome at the start, as the cargoes began falling off before we got out of camp, and during all that day the mules straggled badly. After that day, however, they were placed under the charge of Lieutenant Mathey, who was directed to report at the end of each day's march the order of merit of the efficiency of the troop packers. Doubtless, General Custer had some ulterior design in this. It is quite probable that if he had had occasion to detach troops requiring rapid marching, he would have selected those troops whose packers had the best records. At all events the efficiency was much increased, and after we struck the Indian trail the pack-trains kept well closed. We went into camp about 4 p.m., having marched twelve miles. About sunset "officers' call" was sounded, and we assembled at General

Custer's bivouac and squatted in groups about the General's bed. It was not a cheerful assemblage; everybody seemed to be in a serious mood, and the little conversation carried on, before all had arrived, was in undertones. When all had assembled, the General said that until further orders, trumpet calls would not be sounded except in an emergency; the marches would begin at 5 a.m. sharp; the troop commanders were all experienced officers, and knew well enough what to do, and when to do what was necessary for their troops; there were two things that would be regulated from his headquarters, *i.e.* when to move out of and when to go into camp. All other details, such as reveille, stables, watering, halting, grazing, etc., on the march would be left to the judgment and discretion of the troop commanders; they were to keep within supporting distance of each other, not to get ahead of the scouts, or very far to the rear of the column. He took particular pains to impress upon the officers his reliance upon their judgment, discretion, and loyalty. He thought, judging from the number of lodge-fires reported by Reno, that we might meet at least a thousand warriors; there might be enough young men from the agencies, visiting their hostile friends, to make a total of fifteen hundred. He had consulted the reports of the Commissioner of Indian Affairs and the officials while in Washington as to the probable number of "Hostiles" (those who had persistently refused to live or enroll themselves at the Indian agencies), and he was confident, if any reliance was to be placed upon these reports, that there would not be an opposing force of more than fifteen hundred. General Terry had offered him the additional force of the battalion of the 2nd Cavalry, but he had declined it because he felt sure that the 7th Cavalry could whip any force that would be able to combine against him, that if the regiment could not, no other regiment in the service could; if they could whip the regiment, they would be able to defeat a much larger force, or, in other words, the reinforcement of this battalion could not save us from defeat. With the regiment acting alone, there would be sure harmony, but another organization would be sure to cause jealousy or friction. He had declined the offer of the Gatling guns for the reason that they might hamper our movements or march at a critical moment, because of the inferior horses and of the difficult nature of the country through which we would march. The marches would be from twenty-five to thirty miles a day. Troop officers were cautioned to husband their rations and the strength of their mules and horses, as we might be out for a great deal longer time than that for which we were rationed, as he intended to follow the trail until we could get the Indians, even if it took us to the Indian agencies on the Missouri River or in Nebraska. All officers were requested to make to him any suggestions they thought fit.

This "talk" of his, as we called it, was considered at the time as something extraordinary for General Custer, for it was not his habit to unbosom himself to his officers. In it he showed concessions and a reliance on others; there was an indefinable something that was *not* Custer. His manner and tone, usually brusque and aggressive, or somewhat curt, was on this occasion conciliating and subdued. There was something akin to an appeal, as if depressed, that made a deep impression on all present. We compared watches to get the official time, and separated to attend to our various duties. Lieutenants McIntosh, Wallace (Killed at the Battle of Wounded Knee, December 29, 1890.), and myself walked to our bivouac, for some distance in silence, when Wallace remarked: "Godfrey, I believe General Custer is going to be killed." "Why? Wallace," I replied, "what makes you think so?" "Because," said he, "I have never heard Custer talk in that way before."

I went to my troop and gave orders what time the "silent" reveille should be and as to other details for the morning preparations; also the following directions in case of a night attack: The stable guard, packers, and cooks were to go out at once to the horses and mules to quiet and guard them; the other men were to go at once to a designated rendezvous and await orders; no man should fire a shot until he received orders from an officer to do so. When they retired for the night they should put their arms and equipments where they could get them without leaving their beds. I then went through the herd to satisfy myself as to the security of the animals. During the performance of this duty I came to the bivouac of the Indian scouts. "Mitch" Bouyer, the half-breed interpreter, "Bloody Knife," the chief of the Ree scouts, "Half-Yellow-Face," the chief of the Crow scouts, and others were having a "talk." I observed them for a few minutes, when Bouyer turned toward me, apparently at the suggestion of "Half-Yellow-Face" and said: "Have you ever fought against these Sioux?" "Yes," I replied. Then he asked: "Well, how many do you expect to find?" I answered, "It is said we may find between one thousand and fifteen hundred." "Well, do you think we can whip that many?" "Oh, yes, I guess so." After he had interpreted our conversation, he said to me with a good deal of emphasis, "Well, I can tell you we are going to have a damned big fight." At five o'clock sharp, on the morning of the 23rd, General Custer mounted and started up the Rosebud, followed by two sergeants, one carrying the regimental standard, and the other his personal or headquarters flag, the same kind of flag he used while commanding his cavalry division during the Civil War. This was the signal for the command to mount and take up the march. Eight miles out we came to the first of the Indian camping-places. It certainly indicated a large village and numerous population. There were a great many "wickiups" (bushes stuck in the ground with the tops drawn together, over which they placed canvas or blankets.) These we supposed at the time were for the dogs, but subsequent events developed the fact that they were temporary shelters of the transients from the agencies. During the day we passed through three of these camping-places and made halts at each one. Everybody was busy studying the age of the pony droppings and tracks and lodge trails, and endeavoring to determine the number of lodges. These points were all-absorbing topics of conversation. We went into camp about five o'clock, having marched about thirty-three miles.

June 24th we passed a great many camping-places, all appearing to be of nearly the same strength. One would naturally suppose these were the successive camping-places of the same village, when, in fact, they were the continuous camps of the several bands. The fact that they appeared to be of nearly the same age, that is, having been made at the same time, did not impress us then. We passed through one much larger than any of the others. The grass for a considerable distance around it had been cropped close, indicating that large herds had been grazed there. The frame of a large "Sun Dance" lodge was standing, and in it we found the scalp of a white man. It was whilst here that the Indians from the agencies had joined the Hostiles' camp. The command halted here and the "officers' call" was sounded. Upon assembling we were informed that our Crow scouts, who had been very active and efficient, had discovered fresh signs, the tracks of three or four ponies and one Indian on foot. At this point a stiff southerly breeze was blowing; as we were about to separate, the General's headquarter's flag was blown down, falling toward our rear. Being near the flag I picked it up and stuck the staff in the ground, but it again fell to the rear. I then bored the staff into the ground where it would have the support of a sage-brush. This circumstance made no impression on me at the time, but after the battle, an officer, Lieutenant Wallace, asked me if I remembered the incident. He had observed, and regarded the fact of its falling to the rear as a bad omen, and felt sure we would suffer a defeat.

The march during the day was tedious. We made many long halts, so as not to get ahead of the scouts, who seemed to be doing their work thoroughly, giving special attention to the right, toward Tulloch's Creek, the valley of which was in general view from the divide. Once or twice signal smokes were reported in that direction, but investigation did not confirm the reports. The weather was dry and had been for some time, consequently the trail was very dusty. The troops were required to march on separate trails, so that the dust clouds would not rise so high. The valley was heavily marked with lodge-pole trails and pony tracks, showing that immense herds of ponies had been driven over it. About sundown we went into camp under the cover of a bluff, so as to hide the command as much as possible. We had marched about twenty-eight miles. The fires were ordered to be put out as soon as supper was over, and we were to be in readiness to march again at 11:30 p.m.

Lieutenant Hare and myself lay down about 9:30 to take a nap. When comfortably fixed, we heard some one say, "He's over there by that tree." As that described my location pretty well, I called out to know what was wanted, and the reply came: "The General's compliments, and he wants to see all the officers at headquarters immediately." So we gave up our much-needed rest and groped our way through horse herds, over sleeping men, and through thickets of bushes trying to find headquarters. No one could tell us, and as all fires and lights were out we could not keep our bearings. We finally espied a solitary candle-light, toward which we traveled and found most of the officers assembled at the General's bivouac. The General said that the trail led over the divide to the Little Big Horn; the march would be taken up at once, as he was anxious to get as near the divide as possible before daylight, where the command would be concealed during the day, and give ample time for the country to be studied, to locate the village, and to make plans for the attack on the 26th. We then returned to our troops, except Lieutenant Hare, who was put on duty with the scouts. Because of the dust, it was impossible to see any distance and the rattle of equipments and clattering of the horses' feet made it difficult to hear distinctly beyond our immediate surroundings. We could not see the trail and we could only follow it by keeping in the dust cloud. The night was very calm, but occasionally a slight breeze would waft the cloud and disconcert our bearings; then we were obliged to halt to catch a sound from those in advance, sometimes whistling or hallooing, and getting a response we would start forward again. Finally, troopers were put ahead, away from the noise of our column, and where they could hear the noise of those in front. A little after 2 a.m., June 25th, the command was halted to await further tidings from the scouts; we had marched about ten miles. Part of the command unsaddled to rest the horses. After daylight some coffee was made, but it was impossible to drink it. The water was so alkaline that the horses refused to drink.

Some time before eight o'clock, General Custer rode bareback to the several troops and gave orders to be ready to march at eight o'clock, and gave information that scouts had discovered the locality of the Indian villages or camps in the valley of the Little Big Horn, about twelve or fifteen miles beyond the divide. Just before setting out on the march, I went to where General Custer's bivouac was. The General, "Bloody Knife," and several Ree scouts and a half-breed interpreter were squatted in a circle, having a "talk" after the Indian fashion. The General wore a serious expression and was apparently abstracted. The scouts were doing the talking, and seemed nervous and disturbed. Finally "Bloody Knife" made a remark that recalled the General from his reverie, and he asked in his usual quick, brusque manner, "What's that he says!" The interpreter replied: "He says we'll find enough Sioux to keep us fighting two or three days." The General smiled and re-marked, "I guess we'll get through with them in one day."

We started promptly at eight o'clock and marched uninterruptedly until 10:30 a.m. when we halted in a ravine and were ordered to pre-serve quiet, keep concealed, and not do anything that would be likely to reveal our presence to the enemy. We had marched about ten miles.

It is a rare occurrence in Indian warfare that gives a commander the opportunity to reconnoiter the enemy's position in daylight. This is par-ticularly true if the Indians have a knowledge of the presence of troops in the country. When following an Indian trail the "signs" indicate the length of time elapsed since the presence of the Indians. When the "signs" indicate a "hot trail" *i.e.* near approach, the commander judges his distance and by a forced march, usually in the night time, tries to reach the Indian village at night and make his disposition for a surprise attack at daylight. At all events his attack must be made with celerity, and generally without other knowledge of the numbers of the opposing force than that discovered or conjectured while following the trail. The dispositions for the attack may be said to be "made in the dark," and successful surprise to depend upon luck. If the advance to the attack be made in daylight it is next to impossible that a near approach can be made without discovery. In all our previous experiences, when the immediate presence of the troops was once known to them, the warriors swarmed to the attack, and resorted to all kinds of ruses to mislead the troops, to delay the advance toward their camp or village while the squaws and children secured what personal effects they could, drove off the pony herd, and by flight put themselves beyond danger, and then scattering, made successful pursuit next to impossible. In civilized warfare the hostile forces may confront each other for hours, days or weeks, and the battle may be conducted with a tolerable knowledge of the numbers, positions, etc., of each other. A full knowledge of the immediate presence of the enemy does not imply immediate attack. In Indian warfare the rule is "touch and go." In fact, the firebrand nature of Indian warfare is not generally understood. In mediating upon the preliminaries of an Indian battle, old soldiers who have participated only in the battles of "civilized" war are apt to draw upon their own experiences for comparison when there is no comparison.

Troops Discovered

It was well known to the Indians that the troops were in the field, and a battle was fully expected by them; but the close proximity of our column was not known to them until the morning of the day of the battle. Several young men had left the hostile camp on that morning to go to one of the agencies in Nebraska. They saw the dust made by the column of troops; some of their number returned to the village and gave warning that the troops were coming, so the attack was not a surprise. For two or three days their camp had been pitched on the site where they were attacked. The place was not selected with the view to making that the battle-field of the campaign, but, whoever was in the van on their march thought it a good place to camp, put up his tepee, and the others as they arrived followed his example. (NOTE: This was Gall's explanation.) It is customary among the Indians to camp by bands. The bands usually camp some distance apart, and Indians of the number then together would occupy a territory of several miles along the river valley, and not necessarily within supporting distance of each other. But in view of the possible fulfillment of Sitting Bull's prophecy the village had massed.

The Little Big Horn River, or the "Greasy Grass" as it is known to the Indians, is a rapid, tortuous mountain stream from twenty to forty yards wide, with pebbled bottom, but abrupt, soft banks. The water at the ordinary stage is from two to five feet in depth, depending upon the width of the channel. The general direction of its course is northeasterly down to the Little Big Horn battle-fields, where it trends northwesterly to its confluence with the Big Horn River. The other topographical features of the country concern us in this narrative may be briefly described as follows: Between the Little Big Horn and Big Horn Rivers is a plateau of undulating prairie; between the Little Big Horn and the Rosebud are the Little Chetish or Wolf Mountains. By this it must not be misunderstood as a rocky upheaval chain or spur of mountains, but it is a rough, broken country of considerable elevation, of high precipitous hills and deep, narrow gulches. The command had followed the trail up a branch of the Rosebud to within say, a mile of the summit of these mountains, which form the "divide." Not many miles to our right was the divide between the Little Big Horn and Tulloch's Fork. The creek that drained the watershed to our right and front is now variously called "Sun Dance," Benteen's, or Reno's Creek. The trail, very tortuous, and sometimes dangerous, followed down the bed and valley of the [middle] branch of this creek, which at that time was dry for the greater part of its length. It was from the divide between the Little Big Horn and the Rosebud that the scouts had discovered the smoke rising above the village, and the pony herds grazing in the valley of the Little Big Horn, somewhere about twelve or fifteen miles away. It was to their point of view that General Custer had gone while the column was halted in the ravine. It was impossible for him to discover more of the enemy than had already been reported by the scouts. In consequence of the high bluffs which screened the village, it was not possible in following the trail to discover more. Nor was there a point of observation near the trail from which further discoveries could be made until the battle was at hand.

Our officers had generally collected in groups and discussed the situation. Some sought solitude and sleep, or meditation. The Ree scouts, who had not been very active for the past day or two, were together and their "medicine man" was anointing them and invoking the Great Spirit to protect them from the Sioux. They seemed to have become satisfied that we were going to find more Sioux than we could well take care of. Captain Yates' troop had lost one of its packs of hard bread during the night march from our last halting place on the 24th. He had sent a detail back on the trail to recover it. Captain Keogh came to where a group of officers were and said this detail had returned and Sergeant Curtis, in charge, reported that when near the pack they discovered an Indian opening one of the boxes of hard bread with his tomahawk, and that as soon as the Indian saw the soldiers he galloped away to the hills, out of range and then moved along leisurely. This information was taken to the General at once by his brother, Captain Tom Custer. The General came back and had "officers' call" sounded. He recounted Captain Keogh's report, and also said that the scouts had seen several Indians moving along the ridge overlooking the valley through which we had marched, as if observing our movements; he thought the Indians must have seen the dust made by the command. At all events, our presence had been discovered and further concealment was unnecessary; that we would move at once to attack the village; that he had not intended to make the attack until the next morning, the 26th, but our discovery made it imperative to act at once, as delay would allow the village to scatter and escape. Troop commanders were ordered to make a detail of one non-commissioned officer and six men to accompany the [packs]; to inspect their troops and report as soon as they were ready to march; that the troops would take their places in the column of march in the order in which reports of readiness were received; the last one to report would escort the pack-train.

The Division of Troops

The inspections were quickly made and the column was soon en route. We crossed the dividing ridge between the Rosebud and Little Big Horn valleys a little before noon. Shortly afterward the regiment was divided into battalions. The advance battalion, under Major Reno, consisted of troop "M," Captain French; troop "A," Captain Moylan and

Lieutenant De Rudio; troop "G," Lieutenants McIntosh and Wallace; the Indian scouts under Lieutenants Varnum and Hare, and the interpreter Girard; Lieutenant Hodgson was Acting Adjutant, and Doctors DeWolf and Porter were the medical officers. The battalion under General Custer was composed of troop "I," Captain Keogh and Lieutenant Porter; troop "F," Captain Yates and Lieutenant Reily; troop "C," Captain Custer and Lieutenant Harrington; troop "E," Lieutenants Smith and Sturgis; troop "L," Lieutenants Calhoun and Crittenden; Lieutenant Cook was the Adjutant, and Captain G. E. Lord was medical officer. (It is thought by some that Custer's troops were divided into two battalions, one under Captain Keogh and one under Captain Yates.) The battalion under Captain Benteen consisted of troop "H," Captain Benteen and Lieutenant Gibson; troop "D," Captain Weir and Lieutenant Edgerly, and troop "K," Lieutenant Godfrey. The pack-train, Lieutenant Mathey in charge, was under escort of troop "B," Captain McDougall.

Major Reno's battalion marched down a valley that developed into the [middle] branch of the small tributary to the Little Big Horn, now called the "Sun Dance," Benteen's, or Reno Creek. The Indian trail followed the meanderings of this valley. Custer's column followed Reno's closely, bearing to the right and rear. The pack-train followed their trail.

Benteen's Route

Benteen's battalion was ordered to the left and front, to a line of high bluffs about three or four miles distant. Benteen was ordered if he saw anything, to send word to Custer, but to pitch into anything he came across; if, when he arrived at the high bluffs, he could not see any enemy, he should continue his march to the next line of bluffs and so on until he could see the Little Big Horn Valley.

There is no doubt that Custer was possessed with the idea that the Indians would not "stand" for a daylight attack, that some of them would try to escape up the valley of the Little Big Horn with families, ponies and other impedimenta, and if so, he wanted them intercepted and driven back toward the village. This idea and another that the village might be strung out along the valley for several miles were probably the ones that influenced him to send Benteen's battalion to the left. Benteen marched over a succession of rough steep hills and deep valleys. The view from the point where the regiment was organized into battalions did not discover the difficult nature of the country, but as we advanced farther, it became more and more difficult. To save the strain on the battalion, Lieutenant [Gibson] was sent some distance in advance, but saw no enemy, and so signaled the result of his reconnaissance to Benteen. The obstacles threw the battalion by degrees to the right until we came in sight of and not more than a mile from the trail. Many of our horses were greatly jaded by the climbing and descending, some getting far into the rear of the column. Benteen very wisely determined to follow the trail of the rest of the command, and we got into it just in advance of the pack-train. During this march on the left, we could see occasionally the battalion under Custer, distinguished by the troop mounted on gray horses, marching at a rapid gait. Two or three times we heard loud cheering and also some few shots, but the occasion of these demonstrations is not known. Some time after getting on the trail we came to a water hole, or morass, at which a stream of running water had its source, Benteen halted the battalion. While watering, we heard some firing in advance, and Weir became impatient at the delay of watering and started off with his troop, taking the advance, whereas his place in the column was second. The rest of the battalion moved out very soon afterward and soon caught up with him. We were now several miles from the Reno battle-field or the Little Big Horn. Just as we were leaving the water hole, the pack-train was arriving, and the poor thirsty mules plunged into the morass in spite of the efforts of the packers to prevent them, for they had not had water since the previous evening. We passed a burning tepee, fired presumably by our scouts, in which was the body of a warrior who had been killed in the battle with Crook's troops on the Rosebud on the 17th of June.

Reno's Route

The battalions under Reno and Custer did not meet any Indians until Reno arrived at the burning tepee; here a few were seen. These Indians did not act as if surprised by the appearance of troops; they made no effort to delay the column, but simply kept far enough in advance to invite pursuit. Reno's command and the scouts followed them closely until he received orders to "move forward at as rapid a gait as he thought prudent, and charge the village afterward, and the whole outfit would support him." According to Reno's official report this order was given him near this burning tepee. He says: "Lieutenant Cook, adjutant, came to me and said the village was only two miles above, and running away," and gave the above order.

The Little Big Horn bottom, down which the trail led, is generally flat, and from one to two miles wide; along the stream, especially in the bends at the time of the fight, it was heavily timbered, principally large cotton woods, and obstructed a view of the main villages until Reno got to where he made his farthest advance down the valley; here the village loomed up large among the cotton woods below. Reno following the Indian trail, crossed at a ford; about three and a half miles below it, in a direct line, is a second ford; between these fords, skirting the right bank and paralleling the river is a ridge from one hundred to three hundred feet above the valley, which rises abruptly from river and valley. In following the summit of this ridge the travel distance is considerably increased. The northeast slope declines rather gently at the upper end, but more abruptly at the lower end, and drains into a usually dry stream bed which joins the river at the second ford. About two miles below this ford is another. These lower fords were used by the Hostiles in swarming to the attack on Custer's troops. (NOTE: This valley was almost denuded of timber to furnish lumber for the building of Fort Custer in 1877 and 1878.)

Reno's Fight in the Valley

Reno's battalion moved at a trot to the river, where he delayed about ten or fifteen minutes watering the horses and reforming the column on the left bank of the stream. Both Captain Keogh and Lieutenant Cook were at this crossing for a short time. Reno now sent word to Custer that he had everything in front of him, and that the enemy was strong. Custer had moved off to the right, being separated from Reno by a line of high bluffs and the river. Reno moved forward, in column of fours about half a mile, then formed the battalion in line of battle across the valley with the scouts on the left; after advancing about a mile further he deployed the battalion as skirmishers. In the meantime, the Hostiles, continually reinforced, fell back, firing occasionally, but made no decided effort to check Reno's advance. The horses of two men became unmanageable and carried them into the Indian camp. The Indians now developed great force, opened a brisk fire, mounted, and made a dash toward the foothills on the left bank where the Ree scouts were. The scouts ignominiously fled, most of them abandoning the field altogether. Reno says in his report: "I, however, soon saw that I was being drawn into some trap, as they would certainly fight harder and especially as we were nearing their village which was still standing; besides, I could not see Custer or any other support, and at the same time the very earth seemed to grow Indians. They were running toward me in swarms and from all directions. I saw I must defend myself and give up the attack mounted. This I did."

During this advance the troops began to cheer in answer to the "whoops" of the Hostiles, and Reno yelled, "Stop that noise!" Reno, not seeing the "whole outfit" within supporting distance, did not obey his orders to charge the village, but dismounted his command to fight on foot. The movements of the Indians around the left flank and the flight of the scouts caused the left to fall back until the command was on the defensive in the timber and covered by the bank of the old river bed. Reno's loss thus far was one wounded. The position was a strong one, well protected in front by the bank and fringe of timber, somewhat open in the rear, but sheltered by timber in the bottom. Those present differ in their estimates of the length of time the command remained in the bottom after they were attacked in force. Some say "a few minutes;" others "about an hour." While Reno remained there his casualties were few. The Hostiles had him nearly surrounded, and there was some firing from the rear of the position by Indians on the opposite bank of the river, and directly afterward Reno gave orders to those near him to "mount and get to the bluffs." This order was not generally heard or communicated; while those who did hear it were preparing to execute it, he countermanded the order, but soon afterward repeated the same order "to mount and get to the bluffs," and again it was not generally understood. Individuals, observing the preparations of those of the left, near Reno, informed their troop commanders who then gave orders to mount. Owing to the noise of the firing and to the absorbed attention they were giving to the enemy many did not know of the order until too late to accompany the command. Some remained concealed until the Indians left and then came out. Four others remained until night and then escaped. Reno's command left the bottom by troop organizations in column, but in a straggling formation. Reno was the foremost in this retreat, or "charge," as he termed it in his report, and after he had exhausted the shots of his revolvers he threw them away. The Hostile strength pushed Reno's retreat to the left, so he could not get to the ford where he had entered the valley, but they were fortunate in striking the river at a fordable place; a pony-trail led up a funnel-shaped ravine into the bluffs. Here the command got jammed and lost all semblance of organization. The Indians fired into them, but not very effectively. There does not appear to have been any resistance, certainly no organized resistance during this retreat. On the right and left of the ravine into which the pony-path led were rough precipitous clay bluffs. It was surprising to see what steep inclines men and horses clambered up under the excitement of danger.

Lieutenant Donald McIntosh was killed soon after leaving the timber. Dr. De Wolf was killed while climbing one of the bluffs a short distance from the command. Lieutenant B. H. Hodgson's horse leaped from the bank into the river and fell dead; the lieutenant was wounded in the leg, probably by the same bullet that killed the horse. Hodgson called out, "For God's sake, don't abandon me;" he was assured that he would not be left behind. Hodgson then took hold of a comrade's stirrup-strap and was taken across the stream, but soon after was shot and killed. Hodgson, some days before the battle, had said, that if he were dismounted in battle or wounded, he intended to take hold of somebody's stirrup to assist himself from the field. During the retreat Private Dalvern, troop "F," had a hand-to-hand conflict with an Indian; his horse was killed; he then shot the Indian, caught the Indian's pony, and rode to the command. Reno's casualties thus far were three officers, including Dr. J. M. De Wolf, and twenty-nine enlisted men and scouts killed; seven enlisted men wounded; and one officer, one interpreter and fourteen soldiers and scouts missing. Nearly all the casualties occurred during the retreat and after leaving the timber. Scout Charlie Reynolds (white), and Isaiah Dorman (negro), interpreter from Fort Rice, were killed in the timber on the right of Reno's second position. "Bloody Knife" (Ree) was killed by Reno's side. The Ree scouts continued their flight until they reached the supply camp at the mouth of the Powder, on the 27th. The Crow scouts remained with the command. Mr. F. F. Girard, interpreter, informs me that it is his recollection that only one Crow scout "Curley," and "Mitch" Boyer, Crow interpreter, accompanied Custer's immediate command and that all the other Crow scouts were with Reno. "Curley" probably did not go into the fight at all, but left Custer just before the fighting commenced and went to the high ridge back of the Custer ridge, watched the battle long enough to see that Custer would be defeated and then worked his way to [the mouth of] the Big Horn River and waited for the coming of the steamboat *Far West* the smoke of which could undoubtedly be seen for a long distance. [Then he communicated the defeat at the Little Big Horn.] [NOTES: Garrard told me that it was his belief that Mitch Bouyer and Curley were the only Crow scouts who went with Custer's command. I do not believe that White-Man-Runs-Him, Hairy Moccasin and Goes Ahead were with Custer's command.—E.S.G.]

Benteen Joins Reno

We will now go back to Benteen's battalion. Not long after leaving the water-hole Sergeant Knipe, troop "C," met him with an order from Custer to the commanding officer of the pack-train to hurry it up. The sergeant was sent back to the train with the message; as he passed the column he said to the men, "We've got 'em boys." From this and other remarks we inferred that Custer had attacked and captured the village.

Shortly afterward we were met by a trumpeter, Martin, troop "H," bearing this message signed by Colonel Cook, Adjutant: "Benteen, come on. Big village. Be quick. Bring packs," with the postscript "bring packs."

A riderless horse was the only living thing to be seen in our front. Benteen asked the trumpeter what had been done and Martin informed him that "Indians had 'skedaddled,' abandoning the village." The column had been marching at a trot and walk, according as the ground was smooth or broken. We now heard firing, first straggling shots, and as we advanced, the engagements became more and more pronounced and appeared to be coming toward us. The column took the gallop with pistols drawn, expecting to meet the enemy which we thought Custer was driving before him in his effort to communicate with the pack train, never suspecting that our forces had been defeated. We were forming in line to meet our supposed enemy, when we came in full view of the valley of the Little Big Horn. The valley was full of horsemen riding to and fro in clouds of dust and smoke, for the grass had been fired by the Indians to drive the troops out and cover their own movements. On the bluffs to our right we saw a body of troops and that they were engaged. But an engagement appeared to be going on in the valley too. Owing to the distance, smoke and dust, it was impossible to distinguish if those in the valley were friends or foes. There was a short time of uncertainty as to the direction in which we should go, but some Crow scouts came by, driving a small herd of ponies, one of whom said "Soldiers" and motioned for the command to go to the right. Following his direction, we soon joined Reno's battalion, which was still firing. Reno had lost his hat and had a handkerchief tied about his head, and appeared to be very much excited. Benteen's battalion was ordered to dismount and deploy as skirmishers on the edge of the bluffs overlooking the valley. Very soon after this the Indians withdrew from the attack. Lieutenant Hare came to where I was standing and, grasping my hand heartily, said with a good deal of emphasis: "We've had a big fight in the bottom, got whipped, and I am ———— glad to see you." I was satisfied that he meant what he said, for I had already suspected that something was wrong, but was not quite prepared for such startling information. Benteen's battalion was ordered to divide its ammunition with Reno's men, who had apparently expended nearly all in their personal possession. It has often been a matter of doubt whether this was a fact or the effect of imagination. It seems most improbable in view of their active movements and the short time the command was firing, that the "most of the men" should have expended one hundred and fifty rounds of ammunition per man. Lieutenant Hare was ordered to go back and bring up the ammunition pack-mules. Luckily for us the Indians had not gone back on our trail and discovered and waylaid the pack-train. While waiting for the ammunition pack-mules, Major Reno concluded to make an effort to recover and bury the body of Lieutenant Hodgson. Reno asked for a carbine, saying that he had lost his pistols in the charge. At the same time we loaded up a few men with canteens to get water for the command; they were to accompany the rescuing party. The effort was futile; the party was ordered back after being fired upon by some Indians, who doubtless were scalping the dead near the foot of the bluffs.

A number of officers collected on the edge of the bluff overlooking the valley and were discussing the situation. At this time there were a large number of horsemen, Indians, in the valley. Suddenly they all started down the valley, and in a few minutes scarcely a horseman was to be seen. Heavy firing was heard down the river. During this time the questions were being asked: "What's the matter with Custer, that he don't send word what we shall do?" "Wonder what we are staying here for?" etc., thus showing some uneasiness, but still no one seemed to show great anxiety, nor do I know that any one felt any serious apprehension but that Custer could and would take care of himself. Some of Reno's men had seen Custer's headquarters party, including Custer himself, on the bluffs about the time the Indians began to develop in Reno's front. This party was heard to cheer, and seen to wave their hats as if to give encouragement, and then they disappeared behind the hills or escaped further attention from those below. Major Moylan thinks that the last he saw of Custer's party was about the position of Reno Hill. Major De Rudio thinks he saw Custer on the ridge about opposite where Dr. De Wolf was killed. He says Custer and Tom were dismounted apparently looking at them through field glasses. Reno was then developing into line of skirmishers. He saw them mount and disappear. Custer's battalion was not seen by Reno's troops after the separation.

It was about the time Custer was last seen that Trumpeter Martin (for the Indians were "skedaddling"), left Cook with Custer's last orders to Benteen, viz: "Benteen, come on. Big village. Be quick. Bring packs. Cook, Adjutant. P. S.: Bring packs." The repetition in the order would seem to indicate that Cook was excited, flurried, or that he wanted to emphasize the necessity for escorting the packs. It is possible that from a high point Custer had seen nearly the whole camp and force of the Indians and realized that the chances were desperate; but too late to reunite his forces for the attack. [If Gen. Custer could see the village when Trumpeter Martin left him with the dispatch, it seems to me that he must have been on Hill F, as the village was shut off by the intervening hills and timber.] Reno was already in the fight and his (Custer's) own battalion was separated from the attack by a distance of two and a half to three miles. He had no reason to think that Reno would not push his attack vigorously. A commander seldom goes into battle counting on the failure of his lieutenant; if he did, he would provide that such a failure should not turn into disaster.

During a long time after the junction of Reno and Benteen we heard firing down the river in the direction of Custer's command. We were satisfied that Custer was fighting the Indians somewhere, and the conviction was expressed that "our command ought to be doing something or Custer would be after Reno with a sharp stick." We heard two distinct volleys which excited some surprise, and, if I mistake not, brought out the remark from some one that "Custer was giving it to them for all he is worth." I have but little doubt now that these volleys were fired by Custer's orders as *signals of distress* and to indicate where he was.

Captain Weir and Lieutenant Edgerly, after driving the Indians away from Reno's command, on their side, heard the firing, became impatient at the delay, and thought they would move down that way, if they should be permitted. Weir started to get this permission, but changed his mind and concluded to take a survey from the high bluffs first. Edgerly, seeing Weir going in the direction of the firing, supposed it was all right and started down the ravine with the troop. Weir, from the high point saw the Indians in large numbers start for Edgerly, and signaled for him to change his direction, and Edgerly went over to the high point where they remained, not seriously molested, until the remainder of the troops marched down there. The Indians were seen by them to ride about what afterward proved to be Custer's battlefield, shooting into the bodies of the dead men or killing wounded men.

McDougall came up with the pack-train and reported the firing when he reported his arrival to Reno. I remember distinctly looking at my watch at twenty minutes past four, and made a note of it in my memorandum book, and although I have never satisfactorily been able to recall what particular incident happened at that time, it was some important event before we started down the river. It is my impression, however, that it was the arrival of the pack-train. It was at about this time that thirteen men and a scout named Herendeen rejoined the command. They had been missing since Reno's flight from the bottom. Several of them were wounded. These men had lost their horses in the stampede from the bottom and had remained in the timber. When leaving the timber to rejoin, they were fired upon by five Indians, but they drove them away.

Reno Attempts to Find Custer

My recollection is that it was about half-past two when we joined Reno. About five o'clock the command moved down toward Custer's supposed whereabouts, intending to join him. The advance went as far as the high bluffs ["A" on map] where the command was halted. Persons who have been on the plains have seen stationary objects dancing before them, now in view and now obscured, or a weed on the top of a hill, projected against the sky, magnified to appear as a tree, will readily understand why our views would be unsatisfactory. The air was full of dust. We could see stationary groups of horsemen, and individual horsemen moving about. From their grouping and the manner in which they sat their horses we knew they were Indians. On the left of the valley a strange sight attracted our attention. Some one remarked that there had been a fire that scorched the leaves of the bushes, which caused the reddish-brown appearance, but this appearance was changeable. Watching this intently for a short time with field-glasses, it was discovered that this strange sight was the immense Indian pony-herds.

Looking toward Custer's field, on a hill two miles away we saw a large assemblage. At first our command did not appear to attract their attention, although there was some commotion observable among those near to our position. We heard occasional shots, most of which seemed to be a great distance off, beyond the large groups on the hill. While watching this group, the conclusion was arrived at that Custer had been repulsed, and the firing we heard was the parting shots of the rear guard. The firing ceased, the groups dispersed, clouds of dust arose from all parts of the field, and the horsemen converged toward our position. The command was now dismounted to fight on foot.

Reno Falls Back

Weir's and French's troops were posted on the high bluffs and to the front of them; my own [troop] along the crest of the bluffs next to the river; the rest of the command moved to the rear, as I supposed to occupy other points in the vicinity, to make this our defensive position. Busying myself with posting my men, giving direction about the use of ammunition, etc. I was a little startled by the remark that the command was out of sight. At this time Weir's and French's troops were being attacked. Orders were soon brought to me by Lieutenant Hare, Acting Adjutant, to join the main command. I had gone some distance in the execution of this order when, looking back, I saw French's troop come tearing over the bluffs, and soon after Weir's troop followed in hot haste. Edgerly was near the top of the bluff, trying to mount his frantic horse, and it did seem that he would not succeed, but he vaulted into his saddle and then joined the troop. The Indians almost immediately followed to the top of the bluff, and commenced firing into the retreating troops, killing one man, wounding others and several horses. They then started down the hillside in pursuit. I at once made up my mind that such a retreat and close pursuit would throw the whole command into confusion, and, perhaps, prove disastrous. I dismounted my men to fight on foot, deploying as rapidly as possible without waiting for the formation laid down in tactics. Lieutenant Hare expressed his intention of staying with me "Adjutant or no Adjutant." The led horses were sent to the main command. [Both troops commanded by Edgerly and French went by us at a fast gallop to Reno's position.] Our fire in a short time compelled the Indians to halt and take cover, but before this was accomplished a second order came for me to fall back as quickly as possible to the main command. Having checked the pursuit we began our retreat, slowly at first, but kept up our firing. After proceeding some distance the men began to group together, and to move a little faster and faster, and our fire slackened. This was pretty good evidence that they were getting demoralized. The Indians were being heavily reinforced and began to come from their cover, but kept up a heavy fire. I halted the line, made the men take their intervals, and again drove the Indians to cover; then once more began the retreat. The firing of the Indians was [now] heavy. The bullets struck the ground all about us; but the "ping-ping" of the bullets overhead seemed to have a more terrifying influence than the "swish-thud" of the bullets that struck the ground immediately about us. When we got to the ridge in front of Reno's position I observed some Indians making all haste to get possession of a hill to the right. I could [now] see the rest of the command, and I knew that that hill would command Reno's position. Supposing that my troop was to occupy the line we were then on, I ordered Hare to take ten men and hold the hill, but, just as he was moving off, an order came from Reno to get back as quickly as possible; so I recalled Hare, again drove the Indians to cover, and ordered the men to run to the lines. This movement was executed, strange to say, without a single casualty. [Not a shot had been fired at Reno's command 'till after this troop arrived at position.]

On Reno Hill

The Indians now took possession of all the surrounding high points, and opened a heavy fire. They had in the meantime sent a large force up the valley, and soon our position was surrounded. It was now about seven o'clock.

Our position next to the river was protected by the rough, rugged steep bluffs which were cut up by irregular deep ravines. From the crest of these bluffs the ground gently declined away from the river. On the north there was a short ridge, the ground sloping gently to the front and rear. This ridge, during the first day, was occupied by five troops. Directly in the rear of the ridge was a small hill; in the ravine on the south of this hill our hospital was established, and the horses and pack-mules were secured. Across this ravine one troop, Moylan's was posted, the packs and dead animals being utilized for breastworks. The high hill on the south was occupied by Benteen's troop. Everybody now lay down and spread himself out as thin as possible. After lying there a few minutes I was horrified to find myself wondering if a small sagebrush, about as thick as my finger, would turn a bullet, so I got up and walked alongside the line, cautioned the men not to waste their ammunition; ordered certain men who were good shots to do the firing, and others to keep them supplied with loaded guns.

The firing continued till nearly dark (between nine and ten o'clock), although after dusk but little attention was paid to the firing, as everybody moved about freely.

Of course, everybody was wondering about Custer—why he did not communicate by courier or signal. But the general opinion seemed to prevail that he had been defeated and driven down the river, where he would probably join General Terry, and with whom he would return to our relief. Quite frequently, too, the question, "what's the matter with Custer?" would evoke an impatient reply.

Indians are proverbial economists of fuel, but they did not stint themselves that night. The long twilight was prolonged by numerous bonfires, located throughout their village. The long shadows of the hills and the refracted light gave a supernatural aspect to the surrounding country, which may account for the illusions of those who imagined they could see columns of troops, etc. Although our dusky foes did not molest us with obtrusive attentions during the night, yet it must not be inferred that we were allowed to pass the night in perfect rest; or that they were endeavoring to soothe us into forgetfulness of their proximity, or trying to conceal their situation. They were a good deal happier than we were; nor did they strive to conceal their joy. Their camp was a veritable pandemonium. All night long they continued their frantic revels: beating tom-toms, dancing, whooping, yelling with demoniacal screams, and discharging firearms. We knew they were having a scalp dance. In this connection the question has often been asked, "If they did not have prisoners at the torture?" The Indians deny that they took any prisoners. We did not discover any evidence of torture in their camps. It is true that we did find human heads severed from their bodies, but these had probably been paraded in their orgies during that terrible night.

Our casualties had been comparatively few since taking position on the hill. The question of moving was discussed, but the conditions coupled with the proposition caused it to be indignantly rejected. Some of the scouts were sent out soon after dark to look for signs of Custer's command, but they returned after a short absence, saying that the country was full of Sioux. Lieutenant Varnum volunteered to go out, but was either discouraged from the venture or forbidden to go.

Soon after all firing had ceased the wildest confusion prevailed. Men imagined they could see a column of troops over on the hills or ridges, that they could hear the tramp of the horses, the command of officers or even the trumpet-calls. Stable-call was sounded by one of our trumpeters; shots were fired by some of our men, and familiar trumpet-calls were sounded by our trumpeter immediately after, to let the supposed marching column know that we were friends. Every favorable expression or opinion was received with credulity, and then ratified with a cheer. Somebody suggested that General Crook might be coming, so some one, a civilian packer, I think, mounted a horse, and galloping along the line yelled: "Don't be discouraged, boys, Crook is coming." But they gradually realized that the much-wished-for reinforcements

were but the phantasma of their imaginations, and settled down to
their work of digging rifle pits. They worked in pairs, in threes and
fours. The ground was hard and dry. There were only three or four
spades and shovels in the whole command; axes, hatches, knives, table-
forks, tincups, and halves of canteens were brought into use. However,
everybody worked hard, and some were still digging when the enemy
opened fire at early dawn, between half-past two and three o'clock, so
that all had some sort of shelter, except Benteen's men. The enemy's
first salutations were rather feeble, and our side made scarcely any
response; but as dawn advanced to daylight their lines were heavily
reinforced, and both sides kept up a continuous fusillade. Of course it
was their policy to draw our fire as much as possible to exhaust our
ammunition. As they exposed their persons very little we forbade our
men, except well-known good shots, to fire without orders. The Indians
amused themselves by standing erect, in full view for an instant, then
dropping down again before a bullet could reach them, but of that they
soon seemed to grow tired or found it too dangerous. Then they resorted to the old ruse of raising a hat and blouse, or a blanket, on a stick
to draw our fire; we soon understood their tactics. Occasionally they
fired volleys at command. Their fire, however, was not very effective.
Benteen's troop suffered greater losses than any other, because their
rear was exposed to the long-range firing from the hills on the north.
The horses and mules suffered greatly, as they were fully exposed to
the long-range fire from the east.

Benteen came over to where Reno was lying, and asked for reinforcements to be sent to his line. Before he left his line, however, he ordered
Gibson not to fall back under any circumstances, as this was the key of
the position. Gibson's men had expended nearly all their ammunition,
some men being reduced to as few as four or five cartridges. He was
embarrassed, too, with quite a number of wounded men. Indeed, the
situation here was most critical, for if the Indians had made a rush a
retreat was inevitable. Private McDermott volunteered to carry a message from Gibson to Benteen urging him to hasten the reinforcements.
After considerable urging by Benteen, Reno finally ordered French to
take "M" troop over to the south side. On his way over Benteen picked
up some men then with the horses. Just previous to his arrival an Indian
had shot one of Gibson's men, then rushed up and touched the body
with his "coup-stick," and started back to cover, but he was killed. He

was in such close proximity to the lines and so exposed to the fire that the other Indians could not carry his body away. This, I believe, was the only dead Indian left in our possession, that is, at Reno Hill.

This boldness determined Benteen to make a charge, and the Indians were driven nearly to the river. On their retreat they dragged several dead and wounded warriors away with them.

The firing almost ceased for a while, and then it recommenced with greater fury. From this fact, and their more active movements, it became evident that they contemplated something more serious than a mere fusillade. Benteen came back to where Reno was, and said if something was not done pretty soon the Indians would run into our lines. Waiting a short time, and no action being taken on his suggestion, he said rather impatiently: "You've got to do something here on the north side pretty quick; this won't do, you must drive them back." Reno then directed us to get ready for a charge, and told Benteen to give the word. Benteen called out, "All ready now, men. Now's the time. Give them hell. Hip, hip, here we go!" And away we went with a hurrah, every man of the troops "B," "D," "G" and "K" but one, who lay in his pit crying like a child. The Indians fired more rapidly than before from their whole line. Our men left the pits with their carbines loaded, and they began firing without orders soon after we started. A large body of Indians had assembled at the foot of one of the hills on the north intending probably to make a charge, as Benteen had divined, but they broke as soon as our line started. When we had advanced 70 to 100 yards, Reno called out "Get back, men, back," and back the whole line came. A most singular fact of this sortie was that not a man who had advanced with the lines was hit; but directly after everyone had gotten into the pits again, the one man who did not go out was shot in the head and killed instantly. The poor fellow had a premonition that he would be killed, and had so told one of his comrades.

Up to this time the command had been without water. The excitement and heat made our thirst almost maddening. The men were forbidden to use tobacco. They put pebbles in their mouths to excite the glands; some ate grass roots, but did not find relief. Some tried to eat hard bread, but after chewing it awhile would blow it out of their mouths like so much flour. A few potatoes were given out and afforded some relief. About 11 a.m. the firing was slack, and parties of volunteers were formed to get water under the protection of Benteen's lines.

The parties worked their way down the ravines to within a few yards of the river. The men would get ready, make a rush for the river, fill the camp kettles, and return to fill the canteens. Some Indians stationed in a copse of the woods, a short distance away, opened fire whenever a man exposed himself, which made this a particularly hazardous service. Several men were wounded, and the additional danger was then incurred of rescuing their wounded comrades. I think all these were rewarded with Medals of Honor. [That was done to all in the regiment when a Board convened at Camp Sturgis, October, 1878, Black Hills.] By about one o'clock the Indians had nearly all left us, but they still guarded the river. By that time, however, we had about all the water we needed for immediate use. About two o'clock the Indians came back, opened fire, and drove us to the trenches again, but by three o'clock the firing had ceased altogether.

The Hostiles March Away

Late in the afternoon we saw a few horsemen in the bottom apparently to observe us, and then fire was set to the grass in the valley. About 7 p.m. we saw emerge from behind this screen of smoke an immense moving mass crossing the plateau, going toward the Big Horn Mountains. This moving mass was distant about five or six miles, but looked much nearer, and almost directly between us and the setting sun, now darkened by the smoke and dust ladened atmosphere; the travois with families and belongings and the pony herds were massed, the long column with wide front was skirted by the warriors on guard; thus silhouetted against the red-lined western sky-line, their departure was to us a gladsome sight. A fervent "Thank God" that they had at last given up the contest was soon followed by grave doubts as to their motive for moving. Perhaps Custer had met Terry, and was coming to our relief; perhaps they were short of ammunition and were moving their village to a safe distance before making a final desperate effort to overwhelm us; perhaps it was only a ruse to get us on the move and then clean us out, were the conjectures.

The stench from the dead men and horses was now exceedingly offensive, and it was decided to take up a new position nearer the river. The companies were assigned to positions, and the men were put to work digging pits with the expectation of a renewal of the attack. Our loss on the hill had been eighteen killed and fifty-two wounded [including the wounded in Reno's retreat from the valley].

During the night of June 26th, Lieutenant De Rudio, Private O'Neal, Mr. Girard, the interpreter, and Jackson, a half-breed scout, came to our line. They had been left in the bottom when Reno made his retreat. In attempting to rejoin on the night of the 25th they found the approaches guarded by Indians, so they concealed themselves in the brush some distance up the valley.

Gall at the Reunion, 1886

In this narrative of the movements immediately preceeding, and resulting in, the annihilation of the men with Custer, I have related facts substantially as observed by myself or as given to me by Chief Gall of the Sioux. His statements have been corroborated by other Indians, notably the wife of "Spotted Horn Bull" an intelligent Sioux squaw, one of the first who had the courage to talk freely to any one who participated in the battle.

In 1886, on the tenth anniversary, an effort was made to have a reunion of the survivors at the battle-field. Colonel Benteen, Captains McDougall and Edgerly, Dr. Potter, Sergeant Hall, Trumpeter Penwell and myself met there on the 25th of June. Through the kind efforts of the officers and of the ladies at Fort Custer our visit was made as pleasant as possible. Through the personal influence of Major McLaughlin, Indian Agent at Standing Rock, Chief Gall was prevailed upon to accompany the party and describe Custer's part in the battle. We were unfortunate in not having an efficient and truthful interpreter on the field at the reunion. The statements I have used were, after our return to the agency, interpreted by Mrs. McLaughlin and Mr. Farribault, of the agency, both of whom are perfectly trustworthy and are familiar with the Sioux language.

At the reunion, 1886, a number of us were sitting near the monument asking questions of Gall. From the volubility of the answers by the interpreter nearly all, including Gall, became satisfied that the interpreter was "padding" and I could see that Gall was quite restive. Finally, Gall, giving me a significant glance and toss of his head and quirt, got up, went to his horse and mounted. Waiting a moment, so as not to attract attention, as I could see he did not want the interpreter with us, my orderly and I mounted and followed Gall over to Calhoun's Knoll. Gall silently surveyed the surroundings for a few moments, then he pointed out the direction of Custer's approach, indicating now rapid and now slow march, according to the ground; then the halt, the dismounting of a part and the forward movement of the other troops deploying as skirmishers, opening out his fingers to show this movement, the other troops following, then these latter made a rapid move to the right front toward Custer Hill. Turning to me, he told me to dismount; then he said: "You soldier; me Sioux," and put me in the several positions of the troops, indicating them; during this he indicated the lines of approach of his own warriors, the stampede of the led horses, the driving back of the soldiers, the final stand. Then the disposition of his warriors; some dismounted near the crest, rising and dropping to draw the fire to cause waste of ammunition; the mounted warriors were lower down on the hill side. Then he imitated the war whoop in a low tone, the quirting of the ponies and then the final charge!

All this was graphically told by the sign language with the occasional interpolation of an English or Sioux word. The old Chief was himself again—it was intensely dramatic! The subsequent relation of the same story through the interpreter after our return to Standing Rock seemed tame indeed.

Custer's Trail

It has been previously noted that General Custer separated from Reno before the latter crossed the Little Big Horn under orders to charge the village. Custer's column bore to the right of the river (a sudden change of plan, probably); a ridge of high bluffs and the river separated the two commands and they could not see each other. On this ridge, however, Custer and staff were seen to wave their hats, and heard to cheer as Reno was beginning the attack; but Custer's troops were at that time a mile or more to his right.

It was about this time that the trumpeter was sent back with Custer's last order to Benteen. From this place Custer could survey the valley for several miles above and for a short distance below Reno; yet he could only see a part of the village; he must, then, have felt confident that all the Indians were below him, hence, I presume, his message to Benteen. The view of the main body of the village was cut off by the highest points of the ridge, a short distance from him. Had he gone to this high point he would have understood the magnitude of his undertaking, and it is probable that his plan of battle would have been changed. We have no evidence that he did not go there. He could see, however, that the village was not breaking away toward the Big Horn Mountains. He must, then, have expected to find the squaws and children fleeing to the bluffs on the north, for in no other way do I account for his wide detour to the right. He must have counted upon Reno's success, and fully expected the "scatteration" of the non-combatants with the pony herds. The probable attack upon the families and the capture of the herds were in that event counted upon to strike consternation into the hearts of the warriors, and were elements for success upon which Custer counted in the event of a daylight attack.

When Reno's advance was checked, and his left began to fall back, Chief Gall started with some of his warriors to cut off Reno's retreat to the bluffs. On his way he was excitedly hailed by "Iron Cedar" one of his warriors, who was on the high point, to hurry to him, that more soldiers were coming. This was the first intimation the Indians had of Custer's column; up to the time of this incident they had supposed that all the troops were in at Reno's attack. Custer had then crossed the valley of the dry creek, and was marching along and well up the slope of the bluff forming the second ridge back from the river and nearly parallel to it. The command was marching in column of fours, and there was some confusion in the ranks, due probably to the unmanageableness of excited horses.

The accepted theory for ten years after the battle, and still persisted in by some writers, was that Custer's column had turned the high bluffs near the river, moved down the dry coulee and attempted to ford the river near the lowest point of these bluffs; that he was there met by an overpowering force and driven back; that he then divided his battalion, moved down the river with the view of attacking the village, but met with such resistance from the enemy posted along the river bank and ravines that he was compelled to fall back, fighting, to the position on the ridge. The numerous bodies found scattered between the river and the ridge were supposed to be the first victims of the fight. I am now satisfied that these were bodies of men who either survived those on the ridge or attempted to escape the massacre.

Custer's column was never nearer the river or village than his *final position on the ridge.* The wife of Spotted Horn Bull, when giving me her account of the battle, persisted in saying that Custer's column did not attempt to cross at the ford, and appealed to her husband, who supported her statement. On the battle-field, in 1886, Chief Gall indicated Custer's route to me, and it then flashed upon me that I, myself had seen Custer's trail. On June 28th, while we were burying the dead, I asked Major Reno's permission to go on the high ridge east or back of the field to look for tracks of shod horses to ascertain if some of the command might not have escaped. When I reached the ridge I saw this trail, and wondered who could have made it, but dismissed the thought that it had been made by Custer's column, because it did not accord with the theory with which we were then filled, that Custer had attempted to cross at the ford, and this trail was too far back and showed no indication of leading toward the ford. Trumpeter Penwell was my orderly and accompanied me. It was a singular coincidence that in 1886 Penwell was stationed at Fort Custer, and was my orderly when visiting the battle-field. Penwell corroborated my recollection of the trail.

The ford theory arose from the fact that we found there numerous tracks of shod horses, but they evidently had been made after the Indians had possessed themselves of the cavalry horses, for they rode them after capturing them. *No bodies of men or horses were found anywhere near the ford, and these facts are conclusive to my mind that Custer did not go to the ford with any body of men.*

Custer's Battle

As soon as Gall had personally confirmed Iron Cedar's report he sent word to the warriors battling against Reno, and to the people of the village. The greatest consternation prevailed among the families, and orders were given for them to leave at once. Before they could do so the great body of warriors had left Reno and hastened to attack Custer. This explains why Reno was not pushed when so much confusion at the river crossing gave the Indians every opportunity of annihilating his command. Not long after the Indians began to show a strong force in

Custer's front, Custer turned his column to the left, and advanced in the direction of the village to near a place now marked as a spring, halted at the junction of the ravines just below it, and dismounted two troops, Keogh's and Calhoun's to fight on foot. These two troops advanced at double-time to a knoll, now marked by Crittenden's monument. The other three troops, mounted, followed them a short distance in the rear. The led horses remained where the troops dismounted. When Keogh and Calhoun got to the knoll the other troops marched rapidly to the right; Smith's troops deployed as skirmishers, mounted, and took position on a ridge, which, on Smith's left, ended in Keogh's position (now marked by Crittenden's monument), and on Smith's right, ended at the hill on which Custer took position with Yates and Tom Custer's troops, now known as Custer's Hill, and marked by the monument erected to the command. Smith's skirmishers, holding their gray horses, remained in groups of fours. Twenty-eight bodies, mostly belonging to this troop were found in a big gully near the river, and I firmly believe that these men belonged to Lieutenant Sturgis' Platoon and had been ordered to locate a ford for crossing the river.

The line occupied by Custer's battalion was the first considerable ridge back from the river, the nearest point being about half a mile from it. His front was extended about three-fourths of a mile. The whole village was in full view. A few hundred yards from his line was another but lower ridge, the further slope of which was not commanded by his line. It was here that the Indians under Crazy Horse from the lower part of the village, among whom were the Cheyennes, formed for the charge on Custer's Hill. All Indians had now left Reno. Gall collected his warriors, and moved up a ravine south of Keogh and Calhoun. As they were turning this flank they discovered the led horses without any other guard than the horse-holders. They opened fire on the horse-holders, and used the usual devices to stampede the horses—that is, yelling, waving blankets, etc.; in this they succeeded very soon, and the horses were caught up by the squaws. In this disaster Keogh and Calhoun probably lost their reserve ammunition, which was carried in the saddle-bags. Gall's warriors now moved to the foot of the knoll held by Calhoun. A large force dismounted and advanced up the slope far enough to be able to see the soldiers when standing erect, but were protected when squatting or lying down. By jumping up and firing quickly, they exposed themselves only for an instant, but drew the fire of the soldiers, causing a waste of ammunition. In the meantime Gall was massing his mounted warriors under the protection of the slope. When everything was in readiness, at a signal from Gall, the dismounted warriors rose, fired, and every Indian gave voice to the war whoop; the mounted Indians gave whip to their ponies, and the whole mass rushed upon and crushed Calhoun. The maddened mass of Indians was carried forward by its own momentum over Calhoun and Crittenden down into the depression where Keogh was, with over thirty men, and all was over on that part of the field.

In the meantime the same tactics were being pursued and executed around Custer's Hill. The warriors, under the leadership of Crow King, Crazy Horse, White Bull, "Hump," Two Moon, and others, moved up the ravine west of Custer's Hill, and concentrated under the shelter of the ridges on his right flank and back of his position. Gall's bloody work was finished before the annihilation of Custer was accomplished, and his victorious warriors hurried forward to the hot fight then going on, and the frightful massacre was completed.

Smith's men had disappeared from the ridge, but not without leaving enough dead bodies to mark their line. About twenty-eight bodies of men belonging to this troop and other organizations were found in one ravine nearer the river. Many corpses were found scattered over the field between Custer's line of defense, the river, and in the direction of Reno's Hill. These, doubtless, were of men who had attempted to escape; some of them may have been sent as couriers by Custer. One of the first bodies I recognized and one of the nearest to the ford was that of Sergeant Butler of Tom Custer's troop. Sergeant Butler was a soldier of many years' experience and of known courage. The indications were that he had sold his life dearly, for near and under him were found many empty cartridge shells. From knowledge of his personality, and his detached position, I believe he had been selected as courier to communicate with Reno.

All the Indian accounts that I know of agree that there was no organized close-quarter fighting, except on the two flanks; that with the annihilation at Custer's Hill the battle was virtually over. It does not appear that the Indians made any advance to the attack from the direction of the river; they did have a defensive force along the river and in the ravines which destroyed those who left Custer's line.

There was a great deal of firing going on over the field after the battle by the young men and boys riding about and shooting into the dead bodies.

Another Account

In 1877 a party including Captain Philo Clark, the noted authority on "Indian Sign Language" and Col. J. W. Pope (then Lieutenant 5th Infantry) went over the battle-field with two Indians who were with the Hostiles in the fight, and an Indian scout who was with Reno's command. "We were then led over Custer's trail a distance of [two] miles away to the spot where he was killed. [In '76, with my trumpeter, I saw the *end* of this trail indicating very rapid gait. In 1886 Chief Gall indicated where the trail led; conforming to what Trumpeter Penwell and I saw in 1876.] This trail was in the valley north of the line of bluffs, on the north bank of the Little Big Horn. These two Indians, one of whom may have been "Iron Cedar," stated that after they had followed Reno's command to the hills, they passed on to the north and there saw Custer's command coming down the valley. They hastened and gave the alarm, this being the first intimation they had of Custer's approach. They said that Custer, when he came out in full view of the village, dismounted and formed line; "one troop was formed well forward, making an angle forward with the other troops along the Custer ridge; that this troop ["E" or "I"?] made a considerable fight and that nearly all of the Indians killed fell at this fight. (They estimated the loss at thirty or forty.) That this troop was soon driven back to the position where it was overwhelmed with the whole command; that when nearly all the command had been killed, a few men ran down to get shelter in the timber or ravines." (Extracts from letters from Colonel Pope, 1892.)

After the Battle

Tuesday morning, June 27th, we had reveille without the "morning guns," enjoyed the pleasure of a square meal, and had our stock properly cared for. Our commanding officer [Reno] seemed to think the Indians had some "trap" set for us, and required our men to hold themselves in readiness to occupy the pits at a moment's notice. Nothing seemed determined except to stay where we were. Not an Indian was in sight, but a few ponies were seen grazing down in the valley.

At 9:30 a.m. a cloud of dust was observed several miles down the river. The assembly was sounded, the horses were placed in a protected situation, and camp kettles and canteens were filled with water. An hour of suspense followed; but from the slow advance we concluded that they were our own troops. "But whose command is it?" We looked in vain for a gray-horse troop. It could not be Custer; it must then be Crook, for if it were Terry, Custer would be with him. Cheer after cheer was given for Crook. A white scout, Muggins Taylor, came up with a note from General Terry, addressed to General Custer, dated June 26th, stating that two of our Crow scouts had given information that our column had been whipped and nearly all had been killed; that he did not believe their story, but was coming with medical assistance. The scout said that he could not get to our lines the night before, as the Indians were on the alert. Very soon after this Lieutenant Bradley, 7th Infantry, came into our lines, and asked where I was. Greeting most cordially my old friend, I immediately asked: "Where is Custer?" He replied: "I don't know, but I suppose he was killed, as we counted 197 dead bodies. I don't suppose any escaped." We were simply dumbfounded. This was the first intimation we had of his fate. It was hard to realize; it did seem impossible. Then I took him to Major Reno and there introduced him to the officers.

[Insert by General Godfrey]

[Remarks of Brig. Gen. Edward S. Godfrey at Annual Dinner of Order Of Indian Wars, January 25, 1930.

Mr. Toastmaster, Companions and guests—

I am not going to tell you anything about the details of the campaign in '76, as far as I was concerned. It has only been three or four years since the country resounded with editorials, etc., on the battle of the Little Big Horn, and I suppose you have been fed up on it. So I will just relate one incident connected with it.

On the night of the 25th of June, after it became dark, Colonel Weir crawled up to me and, after some complimentary remarks about saving his troop, etc., he hesitated a while and said: "Godfrey, suppose there should be a clash of opinion as to what we should do, as between Major Reno and Captain Benteen, whose judgment would you follow?" I said, "Benteen's." He drew a long breath, said "all right, all right," and went away.

On the 28th, on our way to bury the dead on the Custer Battlefield, Captain Benteen and I were riding along, looking at the valley where Reno had made his retreat on the 25th. I said to Benteen, after we had scanned the country, "It's pretty damn bad." He turned to me and said, "What do you mean?" I replied, "Reno." He said, "God, I could tell you things that would make your hair stand on end." Just at that instant an orderly came up and joined the men behind, and Benteen said, "I cannot tell you now." I said, "Will you tell me sometime?" He replied, "Yes." Time and time again I asked him to tell me what he meant on that occasion, and always something came up for an excuse to delay him, as somebody came in the vicinity. I waited and made it my point to keep at him.

In '81, after I had read my paper on the Little Big Horn to the officers and cadets at the Military Academy, Benteen came up and paid me a visit. We were sitting out on the porch of double quarters, and I went at him again. Just as I got through, a young lady stepped out on the other side of the house. So that gave him an excuse again.

Sometime during the summer following we had a fishing excursion on the Jersey coast, and one evening everybody, except Benteen and myself, went down to the beach. I said, "Now, Benteen, there is no one around for a mile of us and there is no getting out of your promise to tell me; are you going to pay the debt?" He said, "God, let bygones be bygones." But I said, "No, you promised and I want to know it because I am interested in the history." Well, he hesitated quite a long time. Finally, he said, "On the evening of the 25th, Reno came to me and told me of his plan of getting away. He said, 'I propose to mount all my men that can ride on horses and mules, and destroy the property that we cannot take with us, and make a retreat to the wagon train at the mouth of the Powder River.' I said, 'What are you going to do with the wounded that cannot ride?' He said, 'We will have to abandon them.' I said, 'You can't do that.'" That was the end of it.]

Terry's Arrival

General Terry and staff, and officers of General Gibbon's column, soon after approached and their coming was greeted with prolonged hearty cheers. The grave countenance of the General awed the men to silence. The officers assembled to meet their guests. There was scarcely a dry eye; hardly a word was spoken, but quivering lips and hearty grasping of hands gave token of thankfulness for the relief and grief for the dead.

During the rest of the day we were busy collecting our effects and destroying surplus property. The wounded were cared for and taken to the camp of our new friends of the Montana column. Among the wounded was Saddler "Mike" Madden of my troop, whom I promoted to be sergeant, on the field, for gallantry. Madden was very fond of his grog. His long abstinence gave him a famous thirst. It was necessary to amputate his leg, which was done without administering any anesthetic; but after the amputation the surgeon gave him a good, stiff drink of brandy. Madden eagerly gulped it down, and his eyes fairly danced as he smacked his lips and said: "M-eh, doctor, cut off my other leg."

On the morning of the 28th, we left our intrenchments to bury the dead of Custer's command. The morning was bright, and from the high bluffs we had a clear view of Custer's battle-field. We saw a large number of objects that looked like white boulders scattered over the field. Glasses were brought into requisition, and it was announced that these objects were the dead bodies. Captain Weir exclaimed: "Oh, how white they look!"

All the bodies, except a few, were stripped of their clothing, according to my recollection nearly all were scalped or mutilated, but there was one notable exception, that of General Custer, whose face and expression were natural; he had been shot in the [left] temple and in the left side. Many faces had a pained, almost terrified expression. It is said that "Rain-in-the-Face," a Sioux warrior, has gloried that he had cut out and eaten the heart and liver of Captain Tom Custer. Other bodies were mutilated in a disgusting manner. Much has been said and many times I have been asked about the mutilations of General and Tom Custer's bodies. When we got to the battle-field to bury the dead, the regiment was deployed by troop so as to cover the whole front embracing the battle-ground, and each troop was apportioned a part of this front with orders to bury the dead on its territory. The ground covered by my troop took me two or three hundred yards below the monument. I had just identified and was supervising the burial of Boston Custer, when Major Reno sent for me to help identify the dead at Custer Hill. When I arrived there General Custer's body had been laid out. He had been shot in the left temple and the left breast. *There were no powder marks or signs of mutilation.* Mr. F. F. Girard, the interpreter, informed me that he preceded the troops there. He found the naked bodies of two soldiers, one across the other and Custer's naked body in a sitting posture between and leaning against them, his upper right arm along and on the topmost body, his right forearm and hand supporting his head in an inclining posture like one resting or asleep. There was no sign for the justification of the theory, insinuation or assertion that he committed suicide. When I asked Chief Gall if he knew why General Custer was not scalped, he replied that he "didn't know unless it was because he was the Big Chief, that they respected his rank and his bravery."

When I went to Tom Custer's body it had not been disturbed from its original position. It was lying downward, all the scalp was removed, leaving only tufts of his fair hair on the nape of his neck. The skull was smashed in and a number of arrows had been shot into the back of the head and in the body. I remarked that I believed it was Tom as he and I had often gone in swimming together and the form seemed familiar. We rolled the body over; the features where they had touched the ground were pressed out of shape and were somewhat decomposed. In turning the body, one arm which had been shot and broken, remained under the body; this was pulled out and on it we saw "T.W.C." and the goddess of liberty and flag. This, of course, completed our identification. His belly had been cut open and his entrails protruded. No examination was made to determine if his vitals had been removed.

There were forty-two bodies and thirty-nine dead horses on Custer's Hill. The bodies of Dr. Lord and Lieutenants Porter, Harrington, and Sturgis were not found, at least not recognized. The clothing of Porter and Sturgis I found in the village, and they showed that they had been killed. We buried according to my memoranda, 212 bodies. The killed of the entire command was 265, and of wounded we had fifty-two. The killed included sixteen officers, seven civilians, and three Indian scouts.

The loss of the Hostiles has never been determined. Thirty-eight dead were found in the village, some of them were killed in the Rosebud fights, one at Reno Hill and on the reconnaissance up the Little Big

Horn valley, numerous bodies were found sepultured in trees and on scaffolds. They had no statistics of their dead and wounded.

A "marker" in the battle-field cemetery, as a rule, shows where a body was buried; some bodies were moved from where they fell; they were not buried in deep graves or trenches as we did not have the tools necessary to dig them in the hard, dry ground.

In 1877 the bones of the men were collected and deposited where the monument now is; stakes were driven to show where the bodies or graves had been. Some years later a marker was put up where the stake indicated a grave, but some of these stakes had been taken away; some places were marked where vegetation grew rank or there was a depression to give a clue to a former grave. It is reasonable to suppose that the elements destroyed evidences of some graves before markers were placed, and consequently that all graves are not marked. [When the "markers" were received at Fort Custer the number corresponded to the whole number killed, including Reno's dead, but the officer in charge of installing these markers scattered the surplus over Custer's dead (those of Reno's dead) over the Custer Battlefield.]

The remains of Lieutenant Crittenden were left on the field where he fell. The remains of General Custer were buried at West Point, New York; those of the other officers were buried in the Post Cemetery at Fort Leavenworth, Kansas. Captain Keogh's remains were subsequently removed to Fort Hill Cemetery, Auburn, New York.

The question has often been asked if any soldier escaped. In August we camped at the mouth of the Rosebud where we found the carcass of a horse *shot in the head;* near the horse was a carbine; on the saddle was a small grain sack made of canvas and used by the 7th Cavalry only to carry oats during the march, when detached from the wagons. At the time of the discovery we conjectured that some man had escaped, and on reaching the river had killed his horse for meat and used the saddle straps to tie together a raft. An Indian would not have left the carbine but the man may have abandoned it, either because he was out of ammunition or could not risk the extra weight on his raft.

The question has often been asked: "What were the causes of Custer's defeat?"

I should say:

First. The overpowering numbers of the enemy and their unexpected cohesion.

Second. Reno's panic route from the valley.

Third. The defective extraction of the empty cartridge-shells from the carbines.

On the first, I will say that we had nothing conclusive on which to base calculations of the numbers, and to this day it seems almost incredible that such great numbers of Indians should have left the agencies, to combine against the troops, without information relating thereto having been communicated to the commanders of troops in the field, further than heretofore mentioned. The second has been mentioned incidentally. The Indians say if Reno's position in the valley had been held, they would have been compelled to divide their strength for the different attacks, which would have caused confusion and apprehension, and prevented the concentration of every able-bodied warrior upon the battalion under Custer; that, at the time of the discovery of Custer's advance to attack, the chiefs gave orders for the village to move, to break up; that at the time of Reno's retreat, this order was being carried out, but as soon as Reno's retreat was assured, the order was countermanded, and the squaws were compelled to return with the pony herds; that the order would not have been countermanded had Reno's forces remained fighting in the bottom. Custer's attack did not begin until after Reno had reached the bluffs.

Of the third we can only judge by our own experience. When cartridges were dirty and corroded, the ejectors did not always extract the empty shells from the chambers, and the men were compelled to use knives to get them out. When the shells were clean no great difficulty was experienced. To what extent this was a factor in causing the disaster we have no means of knowing.

A possible fourth cause was the division of the command. With all the regiment under Custer's personal direction, the results might have been different; but, on the other hand, the whole command might have been wiped out.

The division of the command was not in itself faulty. The same tactics were pursued at the battle of Washita and were successful. That was a surprise attack and there was *full co-operation* of the separate commands; each commander carried out his instructions. My studies of the battle of the Little Big Horn leave me in little doubt that had Reno made his charge as ordered, or made a bold front even, the Hostiles would have been so engaged in the bottom that Custer's approach from the

Northeast would have been such a surprise as to cause the stampede of the village and would have broken the morale of the warriors.

On the other hand, with the entire command concentrated under Custer's leadership the charge would have been carried *home*, and, I believe, successfully.

General Custer has been accused of selfish motives in refusing to take the additional forces said to have been offered him while at the mouth of the Rosebud. It is a very delicate matter to analyze motives. In going over letters and diary written during the campaign I find references that may help. General Terry, in his official report makes no mention of the offer, but he says: "It was believed to be impracticable to join Colonel Gibbon's troops to Lieutenant-Colonel Custer's forces; for more than one-half of Colonel Gibbon's troops were infantry who would be unable to keep up with cavalry in a rapid movement; while to detach Gibbon's mounted men and add them to the 7th Cavalry would leave his force too small to act as an independent body." Thus, it is seen that General Terry had his own reasons for not sending them.

In a letter dated June 10, 1876, I find: "The 2nd Cavalry officers are greatly disgusted; one company has to be mounted all the time; the C.O. selects very poor camps for cavalry and *their horses are in very poor condition.*"

The Gatling guns were each hauled by four *condemned* cavalry horses. They were unfitted for long rapid marches and would have been unable to keep up if there had been such a demand upon them. The poor condition of the horses in the 2nd Cavalry and in the Gatling gun battery may have decided against both of them.

Colonel Gibbon in his report says: "The first intimation we had of the force and strategy opposed to us was the check given to Custer's column . . ."

Major Brisbin, 2nd Cavalry, in a letter to me, January, 1892, says he was present at the conference on the steamboat *Far West*; that at General Terry's request he traced the routings of the troops on the map and placed pins to show their probable places en route; that Custer turned to the right and left of the Rosebud just twenty miles short of his further most point on the Rosebud routing.

General Terry says in his report that at the conference he communicated his plan of operations. "It was that Colonel Gibbon's column should cross the Yellowstone near the mouth of the Big Horn, and, thence up that stream with the expectation that it would arrive at the mouth of the Little Big Horn by the 26th. That Lieutenant-Colonel Custer with the whole 7th Cavalry should proceed up the Rosebud until he should ascertain the direction in which the trail discovered by Major Reno led; that if it led to the Little Big Horn it should not be followed (NOTE: Compare with written instructions, wherein Custer is given discretion when so nearly in contact with the enemy, etc.) but that Lieutenant-Colonel Custer should keep still farther to the south before turning toward that river, in order to intercept the Indians should they attempt to pass around his left, and in order, by a longer march, to give time for Gibbon's column to come up. This plan was founded on the belief that the two columns might be brought into co-operating distance of each other, so either of them which should be first to engage might, by a "waiting fight" give time for the other to come up."

The length of the marches has been a subject of comment, it being asserted that the command was subjected to long and exhausting marches. They were: June 22nd, 12 miles; June 23rd, 33 to 35 miles; June 24th, 28 miles; then June 24th at 11:30 p.m. [about 10 miles and from 8:00 a.m. to the divide], about 8 miles; then from the divide between the Rosebud and the Little Big Horn to the battle, about 20 miles; in all about 113 miles [in 4 days].

The battle was unavoidable. Every man in Terry's and Custer's commands expected a battle; it was for that purpose, to punish the Indians, that the command was sent out, and with that determination Custer made his preparations. Had Custer continued his march southward— that is, left the Indian trail—the Indians would have known of our movement on the 25th, and a battle would have been fought very near the same field on which Crook had been attacked and forced back only a week before; the Indians never would have remained in camp and allowed a concentration of the several columns to attack them. If they had escaped without punishment of battle Custer would undoubtedly have been blamed.

The 29th and 30th of June were occupied in destroying property left in the Indian village, preparing litters to carry the wounded and transporting them at night to the Big Horn, where they were placed aboard the *Far West*.

Captain Grant Marsh, master of the *Far West*, was the pioneer navigator of the Big Horn and had courageously held his boat there in the face of receding waters, taking chances of stranding his boat on the rocks and shoals of the treacherous river. But Grant Marsh was always ready to take any chances when the services of his government demanded them. He was a man of tremendous energy and resources to fight and overcome all obstacles. July 1st and 2nd the command marched to, and crossed, the Yellowstone and camped on "Pease Bottom," the [scene] of our fight with the Hostiles in 1873.

At noon July 3rd, the *Far West* loaded with the wounded, Captain Baker's company as escort, and Captain Smith, General Terry's aide-de-camp, and Assistant-Adjutant General of the expedition, with dispatches, etc., cast off, swung into mid-stream, and with "full steam ahead" crashing through willows and caroming against mud banks, made her memorable voyage down the Yellowstone and Missouri rivers, reaching Bismarck 11:30 p.m. July 5th, and then giving to the thirty-nine widows at Fort Lincoln, and to the world, the astounding news of Custer's Last Battle.

Postscript

Recent publications of comments on the movements of the troops and the conduct and characteristics of officers prompts me to add to the foregoing account.

Disobedience of Orders. A careful perusal of the orders issued to General Custer will show that the General was given practically a *free hand.* If any supplemental instructions were given, they were never revealed to the public. General Terry had had no practical experience in Indian warfare. General Custer had that practical experience; he was a student on Indian characteristics; had intimate observations, both in peace and war. He knew that in our centuries of Indian warfare there were more escapes than punishments inflicted for outrages and depredations; that most of these escapes resulted from failure to give vigorous pursuits in following the Hostiles; that the way to find the Hostiles was to follow the trail, stay with it; that success usually depended on surprise attacks; that the most successful surprises came with night approaches and day-break attacks; that forewarned approaches resulted in scatteration into groups or by families and thus escaped punishment, and pursuit apt to be disorganized.

It was an absurdity to think that two commands, of 700 and 400, separated by from fifty to one hundred miles, could co-ordinate their movements in that open country and hold the Hostiles for a co-operative attack. In such a case, and the Hostiles had escaped, who would have shouldered the blame?

In the text I have shown that the country toward Tulloch's Fork was under surveillance, and it is reasonable to suppose that had circumstances not caused a change of plans for a daybreak attack on the 26th, that Scout Herendeen would have been sent to Gen. Terry's headquarters with information as to plans, etc.

There could not have been any understanding, as contended by some, that the two commands of Custer and Gibbon were to meet at or near the mouth of the Little Big Horn on June 26th.

Rashness. The number of probable Hostiles, one thousand to fifteen hundred, did not cause any dismay in the command. We knew, of course, that there would be many casualties, which would be the misfortune of individuals, but that there would be a disaster was not considered probable. General Custer had no reason to think that there would be a general exodus from the Indian agencies on the Missouri River and from Nebraska to join the Hostile camps without warning being given in ample time by the Agents, the Bureau of Indian Affairs or Interior Department to the military authorities. Such a warning from General Sheridan, via Fort Lincoln, by courier was received about [July 14th], too late to avert disaster.

Drunkenness. I have seen articles imputing wholesale drunkenness to both officers and enlisted men, including General Custer who was absolutely abstemious. I do not believe that any officer, except Major Reno, had any liquor in his possession. Major Reno had half a gallon keg that he took with him in the field, but I don't believe any other officer sampled its contents. I saw all the officers early in the morning and again at our halt at the divide and when officers' call was sounded to announce the determination to attack, and I saw no sign of intoxication; all had that serious, thoughtful mien, indicating that they sensed the responsibilities before them.

Reno's Leadership

Among the questions propounded has been this one: "If" Reno had advanced "to the sound of the guns" when we heard the firing on Custer's field, would he have rescued Custer's command? Frankly, I do not believe Custer's command would have been rescued under Reno's leadership. At no time during the battle was his conduct such as to inspire confidence. His faltering advances down the valley, his halting, his falling back to the defensive position in the woods in the old river bed before his command had suffered a single casualty in the ranks; his disorganized, panic retreat to the bluffs with practically no resistance, his conduct up to and during the siege, and until the arrival of General Terry was not such as to inspire confidence or even respect, except for his authority; and there was a time during the night of the 25th, when his authority under certain conditions, was to be ignored. We thought he ought to go, his attention was called to the firing on the Custer field; it was suggested that he go; he was waiting for the ammunition packs to replenish the ammunition; then he waited for the delayed pack-train. We started and marched as far as the first ridge when we beheld the dismounted men crossing the valley, men that had been left when he made his retreat. We halted and waited for them to join, to be mounted and have their ammunition replenished; then we advanced to the high point where we could overlook the Custer battle-field. We saw the commotion on that field when the Hostiles started in our direction. Three troops, D, K and [M] were then ordered to take positions and hold their ground; with the other four and the pack train Reno returned to our first position on the bluffs, nearly two miles away. Then he ordered the troops in position to fall back at once.

"Comanche"

The horse "Comanche," found badly wounded on the site of the Hostile village after the battle of the Little Big Horn, and said to be the only living thing that escaped, was a claybank gelding, ridden by Captain and Brevet Lieutenant-Colonel Myles W. Keogh, 7th Cavalry.

He was purchased in [August] of [1867] at St. Louis, Mo., and [was assigned to troop I]. He was then [6] years old.

When Sully's expedition against the southern Indians was organized at Fort Dodge, Kansas, September, 1868, Captain Keogh was acting Inspector-General on General Sully's staff. He chose this horse for his field mount. During one of our engagements with the Comanche Indians on the Cimarron River or the Beaver Fork, the horse was wounded [in the hip] while Keogh was riding him. Thereupon, the horse was named "Comanche." Keogh became very much attached to him, and thereafter he was known as the "captain's mount," and Keogh rode him at the battle of the Little Big Horn.

When General Terry's troops arrived on the site of the hostile village, June 27th, Lieutenant H. J. Nowlan, 7th Cavalry, who was field quartermaster on General Terry's staff, and an intimate friend of Keogh (both were Irishmen) recognized "Comanche," took him in charge and sent him on the steamer *Far West* with the wounded men to Fort Lincoln, where he was nursed back to health. After his restoration he was in great demand for a ladies' riding horse. The rivalry among the young ladies of the garrison at Fort Lincoln as to whom should be awarded the privilege of riding him, on several occasions when riding parties went out from the post, caused some heart-burnings. The Colonel, to solve the vexatious problem, ordered that "Comanche" be retired from active service, and be no longer ridden; that when the troop was paraded on ceremonial occasions "Comanche" should be led with the troop.

After "Comanche" died at Fort Riley, Kan., [7th] November, 1891, Prof. Dyche, a naturalist, connected with the University of Kansas, made a proposition to the officers of the 7th Cavalry to mount "Comanche" for $400, and the officers retain him, or he would mount him for the University and would put him in the University museum. Captain Nowlan called the officers together and they decided to let the University have him, principally because they had no way of transporting him when changing stations.

Prof. Dyche took him to Lawrence and mounted him in a very creditable manner, and the horse is there now, so far as I know. He was exhibited at the World's Fair in 1893. "Comanche" was 28 years old when he died. "He still lives!"

THE CAVALRY CAMPAIGN OUTFIT AT THE LITTLE BIG HORN

JAMES S.

HUTCHINS

Forever bright in the American legend is the spectacle of Brevet Major General George Armstrong Custer standing at bay with a handful of liege men grouped about him, pouring their last shots into the faces of pressing Indian warriors. Behind this tumultuous scene lies that highly controversial engagement known as the Battle of the Little Bighorn or as the Custer Battle, wherein on 25 June 1876, the enterprising Custer launched the 7th Regiment of U.S. Cavalry in attack upon the vast camps of allied Sioux and Northern Cheyenne Indians lying along the Little Bighorn River in southeastern Montana Territory. In the resultant disaster five companies of the 7th, under Custer's personal leadership, were surrounded and killed to the last man. The balance of the shattered regiment managed, although hard pressed, to avoid a similar end. For 79 years "Custer's Last Fight" has beguiled the brushes of as many artists as has any other combat in American military history. Yet an inspection of even a few of the numerous pictorial representations will disclose varied misconceptions of the appearance of the 7th Cavalry—and the U.S. Cavalry in general—on campaign in the summer of the Centennial Year. The purpose of this essay is to present a reconstruction of the campaign outfit—equipment, weapons, and dress—of the 7th at the time of its epic defeat at the Little Bighorn.

But if we wish to visualize accurately the appearance of the 7th on that June afternoon, we should first get a historical view of the efforts of the Ordnance Department to improve cavalry and horse equipments during the decade following the Civil War. The succeeding Chiefs of Ordnance during those years were not unaware of the need for bettering much of the equipment, to say nothing of the armament, in use by troops serving on the far-away frontier. The design of cavalry and horse equipments which would best meet the peculiar conditions imposed upon the Cavalry in service in the West where the bulk of that arm was employed for many years following 1865—posed numerous problems, the solution of one of which quite often created another and some of which were never really solved to the satisfaction of all. Boards of officers convened at the instance of the Chief of Ordnance in 1872 and 1874 gave considerable attention to these problems and made recommendations for the re-design of both cavalry and horse equipments.[1] But penny-pinching economy was the rule in military expenditures during the period and the Ordnance Department, faced with the prospect of continuingly meager appropriations, could scarcely ever afford to forget its large stores of serviceable equipments left over from the Civil War. A recent study made of the correspondence of the Office of the Chief of Ordnance during the period (preserved in the National Archives) shows conclusively that nearly all arsenal manufacture of new and improved patterns of cavalry and horse equipments was forestalled until after the close of 1876.

The only major exception was the experimental cavalry equipment based on what was termed the "brace system" recommended by a board convened early in 1872. This equipment consisted of a special saber belt to which was attached a "brace yoke" composed of leather suspenders which passed over the wearer's shoulders and crossed in back. A special carbine sling, 1 ¾ inches wide, was attached by its ends to the suspenders at front and back so as to form a loop under the right arm to support the swivel. This equipment had its origin in an experimental infantry equipment (based on one which had found some favor in the British Army) whereby the foot soldier's marching load was to be better distributed. Approximately 2,000 sets of this equipment were manufactured at Watervliet Arsenal and distributed for trial among all the cavalry regiments during the first half of 1873. The 7th, for example, was required to accept 500 sets, which were apportioned among Companies B, C, F, H, I, and K.[2] The "brace system" for the Cavalry proved a dismal failure in actual service. Men and officers deemed it "bulky" and "cumbersome" and at least one company commander in the 7th alleged that it would cause his men to become round-shouldered.[3] The Chief of Ordnance soon found himself all too aware of such widespread distaste and at length gave sanction for the approval of requests by company commanders to turn in the trial sets. By the close of 1874 the ill-conceived and costly "brace system" equipment had practically disappeared from the quarterly returns of ordnance property of every cavalry regiment.[4]

Later in 1872 another board recommended a series of modifications embracing many component parts of both cavalry and horse equipments. These recommendations, approved by the War Department, were announced to the Army in G. O. 60, A. G. O., 29 June 1872, the appearance of which resulted in many requisitions from optimistic cavalry commands. The Ordnance Department was at that time, however, already committed to manufacture of the experimental "brace system" equipment and, regarding the items described in G. O. 60, the Army was advised in an unnumbered circular issued by the Adjutant General on 20 March 1873:

> Requisitions should not be made for any of the horse equipments, Cavalry accoutrements, materials, or tools enumerated in General Orders No. 60 . . . 1872, from this office, except to replace stores worn out in service or to supply deficiencies. The order was not intended to direct or authorize a general refitting of companies, the limited appropriation available for this purpose not permitting such a change.

Whatever quantities were received by cavalry commands of the various items listed in G. O. 60 were, with one exception, so small as to be practically negligible. When in 1874 subsequent board, occupied with re-design of horse equipment, requested the Chief of Ordnance to furnish reports from officers who had used the 1872 modified horse equipment in their commands, the board was told that no complete sets of such equipment had yet been issued.[5] There were, however, issued in 1873, along with the trial sets of "brace system" equipment, two patterns of carbine cartridge boxes and a carbine cartridge pouch, all experimental, mentioned in G. O. 60, 1872, as of "the patterns now being prepared for trial." Boxes and pouch were designed to be worn on the waist belt. The boxes were designated "No. 1" and "No. 2," each containing 24 canvas loops to hold .50 cal. metallic cartridges. The pouch, fleece-lined, was a modification of the original Dyer pouch, carried by means of a shoulder sling, which had, earlier in the 1870's, seen some use by certain cavalry companies including several of the 7th. The modified Dyer pouch found some favor whereas the boxes were considered unsatisfactory because they would not retain cartridges when worn by mounted men. Another deterrent to their use was the introduction of the .45 cal. cartridge in 1874. Anyway, neither boxes nor pouch could stand long before the more efficient looped cartridge belt which, although necessarily improvised, was finding favor among ever-increasing numbers of soldiers in the West during these years.

As early as 1872 at least one cavalry regiment, the 3d, stationed in the Southwest, was reported to be using the cartridge belt to the utter exclusion of cartridge boxes or pouch.[6] Statements received by the Chief of Ordnance in 1873 from representative officers throughout the cavalry regiments indicate that approximately 67 per cent of these then favored the pouch for field service, ten per cent Box No. 1 or Box No. 2, and 23 per cent the cartridge belt.[7] When the Cavalry Equipment Board of 1874 requested recommendations in regard to carrying carbine ammunition in the field, almost two-thirds of 102 cavalry officers responding preferred the cartridge belt.[8] A very good index of the extent to which the looped belt had come into use by troops serving in the Northwest by 1876 is given in a letter to the Chief of Ordnance from Captain C. E. Dutton, Chief Ordnance Officer of the Department of the Platte, dated at Omaha, 14 January 1877:

> I have recently been to Cheyenne for the purpose of making inquiry among the officers returning from the Sioux campaign concerning the deportment of the supplies furnished by the Ordnance Department. The unusually large number of officers collected at that place & passing through it has given me a good opportunity to collect a considerable mass of *individual* opinion & experience . . . upon a few points I received information sufficiently definite to induce me to report it at once . . . The first point relates to the difficulty of extracting cartridge shells from the carbine . . . It arises from the corrosion of the copper by contact with the leather of the belts in which the soldiers carry their cartridges when in

the field . . . This was believed by both officers & men & the remedy was soon found. The belts being considered very much more suitable than cartridge boxes for active service the men made for themselves cartridge belts out of canvas or any other strong fabric which could be procured & fastened them with large buckles or sundry improvised devices & the difficulty at once disappeared. Those who could not find strong cloth & who for various reasons retained the leather belts were in the habit of scouring their cartridges every day or twice a day . . . would [it] not be advisable that both Infantry & Cavalry be allowed to draw from the Ordnance Dept. thimblebelts of canvas or other textile material for use in active campaigns in the Indian country . . . The officers & soldiers *will not use* the cartridge box & *will* use the belt & if they cannot obtain canvas belts from the Ord. Dept. they will improvise them. I should add however that some Cavalry Captains prefer the fleece-lined pouch but certainly not a majority of them.[9]

While it seems unlikely that any officers of the 7th Cavalry were among the individuals interviewed by Captain Dutton at Cheyenne that winter, it is nevertheless interesting to compare the preference then still expressed by some cavalry officers to a similar preference stated by officers of the 7th two years earlier. In contrast to the preference for the cartridge belt on the part of the majority of cavalry officers queried in 1874, of fifteen 7th officers who expressed themselves on the subject at that time, all save one favored the pouch for field service, including General Custer and those officers who were to command Companies A, B, C, F, and G, in the spring of 1876.[10]

The actual extent to which the cartridge belt was in use by the 7th by mid-1876 remains rather obscure. An enlisted (Company C) survivor of the Custer Battle stated in describing the fight that, while he himself wore a "prairie belt," he noticed that "belts for carrying ammunition were . . . just coming into use, and a great many of us had nothing but a small cartridge box as means for carrying our ammunition when away from our horses."[11] It should be remembered that it was a very rare occurrence for a cavalry regiment to be assembled in its entirety as was the 7th in the spring of 1876. Ordinarily the regiment was scattered far and wide in detachments composed of small groups of companies or even single companies, a fact which would surely contribute to varying degrees of progress among different companies toward uniformity in those parts of a campaign outfit where there was any choice.

In the opinion of the author most companies of the 7th were by 1876 equipped in the main with the cartridge belt while in a few companies the pouch was still in use to a considerable extent. The pouches probably numbered some of the experimental modified Dyer pattern issued in 1873 but the majority of them were in all likelihood the pouch recommended for general issue by the Cavalry Equipment Board of 1874. This pouch was evidently quite similar in appearance to the experimental pattern of 1873. It was often termed "Dyer's Pattern" or "Dyer's, modified." It was to contain forty cartridges.[12]

On 24 April 1874, Captain Clifton Comly, writing to the Chief of Ordnance from San Antonio Arsenal, requested that "2,000 carbine cartridge pouches (wool lined) be sent to him for issue to the 4th & 10th Cavalry [because] the carbine cartridge boxes (Sharps) on hand are unsuitable for cal. .45 ammunition." On 17 June Watervliet Arsenal was instructed by the Chief of Ordnance to "issue pouches as called for—made to conform strictly to the recommendations of the Board [adjourned 5 May]." The pouches were on their way to Captain Comly by the end of August 1874.[13] According to the annual reports of the Chief of Ordnance, nearly 4,000 such pouches were issued to cavalry commands up to 30 June 1876. This pouch was always issued when called for.[14] Except for the pouch, manufacture of the patterns of cavalry and horse equipments recommended by the Cavalry Equipment Board of 1874 was confined until late 1876 to a few "sample sets" intended for issue to chief ordnance officers of military departments.[15]

In 1876 the carbine cartridge pouch would be worn on the black leather saber belt with rectangular brass belt plate bearing the U.S. coat of arms and German silver wreath as described in the 1861 *Ordnance Manual*.[16] The issue pistol cartridge pouch consisted of the old percussion cap pouch.[17] Most if not all of the men of the 7th were equipped with the carbine sling, 2½ inches wide with 2-prong brass buckle, although at least some must have carried their carbines across the pommel on the march, after the almost universal habit of civilian plainsmen and Indians.[18] The issue belt holster was still the pattern having a wide semi-circular flap now usually associated with the Civil War, although holsters of various non-regulation patterns were very likely worn by some officers and perhaps a few of the men. In regard to the issue holster, it should be borne in mind that its belt loop was designed to accommodate the regulation leather waist belt, 1.9 inches wide, and no more. Thus an individual seeking to use this holster in conjunction with a cartridge belt was forced to adopt some expedient, either altering the holster's belt loop or providing the belt with some special means of attachment for the holster. This deficiency in the holster went unrecognized by the Ordnance Department when it manufactured and issued the first uniform cartridge belts in 1877.

From the 7th's organization in 1866 it used the McClellan saddle. The leather-covered saddle tree was first introduced in the regiment in 1869[19] and in 1876 all of the saddles in the regiment contained this feature, although the plain rawhide covered tree did not disappear entirely from use in any of the cavalry regiments until the close of 1875.[20] Leather hoods were absent from the stirrups of the enlisted men of the 7th at the Little Bighorn, although this was not characteristic of all cavalry units at that period. Early in 1876 Watervliet Arsenal constructed, for trial in the field, twenty saddles bearing certain features invented by First Lieutenant G. E. Albee, 24th Infantry, with the object of making the saddle "girt . . . upon the animal more easily, quickly, and securely than is possible by the ordinary means now in use."[21] On 14 May 1876, three days before the 7th marched forth from Fort Abraham Lincoln as part of Brigadier General A. H. Terry's "Dakota Column," one each of the experimental Albee saddles were issued to Captains T. B. Weir, F. W. Benteen, G. W. Yates, and M. W. Keogh (master of the celebrated "Comanche"), all of whom were company commanders in the regiment.[22] It appears reasonable to assume that these officers or perhaps members of their companies used the Albee saddles during the campaign that lay ahead.

The girth used by the 7th in 1876 was of blue woolen webbing. The woolen saddle blanket, indigo-blue with orange border, was still the standard for cavalry. It was not until September 1876 that the initial issue of new pattern "dark gray" saddle blankets was made (to the 4th Cavalry). The Model 1863 curb bit was in general use throughout the Cavalry in 1876. Of the Shoemaker curb bit, recommended for adoption in 1874, the first specimens, totalling sixty, were manufactured at Watervliet Arsenal in 1876, most of them intended for trial at West

Point. Headstall and halter issue at the close of the Civil War remained standard. The leather halter strap was used in the field, the halter chain, while it was on hand in the 7th, being reserved for garrison use.

Nose bag and picket pin were still as described in the 1861 *Ordnance Manual*. The first picket pins to bear the Lyon's patent swivel feature, recommended for adoption in 1874, were constructed at Watervliet Arsenal in 1876 by altering a large quantity of unserviceable picket pins of the preceding pattern. The small carbine socket and the Model 1859 saddlebags were standard throughout 1876 and for some time thereafter,[23] although the saddlebags were the source of continual complaints from officers who considered them too small. Captain Dutton, further along in his letter of 14 January 1877, stated the case to the Chief of Ordnance:

> Cavalry officers are in great want of the new saddle-bags. The old pattern (small size) are almost useless to them. The leather bags [Model 1874] would be preferred though the linen bags [Model 1872] would be satisfactory. I think that if the Cavalry could be supplied at once or before the spring campaign opens with large saddle-bags that branch of the service would be most highly delighted.

On February 23, 1877, Captain J. W. Reilly, Chief Ordnance Officer of the Military Division of the Missouri, wired the Chief of Ordnance from Chicago: "Larger saddle bags than old pattern leather ones badly needed. Is it possible to furnish them?" The reply, sent the same day, was that ". . . . it is impossible to supply large saddle bags."[24]

The 7th Cavalry bore full field equipment when it left Fort Lincoln in mid-May. However, when the regiment was camped between 11–16 June at the supply depot established at the junction of the Yellowstone and the Powder Rivers, it stripped to "light marching order" in accord with general practice when rapid marches and the probability of action promised. Here all sabers were boxed and stored. Superfluous clothing, extra blankets, and tentage, were ordered left behind, although officers retained tent flies and some amount of bedding for themselves. Thenceforth the enlisted men were to snatch their rest wrapped in saddle blanket and overcoat with the saddle for a pillow.

The saddle pack of the average trooper was from that time forward constituted as follows. The sky-blue mounted overcoat was folded and strapped to the pommel, although some of the men, to lighten their horses' loads, abandoned their overcoats at the point of commencing the regiment's march up the Rosebud on 22 June.[25] The lariat, rolled or coiled, with picket pin attached, hung from the near pommel ring while the nose bag was suspended from the ring opposite. Strapped to the cantle was the "small . . . canvas . . . grain bag . . . about 20 inches long . . . with which the Seventh had provided itself,"[26] filled on 22 June with twelve pounds of oats. Sidelines also were probably secured to the cantle. The tin cup was fastened by its handle to the near saddlebag strap or, possibly, to one of the coat straps on the cantle. The canteen hung down the near side, its cloth sling apparently looped about the saddlebag stud on the cantle arc. The covering of the canteen upon issue was of gray felt, regarding which Captain Dutton commented in his letter of 14 January 1877:

> There is a very general complaint against the felt covering of canteens. It is very perishable & wears out very rapidly. Hundreds of canteens were covered with fragments of blanket rudely sewed on & these were found to be much more serviceable. I might add my own experience with a blanket-covered canteen which I have carried upon my saddle & shoulder for two summers & the cover is good yet.[27]

Most of the men carried their rations of hardtack and bacon in haversacks, which in many cases were evidently suspended from the saddle.[28]

During the first half of 1874 the 7th had turned in an assortment of revolvers, two-thirds of which consisted of much-worn Colt and Remington percussion models using paper cartridges, to be rearmed throughout with the Model 1872 Colt Army Revolver, .45 cal., the famous "Peacemaker."[29] This was the sidearm of the regiment in 1876, carried by men and officers alike with the exception of General Custer, who evidently carried a brace of stubby English revolvers,[30] and perhaps a few others. By mid-1875 the entire regiment had received the Model 1873 Springfield Carbine.[31] Evidently most of the men of the 7th were equipped with thong and brush wipers for the purpose of cleaning their arms.[32] At this period it was customary to provide wooden ramrods with carbines, in the ratio of one to ten.[33] Some of the officers carried the issue carbine in the field but by no means all of them. General Custer, an ardent huntsman, used a Remington sporting rifle,

J.S.HUTCHINS

*Mounted private of the 7th Cavalry in full campaign kit as drawn
by the author. This trooper obviously preferred the cartridge
belt to either box or pouch.*

while his brother, Captain T. W. Custer, appears to have carried the
Model 1873 Springfield Officer's Rifle. Captain T. H. French preferred
"a Springfield rifle, caliber .50, breech-loader" (referred to by the men
as a "Long Tom"), while his veteran First Sergeant used "a 15-pound
Sharps' telescope rifle, caliber .45," made to his order at Bismarck,
Dakota Territory, for $100.[34] Most members of the 7th rounded out
their armament with "butcher knives," carried in their belts.

All of the men wore a soft broad-brimmed hat, either a gray slouch,
purchased by the individual, or the issue campaign hat of black wool
felt, regarding which an experienced officer observed at its introduction in 1873: ". . . lasts in the field about three weeks; it then becomes
the most useless, uncouth rag ever put upon a man's head."[35] However,
the Quartermaster General seems to have effected some improvement
in its quality by 1876.[36] A soldier participant (Company H) at the Little
Bighorn recalled that Companies C, E, F, I, and L (those companies
wiped out with Custer), wore gray hats into the fight, while the balance

JSH

First Lieutenant William W. Cooke, Adjutant, 7th Cavalry depicted by the
author from contemporary photographs.

of the regiment wore the issue black.[37] A civilian scout with the 7th
stated a few years later in describing the battle: "Occasionally a man
had a letter on his cap [sic], but they generally wore what kind of hat
they pleased, and not all had letters on their hats."[38] At this period,
brass branch insignia, regimental numerals, and company letters, were
issued as separate items.

Most of the men wore the regulation 5-button fatigue blouse of dark
blue flannel with falling collar. But there is every probability that some
wore the "old pattern" 12-button cavalry jacket with yellow trim, some
of which were still in store and, per G.O. 58, A.G.O., 1874, were to
be issued until stocks were exhausted. Judging from contemporary
photographs of cavalrymen on campaign it appears that the original
standing collars of these jackets were altered to the falling pattern,
probably by tailors among the men.[39] During daytime heat the blouse
was usually removed and secured to the saddle. Beneath the blouse
was a flannel shirt, generally the issue navy-blue, although some of

the men doubtless wore shirts of the checkered "hickory" variety purchased from civilian traders. Trousers were generally of the "mixture" sky-blue kersey, the seats and insides of the legs customarily being reinforced with canvas.[40] The issue top-boot of 1876 did not reach the knee. Trouser legs were stuffed into boot tops or were allowed to hang at full length over boot legs at the whim of the individual. Gauntlets, other than ones of sealskin for winter use, were not an item of issue and very few enlisted men, in some contrast to officers, appear to have worn gauntlets of any sort on other than winter campaigns. Few, if any, cavalrymen of those days appear to have flaunted the large yellow neckerchief conspicuous on movie "troopers," although some officers wore cravats with broad running ends when in the field.

In the campaign garb of the officers, especially, informality was the keynote. General Custer as usual set the pace for the regiment with a light gray low-crowned hat, blouse and trousers of fringed buckskin, a navy-blue shirt with its wide collar probably secured by a scarlet cravat, and topboots. About his waist was a canvas cartridge belt from which were suspended his holsters and a knife in a fringed and beaded case.[41] Going into his last battle, Custer carried field glasses [42]—many of the officers carried glasses—and a map case.[43] A number of the officers wore buckskin blouses in emulation of their chief while others, such as Major M. A. Reno, wore the regulation fatigue blouse.[44] All of the officers wore navy-blue shirts, often cut double-breasted and sometimes trimmed with white or yellow braid. The points of the collars usually bore, worked in yellow silk, crossed sabers and the numeral "7."[45] Judging from a photograph of a large group of officers of the regiment made in the Black Hills in 1874, it was the exaggerated fashion of some of them during the period to hook up the wide brims quite close about the crowns of their campaign hats. Second Lieutenant W. S. Edgerly stated afterward that he wore such a hat at the Little Bighorn.[46] Major Reno observed in 1879: "Previous to leaving the mouth of the Rosebud I had been wearing a felt hat, and it was dusty and dirty, and some officers went on a boat to where a trader had some broad brimmed straw hats, which we paid 25 or 50 cents for. They had no band, but they were a very good shelter from the sun. I wore one of those."[47] It is not improbable that some of the enlisted men also purchased straw hats at such an opportunity. A few of the officers wore the Wellington boot with white canvas leggings.[48]

Such was the campaign outfit of the immortal 7th Cavalry as it went into action at the Little Bighorn. It is ironic to view the natty uniforms, gleaming equipments, and sleek mounts, which often appear in fanciful paintings and in movie versions of "Custer's Last Fight." The five-weeks old campaign had carried the regiment through scorching heat, rain, and even snow. The sweat-soaked clothing and the equipments were coated with dust and splotched with accumulated dried mud and grease. Faces, burned to mahogany by sun and wind, were blurred by scrubby beards. The cheeks of more than a few were distended by a "chew" of precious plug tobacco. Among Major Reno's ragged powder-stained survivors, hats were missing and boots cracked. Much of the equipments had been broken, worn out, or lost in the struggle. As one of Brevet Major General John Gibbon's infantrymen who viewed the remnant of the 7th on June 27 put it: "Many of the soldiers that came down from . . . [Reno] hill were without shoes, some using gunnysacks to cover their feet. Their clothes were torn. They had been a long time on the march. They were a sorry looking lot." [49]

Notes

1. The proceedings of these boards are contained in *Ordnance Memoranda No. 13* and *Ordnance Memoranda No. 18*, published at Washington in 1872 and 1874, respectively.

2. "Summary Statements of Ordnance & Ord. Stores in the Hands of Troops, 1st Quarter ending March 31, 1872, to 1st Quarter ending March 31, 1876," 2 vols., National Archives (hereafter cited as "Summary"). Also letter: Hq. Dept. of the South to C.O. 7th Cav., December 24, 1872, located at Custer Battlefield National Monument.

3. "Inventory & Inspection Report of Ordnance & Ord. Stores for which Capt. G. W. Yates, 7th Cav., is responsible, Dec. 31, 1873," National Archives. Here Capt. Yates was in the process of ridding himself of the 76 sets of "brace system" equipment he had received 11 months earlier. Gen. Custer, who signed this report as Special Inspector, stated thereon:

"The equipments . . . are new, having been worn only sufficient to enable the Company Commander to fully test their merits. The universal opinion of officers & men is in favor of the discontinuance of the new Cavalry Equipment & a return to the old carbine sling belt and swivel, with which the larger portion of this command is supplied."

4. "Summary."

5. Correspondence between Presi-

dent Cav. Equipt. Board, Ft. Leavenworth, Kan., and Chief of Ord., January 1874, National Archives.

6. Letter: C.O. Benicia Arsenal,
Cal., to Chief of Ord., July 5, 1872,
National Archives.

7. Ordnance Memoranda No. 18, pp.
88–89.

8. Ibid., 103–5.

9. Letter: Capt. C. E. Dutton,
Chief Ord. Officer Dept. of the Platte,
to Chief of Ord., January 14, 1877,
National Archives.

10. Ordnance Memoranda No. 18,
pp. 103–5.

11. Jesse Brown and A. M. Willard,
Black Hills Trails (Rapid City, S.D.:
Rapid City Journal Co., 1924), 159.

12. In the National Archives are
located "Inventory & Inspection Reports of Ordnance & Ord. Stores"
forwarded by three company commanders of the 7th during winter 1876–1877,
itemizing various articles of equipment
worn out or broken in service. Capt.
T. H. McDougall, C.O., Co. B, on February 14, 1877, listed 50 "Cartridge
Pouches Dyers Pat." and 8 "Carbine
Cartridge Boxes," all of which he had
received from 2d Lt. B. H. Hodgson
on November 13, 1876. Since Hodgson
was assigned to Co. B for some time
up to his death at the Little Bighorn, it
may be assumed that the pouches and
boxes were on hand in this company for
some time prior to that fight. McDougall stated that these items were worn
out because of "constant use in service"
at the time he assumed responsibility
for them. Capt. Myles Moylan, C.O.,
Co. A, on November 10, 1876, included

in a lengthy inventory but 2 "Carbine
Cartridge Boxes," received in January
1873 and since "worn out in service."
1st Lt. C. C. DeRudio, assigned as
C.O., Co. E after the Custer Battle,
listed on April 22, 1877, 2 "Carb.
Cart'ge. Boxes" which he found "in
possession of men of E Co" during the
4th Quarter 1876, both "worn out in
service."

13. Letter: Chief of Ord. to Watervliet Arsenal, June 17, 1874, National
Archives.

14. Manuscript Letter: Chief Ord.
Officer Mil. Div. of the Missouri to
Chief of Ord., May 9, 1876, National
Archives.

15. Such as 1st Lt. O. E. Michaelis,
Chief Ord. Officer Dept. of Dakota,
who received a set early in May 1876.
Michaelis was to accompany Brig. Gen.
A. H. Terry, the Dept. Commander,
into the field for the campaign against
the Sioux. Michaelis notified the Chief
of Ord. on May 8 (letter in National
Archives): ". . . I take with me the complete set of Cavalry Equipments and
accoutrements sent me as a sample . . .
in order to get the opinions of cavalry
officers on their wants. We shall have
with us . . . the 7th Cavalry, and shall
probably meet a portion of the 2nd Cavalry . . . It is further not impossible
that we may meet some of the mounted
troops from the Dept. of the Platte.
The opportunity for obtaining a free
expression was too good to be lost . . ."

16. Two belt plates of this pattern
have been found in the vicinity of
Custer Battlefield and are preserved in
the Natl. Park Service museum there.

One of these was found along Custer's route from Reno Creek to his battlefield, the other at the site of Reno's fight in the valley.

17. "Report of the principal operations at Watervliet Arsenal, N.Y., during the Fiscal Year ending June 30th, 1876," National Archives. Among numerous items listed under "New Fabrications" were 1,070 "Pistol Cartridge pouches (altered from Cap pouches)."

18. A photograph by S.J. Morrow, in the collection of the South Dakota State Historical Society, shows Capt. James Egan's "Gray Horse Company" (K), 2d Cav., mounted in column of two's on a street of Custer City, Dakota Territory, about September 18, 1876. All (including officers) carry their carbines across the pommel. Of some 30 men only one appears to wear a carbine sling.

19. Manuscript Letter: Hq. Dept. of the Missouri to C.O. 7th Cav., August 30, 1869, located at Custer Battlefield National Monument. Refers to a recent request by Capt. T. B. Weir, 7th Cav., for leather with which to cover the saddles of his company. The views of the Chief of Ord. (to whom Weir's request had been referred) are quoted in this letter: "For several years saddle trees covered with leather have been used by some of the Cavalry serving in New Mexico, and with satisfactory results. It is believed by this Bureau that the plan . . . is good. The Commanding Officer of Leavenworth Arsenal will be directed to furnish Captain Weir . . . such material as he may require for covering his saddles and also to cover five hundred saddles . . . to be in readiness for issue." Also see "Summary."

20. "Summary."

21. For specifications and diagram of Albee saddle, see Letters Patent No. 165,973, granted July 27, 1875. Albee's improvements were installed on the McClellan tree.

22. Endorsement by C.O. Rock Island Arsenal, December 5, 1876, on letter Lt. Albee to Chief of Ord., December 20, 1875, National Archives.

23. In the Marquis Collection, housed at Custer Battlefield National Monument, is a complete pair of Model 1859 saddlebags and also a pouch made from one of the pockets of bags of this model. These were secured by the late T. B. Marquis, M.D., from old Cheyenne Indians residing on Tongue River Reservation, Mont., who stated that these articles were captured at the Custer Battle. Dr. Marquis' tag on the pair of bags reads in part: "Saddlebags captured by Bobtailed Horse, Cheyenne Warrior, at Custer's Last Battle. He gave them to the wife of Hollow Wood. She kept them hidden through 51 years. Obtained from her, August 18, 1927 . . ." Displayed in the museum at the site of Ft. Lincoln, near Bismarck, N.D., is a pair of saddlebags of this model, said to be relics of the Little Bighorn.

24. Telegram: Capt. J. W. Reilly, Chief Ord. Officer Mil. Div. of the Missouri to Chief of Ord., February 23, 1877, National Archives.

25. Brown and Willard, *Black Hills*, 144. For a similar occurrence dur-

ing the Nez Perce campaign, summer 1877, see Ami Frank Mulford, *Fighting Indians in the Seventh United States Cavalry*, rev. ed. (Corning, N.Y.: P. L. Mulford, 1925), 107.

26. E. A. Brininstool, *Troopers with Custer: Historic Incidents of the Battle of the Little Big Horn* (Harrisburg, Pa.: Stackpole Co., 1952), 247; W. A. Graham, *The Custer Myth: A Source Book of Custeriana* (Harrisburg, Pa.: Stackpole Co., 1953), 346.

27. Letter: Capt. C. E. Dutton, Chief Ord. Officer Dept. of the Platte, to Chief of Ord., January 14, 1877, National Archives.

28. Circular No. 3, June 5, 1878, contained in "Post & Regtl. Order Book, Hq. 7th Cav., Jan. 1878–Dec. 1881," located at Custer Battlefield National Monument, states: "Notification has been received from the Chief Ordnance Officer of the Dept., that Spring Snaps for attaching Canteens and Haversacks to the saddle can be obtained by making requisitions for them." The arrangement of the saddle pack is based principally upon a photograph by W. H. Illingworth made during the Black Hills Expedition of 1874. The photograph includes a number of 7th Cav. horses grazing during a mid-day halt in the valley of Heart River, Dakota Territory. The author would not pretend to assert that all saddle packs of the 7th on campaign in 1876 were composed exactly as given here. No doubt there were variations in the arrangement, made to suit the individual's idea of convenience, to favor a sore back, or for any number of reasons.

29. Letters: C.O.'s various companies 7th Cav. to Regtl. Adjt., of different dates in March, 1874, stating "class and character" of the arms in the hands of the men (letters located at Custer Battlefield National Monument). John E. Parsons and John S. du Mont, *Firearms in the Custer Battle* (Harrisburg, Pa.: Stackpole, 1953), gives excellent coverage of the 7th's armament and of Indian weapons.

30. Per Gen. E.S. Godfrey (a company commander at the Little Bighorn) in letter written to an artist in 1896, published in Parsons and du Mont, *Firearms*, 48–52, and in Graham, *Custer Myth*, 345–46. On the other hand John Ryan (1st Sgt., Co. M at the battle) stated in 1923 (see Graham, *Custer Myth*, 346): "He [Custer] also carried in his belt two pistols, one a .45-caliber Colt, and the other a French Navy . . ." Godfrey is thought to be the better source.

31. "Summary."

32. Capt. Moylan, Co. A (see note 12), listed "26 Thong & Brush wipers," received new on May 22, 1874, and now "Broken . . . by use in service."

33. Endorsement by C.O. National Armory, August 8, 1876, on letter Chief Ord. Officer Mil. Div. of the Missouri, to Chief of Ord., August 2, 1876, National Archives.

34. Graham, *Custer Myth*, 244, 345–47.

35. *Personal Memoirs of Major General David S. Stanley* (Cambridge: Harvard University Press, 1917), 268.

36. *Circular No. 8: A Report on the Hygiene of the U.S. Army . . . Surgeon-*

General's Office, *May 1, 1875* (Washington, D.C.: Government Printing Office, 1875), 1.

37. Related by the late Charles A. Windolph, last white survivor of the Custer Battle, to his longtime friend, Ralph G. Cartwright, of Lead, S.D.

38. W. A. Graham, ed., *The Official Record of a Court of Inquiry convened . . . upon request of Major Marcus A. Reno . . . to investigate his conduct at . . . the Little Bighorn, June 25–26, 1876* (Pacific Palisades, Calif.: Privately printed, 1951), 228.

39. For example see the jacket worn by a 7th Cav. private, third from left in a hunting party photographed during the Black Hills Expedition, 1874, reproduced on p. 10 of Parsons and du Mont, *Firearms*.

40. See Gen. Godfrey's letter of 1896 (note 30).

41. Godfrey (ibid.) gives details of the attire of a number of individual officers.

42. Borrowed from 1st Lt. C. C. DeRudio, attached to Co. A this campaign. Graham, *Official Record of a Court of Inquiry*, 509.

43. Descriptive pamphlet, "Cyclorama of Gen. Custer's Last Fight Against Sioux Indians . . . with Grand Musée of Indian Curios" (Boston, Mass., 1889), 17. Here Mrs. G. A. Custer states in letter to Proprietors Boston Cyclorama Co., "The only memento I have ever received is the map-case which my husband carried . . . on the 25th of June . . . General Nelson Miles obtained this from the Indians, and gave it to me on the fifth anniversary of the battle." The map it contained is now in the West Point Museum.

44. Graham, *Official Record of a Court of Inquiry*, 511.

45. Godfrey letter (note 30).

46. Information furnished the author by 2d Lt. Robert M. Utley from letter received by him from the late Col. Louis Brechemin, U.S.A. Ret., dated July 25, 1949. "Years ago I pumped General Edgerly . . . about the uniforms of the 7th . . . in that campaign. He spoke of that outrageous Black Hat that looked like Napoleon's Chapeau . . . He said he threw his away at the Custer Fight but could never remember what hat he put on afterward." An example of a hat arranged for wearing in this fashion, labelled "7th Cavalry Campaign Hat. Found on the Custer Battlefield . . . ," is displayed in the museum at Ft. Lincoln, Bismarck, N.D. The hat, of black felt, has two pairs of metal hooks and eyes sewed at points along the edge of the brim to accomplish the arrangement described.

47. Graham, *Official Record of a Court of Inquiry*, 509.

48. Godfrey letter (note 30).

49. Brininstool, *Troopers*, 303.

THE BATTLE OF THE LITTLE BIGHORN

CHIEF JOSEPH

WHITE BULL,

as told to

Stanley Vestal

The morning of June 25, 1876, that fatal day on which General George Armstrong Custer and five troops of the Seventh United States Cavalry rode to their doom, dawned brightly, giving no hint of the bloody scenes that were to make it memorable. During the ten years since the Fetterman fight at Fort Phil Kearny, White Bull had been constantly on the warpath, fighting the whites and neighboring tribes, killing enemies, counting *coups*, stealing horses by the score. That morning he was twenty-six years old, and already a famous warrior.

It was not yet sunup when White Bull stepped out of his wife's tepee in the Sans Arc Sioux camp circle, loosened the picket-ropes of the family horses, and drove his ponies to the river for water.

The Sioux and Cheyennes had pitched their camps, three miles of tepees, circle on circle, in the wide flats along the west bank of the Little Bighorn River. There they rested after the fight with General George Crook on the Rosebud only a week before. Their scouts reported that Crook was retreating, and though they knew that other troops were in their country, they did not expect them that day. Besides, they were not afraid; there were too many Indians in the camp.

The Little Bighorn flowed to the north, its shallow winding course marked by clumps of tall cottonwood timber, above which White Bull could see the abrupt bluffs, scarred by ravines, rising steeply from the eastern bank. When the horses would drink no more, he drove them north of the camp to grass, and when they had settled down to graze, left them and went home for breakfast. Later he returned, trying to keep them in a bunch about a hundred yards west of the river. As usual, he carried his seventeen-shot rifle, and wore two loaded cartridge-belts.

It was a hot, lazy day, almost windless, and the trails were dusty. White Bull remained herding his horses without a thought of any danger, though all that while General Custer's command was rapidly approaching. Custer's scouts had warned him that he would find more Sioux on the Little Bighorn than he could handle, but he refused to be frightened, divided his command into three bodies, and pushed on. Captain Frederick W. Benteen had orders to strike the village from the west; Major M. A. Reno was to attack on the south, while Custer rode over the bluffs to jump the Sioux from the east bank of the stream.

The General expected the Indians to run, and he was anxious to prevent their escape.

It was not yet time for the midday watering when White Bull, watching his horses north of the camp, heard a man yelling the alarm. Immediately he jumped on his best running horse, a fast bay, and ran his ponies back to camp. Before he reached it, everyone in camp had seen the tower of dust coming from the south, and below it the blue shirts of soldiers, the flash of rifle-barrels in the bright sunshine. The column of soldiers spread into a line; smoke burst from it; and White Bull heard the noise of the carbines.

All through that great camp was the confusion of complete surprise. Old men were shouting commands and advice, young men running to catch up their horses, women streaming away to the north afoot and on horseback, trying to escape the soldiers. They abandoned their tents, snatched up their babies and called their children. White Bull saw young girls clutching shawls over their frightened heads, fat matrons puffing and perspiring, and old women, shriveled as mummies, hobbling along with their sticks, trying to save themselves.

White Bull saw his own family started to safety, then sped up-river hard as he could ride, to the camp of his uncle, Sitting Bull, which the soldiers were already nearing. There, he knew, his father's tepee stood on the north side of the circle. By the time he arrived, the women and children had fled, and about a thousand warriors were gathering to resist the troops, whose bullets were already crashing through the tepees, too high to hurt anyone. When White Bull reached the south end of the great camp, he saw a lively fight going on in the open, where the Ree and Crow Government Indian scouts were trying to run off the Sioux ponies. Everything was smothered in a great cloud of dust and smoke, as the Indians on both sides dashed back and forth, fighting for their horses. Already some of the Cheyennes and Sioux had been shot down by the Rees; and the white soldiers, firing from the saddle, kept advancing, pushing the Sioux back. But before long the Sioux had gathered in such numbers that the Rees retreated, leaving most of the ponies to their enemies. Immediately after, the soldiers dismounted and formed a line in the open, facing the north. White Bull saw them set up a flag (guidon).

White Bull yelled aloud: "Whoever is a brave man will go get that flag." But everyone was busy. Nobody volunteered, and before he himself could do anything, the soldiers moved the flag, falling back into the timber which bordered the river.

By this time great numbers of Indians had gathered, and some of them made charges toward the troops, while others stood and fired. After some hot fighting on foot in the timber, Major Reno's troopers climbed into their saddles and rode south up the river, looking for a place to cross. The moment they turned about, the swarming Sioux were on their heels, striking with warclubs and the butts of their guns, shooting arrows into them, riding them down. The soldiers went plunging through the river and up the steep sprawling ridges of the high bluff to the top. Most of them got over, ran up the bluff and dug in. But three soldiers kept up the west bank on the level. White Bull took after these. There was one soldier on a gray horse. White Bull singled him out for his victim and fired, but failed to hit him. Reno had left behind him three officers and twenty-nine men killed.

Just then the foremost Indians halted; White Bull heard some one behind him yelling that troops were coming from the east toward the north end of the camp, three miles down-river. White Bull was near the water and turned downstream with the rest to meet this new danger. Some of the Indians rode through all the camps and crossed the stream above them to block Custer's advance. White Bull and many others crossed almost at once, streaming up the ravine to strike Custer on the flank. As he advanced, he saw Custer's five troops trotting along the bluffs parallel to the river.

White Bull saw that there would be a big fight. He stopped, un-saddled his horse and stripped off his leggings. He thought he could fight better so.

The Indians rode in many small parties, streaming northeast up the ravine toward the troops passing along the ridge.

With White Bull there rode Iron Lightning, Owns-Horn, Shoots-Bear-as-He-Runs, and two Cheyennes. They rode up the ravine with a great horde of warriors. Most of Custer's five troops of cavalry had passed the head of the ravine by the time White Bull was near enough to shoot at the soldiers. From where he was, the soldiers seemed to form four groups of mounted men, heading northwest along the ridge. He was shooting at the group in the rear (Lieutenant James Calhoun's command).

All the Indians were shooting, and White Bull saw two soldiers fall from their horses. The soldiers fired back from the saddle. Their fire was so effective that some of the Indians, including White Bull, fell back to the south. Soon after, the white men halted. Some of them got off their horses to fight. By this time the Indians were all around the soldiers. Many were between the camp and the troopers, ready to defend the ford. Others took their stand wherever they could obtain cover, each small party acting independently.

When White Bull was driven out of the ravine by the fire of Lieutenant Calhoun's men, he rode south and worked his way over to the east of that officer's command, and there joined a party of warriors with Crazy Horse. By this time a large number of Indians were gathering around Calhoun's troops. They were particularly numerous south of him. The troopers at the tail of the column were falling back along the ridge, leaving their dead and wounded behind them, trying to join forces with Keogh's troop. Keogh's men were fighting on foot.

Seeing these soldiers on the run, White Bull, in bravado, dashed across their line between the two troops, hugging the neck of his fleet pony. They fired at him, but missed him. He circled back to his com-rades. Encouraged by his success in this desperate stunt, he called out, "This time I will not turn back!" and charged at a run on the troopers of the last company. When the Sioux heard him yelling and saw him dash-ing forward, many of them followed. This charge seemed to break the morale of the survivors of Calhoun's troop. They all ran to join Keogh, every man for himself, afoot and on horseback. All around, the Sioux were firing, dropping the soldiers.

One of the Sioux shot a mounted trooper. White Bull saw the man waver in his saddle, and quirting his pony, raced forward to strike the man and count the first *coup*. Before he could reach the trooper, the dying man fell from his saddle. White Bull reined in his pony, jumped down and struck the body with his quirt, yelling, "*Onhey!* I have overcome this one." He took the man's revolver and cartridge-belt. Did-Not-Go-Home struck this enemy immediately after; he counted the second *coup*. Then White Bull leaped on his barebacked bay and dashed on with the charging, yelling warriors through the dust and smoke drifting down the bluffs.

By that time the last of Calhoun's men had joined Keogh's troopers, and all together they were falling back northwestward along the ridge to their comrades of the third group. A bugle blared. Those soldiers who still had horses mounted.

White Bull found himself side by side with Chief Crazy Horse. Knowing him for one of the bravest of the Sioux, White Bull dared Crazy Horse to lead a charge. Crazy Horse refused. White Bull led the charge himself.

He saw a mounted trooper left behind; his horse had played out. White Bull charged this man; Crazy Horse followed him. As White Bull dashed up from the rear, the trooper tried to turn in his saddle and bring his carbine to bear on White Bull. But before he could shoot, White Bull was alongside, seized him by the shoulders of his blue coat, and jerked furiously, trying to unhorse the man. The soldier fired in the air, and fell from his horse. Crazy Horse struck this man second. White Bull had outdone the famous chief.

Some troopers were left afoot. One of these, with Indians all around him, stood turning from side to side, threatening them with his carbine. In that way he kept his enemies at a distance. However, White Bull was not daunted. He rode straight for the soldier. At close quarters the trooper fired. White Bull dodged, and the ball missed him. A moment later he flung the shoulders of his horse against the trooper and rode him down. Bear Lice counted the second *coup*.

The remnants of Calhoun's and Keogh's troops had now joined the troopers around Custer to the north and west, near where the monument is now. The fourth mass of soldiers (the commands of Captain G. W. Yates, Captain Tom Custer and Lieutenant A. E. Smith) was then below these, down the hill toward the river. The air was full of dust and smoke. Here and there a wounded man had been unhorsed and left behind.

One of these men, bleeding from a wound in the left thigh, with a revolver in one hand and a carbine in the other, stood all alone, shooting at the Indians. They could not get at him. White Bull dashed up behind the man, who did not see him come. White Bull rode him down. Brave Crow counted the second *coup* on this enemy.

By this time all the troopers on the hill had let their horses go. They lay down and kept shooting. White Bull was to the east of them, Crazy Horse at his side.

Then White Bull charged alone through the body of soldiers at a gallop. It was all open ground. He lay close to his horse's neck, and passed the troopers within a dozen feet, but was not hit.

The horses turned loose by the soldiers—bays, sorrels and grays—were running in all directions. Many of the Indians stopped shooting and chased these loose horses. White Bull tried to head some off, but the Indians swarmed in ahead of him. He caught only one sorrel. The firing was very hot, so hot that immediately after, White Bull's horse was shot down. The animal was shot through the shoulder and chest, through the ribs, and through the head just behind the ears. White Bull was left afoot. Other Indians had dismounted. It was hand-to-hand fighting by that time. White Bull rushed in.

A tall, well-built soldier on foot tried to bluff White Bull, aiming his carbine at him. But when White Bull rushed the man, he threw his gun at him without shooting. They caught hold of each other and wrestled together there in the twilight of the dust and smoke. The soldier was brave and strong. He tried to wrest White Bull's gun from him, and almost succeeded. But White Bull lashed the enemy across the face with his quirt. The soldier let go, then grabbed White Bull's gun with both hands, until White Bull struck him again. But the soldier was desperate: he struck White Bull with his fists on the jaw and shoulders; seized him by his long hair with both hands, drew his face close, and tried to bite his nose off. White Bull thought his time had come. He yelled for help: "Hey, hey, come over and help me!" He thought the soldier would kill him.

Bear Lice and Crow Boy heard his call and came running to his aid. They tried to hit the soldier, but in the rough-and-tumble most of their blows fell on White Bull. He was dizzy from the blows, but yelled as loud as he could to scare his enemy. At last he freed himself, struck the soldier several times on the head with his pistol, knocked him over, took his gun and cartridge-belt. Hawk-Stays-Up struck second. That was a close shave, a hard fight, but White Bull says: "It was a glorious battle; I enjoyed it. I was picking up headfeathers right and left that day."

For a time all the soldiers stood together on the hill near where the monument is now, ringed in by the Sioux, dying bravely one by one, as the Indians poured a hail of lead and arrows into their dwindling strength. They lay or knelt on the bare ridge, firing across the bodies of dead horses or taking cover behind the shallow shelter of a fallen comrade, selling their lives dearly until only a few remained alive.

A Cheyenne named Bearded Man charged these soldiers. He rushed right in among them and was killed there. His body lay in the midst of the soldiers. When the fight was over, the Sioux found him there. They did not recognize his body. They thought he was an Indian Government scout. Little Crow, brother of Chief Hump, scalped Bearded Man. Afterward, when Little Crow realized his mistake, he gave the scalp to the dead man's parents.

By this time many of the Indians had armed themselves with carbines and revolvers taken from the dead troopers, and had filled their belts with cartridges found in the saddle-bags of captured horses. The volume of their fire constantly increased as that of the soldiers diminished. White Bull lay in a ravine pumping bullets into the crowd around Custer, aiming always at the heart. He was one of those who shot down the group in which Custer made his last stand.

All this time White Bull was between the river and the soldiers on the hill. The few remaining troopers seemed to despair of holding their position on the hilltop. Ten of them jumped up and came down the ravine toward White Bull, shooting all the time. Two soldiers were in the lead, one of them wounded and bleeding from the mouth. White Bull and a Cheyenne waited for them. When they came near, he shot one; the Cheyenne shot the other. Both ran forward. White Bull struck first on one soldier, but the Cheyenne beat him to the other one. He got only the second *coup*. The eight remaining soldiers kept on coming, forcing White Bull out of the ravine onto the ridge.

White Bull snatched up the soldier's gun and started up the hill. Suddenly he stumbled and fell. His leg was numb, it had no feeling in it. He searched himself for wounds, but could find none. Then he saw that his ankle was swelling. The skin was not broken, only bruised. He had been hit by a spent ball.

He found a shallow ditch, crawled into it, and lay there until all the soldiers were killed. At the time he stopped fighting, only ten soldiers were on their feet. They were the last ones alive. The fight began before noon and lasted only about an hour, he says.

White Bull found very few cartridges in the belts he captured. Though he was in the thick of the fighting from start to finish, he did not see a single soldier commit suicide.

"The soldiers seemed tired," he says, "but they fought to the end."

Soon after, With-Horns found White Bull, put him on his horse, and led him back across the river. The tepees had not been moved up there. The people had rigged up tent-flies, and were camping as best they could on the open flat.

Makes-Room made his son White Bull lie down under a shade tree, and sent for Sitting Bull. Sitting Bull put "wounded medicine" on White Bull's ankle and wrapped the swelling in buffalo wool. Sitting Bull said: "Nephew, you had better be careful. One of these times you might be killed." Meanwhile the herald was calling out that the camp must be moved to where the people were. The women went after their tepees and moved them.

After a while the Indians had lunch. Then White Bull asked for his horse. They brought it, and helped him upon its back. He crossed the river to get his leggings and the saddle he had left there, and afterward went over the battlefield to see the dead. He says he did not see anyone mutilating the dead. He thinks that the parents of Indians killed in the fight must have gone up there later and mutilated some of the soldiers. On the hilltop he met his relative Bad Soup. Bad Soup had been around Fort Abraham Lincoln and knew Long Hair (General Custer) by sight. The two of them found Custer lying on his back, naked. Bad Soup pointed him out and said: "Long Hair thought he was the greatest man in the world. Now he lies there." They did not scalp Custer, for his hair was cut short.

White Bull took two pairs of trousers from the soldiers. On his way home he washed them in the river. He gave them to his father.

After White Bull reached camp with his saddle and leggings, he rode up to the bluff and took part in the fight with Reno's men, remaining there all night.

About the middle of the morning White Bull went home and took a nap. In the afternoon he rode north downriver to meet the troops coming under General Alfred H. Terry and General John Gibbon. He was successful in stealing eleven horses from these troops.

The Custer fight was over. In that fight, White Bull had counted seven *coups*, six of them "firsts," had killed two men in hand-to-hand combat, captured two guns and twelve horses, had had his horse shot under him, and had been wounded in the ankle. Few if any of the Sioux or Cheyennes in that fight could show such a record of reckless bravery and good fortune.

Because of his bravery and his success on that bloody field, White Bull was chosen from all the Indians on the plains as the representative of the red race in the peace ceremonies held on the Custer Battlefield on the fiftieth anniversary of that fatal day, June 25, 1926. On that day he rode to the monument on the battlefield at the head of hundreds of Indians to exchange gifts and shake hands with Brigadier General E. S. Godfrey, U.S.A. Retired, who, as a first lieutenant, had commanded Company K of the Seventh Cavalry under [Captain] Frederick W. Benteen.

On this anniversary White Bull gave General Godfrey a fine blanket; the General presented White Bull with a large United States flag. That day both the white men and the Indians recognized Chief Joseph White Bull, nephew of Sitting Bull, as the leading chief and bravest man of all the Sioux and Cheyennes.

There are those who believe that White Bull is the man who shot General Custer. Certainly he was among those Indians who fired into the group around Custer, and when asked to point out the place where he saw the body of the General lying, he indicated the exact spot where the body of General Custer was found by his comrades after the battle.

CUSTER'S LAST BATTLE

CHARLES KING

I t is hard to say how many years ago the Dakotas of the upper Mississippi, after a century of warring with the Chippewa nation, began to swarm across the Missouri in search of the buffalo, and there became embroiled with other tribes claiming the country farther west. Dakota was the proper tribal name, but as they crossed this Northwestern Rubicon into the territory of unknown foemen they bore with them a title given them as far east as the banks and bluffs of the Father of Waters. The Chippewas had called them for years "the Sioux" (Soo), and by that strange un-Indian-sounding title is known to this day the most numerous and powerful nation of red people—warriors, women, and children—to be found on our continent.

They were in strong force when they launched out on their career of conquest west of the Missouri. The Yellowstone and its beautiful and romantic tributaries all belonged to the Absarakás, or Crows; the rolling prairies of Nebraska were the homes of the Pawnees; the pine-crested heights of the Black Hills were claimed as the head-quarters of the Cheyennes and Arrapahoes; the western slopes of the Big Horn range and the broad valleys between them and the Rockies were owned by the Shoshones, or Snakes; while roving bands of Crees swarmed down along the north shore of the Missouri itself.

With each and all of these, with the Chippewas behind them, and eventually with the white invaders, the Dakotas waged relentless war. They drove the Pawnees across the Platte far into Kansas; they whipped the Cheyennes and Arrapahoes out of the Black Hills, and down to the head waters of the Kaw and the Arkansas; they fought the Shoshones back into the Wind River Valley, with orders never again to cross the "dead line" of the Big Horn River; and they sent the Crows "whirling" up the valley of the Yellowstone (which they proceeded to call the Elk); and when our great war broke out in 1861 they lent valuable aid and comfort to the rebellion by swooping down on our settlements in Minnesota without the faintest warning, and slaughtering hundreds of defenceless women and children, from whom they were begging or stealing but the day before. General Sully, with a strong command, was sent to give them a severe lesson in payment for their outrages, and he marched far into their territory, and fought them wherever they would assemble in sufficient force to block his way, but it did no lasting good. When '66 came, and our emigrants began settling up the West, they found the Sioux more hostile and determined than ever. The army was called on to protect the settlers, and to escort the surveyors of the transcontinental railways. Not a stake was driven, not an acre cleared, except under cover of the rifles of the regulars, and while the nation seemed rejoicing in unbroken peace and increasing prosperity, its little army was having anything but a placid time of it on the frontier. In the ten years that immediately preceded the centennial celebration at Philadelphia, the cavalry regiments had no rest at all; they were on the war-path winter and summer; and during those ten years of "peace" more officers of the regular army were killed or died of wounds received in action with the Indians than the British army lost in the entire Crimean war, with its bloody battles of the Alma, Balaklava, Inkerman, and the assaults on Sebastopol. The Indians were always scientific fighters, but when, in '74 and '75, they succeeded in arming themselves with breech-loaders and magazine rifles, the Sioux of the Northern plains became foemen far more to be dreaded than any European cavalry.

Treaties had been made and broken. A road had been built through the heart of the country they loved the best—the northeastern slope and foot-hills from the Big Horn to the Yellowstone; and far up in this unsettled region, surrounded by savages, little wooden stockaded forts had been placed and garrisoned by pitifully small detachments of cavalry and infantry. From Fort Laramie down on the Platte far up to the rich and populous Gallatin Valley of Montana only those little forts, Reno, Phil Kearny, and C. F. Smith, guarded the way. One day vast hordes of Sioux gathered in the ravines and cañons around Phil Kearny. Machpealota (Red Cloud) was their leader. They sent a small party to attack the wood-choppers from the fort, who were working with their little escort. Two companies of infantry and one of cavalry went out to the rescue. These were quickly surrounded and hemmed in, then slowly massacred. After that for ten long years the Sioux held undisputed sway in their chosen country. Our forts were burned and abandoned. The Indian allies of the Dakotas joined hands with them, and a powerful nation or confederacy of nearly 60,000 souls ruled the country from the Big Horn River on the northwest down to the Union Pacific Railway. No longer dared they go south of that. Taking with them the Cheyennes and Arrapahoes, who had intermarried with them, the Sioux fell back to the North Platte and the territory beyond. From there they sent raiding parties in every direction. One Secretary of the Interior after another had tried the experiment of feeding, clothing, *bribing* them to be good. Agencies and reservations were established at convenient points. Here the old chiefs, the broken-down men, and the non-combatant women and children made their permanent homes, and here the bold and vigorous young chiefs and warriors, laughing at the credulity of the Great Father, filled up their pouches and *parflèches* with rations and ammunition, then went whooping off on the war-path against the whites wherever found, and came back scalp-laden to the reservation when they needed more cartridges or protection from the pursuing soldiery, who could fire on them only when caught outside the lines.

Two great reservations were established southeast of the Black Hills in the valley of the White River. One of these was the bailiwick of the hero of the Phil Kearny massacre, old Red Cloud, and here were gathered most of his own tribe (the Ogalallas) and many of his chiefs; some "good," like Old-Man-Afraid-of-His-Horses and his worthy son, but most of them crafty, cunning, treacherous, and savage, like Red Dog, Little-Big-Man, American Horse, and a swarm of various kinds of Bulls and Bears and Wolves. Further down the stream, twenty miles away, were the head-quarters of the Brulés, Spotted Tail's people, and "Old Spot" was loyal to the backbone, though powerless to control the movements of the young men. Other reservations there were along the Missouri, and into these reservations the Department of the Interior strove to gather all the Sioux nation, in the vague hope of keeping them out of mischief.

But the young Indian takes to mischief of that description as the young duck to the water. The traditions of his people tell of no case where respect was accorded to him who had not killed his man. Only in deeds of blood or battle could he hope to win distinction, and the vacillating policy of the government enabled him to sally forth at any time and return at will to the reservations, exhibiting to the admiring eyes of friends and relations the dripping scalps of his white victims. The fact that the victims were shot from ambush, or that the scalps were solely those of helpless women and children, detracted in no wise from the value of the trophies. The perpetrator had won his spurs according to the aboriginal code, and was a "brave" henceforth.

But there were those who never would come in, and never signed a treaty. Herein they are entitled to far more respect than those who came, saw, and conquered—by fraud; and one of those who persistently refused, and whose standard was a rallying-point for the disaffected and treacherous of every tribe, was a shrewd "medicine chief" of the Uncapapas, a seer, prophet, statesman, but in no sense a war chief, the now celebrated Tatonka-e-Yotanka—Sitting Bull.

Far out in the lovely fertile valleys of the Rosebud, the Tongue, the Little Big Horn, and the Powder rivers, Sitting Bull and his devoted followers spent their days. Sheltered from storm and tempest by the high bluffs through long, hard winters, living in the midst of untold thousands of buffalo, elk, mountain sheep, antelope, and deer, rejoicing in the grandest scenery on the continent, and in a climate that despite its rigor during the midwinter months is unparalleled for life-giving qualities, it is no wonder they loved and clung to it—their "Indian story land"—as they did to no other. But here flocked all the renegades from other tribes. Here came the wild and untamable Ogalalla, Brulé, Minneconjou, Sans Arc, Uncapapa, Blackfoot; here were all warriors welcomed; and from here time and again set forth the expeditions that spread terror to settler and emigrant, and checked the survey of the Northern Pacific Railroad.

Eighteen hundred and seventy-five found trouble everywhere. White settlers swarmed in the Black Hills in search of gold. Ogalallas and Brulés stole their stock and killed their herders, claiming that the land was theirs and the whites were invaders. Sitting Bull's ranks swarmed with recruits from far to the southeast. The Interior Department found it useless to temporize. Orders were given to the army to bring him in or "snuff him out." Early in March, '76, General George Crook, famous for his successes with the Indians in Oregon and Arizona, was started up into the Sioux country with a strong force of cavalry and infantry. On "Patrick's Day in the morning," long before he was anywhere near Sitting Bull himself, his advance struck a big Indian village deep in the snows of the Powder River. It was 30° below zero; the troops were faultily led by the officer to whom he had intrusted the duty, and the Sioux developed splendid fighting qualities under a new and daring leader, "Choonka-Witko"—Crazy Horse. Crook's advance recoiled upon the main body, practically defeated by the renegades from the Red Cloud and Spotted Tail agencies. Early in May, warned by this lesson, three great expeditions pushed forward into the "Indian story land," where by this time full six thousand warriors had rallied around Sitting Bull. From the south came General Crook, with nearly twenty-five hundred men. From the east marched General Terry, with almost as many infantry and cavalry as had Crook, and a few light pieces of artillery. Down the Yellowstone from the west General Gibbon led a little band of long-trained frontier soldiers, scouting by the way, and definitely "locating" the Indians over on the Rosebud before forming his junction with General Terry near the mouth of the Tongue. If Sitting Bull had been alive to the situation, Gibbon's small force could never have finished that perilous advance, though they might have stood and defended themselves; but Bull was not a general; his talents lay elsewhere.

Early in June Crook's command was on the northeast slope of the Big Horn, and General Sheridan, planning the whole campaign, saw with anxiety that vast numbers of Indians were daily leaving the reservations south of the Black Hills and hurrying northwestward around Crook to join Sitting Bull. The Fifth Regiment of Cavalry was then sent up by rail from Kansas to Cheyenne, and marched rapidly to the Black Hills to cut off these re-enforcements. The great mass of the Indians lay uneasily between Crook at the head waters of Tongue River and Terry and Gibbon near its mouth, watching every move, and utterly cutting off every attempt of the commanders to communicate with each other. They worried Crook's pickets and trains, and by mid-June he determined to pitch in and see what force they had. On June 17th the General grappled with the Sioux on the bluffs of the Rosebud. He had several hundred Crow allies. The stirring combat lasted much of the day; but long before it was half over Crook was fighting on the defensive and coolly withdrawing his men. He had found a hornets' nest, and knew it was no place for so small a command as his. Pulling out as best he could, he fell back to the Tongue, sent for the entire Fifth Cavalry and all his available infantry, and lay on his arms until they could reach him. He had not got within sight of the great Indian village—city it should be called—of Sitting Bull.

Meantime Terry and Gibbon sent their scouts up stream. Major Reno, with a strong battalion of the Seventh Cavalry, left camp on the Yellowstone to take a look up toward the Cheetish or Wolf Mountains. Sitting Bull and his people—men, women, and children—after their successful defence of the approaches to their home on the Rosebud on June 17th, seem to have bethought themselves of roomier and better quarters over in the broader valley of the Little Big Horn, the next stream to the west. Their "village" had stretched for six miles down the narrow cañon of the Rosebud; their thousands of ponies had eaten off all the grass; they were victorious, but it was time to go.

Coming up the Rosebud, Major Reno was confronted by the sight of an immense trail turning suddenly west and crossing the great divide over toward the setting sun. Experienced Indian fighters in his command told him that many thousand Indians had passed there within the last few days. Like a sensible man, he turned about and trotted back to report his discovery to his commander. Then it was that the tragedy of the campaign began.

At the head of Terry's horsemen was the lieutenant-colonel commanding the Seventh Regiment of Cavalry, Brevet Major-General George A. Custer, United States Army, a daring, dashing, impetuous trooper, who had won high honors as a division commander under Sheridan during the great war of the rebellion, who had led his gallant regiment against the Kiowas and the Cheyennes on the Southern plains, and had twice penetrated the Sioux country in recent campaigns. Experience he certainly had, but there were those, superiors and subordinates both, who feared that in dealing with so wily and skilful a foe Custer lacked judgment. All had not been harmonious in his relations with his commanders in the Department of Dakota, nor was there entire unanimity of feeling toward him in the regiment itself, but all men honored his unquestioned bravery, and when General Terry decided to send his cavalry at once to "scout the trail" reported by Reno, the command of the expedition fell naturally to Custer.

Terry had promptly arrived at the conclusion that the Indians had simply moved their villages over into the valley of the Little Big Horn, and his plan was to send Custer along the trail to hold and hem them from the east, while he, with all his own and Gibbon's command, pushed up the Yellowstone and Big Horn in boats; then, disembarking at the junction of the Big and Little Big Horn, to march southward until he struck the Indians on that flank. His orders to Custer displayed an unusual mingling of anxiety and forbearance. He seems to have feared that Custer would be rash, yet shrank from issuing a word that might reflect upon the discretion or wound the high spirit of his gallant leader of horse. He warned him to "feel" well out toward his left as he rode westward from the Rosebud, in order to prevent the Indians slipping off southeastward between the column and the Big Horn Mountains. He would not hamper him with positive orders as to what he must or must not do when he came in presence of the enemy, but he named the 26th of June as the day on which he and Gibbon would reach the valley of the Little Big Horn, and it was his hope and expectation that Custer would come up from the east about the same time, and between them they would be able to soundly thrash the assembled Sioux.

But Custer disappointed him in an unusual way. He got there a day ahead of time, and had ridden night and day to do it. Men and horses were wellnigh used up when the Seventh Cavalry trotted into sight of the city on the Little Big Horn that cloudless Sunday morning of the 25th. When Terry came up the valley on the 26th, it was all over with Custer and his pet troops (companies) of the regiment.

He started on the trail with the Seventh Cavalry, and nothing but the Seventh. A battalion of the Second was with Gibbon's column; but, luckily for the Second, Custer would have none of them. Two field guns, under Lieutenant Low, were with Terry, and Low begged that he and his guns might be sent, but Custer wanted only his own people. He rode sixty miles in twenty-four hours. He pushed ahead on the trail with feverish impatience, and he created an impression that it was his determination to get to the spot and have one battle royal with the Indians, in which he and the Seventh should be the sole participants on our side, and by consequence the sole heroes. The idea of defeat seems never to have occurred to him, despite his experience with old "Black Kettle's" bands down on the Washita.

Only thirty miles away on his left, as he spurred ahead with his weary men that Sunday morning, over two thousand soldiers under Crook were in bivouac on Goose Creek. Had he "felt" any great distance out there the scouts would have met, and Crook would eagerly have reenforced him, but he wanted nothing of the kind. At daybreak his advance, under Lieutenant Varnum, had come upon the scaffold sepulchres of two or three warriors slain in the fight of the 17th, and soon thereafter sent back word that the valley of the Little Horn was in sight ahead, and there were "signs" of the village.

Then it was that Custer made the division of his column. Keeping with himself the five companies whose commanders were his chosen friends and adherents, and leaving Captain Macdougall with his troops to guard the mule pack train in rear, he divided the six remaining companies between Major Reno and Captain Benteen, sending the latter some two miles off to the extreme left, while Reno moved midway between. In this order of three little parallel columns the Seventh Cavalry swept rapidly westward over the "divide."

Unlike the Second, Third, or Fifth Regiment when on Indian campaign, Custer's men rode into action with something of the pomp and panoply of war that distinguished them around their camps. Bright guidons fluttered in the breeze; many of the officers and men wore the natty undress uniform of the cavalry. Custer himself; his brother, Captain Tom Custer; his adjutant, Lieutenant Cooke; and his old Army of the Potomac comrade, Captain Myles Keogh—were all dressed nearly alike in coats of Indian-tanned, beaver-trimmed buckskin, with broad-brimmed scouting hats of light color, and long riding-boots. Captain Yates seemed to prefer his undress uniform, as did most of the lieutenants in Custer's column. The two Custers and Captain Keogh rode their beautiful Kentucky sorrel horses, and the adjutant was mounted on his long-legged gray. The trumpeters were at the heads of columns with their chiefs, but the band of the Seventh, for once, was left behind, Custer's last charge was sounded without the accompaniment of the rollicking Irish fighting tune he loved. There was no "Garry Owen" to swell the chorus of the last cheer.

Following Custer's trail from the Rosebud, one comes in sight of the Little Big Horn, winding away northward to its junction with the broader stream. South are the bold cliffs and dark cañons of the mountains, their foot-hills not twenty miles away. North, tumbling and rolling toward the Yellowstone in alternate "swale" and ridge, the treeless, upland prairie stretches to the horizon. Westward, the eye roams over what seems to be a broad flat valley beyond the stream; but the stream itself—the fatal "Greasy Grass," as the Sioux called it—is hidden from sight under the steep bluffs that hem it in. Coming from the mountains, it swings into sight far to the left front, comes rippling toward us in its fringe of cottonwoods and willows, and suddenly disappears under or behind the huge rolling wave of bluff that stretches right and left across the path. For nearly six miles of its tortuous course it cannot be seen from the point where Custer drew rein to get his first view of the village. Neither can its fringing willows be seen, and—fatal and momentous fact—neither could hundreds of the populous "lodges" that clustered along its western bank. Eagerly scanning the distant "tepees" that lay beyond the northern point where the bluff dipped to the stream, and swinging his broad-brimmed hat about his head in an ecstasy of soldierly anticipation, he shouted: "Custer's luck! The biggest Indian village on the continent!" And he could not have seen one-third of it.

But what he saw was enough to fire the blood of any soldier. Far to the northwest and west huge clouds of dust rose billowing from the broad valley. Far across the hidden stream could be seen the swarming herds of ponies in excited movement. Here, there, and everywhere tiny dots of horsemen scurrying away could be readily distinguished, and down to the right front, down along what could be seen of the village around that shoulder of bluff, all was lively turmoil and confusion; lodges were being hurriedly taken down, and their occupants were fleeing from the wrath to come. We know now that the warriors whom he saw dashing westward were mainly the young men hurrying out to "round up" the pony herds; we know now that behind those sheltering bluffs were still thousands of fierce warriors eager and ready to meet "Long Hair"; we know that the signs of panic and retreat were due mainly to the rush to get the women and little children out of the way; ponies and dogs, hastily hitched to the dust-raising *travois*, dragged the wondering pappooses and frightened squaws far out over the westward slopes; but seeing the scurry and panic, Custer seems to have attached only one meaning to it. They were all in full retreat. The whole community would be on the run before he could strike them. Quickly he determined on his course. Reno should push straight ahead, get down into the valley, ford the stream, and attack the southern end of the village, while he with his pet companies should turn into the long winding ravine that ran northwestward to the stream, and pitch in with wild charge from the east. To Reno these orders were promptly given. A courier was sent to Benteen, far off to the left, notifying him of the "find"; and another galloped to Macdougall with orders to hurry up with the pack trains where the extra ammunition was carried. Custer knew it would be needed.

Then the daring commander placed himself at the head of his own column, plunged down the slope, and, followed by his eager men, was soon out of sight, perhaps out of hearing of what might be taking place over in the valley behind the bluffs that rose on his left higher with every furlong trotted. The last that Reno and his people ever saw of them alive was the tail of the column disappearing in a cloud of dust; then the cloud alone was to be seen, hanging over their trail like a pall.

Pushing forward, Reno came quickly to a shallow "cooley" (frontierism for gully) that led down through the bluff to the stream. A brisk trot brought him to the ford; his troopers plunged blithely through, and began to clamber the low bank on the western shore. He expected from the tenor of his orders to find an open, unobstructed valley, down which, five miles away at least, he could see the lodges of the Indian village. It was with surprise, not unmixed with grave concern, therefore, that, as he urged his horse through the willows and up to the level of the low "bench" beyond, he suddenly rode into full view of an immense township, whose southern outskirts were not two miles away. Far as he could see, the dust cloud rose above the excited villages; herds of war ponies were being driven in from the west on a mad run; old men, squaws, children, draught ponies, and *travois* were scurrying off toward the Big Horn, and Reno realized that he was in front of the assembled warriors of the whole Sioux nation.

What Custer expected of Reno was, is generally believed, a bold, dashing charge into the heart of the village—just such a charge as he, Custer, had successfully led at the Washita, though it cost the life of Captain Hamilton, and eventually of many others. But Reno had no dash to speak of, and the sight that burst upon his eyes eliminated any that might be latent. He attacked, but the attack was nevertheless spiritless and abortive. Dismounting his men, he advanced them as skirmishers across the mile or more of prairie, firing as soon as he got within range of the village. No resistance of any consequence was made as he pushed northward, for the sudden appearance of his command was a total surprise to the Uncapapas and Blackfeet, whose villages were farthest south. Their scouts had signalled Custer's column trotting down the ravine, and those who had not rushed for safety to the rear were apparently rushing toward the Brulé village in the centre as the point which Custer would be apt first to strike. Reno could have darted into the south end of the village, it is believed, before his approach could have been fairly realized. As it was, slowly and on foot, he traversed the prairie without losing a man, and was upon the lodges when a few shots were fired from the willows along the stream, and some mounted Indians could be seen swooping around his left flank. He had had no experience in Indian fighting. He simply seemed to feel that with his little command of two hundred men he could not drive the whole valley full of warriors, and in much perturbation and worry he sounded the halt, rally, and mount. Then for a few moments, that to his officers and men must have seemed hours, he paused irresolute, not knowing what to do.

The Indians settled it for him. They well interpreted his hesitation. "The White Chief was scared"; and now was their chance. Man and boy they came tearing to the spot. A few well-aimed shots knocked a luckless trooper or two out of the saddle. Reno hurriedly ordered a movement by the flank toward the high bluffs across the stream to his right rear. He never thought to dismount a few cool hands to face about and keep off the enemy. He placed himself at the new head of column, and led the backward move. Out came the Indians, with shots and triumphant yells, in pursuit. The rear of the column began to crowd on the head; Reno struck a trot; the rear struck the gallop. The Indians came dashing up on both flanks and close to the rear; and then—then the helpless, horribly led troopers had no alternative. Discipline and order were all forgotten. In one mad rush they tore away for the stream, plunged in, sputtered through, and clambered breathlessly up the steep bluff on the eastern shore—an ignominious, inexcusable panic, due mainly to the nerveless conduct of the major commanding.

In vain had Donald McIntosh and "Benny" Hodgson, two of the bravest and best-loved officers in the regiment, striven to rally, face about, and fight with the rear of column. The Indians were not in overpowering numbers at the moment, and a bold front would have "stood off" double their force; but with the major on the run, and foremost in the run, the lieutenants could do nothing—but lose their own gallant lives. McIntosh was surrounded, dragged from his horse and butchered close to the brink. Hodgson, shot out of saddle, was rescued by a faithful comrade, who plunged into the stream with him; but close to the farther shore the Indians picked him off, a bullet tore through his body, and the gallant little fellow, the pet and pride of the whole regiment, rolled dead into the muddy waters.

Once well up the bluffs, Reno's breathless followers faced about and took in the situation. The Indians pursued no further, and even now were rapidly withdrawing from range. The major fired his pistol at the distant foe in paroxysmal defiance of the fellows who had stampeded him. He was now up some two hundred feet above them, and it was safe—as it was harmless. Two of his best officers lay dead down there on the banks below; so, too, lay a dozen of his men. The Indians, men and even boys, had swarmed all around his people, and slaughtered them as they ran. Many more were wounded, but, for the present at least, all seemed safe. The Indians, except a few, had mysteriously withdrawn from their front. What could that mean? And then, what could have become of Custer? Where, too, were Benteen and Macdougall with their commands?

Over toward the villages, which they could now see stretching for five miles down the stream, all was shrill uproar and confusion; but northward the bluffs rose still higher to a point nearly opposite the middle of the villages—a point some two miles from them—and beyond that they could see nothing. Thither, however, had Custer gone, and suddenly, crashing through the sultry morning air, came the sound of fierce and rapid musketry—whole volleys—then one continuous rattle and roar. Louder, fiercer, it grew for full ten minutes. Some thought they could hear the ringing cheers of their comrades, and were ready to cheer in reply; some thought they heard the thrilling charge of the trumpets; many were eager to mount and rush to join their colonel, and with him to avenge Hodgson and McIntosh, and retrieve the dark fortunes of their own battalion. But, almost as suddenly as it began, the heavy volleying died away; the continuous rattle broke into scattering skirmish fire, then into sputtering shots, then only once in a while some distant rifle would crack feebly on the breeze, and Reno's men looked wonderingly in each other's faces. There stood the villages plain enough, and the firing had begun close under the bluffs, close to the stream, and had died away far to the north. What could it mean?

Soon, with eager delight, the little commands of Benteen and Macdougall were hailed coming up the slopes from the east.

"Have you seen anything of Custer?" was the first anxious inquiry.

Benteen and Weir had galloped to a point of bluff a mile or more to the north, had seen swarms of Indians in the valley below, but not a sign of Custer's people. They could expect no aid from Custer, then, and there was only one thing left—intrench themselves, and hold out as best they could till Terry and Gibbon should arrive. Reno had now seven "troops" and the pack train, abundant ammunition and supplies. The chances were in his favor.

Now what had become of Custer? For him and his there was none left to tell the story except the Crow scout "Curley," who managed to slip away in a Sioux blanket during the thick of the fight, and our sources of information are solely Indian. The very next year a battalion of the Fifth Cavalry passed the battle-ground with a number of Sioux scouts who but a twelvemonth previous were fighting there the Seventh Cavalry. Half a dozen of them told their stories at different times and in different places, and as to the general features of the battle, they tallied with singular exactness. These fellows were mainly Brulés and Ogalallas. Afterward we got the stories of the Uncapapas—most interesting of all—and from all these sources it was not hard to trace Custer's every move. One could almost portray his every emotion.

Never realizing, as I believe, the fearful odds against him, believing that he would find the village "on the run," and that between himself and Reno he could "double them up" in short order, Custer had jauntily trotted down to his death. It was a long five-mile ride from where he sighted the northern end of the village to where he struck its centre around that bold point of bluff, and from the start to the moment his guidons whirled into view, and his troopers came galloping "front into line" down near the ford, he never fairly saw the great village—never dreamed of its depth and extent. Rounding the bluff, he suddenly found himself face to face with thousands of the boldest and most skilful warriors of the prairies. He had hoped to charge at once into the heart of the village, to hear the cheers of Reno's men from the south. Instead he was greeted with a perfect fury of flame and hissing lead from the dense thicket of willow and cottonwood, a fire that *had* to be answered at once. Quickly he dismounted his men and threw them forward on the run, each fourth man holding, cavalry fashion, the horses of the other three. The line seems to have swept in parallel very nearly with the general course of the stream, but to no purpose. The foe was ten to one in their front. Boys and squaws were shooting from the willows ("Oh, we had plenty guns!" said our story-tellers); and worse than that, hundreds of young warriors had mounted their ponies and swarmed across the stream below him, hundreds more were following and circling all about him. And then it was that Custer, the hero of a hundred daring charges, seems to have realized that he must cut his way out. "Mount!" rang the trumpets, and leaving many a poor fellow on the ground, the troopers ran for their horses. Instantly from lodge and willow Ogalallas and Brulés sprang to horse and rushed to the ford in mad pursuit. "Make for the heights!" must have been the order, for the first rush was eastward; then more to the left, as they found their progress barred. Then, as they reached higher ground, all they could see, far as they could see, circling, swooping, yelling like demons, and all the time keeping up their furious fire, were thousands of the mounted Sioux. Hemmed in, cut off, dropping fast from their saddles, Custer's men saw that retreat was impossible. They sprang to the ground, "turned their horses loose," said the Indians, and by that time half their number had fallen. A skirmish line was thrown out down the slope, and there they dropped at five yards' interval; there their comrades found them two days after. Every instant the foe rode closer and gained in numbers; every instant some poor fellow bit the dust. At last, on a mound that stands at the northern end of a little ridge, Custer, with Cooke, Yates, and gallant "Brother Tom," and some dozen soldiers, all that were left by this time, gathered in the last rally. They sold their lives dearly, brave fellows that they were; but they were as a dozen to the leaves of the forest at the end of twenty minutes, and in less than twenty-five— all was over.

Keogh, Calhoun, Crittenden, had died along the skirmish lines; Smith, Porter, and Reily were found with their men; so were the surgeons, Lord and De Wolf; so, too, were "Boston" Custer and the *Herald* correspondent; but two bodies were never recognized among the slain—those of Lieutenants Harrington and "Jack" Sturgis. Down a little "cooley" some thirty men had made a rush for their lives; the Sioux had simply thronged the banks shooting them as they ran. One trooper—an officer, said the Sioux—managed to break through their circle, the only white man who did, and galloped madly eastward. Five warriors started in pursuit—two Ogalallas, two Uncapapas, and a Brulé, all well mounted. Fear lent him wings, and his splendid horse gained on all but an Uncapapa, who hung to the chase. At last, when even this one was ready to draw rein and let him go, the hunted cavalryman glanced over his shoulder, fancied himself nearly overtaken, and placing the muzzle of his revolver at his ear, pulled the trigger, and sent his own bullet through his brain. His skeleton was pointed out to the officers of the Fifth Cavalry the following year by one of the pursuers, and so it was discovered for the first time. Was it Harrington? Was it Sturgis? Poor "Jack's" watch was restored to his father some two years after the battle, having been traded off by Sioux who escaped to the British possessions; but no mention was made by these Indians of a watch thus taken. Three years ago there came a story of a new skeleton found still further from the scene. Shreds of uniform and the heavy gilding of the cavalry buttons lying near, as well as the expensive filling of several teeth, seem to indicate that this too may have been an officer. If so, all the missing are now accounted for. Of the twelve troops of the Seventh Cavalry, Custer led five that hot Sunday into the battle of the Little Big Horn, and of his portion of the regiment only one living thing escaped the vengeance of the Sioux. Bleeding from many wounds, weak and exhausted, with piteous appeal in his eyes, there came straggling into the lines some days after the fight Myles Keogh's splendid sorrel horse Comanche. Who can ever picture his welcome as the soldiers thronged around the gallant charger? To this day they guard and cherish him in the Seventh. No more duty does Comanche perform; no rider ever mounts him. His last great service was rendered that Sunday in '76, and now, sole living relic of Custer's last rally, he spends his days with the old regiment.

But I have said that Sitting Bull was not the inspiration of the great victory won by the Sioux. With Custer's people slaughtered, the Indians left their bodies to the plundering hands of the squaws, and once more crowded upon Reno's front. There were two nights of wild triumph and rejoicing in the villages, though not one instant was the watch on Reno relaxed. All day of the 26th they kept him penned in the rifle pits, but early on the 27th, with great commotion, the lodges were suddenly taken down, and tribe after tribe, village after village, six thousand Indians passed before his eyes, making off toward the mountains. Terry and Gibbon had come; Reno's relic of the Seventh was saved. Together they explored the field, and hastily buried the mutilated dead; then hurried back to the Yellowstone while the Sioux were hiding in the fastnesses of the Big Horn. Of the rest of the summer's campaign no extended mention is needed here. The Indians were shrewd enough to know that now at least the commands of Crook and Terry would be heavily re-enforced, and then the hunt would be relentless. Soon as their scouts reported the assembly of new and strong bodies of troops upon the Yellowstone and Platte, the great confederation quietly dissolved. Sitting Bull, with many chosen followers, made for the Yellowstone, and was driven northward by General Miles. Others took refuge across the Little Missouri, whither Crook pursued, and by dint of hard marching and fighting that fall and winter many bands and many famous chiefs were whipped into surrender. Among these, bravest, most brilliant, most victorious of all, was the hero of the Powder River fight on Patrick's Day, the warrior Crazy Horse.

The fame of his exploit had reached the Indian camps along the Rosebud before this young chief, with his followers, Ogalalla and Brulé, came to swell the ranks of Sitting Bull. Again, on the 17th of June, he had been foremost in the stirring fight with Crook, and when the entire band moved over into the valley of the Little Big Horn, and the Brulés, Ogalallas, and Sans Arcs pitched their tepees in the chosen ground, the very centre of the camp, it is safe to say that among the best and experienced fighters, the tribes from the White River and their neighbors the Cheyennes, no chief was so honored and believed in as Crazy Horse.

In pitching the new camp, the Blackfeet were farthest south—up stream; next came the Uncapapas, with their renowned medicine-man, Sitting Bull; then the Ogalallas, Brulés, and Cheyennes, covering the whole "bottom" opposite the shoulder of bluff around which Custer hove in sight; farthest north were the Minneconjoux; and the great village contained at least six thousand aboriginal souls.

Now up to this time Sitting Bull had no real claims as a war chief. Eleven days before the fight there was a "sun dance." His own people have since told us these particulars, and the best story-teller among them was that bright-faced squaw of Tatonka-he-gle-ska—Spotted Horn Bull—who accompanied the party on their Eastern trip. She is own cousin to Sitting Bull, and knows whereof she speaks. The chief had a trance and a vision. Solemnly he assured his people that within a few days they would be attacked by a vast force of white soldiers, but that the Sioux should triumph over them; and when the Crows and Crook's command appeared on the 17th, it was a partial redemption of his promise.

Wary scouts saw Reno's column turning back down the Rosebud after discovering the trail, and nothing, they judged, would come from that quarter. All around Crook's camp on Goose Creek the indications were that the "Gray Fox" was simply waiting for more soldiers before he would again venture forth. Sitting Bull had no thought of new attack for days to come, when, early on the morning of the 25th, two Cheyenne Indians who had started eastward at dawn came dashing back to the bluffs, and waving their blankets, signalled, "White soldiers—heaps—coming quick." Instantly all was uproar and confusion.

Of course women and children had to be hurried away, the great herds of ponies gathered in, and the warriors assembled to meet the coming foe. Even as the chiefs were hastening to the council lodge there came the crash of rapid volleys from the south. It was Reno's attack—an attack from a new and utterly unexpected quarter—and this, with the news that Long Hair was thundering down the ravine across the stream, was too much for Sitting Bull. Hurriedly gathering his household about him, he lashed his pony to the top of his speed, and fled westward for safety. Miles he galloped before he dare stop for breath. Behind him he could hear the roar of battle, and on he would have sped but for the sudden discovery that one of his twin children was missing. Turning, he was surprised to find the firing dying away, soon ceasing altogether. In half an hour more he managed to get back to camp, where the missing child was found, but the battle had been won without him. Without him the Blackfeet and Uncapapas had repelled Reno and penned him on the bluffs. Without him the Ogalallas, Brulés, and Cheyennes had turned back Custer's daring assault, then rushed forth and completed the death-gripping circle in which he was held. Again had Crazy Horse been foremost in the fray, riding in and braining the bewildered soldiers with his heavy war club. Fully had his vision been realized, but—Sitting Bull was not there.

For a long time it was claimed for him by certain sycophantic followers that from the council lodge he directed the battle; but it would not do. When the old sinner was finally starved out of her Majesty's territory, and came in to accept the terms accorded him, even his own people could not keep straight faces when questioned as to the cause of the odd names given those twins—"The-One-that-was-taken" and *"The-One-that-was-left."* Finally it all leaked out, and now "none so poor to do him reverence."

Of course it was his rôle to assume all the airs of a conqueror, to be insolent and defiant to the "High Joint Commission," sent the following winter to beg him to come home and be good; but the claims of Tatonka-e-Yotanka to the leadership in the greatest victory his people ever won are mere vaporings, to be classed with the boastings of dozens of chiefs who were scattered over the Northern reservations during the next few years. Rain-in-the-Face used to brag by the hour that he had killed Custer with his own hand, but the other Indians laughed at him. Gall, of the Uncapapas, Spotted Eagle, Kill Eagle, Lame Deer, Lone Wolf, and all the varieties of Bears and Bulls were probably leading spirits in the battle, but the man who more than all others seems to have won the admiration of his fellows for skill and daring throughout that stirring campaign, and especially on that bloody day, is he who so soon after met his death in desperate effort to escape from Crook's guards, the warrior Crazy Horse.

SHE WATCHED CUSTER'S LAST BATTLE

KATE BIGHEAD,

as told to

Thomas B. Marquis

Eighty years ago I was born when my people were in camp near Geese river (North Platte river). I am of the Cheyenne tribe, and am now living with the Northern Cheyennes, in Montana. My name on the agency roll is Kate Bighead.

I was with the Southern Cheyennes during most of my childhood and young womanhood. I was in the camp beside the Washita river, in the country the white people call Oklahoma, when Custer and his soldiers came there and fought the Indians (November, 1868). Our Chief Black Kettle and other Cheyennes, many of them women and children, were killed that day. It was early in the morning when the soldiers began the shooting. There had been a big storm, and there was snow on the ground. All of us jumped from our beds, and all of us started running to get away. I was barefooted, as were almost all of the others. Our tepees and all of our property we had to leave behind were burned by the white men.

The next spring Custer and his soldiers found us again (March, 1869). We then were far westward, on a branch of what the white people call Red river, I think. That time there was no fighting. Custer smoked the peace pipe with our chiefs. He promised never again to fight the Cheyennes, so all of us followed him to a soldier fort (Fort Sill). Our people gave him the name Hi-es-tzie, meaning Long Hair.

I saw Long Hair many times during those days. One time I was close to where he was mounting his horse to go somewhere, and I took a good look at him. He had a large nose, deep-set eyes, and light-red hair that was long and wavy. He was wearing a buckskin suit and a big white 363 hat. I was then a young woman, 22 years old, and I admired him. All of the Indian women talked of him as being a fine-looking man.

My cousin, a young woman named Me-o-tzi, went often with him to help in finding the trails of Indians. She said he told her his soldier horses were given plenty of corn and oats to eat, so they could outrun and catch the Indians riding ponies that had only grass to eat. All of the Cheyennes liked her, and all were glad she had so important a place in life. After Long Hair went away, different ones of the Cheyenne young men wanted to marry her. But she would not have any of them. She said that Long Hair was her husband, that he had promised to come back to her, and that she would wait for him. She waited seven years. Then he was killed.

Me-o-tzi mourned when she learned of his death. I was not then with those people, but I heard that she cut off her hair and gashed her arms and legs, for mourning. Her heart was much the more sad on account of his having been killed in a battle where the Northern Cheyennes fought against him. About a year later she married a white man named Isaac. They had several children. One of her daughters is now a middle-aged woman living with us Northern Cheyennes on Tongue river. The mother lived to old age and died in Oklahoma six years ago, some time after Christmas (in January, 1921). But her name is continued among us. A little granddaughter of mine is known to us as Me-o-tzi. At times the young people joke her: "You are Custer's Indian wife."

I came to the Northern Cheyennes when their reservation was in the Black Hills country (1868–1874). White people found gold there, so the Indians had to move out. The Cheyennes were told they must go to another reservation, but not many of them made the change. They said it was no use, as the white people might want that reservation too. Many Cheyennes, and many Sioux also, went to live in the hunting ground between the Powder and Bighorn rivers. White Bull and White Moon, my two brothers, left to go to the hunting ground, and I went with them. Word was sent to the hunting Indians that all Cheyennes and Sioux must stay on their reservations in Dakota. But all who stayed on the reservations had their guns and ponies taken from them, so the hunters quit going there.

The band of Cheyennes where I dwelt had forty family lodges. In the last part of the winter we camped on the west side of Powder river, not far above the mouth of Little Powder river. Soldiers came early in the morning (March 17, 1876). They got between our camp and our horse herd, so all of us had to run away afoot. Not many of our people were killed, but our tepees and everything that was in them were burned. Three days later, all of us walking, we arrived at Crazy Horse's camp of Ogallala Sioux.

The Ogallalas gave us food and shelter. After a few days the two bands together went northward and found the Uncpapa Sioux, where Sitting Bull was the chief. The chiefs of the three bands decided that all of us would travel together for the spring and summer hunting, as it was said that many soldiers would be coming to try to make us go back to the reservations.

The three tribal bands grew larger and larger, by Indians coming from the Dakota reservations, as we traveled from place to place and as the grass came up. Other tribal bands—Minneconjoux Sioux, Blackfeet Sioux, Arrows All Gone Sioux—came to us. There were then six separate tribal camp circles, each having its own chiefs, wherever we stopped. In some of the six camp circles were small bands of other Sioux—Burned Thigh, Assiniboines, and Waist and Skirt people.

All of us traveled together to the west side of lower Powder river, on west across Tongue river, and to the Rosebud valley. The grass grew high and our ponies became strong. Our men killed many buffalo, and we women tanned many skins and stored up much meat, as we camped from place to place up the Rosebud valley. We left the Rosebud where the Busby store now is, and our camps were set up five nights at the forks of what the white people now call Reno creek, near the Little Bighorn river.

Hunters from that camp saw soldiers far southward. During the night all of our young men went to fight them. The next day there was a big fight (Crook, June 17, 1876) on upper Rosebud creek. The Indian dead, one Cheyenne among them, were brought back that night.

The six camps moved the next morning down to the east side of the Little Bighorn, above the mouth of Reno creek. We stayed there five nights. There were more Indians in those six camps than I ever saw together anywhere else. Only a few of our Northern Cheyenne people were absent, and we had with us a few families of Southern Cheyennes.

The chiefs from all the camps, in council, decided we should move down the Little Bighorn river to its mouth, so our hunters could go across to the west side of the Bighorn and kill antelope in the great herds they had seen there. All of the Indians crossed to the west side of the Little Bighorn and moved the first part of the expected journey to the mouth of this stream. The plan was to stay at this camp but one night, and to go on down the valley the next day.

The next morning (June 25, 1876) I went with an Ogallala woman to visit some friends among the Minneconjoux Sioux, up the valley toward where was the Uncpapa camp circle, at the upper or south end of the camps. We found our women friends bathing in the river, and we joined them. Other groups, men, women and children, were playing in the water at many places along the stream. Some boys were fishing. All of us were having a good time. It was somewhere past the middle of the forenoon. Nobody was thinking of any battle coming. A few women were taking down their lodges, getting ready for the move on down the valley that day. After a while two Sioux boys came running toward us. They were shouting:

"Soldiers are coming!"

We heard shooting. We hid in the brush. The sounds of the shooting multiplied—pop—pop—pop—pop! We heard women and children screaming. Old men were calling the young warriors to battle. Young men were singing their war songs as they responded to the call. We peeped out. Throngs of Sioux men on horses were racing toward the skirt of timber just south of the Uncpapa camp circle, where the guns were clattering. The horsemen warriors were dodging through a mass of women, children and old people hurrying afoot to the benchland hills west of the camps.

From our hiding place in the brush we heard the sounds of battle change from place to place. It seemed the white men were going away, with the Indians following them. Soon afterward we got glimpses of the soldiers crossing the river above us. Many of them were afoot. Then we saw that the Indians were after all of them, shooting and beating them.

I came out and set off at running toward our Cheyenne camp circle, the last one, at the north end down the river, more than a mile from where I had been hiding. In all of the camps, as I went through them, there was great excitement. Old men were helping the young warriors in dressing and painting themselves for battle. Some women were bringing war horses from the herds. Other women were working fast at taking down their tepees. A few were loading pack horses with tepee belongings, while others were carrying heavy burdens on their backs.

Many were taking away nothing leaving the tepees and everything in them, running away with only their children or with small packs in hands. I saw one Sioux woman just staying at one spot, jumping up and down and screaming, because she could not find her little son.

Clouds of dust were kicked up by the horse herds rushed into the camp circles, as well as by the horses that had been picketed near at hand by the Indian camp policemen and had been mounted and ridden to fight when came the first alarm. The mounted Indians were still going to the place where had been the fighting, south of the Uncpapa camp. But before I got to my home lodge all of them were riding wildly back down through the camps. It appeared they had been beaten and were running away. But I soon learned what had happened. I heard a Cheyenne old man calling out:

"Other soldiers are coming! Warriors, go and fight them!"

On a high ridge far out eastward from the Cheyenne camp circle I saw those other soldiers. A few Indians were out there, and shots were being exchanged at long distance. Great throngs of other Indians, many more Sioux than Cheyennes, were lashing their ponies through the waters of the river or had crossed it and were on their way up the coulee valley toward the high ridge. It appeared there would be no end to the rushing procession of warriors. They kept going, going, going. I wanted to go too.

"Let me have a horse," I begged my elder brother, White Bull.

I had seen other battles, in past times. I always liked to watch the men fighting. Not many women did that, and I often was teased on account of it. But this time I had a good excuse, for White Bull's son, my nephew, named Noisy Walking, had gone. I was but twenty-nine years old, so I had not any son to serve as a warrior, but I would sing strongheart songs for the nephew. He was eighteen years old. Some women told me he had expected me to be there, and he had wrapped a red scarf about his neck in order that I might know him from a distance.

I crossed the river and followed up the broad coulee where the warriors had gone and were still going. The soldiers had lined themselves out on a long ridge nearer to the river and a little lower than the ridge far out where we first had seen them. By the time I got close enough to see well, the Indians were all around the soldiers, I think. Most of the warriors, when they got where they wanted to go, left their ponies back in gulches and hid themselves for crawling forward along little gullies or behind small ridges or knolls. The soldiers also got off their horses. The getting off the horses was good for both the Indians and the soldiers. A man on a horse can be seen better for shooting at him, while it is hard for him to do good shooting, as his horse will not stand still for him to make a good aim, especially if much shooting is being done.

I rode to the right, keeping far from the soldiers and going on to the north side of them. Some of the warriors were yet on their ponies, but there were lots of loose ponies there, so I knew there were lots of Indian young men hidden near by, although I could not see many of them. The Indians mostly were in warrior society bands at different places, because the men of each warrior society understood each other's ways. But all of them I could see on that side were Sioux, no Cheyennes. I kept on going around, searching the north side, then the west side. At the south side, in the deep gulches and behind the ridges between the soldiers and the river, I found none but Cheyennes and Ogallala Sioux. Keeping myself all the time out of bullet range, I looked and looked among them for Noisy Walking. But I could not find him.

The Indians were using bows and arrows more than they were using guns. Many of them had no guns, and not many who did have them had also plenty of bullets. But even if they had been well supplied with both guns and bullets, in that fight the bow was better. As the soldier ridge sloped on all sides, and as there were no trees on it nor around it, the smoke from each gun fired showed right where the shooter was hidden. The arrows made no smoke, so it could not be seen where they came from. Also, since a bullet has to go straight out from the end of a gun, any Indian who fired his gun had to put his head up so his eyes could see where to aim it. By doing this his head might be seen by a soldier and hit by a soldier bullet. The Indian could keep himself at all times out of sight when sending arrows. Each arrow was shot far upward and forward, not at any soldier in particular, but to curve down and fall where they were. Bullets would not do any harm if shot in that way. But a rain of arrows from thousands of Indian bows, and kept up for a long time, would hit many soldiers and their horses by falling and sticking into their heads or their backs.

The Indians all around were gradually creeping closer to the soldiers, by following the gullies or dodging from knoll to knoll. On the southern side, where I stopped to watch the fight, almost all of the Cheyennes and Ogallala Sioux had crawled across a deep gulch at the bottom of a broad coulee south of the ridge where were the soldiers, and about half way between them and the river. There was a long time—the old men now say they think it must have been about an hour and a half—of this fighting slowly, with not much harm to either side. Then a band of the soldiers on the ridge mounted their horses and came riding in a gallop down the broad coulee toward the river, toward where were the Cheyennes and the Ogallalas. The Indians hidden there got back quickly into the deepest parts of the gulch or kept on going away from it until they got over the ridge just south of it, the ridge where I was watching. The soldiers who had come galloping stopped and got off their horses along another ridge, a low one just north of the deep gulch.

Lame White Man, the bravest Cheyenne warrior chief, stayed in hiding close to where the small band of soldiers got off their horses. From there he called to the young men, and they began creeping and dodging back to him. The Ogallala Sioux chiefs also called to their young men, and these also returned to the fight. Within a few minutes there were many hundreds of warriors wriggling along the gullies all around those soldiers.

I saw one of the white men there kill himself, with his own gun, just after they got off their horses. Soon afterward I saw another one do the same act. From where I was I had a clear view of the soldiers, and their saddled horses standing near them showed all of the warriors where the white men were. I think that only a few soldiers, maybe not any of them, were killed by the Indians during the few minutes of fighting there. I could not see the creeping Indians well enough to know when any one or another of them might have been killed or wounded. After a little while I heard Lame White Man call out:

"Young men, come now with me and show yourselves to be brave!"

On all sides of this band of soldiers the Indians jumped up. There were hundreds of warriors, many more than one might have thought could hide themselves in those small gullies. I think there were about twenty Indians to every soldier there. The soldier horses got scared, and all of them broke loose and ran away toward the river. Just then I saw a soldier shoot himself by holding his revolver at his head. Then another one did the same, and another. Right away, all of them began shooting themselves or shooting each other. I saw several different pairs of them fire their guns at the same time and shoot one another in the breast. For a short time the Indians just stayed where they were and looked. Then they rushed forward. But not many of them got to strike coup blows on living enemies. Before they could get to them, all of the white men were dead.

The horses were driven on to the river, where they wanted to go anyway, as the day was hot and they were thirsty. There they were captured by warriors or by women and old men. The warriors were most glad at getting the guns and cartridges from the dead soldiers. With these they went crawling toward the different parts of the ridge where were yet the main body of soldiers. Although I had been singing strongheart songs, thinking Noisy Walking might hear me, I had not seen him. My heart thumped hard when I saw an Indian leading a horse bearing a rider who appeared to be wounded. The rider resembled my nephew. I whipped my pony into a gallop and caught up with the two men, but I found that both of them were Sioux, so I went back to the fight.

I started to go around the east end of the soldier ridge. Just then I saw lots of Indians running toward that end of the ridge, and the soldier horses there were running away. Pretty soon I saw that all of the white men were dead and the warriors were among them getting their guns. I did not see how they were killed, but I think they must have killed themselves. The Indians crowded on westward along the ridge and along its two sides. I followed, but keeping myself back so I would not be hit by a bullet. I stopped to look over a little hill and watch a band of soldiers on the ground at the north slope of the ridge. Warriors were all around those men, creeping closer and closer. The white men's horses were all gone from there. After I had been looking but a few minutes at those men I saw them go at shooting each other and shooting themselves, the same as I had seen it done by the soldiers down toward the river.

The remaining white fighters collected in a group at the west end of the ridge, where our men say there now is a big stone having an iron fence around it. At that time there must have been hundreds of warriors for every white soldier left alive. The warriors around them were shifting from shelter to shelter, each one of them trying to get close enough to strike a coup blow of some kind upon a living enemy, as all warriors try to do when in a fight. Many hundreds of Indian heads were being popped up for a quick look and then jerked down again for a movement forward a little farther. The soldiers must have seen many of those heads, but they must have been puzzled as to which ones to shoot at. The remaining soldiers were keeping themselves behind their dead horses. The Indians could get only some glimpses of the white men, but it was easy enough to see where they were.

A great crowd of Indian boys had been on their horses on the surrounding hills and watching from there all during the battle. Many old men were there with them. The old men, being where they could get a good view, were calling out helpful advice to the warriors who were hidden. These who had been keeping at a distance began to come closer. Some of the youths got too close, wanting to strike coups. I saw a Sioux boy pitch forward, killed. The men kept calling out:

"Be careful. Wait."

The shots quit coming from the place where the soldiers were lying behind their dead horses. All of the Indians jumped up and ran toward them, supposing all of them were dead. But there were seven of the white men who sprang to their feet and went running toward the river. All of the hundreds of boys came tearing in on their horses, to strike blows upon the dead white men, as that was considered a brave deed for a boy. There was such a rush and mixup that it seemed the whole world had gone wild. There was such a crowd, and there was so much dust and smoke in the air, that I did not see what happened to the seven men who ran down the hillside. Hundreds of Sioux and Cheyenne warriors were after them. The talk I heard afterward was that all of them, and all of the others who had been hidden behind the horses, killed themselves. The Indians believe that the Everywhere Spirit made all of them go crazy and do this, in punishment for having attacked a peaceful Indian camp.

When I was looking at the last fighting, I saw back along the ridge a living soldier sitting on the ground, in plain view. He was just sitting there and rubbing his head, as if he did not know where he was nor what was going on in the world. While I was watching him, three Sioux men ran to him and seized him. They stretched him out upon his back. They went at this slowly, and I wondered what they were going to do. Pretty soon I found out. Two of them held his arms while the third man cut off his head with a sheath-knife.

I went riding among the Indians at different places on the battlefield, in search of Noisy Walking. I saw several different ones of the soldiers not yet quite dead. The Indians cut off arms or legs or feet of these, the same as was done for those entirely dead. A Cheyenne told me where was my nephew, down in the deep gulch half way to the river, where had been most of the Cheyennes and Ogallalas during all of the first part of the battle. I went down there and found him. He had been shot through the body and had been stabbed several times. I stayed with him while a young man friend went to the camps to tell his mother.

Women from many families brought lodgepole travois, dragged by ponies, to take away the dead or wounded Indians. Some of the women, mourning for their own dead, beat and cut the dead bodies of the white men. Noisy Walking's mother and her sister came to get him. We put him upon the travois bed and took him across the river to our camp.

All of the lodges in the six camp circles were taken down as soon as the dead warriors were taken there. New camp spots were chosen, all of them back from the river and down the valley below the first location. The Indian regular custom was to move camp right away when any death occurred among the people in the camp. Not many of the big tepee lodges were set up at the new camp spots. Instead, the poles and skins for them were packed for moving away quickly if necessary. The women gathered willow wands and built little dome shelters, or the people slept that night without any shelter except robe bedding.

The Indians got guns, cartridges, horses, saddles, clothing, boots, everything the soldiers had with them. During the battle, all of the women and children and old people had been watching from the western hills across the valley. They kept themselves ready to run away if their warriors should be beaten, or to return to the camps if their side should win.

After a long time of this watching, all the time in doubt, they saw a band of horsemen coming across the river and toward them. As the horsemen got into good view it was seen that all of them had on blue clothing and were mounted on soldier horses. It appeared the Indian Warriors all had been killed, and these men were soldiers coming to kill the families. Women shrieked, some of them fainted. Mothers and children ran away into hiding. One woman grabbed her two little boys and set out running up a gulch. She was so excited that in picking them up she seized their feet and slung them upside down over her shoulders. It soon became known, though, that these men were our own warriors bringing the horses and the clothing of the dead soldiers.

Noisy Walking died that night. Six of our Cheyenne young men now were dead. Twenty-four Sioux warriors had been killed. Many more Indians would have been killed if the Everywhere Spirit had not caused the white men to go crazy and turn their guns upon themselves. Even as it was in all of the camps there was much mourning and sadness of heart. The night before, there had been dancing and the usual gayety of Indian young people. But on this night there were so many sorrowing people that all feelings of joy were forgotten.

We Cheyennes buried our dead that afternoon. We placed them in hillside caves out from the camps. Some of the Sioux left their dead warriors in burial tepees set up as they had been when in use by the living people. Other Sioux put their dead on scaffolds, near the camps. One of our lost warriors was Chief Lame White Man, the most important war leader among the Cheyennes. He was killed soon after I last had seen him when he called the young men for fighting the soldiers who rode down toward the gulch near the river. Although I had seen him just before his death, I did not learn of it until after I got back to our home camp. He was 37 years old, and he left a widow and two daughters. Each of the other five dead Cheyennes was a young and unmarried man.

Not many Cheyennes got into the first fight up the valley, where the soldiers first shot into the camps, when I was with the women in the river. I think the Uncpapas did the most fighting there, as that was their end of the camps. But there were two Cheyennes killed there. One was named Whirlwind. He was 16 years old. The other was named Hump. He was about 16 or 17, I believe. Some older men said they acted foolish in going too close when there was no need for it. I saw the soldiers there in the river, with the Indians knocking them from their horses. I think there must be yet some soldier guns at the bottom of that river.

A Cheyenne named Scabby showed his spirit powers during the time of that first fighting. The white men were off their horses and were lying down in a long line and shooting toward the Indians, who kept far away just then. But Scabby stripped off all of his clothing, wrapped a flag around his body, mounted his pony and raced it five times back and forth in front of those soldiers. All of them shot at him, but not a bullet touched him. His Medicine powers prevented his being hit by them.

The Cheyennes were considered the special fighters at the battle against the Custer soldiers, where I rode out to watch all of it. This was because those soldiers were trying to get to our end of the camps. The Ogallala Sioux did most of helping the Cheyennes there, but all of the other Sioux got around those soldiers and helped also. Four Cheyennes were killed there, and one of our wounded died three weeks afterward.

The sun was hot that day. I believe there were no clouds, and I know there was not any rain. There were clouds of dust when the soldier horses were running loose toward the river. There was almost enough dust to choke me when all of the old men and boys came tearing in on their ponies after the calls went out that all of the white men were dead.

A few women besides me were out watching the battle. We were not there to do any fighting, were just looking and cheering the men with our songs. All of us had sheath-knives, and some of us had hatchets. But these were carried in our belts all the time, to use in doing our work, not to use for hurting people. Most of the women looking at the battle stayed out of reach of the bullets, as I did. But there was one who went in close at times. Her name was Calf Trail Woman.

Calf Trail Woman had a six-shooter, with bullets and powder, and she fired many shots at the soldiers. She was the only woman there who had a gun. She stayed on her pony all the time, but she kept not far from her husband, Black Coyote, who was one of the warriors creeping along the gulches. At one time she was about to give her pony to a young Cheyenne who had lost his own, but I called out to them: "Our women have plenty of good horses for you down at the river." I was speaking of the soldier horses that had run to the river for water and had been caught there by our people. She took the young Cheyenne up behind her on her pony and they rode away toward the river. This same woman was also with the warriors when they went from the Reno creek camp to fight the soldiers far up Rosebud creek about a week before the battle at the Little Bighorn. She was the only woman I know of who went with the warriors to that fight.

After the big battle on and around the ridge had ended, most of the warriors went to fight again the first soldiers up the valley. Those soldiers then were on a hill just across the river from where had been the valley fight at the time I was in the water and hidden in the brush with other women. All through the remainder of that afternoon, and until darkness came, the Indians fought those soldiers on that hill. Early the next morning that battle started again, and it was kept up most of that day.

Late in the afternoon of the second day the men heralds rode about the willow dome camps and called out to the people that other soldiers were coming up the Little Bighorn valley (Gibbon's men). The chiefs had decided that too many young men had been killed already, that we must go away from there. So all of us women began to hurry at getting ready to go. That did not take long, and before the sun went down all of the Indians were on their way up the Little Bighorn valley.

We traveled during most of that night and for a part of the next day. The first stop for camping was below the mouth of Greasy Grass creek. From day to day afterward we continued on up the Little Bighorn, over to the head of the Rosebud, down that valley, over eastward to Tongue river, and on eastward to and beyond Powder river. Each night during this journey all of the six tribal camps were set up. At each stopping place we stayed but one night. All of the Indians stayed together, none left us, I believe. Another Cheyenne, who had been wounded in the big battle, died after we crossed Powder river. That brought the Cheyenne loss up to seven men. We were about sixteen sleeps in going all the way from the place of the big battle to where we all stopped together east of Powder river. There the six tribes separated, each tribe to go its own way.

The Cheyennes went down to the mouth of Powder river. There we found much food that white men had hidden in holes dug into the ground. We opened the holes and took whatever we wanted. There were bacon, beans, rice, sugar, coffee, crackers, dried apples and corn for horses. Two fireboats (steamboats) went up the Elk river (Yellowstone) past us while we were getting the food. Our men shot at them, just for fun, but I think nobody was hit. Some months afterward, when we learned that Long Hair was chief of the white men soldiers killed at the Little Bighorn, we joked among ourselves by saying: "It is too bad we killed him, for it must have been him, our friend, who left all of the good food for the Cheyennes, his relatives."

Our men hunted all during the rest of the summer, and our women tanned skins and stored up meat for winter use. When came winter, the Cheyenne tribal camp was set up on a little stream far up Powder river on its west side and close to the Bighorn mountains. Soldiers came there, killed many of our people and burned all of our lodges (McKenzie's troops, November 26, 1876). That was a hard winter for us. Other soldiers fought us on Tongue river, at the mouth of Hanging Woman creek (Miles' troops, early January, 1877). These soldiers caught three of our women and four of our children. That night some of our Cheyenne wolf warriors—what the white people call scouts— heard an Indian woman singing in the soldier camp. "That sounds like a Cheyenne song," they said among themselves. They listened carefully and heard: "Get ready to go with the soldiers. There are too many of them for you to fight. They are feeding us and treating us well." But the Cheyennes would not surrender then to the soldiers. Instead all of us went to the Bighorn valley and stayed there on Rotten Grass creek the remainder of that winter.

When spring came, one of the captured women, the eldest one, named Sweet Woman, was sent to tell us that all of our people who would sur- render to Bear Shirt (General Miles) would be treated kindly. She said that she and the other captives had been well cared for. They had been given a tent for themselves, and the soldier guards kept them from being bothered by anybody. Some of our people started right away to go to Bear Shirt's soldier houses (Fort Keogh) at the mouth of Tongue river. White Bull my elder brother, went with them. Not long after- ward my younger brother, White Moon, went there with a big band of our people, and I went too. White Bull had enlisted as a scout for the soldiers. Other Cheyennes enlisted later, but he was the first one.

I may have seen Custer at the time of the battle or after he was killed. I do not know, as I did [not] then know of his being there. All of our old warriors say the same—none of them knew of him being there until they learned of it afterward at the soldier forts or the agencies or from Indians coming from the agencies.

But I learned something more about him from our people in Okla- homa. Two of those Southern Cheyenne women who had been in our camp at the Little Bighorn told of having been on the battlefield soon after the fighting ended. They saw Custer lying dead there. They had known him in the South. While they were looking at him some Sioux men came and were about to cut up his body. The Cheyenne women, thinking of Me-o-tzi, made signs, "He is a relative of ours," but telling nothing more about him. So the Sioux men cut off only one joint of a finger. The women then pushed the point of a sewing awl into each of his ears, into his head. This was done to improve his hearing, as it seemed he had not heard what our chiefs in the South said when he smoked the pipe with them. They told him then that if ever afterward he should break that peace promise and should fight the Cheyennes the Everywhere Spirit surely would cause him to be killed.

Through almost sixty years, many a time I have thought of Hi-es-tzie as the handsome man I saw in the South. And I often have wondered if, when I was riding among the dead where he was lying, my pony may have kicked dirt upon his body.

Lieutenant Colonel George Armstrong Custer posed in dress uniform for Jose M. Mora's camera while visiting New York City in March 1876. He had less than four months to live (Everhard Collection, Amon Carter Museum, Fort Worth, Texas). *379*

Informality marked the Seventh Cavalry campaign outfit, carefully reconstructed by James S. Hutchins (top). Many officers wore versions of the then popular "fireman's shirt," with wide falling collar, and the 1872-pattern black campaign hat with the brim hooked up. Each company carried a silk, swallow-tailed guidon with stars and stripes (Courtesy James S. Hutchins and the Company of Military Historians). Custer waves his hat and gleefully exclaims "Hurrah, boys, we've got them!" on finally coming in sight of the great village on the Little Big Horn (bottom). The artist Gary Zaboly captured the moment as reported by Corporal John Martin, who was shortly thereafter sent back with Custer's last message to Captain Benteen (Courtesy Gregory J. W. Urwin).

Captain Myles W. Keogh (left), a hard-drinking Irish soldier of fortune, commanded Company I and was one of the most romantic and enigmatic officers in the Seventh. Before emigrating to the United States to fight for the Union he had battled for Pope Pius IX in the Papal Army. The Pope awarded him the *Medaglia di Pro Petri Sede* for gallantry, and he carried it thereafter in a leather pouch around his neck. At the Little Big Horn it saved his body from mutilation when the Indians respected it as a powerful medicine token. Captain Thomas W. Custer (middle) commanded Company C. He was as recklessly brave as his older brother, having won two medals of honor in the Civil War. They were inseparable in life and perished literally side by side at the Little Big Horn. So torn and mutilated was his corpse that he was identifiable only by a tattoo on his arm. First Lieutenant William W. Cooke, the regimental adjutant (right), was a Canadian known in the Seventh as "Queen's Own" in honor of his resplendent side whiskers. He fell near the Custer brothers on Last Stand ridge, and his characteristic beard provided the Cheyenne warrior Wooden Leg with a unique scalp (all photos, Custer Battlefield National Monument).

Custer's subordinate wing commanders failed him in every way. Major Marcus
Reno (top left) proved weak, indecisive, and timid. Captain Frederick W. Benteen (top right), though indisputably brave, proved willfully negligent. He first
dawdled on his scout to the south and then disobeyed Custer's written order to
join him. Their actions kept seven companies and the packtrain out of action
while the Indians concentrated their formidable power on Custer's command
(both photos, Custer Battlefield National Monument). Edward S. Godfrey (bottom
right) served as a first lieutenant commanding Company K under Benteen at the
Little Big Horn. In his classic account of the battle he covered up the grave errors
of his superiors, undoubtedly to protect the honor of the regiment. He is shown
here as colonel, Ninth Cavalry, not long before he rewrote his famous essay in
1908 (U.S. Signal Corps photo no. 111-sc-90148, National Archives).

Sitting Bull (top) was the very soul of the nonreservation Sioux. The Hunkpapa spiritual leader refused to bend to government demands and became a symbol of bold resistance to both the Indian and the white world. He was the spiritual and political leader of the great village on the Little Big Horn (Custer Battlefield National Monument). His nephew, White Bull, took an active role in the fight against Custer and, with the help of the white historian Walter Campbell (Stanley Vestal), became the great chronicler of his people's final struggle. He is pictured (bottom) in the 1930s with Campbell (Western History Collections, University of Oklahoma Library).

The Battle of the Little Big Horn as depicted by the Sioux warrior Red Horse in 1881 (top). His striking drawing owes nothing to white conceptions of the battle, which he depicts with a gritty, hard-edged realism that white artists avoided for a century. Richard Lorenz's 1914 painting, *The Last Glow of a Passing Nation* (bottom), presents a far more romantic image while thoughtfully commenting on the irony of the battle as a last stand for the Sioux and Cheyennes as well as for Custer (both illustrations, Custer Battlefield National Monument).

THE CUSTER MYTH

Custer 1876—*Armour's Spirit of the Century Calendar, 1901*
(Courtesy John M. Carroll Collection)

INTRODUCTION

The news broke, suddenly and violently like a summer thunderstorm out of the West, and rained on the biggest parade of the century. On July 4, 1876, an Associated Press wire story originating in Salt Lake City made the astonishing report that Custer and every man of five companies of the Seventh Cavalry had perished at the hands of Indians. Generals William T. Sherman, the commander of the army, and Phil Sheridan, commanding the frontier Division of the Missouri, who were both attending the Centennial Exposition in Philadelphia, responded as one that the preposterous tale was false.

The following day, however, Sheridan received a telegram from General Terry confirming the disaster. Instead of an official report of the battle listing casualties, Terry's telegram was a defense of his campaign strategy implying that Custer had disobeyed orders. Sheridan was enraged that such a self-serving missive should reach him before even a list of the dead and wounded. To make matters worse, a staff officer leaked the confidential telegram to the press, so that newspapers around the country soon echoed Terry's rather twisted version of the events leading up to the Little Big Horn. Another high-ranking officer in Philadelphia criticized Custer in a rather insightful but devastating account that was published in the July 7 *New York Herald* and elsewhere:

> The truth about Custer is that he was a pet soldier who had risen not above his merit but higher than men of equal merit. He fought with Phil Sheridan and through the patronage of Sheridan he rose, but while Sheridan liked his valor and his dash he never trusted his judgment. . . . While Sheridan is always cool, Custer was always aflame. He was like a thermometer. . . . Rising to high command early in life he lost the repose necessary to success in high command . . . but you see we all liked Custer and did not mind his little freaks in that way any more than we would have minded temper in a woman. . . . We all think, much as we lament Custer . . . that he sacrificed the Seventh cavalry to ambition and wounded vanity.[1]

President Grant was quite blunt: "I regard Custer's Massacre as a sacrifice of troops, brought on by Custer himself, that was wholly unnecessary—wholly unnecessary."[2] Even the grief-stricken Sheridan had to concede that the Little Big Horn "was an unnecessary sacrifice due to misapprehension and superabundant courage—the latter extraordinarily developed in Custer."[3]

National opinion, at least that which counted, seemed to have no problem accepting these characterizations of the catastrophe. It was perfectly logical to most to blame the defeat on the man who was in command. The Democratic press briefly used Custer's defeat to castigate the already faltering Republican administration's Indian and military policies, but the 1876 election provided far greater issues for them to better exploit.[4]

And then it began. The poets, the writers, the painters, and the popularizers of every stripe seized on the story. In that centennial summer, while proudly celebrating "A Century of Progress," Americans found in Custer's Last Stand a powerful if somewhat anachronistic symbol of just how far they had come as a nation—and just how far they still had to go. He was their golden sacrifice to progress; a martyred symbol of all the great struggles gone by. The beautiful irony of the conquerors being conquered was lost on them. They were blinded by the shining image of the spotless soldier alone on a wilderness hilltop, surrounded by a fiendish foe. It was so perfect, so sublime, and it belonged to them alone as yet another facet of what made America unique.

The poets came first. Walt Whitman had his "A Death Song for Custer" in the mail to the *New York Tribune* the day after first hearing of the battle. Henry Wadsworth Longfellow quickly followed suit with "The Revenge of Rain-in-the-Face."

> Whose was the right and the wrong?
> Sing it, O funeral song,
> With a voice that is full of tears,
> And say that our broken faith,
> Wrought all this ruin and scathe,
> In the year of a Hundred Years![5]

Frederick Whittaker scribbled out his massive *A Complete Life of Gen. George A. Custer* in record time, publishing the tome in December 1876. It elevated a rash, ever-so-human young soldier into the pantheon of America's greatest heroes. Others, working in many media, followed Whittaker's lead, so that Custer and his final battle became a towering international legend within a few years. It is perhaps the single event from America's frontier past that most foreigners recognize.

The remarkable evolution of the Custer myth from Whittaker until the centennial of the Battle of the Little Big Horn is detailed in my 1976 essay "From Little Bighorn to Little Big Man: The Changing Image of a Western Hero in Popular Culture," reprinted from the *Western Historical Quarterly*. The harshly negative image of Custer so prevalent at the time that article was first published held sway for another decade until the surprise success of Evan S. Connell's *Son of the Morning Star* in 1984. Custer's public rehabilitation was further encouraged by Robert M. Utley's 1988 biography *Cavalier in Buckskin* and by the 1991 ABC television miniseries based on *Son of the Morning Star*, starring Gary Cole and Rosanna Arquette as George and Elizabeth Custer.

Robert Taft explores the origins of the artists' Custer in "The Pictorial Record of the Old West: Custer's Last Stand—John Mulvany, Cassilly Adams, and Otto Becker," reprinted from the November 1946 *Kansas Historical Quarterly*. Taft initiated the serious study of paintings of Custer's Last Stand as cultural artifacts.[6] He was for many years before his death a professor of chemistry at the University of Kansas and the author of *Photography and the American Scene* (1938) and *Artists and Illustrators of the Old West, 1850–1900* (1953). The latter contains an excellent chapter on Custer paintings.[7]

Eric von Schmidt provides an intimate view of the creative process in his enlightening essay "Sunday at the Little Big Horn with George," published here for the first time. Originally presented at the 1987 Los Angeles Western History Association meeting, this entertaining memoir chronicles the travail of the artist in composing his monumental *Here Fell Custer*. The painting, generally regarded as the most accurate and evocative modern version of the battle, was featured in a 1976 *Smithsonian* essay and presently graces the National Park Service's brochure for Custer Battlefield National Monument. The painting hangs in the permanent collection of the Ulrich Museum of Art in Wichita, Kansas.[8]

Von Schmidt lives in Westport, Connecticut, and continues to paint in the same studio once used by his father, the noted artist Harold Von Schmidt. His father, best known today for his marvelous *Satur-*

day Evening Post illustrations, also tackled Custer in a dramatic, and quite heroic, canvas—now on display in the library of the United States Military Academy at West Point—as well as in the advertising art and poster for John Ford's 1948 film *Fort Apache*.[9]

Eric von Schmidt is renowned not only as a painter and book illustrator but also as a folk and blues singer with several albums to his credit. He illustrated the songbook of his friend Joan Baez and coauthored a classic history-memoir of the Cambridge folk-music movement.[10] He recently completed another epic historical painting entitled *The Storming of the Alamo*, which was also featured in a *Smithsonian* article and was the centerpiece of a major exhibit on the Alamo at the Witte Museum in San Antonio, Texas.[11]

The Custer saga has proven as attractive to novelists as it has to artists. Using Thomas Berger's 1964 novel *Little Big Man* as a point of departure, Brian W. Dippie, in "Jack Crabb and the Sole Survivors of Custer's Last Stand," explores the wide range of Custer fiction.[12] Nor has the popularity of Custer novels given any sign of slackening since Dippie published his essay in *Western American Literature* in 1969, with writers regularly producing them, especially for the paperback trade.[13]

Even more influential in defining Custer's historical image than novels have been films. There have been at least forty-seven motion pictures made concerning Custer or his last battle. The evolution of Custer's cinematic image is discussed in my 1991 essay from *Montana the Magazine of Western History*: "'Correct in Every Detail': General Custer in Hollywood." Hollywood's impact on Custer's image has been decisive, for if Errol Flynn in *They Died with Their Boots On* defined the Custer image for several generations after 1941, Richard Mulligan's devastatingly negative Custer in *Little Big Man* determined the popular conception of this soldier for the two decades after 1970. Television has breathed new life into these celluloid depictions, rebroadcasting them over and over again to new audiences in a manner impossible before the 1950s. The proliferation of prerecorded videos in the 1980s has provided an additional marketplace for these films. It appears, however, that the 1991 ABC television production of *Son of the Morning Star* will not dramatically rehabilitate Custer's popular image.[14]

Finally, in our last essay, the folklorist Bruce A. Rosenberg discusses the Custer myth in light of its international antecedents in his

1972 essay "Custer: The Legend of the Martyred Hero in America," first published in the *Journal of the Folklore Institute* at Indiana University. Rosenberg, a professor of English and American civilization at Brown University, is a noted folklorist and author of *Custer and the Epic of Defeat* (1974), *The Code of the West* (1982), and *The Art of the American Folk Preacher* (1970). Rosenberg received the James Russell Lowell Prize for the last.[15] In the essay reprinted here he argues that despite the many parallels between the Custer myth and similar tales from other lands, the Custer story remains distinctly a product of the American imagination. It nevertheless shares similar principles of narrative composition that place it in a grand tradition of folktales of European civilization. Custer's survival as a major hero of the American people, despite his fluctuating popular image, is a testament to the powerful symbolic content and remarkable narrative structure of his story—both so clearly documented in the pages of this anthology.

Notes

1. Quoted in Oliver Knight, *Following the Indian Wars: The Story of the Newspaper Correspondents among the Indian Campaigners* (Norman: University of Oklahoma Press, 1960), 219.

2. Quoted in Robert M. Utley, *Custer and the Great Controversy: The Origin and Development of a Legend* (Los Angeles: Westernlore Press, 1962), 44.

3. Quoted in Paul Andrew Hutton, *Phil Sheridan and His Army* (Lincoln: University of Nebraska Press, 1985), 318.

4. Brian W. Dippie, "Southern Response to Custer's Last Stand," *Montana the Magazine of Western History* 21 (April 1971): 18–31.

5. Longfellow's poem is in Brian W. Dippie, *Custer's Last Stand: The Anatomy of an American Myth* (Missoula: University of Montana, 1976), 7.

6. For more on Custer art, see Harrison Lane, "Brush, Palette, and the Little Big Horn," *Montana the Magazine of Western History* 23 (July 1973): 66–80; Brian W. Dippie, "Brush, Palette, and the Custer Battle: A Second Look," *Montana the Magazine of Western History* 24 (January 1974): 55–67; Judy Henry, "A Centennial Commemoration of the Custer Battle," *Southwest Art* 5 (May 1976): 70–81; James S. Hutchins, "Still Dodging Arrows," *Gateway Heritage* 1 (Winter 1980): 18–27; John M. Carroll, "Anheuser-Busch and Custer's Last Stand," *Greasy Grass* 3 (May 1987): 25–

28; Christopher M. Summitt, "Apologia Pro Custer's Last Stand," *Greasy Grass* 5 (May 1989): 20–29; and most important, the wonderful book by Don Russell, *Custer's Last* (Fort Worth: Amon Carter Museum of Western Art, 1968). Russell also compiled two useful Custer art checklists. See Don Russell, *Custer's List: A Checklist of Pictures Relating to the Battle of the Little Big Horn* (Fort Worth: Amon Carter Museum of Western Art, 1969), and Don Russell, "Custer's List—Continued," in Paul A. Hutton, ed., *Garry Owen 1976: Annual of the Little Big Horn Associates* (Seattle: Little Big Horn Associates, 1977), 196–215. Also see John M. Carroll, *Cyclorama of Gen. Custer's Last Fight* (El Segundo, Calif.: Upton and Sons, 1988), and William Reusswig, *A Picture Report of the Custer Fight* (New York: Hastings House, 1967).

7. Robert Taft, *Artists and Illustrators of the Old West, 1850–1900* (New York: Charles Scribner's Sons, 1953), 129–48.

8. Eric von Schmidt, "Custer, Dying Again at That Last Stand, Is in a New Painting," *Smithsonian* 7 (June 1976): 58–65.

9. See Walt Reed, *Harold Von Schmidt Draws and Paints the Old West* (Flagstaff: Northland Press, 1972).

10. Eric von Schmidt and Jim Rooney, *Baby, Let Me Follow You Down: The Illustrated History of the Cambridge Folk Years* (New York: Anchor Press/Doubleday, 1979).

11. Eric von Schmidt, "The Alamo Remembered—from a Painter's Point of View," *Smithsonian* 16 (March 1986): 54–67. For von Schmidt as book illustrator, see Richard O'Connor, *Sitting Bull: War Chief of the Sioux* (New York: McGraw-Hill Book Co., 1968).

12. Dippie, whose *Custer's Last Stand* remains the standard history of the Custer myth, has published widely on the topic. Also see Brian W. Dippie and John M. Carroll, *Bards of the Little Big Horn* (Bryan, Tex.: Guidon Press, 1978); Brian W. Dippie and Edward T. LeBlanc, "Bibliography of Custer Dime Novels," *Dime Novel Roundup* 38 (July 15, 1969): 66–70; Brian W. Dippie and Paul A. Hutton, *The Comic Book Custer: A Bibliography of Custeriana in Comic Books and Comic Strips* (Bryan, Tex.: Brazos Corral of the Westerners, 1983); Brian W. Dippie and Paul A. Hutton, "Custer and Pop Culture," in Gregory J. W. Urwin, ed., *Custer and His Times: Book Three* (Conway: University of Central Arkansas Press, 1987), 255–71; Brian W. Dippie, "Why Would They Lie? or, Thoughts on Frank Finkel and Friends," in Paul A. Hutton, ed., *Custer and His Times* (El Paso: Little Big Horn Associates, 1981), 209–28; Brian W. Dippie, *Custer's Last Stand* (New York: Viking Press, 1977); Brian W. Dippie, "A Glance at Custer Humor," in Hutton, *Garry Owen 1976*, 183–94; and Brian W. Dippie, "Bards of the Little Big Horn," *Western American Literature* 1 (Fall 1966): 175–95.

13. The following list of Custer fiction, by no means exhaustive, makes clear the continuing fascination writers

have for this story. The Custer saga has proven especially popular among writers of romance novels. See, for example, Stephanie Blake, *A Glorious Passion* (New York: Jove Publications, 1983); Rebecca Drury, *Savage Beauty* (New York: Dell, 1982); Paula Fairman, *The Tender and the Savage* (Los Angeles: Pinnacle Books, 1980); Catherine Hart, *Summer Storm* (New York: Leisure Books, 1987); Michalann Perry, *Captive Surrender* (New York: Zebra Books, 1987); and Janelle Taylor, *Savage Conquest* (New York: Zebra Books, 1985). Custer has also been used by authors of new adult-oriented paperbacks, such as John Benteen, *Taps at Little Big Horn* (New York: Leisure Books, 1973); John Benteen, *Dakota Territory* (New York: Leisure Books, 1972); E. J. Hunter, *White Squaw: Horn of Plenty* (New York: Zebra Books, 1985); Jake Logan, *Slocum's Run* (New York: Playboy Paperbacks, 1981); and Dean L. McElwain, *Preacher's Law: Trail of Death* (New York: Leisure Books, 1987).

If that is not enough, then sample any of the following: Del Barton, *A Good Day to Die* (Garden City, N.Y.: Doubleday, 1980); Matthew Braun, *The Second Coming of Lucas Brokaw* (New York: Dell, 1977); Jackson Cain, *Hellbreak Country* (New York: Warner Books, 1984); Chet Cunningham, *Pony Soldiers: Battle Cry* (New York: Leisure Books, 1989); E. M. Corder, *Won Ton Ton: The Dog Who Saved Hollywood* (New York: Pocket Books, 1976); Kathleen N. Daly, *Tonka* (New York: Pyramid Books, 1976);

George MacDonald Fraser, *Flashman and the Redskins* (New York: Alfred A. Knopf, 1982); John Jakes, *Heaven and Hell* (San Diego: Harcourt, Brace, Jovanovich, 1987); H. Paul Jeffers, *Morgan* (New York: Zebra Books, 1989); Dorothy M. Johnson, *Buffalo Woman* (New York: Dodd, Mead and Co., 1977); Douglas C. Jones, *The Court-Martial of George Armstrong Custer* (New York: Charles Scribner's Sons, 1976); Leo P. Kelley, *Luke Sutton Indian Fighter* (Garden City, N.Y.: Doubleday, 1982); Gary McCarthy, *The Legend of the Lone Ranger* (New York: Ballantine Books, 1981); Donald MacRae, *Conflict of Interest* (New York: Tor, 1989); Jim Miller, *That Damn Single Shot* (New York: Fawcett, 1988); Charles K. Mills, *A Mighty Afternoon* (Garden City, N.Y.: Doubleday, 1980); Chad Oliver, *Broken Eagle* (New York: Bantam Books, 1989); Lewis B. Patten, *Cheyenne Captives* (New York: Signet, 1979); Kevin Randle and Robert Cornett, *Remember the Little Bighorn!* (New York: Charter Books, 1990); Jory Sherman, *Red Tomahawk* (New York: Zebra Books, 1984); Jonathan Scofield, *The Frontier War* (New York: Dell, 1981); Robert J. Steelman, *Cheyenne Vengeance* (Garden City, N.Y.: Doubleday, 1974); Robert J. Steelman, *Surgeon to the Sioux* (Garden City, N.Y.: Doubleday, 1979); Colin Stuart, *Walks Far Woman* (New York: Dial Press, 1976); Robert Vaughan, *A Distant Bugle* (New York: Dell, 1984); and G. Clifton Wisler, *Lakota* (New York: Evans, 1989).

14. For more on Custer films, see Paul A. Hutton, "The Celluloid Custer," *Red River Valley Historical Review* 4 (Fall 1979): 20–43; Paul A. Hutton, "Custer As Seen in Hollywood Films," *True West* 31 (June 1984): 22–28; Paul Andrew Hutton, "Hollywood's General Custer: The Changing Image of a Military Hero in Film," *Greasy Grass* 2 (May 1986): 15–21; Brian W. Dippie, "Popcorn and Indians: Custer on the Screen," *Cultures* 2, no. 1 (1974): 139–68; Brian W. Dippie, "The Many Faces of General Custer," *Fanfare* 1 (January 1978): 4–22; John Phillip Langellier, "Custer's Last Fight and the Silver Screen," *Gateway Heritage* 2 (Winter 1981): 16–21; John P. Langellier, "Movie Massacre: The Custer Myth in Motion Pictures and Television," *Research Review: The Journal of the Little Big Horn Associates* 3 (June 1989): 20–31; Tom O'Neil, "The Making of *They Died with Their Boots On*," *Research Review: The Journal of the Little Big Horn Associates* 4 (June 1990): 22–30; Ronald W. Reagan, "Looking Back at *Santa Fe Trail*," *Greasy Grass* 6 (May 1990): 2–5; and John P. Langellier, *"Santa Fe Trail*: Custer's Image on the Eve of World War II," *Greasy Grass* 6 (May 1990): 6–8; Dan Gugliasso, "Custer's Last Stand on Celluloid," *Persimmon Hill* 19 (Spring 1991): 4–12.

15. There is a chapter on Custer in Bruce A. Rosenberg, *The Code of the West* (Bloomington: Indiana University Press, 1982). Perhaps the most impressive work by this distinguished folklorist remains his *Custer and the Epic of Defeat* (University Park: Pennsylvania State University Press, 1974). For another interesting study along similar lines, see the Custer chapters in Edward Tabor Linenthal, *Changing Images of the Warrior Hero in America: A History of Popular Symbolism* (New York: Edwin Mellen Press, 1982), and Edward Tabor Linenthal, *Sacred Ground: Americans and Their Battlefields* (Urbana: University of Illinois Press, 1991), 127–71.

FROM LITTLE BIGHORN
TO LITTLE BIG MAN:
THE CHANGING IMAGE OF
A WESTERN HERO IN
POPULAR CULTURE

PAUL ANDREW HUTTON

Heroes are not born, they are created. Their lives so catch the imagination of their generation, and often the generations that follow, that they are repeatedly discussed and written about. The lives of heroes are a testament to the values and aspirations of those who admire them. If their images change as time passes they may act as a barometer of the fluctuating attitudes of a society. Eventually, if certain attitudes change enough, one hero myth may replace another. Such is the case with George Armstrong Custer. Once a symbolic leader of civilization's advance into the wilderness, within one hundred years he came to represent the supposed moral bankruptcy of Manifest Destiny.

The historical literature on Custer is voluminous and can be divided into strongly pro or con factions with few moderate voices. Nearly a century of scholarship has resolved little of the controversy surrounding the general or his last campaign, although the latest major scholarly works, Edgar I. Stewart's *Custer's Luck* (1955) and Jay Monaghan's biography, *Custer: The Life of General George Armstrong Custer* (1959), are sympathetic toward the controversial cavalryman.[1] As is often the case, the work of diligent historians seems to have had only marginal effect upon the public mind. Most of the conventional information, or misinformation, about Custer comes from elements of popular culture rather than scholars. It is through novels, motion pictures, newspapers, paintings, television, and mass circulation magazines that one can best trace how the changing image of Custer has partially reflected American opinions and values.

Custer had all the qualities of greatness admired by Americans of the late nineteenth century. A son of the Middle Border, he had firm Anglo-Saxon roots, was born into a modest social position, and rose to be a flamboyant general of extraordinary courage and individualism. He was the perfect hero for a people whose ideal characters were Napoleon and Horatio Alger, Jr. They craved the solace of believing that the individual was all-important, that he could climb to success through his own abilities, and could master other men and his own environment.[2]

Long before his death Custer noted what the people expected of a hero and attempted to conform to that image. As the son of an Ohio blacksmith the young Custer was faced with social and economic barriers to success. He overcame many of these obstacles by obtaining an appointment to West Point in 1857. After squeaking through the academy at the bottom of his class he was thrust into combat at Bull Run. Custer's dominating personality and aggressive spirit won him the admiration of Gen. George McClellan, whom he served as an aide, and then of Gen. Alfred Pleasonton, who promoted him in 1863 from captain to brigadier general. Custer made his debut at Gettysburg sporting a floppy, broad-brimmed hat, crimson scarf, and a black velvet jacket trimmed with gold braid onto which flowed his shoulder-length hair. He had studied the life of Napoleon's flamboyant cavalry leader Murat and understood the usefulness of dramatic flair to impress soldiers and civilians. The press was drawn to him and avidly reported the exploits of the Boy General—he was only twenty-three in 1863. They followed him from charge to charge until he helped cut off Lee's retreat and personally received the white flag at Appomattox. When the war ended he wore the stars of a major general and commanded a division of Philip Sheridan's cavalry.

The army was reorganized after the war, and Custer accepted a commission as lieutenant colonel of the new Seventh Cavalry. Although technically second in command, he actually ran the regiment since the colonels in charge were usually on detached duty. With his bride of two years, Elizabeth Bacon Custer, the new colonel set up headquarters at Fort Riley, Kansas, and began whipping his motley troops into shape. Custer, ever conscious of his image, now adopted the fringed buckskin suit of the frontiersman, but kept his favored wide-brimmed hat and crimson scarf.

In the spring of 1867 the Seventh Cavalry joined the expedition of

Gen. W. S. Hancock against Indians of the southern plains who were harassing the crews building the transcontinental railroad. The expedition ended in failure and Custer was court-martialed for being absent without leave to visit his wife during the campaign. He was suspended from rank and pay for one year but was recalled by General Sheridan for a winter campaign in 1868. Along the Washita River in Oklahoma the Seventh Cavalry wiped out the Cheyenne village of Chief Black Kettle. Although some characterized the battle as a massacre, the reputation of Custer and his regiment as great Indian fighters was firmly established in the popular mind.

Throughout the next eight years Custer's name was kept before the public in press accounts of his expeditions into the Yellowstone region and the Black Hills, in his own articles that appeared in *Galaxy* magazine, and in his memoirs, *My Life on the Plains*, published in 1874.

In 1876 Custer became involved in political controversy when his testimony on government corruption before a congressional committee proved embarrassing to President Grant and Secretary of War Belknap. In retaliation Grant stripped Custer of the command of a proposed expedition against renegade Sioux. Only the intercession of Gens. Alfred Terry and Philip Sheridan saved Custer from the humiliation of having his regiment go into battle without him.

The plan of attack required that three columns converge on the region in southern Montana where the Sioux were expected to be. But Custer, often night marching his troops, reached the Indian encampment ahead of the other columns. Disregarding the advice of his scouts, he divided his regiment into three prongs, just as he had done so successfully at Washita, and attacked. But everything went wrong. The center column, under Maj. Marcus Reno, was routed after attacking the Indian village and was saved only by the timely arrival of the left column under Capt. Frederick Benteen. Although firing was heard in the distance and enemy pressure on their position slackened, Reno and Benteen made only one effort to join Custer, even though Benteen had earlier received written orders to do so. When their one effort failed they dug in and withstood two days of Indian siege until General Terry arrived with the main body of troops and the Indians triumphantly withdrew.[3]

They found Custer and his two hundred men scattered along the hills above the Little Bighorn River. The Boy General lay with fifty of his troopers inside a twisted circle of horses just below the crest of the battlefield's highest hill. His once proud regiment was shattered, the victim of the army's ignorance of the size of the enemy force and of his own rash overconfidence.

The mystery and tragedy of Little Bighorn immediately captured the nation's imagination. The press, and especially the papers controlled by Democrats, turned from singing the praises of the United States on its centennial to singing Custer's praises. With a presidential election coming in November, the battle quickly became a club for the opposition to beat Grant and his faltering party. The *Dallas Daily Herald* may have had problems with its spelling, but its sentiments came across plainly: "Grant exiled Custar and doubtless is glad that fear[less] soldier and unpurchaseable patriot is dead."[4] In the debate over who was to blame for the disaster, the publicity given the battle by the press led to vicious denunciations of almost everyone involved in the campaign, and especially of Grant, Terry, and Reno. The groundwork was then laid for a historical debate unsettled to this day.[5]

The wide press coverage of the battle also created many of the myths that surround the last stand and contributed greatly to Custer's heroic image. The *New York Herald* reported that the troopers had "died as grandly as Homer's demigods." In deference to the democratic tradition the paper noted that "as death's relentless sweep gathered in the entire command, all distinctions of name and rank were blended," but then added that "the family that 'died at the head of their column' will lead the throng when history recalls their deed."[6] Some newspapers were not so generous. The Republican *Chicago Tribune* editorialized that Custer had needlessly brought on the disaster because he "preferred to make a reckless dash and take the consequences, in the hope of making a personal victory and adding to the glory of another charge, rather than wait for a sufficiently powerful force to make the fight successful and share the glory with others."[7] President Grant was just as blunt, telling a reporter that he regarded the battle "as a sacrifice of troops, brought on by Custer himself, that was wholly unnecessary— wholly unneccessary."[8] The official military reports of Terry and Reno echoed Grant.

A hack writer named Frederick Whittaker then appeared on the scene to champion the cause of the "dead lion." Such a champion would seem as necessary to the creation of a hero as the "great man" himself. Many historic characters from the past have had their architects of glory: George Washington had Parson Weems, Paul Revere was selected for immortality by Longfellow, Daniel Boone owes his legend to Timothy Flint and James Fenimore Cooper, Kit Carson was blessed by the writings of John C. Frémont, and Buffalo Bill Cody burst from the fanciful pens of Ned Buntline, Prentiss Ingraham, and John Burke.[9] In that pantheon of mythmakers Whittaker ranks among the best. The dust had barely cleared on the battlefield before Whittaker began work on his biography of Custer. Using newspaper reports and Custer's own writings as his sources, he turned the book out with remarkable speed, publishing it in December 1876. The hero who emerged from the pages of Whittaker's *A Complete Life of Gen. George A. Custer* was a figure of epic proportions, no less than "one of the few really great men that America has produced," and "as a soldier there is no spot on his armor."[10] As might be expected, he was compared favorably to the great Napoleon.[11]

Whittaker's biography was more drama than history and every good drama naturally required villains. There were three in his book: Grant, Reno, and the Sioux warrior Rain-in-the-Face. The author, a Democrat, asserted that Grant wanted to humiliate Custer because of his testimony against Belknap. In Whittaker's eyes the president's revenge proved disastrous, for if Custer had commanded the expedition as originally planned it would have been a success. Furthermore, he stated that "Reno and Benteen would never have dreamed of disobeying their chief, had they not known he was out of favor at court."[12]

This latter charge was widely accepted and repeated. Whittaker made Reno his special target and repeatedly urged his court-martial. Getting no response from the military he turned to Congress and in 1878 managed to get a petition introduced seeking a court of inquiry against Reno. Even though the petition was not voted on, Reno, hounded by Whittaker's accusations, asked President Hayes to appoint a court to investigate the charges against him. Although the military court of inquiry, which met in Chicago for four weeks in 1879, damned Reno with faint praise, Whittaker declared it a whitewash and continued his one-man crusade. Such a crusade, after all, was worth considerable free publicity which aided lagging book sales. The unfortunate Reno, court-martialed twice on other charges, was dismissed from the army in 1879 and died ten years later.[13] To the time of his death he was still attempting to clear his name, but the growing legend was too much for him to fight.

Whittaker discovered his Indian villain, Rain-in-the-Face, in the lurid newspaper reports that followed the slaughter. The story, as reported in the press and repeated by Whittaker, was that Rain-in-the-Face held a grievance against Custer for an 1874 imprisonment and so avenged himself by killing Custer at Little Bighorn and then cutting out his heart. This occurred only after Custer, his pistol empty, fighting "like a tiger . . . killed or wounded three Indians with his saber." [14]

Whittaker's spotless hero, a poor boy who rose through his own efforts to stand in greatness with Napoleon, was finally betrayed by evil politicians and jealous subordinates and died gallantly facing a savage foe. This interpretation, along with numerous factual errors in the book, was repeated over and over in the next fifty years. Popular histories such as D. M. Kelsey's *Our Pioneer Heroes and Their Daring Deeds* (1888), J. W. Buel's *Heroes of the Plains* (1881), John Beadle's *Western Wilds and the Men Who Redeem Them* (1881), and W. L. Holloway's *Wild Life on the Plains and Horrors of Indian Warfare* (1891) followed Whittaker closely and sometimes plagiarized his work.

As important to Custer's growing legend as the bitter work of Whittaker were the loving writings of Mrs. Custer, who devoted the rest of her long life to perpetuating a shining image of her dead husband. Her first book, *Boots and Saddles* (1885), was a great success, selling over twenty-two thousand copies. The reception of that work encouraged her to continue writing, publishing *Tenting on the Plains* in 1887 and *Following the Guidon* in 1890. Custer emerged from her books as a man who found it impossible to hate or hold a grudge, who was devoted to his family, loved children, and who was a great patron of the arts. Although a superb marksman and hunter, he had respect for all living creatures, and although a bold man of action, he was never impetuous, simply quick of mind. [15] In short, he was a saintly hero who was entirely capable of accomplishing all the deeds attributed to him by Whittaker and the pulp writers.

The poets of the day tendered considerable assistance to Mrs. Custer in memorializing her husband. Within twenty-four hours of receiving the news of Custer's fall Walt Whitman had a poetical tribute in the mail, accompanied by his bill for ten dollars. On July 10 the *New*

York Tribune published "A Death Song for Custer" (the title was later changed to "Far from Dakota's Canyons").[16]

> Thou of the tawny flowing hair in battle,
> I erewhile saw with erect head, passing ever in
>   front, bearing a bright sword in thy hand,
> Now ending well in death the splendid fever of
>   thy deeds.

It mattered little that Custer's hair was closely cropped before the campaign and that no one carried a saber; these were the props of high drama and would be called into use again and again.

Not to be outdone, Henry Wadsworth Longfellow hurried into print his version of the tragedy, entitled "The Revenge of Rain-in-the-Face."[17]

> "Revenge!" cried Rain-in-the-Face,
> "Revenge upon all the race
>   Of the white chief with yellow hair!"
> And the mountains dark and high
> From their crags reëchoed the cry
>   Of his anger and despair.

The poem proved to be quite popular and the soldiers' repeated testimony that Custer's body was found unmutilated could not dispel the myth that Rain-in-the-Face had cut out the general's heart.

In 1887 the *Atlantic Monthly* published "On the Big Horn" by John Greenleaf Whittier in which the poet pleaded for the nation to forget Rain-in-the-Face's past deeds and allow him to enter General Armstrong's Industrial School at Hampton, Virginia.[18]

> The years are but half a score,
> And the war-whoop sounds no more
>   With the blast of bugles, where
> Straight into a slaughter pen,
> With his doomed three hundred men,
>   Rode the chief with the yellow hair.
>
> O Hampton, down by the sea!
> What voice is beseeching thee

For the scholar's lowliest place?
Can this be the voice of him
Who fought on the Big Horn's rim?
Can this be Rain-in-the-Face?

Whittier's efforts were to no avail, and the old warrior was not afforded the blessing of a white education. He eventually met the same
fate as many other Indians of note by being displayed as a curio for
white audiences. At Coney Island in 1894 a pair of sensation-seeking
reporters got him drunk and he "confessed" to his part in the fight.
Rain-in-the-Face claimed it was Thomas Custer, the general's brother,
he had mutilated. "The long sword's blood and brains splashed in my
face . . . ," he told them, "I leaped from my pony and cut out his heart
and bit a piece out of it and spit it in his face."[19]

The reporters had gotten just what they wanted and published it as
documented fact. Rain-in-the-Face had not come to believe the legend
but he had come to realize the futility of denying it. Just before his
death in 1905 he told a fellow Sioux, Dr. Charles Eastman, that he had
done none of the acts attributed to him. "Many lies have been told of
me," he said.[20] It was a fitting epitaph.

Unlike Rain-in-the-Face and Reno, William "Buffalo Bill" Cody actively sought identification with the Custer fight and greatly benefited
by it. Cody, already immortalized in the dime novels of Ned Buntline
and others, had been busy since 1872 inventing the Wild West on eastern stages. Upon receiving word of the Indian war, he closed his show
and informed his audience that he was needed far more in the West
than on the stage. That was debatable, but the army seemed to want
him and he was soon scouting for the Fifth Cavalry. At War Bonnet
Creek on July 17, 1876, Cody was given an opportunity to exhibit his
prowess as a scout and abilities as a showman when challenged to a duel
by the Cheyenne warrior Yellow Hand. Between a line of Indians on
the one side and troopers and reporters on the other Cody rode out and
promptly shot the Indian. It was quite a sight as the long-haired scout,
dressed in a silver trimmed and red sashed suit of black velvet, lifted
his fallen foe's topknot and triumphantly proclaimed it to be "the first
scalp for Custer!" This accomplishment was worth nearly a column in
the *New York Herald*.

Having done his duty, Cody quickly returned to the stage to reenact his duel in *The Red Right Hand; or, Buffalo Bill's First Scalp for Custer*, exhibiting Yellow Hand's scalp to the audiences.[21] It was one of his most successful seasons.

The ever popular dime novel also helped to identify Cody with Custer. In Prentiss Ingraham's *Buffalo Bill with General Custer* the scout was depicted as the battle's only survivor. Just as fantastic was *Buffalo Bill's Grip; or, Oath-bound to Custer*, in which Cody arrives on the field while the bodies are still warm. Captured by the white renegade who had led the Sioux against Custer, the scout's life is saved by one of the scores of beautiful Indian girls who have populated our frontier regions since the days of Pocahontas. Upon his escape he engages in a knife duel with Yellow Hand and avenges Custer.[22] Only the most unsophisticated of readers would have accepted the events of the dime novels as fact, but since they were based on historical fact such works aided in the creation of lasting myths.

The last stand itself became a standard attraction in many of the wild west shows. Adam Forepaugh staged "Custer's Last Rally" as part of his show's "Progress of Civilization" pageant.[23] Buffalo Bill, who had exhibited Sitting Bull for a season as Custer's conqueror, used the last stand as his show's climax. Buck Taylor played the general whose tiny group of men were reduced to an ever tightening circle in the middle of the great arena. When the last trooper had fallen the spotlight moved to Buffalo Bill who slowly approached the scene of carnage, removed his hat, and sadly bowed his head. Projected on a screen at the end of the arena were the words, Too Late![24]

It was only natural that, when the popularity of the wild west shows declined after the first decade of this century, Cody would turn his attention to motion pictures. The early western film was a direct descendant of the wild west show, retaining many of its conventions and stereotypes. Cody's 1913 film effort to recreate the Indian wars was not successful either commercially or artistically, but others were also eager to apply themselves to the task. Custer's last stand became a popular subject on the silent screen. The portrayal of Custer, when character was allowed to intrude, was invariably heroic.

The first Custer film was most likely William Selig's 1909 one-reeler, *Custer's Last Stand*. Thomas Ince's 1912 version of *Custer's Last Fight* concentrated on the Rain-in-the-Face myth and starred Francis Ford as Custer. In that same year D. W. Griffith turned his talent to a loose interpretation of the battle entitled *The Massacre*. Two Custer films, *Campaigning with Custer* and *Camping with Custer*, were released in 1913. Thereafter no Custer movies were made until Marshall Neilan filmed *Bob Hampton of Placer* in 1921. As the fiftieth anniversary of Custer's death approached movie producers commemorated the occasion with a bumper crop of Custer films. J. G. Adophe's 1925 nine-reeler, *The Scarlet West* with Clara Bow and Johnnie Walker, was the first of a string of Custer films, which included *The Last Frontier, With General Custer at Little Big Horn*, and *The Flaming Frontier*, all released in 1926.[25] The last named was billed as the epic of the group and featured Hoot Gibson as its hard riding hero and Anne Cornwall as his sweetheart. Their attempts to warn Custer of the trap awaiting him are foiled by the film's black-mustachioed villain. Dustin Farnum portrayed Custer, who was labeled in the film's advertising as "the bravest man that ever lived."[26] Although commercially successful, *The Flaming Frontier* was the last silent film tribute to Custer.

An event occurred in 1890 that had more influence upon Custer's heroic image than all the dime novels, stage shows, and motion pictures combined. This was the bankruptcy of John G. Furber's Saint Louis saloon, in which hung Cassily Adams's twelve-by-thirty-two-foot painting, *Custer's Last Fight*. The Anheuser-Busch Brewing Company acquired the canvas as a creditor's asset and eventually gave it to the Seventh Cavalry. Before making this donation the company employed F. Otto Becker of Milwaukee to copy the painting and reduce it to a manageable size for lithography.[27] Becker, however, made numerous changes in Adams's painting so that the end result could easily be accepted as a different work. Adams's painting complied with Whittaker's fanciful account of Custer's death, and the buckskin clad, long-haired soldier was portrayed just as he dispatched the last of three bold warriors who had dared approach him. Rain-in-the-Face was painted aiming his pistol from a safe distance to kill Custer, as hundreds of other warriors advanced in parade ground ranks. Becker retained all the errors of Adams's painting by depicting Custer as long-haired, fighting with a sword, and the last man standing. But he added a greater sense of confusion and carnage by filling the Little Bighorn Valley behind Custer with hordes of Indians rushing in all directions. Custer was portrayed in much the same way as in the Adams version, although with sword upraised instead of in a lunging position. No less than five warriors are dead around the general while four others take aim to kill him. The foreground of the picture is filled with savages hacking and carving at dead or dying troopers. It is not difficult to discern the representatives of progress and civilization in the painting.

The lithograph was copyrighted in 1896 and over 150,000 copies were distributed by the brewing company as an advertising gimmick.[28] Soon it became a standard prop of saloon furnishing and remained so for at least fifty years. Possibly only Gilbert Stuart's *Washington* has been reproduced more, and in that case only because of efforts to put a print in every schoolroom in the country.[29] While the children labored under the dour visage of the nation's father, their elders consumed alcohol and contemplated the nuances of Becker's *Custer's Last Fight*. As Robert Taft aptly stated, the print "has been viewed by a greater number of the lower-browed members of society—and by fewer art critics—than any other picture in American history."[30] Thus Anheuser-Busch was aided in becoming a corporate giant and Custer a heroic legend in a partnership that must rank as one of the great triumphs of American capitalism.

The Becker lithograph became so identified with the last stand that it was repeatedly invoked when someone wanted to instantly convey an image of the battle. Film producers paid particular attention to it. Thomas Ince posed a number of actors in a photographed copy of the Becker lithograph that was released as a still for his 1912 Custer film. As part of prerelease publicity for *They Died with Their Boots On*, Warner Brothers announced that the last stand in the movie would be carefully based on the picture, a decision which probably contributed to the film's many historical errors.[31] The advertising campaign for the 1951 film, *Little Big Horn*, was based entirely on a reproduction of Becker's print, below which were the words "fifty painted Sioux to every one of their gallant few." The "gallant few" referred to a squad of troopers trying to warn Custer since the general and his last stand were not depicted in the film.

The Adams-Becker version of the last stand was, of course, not the first, and far from the last, painting of the battle. Many early depictions were made to illustrate accounts of the slaughter in newspapers and magazines, and a number, most notably John Mulvaney's epic canvas, were painted for exhibition around the country. Mulvaney's twenty-by-eleven-foot canvas, which depicted a spotlessly attired Custer surrounded by a few kneeling men and encircled by a moving horde of war bonneted savages, was a great commercial success on tour and received laudatory reviews in the press. One such review by Walt Whitman in the August 15, 1881, edition of the *New York Tribune*, clearly shows the nationalistic and chauvinistic manner in which nineteenth-century Americans viewed Custer's stand: "Nothing in the books like it, nothing in Homer, nothing in Shakespeare; more grim and sublime than either, all native, all our own and all fact."[32]

Whitman might well have been speaking of all the Custer paintings that would appear over the next fifty years, for they reflected the high drama and heroic romance of that struggle. In most of them Custer is the dominant figure; usually wielding a saber, his long locks blowing in the wind, standing alone while his comrades kneel at his feet to fire. The dramatic scene would attract artists of all nations and varying degrees of talent, and when a checklist was compiled in 1969 nearly a thousand depictions of the battle were counted. Over the years, even as Custer's public image changed radically, there was no slackening in the production of pictures, not only as paintings, but as book and magazine illustrations, advertisements for motion pictures, pageants, and television programs, comic book illustrations, political and humorous cartoons, posters, play money, bubblegum, greeting, and post cards, record album covers, and advertisements for products ranging from whiskey to children's cereal.[33] Little wonder that Custer's last stand is an event known throughout the western world.

The drama of Little Bighorn also proved fertile territory for novelists. One of the earliest and worst full-length treatments was Herbert Myrick's *Cache la Poudre: The Romance of a Tenderfoot in the Days of Custer* (1905). The book, which concerns the adventures of a New York stockbroker who goes west and joins the Seventh Cavalry, typically contains great doses of editorializing. The following year saw the publication of Randall Parrish's *Bob Hampton of Placer*, a much better novel which introduced into Custer fiction a character who was repeated often enough to become a stereotype—the cashiered officer attempting to regain his honor. Parrish, a prolific and capable writer of historical romances, was even more laudatory of Custer than Myrick had been. The famed Indian fighter is depicted as the "proud, dashing leader of light cavalry, that beau ideal of the 'sabreur'," whose last stand represents the boldest, noblest deed of arms ever known.[34] Reno is presented as a "cowardly fool" who holds his troopers "skulking under cover while Custer begs help."[35] While Reno loses his reputation, the book's hero regains his by fighting with the doomed Seventh Cavalry "to defend its chief and to die for its honor."[36]

Cyrus Townsend Brady's *Britton of the Seventh* (1914) also portrayed a disgraced officer who redeems himself at Little Bighorn. Brady's description of Custer is typical of the early novelists:[37]

> His eyes were of the bright clear blue color characteristic of the fighting, masterful face; his glance was piercing, keen, watchful, observant on occasion. . . . And no one who had ever seen them alight with battle fire in the mad rush of the charge, his long bright golden hair streaming in the wind would ever forget it—a Viking of old, a knight of ancient and chivalric days reincarnated!

Such flowery comparisons of modern heroes with ancient warriors, knights, and especially with Homeric characters were common in the literature of the period. In his autobiography Cody had a long chapter on Custer's last battle in which he compared the general with "Spartacus fighting the legions about him, tall, graceful, brave as a lion at bay, and with thunderbolts in his hands."[38] And when Gen. James Grant Wilson wrote an article about Custer and naval hero William Cushing for an 1891 issue of *Cosmopolitan*, he entitled it "Two Modern Knights Errant."[39] An even more fantastic example of this "ancients" complex is found in Ella Wheeler Wilcox's 1896 poem, "Custer." Wilcox called on the muses to aid her in paralleling Custer's last stand with the ancient siege immortalized by Homer. Calliope seems not to have heeded her call, although, with over a hundred stanzas, the poem is interesting as an example of the limits to which the heroic tradition can go. The poem's climax comes as a scout offers Custer a swift horse on which to escape:[40]

> A second's silence, Custer dropped his head,
> His lips slow moving as when prayers are said—
> Two words he breathed—"God and Elizabeth,"
> Then shook his long locks in the face of death,
> And with a final gesture turned away,
> To join the fated few who stood at bay.
> Oh! deeds like that the Christ in man reveal

Let Fame descend her throne at Custer's shrine
   to kneel.

Too late to rescue, but in time to weep,
His tardy comrades came. As if asleep
He lay, so fair, that even hellish hate
Withheld its hand and dared not mutilate.
By fiends who knew not honor, honored still
He smiled and slept on that far western hill.
Cast down thy lyre, oh Muse! thy song is done!
Let tears complete the tale of him who failed,
   yet won.

By the time of the fiftieth anniversary of the battle in 1926, the heroic legend of Custer was firmly established. That year saw the release of numerous books, articles, and films based on the Custer story. An observance was held at the Little Bighorn on June twenty-fifth with a number of the surviving antagonists of the battle in attendance. As a large crowd applauded and bands played, an Indian and a white officer shook hands next to Custer's monument, signifying that old wounds had healed.[41] However, a full page spread in the *New York Times* of June 20 testified to the fact that some wounds still festered. Praising Custer's skill and daring, the article blamed his defeat on the hatred of Reno and Benteen and credited the defeat with bringing about the reform of the Indian bureau that Custer had long sought.[42] But the days for such an interpretation were numbered as a changing America began to look anew at its heroes and found many of them lacking.

Biographical writing of the late 1920s and 1930s was dominated by a style called debunking, which sought to correct past errors of interpretation by exposing the clay feet of idols. Blessed with a cynical wisdom evidently obtained in the disillusioning years after the first global war, the debunkers concentrated on the human frailties of previously revered individuals. Considering that even George Washington came under attack in 1926, it is a wonder that Custer escaped scrutiny until 1934 when Frederic Van De Water published *Glory-Hunter*.

Van De Water's Custer had little resemblance to the hero of Whittaker or Brady. The new Custer was an immature seeker of fame, a brutal and strict commander, though himself a dangerously insubordinate officer, and one distrusted by most of his officers and men. He

had no military talent, his Civil War victories were the result of providence and more cautious subordinates, and his lone victory over the
Indians was a massacre. A callous, often sadistic egotist, he alone bore
the blame for Little Bighorn, which resulted from a combination of his
military ineptitude and headlong pursuit of fame.[43]

The *New York Times*, which eight years before had unlimited praise
for Custer, now hailed Van De Water's biography as the definitive book
on the subject. As such, the review reflected a growing disenchantment
with "an unjust and unhappy Federal [Indian] policy" in particular and
military leaders in general.[44] This is not to say that Van De Water's
interpretation found universal acceptance. In a long and bitter letter
published in *Today* magazine, Gen. Hugh S. Johnson accused the author
of muckraking and of stooping to "scalp an heroic warrior found dead
on the field of honor."[45] Such complaints were to no avail, however, for
the heroic image of Custer was fading before the widely accepted Van
De Water version.

On the heels of the Van De Water biography came the first anti-
Custer novel, Harry Sinclair Drago's *Montana Road*. In it, a glory-
seeking Custer frustrates the efforts of Indian agent Stephen Glen to
avoid war. Glen rides with Reno's detachment at Little Bighorn and it
is Custer who fails to provide the expected support, not Reno. Drago
echoes Van De Water by having the ambitious Custer disregard his
scout's advice and foolishly lead his men into a trap.[46]

The motion pictures of the period did not share the debunking spirit
of the printed media. The filmmakers, faced with producing for a much
wider and often less sophisticated audience than that of the historians
and novelists, found it safer to concentrate on swashbuckling adventure
than on psychological analysis. Two low budget serials were churned
out in the 1930s dealing sympathetically with Custer—*The Last Frontier* (1932) and *Custer's Last Stand* (1936). In 1937 Cecil B. De Mille
decided to "do justice to the courage of the Plainsmen of the West" in a
film of epic proportions that displayed a remarkable disregard for history.[47] *The Plainsman* told the story of Wild Bill Hickok as scout and
peace officer and brought together in one film nearly every cliché associated with the western genre. John Miljan played Custer as a great
Indian fighter—cool, courageous, and natty in tailored buckskins. At
the last stand he calmly picked off circling redskins until a bullet hit
home and, clutching at his heart, he slowly sank alongside the Ameri-

can flag. As for the Indians in the film, they were presented as nothing more than targets. Naturally the movie was an enormous commercial success.

Heroic Custers also appeared in two films that did not concern the Little Bighorn. Ronald Reagan portrayed a soft-spoken, level headed Custer in Warner Brothers's *The Santa Fe Trail* (1940). In it Custer aided Jeb Stuart in halting the misguided schemes of John Brown at Harpers Ferry. The following year Addison Richards as Custer helped Wild Bill Hickok and Calamity Jane clean up the Black Hills in *Badlands of Dakota*.

Hollywood's pro-Custer era was climaxed in 1941 by Raoul Walsh's *They Died with Their Boots On*. The film demonstrated little regard for historical fact in following Custer's career from West Point to Little Bighorn. Errol Flynn's Custer was a spotless knight, a devil-may-care adventurer who loved a fight for a fight's sake, but who, upon seeing the plight of the Indians resulting from government corruption, sacrifices all in an effort to block the plans of railroad tycoons and dishonest politicians. At Little Bighorn Custer knowingly sacrifices his regiment to halt the Indian advance on General Terry's force of infantry. Custer kidnaps the film's villain and on the eve of battle the terrified captive inquires of their destination. "To hell or to glory—it depends on one's point of view," replies Custer. As the villain dies the next day he confesses to Custer that he "was right—about glory." The general had known that all along, and with his troopers dead around him, his pistol empty, his long hair blown by the western breeze, he draws his saber and falls before a charge of mounted warriors.

Although *Life* magazine lamented that the film "glorifies a rash general" and the *New York Times* accused "writers in warbonnets" of scalping history, the movie was a great success.[48] Walsh never intended for the film to reflect historical fact, but rather to reflect how history should have been. The myth had become more important than the reality, and it was the myth that the public wanted to be entertained by and believe in. Coming as it did on the eve of war, and following years of economic depression, the film's portrayal of villainous businessmen and gallant soldiers struck a responsive chord. As the nation reeled from the shock of Pearl Harbor, Wake, and Bataan, it could easily identify with Custer's last stand. Following the fall of Bataan a cartoon in the syndicated "Out Our Way" series illustrated this identification by depicting Custer and his huddled men awaiting the final charge over the verse:[49]

> My Country
> You can take back
> All you've gave me
> And you'll never
>   Hear a yelp
> For we've let too
> Many heroes die
> A-lookin' back
>   For help.

Ernest Haycox, on the other hand, continued the Van De Water tradition in his novel, *Bugles in the Afternoon* (1944). The story revolves around a disgraced officer attempting to redeem himself and portrays Custer as an irresponsible and often cruel commander who sacrifices his men to advance himself. The novel proved quite popular, being serialized in the *Saturday Evening Post* and then reprinted numerous times in cloth and paper editions.

The first anti-Custer film was John Ford's *Fort Apache* (1948), which changed the locale and names to interpret the Custer story. Henry Fonda played the Custer character, Col. Owen Thursday, as an arrogant, stiff-backed officer contemptuous of his native foe and anxious to regain his Civil War rank of general by some glorious deed. His martinet attitudes antagonize his men, especially his second-in-command, Captain York (John Wayne). His ambition finally leads him to attack a large force of Indians who wipe out his command. Ford, usually a defender of the military and western traditions, had Thursday portrayed as an aberration, representing neither the military nor the government, and thus absolved those groups from blame.

Part of Ford's intent was to convey an idea of the importance of heroes to society. York, now in command, is depicted in the film's last scene discussing an upcoming campaign with a group of reporters. One of them mentions with awe that it must have been an honor to know Thursday. "No man died more bravely," replies York, his voice full of irony, "nor won more honor for his regiment." Another newsman noted that Thursday had become "the hero of every schoolboy in the nation," but that the men who died with him were forgotten. York disagreed, stating that the men live on in the regiment, which was better because of the gallant example set by Thursday. York, who had hated Thursday, realized that society understands little of the true motivation of heroes but still needs to idealize them as figures to emulate. The character of York was obviously based on Captain Benteen, who had expressed the same sentiments, although more bluntly, in an 1879 letter. "Cadets for ages to come will bow in humility at the Custer shrine at West Point," he wrote, "and—if it makes better soldiers and men of them, why the necessity of knocking the paste eye out of their idol?"[50] Ford, like Benteen years earlier, was sensitive to the needs that legends and heroes fill in a society.

The films of the 1950s continued the anti-Custer trend, but for different reasons. The success of Delmar Daves's 1950 film, *Broken Arrow*, which dealt sensitively with the plight of the Indians, proved that a motion picture with Indian heroes could be profitable. It was followed by a number of films which were generally more interested in exploiting a new trend than in righting past wrongs.

In *Sitting Bull* (1954), a film so historically inaccurate it would have made De Mille blush, Douglas Kennedy portrayed Custer as an ambitious, arrogant Indian hater who forces the peace-loving Sioux Chief, Sitting Bull (J. Carrol Naish), into war. The following year a biographical film entitled *Chief Crazy Horse* gave that chief credit for defeating Yellow Hair, although its budget was too small to allow filming of the battle. By 1958 Custer's image had fallen so low that even Walt Disney, as great an upholder of traditional heroes as the movie factories ever produced, turned on him. In *Tonka* (1958), the story of the horse Comanche, the only living creature found on the battlefield, Disney treated Custer as a vain racist. Even the gallant death scenes from *Fort Apache* and *Sitting Bull* were now gone, the Custer of this film being shot early in the battle as he crouched low behind a dead horse. Although perhaps cynically motivated, these films were representative of Hollywood's deepening concern with social problems. They were accepted by a society that had learned in World War II the horrors to which racist dogma could lead, and that was struggling, however timidly, with its own inherent racism.

Custer fared no better with the novelists of the 1950s. In Will Henry's novel, *No Survivors* (1950), Custer was again an incompetent glory hunter but was allowed to redeem himself in the end by realizing his folly (and even dictating a letter during the battle accepting responsibility for the defeat), and then dying gallantly. The same author, writing under the pen name of Clay Fisher, was not so generous in his *Yellow Hair* (1953). Dealing only with Custer's activities on the southern plains, Fisher climaxed his novel with the Washita attack which he characterized as a massacre of innocents.

In the same year Mari Sandoz dealt briefly with Custer in *Cheyenne Autumn*, her tale of the flight of a band of reservation Cheyenne toward their northern homeland. Not only was Washita a massacre, but Sandoz also claimed that the lecherous Custer had bedded the Indian maiden Monahsetah after the battle and that she bore him a son. The story quickly became a popular club with which to beat the Custer legend.

By the time Frank Gruber published *Bugles West* (1954) the glory hunter interpretation was becoming a standard stereotype. His novel had nothing to distinguish it from the others, although his portrait of Reno was sympathetic. As Custer turned from hero to villain it was only natural that Reno would be redeemed. Ken Shiflet's novel, *Convenient Coward* (1961), completed the transformation by having a constantly oppressed Reno as hero and a mentally unstable Custer as his tormentor.

A partisan biography of Reno published in 1966, *Faint the Trumpet Sounds*, told the same story. One of that book's authors, George Walton, along with a great-nephew of Reno and the American Legion, successfully petitioned the army to review the major's dismissal. In May 1967 the army concluded that Reno's dismissal had been "excessive and, therefore, unjust."[51] Reno was restored to rank and given an honorable discharge. Soon after, Reno's body was removed from its unmarked Washington grave and reburied at Custer Battlefield amid much ceremony.

The 1960s gave no respite to the tarnishing of Custer's legend. If the 1950s had seen a budding racial conscience in America, it came to full bloom amid the tumult of the 1960s. The plight of oppressed minorities became the concern of many Americans, and there was no longer room in the pantheon of heroes for those who had engaged in repression. Young people especially began to wonder if the values and heroes of American society were worthwhile and relevant. To an ecology-minded generation the winning of the West became synonymous with environmental exploitation and destruction. The settlement of the frontier was no longer a glorious affair but a murderous conquest accomplished over the dead bodies of innocent Mexicans and Indians. To many, Indian life offered a valid counterculture, a more organic, rational, and natural existence than that of white society. The Vietnam conflict, with its array of political and military blunders, gave rise to a bitter disdain of the military in particular and arrogant leadership in general. By the late 1960s comparisons of the Vietnam War with the Indian wars were becoming commonplace, and Custer, though his image had changed, was still a symbol of those earlier conflicts.

Novelists continued to interpret Custer along the same lines. In William Wister Haines's award winning book, *The Winter War* (1961), the Little Bighorn slaughter is brought on by Custer's "vain stupidity" and flagrant violation of orders.[52] Thomas Berger's *Little Big Man* (1964) portrayed a much more complex Custer than the usual stereotype that had dominated Custer fiction since Van De Water. The book's hero, a frontier Candide named Jack Crabb, starts out hating Custer and attempts to kill him, but finally, after Little Bighorn, gives the dead man a grudging respect. Vain, cruel, and with an irrationality bordering on insanity, Custer leads his men to their deaths in the hope of winning a victory that could lead him to the presidency. In the eyes of Crabb, Custer redeems himself by the strength of his character and the manner of his death. Crabb, who is beside Custer when the general dies, is "imbued with the glory and the tragedy of it all." Upon viewing Custer's body later he concedes the dead man's greatness: "Custer had had to die to win me over, but he succeeded at long last: I could not deny it was real noble for him to be his own monument."[53]

Such sympathies, however limited, were becoming rare. Lewis B. Patten wrote a bitter denunciation of Custer in his novel, *The Red Sabbath* (1968). Once more Custer disobeys orders in his blind search for glory, once more he does not give Reno promised support, and once more he is a cruel and callous commander who sees his men as "tools of his ambition, to be used, dulled, sacrificed and thrown away."[54]

Although television had dealt only sporadically with Custer, a series entitled "Legend of Custer" had a brief run in 1967. The program's producers attempted to exploit one current movement and in the process ran head on into another. Appealing to youth, the show's advertising referred to Custer as a young maverick and a long-haired rebel.

The Tribal Indian Land Rights Association was not impressed and announced that it would petition in the courts for an injunction against the series, claiming that "glamorizing Custer is like glamorizing Billy the Kid" because Custer "endorsed a policy of genocide and massacred village after village of Indians."[55] *Newsweek* magazine, reporting on the furor, noted that Custer "had a reputation for cruelty" and a habit of wenching Indian maidens. *TV Guide* ran an article criticizing the sympathetic image of Custer presented in the show.[56] All the protests were really not necessary since poor quality doomed the show and it went off the air in mid-season.

Four Custer motion pictures were released in this period, and they also conformed to the popular trend. Columbia's *The Great Sioux Massacre* (1965), focused on the efforts of Major Reno and Captain Benteen to dissuade the ambitious and ruthless Custer from bringing on an Indian war in his efforts to win national recognition. They fail when Custer attacks the Indians at Little Bighorn in the hope of winning a victory that could carry him into the White House. In the same year a thinly disguised portrait of an evil Custer was given by Andrew Duggon in Arnold Laven's *The Glory Guys*.

Robert Siodmak's *Custer of the West* (1968) presented the title character as a mass of complexities and contradictions. Custer (Robert Shaw) was a troubled soldier whose only wish was to do battle, yet who loathed the one-sided conflict on the western plains. Although sympathetic to the Indians' plight, he was willing to butcher them mercilessly on orders from Washington. Torn between his sense of humanity and his duty as a soldier, Custer finally decides to use his popularity to inform the nation of the terrible moral price it must pay to conquer the Indians, but his efforts destroy his military career. Frustrated and embittered, Custer knowingly goes to his doom at Little Bighorn. The film's potential to expose the hypocrisy of American Indian policy as seen through Custer's troubled eyes was lost in a jumbled script and poor editing. The film's mediocrity and the complexities of the main character doomed the film to commercial failure. Nor did this film escape litigation from those opposed to even a semipositive view of Custer. Charles Reno, a grandnephew of Major Reno, claimed that his ancestor was slandered in the film. The court backed the film, but that was about all the support it received.[57]

In 1970 Arthur Penn's *Little Big Man* was released and soon proved an immense success, becoming the second biggest money-maker of the film season. Although the film retained much of the humor of Berger's novel, it had none of its realism or deep sense of irony. By patronizing the Indians the film idealized them beyond recognition, and Custer was played in one-dimensional comic book style as a devil in human form.

Penn makes no pretense of objectivity; he envisions Custer as not only vain and ambitious, but also insane. Custer was "so infatuated with his capacity to win, so racially assured that he belonged to a superior breed" that he led his men into a hopeless trap.[58] Penn uses the film as a vehicle to attack the Vietnam War and the arrogant leadership that he felt led America deeper into an Asian quagmire rather than admit a mistake. Contemporary terms such as "higher moral right" and "legal action" appear. In depicting the Washita massacre Penn concentrates on the slaughter of innocent women and children. As a herd of Indian ponies are killed, Custer comments on his humanity in sparing the Indian women who surrendered since "they breed like rats." At Little Bighorn, with all the evidence pointing to a trap, he charges blindly on rather than "change a Custer decision." The last stand is depicted as a rout with no semblance of order, and Custer, entirely mad, wanders about the battlefield ranting until struck down by Cheyenne arrows. There was to be no glory or redemption for this Custer, only a senseless but well-deserved death. The general, however, is not presented as an aberration, for the soldiers under his command are depicted as being just as cruel and racist as their leader. It is a harsh, ideological portrait, as far removed from reality as the early dime novels, yet it seems to have been widely accepted as historical fact.

The increasing media exposure and growing political power of the Indian rights movement also popularized a negative view of Custer. As white Americans became aware of the gross injustices perpetrated on the Indians it became obvious to them that the man who symbolized the Indian fighter in history must himself have been evil since he carried out an immoral policy. Vine Deloria's plea for Indian equality, *Custer Died for Your Sins*, reinforced that view. Custer, Deloria wrote, "represented the Ugly American of the last century and he got what was coming to him."[59]

After the enormous commercial success of Dee Brown's *Bury My Heart at Wounded Knee* (1971) there was an orgy of publication on Indians, much of it of dubious quality. One such work, *The Memoirs of Chief Red Fox*, announced on the cover of the paperback edition "He's 100 years old. And he can tell you the truth about Custer." It became a national bestseller before being exposed as a plagiarized fraud.[60] Still, it seemed that people had an insatiable appetite for the "truth about Custer" and the terrible things he had done to the Indians. Just as Whittaker had needed Rain-in-the-Face and Reno as villains in his drama of Custer's fall, so now the writers turned on Yellow Hair, also finding it necessary to have a villain to offset their Indian heroes.

In a 1971 *Life* article entitled "The Custer Myth," Alvin Josephy quoted an Idaho Nez Percé who summed up the relationship of Custer to the new writings: "The white man's knowledge of Indians is based on stereotypes and false, prejudiced history. Custer is the best known hero of that myth to the whites . . . . Destroy the Custer myth, the biggest one of all, and you'll start getting an understanding of everything that happened and an end to the bias against the Indian people."[61] Josephy then proceeded to aid in that task by labeling Custer a crazed glory hunter and calling his monument in Montana "a sore from America's past that has not healed."[62] The most striking characteristic of the writers of the late 1960s and early 1970s was their commitment to demythologize Custer and finally expose the truth—as if no one had tried before.

So all-pervasive and successfully disseminated was this last burst of anti-Custer feeling that it penetrated to the last bastion of the Custer legend—children's literature. For many years the writers of fiction for youth, and especially for boys, had shared Theodore Roosevelt's assessment of Custer as "a shining light to all the youth of America" and had made certain that that light was not extinguished.[63] The early Custer works were written as historical fiction and usually featured a boy hero who, admiring the example of patriotism and courage set by Custer, somehow managed to ride with the Seventh Cavalry to Little Bighorn. More often than not the book's hero would be a friend of Custer's nephew, Autie Reed, who did accompany the column and died at Little Bighorn. The boy hero would always escape young Reed's fate by being detached with Reno's command. The books were usually, but not always, full of historical errors. Such works include J. M. Travers's dime novel, *Custer's Last Shot; or, The Boy Trailer of the Little Big*

Horn (1883), Elbridge Brooks's well-researched novel, *Master of the Strong Hearts* (1898), Edwin L. Sabin's *On the Plains with Custer* (1913), and Zoa Grace Hawley's *A Boy Rides with Custer* (1938).

After the Second World War the emphasis in children's historical literature changed from fiction to biography. Although the biographies sold as history, they usually contained invented dialogue and numerous historical errors. Examples of this type are Quentin Reynolds's error-filled biography, *Custer's Last Stand* (1951), and another more accurate but no less sympathetic biography by Margaret Leighton, *The Story of General Custer* (1954).

The shining ideal of Custer as a brave and patriotic soldier who sacrificed his life to make the West safe did not begin to change in children's books until the early 1960s. Golden Press was the pacesetter in 1959 with a book based on the Disney film *Tonka*. The book echoed the movie's picture of a Custer consumed by his hatred of Indians. The following year Augusta Stevenson published *George Custer, Boy of Action*, which dealt more realistically with the general than had Leighton or Reynolds, blaming the last stand on his rashness and ambition. Eugene Rachlis's juvenile history for American Heritage, *Indians of the Plains* (1960), accused Custer of slaughtering innocents at Washita and of attacking at Little Bighorn in hopes of attaining the presidency. Even more blunt was the presentation in William K. Power's *Crazy Horse and Custer* (1968). Crazy Horse is presented as a patriot defending his homeland, while Custer appears as a vain martinet who indiscriminately slaughters Indian men, women, and children in pursuit of the presidency. The next year much the same interpretation reappeared in Paul and Dorothy Goble's *Custer's Last Battle*. Such books still serve to teach lessons to youth from the example of history, but the lesson to be learned now from Custer is the evil of vanity and unbridled ambition.

There appears to be a filtering-down process in popular culture whereby interpretation is passed from the more sophisticated medium to the least sophisticated. The comic book, that unsophisticated bulwark of one-dimensional characterization, retained the heroic Custer until the 1970s. Evidence on comics is hard to come by since systematic collections are rare, but those found seem to reflect a definite trend. Custer died with cool bravery facing a savage foe in an issue of *Westerner Comics* (1949), and in two 1950 comics, *Indian Fighter* and

Custer's Last Fight, Massacre at Little Big Horn. Although a darker side was portrayed in Walt Disney's *Tonka* (1958), Custer was back in full glory the following year in Classics Illustrated's *Story of the Army.* In *Famous Indian Tribes* (1962) rashness was hinted at, but Custer was praised for his courage and skill. In the 1970s the shift of sympathy toward the Indian and the negative popular image of Custer emboldened comic book producers to join in the attack on the general's legend. It was a time of new maturity for comics as they began to deal with a number of social issues. The September 1971 issue of *Rawhide Kid* featured a story, "The Guns of General Custer," in which a racist, sadistic Custer disregards the hero's warning and rides to his doom. Only four years earlier in "Massacre at Medicine Bend," the Rawhide Kid had fought alongside Custer whom he considered the "finest battle commander" he had ever seen. The same portrait of a glory-seeking Custer was repeated in the April 1973 issue of *Star Spangled War.*[64]

The Custer legend has thus been completely reversed. What is extraordinary is that over the entire period, long after the clay feet of the idol were exposed, Custer remains an extremely popular figure. The constant production of books and motion pictures on his life and last battle attest to this continuing public interest. Custer's youth, appearance, flamboyance, and adventurous life during a colorful era have all contributed to his popular appeal, but it was the high drama and intrigue about his death that earned him immortality. While few people know of Custer's Civil War exploits, most Americans recognize Custer's last stand. Battles in which one side has been annihilated have long fascinated mankind, and people of many nations point pridefully to such events in their homeland. The leader of the defeated band is often revered as a national hero while the battle becomes a point of cultural pride, an example of patriotism and sacrifice: Leonidas at Thermopylae, Roland at Roncesvalles, Crockett at the Alamo, or Gordon at Khartoum.[65]

Although the last stand assured continuing fame for Custer, it was not enough to guarantee him a perpetual positive image. As the values of society change so does its vision of its history, and one Custer myth is replaced with another. The collective popular mind is unable or unwilling to deal with the complexities of character; its heroes are pure and its villains are evil with no shading in between. As the American view of militarism and Indians changed, so the view of Custer changed. As society's image of the frontier altered from that of a desert stubbornly resisting the progress of civilization to that of a garden of innocence offering refuge from the decadence of civilization, so the expectations for the western hero changed. The conquering military hero was replaced by the frontiersman or Indian who could live in harmony with nature. Thus, from a symbol of courage and sacrifice in the winning of the West, Custer's image was gradually altered into a symbol of the arrogance and brutality displayed in the white exploitation of the West. The only constant factor in this reversed legend is a remarkable disregard for historical fact.

Notes

1. A discussion of the origins and nature of the historical debate on Custer can be found in Robert M. Utley, *Custer and the Great Controversy: The Origin and Development of a Legend* (Los Angeles: Westernlore Press, 1962).

2. Theodore P. Greene, *America's Heroes: The Changing Models of Success in American Magazines* (New York: Oxford University Press, 1970), 110–65.

3. Jay Monaghan, *Custer: The Life of General Armstrong Custer* (Boston: Little, Brown and Co., 1959), is by far the most balanced account of the general's life. Edgar I. Stewart, *Custer's Luck* (Norman: University of Oklahoma Press, 1955), and W. A. Graham, *The Story of the Little Big Horn* (1926; reprint, Harrisburg, Pa.: Stackpole Co., 1945), are the best accounts of the battle.

4. Brian W. Dippie, "The Southern Response to Custer's Last Stand," *Montana the Magazine of Western History* 21 (April 1971): 27.

5. Utley, *Great Controversy*, 29–48.

6. Ibid., 120. "Family" refers to the fact that two of Custer's brothers, a nephew, and a brother-in-law died with him.

7. *Chicago Tribune*, July 7, 1876.

8. Quoted in D. A. Kinsley, *Favor the Bold: Custer, the Indian Fighter* (New York: Holt, Rinehart and Winston, 1968), 233.

9. Two books on the nature of American heroes and their creators are Dixon Wecter, *The Hero in America* (New York: C. Scribner's Sons, 1941), and Marshall W. Fishwick, *American Heroes: Myth and Reality* (Washington: Public Affairs Press, 1954). Especially valuable in understanding the western hero is Henry Nash Smith, *Virgin Land: The American West As Symbol and Myth* (Cambridge: Harvard University Press, 1950). The development of four western myths, including

Custer, is considered in Kent Ladd
Steckmesser, *The Western Hero in History and Legend* (Norman: University
of Oklahoma Press, 1965).

10. Frederick Whittaker, *A Complete Life of Gen. George A. Custer*
(New York: Sheldon and Co., 1876),
628.

11. Ibid., 610–11.

12. Ibid., 608.

13. A detailed account of Whittaker's
crusade against Reno is in Utley, *Great
Controversy*, 51–64.

14. Whittaker, *Custer*, 601.

15. Elizabeth Bacon Custer, *Tenting
on the Plains* (1887; reprint, Norman:
University of Oklahoma Press, 1971),
22–25.

16. Kinsley, *Favor the Bold*, xi.

17. *The Complete Poetical Works of
Henry Wadsworth Longfellow* (Boston:
Houghton, Mifflin and Co., 1880), 272.

18. John Greenleaf Whittier, "On the
Big Horn," *Atlantic Monthly* 59 (April
1887): 433.

19. Utley, *Great Controversy*, 129.

20. Charles A. Eastman, "Rain-in-
the-Face: The Story of a Sioux Warrior," *Outlook* 84 (October 27, 1906):
507–12.

21. Don Russell, *The Wild West:
A History of the Wild West Shows*
(Fort Worth: Amon Carter Museum of
Western Art, 1970), 16.

22. Don Russell, *The Lives and
Legends of Buffalo Bill* (Norman: University of Oklahoma Press, 1960),
407–8.

23. Russell, *Wild West*, 31.

24. Henry Blackman Sell and Victor
Weybright, *Buffalo Bill and the Wild
West* (New York: Oxford University
Press, 1955), 156.

25. Data on some Custer films, but
no commentary, can be found in Allen
Eyles, *The Western: An Illustrated
Guide* (London: Zwemmer, 1967), 44;
Ralph E. Friar and Natasha A. Friar,
*The Only Good Indian . . . The Holly-
wood Gospel* (New York: Drama Book
Specialists, 1972), 321; Don Russell,
*Custer's List: A Checklist of Pictures
Relating to the Battle of the Little
Big Horn* (Fort Worth: Amon Carter
Museum of Western Art, 1969), 64–65.

26. *New York Times*, April 5 and
11, 1926; *Indianapolis Star*, September 23, 1926.

27. Robert Taft, *Artists and Illus-
trators of the Old West, 1850–1900* (New
York: Charles Scribner's Sons, 1953),
142–48; Don Russell, *Custer's Last*
(Fort Worth: Amon Carter Museum of
Western Art, 1968), 31.

28. Taft, *Artists*, 146.

29. Fishwick, *American Heroes*, 48.

30. Taft, *Artists*, 130.

31. *Time* 38 (December 22, 1941): 47.

32. Taft, *Artists*, 138–39.

33. An entertaining and informative
study of Custer paintings is Russell's
Custer's Last. The same author edited
a checklist of Custer pictures, for the
Amon Carter Museum of Western Art,
entitled *Custer's List*. Two more recent works are Harrison Lane, "Brush,
Palette, and the Battle of the Little
Big Horn," *Montana the Magazine of
Western History* 23 (July 1973): 66–
79, and Brian W. Dippie, "The Custer

Battle on Canvas: Reflections and Afterthoughts," *Montana the Magazine of Western History* 24 (January 1974): 55–67.

34. Randall Parrish, *Bob Hampton of Placer* (Chicago: A. C. McClurg and Co., 1906), 360, 367.

35. Ibid., 353.

36. Ibid., 374.

37. Cyrus Townsend Brady, *Britton of the Seventh* (Chicago: A. C. McClurg and Co., 1914), 7.

38. William F. Cody, *Life and Adventures of Buffalo Bill* (Denver: Smith-Brooks Printing Co., 1939), 284.

39. James Grant Wilson, "Two Modern Knights Errant," *Cosmopolitan* 11 (July 1891): 294–302.

40. Ella Wheeler Wilcox, *Custer, and Other Poems* (Chicago: W. B. Conkey Co., 1896), 134.

41. *New York Times*, June 26, 1926.

42. Ibid., June 20, 1926.

43. Frederic Van De Water, *Glory-Hunter* (Indianapolis: Bobbs-Merrill Co., 1934).

44. *New York Times*, November 18, 1934.

45. Utley, *Great Controversy*, 165.

46. Harry Sinclair Drago, *Montana Road* (New York: Doubleday and Co., 1935).

47. Quoted from the preface to the film *The Plainsman*.

48. *Life* 11 (December 8, 1941): 75–78; *New York Times*, November 30, 1941.

49. Russell, *Custer's List*, 48.

50. W. A. Graham, *The Custer Myth: A Source Book of Custeriana* (Harrisburg, Pa.: Stackpole Co., 1953), 325.

51. *New York Times*, June 1, 1967.

52. William Wister Haines, *The Winter War* (Boston: Little, Brown and Co., 1961), 47, 52.

53. Thomas Berger, *Little Big Man* (New York: Dial Press, 1964), 435.

54. Lewis Patten, *The Red Sabbath* (Garden City, N.Y.: Doubleday and Co., 1968), 153.

55. Friar and Friar, *Only Good Indian*, 274–75.

56. *Newsweek* 70 (August 7, 1967): 51; P. M. Clepper, "He's Our George," *TV Guide* (September 23, 1967), 32–34.

57. *New York Times*, October 2, 1967, and March 18, 1968.

58. Gerald Astar, "The Good Guys Wear War Paint," *Look* 34 (December 1, 1970): 60.

59. Vine Deloria, Jr., *Custer Died for Your Sins: An Indian Manifesto* (New York: Macmillan, 1969), 150.

60. *New York Times*, March 11, 1972.

61. Alvin Josephy, "The Custer Myth," *Life* 71 (July 2, 1971): 52–55.

62. Ibid., 55.

63. Quoted in John B. Kennedy, "A Soldier's Widow," *Colliers* 79 (January 29, 1927): 33.

64. "Custer's Massacre," *Westerner Comics* 19 (March 1949); "Chief Crazy Horse's Revenge," *Indian Fighter* 1 (May 1950); *Custer's Last Fight, Massacre at Little Big Horn* 1 (1950); *Walt Disney's Tonka* 966 (1958); "Custer's Last Stand," *Illustrated Story of the Army* 9 (May 1959); "The Sioux Indians," *Famous Indian Tribes* 1 (July-September 1962); "The Guns of General Custer," *Rawhide Kid* 91 (September

1971); "Massacre at Medicine Bend," *Rawhide Kid* 60 (October 1967); "The Little Big Horn," *Star Spangled War* 169 (April 1973).

65. A cross-cultural comparison of the Custer fight with similar battles in other nations is in Bruce A. Rosenberg, *Custer and the Epic of Defeat* (University Park: Pennsylvania State University Press, 1974).

THE PICTORIAL RECORD OF THE OLD WEST: CUSTER'S LAST STAND—JOHN MULVANY, CASSILLY ADAMS, AND OTTO BECKER

ROBERT TAFT

What painting—or its reproduction—has been viewed, commented on and discussed by more people in this country than has any other? Rosa Bonheur's "The Horse Fair"? Landseer's "The Stag at Bay"? The "September Morn" of Paul Chabas? Willard's "Spirit of '76"? "Washington Crossing the Delaware" by Emanuel Leutze? Hovenden's "Breaking Home Ties"?[1] Doubtless each amateur connoisseur will have his own candidate for this position of honor but the writer's nominations for the place are two figure paintings of the same subject, John Mulvany's "Custer's Last Rally" and Cassilly Adams' "Custer's Last Fight" [see page 537]. Mulvany's painting, completed in 1881, was for ten or a dozen years, displayed, known, and admired throughout the country. Chromolithographic copies of the painting can still be occasionally found. The Adams painting, done in the middle 1880's, was lithographed in modified version by Otto Becker and published by the Anheuser-Busch Company of St. Louis in 1896 and is still distributed by that concern. Copies can be viewed in barrooms, taverns, hotels, restaurants, and museums throughout the country. It is probably safe to say that in the 50 years elapsing since 1896 it has been viewed by a greater number of the lower-browed members of society—and by fewer art critics—than any other picture in American history. To be more specific, the writer on a bus trip to St. Louis in the summer of 1940, stopped for rest and refreshment at a tavern in a small mid-Missouri town. On one wall of the tavern, a busy rest stop for bus lines traveling east and west, was "Custer's Last Fight." Each bus that came to rest disgorged its passengers, many of whom found their way into the tavern. As each group entered, some one was sure to see the Custer picture with the result that there were always several people—sometimes a crowd—around it, viewing it, commenting on it, and then hurrying on. Probably hundreds of people saw this picture every month. When one considers that 150,000 copies have been published and distributed since the picture was first published in 1896, it is evident that "Custer's Last Fight" has been viewed by an almost countless throng. Kirke Mechem, secretary of the Kansas State Historical Society, tells me that a reproduction of the painting in the Memorial building close to his work room, is likewise viewed by a constantly changing daily audience. The picture fascinates all beholders, for after viewing it and passing on to examine other pictures and exhibits, return is made to see again "Custer's Last Fight." "It is the most popular by far of all our many pictures," reports Mr. Mechem.

Why? The scene is totally imaginary, for no white witness survived the Custer tragedy. Postponing for the moment the detailed consideration of Mulvany's and Adams' masterpieces, it can be pointed out that the fundamental reason for the popularity of these pieces is the event itself, the event centering around the great climacteric of Custer's life.

Doubtless the name of George Armstrong Custer will be the center of controversy as long as this country honors its military heroes. Few individuals in the nation's history have had the spectacular and varying career that became Custer's lot. At 23 he was a first lieutenant in the United States army assigned to General McClellan's staff who were then assembling the famed Army of the Potomac. Overnight Custer rose from first lieutenant to brigadier general of volunteer cavalry. Two years later, he was a major general. The close of the Civil War brought almost as abrupt downward changes and nearly disaster to his fortunes. From major general to captain, from hero to deserter were his downward steps. The desertion was followed by suspension, but eventually reinstatement to his regiment (the 7th cavalry organized in 1866) started him again on his upward way. At the battle of the Washita against the Plains Indians in 1868 he again gained the eye of the nation. It was not long, however, before he incurred the displeasure of President Grant and was ordered detached from his command. At the last moment the order was rescinded and as lieutenant-colonel in command of the 7th cavalry, he led his command in that long-remembered battle above the Little Big Horn river on July 25, 1876. On the bare Montana uplands of that bright and burning summer day, Custer and his immediate followers entered Valhalla with a drama and suddenness that left the nation shocked. Not a man in that group survived as the Sioux and their allies gave battle. Small wonder that the tragedy of the Little Big Horn has been told by writer, poet and painter in the days since 1876, for here are the elements that should rouse imagination. Indians, the great West, the boys in blue, great tragedy and no living white observer to witness the culmination of a spectacular career.

And imagination has been used. So much so that it is difficult to trace the events of that day. Students of Custer and of the battle of the Little Big Horn have appeared in number. The event still attracts attention and each contribution, as it has appeared, has been almost immediately the subject of extensive adverse criticism or praise.[2]

Pictures of Custer's Last Stand have not often been the subject of serious consideration. The student of art, if he has ever condescended to look at such pictures, politely sniffs the tainted air because, it is true, few of such pictures have any artistic merit. There are, however, some exceptions as will be subsequently pointed out. The professional historian, since such pictures must be, as we have already observed, figments of the imagination, relegates them to the limbo of worthless things. It remains, therefore, for the interested busybody who has nothing else to do to consider their worth, if worth they have. As historical documents, pictures of Custer's Last Stand are admittedly worthless,[3] but any product of man's endeavor which has attracted the attention of millions of his fellows must certainly have some worth. Such pictures have kindled imagination and speculation, have developed observation and criticism[4] and have renewed and aroused interest in our past. In any well-rounded system of history, then, the consideration of such pictures has a place, even if a humble one. Are they not closer and more vital to our American way of life than is Chinese art or the primitive masters? If the art historian or teacher feels that it is his duty to improve the artistic sense and taste of his fellow man, why cannot "popular" pictures—rather than being held up to scorn— be used as a starting point in such a program of education? The wide appeal of such pictures would insure a large audience and therefore a more fertile field for the zealous in art. The strength and weakness of such pictures are easily pointed out and interest in art might be readily stimulated by this method rather than by the use of more conventional ones. Or if this suggestion does not meet the approval of teachers of art, one might make a further suggestion and remark to the reformers: "Here is a subject which has been of national interest for many years. Let's see how your imagination and talents would depict this or similar scenes in a manner befitting the high standards of the profession."

It can, however, be pointed out that there is now available abundant source material for the critical examination of such pictures if the observer is so inclined. Maps and photographs of the terrain upon which Custer fought his last battle are accessible to the interested critic or artist as are details of equipment of both Indians and soldiers.[5] Description of many incidents, for which there is good evidence, are also available.

Dustin, one of the careful students of the battle of the Little Big Horn, writes in this connection:

> Pictures have a proper place in history, provided they are true to life, and many have been painted and drawn of "Custer's Last Battle" and related scenes. In some of the most thrilling, officers and men are represented fighting with sabers and clothed in full dress uniforms, the former with shoulder knots, cords, and aquillettes, and the latter with brass shoulder scales. Custer himself has been depicted arrayed in a short jacket, an enormous red tie, and long red hair falling over his shoulders. In fact, not a saber or sword was carried in this fight, and the dress was the ordinary fatigue uniform, although some of the officers, among them Custer, wore comfortable buckskin coats. The men were armed with the Springfield carbine and Colt or Remington revolver, while many of the officers had rifles of different patterns, belonging to them personally.[6]

Custer's long hair, mentioned above by Dustin, had been cut before his last campaign,[7] and it seems possible from accounts of surviving Indian participants of the battle, that Custer fell early in the final stages of the fight,[8] although some artists have depicted him as the final survivor.[9] It is true that the body of Custer was found near the summit of a ridge overlooking the Little Big Horn river surrounded by the bodies of 40 or 50 of his men and of many horses. Dustin describes the scene as follows:

> Custer himself was lying on the slope just south of the monument, face upwards, head uphill, right heel resting on a dead horse, his right leg over a dead soldier lying close to the horse. The right hand was extended and looked as though something had been wrenched from his grip. The body was stripped but not mutilated in any way, and it was with difficulty that the wounds were found which caused his death. One was in the left side of the head through the ear; another on the same side under the heart, and a third in the right forearm.[10]

For Indian equipment and costumes there is available the extensive description of the Cheyenne warrior, Wooden Leg, who took part in the battle.[11] According to Wooden Leg, warbonnets were worn by 12 of the several hundred Cheyenne warriors present, of which 10 had trails.

> Not any Cheyenne fought naked in this battle. All of them who were in the fight were dressed in their best, according to the custom of both the Cheyennes and the Sioux. Of our warriors, Sun Bear was nearest to nakedness. He had on a special buffalo-horn head-dress. I saw several naked Sioux, perhaps a dozen or more. Of course, these had special medicine painting on the body. Two different Sioux I saw wearing buffalo head skins and horns, and one of them had a bear's skin over his head and body. These three were not dressed in the usual war clothing. It is likely there were others I did not see. Perhaps some of the naked ones were No Clothing Indians.[12]

Wooden Leg also described his own preparations for battle, "I got my paints and my little mirror. The blue-black circle soon appeared around my face. The red and yellow colorings were applied on all of the skin inside the circle. I combed my hair. It properly should have been oiled and braided neatly, but my father again was saying, 'Hurry,' so I just looped a buckskin thong about it and tied it close up against the back of my head, to float loose from there."[13]

For weapons Wooden Leg had a six-shooter and lariat, and his war pony had a blanket strapped upon its back and a leather thong looped through its mouth. Bows and arrows, however, were the usual weapons of the Indians, many securing their first guns from their fallen enemies.[14]

Indian witnesses of the battle have also reported important incidents of the tragic fray which artists of the event could—or have—used in their portrayal. Many of the attacking Indians advanced up numerous side gulleys thus protecting themselves from the fire of the soldiers.[15] In this manner, the total losses among the Indians were kept exceedingly low considering the magnitude of the engagement. Only about 30 Indians were killed,[16] but the portion of the 7th cavalry under Custer's immediate command, which was wiped out, numbered some 220.[17] If many of the Indians fought dismounted, probably a greater number on horseback circled the fight. "We circled all round him [Custer]" is the brief statement of Two Moon, another Indian survivor. Two Moon also recalled that "The smoke [over the battlefield] was like a great cloud, and everywhere the Sioux went the dust rose like smoke."[18]

Several of the paintings of the Custer battle have apparently utilized another recollection of Two Moon. "All along," states Two Moon, "the bugler kept blowing his commands. He was very brave too."[19] The bugler was doubtless Chief Trumpeter Henry Voss, killed in action.[20]

Still another incident of the battle which has not yet found its way into any picturization of Custer's final hour, as far as the writer knows, was the recollection of Rain-in-the-Face, a Sioux, still another survivor. Rain-in-the-Face told Charles A. Eastman, the well-known Sioux writer, that Tashenamani, an Indian maiden whose brother had just been killed in an engagement with General Crook shortly before the battle of the Little Big Horn, took part in one of the charges against Custer. "Holding her brother's war staff over her head, and leaning forward upon her charger, she looked as pretty as a bird. . . . 'Behold, there is among us a young woman,' I shouted. 'Let no young man hide behind her garment.' "[21]

Scalping of the dead and dying soldiers, depicted in some of the pictures of Custer's Last Stand, was a fact. Known mutilation of the dead soldiers' bodies, however, was the work of boys, women and old men when the field was won for the Indians.[22]

Much more might be written concerning factual aspects of the battle but what has been written above will enable us to make some judgment—if we must stick to facts—in the various portrayals of the battle scene; or the brief review, made above, might indicate the way for some artist of the future whose talents, ambition and imagination might lead him to attempt another version of Custer's Last Stand.[23]

Since the Mulvany and Adams paintings and the Becker lithograph are by far the best known of this group of battle paintings, their history, with some information concerning the artists, will be given in some detail. We shall then follow the discussion of these two paintings by a listing, and brief description, of other pictorial records of the same event.

John Mulvany

Mulvany, an Irishman by birth, was born about 1844 and came to this country when 12 years of age. As a boy, after his arrival in New York City, he worked around the old Academy of Design and evidently picked up some training in drawing and sketching. Judging from the meager information concerning his early career, he joined the Union army at the outbreak of the Civil War and continued his sketching in the field. At the close of the war he had enough money to take him abroad, where he became an art student in the famous centers of Dusseldorf, Munich, and Antwerp. He achieved considerable success as a student, winning a medal for excellence at Munich. At Munich he was a student of Wagner and of the famous Piloty, well known for his historical paintings, including a number of battle scenes. Later he went to Antwerp where he studied under De Keyser, the Flemish painter of battle pieces.[24] He returned to this country in the early 1870's and was for a time a resident of St. Louis and Chicago. After the great fire of 1871, Mulvany went farther West and lived near the Iowa-Nebraska border where he began accumulating Western material. His first painting of note, "The Preliminary Trial of a Horse Thief—Scene in a Western Justice's Court," was exhibited before the National Academy of Design in 1876.[25]

As a resident of the West, Mulvany, like countless other Americans of 1876, was shocked by the Custer tragedy and his interest in Western life doubtless led him to contemplate the Custer battle as a theme for his brush. In 1879, after establishing headquarters in Kansas City, he visited the Custer battlefield, made sketches of the terrain and visited the Sioux on reservation. Mulvany also studied, according to his own account, the dress and equipment of the U.S. cavalry and obtained portraits and descriptions of General Custer and his officers. "I made that visit," he stated two years after the trip to the Little Big Horn, "because I wished to rid the painting of any conventionality. Whenever nature is to be represented it should be nature itself, and not somebody's guess. I made myself acquainted with every detail of my work, the gay caparisoning of the Indian ponies, the dress of the Indian chiefs and braves; in fact, everything that could bear upon the work."[26] For two years he worked on his masterpiece which he named "Custer's Last Rally." The work of painting was done in Kansas City, although Mulvany seems to have made other Western trips in this period as well as occasional excursions to nearby Fort Leavenworth for the purpose of consulting army officers at that post.

The painting was nearly complete by the end of March, 1881, for on March 18, the reporters of the Kansas City newspapers, some 20 in number, were invited to view the work.[27] The painting which the 20 gentlemen of the press beheld with awe and admiration was an enormous work, measuring 20 x 11 feet with figures of heroic size. In describing it, one of the journalists wrote:

Custer is, of course, the central figure. He is depicted as standing below, and a little to the right of his favorite horse, in the middle of the barricade formed by the few soldiers who participated in the final hopeless struggle. In his left hand, which is extended at full length, is a revolver, which he is aiming at some unseen foe, while with his right he grasps a glittering saber, holding it tightly at his side. His face expresses all that a man would feel when confronted by certain death. Despair is crowded out by undaunted courage; the thought of personal danger seems to have been sunk in hatred for a bloodthirsty foe, and a subdued expression in the eyes shows that pity for the gallant boys in blue, whom he has hurried to impending doom, is struggling hard for supremacy. His face is flushed with the heat of battle, his broad-brimmed hat lies carelessly on one side, and the long yellow locks, which added so greatly to his manly beauty, are tossed impetuously back. He stands erect, undaunted and sublime. Near him, kneeling upon the ground, and with bandaged head from which blood is spurting, is Capt. Cook, adjutant of the regiment, and a warm friend of Custer's. Cook darts a glance of hatred at the red devils and has his hand upon the trigger of his rifle waiting for a chance to shoot. In the immediate foreground are two Sioux Indians, both dead. One lies with his face turned upward to the June sun, and a more hideous countenance could not be found if a search was made from Dan to Beersheba. The face was covered with paint, the ears and nose are pierced, a gaudy bonnet of eagles' feathers adorns the head, and the features are horribly savage, even in death. The artist has been true to nature in his treatment of the redskin. The breech clout and moccasins and headdress are faithfully delineated.

The general plan of the painting is that of a semi-circle of soldiers intrenched behind dead and dying horses and surrounded by an innumerable horde of Sioux warriors. With the exception of three officers and perhaps half a dozen privates, the soldiers' faces cannot be seen as they are turned to the foe. The barricade is irregular in outline, but preserves some semblance of a circle. The men kneel behind the horses, which have either been killed by the Indians or which the soldiers have themselves killed for shelter, and from this partial cover are making

As Brave a Defense as They Can.

Outside of the enclosure a countless host of savages are pouring a deadly fire upon the little band. The artist has graphically delineated that phase of Indian fighting which is most characteristic of the race. It is well known that an Indian never exposes his person unless the odds are overwhelmingly in his favor. Custer being in such a hopeless minority the foe expose themselves recklessly, and present many fine targets for the blue coats, not seeming to realize that some stray shots may wander that way and hurry them to a timely grave.[28]

Mulvany told his guests that he was planning to take the picture East for exhibition and reproduction, and shortly the painting was in Boston. The fact that such a work of art had been produced in the West itself did not go unnoticed and we find the same journalist commenting, as he brings his description of Mulvany's painting to a close:

That such a work has been produced in Kansas City shows that art is not neglected even in the midst of the great commercial activity that so distinctively marks this growing metropolis. The effect upon other artists here cannot but be beneficial. Of course nothing can be predicated of the reception that Mr. Mulvany's work will meet in the East, but it is fair to presume that it will create the favorable impression that it so richly deserves.[29]

Mulvany, with "Custer's Last Rally" reached Boston in April, 1881, and apparently at the suggestion of friends, some changes in composition were made. Mulvany, therefore, rented a studio in "Kenneday Hall in the Highlands" and proceeded with the suggested alterations. The size of Custer's figure was reduced somewhat; his hair shortened and his face strengthened. After those changes had been made, Mulvany invited the art critics and journalists of the city to examine his work. Edward Clements of the Boston *Evening Transcript* was evidently very favorably impressed after seeing it, for he wrote the following intelligent account:

> The magnificent bravery of the artist's purpose in this picture and the sustained power as well as heroic pluck with which he has bent himself to a great subject are allowed to make their effect upon all who appreciate what it is to project and *carry out* an extended composition like this. . . . To multiply the figure or two of the ordinary achievements of our artists by twenty or forty (as in the case of this huge canvas, containing more than two score of figures) would give but a slight notion of the comparative strength drawn upon to complete such a picture as this of Mulvany's. It is not a mere matter of posing studio models. The subject cannot be posed except in the artist's imagination, and not there until after the creative effort, the "sheer dead lift" of invention which calls it into being. Custer and his command were cut off to the last man, and only the confused boastings of the Indians engaged in the slaughter furnish the material for the artist's detail. To call up the counterpart of the Indians' account, to fill the reflex of their war dance brag with the heroism of the devoted three hundred, must be the work of fervent and sympathetic artistic imagination. . . .
>
> The fighting here portrayed is real, not only in its vigor and desperation, but in fidelity to the facts of modern and contemporary American fighting. Conventional battle-pieces of European art could indeed have furnished but little help in a picture of a death

struggle with Indians, had it not been the artist's chief purpose
to make an original and American composition. It is a grim, dismal melee. No beautiful uniforms, no picturesque flags, no regular
formation of troops into ranks, squares or lines of battle are available to give color, balance and form to the composition, the white
puffs of carbine shots and the dense cloud of dust almost conceal-
ing the overwhelming cloud of savages, whose myriad numbers it
awfully suggests, form the background against which the army-
blue trousers and dark blue flannel shirts of these fighting soldiers
can add but little richness of color. The highest tint is in Custer's
yellow buckskin suit. . . . The picture will go straight to the hearts
of the people, especially in the great West.[30]

Such favorable comment brought the painting its first publicity in
the East and although it was not publicly exhibited in Boston, it was
soon shipped to New York City for exhibition and was there placed on
view in the summer of 1881. No less a personage than Walt Whitman,
that constant protagonist of Americanism, saw it on a day's visit to
New York and was profoundly impressed. What is more important to
us now, Whitman described his impressions, which we shall quote at
length. The quotations which we have already made from the Kansas
City and Boston papers, and which we shall make from the New York
Tribune, in which Whitman's account appears, seem well justified. In
the first place they are intrinsically interesting and important, for they
reveal what was felt and thought at the time Mulvany's picture was
first placed on display. Possibly more important, however, is the concern of the individual writers—possibly an apologetic concern—with
American art and American themes in art. That Whitman showed this
interest and concern is not surprising, for 10 years previously, in 1871,
he had published his *Democratic Vistas* in which was written "I say that
democracy [i.e., America] can never prove itself beyond cavil, until it
founds and luxuriantly grows its own forms of art, poems, schools, the-
ology, displacing all that exists, or that has been produced anywhere
in the past, under opposite influences"; a statement which throws considerable light on the following description of the Mulvany picture,
written in his characteristic and irregular prose style:

I went to-day to see this just-finished painting by John Mulvany,
who has been out in far Montana on the spot at the Forts, and

among the frontiersmen, soldiers and Indians, for the last two or three years on purpose to sketch it in from reality, or the best that could be got of it. I sat for over an hour before the picture, completely absorbed in the first view. A vast canvas, I should say twenty or twenty-two feet by twelve, all crowded, and yet not crowded, conveying such a vivid play of color, it takes a little time to get used to it. There are no tricks; there is no throwing of shades in masses; it is all at first painfully real, overwhelming, needs good nerves to look at it. Forty or fifty figures, perhaps more, in full finish and detail, life-size, in the mid-ground, with three times that number, or more, through the rest—swarms upon swarms of savage Sioux, in their war-bonnets, frantic, mostly on ponies, driving through the background, through the smoke, like a hurricane of demons. A dozen of the figures are wonderful. Altogether a Western, autochthonic phase of America, the frontiers, culminating typical, deadly, heroic to the uttermost; nothing in the books like it, nothing in Homer, nothing in Shakespeare; more grim and sublime than either, all native, all our own and all a fact. A great lot of muscular, tan-faced men brought to bay under terrible circumstances. Death ahold of them, yet every man undaunted, not one losing his head, wringing out every cent of the pay before they sell their lives.

Custer (his hair cut short) stands in the middle with dilated eye and extended arm, aiming a huge cavalry pistol. Captain Cook is there, partially wounded, blood on the white handkerchief around his head, but aiming his carbine [pistol] coolly, half kneeling (his body was afterward found close by Custer's). The slaughtered or half-slaughtered horses, for breastworks, make a peculiar feature. Two dead Indians, herculean, lie in the forground clutching their Winchester rifles, very characteristic. The many soldiers, their faces and attitudes, the carbines, the broad-brimmed Western hats, the powdersmoke in puffs, the dying horses with their rolling eyes almost human in their agony, the clouds of war-bonneted Sioux in the background, the figures of Custer and Cook, with, indeed, the whole scene, inexpressible, dreadful, yet with an attraction and beauty that will remain forever in my memory. With all its color and fierce action a certain Greek continence pervades it. A sunny sky and clear light envelop all. There is an almost entire absence of the stock traits of European war pictures. The physiognomy of the work is realistic and Western.

I only saw it for an hour or so; but it needs to be seen many times—needs to be studied over and over again. I could look on such a work at brief intervals all my life without tiring. It is very tonic to me. Then it has an ethic purpose below all, as all great art must have.

The artist said the sending of the picture abroad, probably to London, had been talked of. I advised him if it went abroad to take it to Paris. I think they might appreciate it there—nay, they certainly would. Then I would like to show Messieur Crapeau that some things can be done in America as well as others.

Altogether, "Custer's Last Rally" is one of the very few attempts at deliberate artistic expression for our land and people, on a pretty ambitious standard and programme, that impressed me as filling the bill.[31]

How long the painting remained on display in New York City we do not know. The next record of its public exhibition comes from Louisville in December, 1881. Here again it met with great popular favor if we may judge by newspaper accounts. The *Courier-Journal* with a fulsome rhetoric that surpassed any of its competitors reports:

A poet of the brush who has walked out to meet the new sun of American art upon the upland lawn of the West has just come back with his inspiration to lay before the country. We refer to John Mulvany and his historical painting of "Custer's Last Rally," now on exhibition at the Polytechnic Library building. We do not care to know just how large the canvas is; it is enough to know that it is large enough to contain the genius of battle. We do not care to lessen the glory of the painter's work by applauding his art. Who would put a rule to the Raphaeles or measure the lines of Homer? These are not results of Art, they are the realizations of genius. And upon Mulvany's canvas one can see the poetical magnificence of that slaughter in the lonely valley of the Little Big Horn as it appeared to the mind of genius. It breathes the spirit of mortal hate, of heroic sullenness, and that matchless courage jeweling the sword of Custer, which even in its fall "Flashed out a blaze that charmed the world."[32]

"Custer's Last Rally" was next reported on exhibit in Chicago where it was shown during August and September of 1882. We could again quote at length from the Chicago press for this period, for the painting and John Mulvany were mentioned many times during the exhibition in Chicago.[33] Enough has already been quoted (the reactions in the Chicago press were similar to those already given) to establish the fact that the Mulvany picture had a wide popular appeal. Indeed, 13 years later the Chicago *Inter Ocean*, when Mulvany stopped off in the Windy City after a visit to the Pacific coast, commented "Mr. Mulvaney [*sic*] needs no introduction to a city in which his magnificent work, 'Custer's Last Charge,' was exhibited. . . ."[34]

One of the Chicago newspaper accounts of 1882, however, mentions another Western painting which should find its way into our record. Mulvany rented a studio while in Chicago and had on display there other pictures in addition to the "Last Rally." One was called "The Scouts of the Yellowstone." The painting depicted in the foreground two kneeling figures, rifles in hand with another scout in the background holding three horses. The figures were set on a hilly landscape with a river in the distance, the highest land represented in the picture just catching the reflection of the sun. The foreground figures were said to be the same as two of the soldiers portrayed in "Custer's Last Rally."[35]

"Custer's Last Rally" was likely exhibited in many other American cities than those already described. It was again on exhibit in Chicago in 1890 and it was probably sent abroad for display.[36] Doubtless on one of its trips to Chicago, the painting was lithographed in color. The Kansas State Historical Society fortunately possesses one of the lithographs which is on display in its museum. The lithographic print itself (without mat) measures 34⅜ inches by 18½ inches. The signature "Jno. Mulvany, 1881" appears (handprinted) in the lower right hand corner of the print and below [in type, also lower right] the name of the lithographer "D. C. Fabronius, Del.," and lower left [in type] "Jno. Mulvany, Pinxt." The copyrighted print (no date) was published by the Chicago Lithographic and Engraving Company. Comparison of this print with a photograph of the original painting in the writer's possession shows that, with minor changes, the figures and surroundings were faithfully copied. The lithograph is subdued in color but whether the original colors are correctly reproduced, I do not know as I have not seen the original painting. I also have no information on the number of copies of the lithograph that were published.

The history of "Custer's Last Rally" from 1890 until the early 1900's is obscure. At the latter date it seems to have been purchased by H. K. Heinz of Pittsburgh[37] and was, in 1940, still in the possession of the H. K. Heinz Company of Pittsburgh which kindly measured the painting.[38] Several years after Mr. Heinz purchased the original painting of "Custer's Last Rally" he commissioned Mulvany to paint a duplicate (for $200) and which Mr. Heinz is reported to have taken to London for exhibition.[39] Mulvany had a long career, but in his later years he seems to have depended upon portrait work for a living. Liquor, however, got the best of him, and in May, 1906, he ended his existence by plunging into the East river. "From a fine physique of a man," reports the New York *Times*, with "handsome features and a kindly countenance, he had sunk to a ragged derelict, uncertain of a night's lodging or a day's food."[40]

Despite Mulvany's tragic end and despite the fact that Mulvany today is virtually unknown, he played a real and not an unimportant part in past American life. The wide response and enthusiastic reception accorded "Custer's Last Rally" is proof enough of the statement above. But Mulvany has other claims to a place in American history. Samuel Isham, the historian of American art, points out that William M. Chase exerted a very considerable influence on American painting during the last quarter of the nineteenth century. Chase was greatly stimulated by examining the work of Mulvany. So much so that Chase went abroad and studied under Piloty and Wagner at Munich, both of whom had been Mulvany's teachers.[41]

More recently, G. V. Millet, an artist of Kansas City, has suggested that Remington, who as a very young man lived in Kansas City in the early 1880's, knew Mulvany and "Custer's Last Rally," and was influenced by these contacts.[42] It does not seem probable that Remington knew Mulvany personally, as Remington did not move to Kansas City until 1884 and Mulvany by that time had moved on.[43] Although Remington was probably not acquainted with Mulvany during his stay in Kansas City it is not at all unlikely that he had seen and marveled at "Custer's Last Rally" as did thousands of other Americans of that day.

It seems reasonable, too, that Mulvany's painting of the Custer tragedy suggested the theme to other artists. It was the first of some 20 attempts with which I am familiar and, being widely known, served as the incentive for subsequent artists, including possibly Cassilly Adams.

Cassilly Adams and Otto Becker

Our fund of information concerning the life and work of Cassilly Adams is not as extensive as is that concerning Mulvany. Adams is not listed in any of the biographical directories of artists but through fortunate contact with a daughter-in-law and a son of Adams, some fundamental information has been secured. Cassilly Adams, a veteran of the Civil War, was born at Zanesville, Ohio, July 18, 1843, the son of a lawyer, William Apthorp Adams, who traced his ancestry back to the John Adams family of Boston. The elder Adams was himself an amateur artist and he saw that his son Cassilly secured an art education at the Boston Academy of Arts. Later (about 1870) Cassilly Adams studied under Thomas S. Noble at the Cincinnati Art School.[44] Some time in the late 1870's, Adams moved to St. Louis where he secured work as an artist and an engraver and for a time had a studio with Matt Hastings, a well-known St. Louis artist.[45]

During the summer of 1940, the writer spent a week in St. Louis making the rounds of the libraries, art galleries, art dealers and art writers of the city newspapers but found no one who had any information concerning Cassilly Adams and his work. I was finally referred to William McCaughen, a retired art dealer of that city. McCaughen told me that he and Adams had belonged to the same social club in the early 1880's but even the information that he could supply me about Adams was meager. McCaughen recalled one other painting (in addition to "Custer's Last Fight") executed by Adams, "Moonlight on the Mississippi." McCaughen also stated that he had arranged the original sale of "Custer's Last Fight" to a saloon owner in St. Louis but could not recall the sale price. For the information available on the painting of this famous piece, we are dependent upon the memory of William Apthorp Adams, son of Cassilly Adams. The son states that he himself saw his father painting the picture in a studio at the corner of 5th and Olive Streets (St. Louis). Over a year was taken in the painting and the figures "were posed by Sioux Indians in their war paint and also by cavalrymen in the costumes of the period."[46] The painting was produced for two associate members of the St. Louis Art Club, C. J. Budd and William T. Richards, who promoted the painting for exhibition purposes, stimulated, no doubt by the success of the Mulvany picture. The date of the painting has not been fixed with certainty but it was made about 1885. The promoters then exhibited it about the country, according to Mr. Adams, in Cincinnati, Detroit, Indianapolis, and Chicago, "at 50¢ admission for adults and 25¢ for children under 15 years of age. Charles Fox, a brother of Della Fox, the actress, was the advance agent. My father traveled with the exhibition part of the time."[47] The exhibition of the painting did not realize the profits expected by the promoters and the sale of the picture was arranged by William McCaughen as noted above. The painting was on display in the saloon for several years and achieved a very considerable local reputation. Here a St. Louis reporter saw it and later commented:

> In 1888, when the writer of these lines was a reporter in St. Louis, the original painting [Custer's Last Fight] . . . hung on the wall of a saloon near Eighth and Olive streets—at the "postoffice corner." The place was a sort of headquarters for city and visiting politicians, and reporters assigned to political work were expected to visit it in their news-gathering rounds; but aside from this fact, there were many who visited the place especially to see the picture, which was a very large one, and was valued at $10,000.[48]

The owner of the saloon died and his heirs unsuccessfully attempted to conduct the business for a time but eventually creditors took over the place. Chief among the creditors was the brewing firm of Anheuser-Busch, Inc., of St. Louis, whose claim against the saloon is said to have amounted to $35,000. Important among the assets of the saloon was the painting of "Custer's Last Fight" which Anheuser-Busch acquired and which has doubtless given rise to the frequently-quoted statement that Adolphus Busch of the Anheuser-Busch company paid the above sum for the painting.[49]

Adams' painting of the Custer fight, like that of Mulvany's, was of large size. The painting proper measured 9'6" by 16'5".[50] There were, however, two end panels when the painting was first displayed. One depicted Custer as a small boy in his father's shop playing with toy soldiers. The other panel portrayed Custer dead on the field of battle and facing the setting sun.[51] The panels soon disappeared after it came into possession of Anheuser-Busch.

Upon acquiring the painting, Adolphus Busch had it lithographed in color and printed for distribution. The lithograph was copyrighted in 1896 so that evidently some time elapsed between the acquisition of the painting and its reproduction. In this interval (*i.e.*, some time between 1888 and 1896) it was presented to the 7th cavalry, then stationed at Fort Riley. It seems probable that the presentation was made about 1895, but from records available at present the exact date is uncertain.[52]

In May, 1895, headquarters of the 7th cavalry was transferred from Fort Riley to Fort Grant at the Carlos Indian Agency, Arizona,[53] and then in the next few years to still other forts. Apparently in these moves the painting was lost and not found again until 1925 when it was rediscovered in bad condition, in an attic of a storage building at Fort Bliss, Texas.[54]

There was some discussion on the part of army officials concerning the restoration and disposition of the painting and it was suggested that it be hung in the office of the chief of cavalry in Washington. Nothing was done and the painting again disappeared from view. In 1934, Col. John K. Herr, commanding the 7th cavalry, took his regiment on a 21-day practice march which included abandoned Fort Grant, Ariz., in its tour. In prowling through the abandoned camp "Custer's Last Fight" was again rediscovered and returned to Fort Bliss, headquarters of the Seventh cavalry.[55] The painting had been folded and torn and its image was badly cracked. Estimates on restoring the painting were secured by officers of the 7th cavalry but as they ranged from $5,000 to $12,000, too great a sum for regimental funds, no immediate steps were taken in its restoration. Finally it was restored by the art division of the W. P. A. in Boston and returned in 1938 to headquarters of the 7th cavalry at Fort Bliss.[56] The painting was then hung until 1946 in the officers' club building at Fort Bliss, Texas. On June 13, 1946, Associated Press dispatches reported that the painting was destroyed by fire.[57]

From this brief history of the painting it can be seen that it never achieved very wide recognition.[58] "Custer's Last Fight" owes its chief claim to fame, however, to the lithographic reproduction published by Anheuser-Busch.

A comparison of the original painting with the lithograph will show immediately that considerable differences exist between the two pictures. As a matter of fact, the lithograph is far more realistic in depicting the topography of the battlefield than is the Adams painting.[59] A number of the figures in the two pictures are similar but the most surprising difference is the fact that the two represent quite different viewpoints. In the lithograph, the background shows the valley of the Little Big Horn river and the river itself while in the painting the slope behind Custer rises abruptly in a steep hill. A comparison of the figure of Custer in the two pictures also shows marked difference. In the painting, Custer is lunging forward with his saber;[60] in the lithograph Custer is swinging the saber back over his shoulder in preparation for a desperate blow.

In considering these—and other—differences, two facts must be kept in mind: First, the lithograph was reproduced on stone by a second artist, and second, the painting was "restored," as pointed out previously, in 1938. The original printing of the lithograph[61] bears as part of the legend (in print) the words "Taken From the Artist's Sketches. The Original Painting by Cassily Adams." The original printings of the lithograph also have the signature (in script and on the print itself) "O. Becker" in the lower right-hand corner. Further, the original lithograph was prepared for publication by the Milwaukee Lithographic and Engraving Company (Milwaukee, Wis.) as is likewise stated in type as part of the legend. A query directed to the Milwaukee Public Library brought the interesting response that Otto Becker, a lithographer by trade, was so listed in the city directories of Milwaukee for the years 1890–1896, inclusive.[62]

Following this lead further, correspondence was established with Miss Blanche Becker of Milwaukee, daughter of Otto Becker. Miss Becker wrote at length concerning the work of her father who was foreman of the art department of the Milwaukee Lithographic and Engraving Company. A letter written by her father in 1933 states "I painted Custer's Last Stand in 1895. The original painting is still in my possession, but unfortunately, I was forced to cut it into pieces so that a number of artists could work on it at the same time, making the color plates."[63] The oil painting was subsequently patched together and restored by Mr. Becker and it was then acquired by Anheuser-Busch. The restored painting measures 24″ by 40″ and is now on display at the offices of Anheuser-Busch in St. Louis.[64] Becker, a one-time resident of St. Louis, had become acquainted with Adolphus Busch and after the acquisition of the Adams painting by Busch, plans were made to lithograph the painting. If we can believe the legend on the original painting "after the artist's sketches," Busch presented several sketches of Adams' work to Becker and Becker would therefore have the right of selecting and making his own composition.[65]

Part of the differences between the two pictures can thus be satisfactorily accounted for. There is, however, the added possibility that in the restoration of the Adams painting in 1938, still other differences were introduced. The painting, after its several discoveries, was admittedly in very bad condition and, since no one was available who knew the original painting,[66] no guide would be available for the restorers. A bad stain or loss of considerable pigment in the background, for example, could be covered by the hill apparent in the painting. Its inclusion would have saved many hours of tedious toil in painting in again (if originally present) the very considerable detail that appears in the background of the lithograph.[67]

It seems probable in considering all of these facts that the differences between painting and lithograph are due to original differences produced in the lithography and to subsequent differences arising in the restoration.

Since the lithograph, however, is the picture that is better known, the differences noted above, after all, are of minor importance. Some 150,000 copies of the large print have been distributed by Anheuser-Busch since the lithograph was first published in 1896, and in 1942, copies were being mailed out to servicemen and others at the rate of 2,000 a month.[68] With this wide distribution of the lithograph it is probably safe to say that few dealers in the products of Anheuser-Busch have been without a copy of the lithograph and doubtless most of them have displayed the print. Some thirst emporiums may have had their original copies on display for the fifty years of the print's existence; especially if they faithfully followed the instructions reportedly sent out with early copies of the lithograph, "Keep this picture under fly-netting in the summer time and it will remain bright for many years."

How many have seen and viewed the lithograph is, of course, any man's guess. An examination, however, will soon show that it is no work of art—if by work of art we mean an object of beauty. But it is indeed a picture that tells a powerful, if melodramatic and horrendous, tale. Be it recalled, however, that it is no more melodramatic or horrendous, however, than was the event itself. Troopers are being brained, scalped, stripped; white men, Indians and horses are dying by the dozens; Custer with flowing red tie[69] and long ringlets is about to deal a terrible saber blow to an advancing Indian who in turn is shot by a dying trooper; and hundreds of Indians are pictured or suggested in the background.[70]

A careful survey of the lithograph is enough to give a sensitive soul a nightmare for a week. No doubt many a well meaning imbiber who has tarried too long with his foot on the rail and his eye on the picture, has cast hurried and apprehensive glances over his shoulder when a sudden yell from a passing newsboy brought him too swiftly back to the day's realities. The writer has one of these lithographs in his back laboratory which is occasionally shown to students, friends, and fellow university professors. The reaction of those who have never seen the picture before is always interesting to observe. Incredulous first glances are always followed by study of all the gory details. "Holy H. Smoke! Was it as bad as that?," was the comment of one university professor as he instinctively rubbed his bald pate. If not the best liked of all American pictures, it doubtless has been the most extensively examined and discussed of any.

Other events have also added to the fame of this remarkable picture. For example, not long after first publication, Adolphus Busch presented a copy of the lithograph to Gov. E. N. Morrill of Kansas. Morrill, who served as governor from 1895 to 1897, upon retiring from office gave the picture to the State Historical Society. Just when it was put on display in that institution there is apparently no definite record, but from the activities of the late Carrie Nation in the early 1900's, there arose a considerable interest because the name of the brewer appeared in large letters beneath the lithographic print of "Custer's Last Fight." The prohibitionists of the state began to sit up and take notice when one of their number called attention to the fact that a beer advertisement was appearing in one of the state's public buildings. The notice became notoriety when on January 9, 1904, Blanche Boies, one of Carrie Nation's faithful followers, entered the State Historical Museum, then in the state house, with an axe in her hand and the light of grim determination in her eye. She advanced on the offensive advertisement of

Messrs. Anheuser and Busch and crashed her axe through the picture. Secretary Martin of the Historical Society hastily called the police who politely escorted Blanche to the city jail where she languished until bailed out by her friends. The Topeka papers gave Blanche a very handsome writeup for her efforts and the press of the state followed suit. One account called attention to the fact, however, that such excursions were nothing unusual for this disciple of Carrie Nation, for she "had wielded her hatchet with destructive effect on numerous occasions in Topeka's illicit pubs."[71]

Blanche's well-intended efforts in protecting the morals of Kansas citizens were, alas, in vain. Some one immediately wired Anheuser-Busch for a new copy of "Custer's Last Fight" and the brewers responded promptly with the copy which now hangs in one of the hallways of the State Historical Society's building. Mr. Martin, however, did have the foresight to opaque out the names of the donors which appear on the legend beneath the picture.

Work of Other Artists

The pictures of Mulvany and Adams have, as our account has shown, attracted wide interest for more than 65 years. Their efforts to recall the Custer tragedy, however, have not been the only ones. Because of the universal interest in this event it seems worth while to make a list of other pictures of Custer's Last Stand. The list as presented below is probably not complete, as new ones—or at least new to the writer— are still being found. Many well-known as well as obscure artists have attempted to portray the event. In the list which follows, some comment on the pictures has been made. Biographical information, when available, also has been included for the lesser known artists. Information about the better known artists can be secured from such useful handbooks as D. T. Mallett's *Index of Artists* (New York, 1935) and *Supplement to Mallett's Index of Artists* (New York, 1940). The list of other Custer pictures follows:

1881. In 1881, Dr. Charles E. McChesney, an army surgeon stationed at the Cheyenne River Agency, South Dakota, secured an account of the Custer battle from Red-Horse, a Sioux chief who took part in the battle. In addition to the narrative, Red-Horse prepared a number of pictographs, many in color, on sheets of manila paper about 24 by 26 inches in size. Although most primitive in design and execution, one can still visualize details of dress, action and incident from the pictographs. Nine of the sheets are reproduced in the *Tenth Annual Report of the Bureau of Ethnology.*[72]

1881. "Death of General Custer," tinted woodcut, unsigned; a crude illustration in J. W. Buel's *Heroes of the Plains* (New York, 1882).

1883. "Custer's Last Fight on the Little Big Horn," a full-page illustration in the 1883 edition of Custer's *Wild Life on the Plains*, signed "Barnsley, del." The illustrations in this book are wood cuts and are for the most part very crudely done.[73]

1884. "Custer's Last Charge," a painting (present location unknown) about four by seven feet in size by John Elder of Richmond, Va. No reproductions are known to the writer.[74]

1888. "Cyclorama of Gen. Custer's Last Fight" painted by E. Pierpont and staff of New York. The cyclorama, one of the popular predecessors of the motion picture in the history of American amusements, depicted many scenes and events of historical interest and it is not surprising that the Custer tragedy found expression in this form of art. The Custer cyclorama was on display in Boston early in 1889, replacing the famous cyclorama of the Battle of Gettysburg. Pierpont, the "executive artist" of the Custer piece, is said to have visited the battlefield on the Little Big Horn before work was begun, and secured photographs, interviewed some of Reno's survivors, and studied official reports. On Pierpont's staff were M. M. Salvador-Mege, Ernest Gros and Emile Merlot who painted the landscape of the cyclorama; the foreground figures on the huge painting were the work of Chas. A. Corwin, Theo. Wendall, and G. A. Travers; E. J. Austin was responsible for many of the distant figures and the Indian village. A number of these artists are said to have worked on the Gettysburg cyclorama as well.[75] There is no record of the fate of this huge canvas.

1889. "The Last Stand," by Rufus Zogbaum, a popular illustrator for *Harper's Weekly* and *Harper's Magazine*. The illustration, of no great merit, shows Custer as the central figure.[76]

1890. "Custer's Last Stand," Frederic Remington. A small pen and ink drawing made for Mrs. Custer.[77] It should be noted that Remington later produced other pictures which were titled "The Last Stand," none of which had reference to the Custer battle. These illustrations, of course, may have been inspired by the Custer tragedy. One depicts a group of dismounted troopers and scouts making their stand at the top of a rocky hill. The main figures are an army officer (with mustache) and a scout.[78] Remington's second "Last Stand" shows a group of troopers on the plains still holding off the attacking Indians.[79]

1891. "Custer's Last Battle," signed only "Williams." This picture, a crude wood cut, will be found in the *Life of Sitting Bull*, by W. Fletcher Johnson.[80]

1893. "Custer's Last Stand," by Edgar S. Paxson [see page 552]. A canvas measuring approximately 5 by 9 feet, now displayed in the entrance of the Natural Science Hall, Montana State University, Missoula. Begun in the early 1890's, it was on display at the Chicago World's Fair of 1893 but it was not brought to its present state for nearly 20 years after Mr. Paxson first began work on it. The painting contains the portraits of 36 members of Custer's command which Paxson secured from photographs. It is one of the most widely known of the Custer pictures.[81]

1897. "We Circled All Round Him," Ernest L. Blumenschein, a full-page decorative illustration showing Custer in the faint background mounted on a horse.[82]

1899. "Gen. Custer's Last Battle," copyright by H. R. Locke. No further information available and it is not even certain from the legend that Locke was the artist.[83]

1902. "Custer's Fight—Little Big Horn River," by Edgar Cameron. One of four paintings prepared by Mr. Cameron for the St. Louis *Globe-Democrat*. The others in the series were "The Discovery of Pike's Peak," "The Burning of Fort Madison" and "The Founding of St. Louis." The Custer piece was reproduced as a color supplement to the *Globe-Democrat* for May 4, 1902. I have been unable to trace the original painting.[84]

1903. "Custer's Last Stand," Charles M. Russell. Reproduced in *Outing*, showing dead and dying troopers, the dim figure of Custer in the center.[85] A color reproduction of another Russell painting, "The Custer Fight" [see page 552], was published in *Scribner's Magazine*.[86] Indians only are distinctly visible, the troopers on the hill being nearly obscured by dust.

1908. "The Custer Battlefield," J. H. Sharp. One of 52 paintings exhibited by Mr. Sharp in St. Louis in 1908. Reproductions and the location of the original painting are unknown to the writer.[87]

1915. "Custer's Last Stand," by W. H. Dunton, reproduced in *The Mentor*. Present location of the painting unknown.[88]

1923. "Custer's Last Stand," by Theodore B. Pitman of Cambridge, Mass. The painting, 25 × 37 inches, was produced originally for illustration in *The Frontier Trail*, by Homer W. Wheeler.[89] It was also reproduced in color as the jacket cover of Stanley Vestal's *Sitting Bull*.[90] The original painting now hangs in Trumbell's "Country Store" in Concord, Mass.[91]

1926. "General Custer's Lekte Schact," by Elk Eber. This painting is reproduced in black and white on the cover of the current descriptive pamphlet of the Custer Battlefield National Cemetery, Montana.[92] The original painting is (or was) in the famous Indian collections of the Karl May Museum in Dresden, Germany. Elk Eber was the son of Herr Eber, a German, and Little Elk, a Sioux woman, who as a young girl witnessed part of the Custer battle. Several years later Little Elk joined Buffalo Bill's Wild West Show and went to Europe where she met and married Herr Eber. Elk Eber's painting is based on his mother's recollections and stories of the Custer battle. Eber himself was recently (February, 1944) reported deceased.[93]

1934. "Custer's Last Stand," a miniature group by Dwight Franklin. A photograph of the group is reproduced in Van de Water's *Glory Hunter*.[94] The original clay figures of the miniature are about a foot high and the group is still owned by the artist who plans to complete the piece and eventually to sell it to a museum.[95] Mr. Franklin states that he obtained much information for the group by interviewing Reno's chief of scouts.

1939. "Custer's Last Fight," by W. R. Leigh, the well-known artist. The original painting, which measures 6½ feet by 10½ feet, is now in the possession of the Woolaroc Museum, Frank Phillips' ranch, Bartlesville, Okla.[96] In the writer's judgment, it is the most satisfactory picture of all the Custer battle scenes. The beautifully modeled foreground figures of Indian warriors and horses are shown realistically, and the imaginative effect in portraying Custer and his command dimmed by the clouds of battle dust is in keeping with the fact that many of the realities of the Custer battle are obscured by the passage of years and the battle of words since 1876.[97]

Notes

1. Note that portraits have not been included in the above list. If such pictures were included, mention should be made of Whistler's "Mother" and Gilbert Stuart's "Washington." The story of Willard's "Spirit of '76" will be found in an interesting privately printed item of Americana by Henry Kelsey Devereux, *The Spirit of '76* (Cleveland, 1926). I mention this fact because "The Spirit of '76" is probably the closest competitor for the author's candidates of popular favor, yet it is not mentioned in such histories of American art as Samuel Isham's *The History of American Painting* (New York: Macmillan Co., 1927), nor in Eugen Neuhaus, *The History and Ideals of American Art* (Stanford: Stanford University Press, 1931). Neuhaus, however, does point out (143) that when Hovenden's "Breaking Home Ties" was exhibited at the great Chicago Fair of 1893 "the carpet in front of it had to be replaced many times; it was easily the most popular picture of that period." Many years later the same picture was exhibited in San Francisco and St. Louis and was apparently as popular as ever.

The "September Morn" of Chabas attracted tremendous attention, partly because of the activities of Anthony Comstock, when it was first exhibited in this country in 1913 as can be seen by examining the *New York Times Index for 1913*. The widespread attention was but temporary, however, for "September Morn" is remembered now only by oldsters who were impressionable youths at the time of its first appearance. The other paintings listed above are such well-known favorites that further comment seems unnecessary.

2. To the writer's mind, the most satisfactory biography of Custer is Frederic F. Van de Water's *Glory-Hunter: A Life of General Custer* (Indianapolis: Bobbs-Merrill Co., 1934). No sooner had it appeared, however, than it was the subject of violent and bitter criticism. No less a person than Gen. Hugh Johnson, of N. R. A. fame, despite a very obvious lack of knowledge, launched an attack on the book. "General Johnson Rides to the Defense," *Today* (December 29, 1934), 16; see also the New York *Times*, December 27, 1934, p. 19, col. 6; December 28, 1934, p. 20, col. 4 (editorial); January 4, 1935, p. 20, col. 6. That the subject of Custer and the battle of the Little Big Horn is one of perennial interest is shown by the fact that in the last 25 years the index of the New York *Times* reveals that discussions, notices, let-

ters, articles, etc., have appeared over 40 times. The most extensive bibliography of Custer material will be found as an appendix to Fred Dustin's *The Custer Tragedy: Events Leading up to and following the Little Big Horn Campaign of 1876* (Ann Arbor: Edwards Brothers, 1939). Mr. Dustin lists nearly 300 items in his bibliography which scarcely touch the truly voluminous mass of newspaper material on Custer which has accumulated since 1876. *The Custer Tragedy* bears evidence of painstaking and exhaustive work and is one of the most valuable sources of information on the battle of the Little Big Horn available to the student. Other Custer items that have come to the writer's attention since the publication of the Dustin book are: Charles J. Brill, *Conquest of the Southern Plains: Uncensored Narrative of the Battle of the Washita and Custer's Southern Campaign* (Oklahoma City: Golden Saga Publishers, 1938), a severe criticism of Custer's Washita campaign; Edward S. Luce, *Keogh, Comanche, and Custer* (St. Louis: John S. Swift Co., 1939); Katherine Gibson Fougera, *With Custer's Cavalry* (Caldwell, Idaho: Caxton Printers, 1940); Charles Kuhlman, *Gen. George A. Custer—* also called *Custer and the Gall Saga* (Billings, Mont.: Privately published, 1940), by a real student of Custer's career; F. W. Benteen, *The Custer Fight* (Hollywood, Calif., 1940), privately published by E. A. Brininstool, another Custer student; William Alexander Graham, *The Story of the Little Big Horn*, 2d ed. (Harrisburg, Pa.:

Military Service Publishing Co., 1941), a standard work the first edition of which was published in 1926; Albert Britt, "Custer's Last Fight," *Pacific Historical Review* 13 (March 1944): 12–20, undocumented; Fred Dustin, "George Armstrong Custer," *Michigan History Magazine* 30 (April–June 1946): 227–54, a biographical review.

3. See the classification of pictures suggested in *Kansas Historical Quarterly* 14 (February 1946): 2. Pictures of the Custer battle would be classed in the second and fourth groups there given.

4. It is worth a few moments of anyone's time to listen to the critical comments and the discussion of detail not immediately apparent, which result as groups of observers, both young and old, cluster around Adams' and Becker's "Custer's Last Rally."

5. For those who wish, examination of the battlefield itself would be in order. According to Dustin, *The Custer Tragedy*, xi, some changes in the course of the Little Big Horn river have occurred since 1876 but the general features of the landscape, of course, remain the same.

6. Ibid., xiv.

7. *Tepee Book* (June 1916), 50.

8. New York *Times*, June 19, 1927, p. 13, col. 2.

9. The absurd pictorial climax of the Warner Brothers picture of 1941, *They Died with Their Boots On*, shows Custer, the final survivor, surrounded by a group of prostrate soldiers arrayed in new and scarcely wrinkled uniforms; see *Life* (December 8, 1941), 75–78.

10. Dustin, *The Custer Tragedy*, 185; see also page 184. The monument mentioned by Dustin is one erected on the summit of the ridge overlooking the valley of the Little Big Horn river and is part of the Custer Battlefield National Cemetery, Crow Agency, Montana. On the monument are inscribed the names of those who fell during the battle. For the topography of the battle site, see the reproduction of the Morrow photograph of 1877 opposite page 376. This photograph, by S. J. Morrow of Yankton, Dakota territory, is one of a group of 12 photographs made by Morrow, at the interment of the Custer soldiers in June and July, 1877. See Robert Taft, *Photography and the American Scene* (New York: Macmillan Co., 1938), 307. The burial party which Morrow accompanied consisted of Company I of the 7th cavalry under the command of Capt. H. J. Nowlan. Captain Nowlan's command reached the military cantonment on the Tongue river on the way to the Custer battlefield on June 20, 1877, and after completing the burial returned to the cantonment on July 13, 1877. 45th Cong., 2d sess., 1877, H. Ex. Doc. 1, pt. 2, vol. 1, pp. 540, 544, 545. Further description of the burial party of 1877 will be found in Joseph Mills Hanson, *The Conquest of the Missouri* (Chicago: A. C. McClurg, 1909), chap. 44.

11. Thomas B. Marquis, *A Warrior Who Fought Custer* (Minneapolis: Midwest Co., 1931). Dr. Marquis has made a contribution of first rate importance to Custer literature in recording in simple language the story of Wooden Leg. Chapters 8, 9, and 10 are devoted to the battle of the Little Big Horn.

12. Ibid., 245.

13. Ibid., 219.

14. Ibid., 224, 230, 243.

15. Ibid., 229–31.

16. Ibid., 274. Marquis also attributed the low losses among the Indians to extensive suicide among the troops.

17. Dustin, *The Custer Tragedy*, 184.

18. Hamlin Garland, "General Custer's Last Fight As Seen by Two Moon," *McClure's Magazine* 11 (September 1898): 443–48.

19. Ibid., 448.

20. Dustin, *The Custer Tragedy*, 225.

21. Charles A. Eastman, "Rain-in-the-Face: The Story of a Sioux Warrior," *Outlook* 84 (October 27, 1906): 507–12. Rain-in-the-Face also stated that Custer fought with "a big knife [saber]." Two Moon (Garland, "Custer's Last Fight") reported a trooper (possibly a scout) who "fought hard with a big knife." These statements, as against the statement of Dustin that no sabers were used, are difficult to reconcile and indicate some of the difficulties in obtaining specific facts with certainty at this late date. It should, of course, be noted, that the statements of Two Moon and Rain-in-the-Face are recollections made many years after the battle of 1876.

22. Dustin, *The Custer Tragedy*, 188; Marquis, *A Warrior*, chap. 10; Eastman, "Rain-in-the-Face."

23. For the reader who wishes to review briefly the main features of the battle of the Little Big Horn the following summary may be useful:

During the summer of 1876, a vigorous and three-pronged campaign was planned by the U.S. army in an attempt to force the Plains Indians back to their reservations. One prong, led by Gen. A. H. Terry, came into present Montana from the east and reached the mouth of the Tongue river, where it empties into the Yellowstone river, early in June, 1876. Here, after some delay, the Seventh cavalry under Lieutenant Colonel Custer (Col. S. D. Sturgis, the commanding officer of the Seventh, was on detached duty) was sent south by Terry to locate any concentrations of hostile tribes supposed to be in the open country of southeastern Montana. It was this move that led to the fateful engagement.

About 12 or 15 miles from the scene of battle General Custer divided his command, the 7th cavalry, into four battalions, two of which were commanded by Custer personally, another was commanded by Major Reno and the fourth by Captain Benteen. At the time the division was made, the 7th cavalry was on a small tributary of the Little Big Horn. Captain Benteen's battalion was detached and ordered to move to the left and to scout and engage any hostiles encountered. Custer's and Reno's battalions proceeded down the tributary toward the Little Big Horn but on its opposite sides. Upon nearing the Little Big Horn, Reno received orders from Custer to advance across that stream and attack the Indians who were now believed to be close at hand in force. Custer turned to the right before reaching the Little Big Horn

and soon found himself cut off from Reno and Benteen and overwhelmed by the Indians in the hills overlooking the river.

Reno, meanwhile, had encountered, after making contact with the Indians, such stiff resistance that he fell back to the river and was finally forced to reford it, taking refuge in the high bluffs above the river where he was joined by Benteen's command. Here the combined battalions were able to hold the Indians at bay for two days until relieved by General Terry and the infantry under his command. Reno's and Benteen's losses amounted to nearly 50 killed and a somewhat larger number wounded. "The defense of the position on the hill [by Reno and Benteen]," reads the official report of the court of inquiry, "was a heroic one against fearful odds."

This brief outline of the action of the 7th cavalry on July 25–27, 1876, is based on "General Orders No. 17," March 11, 1879, a report of the court of inquiry requested by Major Reno. It will be found quoted in Dustin, *The Custer Tragedy*, 210. Casualties of the 7th cavalry during the above days will be found in appendixes 2 and 3 of ibid., 225–30. The dead of Custer's immediate command totaled about 220. Ibid., 184.

Despite Reno's and Benteen's *successful* defensive stand against the overwhelming numbers of the Indians, the heroic action "against fearful odds" has scarcely attracted the attention of any artist.

24. This information on Mulvany's early life comes from obituaries in the

New York *Sun*, May 23, 1906, p. 3, col. 1; New York *Times*, May 23, 1906, p. 9; New York *Tribune*, May 23, 1906, p. 6, col. 6, and the *American Art Annual* 6 (1907–8): 112. The last account states that he was born about 1842 but does not state the source of its information. None of the above accounts specifically states that Mulvany was *born* in Ireland but in an eight-page pamphlet, *Press Comments on John Mulvany's Painting of Custer's Last Rally* (no date, but published about 1882), there is a brief biographical sketch which doubtless was prepared by Mulvany himself and which states that he was "an Irishman by birth."

25. Chicago *Times*, August 13, 1882, supplement, p. 8, col. 8, and the *Art Journal* 2 (1876): 159. The *Times* account above states that "The Trial of a Horse Thief" was "now the property of a Boston gentleman." For reference to Mulvany in St. Louis, see note 41.

26. Kansas City (Mo.) *Daily Journal*, March 2, 1881, p. 5, col. 1. This account is a lengthy description of Mulvany's newly-completed painting as well as an interview with the artist. It is of major importance in any estimate of Mulvany's painting.

27. Kansas City (Mo.) *Times*, March 17, 1881, p. 8, col. 3; March 19, 1881, p. 5, col. 3. Note that the Kansas City *Journal* account had appeared before the reporters as a group viewed the painting. Evidently it was the *Journal* description that whetted their appetites for they addressed a public letter to Mulvany requesting the privilege of seeing the painting.

28. Kansas City *Daily Journal*, March 2, 1881, p. 5, col. 1.

29. Ibid.

30. Boston *Evening Transcript*, June 20, 1881, p. 6, cols. 3, 4. Part of the same account was reprinted (but credited to the Boston *Advertiser*) in the Kansas City *Sunday Times*, June 26, 1881, p. 5, col. 2. I am indebted to the reference department of the Boston Public Library for verifying the location of the Boston *Transcript* account. The account is given in *Press Comments on John Mulvany's Painting*, where it is credited to the *Transcript* of "June 21st, 1881." The pamphlet credits the account to "Ed. Clements."

31. New York *Tribune*, August 15, 1881, p. 5, col. 5. Whitman reprinted this account in his *Specimen Days*, first published in 1883; see Walt Whitman, *Complete Prose Works* (Philadelphia: D. McKay, 1897), 186.

32. Quoted in *Press Comments on John Mulvany's Painting* and credited to "Mr. Allison." The pamphlet dates the account "December 18, 1882." Miss Edna J. Grauman of the reference department, Louisville Free Public Library, has very kindly made an examination of the Louisville newspapers of the above date but could find no reference to the Mulvany picture. An examination of the Louisville *Commercial* for December 18, 1881, p. 2, described the painting and the Louisville *Courier-Journal* for December 18, 1881, p. 4, also had mention of the painting as follows:

CUSTER'S LAST RALLY

This grand work of art is draw-

ing crowds daily to the Polytechnic
Society. At the special request of
nearly all who see it season tickets
have been issued at fifty cents each,
entitling the holder to admission at
all times, visitors on entering the
room stand in awe and admiration
for hours in some instances. It is
truly the most thrilling and realistic
picture ever brought to this city. The
exhibition room adjoins the Polytechnic Library, entrance on the
north side.

Miss Grauman also identified "Mr.
Allison" as Young E. Allison, prominent Louisville writer and editor.

33. Mention and extensive discussion
appear in Chicago *Times*, August 6,
1882, supplement, p. 5, col. 8; August
13, 1882, supplement, p. 8, col. 8;
August 20, 1882, p. 5, col. 8; August 27,
1882, supplement, p. 6, col. 8, and
Chicago *Tribune*, August 13, 1882,
p. 7, col. 7. I am greatly indebted to
Miss Frances Gazda of the Newberry
library, Chicago, for the above extensive array of information. Miss Gazda
writes me that the last mention of
display of the painting is reported on
September 9, 1882. In addition to the
newspaper mention of the painting
given above, *Press Comments on John
Mulvany's Painting* quotes from the
Chicago *Weekly Magazine*, the Chicago
Citizen, and still another account (not
located) from the Chicago *Times*.

34. Chicago *Inter Ocean*, November 24, 1895, p. 35, col. 3, a six-
paragraph account of Mulvany and
his work.

35. Chicago *Times*, August 27, 1882,
supplement, p. 6, col. 8. The *Times*
for August 13, 1882, supplement, p. 8,
col. 8, mentions a painting "On the
Alert," but whether it is a Western
picture is uncertain.

36. Ibid., August 27, 1882, supplement, p. 6, col. 8, reports that "it will
be returned to New York and thence
go to Paris for reproduction in photo-
gravure"; see also Whitman's comment
quoted earlier in this article. Mention
of the exhibition of the painting in Chicago in 1890 is found in the concluding
paragraph of the following account
from the Denver *Republican*, September 23, 1890, p. 8, col. 2, which is
reprinted in full as it gives considerable
additional information on Mulvany's
celebrity as an artist. I am indebted
to Miss Ina T. Aulls, of the Western
History department, Denver Public
Library, for the account:

Mr. John Mulvaney [*sic*], the
artist who painted the celebrated
picture of Custer's rally in the fatal
fight of the Big Horn, is in Denver with friends. He arrived last
Saturday night. For several weeks
past he has been visiting his brother
in Salida. He has been sketching
all through the mountains during
the past summer—up the Shavano
range, along the line of the Colorado
Midland and in the beautiful stretch
of country about Marshall pass.
His sketches, most of them, were
done in colors, and many of them
are paintings in themselves. From
these rough and sketchy studies he

proposes soon to give to the public some oil-paintings, on an elaborate scale, of the picturesque scenery of the Rockies.

He has with him a new painting which he has just finished. It is entitled "McPherson and Revenge." It is an incident from the battles about Atlanta. The most prominent figure in it is General John A. Logan. He is riding down the front of the rifle-pits and the improvised breastworks. He is materializing out of a white cloud of smoke that the guns of both sides have sent rolling across the field of battle. His horse is as black as night; as black as his own tossed hair. He seems a genius or a demon of battle. The soldiers have sprung out [of] the breastworks. They are waving their hats in the air, shouting and yelling their enthusiasm for that splendid leader, who is sweeping down their hue. The picture is full of color; full of action, and the portrait of Logan is a telling likeness. The painting is 12 × 6 feet in dimensions, and is framed in an elegant gilt frame, twelve inches broad. The picture was only finished recently. It was never exhibited before in its finished form. It was on exhibition at the national convention which nominated Harrison for president. Some of the speakers of that memorable convention referred to it. It was only an earnest then of what it would be.

Mr. Mulvaney still has "Custer's Last Rally" in his possession. It made his fame. The picture is now in Chicago on exhibition. It has made a small fortune for its painter.

37. New York *Times*, May 23, 1906, p. 9.

38. Information to the writer from A. L. Schiel, secretary to Howard Heinz, president, in letters dated September 20, September 30, and October 17, 1940. In his last letter Mr. Schiel wrote that the painting was in storage but it was brought out and measured for me. The exact dimensions given by Mr. Schiel were 236 inches by 131 inches.

39. This fact is mentioned in the obituaries of Mulvany appearing both in the New York *Times*, May 23, 1906, p. 9, and in the New York *Sun*, May 23, 1906, p. 3, col. 1.

40. See note 24. Since no other adequate biographical sketch of Mulvany has apparently been attempted, a listing of his paintings as they have been found in my newspaper search seems to be in order. Mulvany's paintings of Western interest have already been described in the text and will not be repeated here. The other titles found include "Love's Mirror" or "Venus at the Bath," "The Old Professor" (Kansas City *Times*, March 19, 1881, p. 5, col. 3; March 31, 1884, p. 8, col. 4; March 1, 1885, p. 2, cols. 1, 2; November 16, 1885, p. 5, col. 2; evidently the latter was quite a remarkable picture for I have seen other favorable comments on it); "A Discussion of the Tariff Question" (Chicago *Times*, August 27, 1882, supplement, p. 6, col. 8, two Southerners and a Negro servant in the living

room of one of the heated debaters); "Sheridan's Ride from Winchester," "Sunrise on Killarney," "Sunrise on the Rocky Mountains" (Chicago *Inter Ocean*, November 24, 1895, p. 35, col. 3); "The Striker" (coal miner), "The Anarchist" (a group of a half dozen men cutting cards to see who would commit murder), "An Incident of the Boer War," "Major Dunne of Chicago" (portrait), "Henry Watterson of Louisville" (portrait), "John C. Breckenridge" (portrait), paid for by Kentucky legislature (New York *Times*, May 23, 1906, p. 9); "The Battle of Aughrin," "The Battle of Atlanta" (New York *Sun*, May 23, 1906, p. 3, col. 1). There were probably many others. The New York *Times* cited above states, "He painted many other Western pictures which he sold for trifling sums."

41. Isham, *American Painting*, 382, 383; Katharine Metcalf Roof, *The Life and Art of William Merritt Chase* (New York: C. Scribner's Sons, 1917), 25. It is apparent that Isham and Roof knew little about Mulvany. Roof even spells the name "Mulvaney" and Isham repeats the error. It should be pointed out that the work of Mulvany seen by Chase did not include "Custer's Last Rally." According to Roof, Chase saw Mulvany's work in St. Louis about 1871 or 1872. If this date is correct, it would suggest that Mulvany lived in St. Louis for a time. Mulvany was evidently a restless spirit, never satisfied for long in one place. The account of Clements in the Boston *Transcript* of 1881 (see note 30) also states that not only was

Mulvany responsible for Chase's trip to Munich but that he also furnished the incentive that sent Frank Duveneck, another important leader in American art, to Munich.

42. Kansas City *Star*, May 3, 1925, magazine section, p. 16.

43. The proprietor of the St. James Hotel of Kansas City brought suit in 1884 against Mulvany to recover judgment for $450, allegedly due "in the shape of borrowed money and an unpaid board bill of four years' standing." Mulvany was reported as being "now in Detroit." Kansas City *Times*, March 31, 1884, p. 8, col. 4. Several of Mulvany's paintings were seized in the court action and sold by the sheriff under the execution to satisfy the judgment obtained by the hotel proprietor. Ibid., March 1, 1885, p. 2, cols. 1, 2.

44. This biographical information was obtained from Mrs. C. C. Adams of Washington, D.C., and William Apthorp Adams of Hammersley's Fork, Pa., a son of Cassilly Adams. Mrs. Adams wrote me that Cassilly Adams' birth date and Civil War record were obtained from the files of the pension office in Washington. Cassilly Adams served as ensign on the U.S.S. *Osage* and was wounded at the battle of Vicksburg.

45. Adams is listed in the St. Louis city directories from 1879 to 1884 at various addresses: sometimes as an artist and sometimes as an engraver. W. A. Adams wrote me that his father lived in St. Louis from 1878 to 1885 and then moved to Cincinnati. Cas-

silly Adams died at Trader's Point (near Indianapolis), Ind., on May 8, 1921. (See death notices of Adams in Indianapolis *News*, May 9, 1921, p. 24, col. 1, and Indianapolis *Star*, May 9, 1921, p. 13, col. 8. I am indebted to the reference department of the Indianapolis Public Library for locating these notices.) Francis O. Healey, a retired art dealer of St. Louis, wrote me under date of October 15, 1940, that Adams and Hastings had a studio together.

46. Letters to the writer, August 1946.

47. Letter to the writer, August 12, 1946. Cassilly Adams, according to his son, also painted many other Western pictures including Indians, buffalo hunting, and other game-shooting scenes. The illustrations for Col. Frank Triplett's *Conquering the Wilderness* (New York and St. Louis: N. D. Thompson and Co., 1883) were drawn in part *on wood* by Cassilly Adams according to W. A. Adams, although they are not so credited in the book itself. The title page of this book credits the *original* illustrations to "Nast, Darley and other eminent artists." As a matter of fact many of the illustrations have been borrowed from other books without the least attempt on the publisher's part to give due credit.

48. Kansas City *Gazette*, August 11, 1903, p. 2, col. 1. In a letter to the writer dated October 3, 1940, Maj. E. C. Johnston, then adjutant of the 7th cavalry, also stated (from the records of the 7th cavalry) that the painting was acquired by a saloon-

keeper. The owner of the saloon was identified as one John Ferber but examination of the city directories of St. Louis for the years 1885–1892 failed to show any listing of Ferber's name. However, in the St. Louis city directories for the years 1885 through 1888, the entry "Furber, John G., saloon, 724 [or 726] Olive" was found for me by the reference department of the St. Louis Public Library. A more positive connection between Furber and the Adams painting is found by the fact that the Library of Congress possesses a four-page pamphlet *Custer's Last Fight* which bears a copyright stamp dated "Apr. 26, 1886," the copyright being issued to John G. Furber, St. Louis. Apparently the pamphlet was published by Furber to accompany copyright of the painting and to use in exhibitions of the painting. The subtitle of the pamphlet reads "Painted by Cassilly Adams—Representing the Last Grand Indian battle that will be fought on this Continent. 12 feet high by 32 feet long, valued at $50,000." The pamphlet is essentially a description of the Custer battle and has little to say about the painting itself.

49. The statement concerning the supposed "cost" of the painting occurs frequently in newspaper comments on the Adams painting (sometimes it is given as $35,000, sometimes as $30,000). The most recent newspaper statement to this effect with which the author is familiar will be found in the Kansas City *Times*, June 14, 1946, p. 1, col. 2. Note that the account

cited above in the Kansas City *Gazette*, August 11, 1903, p. 2, col. 1, states "it [the painting] was valued at $10,000," and in the pamphlet cited in note 48 the claim "valued at $50,000."

50. Information from Maj. E. C. Johnston, Fort Bliss, Tex., in a letter dated October 3, 1940. Major Johnston measured the painting for me. See note 48 for the size of the original painting and panels.

51. Information from W. A. Adams. The end panels are also mentioned by the reporter in the account of the Kansas City *Gazette*, August 11, 1903, p. 2, col. 1, and are briefly described in the pamphlet *Custer's Last Fight* cited in note 48.

52. Maj. E. C. Johnston, then adjutant of the 7th cavalry, wrote me (April 22, 1940) that the records of the 7th cavalry indicated that the painting was presented to the 7th cavalry (then at Fort Riley) some time between September, 1887, and March, 1888. Later (October 3, 1940) Major Johnston wrote me that Adolphus Busch presented it to the 7th cavlary, "at the outbreak of the Spanish-American war. During Mr. Busch's presentation speech he claimed he paid $35,000 for the painting." Evidently the 7th cavalry possessed no clear records of the presentation. The newspaper reporter writing in the Kansas City *Gazette* for August 11, 1903, p. 2, col. 1, wrote, it will be recalled, "In 1888, when the writer of these lines was a reporter in St. Louis, the original painting . . . hung on the wall of a saloon near Eighth and Olive streets—at the 'post-office corner.'" If the reporter's memory was correct, the 7th cavalry didn't come into possession of the painting until 1888 at least. Further the lithographic copy of the painting published by Anheuser-Busch bears the legend under the main title, "The Original Painting has been Presented to the Seventh Regiment U. S. Cavalry," and the notation (lower left), "Entered according to Act of Congress by Adolphus Busch, March 30th, 1896, in the Office of the Librarian of Congress at Washington, D. C." As the picture would have to be published before it was entered for copyright, it is obvious that the 7th cavalry came into possession of the painting before March 30, 1896. An undated newspaper clipping in the Kansas State Historical Society ("Indian Depredations and Battles" clippings, v. 2, p. 140) states with some show of authority that the painting was given the 7th cavalry in 1895. In *Custer's Last Battle*, an 11-page pamphlet published by Anheuser-Busch, Inc. (no date, but probably published within the last eight years), is a frontispiece of Becker's version of "Custer's Last Fight." The legend beneath the illustration reads "The Original Painting Was Presented by Adolphus Busch in 1890 to the Seventh Regiment U. S. Cavalry." There is no indication, however, of the source of this date for correspondence with Anheuser-Busch has produced no contemporary evidence that would substantiate 1890 as the date of acquisition by the 7th cavlry. The pamphlet makes no other comment on the Custer picture but

discusses the Custer battle from well-known accounts by General Fry, Captain Godfrey, Capt. Charles King and others.

53. Junction City *Union*, April 27, 1895, p. 2, col. 2, and May 25, 1895, p. 3, col. 4.

54. Kansas City *Star*, June 22, 1930, p. 16A, col. 3; Harold Evans, "Custer's Last Fight," *Kansas Magazine* (1938), 72–74, gives a somewhat different version. The undated clipping referred to in note 52, indicates that the painting was lost as early as 1903.

55. Information from Supt. E. S. Luce, Custer Battlefield National Monument, Crow Agency, Montana, in a letter to the writer dated July 17, 1946.

56. Information from ibid. and from Maj. E. C. Johnston, the adjutant of the 7th cavalry, in a letter to the writer dated October 3, 1940. Superintendent Luce believes that it cost the WPA some $4,200 to restore the painting.

57. Kansas City *Times*, June 14, 1946, p. 1, col. 2.

58. In an article in the St. Louis *Globe-Democrat*, November 26, 1942, it is reported that in a recent letter of Adams' son written to Anheuser-Busch, Inc., the painting was exhibited, after its completion, "all over the United States." This reference is probably that already described in my article, above. From the fact that the promoters gave up their venture as there described, the Adams painting never achieved the national recognition given to Mulvany.

59. E. A. Brininstool of Hollywood, Cal., long a student of Western history and of Custer in particular, writes me "The lay of the land [in the lithograph] is perfect—I have been over it many times, and can vouch for that part. . . ."

60. See note 21.

61. Copies of the original lithograph, one of which was published as early as 1896, are owned by the Kansas State Historical Society and are those upon which the subsequent remarks in the text are based. Modern printings of the lithograph show the halftone screen very distinctly; the early copies show no screen marks at all.

62. Letter from the reference department of the Milwaukee Public Library dated July 25, 1946. I am indebted to Miss Mamie E. Rehnquist of the Milwaukee Public Library for this information.

63. Miss Becker wrote me under dates of August 9 and 14, 1946. I am greatly indebted to her for her kindness and help in supplying the information concerning her father given above and described subsequently in the text.

64. Information from a letter to the writer by F. W. Webber, of Anheuser-Busch, Inc., July 29, 1946.

65. Otto Becker was born on January 28, 1854, in Dresden, Germany, and as a young man studied in the Royal Academy of Arts in Dresden. He came to New York in 1873 and worked as artist and lithographer in that city as well as in Boston, Philadelphia and St. Louis. In 1880, he went to Milwaukee and was associated with the Milwaukee Lithographic and Engraving Company

for 35 years. In oil and water color, he painted copy for many of the publications of that firm and supervised the work of preparing the copy on stone. On his own account he painted many Western pictures of Indians, cowboys, and portraits of Indian chiefs "after the manner of Remington." Later in life, he supported himself by making city views, religious paintings, marines, and Dutch interior views. Oddly enough, the prolific work of Becker has found no record in one of the most important regional studies of Western art, Porter Butts, *Art in Wisconsin* (Madison, Wis.: Democratic Printing Co., 1936). Mr. Becker died in Milwaukee on November 12, 1945, in his 92d year. This biographical information is, of course, from Miss Blanche Becker.

66. Recall that the painting's whereabouts was practically unknown from at least 1903 to 1934; see note 54.

67. If the original painting was photographed upon its receipt by WPA it could be readily ascertained if such a possibility, as described above, existed. So far, I have been unable to find anyone with knowledge of such a photograph.

68. St. Louis *Globe-Democrat*, November 26, 1942, and letter to the writer from F. W. Webber of the advertising department of Anheuser-Busch, Inc., July 18, 1946.

69. The red tie may have been suggested to Adams or Becker by Mrs. Custer who wrote in a letter dated January 25, 1889, a description of the flowing red merino cravat that Custer wore when with the Third cavalry

division of the Army of the Potomac. See A. J. Donnell, ed., *Cyclorama of Gen. Custer's Last Fight* (Boston: Boston Cyclorama, 1889), 13–17.

70. The legend below the print identifies by name a number of the individuals: "Sioux Warrior Who Killed Custer"; "Rain in the Face"; "Autie Reed, Custer's Nephew"; "Capt. T. W. Custer"; "General Custer"; "Lieut. A. E. Smith"; "Lieut. Cook"; "Lieut. W. Van W. Reily"; "Capt. G. W. Yates"; "Courier From Sitting Bull," etc. It may be noted here that there are at least three printings of the lithograph known to the writer. In the original printing, the print itself measures 24¼″ by 38½″. A modern version on paper, a gift from Anheuser-Busch, Inc., in 1940, shows screen marks (as stated in note 61) and the print measures 23⅞″ by 37¼″. The colors are brighter than the original lithograph but considerable detail has been lost. There apparently is still another printing for E. A. Brininstool writes me that he has a copy printed on *canvas*.

71. Topeka *State Journal*, January 9, 1904, p. 5, col. 1. Miss Boies' attack on the Custer lithograph has been interestingly described by Harold C. Evans in the *Kansas Magazine* (1938), 72–74. Much information on the history of the lithograph will be found in this article. I am also indebted to Mr. Evans for supplying me with additional leads concerning the lithograph.

72. *Tenth Annual Report of the Bureau of Ethnology* (Washington, D.C., 1893), 563–66, and plates 39 to 48. Marquis, *A Warrior*, opposite 220,

reproduces a photograph of Wooden Leg, the Cheyenne survivor of the Battle of the Little Big Horn, making Custer battle drawings but none of the drawings are reproduced save one which shows up faintly in the photograph.

73. George Armstrong Custer, *Wild Life on the Plains* (St. Louis: Excelsior Publishing Co., 1883), 389. There are a number of editions of this book, but the illustrations are all equally poor in the editions I have seen. Many of the illustrations are quite patently copied from those appearing in *Harper's Weekly* and *Leslie's Weekly*. Barnsley's name appears frequently as the delineator of many Western illustrations in this period, but I have been unable to find any information concerning him.

74. *Magazine of American History* 12 (September 1884): 280.

75. Donnelle, *Cyclorama*, 11.

76. *Harper's Magazine* 80 (April 1890): 732, about ½ page.

77. *Cosmopolitan* 11 (July 1891): 302.

78. *Harper's Weekly* (January 10, 1891), 24, 25; also reproduced in Frederic Remington's *Pony Tracks* (New York: Harper, 1895), frontispiece. In the *Harper's Weekly* version (23) the comment is made: "How many scenes of which this is typical have been made on this continent, who can say?"

79. *Mentor* (June 15, 1915), serial no. 85.

80. W. Fletcher Johnson, *Life of Sitting Bull* (Edgewood Publishing Co., 1891), 128.

81. Helen F. Sanders, "Edgar Samuel Paxson," *Overland Monthly*, n.s., 48 (September 1906): 183; see also *American Magazine* 80 (July 1915): 50. I am indebted to Miss M. Catherine White, reference librarian of the Montana State University, Missoula, and to the Historical Society of Montana, Helena, for information concerning Mr. Paxson. A reproduction of the Paxson painting of the Custer battle will be found in Kate Hammond Fogarty, *The Story of Montana* (New York and Chicago: A. S. Barnes Co., 1916), 183.

82. *McClure's Magazine* 11 (September 1898): 447.

83. Annie D. Tallent, *The Black Hills* (St. Louis: Nixon-Jones Printing Co., 1899), opposite 220.

84. Information from the *Globe-Democrat* of the above date and from Mrs. Edgar Cameron, widow of the artist. Mrs. Cameron wrote me under date of July 4, 1946, telling me of her husband's death on November 5, 1944.

85. *Outing* 45 (December 1904): 271. In black and white.

86. *Scribner's Magazine* 37 (February 1945): 158.

87. *Special Exhibition Catalogue*, St. Louis Museum of Fine Arts, November 14, 1908. The Custer piece is No. 46 in the list.

88. Arthur Hoeber, "Painters of Western Life," *Mentor* (June 15, 1915), serial no. 85, p. 10. About ½ page, in black and white.

89. Colonel Homer W. Wheeler, *The Frontier Trail* (Los Angeles: Times-Mirror Press, 1923), opposite 216.

90. Stanley Vestal, *Sitting Bull* (Boston: Houghton Mifflin Co., 1932).

91. I am indebted to Mr. Pitman for this information. E. A. Brininstool of Hollywood, Cal., kindly called my attention to Mr. Pitman's work.

92. U.S. Department of Interior, National Park Service, *Custer Battlefield National Cemetery, Montana* (Washington, D.C.: Government Printing Office, 1942).

93. I am indebted to Supt. E. S. Luce of the Custer Battlefield National Monument for this information. Mr. Luce states that two weeks before he wrote me (June 22, 1946) a correspondent in Zurich, Switzerland, reported that the Dresden Museum was but little damaged by Russian bombing so that Eber's painting may exist. Mr. Luce, through correspondence with Eber prior to the war, had obtained Eber's promise that the painting would be given to the museum at the Custer battlefield but the gift probably will not now materialize. According to Mr. Luce, the Eber painting "is the nearest and most correct conception of what occurred here on this battlefield 70 years ago." The picture was painted, according to Mr. Luce, in either 1926 or 1927. The painting is also reproduced in Mr. Luce's book *Keogh, Comanche, and Custer,* opposite 58.

94. Van de Water, *Glory-Hunter,* opposite 350.

95. Letter of Dwight Franklin to the writer, July 13, 1946.

96. My information concerning the Leigh picture comes from Mr. Leigh himself. Leigh, well known as an artist and student of the Western horse— as well as in other fields—wrote me under dates of October 1, 1940, and July 26, 1946, as follows: "After visiting the battlefield, and spending a summer among the Indian tribes in those parts, I had the head authority, Dr. Whistler of the Museum of Natural History here (New York City), . . . pass upon the picture while it was yet in the charcoal. . . . the bonneted rider in the foreground is Chief Gall, Sioux. The rider further to the left waving a feathered lance is a medicine chief. Custer is seen on the hill, a dim silhouette in the dust and smoke; he is firing a revolver."

97. Other artists who have attempted the depiction of the Custer battle are suggested by Harry B. McConnell, of the Cadiz (Ohio) *Republican,* who wrote me that he has seen calendar illustrations of the scene credited to James Drummond Ball, National Art Company, Boston, and another credited to "Coyle-Harken, 1928"; and still another one he found in an edition of Whittier's poems (one of the poets to write of Custer—as did Longfellow) that is signed "McCracken."

SUNDAY AT THE
LITTLE BIG HORN
WITH GEORGE

ERIC VON SCHMIDT

It seemed like a good idea when I rashly tacked up the canvas in the summer of 1970. Rashness was quite in keeping with the subject-to-be: George Armstrong Custer. Why not do an epic-scale painting of the battle, and perhaps, at long last, *get it right?* I had been reading everything I could get my hands on, but it was W. A. Graham's wonderful hodgepodge, *The Custer Myth*, that had really sucked me in. A delightful stew of fact and fiction, rambling and disorganized, it fitted my mood exactly. The canvas, all five by thirteen feet of it, was so starkly pristine in contrast to Graham's jumbled jigsaw puzzle. What a splendid inducement to begin, especially since this beguiling invitation hung on my studio wall, at that time, directly between the bedroom and the bathroom.

As the months wore on and I learned more and more (and I realized just how much I didn't know), the empty canvas became a deadening reflection of my state of mind. With this monumental salute to blankness, I had created a self-inflicted void, exhausting to contemplate, impossible to ignore.

Usually I make a good many compositional sketches and preliminary drawings for anything I undertake, large or small. In this case I couldn't seem to come up with anything at all. Since no one had commissioned me to do it, nor had anyone expressed the slightest interest in the finished work, I was sorely tempted to pack it in. Still, there was that damned canvas . . . beckoning. Every day it seemed bigger, looking more and more like Herman Melville's Great White Whale.

For a number of years my wife and I had held a January First party on our beach in Sarasota, Florida. It had become a Siesta Key tradition. Soul food for the hangovers, "hoppin' John" for luck in the coming year. It was a big success, and every year it grew bigger. Last time around there were two hundred or more people out there, and we realized there were a whole lot of them we didn't even know. It stopped being fun. End of tradition.

So when I got out of bed on New Year's Day, 1971, the joyous thought hit me on the way to the bathroom: I didn't have to roast a pig, tap beer kegs, provide collard greens for the multitudes. And there it was. The Canvas. Damned expensive rag it was too. Belgian linen, by God! Was it glowing slightly? A mini-epiphany? As I stood there transfixed, it started to look a whole lot less like a whale and a whole lot more like territory. A whole lot of *Dakota* territory. And at that moment I felt like Alphonse Bedoya in *The Treasure of the Sierra Madre*. I may even have said it out loud, *"We* don' need your *stinkin' sketches."*

So I plunged in, painted madly all day, guided only by a three-by-five-inch, black-and-white reproduction of the earliest photograph I could find. When the sun set that night, half of Montana lay between bedroom and bathroom. Indeed, if the battle was unplanned, wild and chaotic, might not my painting itself reflect this fatal disorder?

But the next day when I looked at the huge semiabstract landscape, I was stunned. There was no disorder here; there was a beautiful painting. So good I could hardly bear it. And it was *finished.* I had left nothing unraveled, there was no way to get back in. I was blocked again.

Although my background in painting is academic and traditional, my personal direction has been expressionistic, moving more and more to the abstract over the years. What I had done in that one exuberant day seemed quite complete in itself . . . *Lahkota Alla Prima.* But what then of Colonel Graham's splendid mishmash, all the information I had painstakingly begun to gather? Abandoning all that seemed a waste, yet entering again into my pristine landscape seemed even worse . . . it would amount to rape.

So I digressed. I believe the phrase is "Don't do something, just sit there." I sat there and wrote letters to experts about weapons, buttons, saddlebags, and all that fascinating trivia. I set up a trip to the anthropological archives to look at all forty-two Red Horse drawings of the battle. I persuaded a western painter friend, Gene Shortridge, to take some black-and-white Polaroid snapshots of me running around dressed as either cavalryman or Indian. *Willy-nilly* best describes that particular shoot. Totally unplanned and random, that afternoon's bit of fun was to provide me with the key to getting back into the painting.

Meanwhile, the responses to my letters began to arrive. I had not anticipated such generosity. These people were taking me seriously. I had talked myself into a corner, and now I would have to paint myself out. I was running out of digressions.

It was becoming clear that I had to follow the neatly shod hoofprints of Vic and his charismatic rider into the unknown. It seemed equally obvious that, as an ex-enlisted man myself, a descendant of Europeans, I had to take the viewpoint of the troopers on the ridge. Violating my lovely landscape painting seemed more and more fitting, considering the subject at hand. Finally, in one of Elizabeth Custer's delightful books, I came across the drunken, brawling, original lyrics to "Garry Owen." I knew that was the guidon to follow:

> We'll beat the bailiffs out of fun
> We'll make the mayor and sheriffs run
> We are the boys no man dares dun
> If he regards his whole skin.

I had to be true to that song.

Creative people, I believe, are fortunate in that all areas of personal experience can be used. Pain, heartbreak, failure, can to some extent be redeemed, catharsis achieved. For as long as I can remember, I have had a dream that must be as old as time. In it, *I am fleeing for my life; I try to hide; I am discovered; I am killed.*

Well, one of the little Polaroid photos caught that feeling. It was a snapshot of me, dressed like a trooper and dashing to the right. It looked so real it was quite spooky. There was something about the gait and the look of the man that marked him as doomed. Some of the Indians had spoken with amusement of a few soldiers, near the end of the battle, who had run northward because no enemy could be seen in that direction. The area was, in fact, clogged with warriors taking advantage of the concealment offered by the sloping terrain. So I painted my little "running man" to the far right of the canvas.

The addition of this single figure shattered the unity of the painting. Something else happened too. The defiled landscape gained a raw energy, an emerging scale. *The battle had begun.* Unfortunately, the overall composition remained as much of a mystery as ever. I was left without a clue as to what to do next.

I believe it was around this time that I traveled up to Washington,

D.C., to study the Red Horse drawings firsthand. Red Horse was a Sioux warrior who fought in the battle, gave an early account, and made forty-two drawings five years later. In Washington I met a kindred spirit, Jim Hutchins, a man as fascinated by the battle as I was. His research and encouragement were invaluable. Through him, I got to see the drawings, indeed, *hold them in my hand*, a thrill I will never forget. Though I had come to look for details of dress and equipment, I was struck by page after page of carefully drawn tipis. Nothing but tipis. I guessed that they had never been reproduced because they were repetitious—boring? Old Red Horse was trying to tell us something. We weren't quite getting it.

We shouldn't feel bad. Custer didn't get it either. It wasn't until I got back down to my studio that *I* finally got it. Then I knew I was on the right track. All that territory, that *Lahkota* territory, was fine. Considering that the village was over three miles long, there would have been a whole *lot* of tipis, a *thousand*, give or take a few. Red Horse was telling us in pictographic terms what Custer himself had refused to believe.

True, early on the morning of June 25, 1876, the advance scouts couldn't see the tipis. But from their hidden observation point, fifteen miles away, the Crows began to make out smoke rising from the Little Big Horn Valley. The point of origin was hidden by some bluffs, but directly west of it a huge dark stain spread out across the valley floor. At first the scouts took it to be miles of burned prairie grass. But while the soft blue drained from the dawn sky they watched in awe as the forward edge of the dark mass seemed to shimmer, form, and reform. It was then they knew they were looking at an immense sprawl of grazing ponies. *It was the Sioux horse herd.* One of the interpreters, Mitch Bouyer, reckoned that Custer and the whole command, himself included, were as good as dead. "Lonesome Charlie" Reynolds ("Lucky Man" was one of his Indian names) had expected as much and had given away his belongings the previous night. A hasty note was scribbled; two Arikara scouts rode with it back to the general. They had discovered "a tremendous village."

The Crows tried to point out the herd to their young chief of scouts, Lieutenant Charles Varnum. They told him to "look for worms crawling on the grass." He could see nothing, with or without their "cheap spy glass." Maybe it was his dust-inflamed eyes, the baffling metaphor, the little tricks that scale can play over such vast distances. Whatever it was, I feel for you, Varnum. I've worked the territory. Old Greasy Grass Creek can fool you.

When I returned to Florida I was convinced that I should show as much of this vast encampment on the west side of the river as I could, instead of obscuring it with smoke. Indeed this would have been the first real look many of the ill-fated five companies that rode north with Custer would have had. The view from the ridge would not yet have been clogged with dust and smoke; it must have been paralyzing. Small wonder that some of the troopers took their own lives. My painting includes one of these—a first, I believe, in the thousand-plus depictions of the fight. It is fitting that the "running man" figure later was transformed into the kneeling "suicide" at the far right of the canvas. Although this was done to acknowledge the historical reality, pictorially it allowed me to "stop" the left-to-right movement of the composition.

Near the end of the battle there would have been a good deal of smoke and dust, perhaps even more than I show. As you may have noticed, historical painters love smoke. However, the best of them do not love it for the same reason that some western painters, the ones who have trouble with horses' fetlocks, love tall grass.

Although all the Indian combatants spoke of the diminished visibility that resulted, Red Horse gives no hint of this in his drawings. He presents a pictorial accounting of the event, not the actuality. Beyond even this, a man might be shown in a warbonnet because he owned one, not necessarily because he wore it during the battle. But the very fact that the drawings were quantitative rather than interpretive provided another clue as important as all the tipis: those little knots of slain troopers, so neatly arranged, many stripped, bleeding and dismembered. Now what I needed was the white man's counterpart to these innocent renderings of grotesquely tumbled dead flesh.

Once again I turned to Graham, and he did not disappoint. There was a veritable potpourri of burial reports and testimonies, a good many of them, of course, conflicting. Still, I was able to come up with a workable consensus. When I began to *visualize* who was where, I had the distinct feeling I was finally on my way into the valley of the Little Big Horn.

And by this, I mean a twofold visualization: first, where they were *on the ridge;* then, and *only* then, how they would be placed within the framework of the composition. I had already chosen the psychological concept for the painting (viewpoint of trooper), but the *pictorial* concept remained elusive. Here again, I took my cue from the battle itself: plunge ahead; *something* will turn up.

Meanwhile, back on the ridge. If it was close to the end, Custer would be down, with the chest wound. Real blood would be running out, along with his fabled "luck." Indeed, who in hell would be *standing* as the bullets and arrows poured in? Alive, dying, or already dead, near their stricken leader, would be Robert Hughes, who carried the guidon stitched by Custer's wife; Chief Trumpeter Henry Voss; and Adjutant W. W. Cooke. Brother Tom Custer, Algernon Smith, and George Yates would be as near as they could get. If any man was upright in that deadly hail, he would be seeking better shelter, or like the "running man," attempting to escape in panic, or perhaps going mad.

By this time I had an eight-by-ten glossy of the panoramic view that had gotten the juices flowing that first day. It showed a scattering of wooden stakes serving as grave markers. That was about the only indication of scale I had to work with. The figure of Hughes, holding the guidon, came first. Next was Custer. Slowly, painfully, the foreground figures were established. Then all the soldiers below them down the slope. Dead horses, scattered equipment. It got to be kind of depressing. My one relief was the landscape itself. Since I'd lived in the West from time to time, and had painted and sketched out there in the open, I knew what I was doing.

I slogged along like this for the better part of two years. It was about that time it finally came: the *pictorial* concept. By then, once more, the painting had become my personal reality, not the mental vacuum reflecting the blank canvas but a sense of futility, a heaviness of being. Of course, the Indians were all there in my *mind*. The village too. But none of this was on the canvas—just in my mind. And the mind sometimes has a mind of its own.

There I was, every bloody day, faced by these forlorn and forsaken men as they were relentlessly broken, crushed down by an *unseen* force. All smashed and trampled beneath . . . what? A *landscape*, so tranquil, so utterly sublime. René Magritte, eat your heart out!

I was *not* coming unglued. For I realized that the surreal aspect alone was not what made the canvas unsettling. What I was doing, unconsciously at first, was perverting one of the oldest classical forms: the frieze—the one used with such dignity by the Babylonians and the Egyptians, the one in which a long horizontal space is enlivened by a series of recurring uprights, usually figures. The frieze combines well with formal architecture, the overall effect being graceful, stately, and imposing. Imagine, if you will, Custer and his men standing erect, pondering maps, chatting manfully, taking the occasional potshot. The effect would have been rather elegant, would it not? Downright classical.

But by huddling all the soldiers *below* the horizontal median, the only real vertical being the skinny, sagging guidon, I both confound ordinary visual expectations and further diminish the poor devils. No stately procession here. We are forced to observe a real battle: an obscene jumble of twisted shapes, stripped of dignity, devoid of hope. Pictorially, it is meant to disturb equilibrium, affront sensibility, *spit in your eye.*

If you detect a certain inelegance in that phrase, we are on the right track. Reality is seldom elegant. More often than not the search for historical truth reveals something quite the opposite. As a "warts and all" kind of guy, I think that it might be fitting to share with you a brief list (à la Red Horse) of some of the realities encountered during the search for *Here Fell Custer.*

The painting itself, which I estimated would take two or three months to complete, took over five years of work, about three years of sustained labor. The actual canvas was moved ten times, in and out of three different states. Since I had no "genius grant" to sustain all this activity (an "idiot grant" would have been more appropriate), relationships, private and otherwise, were put to the test. One and a half divorces resulted. Those were the "bad old days."

The strain was far-reaching. My father, a fine painter and illustrator, one of this country's best, came up to New Hampshire to view the work in progress. Old, semi-invalid, sitting in a battered Victorian rocker, he squinted long and hard at the painting. After ten or fifteen minutes, his silence finally drove me out of the room. About ten minutes later, he was still at it. Finally, he turned to me and said, "There is no black in nature." That was it. I swear to God, that was *all* he said.

I admit that I had hoped for a bit more. In fact I had the distinct inclination to haul my sainted father, rocker and all, out into the sun-baked barnyard, poke a loaded .45-caliber Colt pistol in his face, and ask: "Look. See the sun? See the trees? See the leaves? See the *horse-*

shit on the ground? Are we not here together in *nature?* Now, when you *look* into the muzzle of this deadly weapon held by your crazed son, are you absolutely sure that the little round space encompassed by the barrel is not *perfectly* black?"

Well, perhaps it was his way of telling me to get more atmosphere in the painting. I can assure you, such Zen-like pronouncements are more fun for the master than the disciple.

By the third year, I was getting pretty bored with painting white people. I just couldn't take it any more. I had to paint me some *Injuns!* Having grown up around horses and being a fairly good rider, I had all kinds of photographs of me galloping around on borrowed horses, my little pale ass peeking out from under the breechclout. Considering that I still had no better reference than the panoramic view, I knew it would be a rash move to say the least. It was hard enough getting a fix on the stuff that was relatively close, how in hell to determine the rest?

Sagebrush comes in all sizes, cottonwood in all heights. I was still completely at a loss as to how to deal with all those tipis across the river.

I kept wondering why that old-time photographer hadn't sent his assistant down there to the bottom of the ridge to give the thing some scale. Or if the cheap old bastard hadn't had an assistant, why not at least leave his horse down there? Probably too lazy to hike back up. I got pretty exercised about it, started to take it personally. Worse, I started painting Indians in that indefinable middle distance. If only fate had sent me to the right Chinese restaurant. If only I had picked up the right fortune cookie: "Beware the indefinable middle distance."

Every day I studied the photograph. I forced it on friends, mailmen, the occasional Jehovah's Witness. I knew the risk I was taking, but I just couldn't stop painting in Indians. Once you've painted one, you've got to paint more. But I kept searching that photo. I studied in all states—straight, bent, northern, and southern—until one day I found myself in the state of Guanajuato. And would you believe it? I had forgotten to bring the damn thing. Still, I had found my "Jungle-Rites-Bride," and we did together what I should have done in the very beginning.

We drove, in the first flush of love, in her Volkswagen "swayback," CUSTER OR BUSTER lettered on the trunk, directly from central Mexico to the battlefield. We arrived at twilight, and standing on the ridge, I was astonished and delighted at how much the view looked like the old photograph. And in the dim light it was just as hard to make out relative distances. Absurd as it now seems, it took me several minutes to realize the obvious. When I did, I ran down the slope right *into* that tattered old eight-by-ten glossy. I was hollering loud enough to be heard in downtown Hardin. Up on the ridge some guy approached my bride (who was shedding decorous tears of joy) and asked if everything was all right. She told me later that when she answered "Oh, Eric is so happy—he's being an Indian," the guy immediately jumped in his car and burned rubber getting out of there.

The next several days were spent wandering the battlefield, sketching, and taking photographs. I finally hit on a way to solve the problem of relative distances once and for all. First, from the ridge, I painted a carefully accurate landscape that matched the view in the old photograph. Then the park ranger and his wife rode down toward the river, stopping for a minute every fifty yards or so while I quickly sketched them in. When they reached the river, my scale difficulties were over. That was the good news.

On returning east and confronting the actual canvas, I learned the bad. The forty or so Indians I had painted with such loving care (and splendid detail!) as they had galloped across a distant ridge were exactly twice as big as they could have been. Forty men. Forty horses. One hundred and sixty hooves. About six months of work lost. Then, to add insult to injury, one boozy evening as I was brandishing the old photo about, furiously reviling its author with curses now fully justified, I stabbed the indefinable middle distance with a paint-stained finger: "Why didn't he put something RIGHT THERE?" And *there*, right in front of my filthy fingernail, *they* were.

I'd been back from the battlefield for months. Since I now knew the correct scale, and was working from on-site sketches, I'd barely looked at the thing. But there was absolutely no doubt about it: *they were there.* Two men. One standing. The other—would you believe it?—sitting on a *white* horse. Though they were no bigger than the head of a pin, I swear to you, my friends, I had the distinct impression that, at the moment the shutter clicked, *they were laughing!*

So now that you've read my little cautionary tale, please go home and tell your dear ones and loved ones, join the marines, run away with the circus, land your Cessna in Red Square, but don't, *for God's sake,* become a painter of historical themes on the grand scale. There are no courses, no instructors, no texts, no seminars. Not only are there no commissions, *there is no market*. And for those who would still follow, let them ponder these words, as Custer's scouts surely did in the cool of that Sunday morning when grass became ponies: *"How hot will it be by noon?"*

JACK CRABB AND THE SOLE SURVIVORS OF CUSTER'S LAST STAND

BRIAN W. DIPPIE

Thomas Berger's *Little Big Man*, it would seem, has become firmly established as a major Western and American novel. Excerpted in *Esquire*, widely and generally well reviewed in all the right places when it first appeared in 1964, it has since come in for close critical scrutiny, and passed inspection with flying colors. L. L. Lee presented an intelligent appraisal of the novel as a whole;[1] William T. Pilkington placed it in the tradition of Western comedy;[2] Delbert E. Wylder defended it as literature;[3] and Jay Gurian discussed its stylistic achievements.[4] At some point some one might profitably relate the story to its factual sources ("60 or 70 accounts of the Western reality"[5]), if for no other reason than that Berger, unlike Robert Lewis Taylor, has not conveniently listed them at the end of the novel. Moreover, a knowledge of Berger's sources would undoubtedly make the critical task a little easier—and a little surer.

For example, Delbert Wylder was rather taken with *Little Big Man*'s concluding scene, in which hero Jack Crabb's adopted father, Cheyenne chief Old Lodge Skins, shows his "old power to make things happen" by summoning the rain from what was a cloudless sky. "Is the death of Old Lodge Skins a satire on . . . [the] literary treatment of mythology and Indian life?" Wylder wonders, and rather uncertainly concludes: "Apparently it is not, although it could be."[6] Wylder might have been more positive had he compared this episode with the moving postscript to John G. Neihardt's masterpiece, *Black Elk Speaks: Being the Life Story of a Holy Man of the Ogalala Sioux* (1932). It is enough to say that Berger follows Neihardt point by point, and that the tone of both authors is identically one of reverence and awe. This is not to invalidate the parallel which Wylder draws between this scene in *Little Big Man* and the death of Oedipus at Colonnus.[7] Undoubtedly, Neihardt too was mindful of such classic parallels.

Similarly, Wylder's discussion of Crazy Horse's war bonnet would be enriched by reference to Berger's source. In his narrative, Jack Crabb simply states that Crazy Horse "had a face full of sharpened edges, wore no ornamentation whatever, no paint, no feathers; he was like a living weapon."[8] However, Ralph Fielding Snell, "Man of Letters," tells us in his Editor's Epilogue, "As to Crazy Horse's not wearing feathers, we know that statement to be erroneous—his war bonnet . . . presently reposes in my own collection; the dealer who sold it to me is a man of the highest integrity."[9] "Thus," Wylder concludes, "the narrative perspective mirrors absurdity back upon itself and seems to suggest that not only are the details absurd, but that the ultimate vision must also be even more absurd."[10] This is certainly true, but the obvious point is our Man of Letters' gullibility—and Crabb's unexpected veracity. Crazy Horse's biographer has portrayed the chief as an ascetic, a mystical war leader ("the strange man of the Oglalas") who was by nature averse to self-display. There was "nothing about Crazy Horse that bore much resemblance to the gaudy, blood-thirsty Sioux warrior of popular notion," Mari Sandoz wrote. "The man was pale-skinned and had little interest in the things that delighted most of his brother Sioux—paint and feathers, singing, dancing, and recounting the honors of war . . ."[11] Our Man of Letters, then, so eager to demolish others with his solitary weapon, a superior book-learning, is himself the dupe of a swindle. The know-it-all has bought the Indian equivalent of the Brooklyn Bridge, and the reader is invited to share in the joke with Berger. At the same time, a new dimension of credibility is given to Crabb's tale.

In short, in approaching a book such as *Little Big Man*, which is thoroughly grounded in research, a knowledge of the sources can help illuminate the text. Certainly one must grant Berger the artistic license to transform his materials, to fashion them to his own ends, and to create something new with them. But, as A. B. Guthrie, Jr., cautioned, "If we use the record—I'm talking of known events, known people, known words—then, ideally at any rate, we must let ourselves be the prisoners of it."[12] In *Little Big Man*, Berger has been most faithful to history, and it is perhaps this very fidelity which led Robert Edson Lee to dismiss the novel as literature.[13] A well-researched historical novel always runs the risk of failing to rise above the level of a gloss on the sources; while a poorly-researched one simply discredits itself through errors. There is little pleasing the stickler for facts either way: if you are "right," he recalls where you got all of your material; if you are "wrong," he will cite book and verse to prove you so.

I do not propose, then, to be the Dr. Angus McFrisby of Berger's *Little Big Man*.[14] Instead, my intention is a modest one: to place Jack Crabb in his rightful niche in the pantheon of sole survivors of the Battle of the Little Big Horn. The undertaking is worthwhile because of the importance which Berger obviously attaches to the battle. It provides not only the climax to *Little Big Man*, but also the setting for Crabb's most marvelous exploit. It is in becoming the sole survivor of Custer's Last Stand that he assumes epic proportions, and his own legend most effectively fuses with Western myth. When Crabb dismisses the other claimants to the title "Sole Survivor" as "either nuts or just plain liars," and gives us for the first time *his* "true experience," he is perpetuating a venerable literary and historical tradition. For his is the ultimate Western boast: "From here on you have only my word for what happened to Custer and his five troops that Sunday afternoon, *for I am the only man what survived out of them 200-odd who rode down Medicine Tail Coulee towards the ford of the Little Bighorn River.*"[15]

The novelist who would write about Custer's Last Stand faces a logical impasse: for fictional purposes, his hero cannot be killed; yet, for historical purposes, no man can survive. Some authors have focused their stories on Indian or even animal heroes, thereby avoiding the issue altogether. But, since most want their protagonists to be white men, the problem of the survivor-hero remains. Other than the unsatisfactory device of having the hero arrive first on the battlefield and discover the bodies of Custer's slaughtered command, the writer has only four alternatives. He can have his hero reside in the Indian camp either as a prisoner or a renegade; ride with Custer's subordinates, Major Reno and Captain Benteen, whose battalions survived the battle; serve as Custer's final messenger; or, throwing the stipulation about historical plausibility aside, escape death in the Last Stand itself.

A second problem that immediately confronts the Custer novelist is the very real difficulty of outdoing a legion of charlatans who have

paraded themselves about as sole survivors of the fight. "The plains
and Rockies are full of them," an officer who had served under Captain
Benteen at the Little Big Horn remarked in 1918.[16] By 1939 one writer
had collected over seventy survivor tales,[17] and Stewart H. Holbrook
was later led to designate "The Survivor of the Custer Massacre" as
the major species of Northwestern "phony."[18] To this day, survivor
tales are foisted on the public, and *The Casper* (Wyoming) *Star-Tribune*
saluted the ninetieth anniversary of the Little Big Horn with a story
which not only had Custer outliving his own Last Stand, but planning
to attend the semi-centennial observance in 1926![19] In short, the survivors of Custer fiction must compete with an imposing crew of actual
"survivors."

It is an accepted fact that Lieutenant James H. Bradley was the
first white man on the battlefield after the Custer disaster. Yet rivals
for the honor abound. The autobiography of Frank Grouard, a highly-
regarded scout in the 1870's, describes how he stumbled onto the bodies
of Custer's men during the night of June 25. Little credence need be
given this tale, however, for the autobiography was dictated to a news-
paperman, Joe DeBarthe, and between Grouard and DeBarthe history
occasionally suffered.[20] Will Logan recounted in vivid detail how he, as
the first white man on the battleground, strolled among the trampled
roses and the corpses from which "fresh blood . . . in many places . . .
still oozed, bubbled and flowed from gaping wounds."[21] Not to be outdone, "old Indian scout" Bob Nixon told almost gleefully of discovering
the mutilated remains of the General, with the "long dark hair" still
on the severed head.[22] Finally, one must not neglect a fanciful piece of
evidence which "proves" that it was Calamity Jane who actually discovered the gory corpses on the ridge above the Little Big Horn River.
"I went to the battlefield after Custer's battle," Calamity supposedly
wrote her daughter, Janey Hickok, in July, 1879,

> and I never want to see such a sight again. In a horse which had
> been disemboweled was the carcass of a man, apparently hidden
> there to escape the Indians seeking revenge. The squaws had cut
> legs and arms from the dead soldiers. Their heads were chopped . . .
> their eyes poked out. . . . Your Uncle Cy was in that battle, Janey.
> I found him hacked to pieces, his head in one place, legs and arms
> scattered about. I dug a grave and put his poor, poor old body in

my saddle blanket and buried him. I can never think of him without crying. Goodnight, dear, till next time.[23]

All Calamity's letter lacks is "pleasant dreams" at the end.

Such imaginative contenders for the title "First Man on the Battlefield" have left scant room for fictional claimants, though the avid dime novel reader would have learned in 1883 that it was really Buffalo Bill who discovered the General's body.[24] This fact was later reaffirmed at many performances of Cody's Wild West Show, though it was somewhat clouded by a subsequent dime novel, which had him fighting side by side with Custer to the bitter end.[25] But ubiquitousness, after all, as Jack Crabb would confirm, was ever the hallmark of the Western hero.

To digress for a moment, the "First Man on the Battlefield" is but one variety of a species more common on the screen than in novels. Their mission: to warn Custer of impending disaster. Plot: through unavoidable complications, they are detained. Outcome: they always arrive just too late to save the Seventh Cavalry. Scouts Buckskin Joe and Jerome B. James of Herbert Myrick's *Cache la Poudre: The Romance of a Tenderfoot in the Days of Custer* (1905) fit this pattern. Sent out by the General a few weeks before his ill-fated attack to locate and determine the strength of the hostile Indians, the two thrash about in the brush long enough for the Seventh to get annihilated. Then they emerge, breathless, and, before falling into the open arms of their respective girl friends (who happen to be conveniently on hand), manage to gasp out their belated tidings. Buckskin Joe comes up with "Tell Custer—it was lie—thousands of Indians—beware . . . Oh, Milly." Moments later,

an even more gaunt, bloody and bedraggled form staggered into camp from the brush, and clutching by the shoulder the first one he met, whispered hoarsely:

"Where's Custer? Give him this dispatch!"

Too late. The General and his men were by then cold in death on a nearby hill, mercifully oblivious to the scene enacted when Jerome at last spotted his darling Gladys:

"Sweetheart!" was all he said.

"My Jerome"—and Gladys folded the weary frame to her strong, virgin bosom that rose and fell in mighty heartbeats.[26]

At any rate, the reader can find some consolation in the fact that whenever Custer *is* warned, in films and in fiction, he immediately explodes in anger, accuses his informant of lying, places him under arrest as an Indian spy or a renegade, and ignores the proffered advice.[27]

Although the "First Man on the Battlefield" and others of his kind have garnered some notoriety, they are not in the same league with the survivors of the fight itself. To them belongs the lion's share of glory. Certainly the novelists and publicity-seekers alike have always thought so.

While Tom Logan in Frank Gruber's *Bugles West* (1954) and Dick Howard in Joseph A. Altsheler's *The Last of the Chiefs: A Story of the Great Sioux War* (1909) witness parts of the Last Stand as captives in the Indian village, their tales are tepid beside those of "an old trapper" named Ridgely, Walter Winnett, and Willard J. Carlyle. Ridgely not only claimed to have seen the battle, but told how he was later forced to watch the torture of a number of prisoners.[28] Winnett, allegedly a captive of the Sioux for some four years, and sixteen or seventeen years old at the time of the battle, said that he was absent during the fighting, but did see the bodies afterward.[29] Perhaps no such story is quite so marvelous as Carlyle's. At the age of sixteen, while mining gold in the Black Hills, he was shot in the mouth, taken captive by the Sioux, and, after enduring a test of courage, was made a full-fledged member of the tribe.[30] Naturally, he was present at the Little Big Horn. "I am," he wrote Mrs. Custer in 1926, "the only living white man that saw that fight," and he went on to tell her of the General's demise:

> One sweep of his saber and an Indians head was split in two, one flash of his revolver, his last shot, and a red-skin got the bullet between the eyes, then he fell with a bullet in the breast, the last of that brave band.
>
> I saw him within 15 minutes after he was shot, and there was still a smile on his face. Perhaps he was thinking of his home, his beloved wife or Mother. Who can tell.[31]

Obviously just "one of them cranks who wrote letters to poor Mrs. Custer in later years, some of them still children in 1876," as Jack Crabb would have it.[32] All the same, in the face of such competition, a mere novelist must wilt.

A favorite plot of the Custer writers places a renegade white man in the Indian camp. He may join Major Reno, and thus symbolically rejoin his own race, at some crucial point in the fighting (as does Jim Aherne in Leonard L. Foreman's *The Renegade* [1942]), or he may even have a change of heart in time to go into the fray with Reno or Custer (for example, John Clayton in Will Henry's *No Survivors* [1950] and Jack Crabb in *Little Big Man*). Actually, Crabb had been away from the Cheyennes for eight years, but he was still enough the renegade to consider himself "an enemy in this midst" when he rode with the Seventh to the Little Big Horn.[33] There, of course, he fought to the end with Custer. In contrast are Beau Mannix, outcast and artist, who elects to stay with his Indian friends in Robert Steelman's superior Western *Winter of the Sioux* (1959), and Hiram Shaw, adopted son of a Cheyenne chief in Frederic F. Van de Water's *Thunder Shield* (1933). Hiram is killed in a charge led by Crazy Horse, a fitting death, for it crystallizes his decision to remain ever loyal to his chosen people. Bert Raynor, captured and adopted by a band of Oglalas in William O. Stoddard's *Little Smoke: A Tale of the Sioux* (1891), witnesses Custer's Last Stand, but refrains from participating on either side. This leaves him free to rejoin white society without having to repudiate the Indian cause. "Ke-o-na-wagh [Bert's Indian name] go to his own people," he tells his "brother," Little Smoke. "Not Ogalallah. White. Love Little Smoke. Goodby. Keep Pah-sap-pa [the Black Hills]."[34]

The historical question of renegades in the Indian village remains a moot one, muddled in part by Major Reno's own assertion that he was battling every squawman in the country at the Little Big Horn.[35] William A. Graham, a serious Custer student, held the qualified opinion that Frank Huston, an embittered former Confederate officer and a squawman, was in or near the Sioux camp when Custer attacked. Huston himself denied that he took part in the battle, but did admit that, "as a matter of fact, there *were* white men there; *not* with the Sioux, but with other nations present." As Huston so aptly put it, in their place, "would you, *then* or *now*, acknowledge it?"[36]

The most obvious "escape-hatch" for the hero of a Custer novel is with Reno's command. Elbridge S. Brooks' *The Master of the Strong Hearts: A Story of Custer's Last Rally* (1898), Cyrus Townsend Brady's *Britton of the Seventh: A Romance of Custer and the Great Northwest* (1914), Harry Sinclair Drago's *Montana Road* (1935), Zoa Grace Hawley's *A Boy Rides with Custer* (1938), Ernest Haycox's *Bugles in the After-*

noon (1944), and a third-rate imitation of Haycox's book, Charles N. Heckelmann's *Trumpets in the Dawn* (1958), all chose this solution. However, it is a solution with a fundamental drawback, for the story's action is thereby shut off from the central event—Custer's Last Stand. (Only John Clayton of *No Survivors* overcomes this limitation: he fights with Reno in the valley and on the hill; sallies out with the others to Weir Point, Reno's furthest advance toward Custer's position; and then gallops off to join the General in time for the Last Stand.)

An alternative solution particularly favored in juvenile fiction is to have the boy hero carry Custer's last message to Reno or Benteen.[37] Historically, while more than one trooper bore dispatches from Custer, Giovanni Martini (or, in its Americanized form, John Martin) is accepted as Custer's last courier. Both Theodore Goldin and Henry L. Benner aspired to this role, but were convincingly discredited by Colonel Graham.[38] The story of John C. Lockwood, published in 1966, contends not only that he and scout "Lonesome Charley" Reynolds carried the final dispatches ("'Yes,' said Custer, 'Jack has his horse Satan, and the whole Sioux tribe can't catch that horse,' and he handed the other dispatch to me"), but also that he witnessed enough of the action which followed to see Custer fall first.[39] Not without cause, Lockwood's membership in the Veterans of the Indian Wars Association was suspended for "unsubstantiated pretensions" prior to his death in 1928.[40] More plausible is the romantic legend which has grown up about the solitary tombstone of Sergeant James Butler. It marks the deepest penetration made toward Reno Hill by any member of Custer's immediate command, and some believe that Butler died bearing Custer's last, desperate appeal for help. J. K. Ralston's oil painting *Custer's Last Hope* and Usher L. Burdick's novelette *Tragedy in the Great Sioux Camp* (1936) have immortalized this possibility.

Survivors of the Last Stand itself would seem to be within the exclusive province of the novelists. Yet it is precisely here that the competition for the limelight has waxed the hottest. Though Curly, a Crow scout with Custer's detachment, probably saw parts of the fight, he can hardly be termed a survivor of it. (Jack Crabb, with his vested interest in this matter, recalled how Curly "used to be exhibited around as the sole survivor of the battle. Except that Curly was not upon the field, but only watched a portion of the fight from a distant ridge . . ."[41]) In the public's mind, however, Curly remains the "Sole Survivor of the Custer Massacre"—excepting always the horse Comanche. This fact never discouraged the multitude of pretenders to the title. Two qualities, an historian has pointed out, distinguished each one's tale: "There was invariably a very ingenious explanation of how he happened to escape from the field of carnage and an equally ingenious reason for having remained silent so long."[42] Methods of escape ranged from hiding in a hollow log or in a tree[43] to lying under a dead horse[44] or inside the carcass of a buffalo.[45] One inventive soul told how, badly wounded and temporarily deranged, he was taken captive by the Indians and spared because they considered him *wakan*, touched by the gods. Frank Finkel, the man with the soundest case ever advanced by a "Sole Survivor," claimed that he simply outran his pursuers to safety— thereby gaining in credibility what he lost in drama.[46]

In comparison with such exploits, those of the fictional figures necessarily seem tame. Buffalo Bill, John Clayton and Jack Crabb battle to the end with Custer, merely to be revived and rescued by Indian benefactors. Old scout Pandy Ellis fights his way clear of the circle of death, while two other dime novel heroes, Mason Pierrepont and Tom Carleton, fall beside the General.[47] Left for dead on the battlefield, they recover in time to dispatch looters engaged in robbing the corpses, and so make good their escapes.

There are, then, two great traditions of sole survivors of the Battle of the Little Big Horn, those in fiction, and those who claimed to be so in fact. Jack Crabb naturally belongs within the first; but, in the context of *Little Big Man*, as a 111-year old recollecting his youthful adventures, he belongs in the second as well. Thus he is both the fictional hero who alone survives Custer's Last Stand, and the garrulous old claimant to that honor. Berger's Custer, down to such masterly touches as his mad monologue during the Last Stand (lifted verbatim, incidentally, from the real Custer's opus, *My Life on the Plains*), is a triumph, a subtly-shaded portrait of a man usually painted in black or white. But it is Crabb, the perfectly-conceived survivor-hero, who explains why *Little Big Man*, besides its other achievements, is the best Custer novel yet written. The only recognized contenders for the honor previously were Ernest Haycox's *Bugles in the Afternoon* and Will Henry's *No Survivors*.

Bugles in the Afternoon is a success because it is the formula Western fully realized. Its historical setting is unobtrusive; the stereotyped plot moves with mechanical precision to a timeless resolution (boy gets girl), neither disturbing, nor much disturbed by, Haycox's fidelity to historical fact. *No Survivors*, in contrast, is a comparative failure because it aspires to more, but falls far short. The story's hero, Colonel John Buell Clayton, an unreconstructed Reb, goes to live with the Sioux soon after the Fetterman battle of December 21, 1866, and remains with them for nine years, "a 'red' Indian in fact and being," [48] until the very eve of the Battle of the Little Big Horn. Clayton is ubiquitous and indestructible, a super hero with all the potential for becoming a legend. But Henry does not hold a steady course. During much of the novel, Clayton is stranded in the nebulous middle ground between man and myth. As a normal being he is simply unconvincing; his lack of probability is painfully evident, and he seems devoid of motive, logic and life. Clayton's sole reason for joining the Sioux was his love for the beautiful North Star (an obvious *deus ex machina*, since her role in the story thereafter is negligible). His abrupt departure is even less explicable. After living with the Sioux for almost a decade, he is suddenly and very conveniently convinced by the Rosebud battle, fought a week before Custer's Last Stand, that he is still a white man at heart. So Clayton deserts his Indian companions, and ends up with the soldiers at the Little Big Horn. In recounting the Last Stand, Henry reverts to the approach which, consistently followed, might have resulted in a distinguished novel. Clayton, once more, is an epic hero who fights beside Custer until he is "killed"—only to rise again and, on his equally indestructible horse Hussein, ride off in search of the people he had foresaken, into the enfolding mists of legend like a modern El Cid. [49]

Will Henry had the opportunity to write a great Custer novel within his grasp, but he let it slip through his fingers. Fourteen years later, Thomas Berger finished the book that Henry might have written. *Little Big Man* mines the same vein as *No Survivors*, but turns up most of the gold. *No Survivors* is "based" on the journal of the late John Clayton; *Little Big Man* is the firsthand narrative of irrascible, impossibly ancient Jack Crabb. Both men are super heroes, but Crabb does just twice as much as Clayton, and covers twice as much ground in doing it. The real superiority of *Little Big Man*, however, lies in Berger's flawless control of his theme: he is not so much exploding the old legends as, in Granville Hicks' words, "creating a new legend." [50] Crabb, of course, *is* the "new legend," and in himself encompasses most of the old ones.

Fittingly, then, his story breaks off just after Custer's Last Stand, one of America's great "legends of total annihilation."[51]

Jack Crabb is not only the most recent, but also the most arresting, addition to the company of "Sole Survivors." John Clayton is his literary antecedent. The historical antecedent of both might well be Jack Cleybourne. Cleybourne, allegedly captured by the Cheyennes in 1866 and named Chialla (White Cheyenne), witnessed many battles from the Indian side over the years. At the Washita battle in 1868 he tried to save some of the Indian children from the Seventh Cavalry, and he claimed to have seen Custer fall last at the Little Big Horn eight years later.[52] Jack Crabb, John Clayton, Jack Cleybourne. The names blend; the line between possible fact and intentional fiction becomes so indistinct that one can hardly be positive which is which. Caught in this dilemma, an English reader of a popular Western magazine wrote in to the editors to determine if "a Captain or a Colonel S. [*sic*] Clayton, a former Confederate," was with the Indians at the Little Big Horn. Appropriately, no one at the magazine could tell him for certain.[53]

Because there were no survivors, the element of uncertainty is deeply ingrained in all accounts of Custer's Last Stand. But in turn, it is this very uncertainty which permits the legend of a sole survivor to flourish. We do not, *cannot*, know for sure; perhaps there really was a Jack Crabb. Such lingering doubts provide an ideal foundation for the writer to build on. For, as Berger demonstrates in *Little Big Man*, the tradition of a sole survivor at Custer's Last Stand can be a springboard into the realm of Western myth.

A close study of Berger's historical sources would serve to facilitate the critical task to the extent that his meaning can often be more precisely determined from a knowledge of his borrowings. But his sources are two-fold. In *Little Big Man*, Berger is faithful to both the West of history and the West of myth. Each contributes in its own way to the aura of plausibility that so enriches the basic tall tale that he is telling. The surface accuracy, the correctness of detail, the verisimilitude that he conveys, derive from a book-learned, factual knowledge. But *Little Big Man* rests upon a foundation of Western myth. Leslie Fiedler, on the premise that the two kinds of "truth," historical and mythical, are necessarily in conflict, considered *Little Big Man* a "compulsive anti-mythical burlesque," one of the genre of New Westerns which parody the formula Westerns and the myths that they have so self-consciously perpetuated.[54] Berger, however, goes beyond parody to the realization that these myths are now as vital—as *real*—as historical fact. *Little Big Man* itself refutes Fiedler's contentions by showing that it is only by blending the two kinds of truth that one arrives at the West of the American mind. Far from being incompatible, history and myth are the essential elements in a single concept. Thus Berger's use of the tradition of a sole survivor of Custer's Last Stand was particularly appropriate, for it is a myth within a myth grounded in fact. Jack Crabb's saga, then, like the Old West itself, is a compound of history, myth and imagination. All three elements deserve the critic's attention.

Notes

1. L. L. Lee, "American, Western, Picaresque: Thomas Berger's *Little Big Man*," *South Dakota Review* 4 (Summer 1966): 35–42.

2. William T. Pilkington, "Aspects of the Western Comic Novel," *Western American Literature* 1 (Fall 1966): 215–17.

3. Delbert E. Wylder, "Thomas Berger's *Little Big Man* As Literature," *Western American Literature* 3 (Winter 1969): 273–84.

4. Jay Gurian, "Style in the Literary Desert: *Little Big Man*," *Western American Literature* 3 (Winter 1969): 285–96.

5. Thomas Berger, quoted in ibid., 296.

6. Wylder, "Thomas Berger's *Little Big Man* As Literature," 283.

7. Ibid., 279.

8. Thomas Berger, *Little Big Man* (New York: Dial Press, 1964), 433.

9. Ibid., 440.

10. Wylder, "Thomas Berger's *Little Big Man* As Literature," 282.

11. Mari Sandoz, *Crazy Horse: The Strange Man of the Oglalas* (New York: Alfred A. Knopf, 1942), viii–ix. However, this statement should not be taken too literally, since Crazy Horse did wear paint and some ornamentation in battle. See, for example, ibid., 326.

12. A. B. Guthrie, Jr., "The Historical Novel," *Montana Magazine of History* 4 (Fall 1954): 6.

13. Robert Edson Lee, *From West to East: Studies in the Literature of the American West* (Urbana: University of Illinois Press, 1966), 156.

14. Surely no reader of *Western American Literature* has forgotten Dr. Angus McFrisby, "Professor of English at the Upper Pahvant College for Girls and one of the leading authenticators in Western letters," a particular target in Don D. Walker's delightful "The Rise and Fall of Barney Tullus," *Western American Literature* 3 (Summer 1968): 93–102.

15. Berger, *Little Big Man*, 396.

16. "General Denies Suicide Story

Told Here," *Denver Post*, June 23 [?],
1918. Clipping in George A. Custer
folder, B–C 96g, Western History
Research Center,

17. Fred Dustin, *The Custer
Tragedy: Events Leading up to and following the Little Big Horn Campaign
of 1876* (1939; reprint, Ann Arbor:
Edwards Brothers, 1965), 150.

18. Stewart H. Holbrook, "Phonies
of the Old West," *American Mercury*
68 (February 1949): 234.

19. T. J. (Tim) Mahoney, "Was It
Really Gen. Custer's Last Stand?"
Casper Star-Tribune, March 20, 1966.
Edgar I. Stewart discusses two ver-
sions of the Custer survived story in
"Which Indian Killed Custer?" *Mon-
tana the Magazine of Western History* 8
(Summer 1958): 31–32.

20. *Life and Adventures of Frank
Grouard*, ed. Edgar I. Stewart (1894;
reprint, Norman: University of Oklahoma Press, 1958), 123–24. Stewart
also edited James H. Bradley's diary
of the 1876 expedition under the title
*The March of the Montana Column: A
Prelude to the Custer Disaster* (1896;
reprint, Norman: University of Oklahoma Press, 1961). Bradley discovered
the bodies of Custer's men on the
morning of June 27, 1876.

21. Wallace David Coburn, "The
Battle of the Little Big Horn," *Mon-
tana the Magazine of Western History* 6
(Summer 1956): 36.

22. Mrs. A. B. Conway, letter in
Life, July 12, 1948, p. 8. Mrs. Conway
was fortunate enough to have in her
possession an affidavit signed by Nixon
on May 18, 1927, verifying this tale.

23. Kathryn Wright, "The *Real* Calamity Jane," *True West* (December
1957), 25. The letter and the daughter
(by Wild Bill Hickok) are equally spuri-
ous.

24. Prentiss Ingraham, "Buffalo Bill's Grip; or, Oath-Bound to
Custer," *Beadle's Weekly* 1 (January 13–March 10, 1883).

25. Author of Buffalo Bill [Prentiss
Ingraham?], "Buffalo Bill's Gallant
Stand; or, The Indian's Last Vic-
tory," *Buffalo Bill Stories*, no. 95
(March 7, 1903).

26. Herbert Myrick, *Cache la
Poudre: The Romance of a Tender-
foot in the Days of Custer* (New York:
Orange Judd Company, 1905), 177–78.

27. The underlying assumption that
Custer's obstinancy deafened him to
advice receives some support from history. Among others, scouts "Lonesome
Charley" Reynolds, Bloody Knife, Half
Yellow Face and the half-breed Mitch
Bouyer were all extremely pessimistic about the Seventh's chances at the
Little Big Horn, and expressed strong
doubts about the wisdom of attacking
the Indian village. Custer ignored their
warnings, and even taunted Bouyer
with the suggestion that, in consideration of his Sioux blood, he would
perhaps prefer not to fight. His courage
questioned, Bouyer went to the death
with the General. Thus, if they were
not actually threatened with arrest,
Custer's scouts did feel the lash of his
scorn—even Buffalo Bill when, in *Buffalo Bill's Gallant Stand*, his words
of caution were met with the retort,
"What, Cody, are you, too, going to

turn croaker?" So, against his better judgment, Buffalo Bill finds himself knee-deep in Indians at the Last Stand.

28. Because it was among the first of many such tales, Ridgely's was widely reprinted and cited. See, for example, William Blackmore's introduction to Richard I. Dodge, *The Plains of the Great West* (1877; reprint, New York: Archer House, 1959), xxxix–xl.

29. Max Miller, *It Must Be the Climate* (New York: Robert M. McBride and Co., 1941), 95.

30. "Killing of Custer Seen by Saugus Man," unidentified clipping in George A. Custer folder, B–C 96g, Western History Research Center, Laramie, Wyoming.

31. W. A. Graham, *The Custer Myth: A Source Book of Custeriana* (Harrisburg, Pa.: Stackpole Co., 1953), 355.

32. Berger, *Little Big Man*, 396.

33. Ibid., 362.

34. William O. Stoddard, *Little Smoke: A Tale of the Sioux* (New York: D. Appleton and Co., 1891), 288.

35. "Report of Major M. H. [*sic*] Reno," July 5, 1876, in *Annual Report of the Secretary of War* [1876], 44th Cong., 2d sess., 477–78.

36. Graham, *Custer Myth*, 80.

37. See, for example, Noname [Lu Senarens], "Custer's Little Dead-shot; or, The Boy Scout of the Little Big Horn," *Wide Awake Library*, no. 826 (May 16, 1888); Edwin L. Sabin, *On the Plains with Custer* (Philadelphia: J. B. Lippincott Co., 1913); and Jeff Jeffries, *Seventh Cavalry* (London: Children's Press, n.d.).

38. Graham, *Custer Myth*, 267–78,

354–55. The story of John Martin and the last message is told on 287–300.

39. J. C. Ryan, ed., *Custer Fell First* (San Antonio: Naylor Co., 1966), 47–48. The parallels between Lockwood's story and the usual juvenile Custer novel are unmistakable. At the age of fourteen, boy hero (Lockwood) meets Boy General (the chapter is titled "The Little Cowboy Meets the General"); they become fast friends and hunting companions from 1873 on; Lockwood serves as an apprentice scout under "Lonesome Charley" Reynolds and, at the Little Big Horn, carries Custer's last dispatch (note that the General, in keeping with the motif of illogical familiarity, even knows the name of his horse); and, after the battle, at the age of nineteen, Jack decides to enlist in the Seventh Cavalry.

40. Anthony A. Amaral, *Comanche: The Horse That Survived the Custer Massacre* (Los Angeles: Westernlore Press, 1961), 33–34 n. 4.

41. Berger, *Little Big Man*, 396.

42. Edgar I. Stewart, *Custer's Luck* (Norman: University of Oklahoma Press, 1955), 490.

43. Dustin, *Custer Tragedy*, 150.

44. Holbrook, "Phonies of the Old West," 235.

45. Stewart, *Custer's Luck*, 491.

46. Ibid., 491–92. Also see Charles Kuhlman, *The Frank Finkel Story*, ed. Michael J. Koury (Omaha: Citizen Printing Co., 1968).

47. Pandy and Mason are, respectively, old and young heroes of a dime novel by "Custer's Scout" [St. George Henry Rathborne], "Custer's Last

Shot; or, The Boy Trailer of the Little Horn, *Boys of New York* (August 7–September 4, 1876); while Tom Carleton is the young hero of an unknown writer's story, "Sitting Bull on the War Path; or, Custer in the Black Hills," *Fireside Companion* (August 28–December 11, 1876).

48. Will Henry [Henry W. Allen], *No Survivors* (New York: Random House, 1950), 107.

49. Henry W. Allen's work, published under the pen-names Will Henry and Clay Fisher, is intelligently assessed in a long review by Arnold E. Needham in *Western American Literature* 1 (Winter 1967): 297–302. Needham attempts to distinguish between the quality writing and the drivel that Allen, in his prolificity, turns out indiscriminately.

50. Granville Hicks, "Paleface in the Cheyenne Camp," *Saturday Review* (October 10, 1964), 40.

51. D. W. Brogan, *The American Character* (New York: Vintage Books, 1954), 181.

52. Kent Ladd Steckmesser, *The Western Hero in History and Legend* (Norman: University of Oklahoma Press, 1965), 204.

53. N. B. (Essex, England), in *The West* (June 1966), 43.

54. Leslie A. Fiedler, *The Return of the Vanishing American* (New York: Stein and Day, 1968), 161, 164.

"CORRECT IN
EVERY DETAIL":
GENERAL CUSTER
IN HOLLYWOOD

PAUL ANDREW HUTTON

t the conclusion of John Ford's classic film *Fort Apache* (1948), a group of newspaper reporters question Lieutenant Colonel Kirby York (John Wayne) about his forthcoming campaign against Geronimo, while also reflecting on the glorious reputation of his regiment. That glory is chiefly derived from the last stand of the regiment's previous commander, Lieutenant Colonel Owen Thursday (Henry Fonda). Colonel York despised Thursday, who had in reality sacrificed the regiment to racial arrogance, vainglorious pride, and wounded vanity. The last stand had in fact been a near-rout in which Thursday had played little part except to initiate disaster. "No man died more gallantly," York responds to a reporter's praise of Thursday, his voice sad and dripping with irony, "nor won more honor for his regiment." Asked if he has seen the grand painting of "Thursday's Charge" now hanging in the nation's capitol, the colonel answers affirmatively.

"That was a magnificent work," declares an enthusiastic reporter. "There were these massed columns of Apaches in their warpaint and feathered bonnets, and here was Thursday leading his men in that heroic charge."

"Correct in every detail," the colonel responds.

Of course, as Colonel York and the film's audience know only too well, not a single detail of the painting was correct. But York has come to understand that if the sacrifice of his regiment is to have any value it must be as myth. That myth, even if mostly false, can still provide an ideal of courage and sacrifice that will give the new regiment (and the new nation) strength, pride, and a sense of identity.

Director Ford and screenwriter Frank S. Nugent understood that the importance of heroes is not to be found in the often mundane or sordid reality of their lives, but rather in what society makes of them. Ford, who based *Fort Apache* loosely on the Custer story, had no problem in revealing the incompetence, hypocrisy, and brutality of the frontier army or in displaying the honor, dignity, and heroism of the Native Americans twenty years before it became fashionable to do so.

Some critics, who often castigate Ford as a chauvinistic celebrationist, are puzzled by the conclusion of *Fort Apache*. They fail to comprehend its subtlety, which goes, of course, to the heart of understanding and accepting our most cherished national myths for what they actually are. Ford had no problem with the ending.

Critic and filmmaker Peter Bogdanovich questioned Ford about the ending of *Fort Apache* in a 1967 interview, rightly pointing out that it foreshadowed the conclusion of an even darker Ford portrayal of frontier myth in *The Man Who Shot Liberty Valance* (1962):

Bogdanovich: The end of *Fort Apache* anticipates the newspaper
  editor's line in *Liberty Valance*, "when the legend becomes a fact,
  print the legend." Do you agree with that?
Ford: Yes—because I think it's good for the country. We've had a lot
  of people who were supposed to be great heroes, and you know
  damn well they weren't. But it's good for the country to have
  heroes to look up to. Like Custer—a great hero. Well, he wasn't.
  Not that he was a stupid man—but he did a stupid job that day.[1]

Despite Ford's belief that myth was "good for the country," his artistic vision is dedicated in both *Fort Apache* and *The Man Who Shot Liberty Valance* to the explanation of a truth about the past that was lost to most of his Hollywood peers and to many historians as well: that good men, with noble motives, can do evil. His truthful fiction of the Custer battle, *Fort Apache*, remains the best of over forty celluloid portrayals of America's most flamboyant military failure, George Armstrong Custer.[2]

The trick, of course, in reviewing the checkered cinematic career of the enigmatic General Custer is to find a film that is correct in *any* detail, much less one correct in *every* detail. Much like John Wayne's Colonel York in *Fort Apache* we, as the audience viewing these films, must search for a higher correctness in them than a mere adherence to fact—and that can prove a daunting task indeed.

Custer's dead troopers had yet to receive a proper burial before the redoubtable William F. "Buffalo Bill" Cody was amazing eastern audiences with his *The Red Right Hand; or, Buffalo Bill's First Scalp for Custer.* Now, you had to admire Cody's grit, for in the summer of 1876 he had abandoned the eastern stage (where he had been doing good box-office business since 1872) to rejoin his old regiment on the plains. Everyone from General Phil Sheridan on down believed this would be the last great Indian war, and Cody was not about to miss it.

Having heard the shocking news about Custer, the Fifth Regiment was scouting the rolling hills along Warbonnet Creek, Nebraska, on July 17, 1876, when an advance party of Little Wolf's Cheyennes, on their way north to join Sitting Bull, clashed with a small party of soldiers led by Cody. The long-haired scout, garbed in one of his stage costumes of black velvet trimmed with silver buttons and lace, brought down the only casualty in the skirmish, an unfortunately bold Cheyenne warrior with the ironic name of Yellow Hair (the name was in recognition of a blonde scalp he had taken). Cody promptly lifted the fellow's hair, proclaiming his grisly trophy as "the first scalp for Custer." The soldiers then chased the Indians back to the Red Cloud Agency in one of the army's few victories of the Great Sioux War.[3]

Within five weeks Cody left the army, heading eastward where the opportunities for glory before the footlights were far greater than on the plains. The new play, according to Buffalo Bill, was a five-act monstrosity "without head or tail . . . a noisy, rattling, gunpowder entertainment." It was Cody's most successful play.[4]

After Warbonnet Creek it became increasingly difficult to tell if art were imitating life or vice versa. Cody had dressed the morning of July 17, 1876, in his Mexican vaquero stage outfit in anticipation of a battle with the Indians. He was anxious to later tell his eastern audiences that his colorful costume was authentic, for he wanted to shed the drab buckskins he had always worn. Dressed properly for the part he ventured forth and boldly killed an Indian in a frontier ritual that immediately reaffirmed his hero status. He then hurried east, scalp in tow, to exploit this act before audiences hungry for a look at a "real Wild West" as fresh as the morning headlines, but already anachronistic to an increasingly urban, industrial society. It was as if the frontier

West was providing them with living, breathing entertainment. After his premier performance at Warbonnet Creek (and it certainly was a more daunting act than Errol Flynn or John Wayne ever had to perform), Cody simply took the show on the road in *The Red Right Hand*, and the profits were indeed impressive.

When Cody initiated his famous Wild West show in 1883 he continued his personal identification with the Custer story. Sitting Bull toured for a season with the company, and Custer's Last Stand was often reenacted as the climax of the program. As time passed Cody updated the historical pageants, so that the last stand rotated with scenes from the Spanish-American War or the Boxer Rebellion, but Cody's first scalp for Custer remained standard fare throughout the show's long run.[5]

Cody was naturally attracted to the new medium of moving pictures. As early as 1894 his Wild West company was filmed by the Edison Kinetoscope for the peepshow circuit. It was financial disaster, however, that brought Cody into the film business. Fred Bonfils and Harry Tammen, the buccaneering capitalists who owned the Denver *Post*, forced Cody into bankruptcy in 1913 and then used him to form, in collaboration with the Essanay Company, the Colonel W. F. Cody (Buffalo Bill) Historical Pictures Company in September 1913.

The company was to film a historical epic of the Indian wars using many of the actual participants, including Cody, retired Lieutenant General Nelson Miles, Frank Baldwin, Charles King, Dewey Beard, Iron Tail, Short Bull, and Running Hawk. The scenario for *Buffalo Bill's Indian Wars* was by Charles King, a former Fifth Cavalry officer who had been with Cody at Warbonnet Creek and had since become a famous novelist. It included the Battle of Summit Springs, Cody's first scalp for Custer, the death of Sitting Bull, and was climaxed with a re-creation of the tragedy at Wounded Knee. Denver *Post* reporter Courtney Ryley Cooper, who would later ghostwrite the autobiography of Cody's wife and write a 1923 Custer novel, *The Last Frontier*, that would be twice filmed by Hollywood, reported that the picture, thanks to Cody and General Miles, "was historically correct in every detail and that not a feature was forgotten."[6]

The government, having provided six-hundred cavalrymen for the film, may have been unhappy with Cody's determination to portray the massacre at Wounded Knee truthfully. Cody and Miles quarreled bitterly during the filming and their long friendship came to a stormy end.

The government delayed release of the film for almost a year. When it finally played in New York and Denver, Cody and several Sioux appeared on stage to introduce it. The film was rereleased in 1917 after Cody's death but was never widely distributed. "My object of desire," declared Buffalo Bill before his death, "has been to preserve history by the aid of the camera with as many living participants in the closing Indian wars of North America as could be procured."[7] Perhaps in his final foray into show business, Buffalo Bill had, for once, been too truthful. Ben Black Elk, whose father was in the film, claimed that the Interior Department banned it and later destroyed it. No copy is known to exist today.

Even before Cody's film was completed in October 1913, the Custer story had already been told at least four times on film. William Selig's 1909 one-reeler, *Custer's Last Stand (On the Little Big Horn)*, used a reenactment of the battle on the actual site by the Montana National Guard as the centerpiece of its story. More ambitious was Thomas Ince's 1912 three-reeler, *Custer's Last Fight*. Starring as well as directed by Francis Ford, the brother of John Ford, the movie centered on the old tale that Rain-in-the-Face had stalked Custer at the Little Big Horn to avenge his earlier arrest. The film ranks as one of the few Custer movies to treat Indians as vicious savages, leaving no doubt that the Sioux must be swept aside to make way for the greater civilization that Ford's Custer represents. Sitting Bull is portrayed as a coward while Custer appears as a wise, experienced commander. Ford's heroic portrayal of Custer set a pattern unbroken in film until his brother made *Fort Apache* in 1948.[8]

Like *Fort Apache*, D. W. Griffith's 1912 film, *The Massacre*, presented an impressionistic interpretation of the Custer fight far removed from the penchant for historical detail found in the Ince film. The battle is secondary to the primary story of a pioneer family moving West and of the heroic scout who silently loves the pioneer's wife. Unlike the Ince film, the Griffith film treats the Indians heroically. An attractive Indian family is presented in parallel to the pioneer family, but their happy lives are destroyed in a Washita-like massacre led by a long-haired, Custer-like cavalry officer. The Indian father escapes, but his wife and child are slain, and he swears dark revenge. When the Indian leads his warriors against the wagon train, now escorted by the same cavalry troopers who had killed his family, the soldiers and settlers form a ring around the young pioneer's wife and infant. One by one the whites perish—gambler and priest, general and scout—falling side by side. When the young pioneer arrives with a rescue column he finds wife and child alive under the pile of corpses, the men having made human shields of themselves.

Custer is identifiable as the leader of the cavalry, but was not named in the film—possibly because such liberties were taken with the facts of Little Big Horn, and possibly because the Ince film was released at the same time. Nevertheless, *The Massacre* clearly presents the essence of the early Custer myth, both in print and on film: the heroic self-sacrifice of Custer and his men to protect the pioneers and expand civilization's borders.

Bison Films, the releasing company for the Ince film, also released *Campaigning with Custer* in 1913 and *Custer's Last Scout* in 1915. Successful novels were the basis of two more Custer films of that era: Vitagraph's 1916 four-part serial, *Britton of the Seventh*, featuring Ned Finley as Custer, based on Cyrus Townsend Brady's 1914 novel; and Marshall Neilan's *Bob Hampton of Placer* (1921), starring Dwight Crittenden as Custer and based on Randall Parrish's 1906 book. Both films dealt with the theme of a disgraced officer who redeems himself at the Little Big Horn. This plot device became commonplace in Custer fiction and films. Custer appeared briefly in Clifford Smith's *Wild Bill Hickok* (1923), where he persuades William S. Hart as Wild Bill to strap back on his pistols to bring law and order to the frontier. Custer made another cameo in Metropolitan's *The Last Frontier* (1926), this time assisting Wild Bill and Buffalo Bill in a film based on Courtney Ryley Cooper's 1923 novel. RKO remade the film as a serial in 1932 with William Desmond as Custer.[9]

Several Custer films were released to coincide with the fiftieth anniversary of the last stand. The first was J. G. Adophe's 1925 nine-reeler, *The Scarlet West*, which used the unusual plot device of an Indian hero. Robert Frazier portrayed Cardelanche, the educated son of a Sioux chief who attempts to lead his people over to white culture. Frustrated in his efforts, he leaves the Sioux and accepts a commission in the cavalry. He soon falls in love with the post commander's daughter, played by Clara Bow, but the gulf between them proves too great and he returns to his own people after they wipe out Custer's command. Such an involved plot was not allowed to slow the action in Anthony J. Xydias' *With General Custer at Little Big Horn*, released the following year as part of a series of films on American history by Sunset Pictures.[10]

Universal's 1926 film, *The Flaming Frontier* was the best publicized of the rash of Custer films, billed as "the supreme achievement in western epics."[11] Again the story involved a disgraced soldier who wins redemption at Little Big Horn. In this case the soldier was former pony express rider Bob Langdon, played by Hoot Gibson, who is unjustly expelled from West Point. He quite naturally heads West and promptly finds employment as a scout for Custer, played by Dustin Farnum. Corruption on the frontier and ineptitude in Washington undermine the efforts of the heroic Custer to keep peace with the cheated Indians who are finally driven to the warpath. At the last moment, Custer sends scout Langdon for reinforcements, and although he is unable to save the Seventh Langdon does defeat the white villain, rescue the heroine, and get reinstated to West Point.

The last stand was elaborately staged with Farnum, who came out of retirement to portray Custer, giving his role the ultimate hero treatment. One ad for the film simply ran a portrait of Farnum as Custer over the banner—"see his sublime courage in *The Flaming Frontier*."[12] The critic for the New York *Times* was unimpressed, however, noting that Farnum "was in one of his lax moods while impersonating General Custer."[13]

When the film premiered at New York's Colony Theater on April 4, 1926, General Edward S. Godfrey was a special guest of honor.[14] He had distinguished himself as a young lieutenant in Captain Frederick Benteen's detachment at Little Big Horn, and his 1892 article in *Century* magazine had often been praised as the best account of the battle by a participant. He received a standing ovation from the crowd and then settled in to watch the great tragedy of his youth distorted into fanciful entertainment for a people completely divorced from frontier times. One wonders if Custer's widow, Elizabeth, who then lived in New York City, could bring herself to visit Colony Theater.

The Flaming Frontier proved to be the last major silent film on Custer, although the general briefly rode again in Tim McCoy's *Spoilers of the West* in 1927. After the rash of commemorative Custer films, the story was neglected for a decade, had a brief revival of interest in the years just before World War II, then vanished again as a Hollywood subject until 1948.

By the time filmmakers returned to his story, Custer's heroic image was under assault from a variety of sources. Most notable of these was Frederic F. Van de Water's highly successful 1934 biography, *Glory-Hunter*. For fifty-eight years no one had dared to chip away at the hallowed image of Custer, created by the popular press in the decade after Little Big Horn and then carefully nurtured by Elizabeth Custer in a trilogy of bestselling memoirs. Biographies by Frederick Whittaker, Frederick Dellenbaugh, and Frazier Hunt were wildly hagiographic, while for those whose tastes were not literary in nature the Anheuser-Busch Company had more than 150,000 copies of F. Otto Becker's *Custer's Last Fight* distributed as a standard prop of saloon decor. This gaudy print, as close to both history and art as many turn-of-the-century Americans ever got, earnestly reinforced the message of Custer's heroic sacrifice. Custer's critics, and there were many both inside and outside the military, held their tongues so long as his widow lived. But she outlived them all, not dying until 1933.[15]

Van de Water, well known in eastern literary circles as an editor, critic, poet, and novelist, was heavily influenced in his writing by the debunking spirit of the 1920s, best exemplified by Lytton Strachey's pioneering *Eminent Victorians* (1918). Many other writers had followed Strachey's lead, and all were deeply touched by the cynicism growing out of World War I, by a rising spirit of anti-militarism, by the work of Sigmund Freud, and by a new emphasis on social forces at the expense of the previous celebration of the individual. Many heroes besides Custer were reinterpreted to suit the times, but while other reputations survived the attacks, Custer's did not.

Few books have had so immediate and dramatic an impact on both historical interpretation and the popular mind as did Van de Water's *Glory-Hunter*. The biography is simply the most influential book ever written on Custer. Van de Water created a compelling portrait of a man consumed by ambition, driven by demons of his own creation, and finally destroyed by his own hubris. Gone forever was the marble hero of the past.

Within a few years the glory hunter interpretation became the standard portrayal of Custer in the popular press and fiction. It set the tone for novels such as Harry Sinclair Drago's *Montana Road* (1935), Ernest

Haycox's *Bugles in the Afternoon* (1944), Will Henry's *No Survivors* (1950), Frank Gruber's *Bugles West* (1954), Thomas Berger's *Little Big Man* (1964), and Lewis B. Patten's *The Red Sabbath* (1968).[16]

Films were changing as well, and at first it seemed as if Hollywood might follow the cynical lead of the literary elites. Adapting to the revolutionary changes wrought by the coming of sound, films such as *The Dawn Patrol* (1930) and *All Quiet on the Western Front* (1930) exposed the insanity of war; while *Little Caeser* (1930), *The Public Enemy* (1931), and *Scarface* (1931) condemned the power of the underworld while linking it to societal indifference to poverty. Meanwhile, *The Front Page* (1931), *I Am a Fugitive from a Chain Gang* (1932), and *The Dark Horse* (1932) made it clear that corruption was not confined to the mobsters.

As social commentaries such films, combined as they were with a more daring approach to sexuality and violence, enraged conservative segments of the American public. These groups found their voice with the 1933 formation of the Legion of Decency. Will Hays, who had been appointed twelve years earlier by the major film companies to insure the decency of Hollywood's product, now found a powerful ally in the Legion. His job had proved futile until the church-backed Legion gave him the clout to clean up Hollywood. Gone was the sex and violence, but a successful attack was also launched against the cynical irreverence and negative tone of the social commentary films. Censorship triumphed so that the slum problems that produced the gangsters were replaced by the agonies of young Andy Hardy as he learned the social graces, and the corruptions endemic in political life were drowned out by the spirited songs and high-stepping dancers of Busby Berkeley musicals. The only truly serious topics touched upon were in celluloid versions of classic literature, and even they were cleaned up. Thus was the American cinema made safe for every sheltered twelve-year-old in the country.[17]

In such a stifling atmosphere no film was about to attack a national hero like Custer. Furthermore, the very forces in the late twenties that had led to the social commentary films had also left the western in disrepute as simple-minded entertainment for the masses. With the 1929 stock market crash the studios retrenched and proved unwilling to finance films of the magnitude necessary to tell Custer's story. This trend was exacerbated by the coming of sound, for the bulky and expensive sound equipment made outdoor action dramas more difficult and costly to film.

Prestige westerns continued to be made throughout the 1930s, with *Cimarron* in 1931 becoming the only western to date to win the Academy Award for Best Picture, but they were limited to only one or two a year. Instead the genre was dominated by the budget, or B, western. Led by Republic Studio, many independent production companies now rushed to fill the entertainment gap created by the desertion of the western by the majors. Stories became increasingly simple-minded and action-oriented, with the singing cowboy emerging as a Hollywood staple. Gone was the stark western realism pioneered by silent star William S. Hart. In its place came the entertaining froth of Ken Maynard, Buck Jones, Hoot Gibson, and Gene Autry. Not until the commercial and critical success of John Ford's *Stagecoach* in 1939, which also rescued John Wayne from the Republic Bs, was interest in serious, prestige westerns renewed.[18]

Custer thus turned up in only five films in the decade, with three of them low-budget serials for the Saturday-matinee crowd: RKO's 1932 remake of *The Last Frontier* with William Desmond as Custer; the fifteen-episode *Custer's Last Stand* in 1936 with Frank McGlynn, Jr., as a rather elderly-looking Custer (the serial was cut and rereleased as a feature a decade later); and the 1939 Johnny Mack Brown vehicle *The Oregon Trail*, with Roy Barcroft as Custer. Clay Clement had a cameo as Custer in *The World Changes* (1933), a dark tale of the rise of a meat-packing magnate starring Paul Muni. Custer appears only long enough to inform Muni's isolated Dakota family that the Civil War is at last over, but they never knew it started. Finally, Custer is featured in the splashiest epic western of the decade, Cecil B. DeMille's 1937 celebration of Manifest Destiny, *The Plainsman*.

DeMille's film once again brought Custer (John Miljan) together with Wild Bill (Gary Cooper) and Buffalo Bill (James Ellison), this time with a glamorous Calamity Jane (Jean Arthur) thrown in for good measure, in a wild tale remarkable for its fidelity to minute historical detail (the statue on Custer's desk is correct) and its absolute disregard for the broad outlines of the historical record.

Custer appears as something of a domineering father figure to the other characters—scolding, rescuing, ordering. The last stand is briefly depicted in a dream sequence narrated by Anthony Quinn as an Indian warrior captured by Hickok and Cody. Rarely has the usually subtle connection between nineteenth-century artwork and twentieth-century film been so blatantly displayed as in the tableau vivant of the Alfred Waud drawing from Whittaker's biography that composes the last stand sequence in the film. When an Indian bullet finally pierces his ever-so-noble heart, Custer clutches onto the flag he has gallantly defended and slowly sinks from view. The uncharitably correct critic for the New York *Times*, a paper which had long since committed itself to the debunked Custer of the Van de Water camp, noted that "Custer rated no more than he received: a brief fadeout."[19]

Custer was back twice in 1940. First in the person of Paul Kelly in MGM's *Wyoming*, a light but entertaining Wallace Beery oater filmed in Jackson Hole, Wyoming. Beery plays his patented good-badman role, helping Custer clean up a crooked town in a film best remembered as the initial teaming of the affable star with Marjorie Main. More impressive was Warner Brothers' *Santa Fe Trail*, directed by Michael Curtiz and purporting to tell the story of how young Jeb Stuart (Errol Flynn) and George Custer (Ronald Reagan) frustrate John Brown in Kansas then capture him at Harpers Ferry. Raymond Massey's portrayal of Brown as a mad Old Testament prophet steals the show, despite the film's pro-southern posture.

Not the least of the film's inaccuracies was that the real Custer was but sixteen at the time of Brown's Kansas raids. The Robert Buckner script also had Reagan's Custer as thoughtful and introspective, given to furrowing his brow and actually thinking that slavery just might be wrong—none of which characteristics was in keeping with the real Custer. Even Reagan, who had just finished his role as George Gipp in *Knute Rockne—All American*, noticed that the plot was not following his childhood history lessons. "I discovered I would again be playing a biographical role," he noted, "but with less attention to the truth this time."[20] The New York *Times*, later to be at odds with Reagan so often, was in complete agreement this time: "For anyone who has the slightest regard for the spirit—not to mention the facts—of American history, it will prove exceedingly annoying."[21] But while *Santa Fe Trail* may have flunked as history, it got an "A" as rousing entertainment.

There was no slackening of Custer's celluloid appearances in 1941. As the nation warily confronted a world consumed by war, and hesitatingly prepared for its own inevitable entry into conflagration, military heroes became quite popular again. Alfred Green's *Badlands of Dakota* for Universal featured Addison Richards as Custer in yet another horse opera reuniting him with Wild Bill (Richard Dix) and Calamity Jane (Frances Farmer). Robert Stack, then a young contract actor appearing in only his fourth film, remembered it as "one of the most forgettable westerns ever made."[22]

Two powerful Hollywood tycoons clashed early in 1941 over Custer films. Both Jack Warner and Sam Goldwyn developed prestige westerns on Custer, and then argued bitterly over just who had priority rights to the story. Custer belongs to the public domain, of course, so neither possessed exclusive "rights," but Warner triumphed and Goldwyn eventually gave up on his film. He had envisioned *Seventh Cavalry* as a sure-fire box-office winner to follow the success of his 1940 hit *The Westerner* with Gary Cooper and Walter Brennan. Goldwyn planned to reunite these two stars in *Seventh Cavalry*, with Brennan (who had won an Academy Award for his Judge Roy Bean portrayal in *The Westerner*) as a villainous Custer and Cooper as a Captain Benteen-like officer.

It was Warner Brothers' *They Died with Their Boots On* that went into production. The title was from Thomas Ripley's 1935 popular history of western gunfighters, a property purchased by Warners but never developed. It was a major film for Warners, with $1,357,000 eventually budgeted for the production. Michael Curtiz, the director of swashbuckling adventure films such as *Captain Blood, The Charge of the Light Brigade,* and *The Adventures of Robin Hood,* was scheduled to direct the film but was replaced by Raoul Walsh once Errol Flynn was cast as the lead. Flynn and Curtiz had clashed on previous films and would not work together again. Walsh, also a master of the adventure film, with such classics as *What Price Glory?* and *High Sierra* to his credit, was just as importantly a great drinking buddy of Flynn.[23]

The original script by Wally Kline and Aeneas Mackenzie clearly was influenced by the Van de Water biography, but the studio decided to rewrite the script to better fit the Flynn persona. Associate producer Robert Fellows properly characterized it as a "fairy tale, with no attempt at adherence to historical fact." Still, screenwriter Lenore Coffee, called in to punch-up the romantic scenes between George and Elizabeth, was horrified by "really shocking inaccuracies" in the script. She was ignored, and, despite her major contribution to the final script, denied screen credit.[24] Warner Brothers had firmly decided to treat

General Custer in the same swashbuckling manner in which they had handled Robin Hood in 1938. The tenor of the times influenced the decision. "In preparing this scenario," screenwriter Mackenzie assured producer Hal Wallis, "all possible consideration was given the construction of a story which would have the best effect upon public morale in these present days of national crisis."[25] While *Life* magazine lamented that the film "glorifies a rash general," and the New York *Times* accused "writers in warbonnets" of scalping history, the only critics that Warner Brothers cared about lined up in droves to see *They Died with Their Boots On*. It was a huge success at the box-office.[26]

The impressive action sequences in the film were particularly difficult to shoot. Because of the excessive number of injuries to horses caused by the use of the "Running W" in Warners' *The Charge of the Light Brigade* (1936) the American Humane Association had successfully sued the studio to stop the cruel practice.[27] To the increased difficulty in portraying horse falls were added new Screen Extras' Guild rules preventing directors from hiring only experienced riders. Many old cowboys had drifted into the employ of the studios in the silent era and for years they formed a reliable cadre of cheap talent for riding scenes in westerns. Walsh and other directors had been able to hire specific cowboys for action scenes in their films, but the new union rules changed all that.[28]

In the opening days of filming the cavalry charges, more than eighty of the inexperienced riders were injured. Three men were killed. As the buses carrying the extras left the studio for the Lasky Ranch in Agoura, where the battle scenes were shot, they were followed by an ambulance. One day Anthony Quinn hired a hearse to follow the ambulance, which panicked the extras and sent them scurrying back to the studio. Eventually Walsh got the experienced riders he wanted.[29]

The film follows Custer from West Point to Little Big Horn, and only in the opening sequences is the harder edge of the original script still evident. But Custer's vain buffoonery and rashness in the West Point and Civil War sections of the film quickly give way to thoughtful heroism once he reaches the frontier.

Flynn brought his usual charm and elan to the Custer role, of course, and was ably supported by Olivia de Havilland, who had been teamed with him seven times before, as Elizabeth Custer. This is the only film to deal with the relationship of the Custers at great length, with the script displaying a great reliance on Elizabeth's books as source material.[30] Stanley Ridges played Romulus Taipe, the villainous soldier turned politician, who is obviously based on Grant's venal Secretary of War, William W. Belknap. John Litel portrayed Custer's mentor, General Phil Sheridan, while Charley Grapewin was along for comedy relief as a crusty California Joe. G. P. Huntley portrayed Custer's British adjutant, who is called Lieutenant Butler in the film, although named Cooke in the original script. The character is obviously based on Custer's true adjutant, William W. Cooke, who was a Canadian known as "Queen's Own," the same nickname given to the Butler character in the film. Having faced recent lawsuits over historical films, the studios often changed the names of real characters to avoid possible litigation.

The film is one of the few westerns to make the important connection between the Civil War and national expansion. After the Gettysburg sequence, where the inexplicable plot device of an accidental promotion thrusts Custer into high command so that he can save the Union by turning back the rebel cavalry, the war is told through a series of effective montages. The new national hero returns home to Michigan to wed Elizabeth and settle into civilian life. He is approached by Taipe to lend his name to a shady stock deal but angrily rejects the offer, proclaiming: "I'll gamble with anything, my money, my sword and even my life. But there's one thing I won't gamble with, and that is my good name!"

Recalled to active service through the influence of his wife, he quickly organizes the Seventh Cavalry from a band of misfits and outcasts into a crack regiment that breaks the power of the hostile tribes. Custer pledges to Crazy Horse (Anthony Quinn) that in exchange for peace he will guard the sacred Black Hills from white intrusion. In another bow to western art, the scene between Flynn and Quinn is based on Charles Schreyvogel's painting *Custer's Demand*.

This interferes with the railroad-building scheme of Taipe and his accomplice, Ned Sharp (Arthur Kennedy), and they conspire to have Custer recalled to Washington while they plant false rumors of gold in the Black Hills. Custer's attempts to expose their conspiracy before Congress is ruled as hearsay, admissable only as a dying declaration. Frustrated, Custer is finally able to convince President Grant (Joseph Crehan) to restore him to his command. Realizing that the Seventh

Cavalry will have to be sacrificed to give General Sheridan more time to mobilize troops to defeat the enraged and betrayed Indians, Custer marches toward Little Big Horn.

The night before the battle Custer writes a letter exposing Taipe which, as a dying declaration, will be admissable as evidence. He asks his adjutant to carry it back to the fort, explaining that he does not wish a foreigner sacrificed in such a "dirty deal" as the coming battle. Butler indignantly refuses, reminding Custer that the only real Americans present are in the Little Big Horn valley waiting for the Seventh.

Custer then knowingly leads the Seventh Cavalry to its doom. And what a glorious doom it is—enacted against a powerful Max Steiner soundtrack countering "Garry Owen" against a rythmic, ragged Indian theme. With his troopers all dead around him, his pistols empty, his long hair dancing in the western breeze, Custer draws his saber and falls from a shot from Crazy Horse's rifle as a charge of mounted warriors rides over him.

The final victory, of course, belongs to Custer. Elizabeth and Sheridan use his final letter to force Taipe's resignation and to receive a pledge from Grant to return the Black Hills to the Sioux. As Sheridan comforts Elizabeth with the assurance that her husband "won his last battle—after all," Custer and his regiment march off into a celluloid sunset to the strains of "Garry Owen."

If only historical reality could have been so sublime. Novelist and screenwriter George MacDonald Fraser, in his marvelous book *The Hollywood History of the World*, dismisses *They Died with Their Boots On* as "typical Hollywood dream-rubbish of the worst kind," a viewpoint echoed by other critics at the time the film was released and ever since.[31]

The historical errors in this particular film are legion: Custer was not promoted to general by mistake; he was not a civilian after the Civil War; he was more than willing to engage in shady business deals reflective of the Gilded Age in which he lived; he did not organize the Seventh in Dakota, but rather in Kansas; he did not protect the Black Hills but rather opened them up; he was not the enemy of the railroad capitalists but their best friend on the northern plains; he was not a defender of Indian rights; he did not knowingly sacrifice his regiment at Little Big Horn to save others; Custer's hair was cut short at the time of the battle and he did not carry a saber, nor did any of his men; the

Sioux were not protected in their rights to the Black Hills as a result of his sacrifice; and on and on and on. But who is truly surprised by that? It is simply ridiculous to expect films to be true to the facts of history. They are works of fiction. If, by chance, they use a story to tell us a greater truth about ourselves and our past then they have succeeded as art. If they give us a momentary diversion and make us smile or tug at our heart, then they have succeeded admirably at what they are—popular entertainment.

They Died with Their Boots On is wonderful entertainment—a rousing adventure reflective of our dreams of how we wish our past might have been. But there is a veneer of truth—Custer was a dashing, romantic soldier; he and Elizabeth did have a storybook marriage; the Sioux were a terribly wronged people; and the last stand was indeed the result of events set in motion by venal capitalists and inept, corrupt politicians. Perhaps the film's greatest artistic triumph is in cutting to the essence of the American love affair with Custer—that the golden-haired soldier was the best his nation had to offer as the people's sacrifice to somehow atone for the ghastly treatment of the Native Americans. Vine Deloria, Jr., hammered home the same message again in the title to his 1969 bestseller: *Custer Died for Your Sins.*

By chance, the film's release in late November 1941 coincided with American entry into World War II. As the people reeled from the news of Pearl Harbor, Wake Island, and Bataan, they could clearly identify with the heroic self-sacrifice of Custer and the Seventh Cavalry. The greedy capitalists, crooked politicians, and gallant soldiers of *They Died with Their Boots On* made perfect sense to a people marching out of economic depression and into war.

There were dramatic changes in the western film genre during the war years. The major filmmakers tended to produce fewer prestige westerns, lavishing budgets instead on escapist fare (this was the heyday of the MGM musical) or on films concerned with the war effort. The independents, of course, continued to crank out formula westerns at a prodigious rate, with Roy Rogers overtaking Gene Autry in 1943 as the top western money-making star. Several of the prestige westerns that were made foreshadowed the trend toward social and psychological films that followed the war. Most notable among these were William Wellman's *The Ox-Bow Incident* (1942) with its bleak vision of the frontier's moral code; Howard Hughes' *The Outlaw* (1943) and King

Vidor's *Duel in the Sun* (1946) with their preoccupation with eroticism; and Raoul Walsh's *Pursued* (1947), perhaps the first Freudian-inspired western.[32]

While none of these themes is explicit in the first post-war Custer film, John Ford's *Fort Apache* (1948), it is nevertheless clear that much of the glossy veneer that surrounded Custer's image in the past had been worn away. While high courage and self-sacrifice are major themes in Ford's film, just as they were in *They Died with Their Boots On*, this time Custer was not to be the hero.

Unrecognized as such by film critics at the time, *Fort Apache* is a fictionalized telling of the Custer story with the locale shifted to the Southwest to make use of Ford's beloved Monument Valley. By changing the historical setting to the stark moral universe of Monument Valley, by fictionalizing his storyline, and by freeing himself from the shackles of historical detail, Ford saved himself from the kind of factual criticism leveled at the Walsh film and allowed his artistic vision full rein. The result is a masterpiece of this peculiarly American art form that comes closer than any other Custer film to explaining the great contradictions of the protagonist's life, death, and legend.[33]

"A legend is more interesting than the actual facts," Ford once said in commenting on Custer.[34] In *Fort Apache* he does not celebrate that legend, but rather explains it. Henry Fonda's Lieutenant Colonel Owen Thursday is a textbook soldier bitter over his postwar reduction in rank from general and anxious to escape from his new frontier assignment by some glorious deed. His rigidity antagonizes his subordinates, and none more so than John Wayne's Captain Kirby York. When the corrupt practices of Indian agent Silas Meacham (Grant Withers) force Cochise (Miguel Inclan) to bolt the reservation, Thursday sees his chance. Through York's efforts the Apaches are persuaded to return from Mexico to meet with Thursday. But the colonel disregards York's promises to Cochise and prepares to attack. Protesting this duplicity, York is accused of cowardice by Thursday and ordered to the rear to protect the pack train. The troops then follow Thursday into Cochise's ambush, with the colonel unhorsed early in the charge. The wounded Thursday ignores York's offer of escape and rejoins his doomed command.

Thursday's tragic flaw, like that of the real Custer, is that he is unable to restrain an individuality bordering on megalomania. A martinet when it comes to enforcing military regulations, he cannot himself abide by the rules of his community, the cavalry. His every action is directed by personal desires, not community needs or moral values. His contempt for ritual is made apparent in his reluctance to fulfill his duty by dancing with the sergeant-major's wife at the NCO Ball, and by his refusal to engage in courtly discussion with Cochise. In the end he disregards better advice and leads his men into a deadly trap. ("They outnumber us four to one. Do we talk or fight?" asks York just before the battle. "You seem easily impressed by numbers, Captain," Thursday responds.) His soldiers follow Thursday because they are solidly members of the community—he leads them into slaughter because he is not. Yet Thursday, for all his faults, is a leader, and so he ignores escape and rejoins his command.[35]

The Indians remain tangential to the main theme of *Fort Apache*. Cochise is presented as a wise leader who wishes to avoid war while his Apaches are an honorable, cheated people. Unlike other celluloid last stands where the men die spread out as individuals, in *Fort Apache* the little band of soldiers forms a tight knot. Thursday stands with them, finally a member of the community he disdained. A distant rumble of hooves builds to a crescendo as the Apaches suddenly burst onto the scene, ride over the soldiers, and just as quickly vanish into the swirling dust. Their appearance is only fleeting as they claim their victory and affirm both Thursday's dishonor and his heroism.[36]

The Indian victory in *Fort Apache* is turned into a spiritual victory for the defeated soldiers, just as Custer's Last Stand achieved a power as legend far greater than any victory Custer might have won at Little Big Horn. Just as John Wayne's York reaffirms the importance of Thursday's sacrifice at the conclusion of *Fort Apache*, so did soldiers of Custer's generation protect his reputation. General William T. Sherman noted in an 1876 letter that Custer had made several tactical mistakes at Little Big Horn, "but his gallant fight and death spread the mantle of oblivion over such trivial errors."[37] Similar views were expressed by Captain Frederick Benteen, who had commanded a wing of the Seventh at Little Big Horn and who might well have been the model for the York character in *Fort Apache*. Observing that Custer had been enshrined with a monument at West Point, Benteen noted that despite his own contempt for the dead man, Custer's example was good for the cadets: "If it makes better soldiers and men of them, why the necessity of knocking the paste eye out of their idol?"[38] Sherman, Benteen, and many others in the army participated in a quiet coverup of Custer's folly so that the army and the nation might have a glowing myth. Although Ford exposed the truth behind the Custer myth in *Fort Apache* he was not attacking it. On the contrary, he reaffirmed its usefulness.

Ford made no apologies for his treatment of the Indians in his films. He was hardly a romantic in his approach to the Indian wars, often comparing the plight of the Indians to that of the Irish. "Let's face it," Ford told Peter Bogdanovich, "we've treated them very badly—it's a blot on our shield; we've cheated and robbed, killed, murdered, massacred and everything else, but they kill one white man and, God, out come the troops."[39]

Still, Ford approached the plight of the Indians with a balanced perspective. "The Indians are very dear to my heart," Ford declared. "There is truth in the accusation that the Indian has not been painted with justice in the Western, but that is a false generalization. The Indian did not like the white man, and he was no diplomat. We were enemies and we fought each other. The struggle against the Indian was fundamental in the history of the Far West."[40]

Of the major Custer films before *Fort Apache*, only the Ince and DeMille features had dealt insultingly with the Indians, while *The Massacre*, *The Scarlet West*, and *They Died with Their Boots On* had all treated them sympathetically. Hollywood tended to follow the general dichotomy of American literature that alternated between images of the Indian as nature's nobleman and as debased savage. While westerns had long been populated by noble red men (often as trusty side-kicks), crooked Indian agents, whiskey traders, and various types of Indian haters, the vast majority of films in the genre treated the natives as part of a harsh environment that was to be conquered. Few films attempted to develop the basic humanity of Indian characters adequately.[41]

The 1950 box-office success of Delmer Daves' *Broken Arrow* forever altered the Hollywood approach to Indians, however, and resulted in a long string of films with Indian heroes (invariably portrayed by whites).[42] The western was simply following a trend toward social commentary that began immediately following World War II with films like *Lost Weekend* (1945), *The Best Years of Our Lives* (1946), and *The Snake Pit* (1948). Films concerned with racial justice were especially popular, as evidenced by *Gentleman's Agreement* (1948), *Home of the Brave* (1949), *Pinky* (1949), and *No Way Out* (1950). While such message films quickly vanished in the early 1950s as race became a more devisive national issue, the trend toward racial-justice westerns continued throughout the decade. Because Indian people were neither a visible nor politically organized minority at the time, and because the "Indian problem" had already been settled by conquest, little controversy resulted from such films.[43]

It was only natural for Hollywood to demythicize Custer, ever the symbol of the Indian wars and the cavalry, and use him as an evil counter to the new Indian heroes. As such, the moviemakers finally got to the point their literary cousins had reached in the 1930s. With rather monotonous regularity Custer was portrayed in both films and novels throughout the 1950s and 1960s as a vain racist in search of personal glory at the expense of innocent, usually quite peace-loving, natives. This new Custer image was so all-pervasive by 1971 that *Life* magazine labeled the Custer Battlefield National Monument in Montana "a sore from America's past" and suggested its elimination.[44]

The Custer films of the 1950s aided in dramatically altering public perceptions of the Indian wars. The first three Custer films of the decade, however, were quite traditional. Both *Warpath* (1951) and *Bugles in the Afternoon* (1952) used the Little Big Horn battle as a convenient backdrop for conventional revenge sagas. Custer was not an important character in either film. James Millican in *Warpath* portrayed Custer as arrogant and contemptuous of his Indian foe, while Sheb Wooley in *Bugles in the Afternoon* gave no hint of Custer's personal characteristics (even though Custer was a central, and negative, character in the Ernest Haycox novel upon which the film was based). *Little Big Horn* (1951), despite the clever use of Otto Becker's barroom print as an advertising motif, did not portray Custer or his last battle. Instead, the film, produced by Charles Marquis Warren, western novelist turned scriptwriter and director, is a variant on the horror movie in which every member of the cast stupidly goes one-by-one down into the basement. In this case it is a squad of soldiers, led by feuding officers Lloyd Bridges and John Ireland, who ride off to warn Custer only to meet horrible fates one-by-one.

John Ford returned to Custer twice in this period. *She Wore a Yellow Ribbon* (1949) begins with a Seventh Cavalry guidon whipping in the wind as a voice-over narrator informs the audience: "Custer is dead. And around the bloody guidon of the immortal Seventh Cavalry lie two hundred and twelve officers and men." That fact dictates the action that follows in this splendid technicolor western scripted by Frank Nugent and Laurence Stallings and based on the James Warner Bellah short story, "War Party." In Ford's *The Searchers* (1956), again scripted by Nugent, the aftermath of a Washita-like massacre is depicted. Custer's cavalry is seen herding captive women and children through the snow into an army post, while "Garry Owen" plays on the soundtrack. In a scene cut from the final release print, John Wayne as antihero Ethan Edwards confronts Peter Ortiz as an arrogant Custer about the massacre. Only a publicity still and the original script remain to remind us of Custer's fleeting appearance in the single greatest western ever made.

In *Sitting Bull* (1954) a glory hunting, racist Custer played by Douglas Kennedy manages to frustrate the efforts of Dale Robertson as an army officer and J. Carrol Naish as an incredibly noble Sitting Bull to prevent war. The Sidney Salkow and Jack DeWitt script then has Custer disobeying his orders in a headlong rush to destroy the Sioux. After the last stand President Grant comes west to save Robertson from a firing squad and make peace with Sitting Bull. This history rewrite was too much for the New York *Times* film critic, who noted that "Grant was an optimist toward Indians, but he wasn't an absolute fool: and that is apparently what some scriptwriters take the poor public to be."[45] Naish, an Irish-American who had portrayed General Phil Sheridan in *Rio Grande* in 1950 and was to play General Santa Anna in *Last Command* in 1955, seemed to be every casting director's favorite historical character. This was his second outing as Sitting Bull, having played the role in the 1950 musical, *Annie Get Your Gun*.

Crazy Horse is given credit for wiping out the Seventh in the 1955 film, *Chief Crazy Horse*, although the battle is not depicted. Victor Mature, terribly miscast as the mystical Sioux warrior, does the best he can. The Franklin Coen and Gerald Adams script was at least fairly faithful to history. More interesting today is the behind-the-scenes tragedy that accompanied the making of the film. Twenty-three-year-old Suzan Ball, who plays Crazy Horse's wife, went ahead with her role despite having just had a leg amputated because of cancer. She died soon after the film was completed.

Columbia's *Seventh Cavalry*, released the next year, was based on a

Glendon Swarthout story about a cavalry officer accused of cowardice for missing Little Big Horn but who redeems himself by leading a suicide mission to bury Custer's dead. Randolph Scott plays the officer who constantly defends Custer's reputation against the aspersions cast by Major Marcus Reno and others. Such a defense of Custer was already a Hollywood rarity.

Custer, as portrayed by Britt Lomand, was particularly sadistic and racist in Walt Disney's *Tonka* (1958). Lomand played the villain in the successful Disney *Zorro* television series, and he brought the same graceful snarl to his Custer role.

Based on David Appel's novel, *Comanche*, the film purported to tell the story of the only cavalry mount to survive Custer's Last Stand and of the young Indian boy who cared for him. Sal Mineo played the Sioux youth, White Bull, whose love for the stallion, Tonka, causes his banishment when he frees the horse to prevent its mistreatment by a rival brave. The horse eventually becomes the mount of Captain Myles Keogh (Philip Carey), who previously appeared as a particularly vibrant memory in Ford's *She Wore a Yellow Ribbon*. Custer's maniacal hatred of the Indians brings on war, and at Little Big Horn the kindly and heroic Keogh is killed by White Bull's rival. When the Indian attempts to scalp the fallen officer he is trampled to death by the enraged horse. White Bull fights with the Sioux in the battle and is terribly wounded. Found on the battlefield with his horse, they are both nursed back to health by the soldiers. The army seems to hold no grudges in this Disney version of history, for the horse becomes the mascot of the cavalry with White Bull as his uniformed stable attendant.

The battle in *Tonka* is among the best ever filmed, with the terrain fairly correct and troop movements following the sketchy details that are available. Custer does not even get his standard gallant death scene, being shot early in the battle as he huddles behind a dead horse. Of the Custer films to date only *Tonka* and *Little Big Man* have deviated from the stereotypical last stand image.

Philip Carey, who portrayed Captain Keogh in *Tonka*, was promoted to the role of Custer in *The Great Sioux Massacre*. This 1965 Columbia film also marked a return to familiar territory for director Sidney Salkow, who had directed *Sitting Bull*. Also starring in the film was Cherokee actor Iron Eyes Cody, another alumnus from *Sitting Bull*, where he had portrayed Crazy Horse. Cody began his career in pictures in 1912 in Griffith's *The Massacre,* and later appeared in *The Plainsman, They Died with Their Boots On,* and *Fort Apache,* certainly a record for appearances in Custer films.[46]

Carey's Custer begins the film by sympathizing with the plight of the Indians, but his head is soon turned by the blandishments of a conniving politician. Believing that a great victory over the Indians will be his ticket to the White House, Custer disregards the advice of Major Reno (Joseph Cotton) and Captain Benteen (Darren McGavin) and leads the Seventh to its doom. The most interesting aspect of the battle is the ludicrous juxtaposition of long shots of mountain scenery borrowed from *Sitting Bull* with Sonoran desert closeups filmed near Tucson.

Also released in 1965 was Arnold Laven's *The Glory Guys.* Sam Peckinpah's script, based on Hoffman Birney's 1956 novel, *The Dice of God,* has something of the raw realism and violent action that he would bring to the western as a director by decade's end, but for the most part the film remains a pedestrian retelling of the Little Big Horn story. Andrew Duggan's General McCabe is yet another Indian-hating racist blinded by personal ambition who finally gets just what he deserves.

The most impressive Custer film of this period was never made. Wendell Mayes wrote a marvelous script for Twentieth-Century Fox, titled "The Day Custer Fell," and Fred Zinnemann, of *High Noon* fame, was set to direct it. Richard Zanuck approached Charlton Heston to take the Custer part but Heston declined, saying, "I don't see how you can make a serious film about a man who seems to have been not only egocentric, but muddleheaded. He was neither a very good soldier nor a very valuable man."[47] The eighteen-million-dollar project eventually collapsed as a result of the financial debacle that crippled Fox in the wake of the studio's production of *Cleopatra.*

Leslie Nielsen had a cameo as Custer in the 1966 Universal remake of *The Plainsman,* while the Little Big Horn was used as a prelude to the action in *Red Tomahawk,* released by Paramount that same year. The latter has the distinction of being the last of a series of A. C. Lyles' B-westerns, marking the final gasp of that particular film type. Despite this rash of Custer films, the western genre was reaching the end of the celluloid trail, at least temporarily.

The western had thrived during the 1950s, reaching a new maturity and attracting Hollywood's top talents. Major stars appeared regularly

in prestige westerns throughout the decade, with the genre accounting for nearly 30 percent of the major studios' total feature production.
Yet, just as for the Sioux at Little Big Horn, at the western's moment
of greatest triumph the seeds of doom were already sown.[48]

Early television was desperate for programming, and old budget
westerns filled the bill. Features starring Tim McCoy, Hoot Gibson,
and Bob Steele became standard fare while serials such as *Custer's Last
Stand* from 1936 fit particularly well into television time slots. It was
William Boyd, however, who proved just how lucrative television could
be. He stopped making Hopalong Cassidy films in 1948 and promptly
licensed the rights to his sixty-six films to television. By 1950 Boyd
oversaw a Hoppy industry estimated at $200 million as the incredible
success of his television westerns promoted a wide array of merchan-
dising. Gene Autry went over to television in 1950, followed soon after
by Roy Rogers. Their products, and a host of other television westerns, employed the conventions of the B-western and aimed for the
same juvenile audience. The impact on the small independent production companies was devastating. Although they had enjoyed a boom
by selling their products to television in the late-1940s, they were now
consumed by the very medium they had nurtured. In 1958, the greatest
of the independents, Republic, went under.

Walt Disney broke with the major film studios in 1954 and began
producing programs for the fledgling ABC network. His *Disneyland*
television program revolutionized the neophyte medium with a three-
part series on the life of Davy Crockett. By the time the last episode
of the trilogy aired on February 23, 1955, a national craze of unprece-
dented proportions was underway. Soon every moppet in America had
a coonskin cap and every network a stable of horse operas. These
new television westerns, like the Davy Crockett programs, emphasized
high production values and aimed for an audience beyond the kinder-
garten crowd. In the fall of 1955 ABC launched Hugh O'Brien in *The
Life and Legend of Wyatt Earp*. CBS countered with James Arness in
Gunsmoke, and the TV adult western was born. By the 1958–1959 season six of the top seven programs on television were westerns, with
forty-eight western series galloping across the airwaves by 1959.[49]

The overexposure caused by television, a loss of faith in old conventions, and the death or retirement of major stars all contributed to a
stark decline of the western in the 1960s. While 130 western feature

films had been released in 1950, and sixty-eight in 1955, only twenty-eight were released in 1960, down to twenty-two by 1965. Much of what was made simply parodied the genre, such as *Cat Ballou* in 1965 or *Waterhole No. 3* in 1967, or played off the new conventions of violence imported with the Italian westerns of Sergio Leone and others. Other filmmakers became obsessed with the death of the frontier, usually tinged with a romantic nostalgia for what was lost. *Lonely Are the Brave* (1962), *The Man Who Shot Liberty Valance* (1962), *Ride the High Country* (1962), and *Butch Cassidy and the Sundance Kid* (1969) all used this theme, but it was Sam Peckinpah's violent 1969 masterpiece *The Wild Bunch* that most fully realized its potential. The westerns that followed *The Wild Bunch* became so focused on the closing of the West that they helped close out the western.[50]

The dark tragedy and explicit violence of the westerns of the late sixties and early seventies clearly reflected the times in which they were made. While the decade began with a burst of optimism and bright promise with the election of John F. Kennedy and the unveiling of his "New Frontier" assault on poverty and racism, it ended with dark alienation dominating a nation torn asunder by domestic unrest and foreign war. Political assassination, continuing racism, and resultant black militancy, the self-serving deception of the people by two presidential administrations, and above all the frustrating and divisive Vietnam War all tore at the social fabric and undercut national identity. The ecology movement led to a new view of wilderness conquerors as ecological exploiters. Indian civil rights organizations rose to prominence, pointing out that their ancestors had lived in harmony with the land. Many now came to view Indian culture as a more rational, natural way of life. No group was more affected by these new views than the young, who were, of course, also the main patrons of motion pictures.

The new westerns reflected this growing disenchantment with both the present and the past. Heroism and self-sacrifice gave way to greed and self-interest in films like *Hombre* (1967) and *McCabe and Mrs. Miller* (1971). Those who could not adjust to an increasingly corrupt society were destroyed by it, as in *Billy Jack* (1971), *The Life and Times of Judge Roy Bean* (1972), and *Tom Horn* (1980). Racism continued as a major theme, but the triumph of justice that had marked the endings of *Broken Arrow* and *Cheyenne Autumn*, was replaced with tragedy, as in *Tell Them Willie Boy Is Here* (1969), or genocide, as in *Soldier Blue*

(1970). Finally, western heroes were regularly debunked: Wyatt Earp in *Hour of the Gun* (1967) and *Doc* (1971); Jesse James in *The Great Northfield, Minnesota, Raid* (1971) and *The Long Riders* (1980); Buffalo Bill Cody in *Buffalo Bill and the Indians* (1976); Billy the Kid in *Dirty Little Billy* (1972); and Pat Garrett in *Pat Garrett and Billy the Kid* (1973). Custer made perfect grist for the mill of the celluloid debunker.

ABC television, in attempting to exploit the youth fixation of the 1960s, presented a heroic Custer in a 1967 series starring Wayne Maunder. Titled *Custer*, the program's advertising emphasized that its hero was "long-haired, headstrong, flamboyant, and a maverick." Despite the haircut, America's youth did not warm to the program, while Indian groups got rather heatedly outraged. The National Congress of the American Indian demanded equal time to respond to the premiere episode, declaring that "glamorizing Custer is like glamorizing Billy the Kid" because he "endorsed a policy of genocide and massacred village after village of Indians."[51] *Newsweek* criticized the show, pointing out that Custer was not a suitable hero because he "was court-martialed twice, once left his men to die, discarded a son squired through Indian wenching, and had a reputation for cruelty."[52] It was disinterest, however, that finished off Custer in midseason—the ratings were abysmal. Long-haired maverick or not, a heroic Custer was a tough sell in the sixties.

Television had often dealt with the Custer story, most especially during the 1950s western craze. Custer had proven the basis of particularly compelling episodes of *The Twilight Zone, Cheyenne, Gunsmoke, Time Tunnel,* and *Branded*. But after ABC's debacle with Custer the general lost his popularity with producers. When he did appear again, in the 1977 NBC *Hallmark Hall of Fame* teleplay of "The Court-Martial of George Armstrong Custer," it would be as a near-raving lunatic. James Olsen's unhinged Custer was derived from Douglas C. Jones' bestselling fantasy novel in which Custer is the only survivor of Little Big Horn.[53]

Two trends of the dying western genre—the European western and the end-of-the-frontier western—were combined with the gimmickry of cinerama in *Custer of the West* (1968). Filmed in Spain and starring English actor Robert Shaw as the title character, the film made a sincere if misguided effort to deal with the complexities of frontier expansion and the Indian wars. Custer is a hell-for-leather soldier who loves a fight for the sake of a fight, but who finds the one-sided warfare with the Indians troubling. He is even more worried by the onrushing industrial revolution and the impersonal impact it will have on combat. "Trains, steel, guns that kill by thousands—our kind of fighting is done," he tells visiting Indians. In destroying the Indians this Custer is also destroying the only warriors left who are just like himself. Shaw postures, broods, and agonizes until he finally rushes purposefully to his doom at Little Big Horn. Custer is the last man alive on the stricken field, and the Indians pull back to allow him to leave. Unwilling to face life in a corrupt, changing world, Custer places a single bullet in his pistol and shouts the charge.

Custer of the West was a bust at the box office, and critical reviews attacked its semi-positive view of its protagonist. Charles Reno, a grandnephew of Major Marcus Reno, sued the film's producers, claiming his ancestor was slandered by Ty Hardin's portrayal of him in the film. The New York State Supreme Court dismissed the case in Custer's only victory during the sixties.[54]

The 1960s also witnessed a revitalization of interest in the plight of the American Indian, both past and present. Ironically, much of this new sensitivity to past injustice was a direct result of the Vietnam War. The Indian was often used as a vehicle by literary artists to attack American involvement in Vietnam. Arthur Kopit's critically acclaimed play, *Indians* (filmed in 1976 by Robert Altman as *Buffalo Bill and the Indians*) and Ralph Nelson's *Soldier Blue* (1970) use an Indian wars theme to attack the Vietnam War. Indian civil rights groups became increasingly active during this period, encouraged by the national reception of Vine Deloria's bestselling manifesto, *Custer Died for Your Sins*, in 1969. Indian topics became all the rage among eastern publishers, especially after the enormous success of Dee Brown's *Bury My Heart at Wounded Knee* in 1971.

Arthur Penn's 1970 film, *Little Big Man*, fit perfectly into its times, proving to be the second-highest grossing movie of the year. Based on Thomas Berger's deeply ironic novel, the film follows the travail of Jack Crabb (Dustin Hoffman) as he aimlessly moves back and forth between the worlds of the Indians and the whites. Crabb gradually comes to recognize the purity of the simpler Cheyenne way over the decadence of the white world. The leader of the whites is, of course, Custer—bloodthirsty, opportunistic, arrogant, and finally stark raving mad.

Director Penn and screenwriter Calder Willingham made no pretense at objectivity. Penn used his film as a vehicle to attack the arrogant, wrong-headed brand of leadership that prolonged the fighting in Vietnam rather than admit a mistake. Custer, Penn felt, was "so infatuated with his capacity to win, so racially assured that he belonged to a superior breed," that he led his men into a hopeless battle, and thus made the perfect historical metaphor. "Although I am focusing on history," Penn explained in a press release, "I believe that the film is contemporary because . . . history does repeat itself."[55]

The detailed, and fairly accurate, depiction of Custer's attack on Black Kettle's village on the Washita is used as an obvious parallel to the MyLai massacre, even to the casting of oriental actress Amy Eccles as Crabb's Indian wife killed in the slaughter. Sound bytes as if from the Vietnam-era six-o'clock news appear, as when Custer defends the Washita massacre to a shocked subordinate: "This is a legal action, lieutenant. The men are under strict orders not to shoot the women—unless, of course, they refuse to surrender. History will confirm the larger moral right is ours."

At Little Big Horn Custer is trapped by his own arrogance, ignoring evidence of a trap rather than "change a Custer decision." The battle is a rout, with no lines of defense or order. Custer, entirely unhinged, wanders about ranting until struck down by arrows just before he can kill Crabb. This time there is to be no glory, no heroism, no redemptive sacrifice—just a well-deserved and ignoble death.

This harshly ideological portrait, while containing some elements of truth, is ultimately even more wildly inaccurate than *They Died with Their Boots On*. Richard Mulligan's Custer is a preening buffoon who cannot be taken seriously. He is all conceit and bluster, failing entirely as menacing devil or as a particularly dangerous opponent. The sense of irony that marked Thomas Berger's novel, where Custer is always larger than life, is gone entirely from the film version. Finally, the great Indian victory at Little Big Horn is trivialized, for there can be no honor in defeating such a cowardly band of soldiers led by such a complete idiot.

Little Big Man is a disturbing tragedy clothed in the conventions of broad farce. It fed on the conventions of the western genre, holding them up to ridicule and sometimes turning them upside down. Custer, that most famous of all frontier warriors—the hero, the martyr, the sacrifice of his race—was now exposed as a clown dressed up in a soldier suit. *Little Big Man* struck a responsive chord with audiences and for two decades had the final word on General Custer and his celebrated last stand.

Hollywood may have finished with Custer after *Little Big Man*, but he returned in the 1974 French film *Touche pas la femme blanche*. Marcello Mastroianni's Custer was a "milksop braggart and dandy infatuated with his own success." The last stand was filmed in a Paris excavation pit with Vietnamese refugees playing the Sioux. Director Marco Ferreri found it "laughable" that "the conquerors are eventually wiped out too. That's what happened at Little Big Horn and what will happen tomorrow, I hope, everywhere." But Ferreri's Marxist vision of Little Big Horn was never released in the United States.[56]

Hollywood appeared to be finished with the Custer story, and perhaps with the western genre as well. A new, darker vision of the past had settled on a torn and divided nation. Guilt and self-doubt had replaced pride and optimism. The westerns of the 1970s reflected this national malaise, finally cannibalizing themselves and parodying the genre out of existence. At the same time, the old masters left the scene. *Gunsmoke*, the last great television western, was cancelled in 1975. John Ford died in 1973, Howard Hawks in 1977, John Wayne in 1979, Raoul Walsh in 1981, and Sam Peckinpah in 1984. No one stepped forward to take their places. By 1980 only six westerns were released by the studios. Finally, in 1980, the *coup de grace* was applied to the genre by the collapse of United Artists studio after the critical and commercial failure of Michael Cimino's *Heaven's Gate*.

Custer's celluloid career rose and fell with the fortunes of the western film. He persisted as a heroic figure on film far longer than he did in print, but in all cases he proved a remarkably resilient and flexible historical figure. From a symbol of heroic self-sacrifice in the winning of the West, Custer gradually evolved into a symbol of white arrogance and brutality in the conquest and exploitation of the West. As the popular perception of the military, the environment, the Indians, and the West changed, a new Custer myth emerged in place of the old. But always, the fascination with this dashing if misguided soldier held firm—at least so long as the western film prospered.

These Custer films have been like glass windows—sometimes opening up a pathway to an understanding of the past, as in *Fort Apache*—

and other times staying shut to mirror the times in which they were made, as with *They Died with Their Boots On* and *Little Big Man*. We can never hope to discern the facts of history from them, but the best of them can effect a truthful fiction well worth contemplation and perhaps tell us something about ourselves.

The video cassette revolution of the 1980s has given a new life to many of these old features. Major films such as *The Plainsman, They Died with Their Boots On, Fort Apache*, and *Little Big Man* are all now easily accessible on videotape. Even minor titles, such as *Little Big Horn, Bugles in the Afternoon*, and *Seventh Cavalry*, are reaching entirely new audiences as a result of video sales and rental outlets. This, of course, has remarkably increased the audience and influence of older films, so that the impact of a film will no longer be tied only to the generation of its release period. Errol Flynn's Custer can now compete with Richard Mulligan's Custer for the hearts and minds of a vast video audience, both now and far into the future.

We may also assume that Hollywood is not done with General Custer either. The enormous success of *Lonesome Dove* on television, coupled with the recent triumph of Kevin Costner's *Dances with Wolves* at the movie theaters, has heralded to many the return of the western. These two features approached our western heritage from decidedly different points of view, but both dealt with their subjects on a grand scale, treating their material seriously and recreating a compelling past for their audiences.

At the same time there has been a remarkable revival of interest in Custer. Evan S. Connell's free-wheeling exploration of Custer and his singular, epic moment at Little Big Horn, *Son of the Morning Star*, was the surprise bestseller of 1984. *Time* listed it as one of the top books of the decade. Connell's portrait of Custer as a brave, experienced, but driven soldier full of contradictions did much to rehabilitate his reputation. That was followed in 1988 by Robert M. Utley's definitive biography, *Cavalier in Buckskin: George Armstrong Custer and the Western Military Frontier*, which gave an even more positive portrait of its protagonist.

Son of the Morning Star was promptly developed as a television miniseries. Scripted by Melissa Mathison (who wrote *E. T.*), the production initially had Kevin Costner signed to portray Custer. NBC, not feeling that Costner was a big enough star, passed on the project. Costner went on to super stardom and the mini-series finally found a home at ABC. It will air on February 3 and 4 with Gary Cole as Custer, Rosanna Arquette as Elizabeth, Dean Stockwell as Sheridan, and Rodney Grant (who is also featured in *Dances with Wolves*) as Crazy Horse.

Indian war buffs will be enthralled by the program's careful attention to historical detail. Its remarkable fidelity to the historical record marks it as by far the most accurate version of Little Big Horn ever filmed. It will be as drama, however, that the mini-series will have to win over a mass television audience. If the program proves successful it may yet salvage Custer's sullied popular reputation. That will only be fitting, since for eight decades film has been the leading factor in determining the popular perception of this endlessly fascinating frontier soldier.

Whatever the impact of *Son of the Morning Star*, we can be certain that creative artists will continue to interpret and reinterpret the Custer story. It is too powerful a tale to be long ignored. Custer, dying again, and again, and again will continue to provide audiences with lessons about the past, the present, and the future. But, of course, he never really died. Ultimately, that bold young warrior achieved his greatest ambition—immortality.

Notes

1. Peter Bogdanovich, *John Ford* (Berkeley: University of California Press, 1968), 86.

2. When John Ford approached Frank Nugent to write the screenplay Ford gave Nugent a list of some fifty books to read on the Indian wars. Later Ford sent him to Arizona to get a feel for the landscape. "When I got back," Nugent recalled, "Ford asked me if I thought I had enough research. I said yes. 'Good,' he said, 'Now just forget everything you've read, and we'll start writing a movie.'" So much for the impact of scholarship on film. Lindsay Anderson, *About John Ford* (New York: McGraw-Hill Book Co., 1981), 77–79. *Fort Apache*, like the other two films in Ford's cavalry trilogy, *She Wore a Yellow Ribbon* (1949) and *Rio Grande* (1950), was based on a James Warner Bellah short story. Bellah later wrote the scripts for Ford's tale of the Buffalo Soldiers, *Sergeant Rutledge* (1960) and *The Man Who Shot Liberty Valance* (1962). His cavalry short stories, most of them originally published in the *Saturday Evening Post* in the late-1940s, appeared as James Warner Bellah, *Reveille* (Greenwich, Conn.: Fawcett Gold Medal, 1962).

3. Paul L. Hedren, *First Scalp*

for *Custer: The Skirmish at War-bonnet Creek, Nebraska, July 17, 1876* (Glendale, Calif.: Arthur H. Clark Co., 1980).

4. William F. Cody, *The Life of Hon. William F. Cody, Known As Buffalo Bill* (1879; reprint, Lincoln: University of Nebraska Press, 1978), 360; Don Russell, *The Lives and Legends of Buffalo Bill* (Norman: University of Oklahoma Press, 1960), 253–57.

5. The evolution of Cody's show is fully and ably discussed in Don Russell, *The Wild West: A History of the Wild West Shows* (Fort Worth: Amon Carter Museum of Western Art, 1970).

6. Kevin Brownlow, *The War, the West, and the Wilderness* (New York: Alfred A. Knopf, 1979), 232.

7. Ibid., 228. See also Russell, *Buffalo Bill*, 457–58, and William Judson, "The Movies," *Buffalo Bill and the Wild West* (Pittsburgh: University of Pittsburgh Press, 1981).

8. Vincent A. Heier, Jr., "Thomas H. Ince's *Custer's Last Fight*: Reflections on the Making of the Custer Legend in Film," [St. Louis Westerners] *Westward* 5 (May 1976): 21–26; Brownlow, *The War, the West*, 257–60.

9. Data on silent Custer films is in Kenneth W. Munden, ed., *The American Film Institute Catalog of Motion Pictures Produced in the United States: Feature Films, 1921–1930* (New York: AFI, 1971); Edward Buscombe, ed., *The BFI Companion to the Western* (New York: Atheneum, 1988); and Allen Eyles, *The Western*, rev. ed. (New York: A. S. Barnes, 1975).

Camping with Custer, released in 1913, is most likely a variant release title of *Campaigning with Custer* of the same year. Most certainly the 1912 film *Custer's Last Raid* is the same film as Ince's *Custer's Last Fight*. The Ince film is one of the few of these films to have survived; almost all of them have been lost.

10. Munden, *American Film Institute Catalog*, 284, 420, 687; Indianapolis *Star*, December 20, 1925.

11. Indianapolis *Star*, September 26, 1926.

12. Ibid., September 23, 1926.

13. New York *Times*, April 11, 1926.

14. Ibid., April 5, 1926. Despite the epic qualities and enormous budget of *The Flaming Frontier*, no copy of the film is known to exist today.

15. For the evolution of the Custer myth, see Paul A. Hutton, "From Little Bighorn to Little Big Man: The Changing Image of a Western Hero in Popular Culture" [reprinted in this volume]; Brian W. Dippie, *Custer's Last Stand: The Anatomy of an American Myth* (Missoula: University of Montana, 1976); Robert M. Utley, *Custer and the Great Controversy: The Origin and Development of a Legend* (Los Angeles: Westernlore Press, 1962); Bruce A. Rosenberg, *Custer and the Epic of Defeat* (University Park: Pennsylvania State University Press, 1974); Kent Ladd Steckmesser, *The Western Hero in History and Legend* (Norman: University of Oklahoma Press, 1965); and Edward Tabor Linenthal, *Changing Images of the Warrior Hero*

in America: A History of Popular Symbolism (New York: Edwin Mellen Press, 1982).

16. For Custer fiction, see Brian W. Dippie, "Jack Crabb and the Sole Survivors of Custer's Last Stand" [reprinted in this volume].

17. Robert Sklar, Movie-Made America: A Cultural History of American Movies (New York: Random House, 1975), 173–94. So powerful and so attentive to detail did the censorship groups become, that by 1943 they could pressure Producers Releasing Corporation to change the name of the main character of the highly successful Billy the Kid film series from the historical Billy Bonney to the fictional Billy Carson. Thus, matinee-crowd moppets were rescued from the glorification of western outlaws. Paul Andrew Hutton, "Dreamscape Desperado," New Mexico Magazine 68 (June 1990): 44–57.

18. Two invaluable guides to the western genre are Buscombe, BFI Companion, and Phil Hardy, The Western (New York: William Morrow and Co., 1983). Highly opinionated but delightful, is Brian Garfield, Western Films: A Complete Guide (New York: Rawson Associates, 1982), while an equally personal but more anecdotal overview is in Jon Tuska, The Filming of the West (Garden City, N.Y.: Doubleday, 1976). The standard history remains George N. Fenin and William K. Everson, The Western: From Silents to the Seventies (New York: Grossman Publishers, 1973), while two useful anthologies are Jack Nachbar, ed., Focus on the Western (Englewood Cliffs, N.J.: Prentice-Hall, 1974), and Richard W. Etulain, ed., "Western Films: A Brief History," Journal of the West 22 (October 1983).

19. New York Times, January 17, 1937.

20. Michael E. Welsh, "Western Film, Ronald Reagan, and the Western Metaphor," in Archie P. McDonald, ed., Shooting Stars: Heroes and Heroines of Western Film (Bloomington: Indiana University Press, 1987), 153. See also Tony Thomas, The Films of Ronald Reagan (Secaucus, N.J.: Citadel Press, 1980), 109–14; Ronald Reagan, with Richard G. Hubler, Where's the Rest of Me? (New York: Duell, Sloan and Pearce, 1965), 95–96; and Ronald W. Reagan, "Looking Back at Santa Fe Trail," Greasy Grass 6 (May 1990), 2–5.

21. New York Times, December 21, 1940.

22. Robert Stack and Mark Evans, Straight Shooting (New York: Macmillan, 1980), 63.

23. Rudy Behlmer, Inside Warner Bros. (1935–1951) (New York: Viking, 1985), 173–74.

24. Ibid., 175–78; Tony Thomas, Rudy Behlmer, and Clifford McCarty, The Films of Errol Flynn (New York: Citadel Press, 1969), 106–11. See also Kingsley Canham, The Hollywood Professionals: Michael Curtiz, Raoul Walsh, Henry Hathaway (New York: A. S. Barnes, 1973), and Peter Valenti, Errol Flynn: A Bio-Bibliography (Westport, Conn.: Greenwood Press, 1984), 30–31, 72–73.

25. John E. O'Connor, The Hollywood Indian: Stereotypes of Native

Americans in Films (Trenton: New Jersey State Museum, 1980), 42.

26. *Life* 11 (December 8, 1941): 75–78; New York *Times*, November 30, 1941.

27. Fine wires were attached to leg bands on a horse's front legs, with the other ends tied to logs buried in the ground. Slack between the horse and log allowed a strong gallop before the horse's front legs were suddenly jerked from under him. Dramatic scenes of horses plunging forward or turning somersaults were the result. Neither horse nor rider had to be trained for such stunts. Many horses were killed in the fall or had to be destroyed because of broken legs. Anthony Amaral, *Movie Horses: Their Treatment and Training* (Indianapolis: Bobbs-Merrill, 1967), 9–20.

28. Among the old westerners who gravitated to Hollywood were Wyatt Earp, Charlie Siringo, Al Jennings, Emmett Dalton, and Bill Tilghman. For more on the cowboys who provided the essential cadre of rough riders for the movies, see Dianna Serra Cary, *The Hollywood Posse: The Story of the Gallant Band of Horsemen Who Made Movie History* (Boston: Houghton Mifflin, 1975).

29. Richard Schickel, *The Men Who Made the Movies* (New York: Atheneum, 1975), 47–48; Buster Wiles, *My Days with Errol Flynn: The Autobiography of a Stuntman* (Santa Monica: Roundtable Publishing, 1988), 97–100; William R. Meyer, *The Making of the Great Westerns* (New Rochelle, N.Y.: Arlington House, 1979), 108–21.

30. Tony Thomas, *The Films of Olivia de Havilland* (Secaucus, N.J.: Citadel Press, 1983), 181–87.

31. George MacDonald Fraser, *The Hollywood History of the World: From One Million Years B.C. to Apocalypse Now* (New York: William Morrow, 1988), 200. Fraser is the author of several screenplays as well as the successful Flashman series of novels. That series includes one of the best available Custer novels, *Flashman and the Redskins* (New York: Alfred A. Knopf, 1982). Two other critical discussions of the relationship of western films to western history are Jon Tuska, *The American West in Film: Critical Approaches to the Western* (Westport, Conn.: Greenwood Press, 1985), and Wayne Michael Sarf, *God Bless You, Buffalo Bill: A Layman's Guide to History and the Western Film* (Rutherford, N.J.: Fairleigh Dickinson University Press, 1983).

32. Buscombe, BFI *Companion*, 42–45, 426–28. For more on the postwar western, see Philip French, *Westerns* (New York: Oxford University Press, 1977), and Jim Kitses, *Horizons West: Anthony Mann, Budd Buetticher, Sam Peckinpah: Studies of Authorship within the Western* (Bloomington: Indiana University Press, 1969).

33. Few filmmakers have been as discussed as Ford, arguably the greatest director in the history of film. For studies that consider *Fort Apache* in some detail, see Tag Gallagher, *John Ford: The Man and His Films* (Berkeley: University of California Press, 1986); Anderson, *About John Ford*;

J. A. Place, *The Western Films of John Ford* (New York: Citadel Press, 1974); Andrew Sarris, *The John Ford Movie Mystery* (Bloomington: Indiana University Press, 1975); Joseph McBride and Michael Wilmington, *John Ford* (New York: DaCapo Press, 1975); John Baxter, *The Cinema of John Ford* (New York: A. S. Barnes, 1971); Peter Stowell, *John Ford* (Boston: Twayne, 1986); and two more biographical works—Andrew Sinclair, *John Ford* (New York: Dial Press, 1979), and Dan Ford, *Pappy: The Life of John Ford* (Englewood Cliffs, N.J.: Prentice-Hall, 1979). Ford's impressive body of cinematic work on the American frontier experience and on American history in general obviously had a dramatic impact on the nation's collective imagination concerning its past. His work is well worth study as art, as cultural artifact, and as a lesson on popular history.

34. Sinclair, *John Ford*, 142.

35. For more on *Fort Apache*, see Russell Campbell, "Fort Apache," *Velvet Light Trap* 17 (Winter 1977): 8–12; William T. Pilkington, "Fort Apache (1948)," in William T. Pilkington and Don Graham, eds., *Western Movies* (Albuquerque: University of New Mexico Press, 1979), 40–49; and Tony Thomas, *The West That Never Was* (Secaucus, N.J.: Citadel Press, 1989), 104–11.

36. In the original James Warner Bellah short story Thursday arrives on the stricken battlefield after the massacre and commits suicide. James Warner Bellah, "Massacre," *Saturday Evening Post* 219 (February 27, 1947): 18–19, 140–46.

37. Robert M. Utley, ed., "Sherman on Custer at Little Big Horn," *Little Big Horn Associates Newsletter* 9 (October 1975): 9.

38. W. A. Graham, *The Custer Myth: A Source Book of Custeriana* (Harrisburg, Pa.: Stackpole Co., 1953), 325.

39. Bogdanovich, *John Ford*, 104.

40. Sinclair, *John Ford*, 149.

41. For the image of Indians in film, see Gretchen M. Bataille and Charles L. P. Silet, eds., *The Pretend Indians: Images of Native Americans in the Movies* (Ames: Iowa State University Press, 1980), and Ralph E. Friar and Natasha A. Friar, *The Only Good Indian . . . The Hollywood Gospel* (New York: Drama Book Specialists, 1972). For the broader context, see Brian W. Dippie, *The Vanishing American: White Attitudes and U.S. Indian Policy* (Middletown, Conn.: Wesleyan University Press, 1982); Robert F. Berkhofer, Jr., *The White Man's Indian: Images of the American Indian from Columbus to the Present* (New York: Alfred A. Knopf, 1978); Roy Harvey Pearce, *Savagism and Civilization: A Study of the Indian and the American Mind* (Baltimore: Johns Hopkins Press, 1965); Raymond William Stedman, *Shadows of the Indian: Stereotypes in American Culture* (Norman: University of Oklahoma Press, 1982); and Richard Slotkin, *Regeneration through Violence: The Mythology of the American Frontier, 1600–1860* (Middletown, Conn.: Wesleyan University Press, 1973).

42. Some examples include *Battle at Apache Pass* (1952), *Hiawatha* (1952), *Conquest of Cochise* (1953), *Apache* (1954), *Taza, Son of Cochise* (1954), *Broken Lance* (1954), *White Feather* (1955), *The Indian Fighter* (1955), and *The Savage* (1953) which, although based on L. L. Foreman's 1942 Custer novel, *The Renegade*, altered the story and dropped Custer from the film.

43. Sklar, *Movie-Made America*, 279–80.

44. Alvin Josephy, "The Custer Myth," *Life* 71 (July 2, 1971): 55.

45. New York *Times*, November 28, 1954.

46. Iron Eyes Cody and Collin Perry, *Iron Eyes: My Life As a Hollywood Indian* (New York: Everest House, 1982).

47. Charlton Heston, *The Actor's Life: Journals, 1956–1976*, ed. Hollis Alpert (New York: E. P. Dutton, 1976); Wendell Mayes, "The Day Custer Fell" (unpublished screenplay, 1964).

48. John H. Lenihan, *Showdown: Confronting Modern America in the Western Film* (Urbana: University of Illinois Press, 1980); Buscombe, *BFI Companion*, 45–48.

49. J. Fred MacDonald, *Who Shot the Sheriff? The Rise and Fall of the Television Western* (New York: Praeger, 1987), 15–85; Paul Andrew Hutton, "Davy Crockett: An Exposition on Hero Worship," in Michael A. Lofaro and Joe Cummings, eds., *Crockett at Two Hundred: New Perspectives on the Man and the Myth* (Knoxville: University of Tennessee Press, 1989), 20–41.

50. For the films of this period, see Nachbar, *Focus on the Western*, 101–28; French, *Westerns*, 135–67; Hardy, *The Western*, 274–363; Tuska, *Filming of the West*, 559–84; and Buscombe, *BFI Companion*, 48–54.

51. Friar and Friar, *Only Good Indian*, 274–75.

52. *Newsweek* 70 (August 7, 1967): 51; New York *Times*, September 7, 1967; P. M. Clepper, "He's Our George," *TV Guide* (September 23, 1967), 32–34. In an effort to recoup some of their losses, the producers combined several episodes of the television show and released it in Europe as a feature, titled *The Legend of Custer*.

53. Paul A. Hutton, "Custer's Last Stand: Background," *TV Guide* (November 26, 1977), 39–42. See also John P. Langellier, "Movie Massacre: The Custer Myth in Motion Pictures and Television," *Research Review: The Journal of the Little Big Horn Associates* 3 (June 1989): 20–31. Custer appeared again in the 1979 television movie *The Legend of the Golden Gun*, where Keir Dullea portrayed him as a General MacArthur clone complete with sunglasses and pipe. Another television movie, *The Legend of Walks Far Woman* in 1982, featured the Little Big Horn but did not portray Custer.

54. New York *Times*, October 2, 1968, March 18, 1960.

55. Gerald Astar, "The Good Guys Wear War Paint," *Look* 34 (December 1, 1970): 60; *Little Big Man* (Cinema Center Films Pressbook, 1971), 4. See also John W. Turner, "Little Big Man

(1970)," in Pilkington and Graham, *Western Movies*, 109–21.

56. Brian W. Dippie, "Popcorn and Indians: Custer on the Screen," *Cultures* 2, no. 1 (1974): 162–63. Custer returned to the screen in a 1976 spoof of early Hollywood, *Won Ton Ton the Dog Who Saved Hollywood*, where Ron Leibman played the actor Rudy Montague, who portrayed Custer in the film within the film; in the over- blown 1981 western *The Legend of the Lone Ranger*, where Lincoln Tate had a cameo as a rather foolish Custer; and in the 1984 comedy *Teachers*, in which Richard Mulligan reprised his Custer role while portraying an escaped mental patient who dressed up as historical characters. By the 1980s, Hollywood viewed the Custer story only as comic relief.

Movies Concerning Custer

The following theatrical films have concerned Custer or his last battle. Some of the silents, however, may be variant titles of the same film:

Custer's Last Stand [On the Little Big Horn] (1909); *Custer's Last Fight [For the Honor of the Seventh]* and also *Custer's Last Raid* (1912); *The Massacre* (1912); *The Big Horn Massacre* (1913); *Camping with Custer* (1913); *Campaigning with Custer* (1913); *Custer's Last Scout* (1915); *Britton of the Seventh* (1916); *Bob Hampton of Placer* (1921); *Wild Bill Hickok* (1923); *The Scarlet West* (1925); *The Flaming Frontier* (1926); *The Last Frontier* (1926); *With General Custer at Little Big Horn* (1926); *Spoilers of the West* (1927); *The Last Frontier* (1932); *The World Changes* (1933); *Custer's Last Stand* (1936, serial rereleased as feature in 1947); *The Plainsman* (1937); *The Oregon Trail* (1939); *Wyoming* (1940); *Santa Fe Trail* (1940); *Badlands of Dakota* (1941); *They Died with Their Boots On* (1941); *Fort Apache* (1948); *She Wore a Yellow Ribbon* (1949); *Warpath* (1951); *Little Big Horn* (1951); *Bugles in the Afternoon* (1952); *Sitting Bull* (1954); *Chief Crazy Horse* (1955); *Seventh Cavalry* (1956); *Tonka* (1958); *The Canadians* (1961); *The Great Sioux Massacre* (1965); *The Glory Guys* (1965); *Due Sergenti del Generale Custer* (1965); *Red Tomahawk* (1966); *The Plainsman* (1966); *The Legend of Custer* (1967); *Custer of the West* (1968); *Little Big Man* (1970); *Touche pas la femme blanche* (1974); *Won Ton Ton the Dog Who Saved Hollywood* (1976); *The Legend of the Lone Ranger* (1981); and *Teachers* (1984).

CUSTER: THE LEGEND
OF THE MARTYRED HERO
IN AMERICA

BRUCE A. ROSENBERG

Custer has been all but forgotten by professional historians and students of military tactics, and belittled by our generation in its sympathy for the American Indian. The battle in which he lost his life and gained an undying fame was a small one militarily, involving only one regiment of cavalry, about 600 men. It did not decide a campaign or the war against the Sioux. Army colleges now study Custer's tactics mainly to profit by his mistakes; yet despite all this, despite the debunking his memory sustained in Frederic F. Van de Water's acerbic biography, *Glory-Hunter*,[1] and the many books derivative of it, despite the symbol he has become of white suppression of the American Indian, he survives, and he remains far and away the most popular hero of the American people.

More artistic effort—most of it admittedly poor—has been lavished on that one brief skirmish, which was miniscule when compared to the epic bloodshedding of the then recent Civil War, than has been expended on San Juan Hill, Chateau-Thierry, D-Day, Iwo-Jima, and Khe Sahn combined.[2] If this is hyperbole and thus disbelieved because impossible to prove statistically, the claim certainly embodies a poetic truth. Don Russell's *Custer's List*[3] documents 967 paintings and illustrations of Custer and his last battle, and more are reproduced daily. Fred Dustin's bibliography[4] of the early 1950s has over 640 entries, but poetry and fiction—which would surely triple that number—are not included. More than a score of motion pictures are about Custer or else mention him prominently, the best known among them being *They Died with Their Boots On*, *Bugles in the Afternoon*, *Sitting Bull*, *Two Flags West*, and most recently, *Little Big Man*. At least three films, insignificant by any artistic standard, bear the title of *Custer's Last Stand* or *Custer's Last Fight*. And several television shows have been about him directly or else have utilized the story of the Little Bighorn: "Custer," "Branded," "Time Tunnel," and "Cheyenne."

The national park which was built on the site of the battle is one of the only ones to be named for the man and not the place or the event: it is, after all, Custer Battlefield National Monument, and not "Little Bighorn National Park," or some such thing as "Sitting Bull National Monument." Statues of Custer have been erected at West Point, at Monroe, Michigan (the home of his late adolescence and the residence of his wife's family), and at New Rumley, Ohio—his birthplace. Streets, schools, and army camps have been named for him: a park in Hardin, Montana; the airport at Monroe; and numerous towns and counties in Montana and North Dakota, to say nothing of state parks and national highways. Much of southeastern Montana is named for him and his last battle: Garryowen, Reno Creek, Custer City. Dozens of settlements and highway markers proclaim that "Custer Marched Here," or that "Custer Camped Here," evincing a popularity which rivals that of any hero, American or European.

And he lives in our everyday expressions, in our jokes, and on our bumper stickers. If there is any consistent pattern to these varied Custer allusions and references, it is to the implication that the Last Stand was lost because of the overwhelming number of the Indians: he remains in our memory the great soldier who found himself confronting too many of the enemy, even for him. His last words are imagined to be, "where did all the Indians come from," or "remember, men, take no prisoners." One waggish observation has Custer and his men wearing Arrow Shirts. A recent one-line put-down goes: "If you were an Indian, Custer would still be alive."

Comedian Bill Cosby used a routine in which he is the referee at a metaphysical football game between those traditional rivals, the cavalry and the Sioux. The game is about to begin; the coin is tossed, and Cosby tells "Custer" to take his ten men and go to one end of the field. Then he tells "Sitting Bull," the opposing captain, to take his ten thousand braves and go to the other end. Bumper stickers have tended more toward social protest. Vine Deloria's treatise provided the inspiration for one sticker, "Custer Died for Your Sins," and car owners from the Far West are fond of "Custer Had it Coming." A recent anti-war poster from Berkeley, California, shows the 1865 portrait of "Yellow Hair" with his arms akimbo, assuming that everyone will recognize him and his most famous encounter with the enemy: "Let's Win This War and Get The Hell Out." Out of respect for the sensibilities of my readers, I omit the obscene jokes, of which there are many. But what of the real Custer and his last stand? The unhappy fact is that nothing is known of the fate of Lt. Col. (Brevet Major General) George A. Custer and the five companies of the Seventh Cavalry under his immediate command on June 25, 1876, but where there are no ascertainable facts, or few, we have supplied the missing data with a narrative of our own making. Part of this folklore will be the focus of the present essay.

Nearly all of the more than 950 paintings and illustrations show Custer with a sword, but the regiment did not carry this particular weapon into combat on that day, and there is good evidence that it had not been used in battle since the Civil War.[5] Rather, the Seventh was armed with pistols and carbines. Sabre-wearing Errol Flynn, in *They Died With Their Boots On*, is the last of his command to die. The Warner Brothers' director placed Flynn, defiant and undaunted, amid a field strewn with extras; but what testimony we have from the Indians suggests the opposite.[6] When the firing had died down and the braves moved forward to count coups, several troopers are said to have leaped over the barricade they had formed with the bodies of their dead horses, and to have made a frantic dash for the river. They were clubbed down before they could escape; but these, and not the dead men on the hill, were the last whites alive on the field. Custer's body was found on the hill.

The battle of the Little Bighorn is said to have been the easiest and most one-sided victory for the Indians in their plains wars with whites. Yet contemporary newspaper accounts placed the Sioux loss at well over 200, and others, including Captain Benteen (the regiment's third-in-command) believed that Custer had taken more than his own number of the enemy with him.[7] But reconstruction, based on careful interviews with surviving chiefs, have put the Indian loss at about 45 killed, though many more were wounded.[8]

Custer's refusal to accept Gatling guns or the support of a battalion of the Second Cavalry is now famous. But another story, not quite so well-known, also circulated that he was alleged to have sent for aid when the battle was all but lost, and the J. K. Ralston painting captures that imagined moment: Custer and about thirty men have already shot their horses and are organizing a defense at the northern end of "Custer

Ridge." Meanwhile, in the right rear of the painting, heading south-east, Sergeant Butler rides for help. But again, there is no evidence that such a rider was sent for aid, or even that Custer had time to think about such a move: most of the reliable Indians thought that the battle lasted about thirty to forty-five minutes.[9] In any event, the direction of Butler's route in Ralston's painting would lead him directly into the path of Gall's attacking braves who had at that moment, presumably, just overrun Keogh's and Calhoun's position to Custer's rear.

Stories of treachery were at the time rife: various Crow scouts had from time to time been thought to have betrayed the column (to their ancient enemies, the Sioux!). Immediately after the news of the defeat fell upon the United States, General Alfred Terry, Custer's immediate commander, was accused of incompetence, but swiftly the public's accusations shifted to Captain Benteen and finally to the Regiment's second-in-command, Major Marcus A. Reno. Frederick Whittaker, dime novelist of some distinction, onetime captain of the army, and full-time accuser of Reno, brought such public and congressional pressure to bear on that unhappy officer, that he finally asked for, and was granted, a Board of Inquiry to investigate his conduct on the field. The Board exonerated him.[10] Nevertheless, many today still believe that Reno permitted Custer to ride to his death, out of cowardice and hatred, and then withheld assistance. The crime would be all the more heinous since it means that Reno would have allowed more than two hundred of his friends and colleagues to ride to their deaths with Custer.

Probably the most widely-circulated legend about the battle was that of the lone survivor. He was supposed to have lived through the entire battle, to have seen all, and to have given the details of the battle to the waiting world. But we are positive that this detail also is not true. The man most often identified as the lone survivor was a Crow scout named Curly, but he saw only the first shots fired, and never claimed to have witnessed very much.[11] However, a lone survivor was a convenience for newspaper reporters who needed an "authority" for their imaginative accounts of the battle.

Finally, Custer is supposed to have been on the very top of the ridge when he was killed, as many paintings place him. Where Custer, or any of his men, fell is impossible to know, for nearly all of the bodies were stripped and mutilated, and certainly the Indians did not replace the corpses in their original positions when they had removed their uniforms. The bodies were buried shallowly two days later and reinterred a year later. At that time wooden stakes were placed on the gravesites, but several years following when the troopers were again reburied atop the hill under a marble monument and the officers removed for private burial, marble markers were put in the place of the fallen men. But by that time the chance for miscalculation had been compounded several times. Custer's marker is about fifty feet down the slope; this may not be the exact spot where he fell, but it is the only evidence we have.

When we put all of these elements together (the sword, the hilltop, the lone survivor, the traitor, etc.) what emerges is a narrative familiar to us from various eras and diverse parts of the world. It is the story of the death of Saul as told in *First Samuel*; defeated by the Philistines on Mt. Gilboa, Saul sees all of his men and then his three sons fall to the enemy. He orders his armor-bearer to kill him, but that loyal servant cannot bring himself to. As we learn in *Second Samuel* an unnamed Amalekite in the region claimed to have dispatched God's anointed. He is the lone survivor and the traitor, for which sin David slays him.

Roland, too, is pitted against an overwhelming number of the enemy, in his case the Saracens. His betrayer is one of the most famous in Western literature, Ganelon, who has given the route of the Franks' march to the Saracens. The battle takes place in a pass in the Pyrenees, but we are several times told that the Franks are on the hilltop while the pagans swarm through the valley. The end of the battle is inevitable, but before that end the Franks take more than their own number of their foes. Roland, like Saul and Custer, is the last of his command to die. The earliest version of the *Chanson de Roland*, in Digby 23, does not have a lone survivor, a detail reserved for later redactions, particularly the *Pseudo-Turpin*, in which Roland's brother escapes to carry the sad news to Charlemagne.

Leonidas and his Spartans made a heroic defense of the pass at Thermopylae, but he died before the end of the battle. However, most of the other elements we have been considering are present in Herodotus' account. The great horde of Persians drives the allied Greek army back to the narrow pass at Thermopylae where a successful defense is made. But when a peasant in the area betrays his countrymen and shows Xerxes a pass which outflanks the Greek position, Leonidas sends his allies to the rear and remains to fight with his three hundred comrades. Two Spartans were in the rear, but when word of the stand reached them one asked to be led forward; the other—much to his subsequent shame—asked to be led to safety.

When Leonidas dies during the fight, the Spartans are put on their mettle, and they respond nobly, redoubling their efforts against the Persians to save their king from disgrace and defilement. So too with the English at the battle of Maldon: Byrhtnoð dies while many of his men are still alive, and the event tests the character and loyalty of his *comitatus*. A few, like Godric, flee for their lives, an act which at the time was not only cowardice but the worst sort of treason to one's lord. But most, like Ælfwine and Dunnere, remain true to their warrior's code and their obligation to their lord.

Before Arthur can confront Mordred (in the alliterative *Morte Arthure*), Sir Gawain and seven score knights attack the traitor's army of sixty thousand. Like the battle at Maldon, Gawain's last stand is made on a beach, not a hilltop. And no one lives to tell the tale; but there is treason (Mordred himself), great numbers of the enemy dead, and Gawain dies last.

The paradigm works for other heroes and other battles as well. Lazar and his fellow Slavs are defeated by the Turks at the plain of Kosovo, a fourteenth-century struggle which is said to remain in the Yugoslav consciousness yet. Move the battle indoors and it is in most details the Last Stand of Bjarki against the traitors to his king; or it is the story of the Alamo, with the vast Mexican army defeating the Texan contingent, Davy Crockett dying last, and a few women and children surviving to tell the tale. Or move the paradigm to the nineteenth-century novel and it takes form in Flaubert's *Salammbô* in which Polybius' austere and precise account of the Lydian revolt led by Matho is substantially changed: the villains are transformed to heroes, and to make their transformation suitable they are given a last stand on a hilltop where Matho, when all of his fellow rebels have been killed, is taken prisoner, only to die moments later.

I have tried in these few pages to place Custer in a heroic context quite outside of Lord Raglan's paradigm of the hero, a context for which some name ought to be devised: "The Martyred Hero" will do. Yet so many legends and anecdotes have been told of Custer, and they are so diverse, that a case might as well be made for the Raglanite thesis. Custer did come from humble backgrounds, and though he did actually finish last in his class at West Point, more is made of this unpromising

beginning than is appropriate: in view of Custer's end, the implication that his military life was something of a "success story" has to be
seen ironically. Beowulf, Offa, Helgi, Grettir and Percival had slack
and unpromising youths (Professor Felix Oinas reminds me that Marko
Kraljevič was also a dullard as a young man). But the Custer that we
know and love is not the Giver of Laws to his people: he is not King
Arthur, but his trusty vassal Gawain; not Charlemagne, but Roland; a
Saul rather than Samuel.

Such is the fame and respect which the American people have afforded their Martyred Hero that they placed him in a very exclusive
Valhalla reserved, usually, for only one man in a culture's history. And
a further tribute to the hold which this man has upon the imagination
of his countrymen, even a century after his death, is the great number
and variety of traditional stories which have been told about him, and
the comparisons implicit in those stories. Rather than compile an arbi-
trary list of them here, however, I shall mention only a few of the most
popular concerning his death, and then only those with an international
distribution.

One of the most interesting concerns the young Colonel and a comely
Cheyenne maiden, Mo-nah-se-tah. She is said to have been at the battle
with her family and tribe and to have gone to the top of Custer Ridge
when the shooting stopped. It was there, while her tribesmen and allies
were stripping and ceremonially mutilating the fallen soldiers, that she
recognized Custer—the father of her child several years before—and
saved his body from disfiguration. Custer's body was one of the few
found on the ridge which was not mutilated, and almost immediately
fanciful reasons were given to explain this happy exception: that Mo-
nah-se-tah had saved him from this final indignity, that the Sioux had
too great a respect for their fallen foe, and that Custer had shot himself
to avoid capture, thus making his body bad medicine for the Indians.

The Mo-nah-se-tah story was supposed to have begun during the
Seventh's raid on Black Kettle's village in 1868. To achieve surprise,
Custer ordered the regiment to attack at dawn, about the only time
that an Indian village would be vulnerable. The intention of the cavalry
was to round up or drive off the herd of ponies, thus immobilizing the
fighting men, and to capture the women and children of the village.
They were to be brought to a secure reservation in the expectation
that the able-bodied husbands and sons who were left behind would

follow them in. On the morning of the raid in question the Seventh
busied itself in these objectives. But as the day wore on, many of the
warriors who had escaped the first assault and who managed to flee
to neighboring villages, began returning with reinforcements. Major
Joel Elliott and a small detachment rode off in pursuit of several fugitives but they soon found themselves cut off from their unit, and were
eventually destroyed. In the meantime the pressure on the main body
of the attacking force was such that Custer ordered a withdrawal by
early afternoon. A number of squaws who were seized as hostages were
taken by the regiment back to Camp Supply. Major Elliott and his men
were left to their fates.

During the following months, Mo-nah-se-tah became an interpreter
at the post, and allegedly much more than that to Custer. But as with so
many stories which have arisen about him there is simply no evidence
that he became her lover, let alone the father of her child—if she ever
had one. All is hearsay and anecdote. Custer apologists claim that he
would never do such a thing, so great was his love for Elizabeth, surely
the most conjectural and naive kind of evidence.[12] One cannot be certain
that Mo-nah-se-tah bore a child in captivity, despite the respectability
given the story by Mari Sandoz. A variant of this legend, told by Kate
Bighead, has two Cheyenne women save Custer's body from mutilation, but Kate did not identify either of them as Mo-nah-se-tah, and as
usual all that remains is conjecture and fantasy.[13]

Custer's body had been found reclining supine, stripped of his uniform, in an attitude of repose. So many of those around him had been
badly disfigured and maimed that his fate did seem special: why not a
Mo-nah-se-tah, who carried not only the white man's son but a lasting
love for him. The story, after all, is an old one: only a few details are
changed from the salvation of John Smith by Pocahontas in colonial
America. In the Custer version the hero is now dead, and the Cheyenne
maiden cannot save his life: only his body and the memory of what he
had been to her in life. This is surely a variant of the John Smith legend:
what one maudlin poem described of the earlier version could well have
been, with a change of names, said of the latter:

> Then the maiden Pocahontas
> Rushes forward, none can stop her,

> Throws her arms about the captive,
> Cries,—"oh spare him!"[14]

Nausicaa saved the life of the stranger Odysseus, though not by inter-posing her lovely head between the poised clubs and the head of the stranger, and Aeneas had a similar encounter with Lavinia, who dreamed that her husband would come to her from across the seas. Medievalists have named the Pocahontas–Mo-nah-se-tah figure "The Enamored Moslem Princess," as again and again in the romances she saves the life of the Christian captive of her pagan father. The story was told all over central Europe, and made its way down through Turkey and the Balkan peninsula. The *Gesta Romanorum*, that tremendously popular collection of moral tales which entertained centuries of medi-eval people, includes a variant called "Of Fidelity." The story came, as we well know, to the New World as well, but whether it was invented or perpetuated by people who already knew its outlines does not mat-ter so much as the reason for its popularity: it is a simple tale, just an episode really, which has touched upon some fundamental center in the millions who have heard and read and retold it.[15] If the Mo-nah-se-tah story had not been modeled on well-known lines, it might well have been reinvented coincidentally along those same lines.

Those who had not heard of the alleged affair between Custer and his Pocahontas of the plains invented another, perhaps equally romantic, explanation for his unmutilated body, a story that reflected glory upon Custer but also praised the nobility of his assailants: that out of respect for their fallen antagonist, the Sioux and Cheyenne left his body un-defiled. This story was widely circulated at the time and though less popular now, is with us still. But that any of the Indians knew that their attacker was Custer is doubtful. The warrior most frequently accused of killing Custer, Rain-in-the-Face, denied in his most reli-able interview that any of the Indians knew of Custer's presence with the soldiers, and that no Indian knew who killed him.[16] The evidence strongly suggests that Custer's body was untouched by chance, not choice.

Yet the stories of the Indian's nobility toward the body of their fallen foe continued to be as popular as the accounts of his mutilation. On the one hand it was desirable to imagine the enemy as savage and ruthless;

it increased the desire for revenge and reinforced the idea that Custer was at least morally superior to the enemy who defeated him. Yet the sympathetic stories showed the same qualities: even his mortal enemies recognized a great warrior when they had beaten him. Unconsciously or not, however, some of the nobility was reflected on the Sioux who had had the grace, after all, to honor Custer. One such account, which shows more imagination than most, depicted Sitting Bull walking up to Custer Ridge when the fighting had stopped to kneel by the side of his slain enemy. Sitting Bull lamented, and then placed a cloth over the white man's face: "This handkerchief will guard your features against the desert's blackening heat. Farewell, great Custer, till we meet!"[17]

Like T. S. Eliot, who is said to have immortalized a discredited scholarly thesis with his great poem, *The Waste Land*, Henry Wadsworth Longfellow immortalized a discredited anecdote, that in revenge for previous indignities, Rain-in-the-Face cut Custer's heart out of his body and ate it. If the story is not as good as Jesse Weston's book which inspired Eliot, neither is Longfellow's poem as good as Eliot's. The nineteenth-century work tells the following story:

> In his war paint and his beads,
> Like a bison among the reeds,
>   In ambush the Sitting Bull
> Lay with three thousand braves
> Crouched in the clefts and caves,
>   Savage, unmerciful!
>
> Into the fatal snare
> The white chief with yellow hair
>   And his three hundred men
> Dashed headlong, sword in hand;
> But of that gallant band
>   Not one returned again.
>
> But the foemen fled in the night,
> And Rain-in-the-Face, in his flight,
>   Uplifted high in air
> As a ghastly trophy bore
> The brave heart, that beat no more,
>   Of the white chief with yellow hair.[18]

Nearly every major newspaper in the country had carried this story shortly after the first news of the battle. Rain-in-the-Face, allegedly humiliated several years before by Custer's arrest of him at a reservation trading post and his subsequent imprisonment, had sworn revenge. At the Little Bighorn, according to this legend, revenge was his.

One version had it that Rain-in-the-Face cut out Custer's heart and danced with it impaled on the end of his lance around a victory bonfire. In still other versions the victim of revenge was not George A. Custer, but his brother Tom who commanded Company "C," and who fell several feet from his brother down the slope of Custer Ridge. Reports of the actual condition of Tom Custer's body vary, one version even going to the extent of quoting—allegedly—Major Reno on the amount of mutilation.[19]

Again, we are confronted with a very old belief which became attached, in the nineteenth century, to the Custer legend. From the earliest times the blood was thought to be the vehicle of the soul and the heart its seat.[20] The primitive warrior saw that as the blood ran from the wounds of the fallen, the strength, and finally the life, also left the body. As the vehicle of the soul, the blood carries with it the characteristics of its host. Thus, to gain the strength of the bear, Hialto swallowed a bear's heart and drank its blood. Old Norse Ingiald emboldened himself by eating a wolf's heart, a principle also employed by Hagen in the *Kudrun*. Siegfried had made himself invulnerable, except in one part of his body, by bathing in dragon's blood. To heal the Fisher King of his wounds the blood of a pelican—a bird known for its excess of maternal love—was rubbed on them, though in the case of the hapless king, with no success. To eat the heart of man or beast ensures both the eternal death of the owner, and it also imparts its quality to the eater. When Rain-in-the-Face allegedly ate Custer's heart, he was making sure that his fallen foe would never rise again, and that Custer's spirit would not come back from the grave to harm him or his fellow Sioux. But Custer's heart was buried with him, though quite another spirit of Custer's returned to plague his killers.

Yet another revenge story reverses the role of hero and villain, giving Custer only what he had coming. At Fort Lincoln many curious Sioux would watch the locomotives steaming between Bismarck and the fort from a convenient embankment. From a nearby rifle range troopers of the Seventh would snipe at the Indians sitting by the tracks, and

Custer is alleged to have permitted this "target practice." Sioux girls were frequently molested by the soldiers as well as by the General, who in this story is described as "quite a drunkard," who kept stirring up trouble. His barbaric abuse was climaxed one day when, drunk as usual, he shot at a squaw who sat awaiting a train, the bullet passing through the heart of the baby in her arms, killing both mother and child.

It does not matter that Custer was one of the few cavalrymen who did not drink, having given up the habit during his Civil War days. What is important for this story is the motivation it gives the Sioux, to say nothing of moral rectitude: the epilogue of the story has it that this last atrocity of Custer's so angered various Sioux tribes in the area that when the Seventh left Fort Lincoln on its fated mission, they followed him up the Missouri River to Montana.[21] At the Little Bighorn they caught up with him, presumably, though this account also catches up with its own sense of history. Custer is no longer the aggressor, as we have always thought of him, encroaching on Sioux, but the victim of an ambush. This story, which has not had wide circulation, simply replaces one form of white racism with another. No one is the better for it.

Another story that gained currency with those who wished to praise Custer as well as with those who wished to defame him related his suicide. The account, like those above, was invented to explain why the Indians had not violated his body: suicides were supposed to be powerful medicine to the Sioux, and having seen Custer take his own life, none of the attacking braves would risk violating his corpse. The apologists took an entirely different stand based on the same "fact," namely that Custer had obeyed an unwritten law of the West and of Indian-fighting by saving the last bullet for himself. Capture at the hands of the Indians, whose hearts we know to have been "bad" that day, would have been far worse than death. The story also allows Custer to die, like Roland, undefeated: no Indian could kill him (just as Roland's temples burst from blowing the Oliphant too vigorously), and so he died in a very important sense undefeated.

The other side of the story depicts Custer the coward or perhaps even Custer the psychotic who ends his military career not by fighting the enemy but in an act of shame. Now Custer was right-handed, though the two wounds found on his body by the burial detail were on the left side—of his chest and temple. To have killed himself Custer would have had to have done so with considerable perverse flair, with a highly developed sense of irony, to say nothing of phenomenal dexterity. Under fire from several hundred howling Indians, he would have had to reach his revolver across his body to his left side, and then to the temple, to finish the job. Surely there were easier ways. But the story had grown to such proportions and significance that Captain E. S. Godfrey, who survived with Reno and had been with the burial detail, found it necessary to comment on the rumor explicitly: "there was no sign for the justification of the theory, insinuation, or assertion that he committed suicide."[22]

So strong was the medicine of Custer that while the battle raged, his spiritual presence was as powerful as his physical being. In 1938 the *Bismarck Tribune* carried a story about an alleged scene at Fort Lincoln, several hundred miles to the east of the Little Bighorn, which is supposed to have occurred while the battle was being fought. A Reverend Wainwright was leading a service in the Custer home for Elizabeth and the wives of the regiment's officers. At the very moment that the battle was blazing, the congregation sang "Nearer My God to Thee,"[23] the Welsh hymn also sung—according to another legend—by those who were left aboard the *Titanic* when she went down in the Atlantic on her maiden voyage. So too in this great calamity, God visited the widows of the regiment and, unconscious even to them, inspired this favorite hymn.

We see continually that a great many people claim or are said to have missed disasters, such as the people one always hears about who failed to catch a fatal jetliner because their taxicab got caught in traffic, or those who decided to stay an extra day in town and who cancelled their fated reservation at the last minute. The Custer disaster also had its share—the lone survivors—as we have seen.[24] And it also had its portion of omens which always seem, in retrospect, to anticipate major calamities. For instance, several days before the battle, after an officer's call, Custer's personal guidon fell over in the dust. The other officers took it to be an omen of bad luck. Custer's manner impressed Lieutenant Wallace so much that he soon after remarked to Godfrey (the same officer in the burial detail) that he thought that Custer would die.[25] And still others made out their wills as though they had a presentiment of their fate. Even the hero himself is said to have foreseen the end: in a remark made to a friend he lamented that it would take "another Fort Phil Kearney" defeat to arouse Congress sufficiently to appropriate more funds.[26] His subsequent defeat did, in fact, arouse Congress as he had anticipated.

Today the legendary aspects of Custer retain much of their potency, despite the efforts to debunk and belittle him, despite the analyses of later psychologists to "explain" him away, despite our attempts to establish the facts about the man and his most famous battle. He is, in nearly every respect, regarded by many as a hero—in the classical sense. A very active cult celebrates the memory of his life and the fields of his conflicts, vowing "to seek and preserve the truth about the Battle of the Little Big Horn and all of Custeriana." The cult is nationwide, has official annual meetings in the home town of Custer's adolescence (Monroe, Michigan), and has lobbied for such legislation as the expansion of National Park Service jurisdiction over land adjacent to the Little Bighorn Battlefield.

Custer's cult, the "Little Big Horn Associates," publishes a monthly newsletter for the faithful, and a quarterly *Research Review*, a rather unsophisticated hagiography. The "Associates" do not sponsor trips to Montana, but the newsletter makes it clear that many of the members take such pilgrimages, yearly, to the shrine. Such journeys have all the earmarks of the conventional pilgrimage: a worshipful visit to the shrine, the seasonal character of the pilgrimage, and the re-creation of the battle by local Crow Indians and National Park Service employees.

In the shrine the hero's relics are encased in glass. The Custer Battlefield National Monument preserves, in addition to the usual assortment of carbines, bows and arrows, and clothing, Custer's boots, a buckskin jacket he once wore, personal letters, the last message from him ("Benteen: Come on. Big Village. Be quick. Bring packs. P.S. Bring pacs.")[27] and other mementoes. Another shrine, in Monroe, also reveres a buckskin jacket ("once worn by General Custer . . ."), a campaign trunk, and a lock of his hair.

Frederick Whittaker (and he was not alone in this conception) bestowed upon Custer a martyr's death, raising him above the level of ordinary mortals, even ordinary military heroes. The scene is Custer Ridge; all that remains of the five companies are the general and a "little group of men." Curly, the faithful Crow scout, approaches Custer during a lull in the fighting while the encircling Indians gather for one final charge, and offers "Yellow Hair" a chance to escape. A moment's reflection:

> In that moment, Custer looked at Curly, waved him away and rode back to the little group of men, to die with them. How many thoughts must have crossed that noble soul in that brief moment. There was no hope of victory if he stayed, nothing but certain death. With the scout he was nearly certain to escape. His horse was a thoroughbred and his way sure. He might have balanced the value of a leader's life against those of his men, and sought his safety. Why did he go back to certain death? Because he felt that such a death as that which that little band of heroes was about to die, was worth the lives of all the general officers in the world.[28]

The role of ritual, of which the annual re-creation of the battle is only one aspect, should not be underestimated: far more people than the membership of the "Associates" (or other Custer buffs) attend the yearly play battle, making it one of Montana's leading tourist attractions. Among many of these tourists something deeper than historical interest is involved, as the startling popularity of the Custer legend itself attests. This man's act symbolizes the ultimate act of defiance against all our enemies, against all our frustrations which arise simply by living in human society, against all the circumstances, which may or may not have consciously hostile causes, that thwart our desires. Custer is our idealization of defiance ennobled, on both a personal and a national scale, the embodiment of the wish that regardless of the cost we can remain true to our convictions and our principles, that we shall continue to exert our will in the face of society's pressures and counter-desires.

Consciously we may condemn the tragic hero's rashness, as did the press, when the news of the battle was first known, condemn Custer. But in that he succumbs easily to his impulses he achieves our sanction, because such impulses are something we can, on a level other than consciousness, empathize with: on some level we want the hero to yield to his impulses so that we can relish his "transgressions." His courage and dauntlessness reveal the hero's spiritual value, and replenish ours. Obviously, one needs great moral strength to face death without flinching: the hero rises to meet his fate, and in so doing he proves himself the master of it. The Indians killed Custer but, white Americans wanted to believe, in a higher sense he was impervious to their slings and arrows. His calamity tested to the utmost his inner strength.

We admire the brave loser more than the winner. Let me give two illustrations of this principle, one sublime and the other, by comparison, a bit ridiculous. Many more men win the Congressional Medal of Honor posthumously than live to receive it. This is probably so because we tend to think that a man who has given his life in some heroic act is more brave than one who, while performing the same deed, has lived. A sound psychological truth is involved: a man who dies in such an act of bravery has given his "all," he has given the fullest measure of his devotion which, paradoxically, does not quite seem true of the live hero.

My other illustration is from my experience at the Pennsylvania State University, though I can well believe that similar events take place all over the country. In 1971 the Penn State football team won its first ten games, and including the second half of the 1970 season had a winning streak of fifteen games. For the last game of the season in 1971 the team flew to Knoxville where it was decisively beaten by the University of Tennessee. When the team returned to Pennsylvania the bus discharged them, as usual, by the field house where, as it happened, a basketball game was in progress. A few players strolled in to watch the game and as soon as they were seen the fans rose to give them a standing ovation which was cut short by the basketball referee's insistence. From my experience at Penn State, such tributes rarely, if ever, were lavished on winning teams, particularly after any one game. The people in central Pennsylvania, like those in many other areas no doubt, think of themselves as being able to lose with "pride and poise." The previously undefeated team which had lost to Tennessee was somehow the more heroic for having lost the game while retaining its pride.[29]

What may also be involved in our feeling about Custer and the other analogous heroes (Sam Bayard has suggested to me that they be called "The Custer Cluster") is a propitiation of guilt. It is probably true that Custer died for our sins, originally because of racist attitudes toward the Indians and consequent contempt for them as warriors: Custer rode into battle believing that his greatest worry was the Indians' escape, believing (and having so stated publicly) that his regiment could whip all the Indians of the plains. Subsequently there has been guilt enough over our treatment of the Indians, the confiscation of their lands and the squalid life they have had to live, for the most part, on reservations. Custer dies yearly for those sins, too. Marie Bonaparte once commented on stories circulating throughout Europe on the eve of World War II concerning "sacrificial" deaths related to predictions of Hitler's imminent doom: "war . . . must have revivified within us some of humanity's most ancient beliefs; in this case the conviction of the need for a sacrifice, to obtain some great good fortune."[30] If this phenomenon may be applied in any way to Custer—and I would in no way argue that the annual re-enactment is only guilt propitiation—then the American people are the sacrificers who reap the benefits, and Custer is the perpetual sacrifice. The place of the rite is appropriately numinous.[31]

But why was Custer chosen for this great and dubious honor? Several years before the battle of the Little Bighorn a Captain Fetterman and about eighty soldiers were surrounded by Indians, and annihilated, yet we never hear about Fetterman's Last Stand. This was the Ft. Kearney disaster of which Custer had spoken. Aside from the "unromantic" sound of the name, I think there are more cogent reasons. Custer was a charismatic and controversial figure from the moment of his graduation from West Point. He became one of the youngest officers to win a brigadier general's rank—at twenty-three—and at Appomattox had won his second star. He was the darling of the newspapermen with his nonregulation red kerchief, shoulder-length hair, and acerbic comments. After the war he dabbled in politics, though not successfully. In 1872 when the Grand Duke Alexis toured the American West, Custer escorted him. The Seventh, under his leadership, successfully raided Black Kettle's village (where he met Mo-nah-se-tah?); later, he was court-martialled for ordering the execution of deserters without trial, was found guilty, and was suspended for a year. When his regiment was outfitting to march against the Sioux in 1876, Custer was in Washington testifying in the Belknap impeachment proceedings.

In a very similar study of the popular legends of Davy Crockett and Ethan Allen, Horace Beck noted not so much that they were frontiersmen, but self-publicists.[32] Many legitimate heroes, on and off the frontier, are barely heard of during their lives, and never after. Crockett and Allen were flamboyant personalities, as was Custer. Both of them were opportunists, in their case politically oriented, and whatever his motivation "The Boy General" also had the knack of making headlines. But perhaps most important to the legendizing process in at least these two cases, Beck thinks, is publicity. Crockett and Allen were authors of sorts, and whatever shortcomings they may have had, and whatever critics may have assailed them, they were able to defend themselves to a friendly public. So too was Custer an author, having published *My Life on the Plains* in 1874 (which was also serialized), and several articles.

Then, the nature of the battle was one to pique the imagination. Nothing was known of the fate of the five companies under his command and just that fact appeals to the problem-solving propensities in man. Countless historians and fiction-writers have tried to figure out what really happened that day, or in despair of ever knowing (and perhaps secretly glad that no one would ever know) have created their own imagined and imaginative accounts. If the actions and maneuvers of those five companies of the Seventh were unknown in fact, then anything was possible in the imagination; every man could become his own creator of epics since several of the "right" materials were given: the superior numbers of the enemy, the "wild West," an illustrious regiment and its romantic commander killed.

Finally, the times seemed right. 1876 was the centennial year for the new republic, and the nation's eyes were turned towards Philadelphia and the international exposition there. When the Seventh rode out of Bismarck toward the West, royalty and celebrities from all of the Western world were heading toward America to honor England's most successful colony. Hopes were high throughout the United States that good times would once again return and drive away the demons of recession and scandal which then plagued the Grant administration. As Generals Terry and Sheridan planned the three-pronged movement to entrap the hostile Sioux, the folks "back home" confidently expected a speedy end to the Indian problem. The mood of America was expectant and hopeful.

Under such circumstances it is hardly surprising that Americans found the disaster hard to believe, as it was expressed by General Sherman: "I don't believe it, and I don't want to believe it, if I can help it."[33] And few others wanted to believe it. The resulting psychological process has been termed "cognitive dissonance."[34] The fact of the loss to the Indians was painful in many ways, but that basic fact could not be changed or explained: five companies were dead and even all the rhetoric of Cicero could not soften the blow. Newspapers tended to blame Custer for his rashness and impetuosity in leading five companies into what was described as a ravine. But very quickly the idea grew that rather than being ambushed in a ravine, the Seventh had fought like tigers, line behind line, all killed in place, until the last man was struck down. This explanation of the loss relieved the "dissonance": white America may have lost five companies in combat, but in dying the Seventh achieved a moral superiority to the enemy.

This legendizing process began almost immediately, and was in oral circulation as well as in the newspapers simultaneously. The surviving soldiers themselves seem to have believed in the stories about a Crow scout who survived the fighting and the "report" that Custer's men killed more than their own number of Sioux. Newspapers elaborated on the Curly story, and added a heroic defense, "line behind line." Stories of treason seemed to spring up everywhere—quite a natural creation to explain the loss—and Eastern papers carried the first of these. Painters and illustrators put Custer on a hilltop where he would be the most impressive visually. So spontaneous was this legendizing process, speeded but not created by the telegraph, that when Frederick Whittaker drew to the last chapter of his *Life of Custer* still within 1876, nearly all the materials were at hand. Thus, as Jan de Vries has observed, does heroic legend become epic—in the hands of an eclectic artist.[35]

But proximity of the legend to the event seems to have little effect on the accuracy of the former. We tend to think that the closer the epic is to the man or the event it celebrates, the more real or lifelike its form. If the Custer story as it was transformed by the popular imagination and recorded by Whittaker is any model, then time does not appear to be one of the parameters of the imagination. It does not matter to this model that Whittaker's mode is biography and not epic: the factor of talent is secondary, here, to the availability of heroic legend within a very few months of the event. Whittaker's poem, "Custer's Last Charge," published within a month of the battle, is a heroic lay (though again not distinguished) illustrating the main features of the legend, and perhaps will do for a model of the relations between event and poetic eulogy.

Friends have argued with me in private conversations that surely such legends as Custer's developed because those involved knew of the accounts of Leonidas, Saul, Roland, and the others. It seems hard to believe that such a legend could arise spontaneously in the United

States. But this is exactly what I am insisting. The soldiers and reporters who created the legend, each contributing only a small fraction of it until Whittaker put it together, were ignorant of classical and medieval heroic epic. I once conducted an informal (and unpublished) study at the University of Virginia of students who had heard stories that John F. Kennedy was still alive, either at Parkland or Bethesda Naval Hospital, or on Onassis' Island. Some of these students believed the story themselves, but were amazed to learn that King Arthur is also said to have survived his "death" and to be residing on an island across the sea, and that the same stories were told about Nero, Thor, Thomas Paine, Zapata, even Hitler who is alive and well in Argentina. These students did not make up such stories, certainly not those who believed in them. Rather, they "lived" their beliefs; and so it was with the disseminators of the Custer legend.

We all know of the human tendency to dramatize reality, folklorists particularly. Axel Olrik has commented on this perceptively in his "Epic Laws," many of which observations were confirmed in the laboratory of the English psychologist F. C. Bartlett and described in *Remembering*.[36] I would like to use just one of Olrik's "Laws" to demonstrate a final point about the Custer legend, that of contrast. As the Custer legend came to us as recently as 1940, the dashing, young, incomparably brave commander has been contrasted with the plodding, older, and perhaps cowardly Reno. The numbers of the Indians contrasted with the heroism of the small band of troopers. To counter the loyalty of the Seventh to God, Duty, and Country we invent the heinous acts of the traitor. They are savages; we are white Christian champions of civilization. Custer dies on the very top of the hill while the Indians sneak around in gullies and ravines. And so on. Given certain basic facts about the battle—which I have already mentioned—the Custer legend developed with a certain predictability simply because in the West[37] it was the best way to tell the story.

I once had the occasion to argue on these same pages[38] that even though the roles of Unferð (in *Beowulf*) and Euryalus (in the *Odyssey*) are strikingly similar, direct attribution should not be assumed. Both Unferð and his Greek counterpart are courtiers whose carping jibes at the visiting hero (Beowulf and Odysseus) evoke a recounting of the hero's past deeds. Albert B. Lord noted these similarities and guessed that some basic "Indo-European narrative tradition"[39] accounted for these analogues; but what seems to be involved—given the notable failure of scholars to demonstrate a knowledge of classical epic by the *Beowulf* poet—is simply the best way, speaking dramatically, of eliciting information about the heroic past of the champion. One should think of the situation in terms of dramatic problems to be solved; when they are similar, the tactics evolved to solve them may well also be similar, and derived independently.

In discussing this matter with Francis Lee Utley several years ago, several other characters who emerge in similar situations were suggested: Thersites in the *Iliad*, Humbab in *Gilgamesh*, Pandarus in *Troilus and Criseyde*, perhaps even Falstaff in Parts I and II of *Henry IV*. And I might add Satan in *Paradise Lost* and Sir Kay in the Arthurian romances, especially those of Chrétien de Troyes. Although the legend of Custer is quite different from these, I believe that the principle of narrative composition is much the same. Like the *scops, jongleurs,* and minstrels of medieval Europe, like the learned poets of many eras, the unschooled "folk" of nineteenth-century America created a heroic legend which was, for the most part, coincidentally analogous to those of the greatest legends of the Western civilization. The tradition in question appears to be as much a matter of the imagination as of manuscripts.

Notes

1. Frederic F. Van de Water, *Glory-Hunter: A Life of General Custer* (Indianapolis: Bobbs-Merrill Co., 1934).

2. The estimate is basically that of Don Russell, *Custer's Last* (Fort Worth: Amon Carter Museum of Western Art, 1968), 1.

3. Don Russell, *Custer's List: A Checklist of Pictures Relating to the Battle of the Little Big Horn* (Fort Worth: Amon Carter Museum of Western Art, 1969). *Custer's List* is a bibliography of paintings and illustrations; *Custer's Last* is an annotated, and very selective, reprinting of several of the more famous paintings and lithographs.

4. Most accessible in W. A. Graham, *The Custer Myth: A Source Book of Custeriana* (Harrisburg, Pa.: Stackpole Co., 1953), 383–405.

5. Philip M. Shockley, "Sabers of the Seventh," *Little Big Horn Associates Research Review* 5 (Spring 1971): 1–5. See also the statement by one of the survivors, Lt. E. S. Godfrey, in Graham, *Custer Myth*, 127.

6. Kate Bighead, a Cheyenne, claims to have seen several troopers alive

after those in the ring around Custer were dead: cited in Edgar I. Stewart, *Custer's Luck* (Norman: University of Oklahoma Press, 1955), 461.

7. A letter from Benteen to his wife, dated July 4, 1876, is transcribed in Graham, *Custer Myth*, 300: ". . . our men killed a great many of them—quite as many, if not more, than was killed of ours."

8. David Humphreys Miller, *Custer's Fall: The Indian Side of the Story* (New York: Duell, Sloan and Pearce, 1957), 255, puts the number at thirty-two.

9. See, for instance, Graham, *Custer Myth*, 91, for an Indian estimate; similar evaluations by the survivors may be found in W. A. Graham, ed., *Abstract of the Official Record of Proceedings of the Reno Court of Inquiry* (Harrisburg, Pa.: Stackpole Co., 1954).

10. See Graham, *Reno Court.* Among those who still believe in Reno's treason are the guides at the Monroe, Michigan Historical Society.

11. Curly's first report was to Lt. Bradley aboard the "Far West": "I did nothing wonderful—I was not in the fight." Cited in Graham, *Custer Myth*, 9.

12. G. W. Schneider-Wettengel, "Custer's Laying Out," *Little Big Horn Associates Research Review* 4 (Winter 1970): 7–9.

13. Ibid., 7. A lengthy interview with Kate was published in Thomas B. Marquis, *She Watched Custer's Last Battle, Her Story, Interpreted, in 1927* (Hardin, Mont.: Privately printed, 1933).

14. Quoted in Philip Young, "The Mother of Us All: Pocahontas Reconsidered," *Kenyon Review* 24 (Summer 1962): 403. Much of my information about the analogues comes from this excellent study.

15. Philip Young's thesis is that the Pocahontas-figure is "all the 'Dark Ladies' of our culture—all the erotic and joyous temptresses, the sensual brunette heroines, whom our civilization . . . has summoned up to repress." Ibid., 415.

16. Charles A. Eastman, "Rain-in-the-Face: The Story of a Sioux Warrior," *Teepee Book* (June 1916), 101.

17. Milton Ronsheim, *The Life of General Custer* (Cadiz, Ohio: Cadiz Republican*, 1929), n.p.

18. *The Complete Poetical Works of Henry Wadsworth Longfellow* (Boston: Houghton, Mifflin and Co., 1880), 272. The original has eight stanzas; IV, V, and VII are quoted here.

19. Cited in *Americana Magazine*, no date, in the Newberry Library, Ayer Collection (Ayer 228/H 18 b), in a compilation by Eugene D. Hart entitled "The Battle of the Little Big Horn: A Miscellaneous Group of Published Accounts," 57.

20. See Bruce A. Rosenberg, "The Blood Mystique of Gottfried and Wolfram," *Southern Folklore Quarterly* 27 (Fall 1963): 214–22.

21. Richard M. Dorson, *Bloodstoppers and Bearwalkers* (Cambridge: Harvard University Press, 1952), 38–39.

22. Quoted in Graham, *Custer Myth*, 376.

23. Bismarck *Tribune*, August 6,

1938, n.p. (from the Ayer Collection, 228/*k* 43).

24. A discussion of the most prominent "survivors" is found in Robert M. Utley, *Custer and the Great Controversy: The Origin and Development of a Legend* (Los Angeles: Westernlore Press, 1962), 135–45.

25. Recounted by Lt. Godfrey; reprinted in Graham, *Custer Myth*, 135.

26. Chicago *Tribune*, July 18, 1876, p. 1.

27. This message, written by Adjutant W. W. Cooke, is kept in a vault and is not on display to the public.

28. Frederick Whittaker, *A Complete Life of Gen. George A. Custer* (New York: Sheldon and Co., 1876), 599.

29. See also the account of the defeat of Penn State by Colorado in Mervin D. Hyman and Gordon S. White, Jr., *Joe Paterno: "Football My Way"* (New York: Macmillan, 1971), 230–31: "In defeat, Joe Paterno and his team were gallant. They were so humble and faithful to what sportsmanship is supposed to mean that, in the age in which we live, it was almost unbelievable. . . . Penn State students also took the loss in stride. Some 2,000 of them were on hand to greet Joe and his players when they returned to University Park on Sunday at 3 a.m."

30. Marie Bonaparte, *Myths of War*, trans. John Rodker (London: Imago Publishing Co., 1947), 15.

31. Ibid., 21. Or else it is not a sacrifice, but merely murder. Much has been written on the quasi-numinous quality of the American wilderness, particularly George Huntston Williams, *Wilderness and Paradise in Christian Thought* (New York: Harper, 1962), and Henry Nash Smith, *Virgin Land: The American West As Symbol and Myth* (Cambridge: Harvard University Press, 1950).

32. Horace Beck, "The Making of the Popular Legendary Hero," in Wayland Hand, ed., *American Folk Legend: A Symposium* (Berkeley: University of California Press, 1971), 128–30.

33. Quoted in the Chicago *Tribune*, July 7, 1876, p. 1.

34. Leon Festinger, *A Theory of Cognitive Dissonance* (Stanford: Stanford University Press, 1957).

35. Jan de Vries, *Heroic Song and Heroic Legend*, trans. B. J. Timmer (London: Oxford University Press, 1963), 164–79.

36. The relevant chapter is reprinted in Alan Dundes, ed., *The Study of Folklore* (Englewood Cliffs, N.J.: Prentice-Hall, 1965), 243–58.

37. I have not found any analogues in Eastern literature.

38. "The Necessity of Unferth," *Journal of the Folklore Institute* 6 (June 1969): 50–60.

39. "Beowulf and Odysseus," in Robert P. Creed and Jess B. Bessinger, Jr., eds., *Franciplegius: Medieval and Linguistic Studies in Honor of Francis Peabody Magoun, Jr.* (New York: New York University Press, 1965), 86–91.

This imaginative cover illustration on the July 13, 1876, *Illustrated Police News* beat out William M. Cary's July 19 drawing in the *New York Graphic Newspaper* to rank as the very first of over fifteen hundred artistic renderings of Custer's Last Stand (John M. Carroll Collection).

Frederick Whittaker, a veteran of the Sixth New York Cavalry, was a prolific author of dime novels and magazine articles when he met George Custer in the New York offices of *Galaxy* magazine. He later became the dead soldier's champion, with his bulky *A Complete Life of Gen. George A. Custer* on book shelves and selling briskly by December 1876. It was Whittaker's charges of cowardice against Major Marcus Reno that led to the convening of the Reno Court of Inquiry in 1879. *The Dashing Dragoon* dime novel (top) was but one of Whittaker's numerous Custer publications (Courtesy Brian W. Dippie, from the collection of Edward T. LeBlanc). William F. "Buffalo Bill" Cody was another Custer champion. He had known Custer fairly well during the Indian Wars and had left the stage in 1876 to scout for the Fifth Cavalry and take his celebrated "first scalp for Custer." When Cody established his Wild West show in 1883, the Last Stand was often depicted, as this 1904 poster (bottom) attests to (Buffalo Bill Historical Center, Cody, Wyoming).

CUSTER'S LAST FIGHT

ANHEUSER BUSCH BREWING ASSOCIATION.

F. Otto Becker greatly improved on Cassilly Adams's rather crude *Custer's Last Fight* when he copied the painting for lithography. Copyrighted in 1896, it was distributed for advertising purposes by the Anheuser-Busch Brewing Company and quickly became a standard prop of saloon furnishings (top). Few paintings have been so widely viewed (Custer Battlefield National Monument). John Mulvany's twenty-by-eleven-foot oil *Custer's Last Rally* (bottom), completed in 1881, was exhibited around the country for a decade and was widely reproduced as a book illustration (Montana Historical Society Museum).

Two Montana artists who produced quite different paintings of the same event were Edgar S. Paxson and Charles M. Russell. Paxson's cluttered *Custer's Last Stand* (top), finished in 1899 after nearly two decades of research and labor, contains numerous portraits of participants in the battle. Lieutenant William W. Cooke is beside the wounded Custer, and Captain Tom Custer is to the left, with Captain George Yates just below. The scout Mitch Boyer takes aim far to the right. To the right of Tom Custer, with raised war club, is Rain-in-the-Face, and to his left, with upraised rifle, is Gall. Far to the right, Crazy Horse, with club, charges toward Boyer, while just below, Crow King fires his pistol (Buffalo Bill Historical Center, Cody, Wyoming). Russell's *The Custer Fight* (bottom) concentrates not on beleaguered soldiers but on heroic Indian warriors in a 1903 watercolor full of action and movement (National Cowboy Hall of Fame, Oklahoma City).

A certain economy of style marked N. C. Wyeth's nevertheless dramatic *Custer's Last Stand* (top), used in 1932 to promote Lucky Strike cigarettes in color magazine advertisements (Author's Collection). Harold Von Schmidt's *Custer's Last Stand* (bottom) was also meant for use in a magazine, being painted expressly for *Esquire* and appearing as a color foldout in the September 1950 issue. Although the author was no admirer of Custer, he nevertheless painted him as flamboyantly heroic (Courtesy Eric von Schmidt).

The grim realism of Eric von Schmidt's *Here Fell Custer* is in sharp contrast to the romantic Last Stand illustrations painted by his father. Breaking with a century of tradition, von Schmidt created a stark panorama emphasizing the hopeless desperation of the battle's last few minutes. His meticulous research is evident throughout the canvas. He included in the painting several of those known to have fallen near Custer. They are (left to right) Lt. Algernon Smith in the vest; Capt. Tom Custer, wounded and crawling; Capt. George Yates, in buckskin jacket and black hat; Sgt. Robert Hughes holding Custer's personal guidon; Chief Trumpeter Henry Voss sprawling across a clump of sagebrush full of arrows; Lt. William W. Cooke, struck by an arrow just above Voss; and Lt. Col. Custer, clutching his death wound and staring out upon the result of his folly. The artist painted himself, wearing a forage cap and wounded, in between Tom Custer and Hughes (© 1976 Eric von Schmidt, world rights reserved).

William Selig's 1909 one-reeler *Custer's Last Stand* was probably the first Custer film (top). It featured a reenactment of the battle, staged on the actual site by Crow Indians and members of the Montana National Guard (Buffalo Bill Historical Center, Cody, Wyoming). Thomas H. Ince's 1912 *Custer's Last Fight* was far more lavish, featuring hundreds of actors in an impressive recreation of the battle (bottom). Francis Ford's portrayal of Custer set a heroic pattern not broken until his brother John Ford directed *Fort Apache* in 1948 (Author's Collection).

The most impressive of the Custer silent films was undoubtedly Universal's 1926 spectacle *The Flaming Frontier*, starring Dustin Farnum as Custer (top). The first major sound film to deal with Custer was Cecil B. DeMille's 1937 Paramount epic *The Plainsman* (bottom). But John Miljan's Custer, here striking a familiar pose in a studio publicity shot, was a decidedly secondary character to Gary Cooper's Wild Bill Hickok and James Ellison's Buffalo Bill Cody (Author's Collection).

On the eve of World War II, Warner Brothers released two films featuring Custer. In the first the studio massacred history in a rousing 1940 adventure entitled *Santa Fe Trail* (top) and featuring (left to right) Ronald Reagan as Custer, Errol Flynn as Jeb Stuart, and William Lundigan as Bob Halliday. The least of the film's historical inaccuracies is that Custer was but a schoolboy at the time of many of the events depicted. No other actor was ever better equipped to capture the heroic side of Custer's character than Errol Flynn, and his portrayal in *They Died with Their Boots On* (1941) remains a Hollywood classic. In this scene (bottom) he receives his death wound from Crazy Horse's rifle. Flynn's would be the last heroic Custer, as well as the best (Author's Collection).

The director John Ford was the first to break with the heroic Custer tradition in film, but he changed the names and locale to do so in his 1948 Argosy-RKO classic *Fort Apache* (top). Ford used Custer again in *She Wore a Yellow Ribbon* (Argosy-RKO, 1949), where the Last Stand is the backdrop of the film's action, and in *The Searchers* (Warner Brothers, 1956), where Custer's cavalry attacks a Comanche village and then herds Indian prisoners back to an army post. In a scene cut from the final release print (bottom), John Wayne as Ethan Edwards confronts Peter Ortiz as Custer about the Washita-like slaughter (Author's Collection).

Wayne Maunder made a dashing Custer and Slim Pickens a crusty California Joe
Milner in the 1967 ABC television series "Custer" (top), but poor ratings did in the
hero at midseason before Michael Dante's Crazy Horse got a chance to. Episodes
were combined into a 1968 film, *The Legend of Custer*, for release in Europe and
to television. Far more successful was Richard Mulligan's devastating portrayal
of Custer as a racist megalomaniac in Arthur Penn's 1970 film *Little Big Man*. At
the Little Big Horn, Custer (bottom) becomes totally unhinged before meeting a
well-deserved death (Author's Collection).

The international appeal of the Custer story is evident in a German dime novel (top left) and an Italian comic book (bottom right). In the German book, published around 1910, Sitting Bull rescues a young lady disguised as a soldier who had ridden with Custer (Courtesy Brian W. Dippie, from the collection of Edward T. LeBlanc). Custer made several appearances in the wonderful Italian comic book series *Storia Del West*, edited by Sergio Bonelli, published by Daim Press from 1967 to 1980, and reissued by Bonelli in the late 1980s. Gino D'Antonio's story, featuring his superb artwork, tells the tale of a Cheyenne warrior who stalks Custer to avenge the death of his wife at the Washita. They meet at the Little Big Horn and kill each other (Courtesy Sergio Bonelli).

BIBLIOGRAPHICAL ESSAY

The sheer bulk of written material on George Armstrong Custer is astonishing. A 1953 bibliography by Fred Dustin listed 641 items. A 1972 listing of bibliographical "high spots" by Tal Luther ran to 195 entries, whereas John Carroll's exhaustive periodical checklist ran to well over three thousand entries. This essay makes no attempt to be exhaustive in its coverage but instead should guide the interested reader through this morass of publication.

Essays reprinted in *The Custer Reader* are not discussed in this bibliographical essay because their value is made clear in the section introductions. Several detailed studies on sidelights of the Custer story have been mentioned in the notes to section introductions and are not repeated here. Many excellent essays on minor points of Custer's life or on the Battle of the Little Big Horn are also not discussed, for obvious space reasons. Much of the Custer literature, of course, makes no real contribution to our understanding of the man or his era and really deserves no space in any bibliography except one that wishes to be definitive.

The place to begin a more detailed exploration of Custer's storied life is with the biographies. It is rather surprising, considering the extent of the Custer bibliography, just how few good biographies have been written. The first is still worth looking at, for Frederick Whittaker's *A Complete Life of Gen. George A. Custer* (New York: Sheldon and Co., 1876) stood for over a quarter of a century as the only significant biography. It contains much useful information and, more important, was instrumental in transforming Custer into a major American hero. Later heroic biographies by Frederick Dellenbaugh in 1917 and Frazier Hunt in 1928 are not interesting as history or literature. Frederic F. Van de Water's *Glory-Hunter: A Life of General Custer* (Indianapolis: Bobbs-Merrill Co., 1934) broke with the interpretation of over fifty years to dismantle the marble hero and present instead an understandable, if deeply flawed, human being. Few books have had so immediate and dramatic an impact on historical interpretation. Inspired by the works of Sigmund Freud as well as by the debunking biographers of the Lytton Strachey school, Van de Water penned a compelling portrait of a man consumed by ambition, driven by demons of his own making, and finally destroyed by his own hubris. Compellingly written, the book has stood the test of time as high literary biography and remains the most influential book ever written on Custer. In 1988 it was reprinted as a Bison Book by the University of Nebraska Press.

Van de Water had no challenge until Jay Monaghan's *Custer: The Life of General George Armstrong Custer* (Boston: Little, Brown and Co., 1959), also available as a Bison Book from the University of Nebraska Press. Monaghan is far more favorable toward Custer, but his research was hardly exhaustive, and his account of the Little Big Horn is sketchy and inadequate. His Civil War sections, however, are much stronger. But Monaghan fails to penetrate the Custer enigma, and the biography lacks the energy and force of Van de Water's or of later works by Connell and Utley.

D. A. Kinsley's *Favor the Bold*, 2 vols. (New York: Holt, Rinehart and Winston, 1967–68) has some literary pretense but little else of interest or value to the reader. More interesting is Stephen E. Ambrose, *Crazy Horse and Custer: The Parallel Lives of Two American Warriors* (Garden City, N.Y.: Doubleday and Co., 1975), but it ultimately provides nothing new despite the book's innovative organization and the author's distinguished credentials. Charles K. Hofling's *Custer and the Little Big Horn: A Psychobiographical Inquiry* (Detroit: Wayne State University Press, 1981) is certainly an interesting, even provocative, biography but will prove tough going for the nonspecialist reader. It is mostly speculative in content and is difficult to accept as true biography. Far more satisfying, although often equally as speculative, is Evan S. Connell's *Son of the Morning Star* (San Francisco: North Point Press, 1984), the surprise best-seller that partially rehabilitated Custer's reputation. Although the author is occasionally careless with facts, he nevertheless gets to the heart of his subject better than any writer before him. Coming from a literary rather than an academic background, Connell is unshackled by convention and engages in wild digressions across time and space in freewheeling explorations of Custer and his singular, epic moment at the Little Big Horn. At the same time, Connell restores Custer to his proper place in history as a brave, experienced, but driven soldier full of compelling contradictions.

Far more traditional in terms of organization and approach, Robert M. Utley's *Cavalier in Buckskin: George Armstrong Custer and the Western Military Frontier* (Norman: University of Oklahoma Press, 1988) is as definitive a portrait of Custer as we are likely to see for some time, firmly placing its subject within the broader context of national expansion. Although concentrating on Custer's western career, the biography nevertheless handles his Civil War actions admirably. Utley, the dean of frontier military historians, brought a lifetime of careful research to the project. The book has no documentation as a result of the series format that it is part of, but Utley's reputation gives enormous credibility to every word in this graceful, gripping biography. It is *the* Custer book to begin with.

George and Elizabeth Custer both left fine memoirs that are still available in reprint editions. They are often as informative by what they leave out as what they include: George Armstrong Custer, *My Life on the Plains; or, Personal Experiences with Indians*, ed. Edgar I. Stewart (Norman: University of Oklahoma Press, 1962); Elizabeth B. Custer, *"Boots and Saddles"; or, Life in Dakota with General Custer* (New York: Harper and Brothers, 1885); Elizabeth B. Custer, *Tenting on the Plains; or, General Custer in Kansas and Texas*

(New York: Harper and Brothers, 1887); and Elizabeth B. Custer, *Following the Guidon* (New York: Harper and Brothers, 1890). Extracts from the letters of the Custers, although heavily edited, are presented in Marguerite Merington, ed., *The Custer Story: The Life and Intimate Letters of General George A. Custer and His Wife Elizabeth* (New York: Devin-Adair, 1950), which is available as a Bison Book from the University of Nebraska Press. Additional correspondence and much useful information is contained in the encyclopedic and slavishly worshipful biography of Elizabeth by Lawrence A. Frost, *General Custer's Libbie* (Seattle: Superior Publishing Co., 1976).

Lawrence A. Frost, for years the curator of the Custer room of the Monroe County Museum in Custer's boyhood hometown, also compiled an entertaining but hagiographic pictorial biography: *The Custer Album: A Pictorial Biography of General George A. Custer* (Seattle: Superior Publishing Co., 1964). More dependable in terms of captioning and containing far superior photographic reproductions, but limited in content to only Custer, is D. Mark Katz, *Custer in Photographs* (Gettysburg: Yo-Mark Production Co., 1985). Also of interest to photo enthusiasts are Neil C. Mangum, *Register of the Custer Battlefield National Monument Photograph Collection* (Crow Agency, Mont.: Custer Battlefield Historical and Museum Association, 1984), and Neil Mangum, "Solving Custer Photo Puzzles: Some New Dates and Identifications," *Montana the Magazine of Western History* 31 (October 1981).

To focus on Custer's Civil War career, one should begin with Gregory J. W. Urwin, *Custer Victorious: The Civil War Battles of General George Armstrong Custer* (Rutherford, N.J.: Fairleigh Dickinson University Press, 1983), which was reprinted in 1990 as a Bison Book from the University of Nebraska Press. The best memoir by one of Custer's officers is J. H. Kidd, *Personal Recollections of a Cavalryman with Custer's Michigan Cavalry Brigade in the Civil War* (1908; reprint, Grand Rapids, Mich.: Black Letter Press, 1969), and Custer is also featured prominently in Henry Edwin Tremain, *Last Hours of Sheridan's Cavalry: A Reprint of War Memoranda* (New York: Bonnell, Silver and Bowers, 1904). General Sheridan's memoirs also deal at length with Custer both in the Civil War and on the plains, with the best edition being the 1902 enlarged one: Philip Henry Sheridan and Michael V. Sheridan, *Personal Memoirs of Philip Henry Sheridan General United States Army: New and Enlarged Edition with an Account of his Life from 1871 to his Death, in 1888*, 2 vols. (New York: D. Appleton and Co., 1902).

Custer's own aborted Civil War memoirs, though brief, are insightful and useful. They are available in E. Elden Davis, ed., "George A. Custer's War Memoirs," in Paul A. Hutton, ed., *Garry Owen 1976: Annual of the Little Big Horn Associates* (Seattle: Little Big Horn Associates, 1977), 14–97, and in John M. Carroll, ed., *Custer in the Civil War: His Unfinished Memoirs* (San Rafael, Calif.: Presidio Press, 1977). The latter also reprints Custer's Civil War reports.

For two specific campaigns, see David F. Riggs, *East of Gettysburg: Stuart vs. Custer* (Bellevue, Nebr.: Old Army Press, 1970), and Jeffry D. Wert, *From Winchester to Cedar Creek: The Shenandoah Campaign of 1864* (Carlisle, Pa.: South Mountain Press, 1987). For the overall picture, consult Stephen Z. Starr, *The Union Cavalry in the Civil War: The War in the East from Gettysburg to Appomattox, 1863–1865* (Baton Rouge: Louisiana State University Press, 1981).

Custer's Reconstruction duty in Texas is the focus of John M. Carroll, ed., *Custer in Texas: An Interrupted Narrative* (New York: Sol Lewis/Liveright, 1975). Also of interest are William L. Richter, "'A Better Time is in Store for us': An Analysis of the Reconstruction Attitudes of George Armstrong Custer," *Military History of Texas and the Southwest* 11 (1973), and Minnie Dubbs Millbrook, "The Boy General and How He Grew," *Montana the Magazine of Western History* 23 (Spring 1973).

For a superb synthesis of the postwar military frontier, see Robert M. Utley, *Frontier Regulars: The United States Army and the Indian, 1866–1891* (New York: Macmillan Publishing Co., 1973), which is also available in a Bison Book reprint from the University of Nebraska Press. Solid general histories of the war for the southern plains include several excellent essays by Lonnie J. White reprinted in Lonnie J. White, *Hostiles and Horse Soldiers: Indian Battles and Campaigns in the West* (Boulder, Colo: Pruett Publishing Co., 1972); William H. Leckie, *The Military Conquest of the Southern Plains* (Norman: University of Oklahoma Press, 1963); and Wilbur Sturtevant Nye, *Plains Indian Raiders: The Final Phases of Warfare from the Arkansas to the Red River* (Norman: University of Oklahoma Press, 1968). The Indian side of these campaigns is covered in George Bird Grinnell, *The Fighting Cheyennes* (1915; reprint, Norman: University of Oklahoma Press, 1956); Donald J. Berthrong, *The Southern Cheyennes* (Norman: University of Oklahoma Press, 1963); and George E. Hyde, *Life of George Bent: Written from His Letters*, ed. Savoie Lottinville (Norman: University of Oklahoma Press, 1968).

For the formation and history of the Seventh Cavalry, see Melbourne C. Chandler, *Of Garry Owen in Glory: The History of the Seventh United States Cavalry Regiment* (Annandale, Va.: Turnpike Press, 1960), and Charles K. Mills, *Rosters from Seventh U.S. Cavalry Campaigns, 1866–1896* (Bryan, Tex.: J. M. Carroll and Co., 1983). Brief biographies of those who were at the Little Big Horn can be found in Kenneth Hammer, *Biographies of the Seventh Cavalry: June 25th, 1876* (Fort Collins, Colo.: Old Army Press, 1972). This is a particularly useful research tool. John M. Carroll built on and expanded Hammer's research in John M. Carroll, ed., *They Rode with Custer: A Biographical Directory of the Men That Rode with General George A. Custer* (Bryan, Tex.: J. M. Carroll Co., 1987).

The western career of Custer's mentor, with much on their relationship, is covered in Paul Andrew Hutton, *Phil Sheridan and His Army* (Lincoln: University of Nebraska Press, 1985). Profiles of Custer and many of his contemporaries are in Paul Andrew Hutton, ed., *Soldiers West: Biographies from the Military Frontier* (Lincoln: University of Nebraska Press, 1987). Several of Custer's officers have received biographical treatment. Myles Keogh is heroically depicted in Edward S. Luce, *Keogh, Comanche, and Custer* (1939; reprint, Ashland, Oreg.: Lewis Osborne, 1974), and in the more informative pamphlet by G. A. Hayes-McCoy, *Captain Myles Walter Keogh, United States Army, 1840–1876* (Dublin: National University of Ireland, 1965). Another foreign-born Seventh Cavalry officer's career is briefly detailed in Charles K. Mills, *Charles C. DeRudio* (Bryan, Tex.: J. M. Carroll Co., 1983). An apologetic account of Marcus Reno's life can be found in John Upton Terrell and George Walton, *Faint the Trumpet Sounds: The Life and Trial of Major Reno* (New York: David McKay Co., 1966). There is more material on the mercurial Frederick W. Benteen than on any other Seventh Cavalry officer except Custer. Charles K. Mills's *Harvest of Barren Regrets: The Army Career of Frederick William Benteen, 1834–1898* (Glendale, Calif.: Arthur H. Clark Co., 1985) is overly detailed but quite useful. Far more compelling are Benteen's own caustic letters, available in two most revealing volumes: John M. Carroll, ed., *Camp Talk: The Very Private Letters of Frederick W. Benteen of the Seventh U.S. Cavalry to His Wife, 1871 to 1888* (Bryan, Tex.: J. M. Carroll Co., 1983), and John M. Carroll, ed., *The Benteen-Goldin Letters on Custer and His Last Battle* (New York: Liveright, 1974).

Enlisted men rarely rate biographies, but Custer's orderly John Burkman is the subject of a fine anecdotal one, based for the most part on his reminiscences. The 1989 Bison Book edition from the University of Nebraska Press is the most useful because of Brian W. Dippie's fine introduction to Glendolin Damon Wagner, *Old Neutriment* (Boston: R. Hill, 1934). Sergeant Charles Windolph finally rated a biography by managing to outlive all the other white survivors of the Little Big Horn. Neil Mangum provided a new introduction to the 1987 Bison Book reprint of Frazier Hunt and Robert Hunt, *I Fought with Custer* (New York: Charles Scribner's Sons, 1953). Custer's scout on the southern plains, Moses E. Milner, is the subject of Joe E. Milner and Earle R. Forrest, *California Joe: Noted Scout and Indian Fighter* (Caldwell, Idaho: Caxton Printers, 1935), also available as a Bison Book with a new introduction by Joseph G. Rosa. The travail of a Seventh Cavalry wife is related in Katherine Gibson Fougera, *With Custer's Cavalry* (Caldwell, Idaho: Caxton Printers, 1940), reprinted as a Bison Book in 1986.

Custer's own account of his introduction to Indian warfare, presented with considerably more bile than in his later autobiography, is in Brian W. Dippie, ed., *Nomad: George A. Custer in Turf, Field, and Farm* (Austin: University of Texas Press, 1980). Dippie's detailed discursive notes are particularly valuable. Hancock's campaign, as well as the Washita campaign, is covered in the insightful and fascinating Barnitz diaries and letters, reprinted in 1987 as a Bison Book by the University of Nebraska Press. This record of life on the military frontier can scarcely be matched elsewhere and is an invaluable resource. See Robert M. Utley, ed., *Life in Custer's Cavalry: Diaries and Letters of Albert and Jennie Barnitz, 1867–1868* (New Haven: Yale University Press, 1977).

Custer's September 1867 court-martial is detailed in Lawrence A. Frost, *The Court-Martial of General George Armstrong Custer* (Norman: University of Oklahoma Press, 1968), which includes the court proceedings. Two useful articles on the same subject are Robert A. Murray, "The Custer Court Martial," *Annals of Wyoming* 36 (October 1964), and Milton B. Halsey, Jr., "The Court-Martial of Brevet Major General George A. Custer," *Trail Guide* 13 (September 1968). This was Custer's second brush with military justice. For his earlier troubles, see Minnie Dubbs Millbrook, "Cadet Custer's Court-Martial," in Paul A. Hutton, ed., *Custer and His Times* (El Paso: Little Big Horn Associates, 1981).

The official documents of the Washita campaign have been published as John M. Carroll, ed., *General Custer and the Battle of the Washita: The Federal View* (Bryan, Tex.: Guidon Press, 1978), which makes a handy reference work. The best monograph, despite certain limitations, remains Stan Hoig, *The Battle of the Washita: The Sheridan-Custer Indian Campaign of 1867–69* (Garden City, N.Y.: Doubleday and Co., 1976). A particularly fine memoir of the campaign by a volunteer trooper is David L. Spotts, *Campaigning with Custer and the Nineteenth Kansas Volunteer Cavalry on the Washita Campaign, 1868–69*, ed. E. A. Brininstool (Los Angeles: Wetzel Publishing Co., 1928), reprinted in 1988 as a University of Nebraska Press Bison Book. A view from the top is provided by the journalist De B. Randolph Keim, *Sheridan's Troopers on the Borders: A Winter Campaign on the Plains* (Philadelphia: Clayton, Remsen and Habbelfinger, 1870), reprinted in 1985 as a Bison Book with a new introduction by Paul Andrew Hutton.

Custer's Reconstruction duty in Kentucky has been largely ignored except for Theodore J. Crackel, "Custer's Kentucky: General George Armstrong Custer and Elizabethtown, Kentucky, 1871–1873," *Filson Club History Quarterly* 49 (April 1974): 144–55. Custer spent much of his time in Kentucky indulging his love of horse racing, and a history of the various horses owned by this cavalryman is provided by Lawrence A. Frost, *General Custer's Thoroughbreds: Racing, Riding, Hunting, and Fighting* (Bryan, Tex.: J. M. Carroll Co., 1986). The most famous horse connected with Custer did not belong to him but was the mount of Captain Myles Keogh. There is a large body of literature on the horse Comanche, but much of it is summarized in Elizabeth Atwood Lawrence, *His Very Silence Speaks: Comanche—The Horse Who Survived Custer's Last Stand* (Detroit: Wayne State University Press, 1989).

A highlight of Custer's Kentucky sojourn was his participation in General Sheridan's 1872 buffalo hunt for the Russian Grand Duke Alexis. A good brief account of the hunt is in John I. White, "Red Carpet for a Romanoff," *American West* 9 (January 1972). Two nice versions by participants are James Albert Hadley, "A Royal Buffalo Hunt," *Transactions of the Kansas State Historical*

Society 10 (1907–8), and *The Life of Hon. William F. Cody, Known As Buffalo Bill* (1879; reprint, Lincoln: University of Nebraska Press, 1978). Full details of the Grand Duke's tour are in *The Grand Duke Alexis in the United States of America* (New York: Interland Publishing, 1972).

A good monograph of the important 1873 Yellowstone expedition is still needed. Much useful information, however, is contained in Lawrence A. Frost, *Custer's Seventh Cav and the Campaign of 1873* (El Segundo, Calif.: Upton and Sons, 1986). An interesting sidelight to the expedition concerns the killing of two civilians and a trooper by a party of Sioux supposedly led by Rain-in-the-Face. This incident and its consequences are detailed in John S. Gray, "Custer Throws a Boomerang," *Montana the Magazine of Western History* 11 (April 1961). Another controversy growing out of the expedition, concerning the value of Northern Pacific Railroad land on the northern plains, is covered in Edgar I. Stewart, ed., *Penny-an-Acre Empire in the West* (Norman: University of Oklahoma Press, 1968).

Unlike the Yellowstone expedition, the 1874 Black Hills expedition has produced a sizable body of good literature. A fine overview is provided in Donald Jackson, *Custer's Gold: The United States Cavalry Expedition of 1874* (New Haven: Yale University Press, 1966), whereas excellent coverage of newspaper stories and participants' official reports is in Herbert Krause and Gary D. Olson, *Prelude to Glory: A Newspaper Accounting of Custer's 1874 Expedition to the Black Hills.* (Sioux Falls: Brevet Press, 1974). A modern photographic reconstruction of Custer's route, with fascinating insights into changes in the land since 1874, is Donald R. Progulske and Frank J. Shideler, *Following Custer* (Brookings: Agricultural Experiment Station, South Dakota State University, 1974). Two diaries of the expedition are to be found in Lawrence A. Frost, ed., *With Custer in '74: James Calhoun's Diary of the Black Hills Expedition* (Provo, Utah: Brigham Young University Press, 1979), and John M. Carroll and Lawrence A. Frost, eds., *Private Theodore Ewert's Diary of the Black Hills Expedition of 1874* (Piscataway, N.J.: CRI Books, 1976).

There is no single monograph that adequately covers the entire Great Sioux War of 1876–77. The causes of the war are grounded in twenty years of conflict between the Sioux and the expanding United States and, before that, in another hundred years of conflict between the expansive Sioux and other plains tribes. Excellent coverage of Sioux aggression is in Richard White, "The Winning of the West: The Expansion of the Western Sioux in the Eighteenth and Nineteenth Centuries," *Journal of American History* 65 (September 1978). The immediate cause of conflict in 1876 is debated in essays by Mark H. Brown and Harry H. Anderson, reprinted along with several other important articles from *Montana the Magazine of Western History* in Paul L. Hedren, ed., *The Great Sioux War, 1876–77* (Helena: Montana Historical Society Press, 1991).

A particularly fine memoir of the entire war is the *Chicago Times* reporter John F. Finerty's *War-Path and Bivouac; or, The Conquest of the Sioux* (Norman: University of Oklahoma Press, 1961). Not as lively, but still useful, is

Colonel John Gibbon's *Gibbon on the Sioux Campaign of 1876* (Bellevue, Nebr.: Old Army Press, 1970), which reprints two 1877 Gibbon articles that appeared in the *American Catholic Quarterly Review.* The excellent journal of Lieutenant James H. Bradley of Gibbon's command, who discovered the bodies on Custer's battlefield, is reprinted in James H. Bradley, *The March of the Montana Column: A Prelude to the Custer Disaster,* ed. Edgar I. Stewart (Norman: University of Oklahoma, 1961). Two other Montana Column memoirs are Edward J. McClernand, *On Time for Disaster: The Rescue of Custer's Command* (Lincoln: University of Nebraska Press, Bison Book, 1989), and George A. Schneider, ed., *The Freeman Journal: The Infantry in the Sioux Campaign of 1876* (San Rafael, Calif.: Presidio Press, 1977). A good memoir by an enlisted man of the Second Cavalry is Thomas B. Marquis, *Custer, Cavalry, and Crows: The Story of William White As Told to Thomas Marquis* (Fort Collins, Colo.: Old Army Press, 1975).

For the activities of General George Crook's command, the best book remains the memoir by Captain Charles King, *Campaigning with Crook* (Norman: University of Oklahoma Press, 1964). The sorry beginning of the campaign is ably covered in J. W. Vaughn, *The Reynolds Campaign on Powder River* (Norman: University of Oklahoma Press, 1961). Crook's defeat at the Rosebud has been the subject of two solid studies: J. W. Vaughn, *With Crook at the Rosebud* (Harrisburg, Pa.: Stackpole Co., 1956), and Neil C. Mangum, *Battle of the Rosebud: Prelude to the Little Bighorn* (El Segundo, Calif.: Upton and Sons, 1987). The three other major engagements fought by troops under Crook's overall command are covered in Paul L. Hedren, *First Scalp for Custer: The Skirmish at Warbonnet Creek, Nebraska, July 17, 1876* (Lincoln: University of Nebraska Press, Bison Book, 1987); Jerome A. Greene, *Slim Buttes, 1876: An Episode of the Great Sioux War* (Norman: University of Oklahoma Press, 1982); and John G. Bourke, *Mackenzie's Last Fight with the Cheyennes: A Winter Campaign in Wyoming and Montana* (Bellevue, Nebr.: Old Army Press, 1970). A fascinating pictorial account of Crook's campaign is Paul L. Hedren, *With Crook in the Black Hills: Stanley J. Morrow's 1876 Photographic Legacy* (Boulder, Colo.: Pruett Publishing Co., 1985); the same author chronicles the pivotal role of Fort Laramie in the campaign in *Fort Laramie in 1876: Chronicle of a Frontier Post at War* (Lincoln: University of Nebraska Press, 1988).

Crook's unfinished autobiography is not particularly useful for the Great Sioux War, but it contains valuable background material: Martin F. Schmitt, ed., *General George Crook: His Autobiography* (Norman: University of Oklahoma Press, 1946). Also surprisingly sketchy on the Great Sioux War, in which he played an important role, is the otherwise interesting memoir of Anson Mills, *My Story* (Washington, D.C.: Byron S. Adams, 1921). Far more useful is the classic memoir by Crook's aide, John G. Bourke, *On the Border with Crook* (New York: Charles Scribner's Sons, 1891), as well as his biography by Joseph C. Porter, *Paper Medicine Man: John Gregory Bourke and His American West* (Norman: University of Oklahoma Press, 1986). A truly marvelous memoir by one of Crook's enlisted men, focusing on the Powder River expedition, is in Sherry L. Smith, *Sagebrush Soldier: Private William Earl Smith's View of the Sioux War of 1876* (Norman: University of Oklahoma Press, 1989).

In a controversial chapter on the Custer battle, General Nelson A. Miles quotes General Terry as giving Custer wide latitude of action should he strike the Indian trail. Recent evidence has tended to support Miles's long-disputed account of their conversation. His memoirs are particularly valuable on Miles's 1877 campaign: *Personal Recollections and Observations of General Nelson A. Miles* (New York: Da Capo Press, 1969). Miles was vindicated by impressive historical detective work presented in John S. Manion, *Last Statement to Custer* (Monroe, Mich.: Monroe County Library System, 1983). For more on Miles and his campaigns in the Great Sioux War, see Brian C. Pohanka, ed., *Nelson A. Miles: A Documentary Biography of His Military Career, 1861–1903* (Glendale, Calif.: Arthur H. Clark, 1985); Virginia W. Johnson, *The Unregimented General: A Biography of Nelson A. Miles* (Boston: Houghton Mifflin Co., 1962); and M. M. Quaife, ed., *"Yellowstone Kelly": The Memoirs of Luther S. Kelly* (New Haven: Yale University Press, 1926).

The best single volume on the Battle of the Little Big Horn is undoubtedly John S. Gray's *Centennial Campaign: The Sioux War of 1876* (Fort Collins, Colo.: Old Army Press, 1976). As a history of the entire campaign, Gray's book does not succeed, for though his background chapters are strong, the book trails off quickly after Custer's defeat and does not provide adequate coverage of Nelson Miles's important operations. It is the study of Custer's defeat, however, that marks Gray's book as a remarkable accomplishment. Despite an aggravating system of documentation, Gray's impressive research, careful analysis, remarkable time studies, and deductive reasoning have resulted in a persuasive reconstruction of the battle, against which all other accounts must be measured. Gray greatly expanded on that earlier work in a book labeled as "brilliant, revolutionary, and all but unassailable" by Robert M. Utley; see *Custer's Last Campaign: Mitch Boyer and the Little Bighorn Reconstructed* (Lincoln: University of Nebraska Press, 1991). Gray's two books have replaced Edgar I. Stewart's *Custer's Luck* (Norman: University of Oklahoma Press, 1955) as the standard accounts of the battle. Stewart's book, however, remains a nicely written, carefully balanced narrative well worth consulting. The same cannot be said for three earlier reconstructions of the battle that have not stood the test of time: W. A. Graham, *The Story of the Little Big Horn: Custer's Last Fight* (New York: Century Co., 1926); Fred Dustin, *The Custer Tragedy: Events Leading up to and following the Little Big Horn Campaign of 1876* (Ann Arbor, Mich.: Edwards Brothers, 1939); and Charles Kuhlman, *Legend into History: The Custer Mystery* (Harrisburg, Pa.: Stackpole Co., 1952). Dustin is so stridently anti-Custer that it fatally mars his careful analysis of the battle. Kuhlman, on the other hand, presents a defense of Custer's actions that is far too speculative. Of the three, Graham's work is the most useful, although his dismissal of Indian sources is a glaring problem. Nor is his attempt to vindicate Major Reno convincing. The fact that Colonel Robert P. Hughes's 1896 essay "The Campaign against the Sioux in 1876" is reprinted adds to the usefullness of Graham's book, reprinted in 1988 as a Bison Book by the University of Nebraska Press.

A useful compilation of official government documents relating to the battle is John M. Carroll, ed., *General Custer and the Battle of the Little Big Horn: The Federal View* (New Brunswick, N.J.: Garry Owen Press, 1976). Military reports and rosters are in Loyd J. Overfield II, comp., *The Little Big Horn 1876: The Official Communications, Documents, and Reports* (Glendale, Calif.: Arthur H. Clark Co., 1971). James Willert, *Little Big Horn Diary: Chronicle of the 1876 Indian War* (La Mirada, Calif.: James Willert, Publisher, 1977), provides a richly detailed examination of daily activity leading up to the battle.

One of the handful of key books on the battle is the delightful potpourri of original narratives, letters, reports, debates, and tall tales compiled by Colonel W. A. Graham, *The Custer Myth: A Source Book of Custeriana* (Harrisburg, Pa.: Stackpole Co., 1953), reprinted in 1986 by the University of Nebraska Press. The book also contains Fred Dustin's comprehensive, if dated, bibliography. Of equal value are the collected interviews of Walter Camp with Custer battle survivors, both soldier and Indian, in Kenneth Hammer, ed., *Custer in '76: Walter Camp's Notes on the Custer Fight* (Provo, Utah: Brigham Young University Press, 1976).

Much valuable testimony on the battle is contained in the massive *The Reno Court of Inquiry: The Chicago Times Account* (Fort Collins, Colo.: Old Army Press, 1972). A useful shorter version is W. A. Graham, *Abstract of the Official Record of Proceedings of the Reno Court of Inquiry* (Harrisburg, Pa.: Stackpole Co., 1954).

There are a surprising number of diaries and memoirs. Several interesting reminiscences, as well as many reprinted articles by the author, are in E. A. Brininstool, *Troopers with Custer: Historic Incidents of the Battle of the Little Big Horn* (Harrisburg, Pa.: Stackpole Co., 1952). A number of rather cryptic diaries are compiled in Michael J. Koury, *Diaries of the Little Big Horn* (Bellevue, Nebr.: Old Army Press, 1968). The unfinished memoir of Lieutenant Charles Varnum has been published as John M. Carroll, ed., *Custer's Chief of Scouts: The Reminiscences of Charles A. Varnum* (Lincoln: University of Nebraska Press, 1987), first published in a limited edition by the Arthur H. Clark Co. in 1982. The diary of Dr. James DeWolf, who was killed in Reno's retreat, can be found in Edward S. Luce, ed., "The Diary and Letters of Dr. James M. DeWolf . . . ," *North Dakota History* 25 (April–July 1958). Two accounts by enlisted men are Daniel O. Magnussen, *Peter Thompson's Narrative of the Little Bighorn Campaign, 1876* (Glendale, Calif.: Arthur H. Clark Co., 1974), and Bruce R. Liddic, ed., *I Buried Custer: The Diary of Pvt. Thomas W. Coleman, Seventh U.S. Cavalry* (College Station, Tex.: Creative Publishing Co., 1979).

Richard A. Roberts was a friend of the Custers' and the brother-in-law of Captain George Yates. As a youngster, he accompanied the expedition as a herder, along with Custer's teenage nephew Harry Armstrong Reed. Unlike Reed, he survived and left an informative memoir published as *Custer's Last Battle: Reminiscences of General Custer* (Monroe, Mich.: Monroe County Library Systems, 1978). In his defense of Custer, Roberts contends that the cavalryman did not disobey General Alfred Terry's orders, an important question also analyzed by Charles Kuhlman, *Did Custer Disobey Orders at the Battle of the Little Big Horn?* (Harrisburg, Pa.: Stackpole Co., 1957), and Francis B. Taunton, *"Sufficient Reason?" An Examination of Terry's Celebrated Order to Custer* (London: English Westerners' Society, 1977). General Terry's own campaign diary sheds little light on the question, although it does contain useful, if cryptic, information: *The Field Diary of General Alfred H. Terry: The Yellowstone Expedition—1876* (Bellevue, Nebr.: Old Army Press, 1970). A defense of General Terry's actions is in John W. Bailey, *Pacifying the Plains: General Alfred Terry and the Decline of the Sioux, 1866–1890* (Westport, Conn.: Greenwood Press, 1979).

Battle narratives by Custer's Arikara scouts appear in O. G. Libby, ed., *The Arikara Narrative of the Campaign against the Hostile Dakotas, June, 1876* (Bismarck: North Dakota Historical Society, 1920), and accounts from Custer's Crow scouts, as well as narratives by warriors who fought Custer, are in Joseph K. Dixon, *The Vanishing Race* (Garden City, N.Y.: Doubleday, Page and Co., 1913). The story of the scout Goes Ahead appears in a biography of his wife: Frank B. Linderman, *Pretty-shield: Medicine Woman of the Crows* (Lincoln: University of Nebraska Press, 1974). Its original publication in 1932 as *Red Mother* contained the first appearance of the story that Custer was the first to fall, shot from his horse while attempting to ford the river.

The accounts of many of the warriors who fought Custer are pulled together in the well-written and fast-paced narrative by David Humphreys Miller, *Custer's Fall: The Indian Side of the Story* (New York: Duell, Sloan and Pearce, 1957), reprinted in 1985 as a Bison Book by the University of Nebraska Press. Miller claimed to have based his narrative on personal interviews with the aged Indian participants, but his stories bear striking similarities to previously published Indian narratives. The best Indian-based account of Sioux resistance to white aggression remains Stanley Vestal's *Warpath: The True Story of the Fighting Sioux Told in a Biography of Chief White Bull* (Boston: Houghton Mifflin, 1934), reprinted in 1984 as a Bison Book with a new foreword by Raymond J. DeMallie. Another version of White Bull's narrative is in James H. Howard, trans. and ed., *The Warrior Who Killed Custer: The Personal Narrative of Chief Joseph White Bull* (Lincoln: University of Nebraska Press, 1968). Another compelling Sioux narrative, as seen through the poetic eye of John G. Neihardt, is *Black Elk Speaks* (New York: William Morrow and Co., 1932). Several Sioux accounts of the battle were used by James McLaughlin in *My*

Friend the Indian (Lincoln: University of Nebraska Press, Bison Book, 1989), and Indian testimony is also at the heart of Thomas B. Marquis, *Custer on the Little Bighorn* (Lodi, Calif.: Kain Publishing Co., 1969). The best Cheyenne memoir is that of Wooden Leg, presented in Thomas B. Marquis, *A Warrior Who Fought Custer* (Minneapolis: Midwest Co., 1931), reprinted as a Bison Book under the title *Wooden Leg* in 1962. Dr. Marquis' interviews with the Cheyennes led him to conclude that Custer's men committed mass suicides, an interpretation of the battle he presented in *Keep the Last Bullet for Yourself: The True Story of Custer's Last Stand* (New York: Two Continents Publishing/ Reference Publications, 1976). The suicide story was disputed by the Cheyenne historian John Stands in Timber in his exceptionally fine chronicle of his people. The Custer fight and other battles on the northern plains are important features of John Stands in Timber and Margot Liberty, *Cheyenne Memories* (New Haven: Yale University Press, 1967), reprinted in 1972 as a University of Nebraska Press Bison Book.

The leading Indian personalities have received biographical treatment, with the best work being Stanley Vestal's *Sitting Bull*, rev. ed. (Norman: University of Oklahoma Press, 1957). A work of far greater literary than historical merit is Mari Sandoz, *Crazy Horse: The Strange Man of the Oglalas* (New York: Alfred A. Knopf, 1942). Although the great Oglala leader Red Cloud was not at the Little Big Horn, his biography is particularly valuable in providing background and perspective: James C. Olson, *Red Cloud and the Sioux Problem* (Lincoln: University of Nebraska Press, 1965).

Archaeological excavations at Custer Battlefield National Monument in 1984 and 1985 have tended to give additional credibility to Indian narratives of the battle. The refusal of earlier white historians to properly analyze or accept Indian testimony is particularly ridiculous in light of these findings, which often contradict the suppositions of soldiers who went over the field soon after the battle and which support Indian accounts. Although no major new discoveries were made by the excavations, they nevertheless provided an impressive amount of new physical evidence and solved several persistent battle puzzles, such as how well were the Indians armed (quite well, and many with repeating rifles); how important was extraction failure of the soldiers' Springfield carbines in explaining the defeat (not a significant factor); and how accurate was the placement of markers on the battlefield to indicate where soldiers fell (quite accurate, although there are too many markers). The final report of the archaeological team is required reading for the student of the battle: Douglas D. Scott, Richard A. Fox, Jr., Melissa A. Connor, and Dick Harmon, *Archaeological Perspectives on the Battle of the Little Bighorn* (Norman: University of Oklahoma Press, 1989).

Support for the Indian narratives, also based on archaeological evidence, had been provided by a former Custer Battlefield National Monument ranger, Jerome A. Greene, in *Evidence and the Custer Enigma: A Reconstruction of Indian-Military History* (Kansas City: Kansas City Posse of the Westerners,

1973). A revised edition, making use of the later archaeological findings, was published by Outbooks of Golden, Colorado, in 1986. Greene was the first to inventory and map where various battlefield artifacts had been, although his evidence was mainly from Nye-Cartwright Ridge (parallel to Custer Ridge), which is outside the park boundary. Greene's evidence, however, tends to support the evidence from the 1984 and 1985 excavations, and combined, they provide vital clues to the nature of the battle. A similar combination of Indian testimony and physical evidence was employed by Richard G. Hardorff, with intriguing results, in *Markers, Artifacts, and Indian Testimony: Preliminary Findings on the Custer Battle* (Short Hills, N.J.: W. Donald Horn, Publisher, 1985).

The origins of the spectacular legend that grew out of the battle are presented in Robert M. Utley, *Custer and the Great Controversy: The Origin and Development of a Legend* (Los Angeles: Westernlore Press, 1962), the first book to deal with what has come to be called the Custer myth. Utley, for the most part, focuses his study on journalistic controversies and historiographical debates, whereas Kent Ladd Steckmesser, in his pioneering study *The Western Hero in History and Legend* (Norman: University of Oklahoma Press, 1965), deals more with fiction and film in a section on Custer. Considerably more all-inclusive than either Utley or Steckmesser is Brian W. Dippie's *Custer's Last Stand: The Anatomy of an American Myth* (Missoula: University of Montana, 1976). Dippie's delightfully encyclopedic study surveys the entire range of writing and iconography making up the Custer myth—history, poetry, paintings, novels, and movies. For Dippie, the Custer of legend is a far more important figure to America than the real man. In a particularly intriguing and sophisticated study, the folklorist Bruce A. Rosenberg places the Custer myth within an international context, relating it to universal hero myths and heroic legends from other lands, in his *Custer and the Epic of Defeat* (University Park: Pennsylvania State University Press, 1974). Another interpretation of the growth of the legend is in Richard Slotkin, *The Fatal Environment: The Myth of the Frontier in the Age of Industrialization, 1800–1890* (New York: Atheneum, 1985).

In this age of lists, it is perhaps appropriate to conclude this discussion of Custer literature with a top-ten list—the basic books for the Custeriana library. All such lists are highly subjective, but these books will give the interested reader a solid, well-rounded introduction to the vast Custer bibliography.

1. Robert M. Utley, *Cavalier in Buckskin*: the best biography and the book to begin with
2. George Armstrong Custer, *My Life on the Plains*: the story from Custer's own perspective
3. Elizabeth B. Custer, *"Boots and Saddles"*: the poignant memoir of the Custers' last years together
4. Marguerite Merington, ed., *The Custer Story*: despite the heavy hand

of the sanitizing editor, these letters are a treasure trove of insights into both Custers

5. John S. Gray, *Custer's Last Campaign*: the most informative and enlightening book on the Battle of the Little Big Horn

6. Evan S. Connell, *Son of the Morning Star*: as provocative and daring as its protagonist, replete with remarkable insights into the personalities involved in the struggle at the Little Big Horn

7. W. A. Graham, *The Custer Myth*: a wild hodgepodge of often contradictory information and a remarkable sourcebook, the place to begin a more exhaustive personal investigation of the man and his last battle

8. Kenneth Hammer, *Custer in '76*: these interviews by Walter Camp are dramatic, telling, and significant; along with Graham's work, this is essential source material for the serious student

9. Brian W. Dippie, *Custer's Last Stand*: a wonderful exploration of Custer in popular culture, full of delightful surprises and significant insights

10. Paul Andrew Hutton, *The Custer Reader*: the book you have in your hands provides a definitive collection of personal narratives, reprinted scholarship, and the best of current research from top Custer scholars

If all of this is not enough, then jump into the vast Dustin bibliography in Graham's *Custer Myth*; Tal Luther's *Custer High Spots* (Fort Collins, Colo.: Old Army Press, 1972); John M. Carroll's massive *Custer in Periodicals: A Bibliographic Checklist* (Fort Collins, Colo.: Old Army Press, 1975), plus Carroll's numerous published corrections and additions to that list; and Vincent A. Heier's exhaustive Custer bibliographies published in the four annuals of the Little Big Horn Associates (*Garry Owen 1976* and *Custer and His Times*, volumes one through three). The bibliography on this intriguing American and his last battle is as fascinating and contradictory as the subject, and it shows no sign of slackening in terms of production. Custer, and his myth, will be with us so long as humans continue to be drawn to heroism, folly, mystery, and towering legendry.

SOURCES

Previously published selections were originally published in or are reprinted from the following sources:

"From West Point to the Battlefield," by G. A. Custer. Originally published in *Galaxy Magazine* 21 (April 1876).

"Custer's 'Last Stand'—Trevilian Station, 1864," by Jay Monaghan. Reprinted from *Civil War History* 8 (September 1962): 245–58, courtesy of Kent State University Press.

"The Battle of Waynesboro," by Harlan Page Lloyd. Reprinted from W. H. Chamberlain, ed., *Sketches of War History, 1861–1865: Papers Prepared for the Ohio Commandery of the Military Order of the Loyal Legion of the United States, 1890–1896* (Cincinnati: Clarke Company, 1896).

"The West Breaks in General Custer," by Minnie Dubbs Millbrook. Reprinted from *Kansas Historical Quarterly* 36, no. 2 (Summer 1970): 113–48, courtesy of the Kansas State Historical Society.

"Some Reminiscences, Including the Washita Battle, November 27, 1868," by Edward S. Godfrey. Reprinted from *Cavalry Journal* 37, no. 153 (October 1928): 481–500.

"Expedition to the Yellowstone River in 1873: Letters of a Young Cavalry Officer," by Charles W. Larned, edited by George Frederick Howe. Reprinted from *Mississippi Valley Historical Review* 39 (December 1952): 519–34, courtesy of the *Journal of American History* on behalf of the Organization of American Historians.

"Battling with the Sioux on the Yellowstone," by G. A. Custer. Reprinted from *Galaxy Magazine* 22 (July 1876): 91–102.

"Custer's Last Battle," by Edward S. Godfrey. Original version published in *Century Magazine* 43 (January 1892): 358–87. Revised version reprinted from John M. Carroll, ed., *The Two Battles of the Little Big Horn* (New York: Liveright, 1974), 39–125, courtesy of John M. Carroll.

"The Cavalry Campaign Outfit at the Little Big Horn," by James S. Hutchins. Reprinted from *Military Collector and Historian* 7, no. 4 (Winter 1956): 91–101, courtesy of the Company of Military Historians.

"The Battle of the Little Bighorn," by Chief Joseph White Bull, as told to Stanley Vestal. Reprinted from *Blue Book Magazine* 57 (September 1933): 52–58, courtesy of Malory C. Ausland and Dorothy Callaway.

"Custer's Last Battle," by Charles King. Originally published in *Harper's New Monthly Magazine* 81 (August 1890): 378–87.

"She Watched Custer's Last Battle," by Kate Bighead, as told to Thomas B. Marquis. Reprinted from Thomas B. Marquis, *Custer on the Little Bighorn* 575

(Algonac, Mich.: Reference Publications, 1986), 35–43, courtesy of Reference Publications, Inc., 218 St. Clair River Drive, Box 344, Algonac, Michigan 48001.

"From Little Bighorn to Little Big Man: The Changing Image of a Western Hero in Popular Culture," by Paul Andrew Hutton. Reprinted from *Western Historical Quarterly* 7 (January 1976): 19–45, courtesy of the *Western Historical Quarterly*.

"The Pictorial Record of the Old West: Custer's Last Stand—John Mulvany, Cassilly Adams, and Otto Becker," by Robert Taft. Reprinted from *Kansas Historical Quarterly* 14, no. 4 (November 1946): 361–90, courtesy of the Kansas State Historical Society.

"Jack Crabb and the Sole Survivors of Custer's Last Stand," by Brian W. Dippie. Reprinted from *Western American Literature* 4 (Fall 1969): 189–202, courtesy of *Western American Literature*.

" 'Correct in Every Detail': General Custer in Hollywood," by Paul Andrew Hutton. Reprinted from *Montana the Magazine of Western History* 41 (Winter 1991): 28–57, courtesy Montana Historical Society.

"Custer: The Legend of the Martyred Hero in America," by Bruce A. Rosenberg. Reprinted from *Journal of Folklore Research* 9 (Fall 1972): 110–32, courtesy of the Folklore Institute, Indiana University.